UNDERGROUND!

THE DISINFORMATION GUIDE TO ANCIENT CIVILIZATIONS,

ASTONISHING ARCHAEOLOGY AND HIDDEN HISTORY

Edited by Preston Peet

disinformation®

Published by The Disinformation Company Ltd.
163 Third Avenue, Suite 108
New York, NY 10003
Tel.: +1.212.691.1605
Fax: +1.212.691.1606
www.disinfo.com

Cover: Anlända
Layout: Hedi El Kholti

Library of Congress Control Number: 2005930392

ISBN-10: 1-932857-19-2
ISBN-13: 978-1-932857-19-1

Printed in USA

10 9 8 7 6 5 4 3 2 1

Distributed in the USA and Canada by:
Consortium Book Sales and Distribution
1045 Westgate Drive, Suite 90
St Paul, MN 55114
Toll Free: +1.800.283.3572
Local: +1.651.221.9035
Fax: +1.651.221.0124
www.cbsd.com

UNDERGROUND!

THE DISINFORMATION GUIDE TO ANCIENT CIVILIZATIONS, ASTONISHING ARCHAEOLOGY AND HIDDEN HISTORY

Edited by Preston Peet

disinformation®

CONTENTS

7   INTRODUCTION

21   ORIGINS MYTHIC OR HISTORIC

23   Michael A. Cremo—Human Devolution
33   John Anthony West—Consider the Kali Yuga
39   N. S. Rajaram—Ocean Origins of Indian Civilization
50   Acharya S—Deus Noster, Deus Solis: Our God, God of the Sun
57   Dave Dentel—Mysterious Origins—Are Humans Just a Happy Accident?

65   ANCIENT CITIES, ANCIENT PLANS

67   Richard Nisbet—Ancient Walls
77   Gary A. David—Along the 33rd Degree Parallel: A Global Mystery Circle
87   David Hatcher Childress—Did the Incas Build Machu Picchu?
101   Colin Wilson—Summary of Atlantis and the Old Ones: An Investigation of the Age of Civilization
107   Robert M. Schoch with Robert S. McNally—The Meaning of the Pyramids
109   Roy A. Decker—The Secret Land
117   Robert Merkin—Lingering Echoes: Athens, Jerusalem

123   CATACLYSMS AND MIGRATIONS

125   Graham Hancock—Underworld: Confronting Yonaguni
149   Martin Gray—Sacred Geography: Cosmic and Cometary Induced Cataclysms, and the Megalithic Response
162   George Erikson with Ivar Zapp—Atlantis in America: A Summing Up—Awaiting the New Paradigm
169   Frank Joseph—Nan Madol: The Lost Civilization of the Pacific
177   Graham Hancock—Underworld: Confronting Kerama

191   TECHNOLOGIES AND CONTACTS

193   Christopher Dunn—The Giza Power Plant
199   Erich von Däniken—Aviation in Antiquity?
206   Crichton E. M. Miller—The Constantine Conspiracy
215   George T. Sassoon—The Ancient of Days: Deity or Manna-Machine?
220   Giorgio A. Tsoukalos—The Giant Flying Turtles of Guatemala
226   William R. Corliss—Ancient Scientific Instruments

235   RELIGIONS AND WISDOMS

237   Sharon Secor—Creation of a Gifted People: The Mayan Calendar
243   Robert M. Schoch—Ancient Wisdom and the Great Sphinx of Giza
247   Ron Sala—Where is the Holy Grail?
257   Richard Cusick—Journey to Bubastis
265   Dan Russell—Gnosis: The Plants of Truth

283   MODERN EXPLORATIONS, ANOMALIES AND COVER-UPS

285   Preston Peet—A Conversation With Greg Deyermenjian: Lost Cities Sought, Lost Cities Found
297   Mickey Z.—Source of the Blood: Nazi Germany's Search for its Aryan Roots
302   Michael Arbuthnot—Team Atlantis
307   Troy Lovata—Shovel Bum—A Life Archaeologic
317   Will Hart—Archaeological Cover-Ups: A Plot to Control History?

327   RESOURCES

333   ARTICLE HISTORIES

335   CONTRIBUTOR BIOGRAPHIES

342   ACKNOWLEDGMENTS

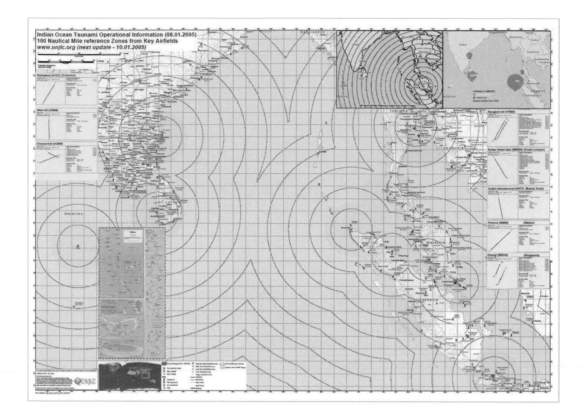

Regional Map of Tsunami-Affected Areas 2. Source: UNOSAT Satellite Imagery for All.

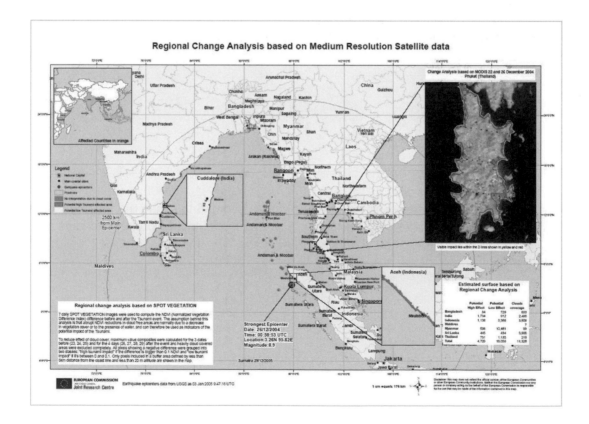

Post Tsunami—Regional Change Analysis based on Medium Rsolution Satellite data. Source: UNOSAT Satellite Imagery for All.

Preston Peet

INTRODUCTION

ON DECEMBER 26, 2004, at 7:58 A.M. local time, an earthquake registering a massive 9.0 on the Richter scale ripped open the sea floor under the Indian Ocean about 100 miles off Northwest Sumatra, Indonesia. According to the National Oceanic and Atmospheric Administration (NOAA), the "Pacific Basin tsunami warning system did not detect a tsunami in the Indian Ocean since there are no buoys in place there." While the NOAA did try to warn the numerous Pacific Rim nations of the incredibly destructive force heading their way, "the tsunami raced across the ocean at speeds up to 500 mph," eventually slamming into coastal communities and tourist havens alike, leaving an eventual death toll that some have estimated surpasses 212,000 people, according to CNN and other news sources. The countries worst hit by the disaster, according to www.reliefweb.int, included India, Indonesia, Kenya, Malaysia, Maldives, Myanmar, Seychelles, Somalia, Sri Lanka, Thailand and the United Republic of Tanzania, with the wave making no distinction between rich and poor, old or young. It wiped out everything in its path and left a scene of devastation and destruction not witnessed by most human beings within living memory (barring victims of atomic blasts and other shock and awe bombardments, perhaps). Similarly, as of this writing, the Gulf Coast of the United States is being buffeted by waves brought about by the relentless force of Hurricane Katrina, with much, if not most, of New Orleans disappearing underwater.

All of these countries and islands lost substantial amounts of not only life, but also vast swaths of land that disappeared underneath the waves. Where just seconds before stood modern hotels, primitive villages, cites and communities full of people busy celebrating a beautiful Christmas holiday, there was suddenly nothing but water, mud and debris—what humans had built was forever wiped clean from the face of the earth, now to be remembered only in stories of that horrible morning that shook the entire world.

Just two groups of living creatures managed to avoid the worst of the disaster. CBS News reported, on January 10, 2005, that many different animals seemed to sense the incoming devastation, from elephants breaking their chains and heading for the hills, to flocks of birds all suddenly taking flight, to dive boat leader Chris Cruz's report of his insistence on following what he described as an ocean erupting with dolphins out into deeper water, where the worst of the wave passed harmlessly underneath them. Did these animals sense warnings, emanations from the earth itself, a talent that pre-historic peoples may have been endowed with as well, but which we have since unlearned or forgotten? We will discuss this possibility within this anthology, but for now, let's get back to the wave.

Beside proving how fast and completely land can disappear underneath the waves, there are other important facts about the 2004 Christmas tsunami that relate to *Underground!—The Disinformation Guide to Ancient Civilizations, Astonishing Archaeology and Hidden History*. Throughout the disaster zone, there were small groups of people who saw the receding waters and remembered ancient tales passed down to them by their ancestors, tales which told of how water that disappeared out to sea would return with the same or greater force and bring death and ruin, and how people would run for the hills, often stopping just long enough to pass on a warning to their neighbors before fleeing to safety. On South Surin

2001, that explorations off the coast to search for a sunken city be undertaken—stood in awe. There, spread over a mile or more just off the coast of their ancient and historic temple-laden city, lay the ruins of an obviously ancient mud-and-barnacle-encrusted city, with "refrigerator sized blocks" laying all over the place, exposed in the moments just before the sea returned.

"You could see the destroyed walls covered in coral, and the broken-down temple in the middle," said Durai, a fisherman quoted by CBS News on March 17, 2005. "My grandfathers said there was a port here once and a temple, but suddenly we could see it was real, we could see that something was out there."

There, spread over a mile or more just off the coast of their ancient and historic temple-laden city, lay the ruins of an obviously mud-and-barnacle-encrusted city, with "refrigerator sized blocks" laying all over the place, exposed in the moments just before the sea returned.

---

in the Andaman Islands, the Morgan sea gypsies remembered these ancient warnings, and managed to save 181 people from the incoming wave. No one knows how long these stories have been passed down from generation to generation or where they originated. What's important is that they were remembered and acted upon by these so-called primitive people who had heard the stories all their lives. The Morgan people did not call these stories myths, or allegories, or interpretations of things their ancestors saw but did not understand—they took the stories at face value and hence saved their lives and those of many others when the chips were down and the waves came to claim huge parts of the land and its inhabitants for their own.

Besides the devastation to land and people wrought by the tsunami, something magical happened directly as a result of this wave.

As the water receded prior to the incoming tidal wave, residents of Mahabalipuram, India—where author Graham Hancock (*Fingerprints of the Gods*) had insisted to archaeologists, back in

While mainstream reports put the city's submergence at just 1,200-1,500 years ago, Hancock points out on his Web site and in his book *Underworld* that there are no contemporary reports from that time describing such a disaster. One would imagine that a large part of an inhabited city being swallowed by the sea might elicit some sort of mention in contemporary chronicles, but there are none—yet there are such tales in Indian "myths" that date back some 5,000 years and more. There is also the evidence from inundation maps created by Dr. Glenn Milne of Durham University—illustrating how much land was covered by the rising seas in stages at the end of the last ice age—which seem to prove there has been no land-subsidence in that area over the last 6,000 years, meaning that whoever built that submerged and briefly exposed ancient city did so a long time ago, in a time when human beings were supposed to still be in the very beginning stages of limited agriculture and small communities. If it was built before the seas rose at the end of the last ice age, that civilization would be thousands of years older than any civilization accepted by the current mainstream archaeological view. The same wave action that temporarily brought the ancient underwater kingdom back to the light of day also, by dredging away huge layers of sand these amazing discoveries and many more were of cities and kingdoms thought for centuries and longer to have been nothing but myth, but strong-willed and imaginative individuals proved them real beyond any shadow of a doubt. These

---

> **All these amazing discoveries and many more were of cities and kingdoms thought for centuries to have been nothing but myth, but strong-willed and imaginative individuals proved them real beyond any shadow of a doubt.**

---

from the beaches, exposed a number of ancient and previously unknown sculptures of lions, flying horses and other figures still being studied.

It took a number of independent explorers and characters to bring cities and cultures that had been widely believed to be merely myth to light over the years. Heinrich Schliemann "discovered" the "mythical" Troy in 1870, after being ridiculed by those in the "know" for years, earning himself fame, fortune and a reputation for life. Sir Arthur Evans undertook excavations near the modern capital of Heraklion on the northern coast of the island of Crete after hearing and, more importantly, *taking seriously* local folk tales, and turned "mythical" Minoan civilization back into "real" history when he uncovered the legendary Palace of Knossos at the tail end of the Nineteenth Century. In 1911, explorer and adventurer Hiram Bingham went searching the jungle-covered mountains of Peru for Vilcabamba, the final stronghold of the last ruler of the Incas, Tupac Amaru. A local farmer told Bingham of a fabulous fortress at the top of the mountain at the foot of which his party was camped. While the rest of his exhausted party remained waiting below, Bingham, along with one member of the accompanying Peruvian military force, climbed with the farmer up the mountain until he beheld—straddling the very top of a mountain with sheer drops to all sides and constructed of megalithic stones cut and fitted with the precision of modern-day masons—the now world-famous and beautiful beyond belief Machu Picchu. All

discoveries were all on land—what lies waiting for us beneath the waves, where even more ancient myths and stories tell of hidden cities and lands built before the flood, in some distant Golden Time?

Incredibly ancient tales and modern claims of finds of lost cities under the sea abound around the world. From the classic and oft-described as fantastical stories about Atlantis and Lemuria, to the possibly man-made or man-altered castle-like monuments discovered in the last 20 years just meters under the waves off Yonaguni, Japan, to an even more mysterious sunken sister city to the already enigmatic Nan Madol of the South Pacific, the sinking of these cities is often explained in myth and folklore as disasters brought about by vengeful gods against people grown cocky, arrogant, warlike or simply unlucky.

Hancock, in his groundbreaking and beautiful book *Underworld*, uses the inundation maps of Dr. Milne to graphically illustrate that as the last ice age ended the waters rose in stages, steadily eating away at shorelines around the world, changing the very shape of the land. Humanity lost up to, and possibly more than, 25 million square kilometers (about 10 million square miles, or five percent, of the earth's surface) of arid, habitable land to the rising waters as the ice caps melted and sea levels drastically changed the landscape all over the globe. As Hancock writes in *Underworld*, "That is roughly equivalent to the combined area of the United States (9.6 million square kilometers) and the whole of South America (17 million square kilometers). It is an area almost three times as large as Canada and much larger than China and Europe combined." The possibility that the sea hides a large amount of human history has to be considered and serious explorations must be undertaken. A few courageous explorers and thinkers are doing just that.

New discoveries are throwing old dogmatic paradigms, and what science thinks it really "knows" about the past, and even the present, into wild disarray on an almost daily basis, as the discovery, mentioned above, that the sunken city long rumored to lie off the coast of Mahabalipuram really *does* exist amply demonstrates. But that's not nearly the only sunken settlement reported discovered in recent years.

flood 7,600 years ago (leading many to believe that this event was the catalyst for the Bible's flood stories, though many others ridicule this idea). In 2000, while exploring the depths of the Black Sea on a *National Geographic*-backed expedition, using side-scan radar, a visual imaging vehicle and a remote robot-like device to collect samples, his team discovered not only five of the best-preserved ancient wooden ships ever found, in the oxygen-deprived waters 656 feet (about 200 meters) below the surface, but at a separate site off the coast of Sinop, Turkey, he found what appeared to be five carved wooden artifacts and the remains of human habitation, a 39 by 13 foot rectangular structure at 311 feet (over 100 meters) under the surface. Further research is still underway as this book goes to press.

"What we see in our high-resolution sonar images are limitless, rolling, white sand plains and, in the middle of this beautiful white sand, there are clear man-made large-size architectural designs. It looks like when you fly over an urban development in a plane and you see highways, tunnels and buildings," Zelitsky told Reuters about their enigmatic deep-water discovery.

Dr. Penny Spikins of Newcastle University, the leader of the multinational research team behind the Submerged Prehistoric Landscapes Project reported Scotsman.com, made discoveries of two separate Stone Age settlements underneath the North Sea off the coast of Scotland (both found in the same general location, near the mouth of the river Tyne), long suspected ever since a Neolithic harpoon was dredged from the sea floor early in the Twentieth Century by a fishing trawler. One site is thought to date to the late Mesolithic period between 5,000 and 10,000 years ago, and the other to the early Mesolithic period, 10,000 years or more.

Respected undersea explorer Robert Ballard, who discovered and extensively photographed the final resting place of the ocean liner *Titanic* at the bottom of the North Atlantic in 1985, located the German WWII battleship *Bismarck* and even found John F. Kennedy's *PT-109*, has postulated that the Black Sea was flooded in a cataclysmic

On May 14, 2001, Reuters reported the alleged discovery, at an almost unbelievable 600-700 meters (about 2,200 feet) below sea level, of a humongous site spread across 20 kilometers that looks remarkably like a human-built city, strewn with huge blocks of stone and what appear to be pyramid-shaped structures, as well as roads and other buildings. Located off the western tip of Cuba, off the Guanahacabibes Peninsula on what's known as the Cuban Shelf, again, as with Ballard's finds in the Black Sea, this is a seriously anomalous discovery made by respected researchers not known for making wild, unsubstantiated claims, and again this was an accidental discovery. Paulina Zelitsky, who with husband Paul Weinzweig owns and operates the Canadian company Advanced Digital Communications (ADC), with offices in both Cuba and Canada, was not seeking sunken cities but was rather engaged in underwater surveying, searching for sunken treasure ships in cooperation with the Cuban government. (In November 2000, they discovered and filmed the U.S. battleship *USS Maine*, which blew up and sank in 1898, instigating the Cuban-American war that brought Theodore Roosevelt military fame and, eventually, the U.S. presidency.) "What we see in our high-resolution sonar images are limitless, rolling, white sand plains and, in the middle of this beautiful white sand, took much imagination on the part of this editor, anyway) to see anything remotely resembling an underwater city, the response of the mainstream press was informative—the story was picked up and given press all over the world both online and in print newspapers, proving that tales of Atlantis and other mysteries of our distant past still intrigue and grab attention.

The study of archaeology is rife with misinterpretation and dogmatic insistence on one view of history, that human beings have only been civilized for the briefest span of time, and that only accredited, "professional" archaeologists are able to reach conclusions that are worth consideration when it comes to our ancient past—and even then the professional label doesn't always help.

---

there are clear man-made, large-size architectural designs. It looks like when you fly over an urban development in a plane and you see highways, tunnels and buildings," Zelitsky told Reuters about their enigmatic, deep-water discovery. Her husband Weinzweig told Reuters, "We had been looking at the images for some months, and keep a picture on the wall showing pyramids in the Yucatán, and let's just say they kept reminding us of these structures. They really do look like an urban development."

Then there's the American explorer Robert Sarmast, who claimed in November 2004 to have discovered the remains of Atlantis 80 kilometers (about 50 miles) southeast of Cyprus. Conducting sonar scanning of the seabed 1.5 kilometers (just under one mile) below the surface between Cyprus and Syria, Sarmast claims to have located man-made walls of incredible dimensions, including one wall said to stretch as long as three kilometers, as well as man-dug trenches. "We found more than 60-70 points that are a perfect match with Plato's detailed description of the general layout of the acropolis hill of Atlantis. The match of the dimensions and the coordinates provided by our sonar with Plato's description are so accurate that, if this is not indeed the acropolis of Atlantis, then this is the world's greatest coincidence," Sarmast told CNN. Although his sonar imaging was hazy (and

HOW FAR BACK DID YOU SAY?

For the past few decades the accepted academic estimates put modern humans appearing on the scene between 100,000 and 150,000 years ago, then spending the next 140,000 to 90,000 years spreading about the globe by land, hunting and gathering, grunting and living in caves all the while, until about 10,000 years ago, when humans suddenly began to practice agriculture and gather into small communities. Then, in February 2005, it was announced on ScienceDaily.com that fossils of anatomically correct "modern" human beings had been found—back in 1967 near Kibish, Ethiopia—and though initially thought to be about 138,000 years old, these were now estimated to be closer to 195,000 years old, "give or take 5,000 years." Those are approximately *200,000-year-old "modern" humans*, in other words. According to research by Frank Brown, the dean of the University of Utah's College of Mines and Earth Sciences, who conducted the newest study along with geologist and geochronologist Ian McDougall of Australian National University in Canberra, and anthropologist John Fleagle of New York state's Stony Brook University (a long-time proponent of the "Clovis-first in North America" theory), the age of modern humans can be pushed back so much further:

...[this] is significant because the cultural aspects of humanity in most cases appear much later in the record—only 50,000 years ago—which would mean 150,000 years of *Homo sapiens* without cultural stuff, such as evidence of eating fish, of harpoons, anything to do with music (flutes and that sort of thing), needles, even tools. This stuff all comes in very late, except for stone knife blades, which appeared between 50,000 and 200,000 years ago, depending on whom you believe.

Fleagle stressed the importance of the anomaly of such ancient and apparently "modern" humans and the seemingly late arrival of any activity even remotely resembling modern civilized activity, despite their "modern" appearance at such an early date:

"There is a huge debate in the archeological literature regarding the first appearance of modern aspects of behavior such as bone carving for religious reasons, or tools (harpoons and things), ornamentation (bead jewelry and such), drawn images, arrowheads. They only appear as a coherent package about 50,000 years ago, and the first modern humans that left Africa between 50,000 and 40,000 years ago seem to have had the full set. As modern human anatomy is documented at earlier and earlier sites, it becomes evident that there was a great time gap between the appearance of the modern skeleton and 'modern behavior.'"

The study of archaeology is rife with misinterpretation and dogmatic insistence on one view of history, that human beings have only been civilized for the briefest span of time, and that only accredited, "professional" archaeologists are able to reach conclusions that are worth consideration when it comes to our ancient past—and even then the professional label doesn't always help. Take for instance the entrance of human beings into North and South America, the "New World." Who was it to first make it into the New World, just how exactly did they do it, from where did they come and where did they arrive? Considering that the oldest "city" found in the New World, a huge complex spread across the 35 square mile Supe Valley in Peru, was flourishing nearly 5,000 years ago, that

"Caral, as the 150-acre complex of pyramids, plazas and residential buildings is known, was a thriving metropolis as Egypt's Great Pyramids were being built," according to a 2002 *National Geographic* report, something about the common views on how and where populations and their civilizations first took root and progressed around the world isn't ringing true.

"Topper is the oldest radiocarbon dated site in North America," said archaeologist Albert Goodyear of the University of South Carolina Institute of Archaeology and Anthropology, quoted by CNN (November 17, 2004). Obtaining radiocarbon dates of 50,000 years at a site of human habitation in South Carolina, along with stone tools shaped by human hands, as claimed by Goodyear to be the case, would be more than 25,000 years older than the still most commonly accepted date by academics and archaeologists

But the evidence that Clovis hunters weren't first to arrive just keeps growing and becoming harder to refute.

of between 13,000-13,500 years ago for the entrance of humans into North America—via the Bering Land Bridge when a narrow corridor was opened by the receding glaciers, and primitive hunters using Clovis points followed roaming herds of game animals into North America until they spread across both continents—thereby blowing the current paradigm clean out of the water. Though more scientists are gradually accepting earlier and earlier dates for the entry of human beings into the Americas, there is still a vocal, and influential, proportion who resist the new paradigm, the idea that people have been traveling and settling everywhere across the globe, by land and by sea, settling in both South and North America for far longer than a measly 13,500 years, as has been the prevailing theory since the late 1930s, when Clovis points were first discovered in New Mexico in 1936 and labeled irrefutable evidence of the oldest inhabitants of the Americas. But the evidence that Clovis hunters weren't first to arrive just keeps growing and becoming harder to refute.

> Yet so often when new, so-called fringe or radical theories are postulated, they are laughed at, denigrated by many of those who make a living promoting only the accepted dogma of the day-who seem to forget that what is considered "fringe science" today is often the "real" science of tomorrow.

Federico Solórzano, a professor of anthropology and paleontology in Guadalajara, Mexico, has made a habit of collecting old bones from the region around the largest lake in Mexico, Lake Chipala (or Chapala), and one day noticed something extremely unusual, "a mineral-darkened piece of brow ridge bone and a bit of jaw that didn't match any modern skulls," according to an October 3, 2004 report at CNEWS.

> But Solórzano found a perfect fit when he placed the brow against a model of the Old World's Tautavel Man—a member of a species, *Homo erectus*, that many believe was an ancestor of modern *Homo sapiens*.
> The catch: *Homo erectus* is believed to have died out 100,000 to 200,000 years ago—tens of thousands of years before men are believed to have reached the Americas.
> And archaeologists have never found a trace of *Homo erectus* in the Americas.

It's going to take more than a few teeny bits of "mineral-darkened bone" to change the minds of those holding to the Clovis First theory, but the evidence that they are not seeing the whole picture is piling up quickly. At Monte Verde, on the southernmost tip of Chile, there is a site that even mainstream, previously extremely skeptical academics have declared genuine, with established signs of human habitation, cooking fires and tools, dating back at least 10,000 years, with one tool even apparently "splattered with blood some 34,000 years ago," according to the aforementioned report by CNEWS, leading some to wonder how humans managed to migrate from the most northern climes to the most southern in so short a time. A second site at Monte Verde seems to date even earlier, to 14,000 years ago,

a good 500 years before any land bridge across the Bering Strait 8,800 miles (14,000 kilometers) had opened. There have been stone tools found and tentatively dated at 40,000 to 50,000 years old in Brazil. With these and many other examples, it's clear that no matter what we think we know about our past, there is still so much more for us to learn, and we're nowhere near any definitive answers. But there are still questions galore that need to be asked and should be asked. Yet so often when new, so-called fringe or radical theories are postulated, they are laughed at, denigrated by many of those who make a living promoting only the accepted dogma of the day—who seem to forget that what is considered "fringe science" today is often the "real" science of tomorrow.

THE "REAL" PAST

"In recent years, archaeology has turned a great deal of its attention to theoretical musings, to examining its most basic assumptions. Are there any 'facts'?" asks Paul G. Bahn in the foreword to his 1995 collection *100 Great Archaeological Discoveries*, which, writes Bahn, details 100 of the most exciting discoveries made by archaeology in the last few centuries. "Can one say anything meaningful and objective about the past when studying (highly incomplete) evidence in the present?" But just a page later, after noting that we cannot possibly really "know" human pre-history, Bahn then goes on to illustrate the way in which the mainstream often ostracizes and ridicules what Barbara Ann Clow, in her 2001 book *Catastrophobia* describes as the "new paradigm researchers," and who is herself definitely a "new paradigm researcher," by writing:

A further motivation for producing a book of this kind is to be found in the recent re-emergence of the von Dänikenesque (*Chariots of the Gods?*) "God is a Spaceman" message. We had hoped that books promoting the theory that anything impressive or bizarre in the archaeological record must be attributable to extraterrestrial visitors were a freak phenomenon of the 1970s, and that, having sold in tens of millions, they had faded away. Now, however, the success of the film *Stargate* (a science-fiction fantasy suggesting that ancient Egyptian civilization was produced by an extraterrestrial) and the unexpected appearance in the 1995 bestseller lists of *Fingerprints of the Gods* (a book arguing that the monuments of the ancient world were built 15,000 years ago by a race of super-beings whose lost civilization now

more than one civilization during those thousands upon thousands of years between the appearance of apparently "modern" humans and what appears to have been cataclysmic changes on the earth at the end of the last ice age about 12,000 or so years ago. Insulting too is Bahn's assertion that von Däniken's idea (and von Däniken is certainly not alone in his suspicions, or he wouldn't have sold those tens of millions of books Bahn almost jealously mentions) that extraterrestrials might have visited and interacted with people in some way on earth at some point in the mists of prehistory as being beyond consideration is merely condescending—with the vast number of stars and possibilities for different cultures having developed throughout the cosmos, who's to say one way or the other

The goal of this anthology is not to present definitive answers to all, or even to any of the myriad mysteries and puzzling questions contained herein. Rather, the goal is to inspire you, the readers, to think and question archaeological and historical orthodoxy on any number of levels by offering alternative possibilities to what are now the "acceptable" theories.

lies in ruins beneath Antarctica) shows that the monster was merely dormant; it can easily awake and devour an army of gullible readers. So we hope a book that sets out the "real past," the astonishing variety of human achievements, the end-products of our ancestors' sweat and ingenuity, will not only help explain what archaeologists do and why (albeit in a very incomplete fashion at that) but also go a little way towards counteracting this resurrected obsession without ascribing our heritage to fantasy super-humans.

Besides his telling readers first that there's no way to "know the real past," then decreeing what should be considered "real" when studying the past, Bahn is blatantly misrepresenting Hancock's theories put forth in *Fingerprints of the Gods*, in which Hancock never wrote anything about "super-humans," but rather examined the possibility that humanity had progressed into a fairly advanced maritime civilization or even

whether such radical theories are wrong or crazy merely because they're so "controversial" or "strange" or unacceptable to the status quo.

In *Underground!—The Disinformation Guide to Ancient Civilizations, Astonishing Archaeology and Hidden History*, my goal is to illustrate that the "monster"—of questioning the established paradigm, and positing radical new ideas and theories—is not dormant nor dying, that it is alive and well, and that mainstream guardians of the status quo resorting to haughty statements of assuredness and sincerity and scorn of the outsider cannot hide the fact that there are unanswered questions and mysteries that abound about our pre-history, questions that haven't come close to being answered by mainstream archaeology. The goal of this anthology is not to present definitive answers to all, or even to any of the myriad mysteries and puzzling questions contained herein. Rather, the goal is to inspire you, the readers, to think and question archaeological and historical orthodoxy on any number of levels by offering alternative possibilities to what are now the "acceptable" theories. Countless are the interpretations of the "extremely limited" evidence at hand, and many the mysteries and anomalies (too many even for a collection as wide and varied as *Underground* to include under one cover), so that any theory or postulation is as valid as the next, since we cannot, as Bahn noted, "really know" our pre-history, that span of 100,000 to 200,000 years (and quite possibly even much longer) when modern humans were walking the earth apparently waiting for that magic moment when civilization's trappings suddenly took root and sprang up across the globe in scattered and supposedly disconnected locations amongst people totally independent of contact between one another on their separate continents. But we can take a look at these mysteries and wonder, postulate, theorize and suggest conclusions from the evidence without having to worry about not being politically correct enough for those academics who insist that pre-history is a cut and dried story just missing a few minor details.

more all examine an incredible number of alternative views to those promoted by the current defenders of mainstream paradigms, who insist that only they can tell us what was happening during our "real" pre-historical stages. The contributors within these pages might not all agree with one another's theories and ideas, but they do prove again and again that we human beings have not necessarily "evolved" from most primitive to most advanced, but have risen and fallen in fits and starts, rising to great heights only to be wiped out by some disaster, like a cometary strike, a massive flood or simply human stupidity, or any number of other great disasters that could have befallen the more advanced and primitive civilizations alike.

CATASTROPHE

"Biblical stories, apocalyptic visions, ancient art and scientific data all seem to intersect at around 2350 B.C., when one or more catastrophic events wiped out several advanced societies in Europe, Asia and Africa," reports Robert Roy Britt at Space.com (November 13, 2001). While some

---

While some sort of strike by a large object from space has long been a theory to explain the sudden decline of many of the great early civilizations of the Ancient World, there was no "smoking gun" until the find by satellite imagery of a gargantuan, two-mile-wide crater left by the impact of an extra-planetary object, either a comet or a comet's "associated meteor storms" which slammed into what is now Iraq.

Contributors such as Graham Hancock (*Underworld, Talisman: Sacred Cities, Secret Faith* and *Sign and the Seal*), Colin Wilson (*The Occult, From Atlantis to the Sphinx* and *The Atlantis Blueprint*, with Rand Flem-Ath), Frank Joseph (*Survivors of Atlantis* and *The Destruction of Atlantis*), William R. Corliss (*The Sourcebook Project, Ancient Man—A Handbook of Puzzling Artifacts* and *Archeological Anomalies: Small Artifacts—Bone, Stone, Metal Artifacts, Footprints, High Technology*), George Erikson (*Atlantis In America*), Christopher Dunn (*The Giza Power Plant—Technologies of Ancient Egypt*) and many

sort of strike by a large object from space has long been a theory to explain the sudden decline of many of the great early civilizations of the ancient world, there was no "smoking gun" until the find by satellite imagery of a gargantuan, two-mile-wide crater left by the impact of an extra-planetary object, either a comet or a comet's "associated meteor storms" which slammed into what is now Iraq. "The Akkadian culture of Iraq, thought to be the world's first empire, collapsed," writes Britt. "The settlements of ancient Israel, gone. Mesopotamia, earth's original breadbasket, dust. Around the same time—a period called the early Bronze Age—apocalyptic writings appeared, fueling religious beliefs that persist today." The *Epic of Gilgamesh*, written at about this time, describes "the fire, brimstone and flood of possibly mythical events." Britt reports, "Omens predicting the Akkadian collapse preserve a record that 'many stars were falling from the sky.' The 'Curse of Akkad,' dated to about 2200 B.C., speaks of 'flaming potsherds raining from the sky.' Roughly 2,000 years later, the Jewish astronomer Rabbi bar Nachmani created what could be considered the first impact theory: That Noah's Flood was triggered by two 'stars' that fell from the sky. 'When God decided to bring about the Flood, He took two stars from Khima, threw them on earth, and brought about the Flood.'"

More ancient Indian myths and histories are explored in detail by N. S. Rajaram and John Anthony West (*Serpent in the Sky: The High Wisdom of Ancient Egypt*), who illustrate why we might benefit by paying more attention to these ancient and venerated tales from India, that tell of peoples in long ago and long-forgotten ages, and possibly foretell our current coming ages too. Records detailed in these "myths" point to not only a much longer span of history in which civilizations reached heights unimagined by mainstream archaeologists, and understood the stars and other sciences to degrees far beyond what they're commonly given credit for. The idea that there was an Aryan "invasion" of India is seriously questioned by Rajaram.

Did ancient navigators sail and map the world's oceans while conducting worldwide trade, including that of cocaine and nicotine, both New World substances that have turned up in hundreds of ancient Egyptian mummies?

If a worldwide calamity took place today, possibly leaving behind a few scattered remnants of more technologically advanced people to rebuild small communities and devices to try and forecast another disaster should it come, as survivors of ancient advanced civilizations perhaps did when building the now enigmatic and mysterious megalithic temples and observatories around the globe, but mainly left those primitive peoples who, as is still the case today, in early 2005, live in Stone Age conditions in the remotest parts of the world, to tell the tale of what came before, to describe for their children and grandchildren the vast modern cities and technologies that were utterly destroyed in fiery cataclysm or sunk beneath the waves, how would future scientists interpret their stories, which would eventually become their myths? Would they do any better a job then we have?

Michael A. Cremo (*Forbidden Archaeology* and *Hidden History of the Human Race*) questions not *when* humans became modern humans, but *what exactly* makes modern humans *human*—are we creatures of merely matter and chemical reactions, or do we have a soul as so many ancient texts describe? Dave Denton asks if Darwin's version of evolution is correct and if human beings are who and what we are by simple "happy accident"—or if there really is some kind of design to who and what we are. Dan Russell discusses the possible plants that originally brought *gnosis* to the ancients.

Professor Robert M. Schoch, author of *Voice of the Rocks* and *Voyages of the Pyramid Builders,* not only explains why he thinks the Great Sphinx on the Giza Plateau (and hence ancient Egyptian civilization itself) goes back much further in time than the current archaeological paradigm permits, but also describes, with co-author Robert S. McNally, why he thinks that worldwide pyramid building stems from a common source from deep in the mists of pre-history.

Michael Arbuthnot, founder of Team Atlantis, a group dedicated to searching out anomalous and mysterious archaeological reports and discoveries, explains why the Bering land crossing theory might not be entirely correct, and why it's more than reasonable to assume there very well could have been diffusion between the Old and New Worlds from both East and West pre-Columbus cultures, while Roy A. Decker points out numerous examples of anomalous finds that point to explorations of and even settlements in the New World by ancient cultures such as the Carthaginians, Romans, Phoenicians and many more.

Richard Nisbet takes us on an incredibly beautiful photographic tour of megalithic architecture in Peru that simultaneously inspires awe while defying explanation, while David Hatcher Childress, author of the *Lost Cities* series, and founder of the World Explorers Club, asks if anyone can seriously believe that the Incas really built Machu Picchu. I also interview intrepid explorer Greg Deyermenjian about his explorations in the hostile and uninviting jungles of Peru in search of the fabled lost city Paititi and the enigmatic "dots" that might or might not be undiscovered massive pyramids. William R. Corliss examines some anomalous toys and scientific equipment that should not exist according to the mainstream paradigm, while Erich von Däniken asks if ancient humans had devices with which they could fly.

Robert Merkin examines the results of two ancient cultures meeting and mixing—ancient Greece, cosmopolitan and liberal, and ancient Israel, theocratic and religiously intolerant—and the sometimes drastic and dramatic results of that meeting. George T. Sassoon questions whether the wandering Israelites were obtaining "mana" from a machine called the Ancient of Days.

Could the ancients sense and utilize earth's vibrations and energies, placing their menhirs and building their stone circles upon "sacred places" not only to mark the spots but to harness the energies in those locations? Did ancient navigators sail and map the world's oceans while conducting worldwide trade, including that of cocaine and nicotine, both New World substances that have turned up in hundreds of ancient Egyptian mummies? Did ancient peoples mirror the stars here on earth and, if so, for what purpose? Was the earth really visited by extraterrestrials and did they influence our development towards civilization? Did Atlantis and Lemuria exist, and if so, where did the survivors head when their homelands were destroyed? Did a series of cometary strikes wipe out more than one early, advanced civilization and was there more than one catastrophic event within human memory, including a cataclysm that became the worldwide flood myths of which Noah's is most famous? What were the Nazis looking for during their extensive archaeological adventures before and during WWII? What was the Holy Grail and why were so many looking for it? Do academics and archaeologists actively work to suppress new, controversial archaeological finds and ruin those who insist on reporting their anomalous results?

There is no way to fit every astonishing archaeological find, puzzling ancient civilization and theory about hidden history within this book—it would take thousands of pages. But it is hoped that by reading the many theories contained herein that you will find yourselves more curious to examine the many alternatives to what your professors and pundits say about our distant past and the awesome achievements of our so-called primitive ancestors, that you'll realize the mysteries about our ancient past and our ancestors are far greater and far deeper than you've ever imagined possible. It must be stressed that there are many divergent viewpoints expressed inside this book, and very few of the contributors know who the other contributors are—and as will be obvious as you read this book, they do not all agree with one another, which is representative of the archaeological world at large

SHIFTING OF THE PARADIGM HAPPENS ALL THE TIME

For two last glaring examples of exactly how little scientists and archaeologists really do know and how quickly viewpoints and paradigms and so-called "facts" about the ancient past and scientific knowledge can change, let's consider the following reports.

The first comes from the March 25, 2005 edition of the *Los Angeles Times*:

In bone blasted from Montana sandstone, fossil hunters for the first time have discovered the microscopic soft tissue of a *Tyrannosaurus rex*, preserved almost unaltered inside a bone since the dinosaur died 70 million years ago, scientists announced Thursday.

Scientists at North Carolina State University and at Montana State University's Museum of the Rockies in Bozeman found brownish oblong cells, elastic threads of veins and pliable dabs of red bone marrow in the core of a stout hind leg, the researchers reported in the journal *Science*.

The translucent vessels were so elastic that when one was stretched out and then released, it snapped back like a rubber band.

"To my knowledge, preservation to this extent has not been noted in dinosaurs before," said Mary H. Schweitzer, a paleontologist at North Carolina State University in Raleigh. "The tissues are still soft," said Schweitzer, who led the research team. "The microstructures that look like cells are preserved in every way."

Under a scanning electron microscope, these dinosaur tissues—minute remains of the mightiest of earth's ancient carnivores—were 'virtually identical' to those of a modern ostrich."

Even this stupendous discovery was the result of an accident, the minute tissue samples noticed only because workers had to break a precious dinosaur leg bone to get it onto a helicopter to move it from the excavation's remote location. These 70 million-year-old organic remains go against all prevailing knowledge about how fossils form, which say organic material could not last more than 100,000 years at maximum—but because science insisted this was impossible, how many other traces have been missed over the years, simply because scientists weren't looking for it, so set was their way of thinking? So once again the modern prevailing scientific paradigm is proven not only wrong, but quite dramatically so.

The second incredible, paradigm-shifting story comes from the April 2005 edition of *National Geographic* magazine.

In the large, cathedral-like Liang Bua ("meaning 'cool cave' in the local Manggarai language") cavern on the 220-mile Indonesian island of Flores, which sits between the mainland of Asia and Australia, scientists have found the remains of tiny human beings, labeled *Homo floresiensis*, standing only three feet tall as full grown adults, which they've affectionately called "hobbits." To get to the island involved crossing at least 15 miles of sea, until very recently considered impossible for primitive humans. In the 1950s and 1960s, an amateur archaeologist and part-time priest named Theodor Verhoeven found in the Sea Basin of Flores the remains of primitive stone implements near stegodont (a now extinct species of miniature elephant) fossils thought to be at least 750,000 years old. Since he knew that *Homo erectus* was known to have inhabited nearby Java 1.5 million years ago, Verhoeven "concluded that *erectus* somehow crossed the sea" separating the two islands, called the "Wallace Line," at a much earlier date. Verhoeven's hypothesis, since he was merely an amateur with no scholarly training in archaeology, was scoffed at and ridiculed by mainstream professional archaeologists. Then scientists in the 1990s dated the tools to be even older, nearly 840,000 years old. That meant that Verhoeven was correct about *erectus* making the crossing. But more fascinating to scientists were the newly discovered *floresiensis*. Still existing at the same time as modern human beings, inhabiting Flores from as long ago as 95,000 years ago to as recently as 13,000 years ago, these previously unknown people were descended from *erectus*, which arose nearly two million years ago. Although *floresiensis*' brains were tiny, "small even for a chimpanzee," they were making tools, hunting prey and living and cooperating in organized groups, and though much smaller in stature and brain size than their *erectus* ancestors, they were apparently much smarter. As *National Geographic* points out, this discovery of a different species of human being sharing the planet with modern *Homo sapiens* is mind boggling, but isn't the only mystery. How did these primitive people get to Flores so many thousands of years ago?

"Was *Homo erectus* a better mariner than anyone suspected, able to build rafts and plan voyages?" asks *National Geographic*, to which many of the contributors in this book would reply with a resounding "Yes!" There's more to this story than just this question of ancient navigation too. "And it raises a new and haunting question. Modern humans colonized Australia from mainland Asia about 50,000 years ago, populating Indonesia on their way. Did they and the hobbits ever meet?" There are no signs of modern humans on Flores until about 11,000 years ago, but it is possible that some *floresiensis* had managed to survive in remote areas of the island. "A clue may come from local folktales about half-size, hairy people with flat foreheads, stories the islanders tell even today. It's breathtaking to think that modern humans may still have a folk memory of sharing the planet with another species of human, like us but unfathomably different." So once again, it took nearly 20 years for mainstream archaeologists to catch up to the amateur's hypothesis, which turned out to be correct despite the nay-sayers who insisted it was impossible, that there was no way humans of any kind had reached Flores so many thousands of years earlier than accepted dogma gave them credit for. To their shame, these nay-sayers held up solid research by their insistent clinging to the established viewpoint, until finally the paradigm shifted and scientists became more open to yet another new, previously ridiculed idea.

Maybe you, dear reader, will make the next astonishing discovery, or unlock the secret code that deciphers some ancient language and gives us back more of our long lost history. Perhaps you will find that jungle-covered temple, sunken city or forgotten race that returns to us some of our ancient lost memories, our forgotten links to our ancestors who came before and left such enigmatic clues to their existence across the globe. Whether you are an armchair explorer or an active jungle trekker and trail blazer, an idealist or pragmatist, the following pages promise to take you on a wild ride through alternative landscapes, to visit and examine the remnants that our ancient ancestors left behind. So put on your bush hat and take out your compass, because we're about to head into parts unknown, where the maps are marked *Datos Insuficientes*, or "insufficient data," where monsters dwell, lost cities lie crumbling, buried under jungle and sand, and mind-boggling, enigmatic mysteries still lie awaiting discovery.

1

ORIGINS MYTHIC OR HISTORIC

Michael A. Cremo

HUMAN DEVOLUTION

MY BOOK *Forbidden Archeology*, co-authored with Richard L. Thompson, documents archaeological evidence for extreme human antiquity, consistent with the *Puranas*, the historical writings of ancient India. This evidence places a human presence so far back in time as to call into question the Darwinian account of human origins.

Kenneth Feder, in his review of *Forbidden Archeology*,[1] said:

> When you attempt to deconstruct a well-accepted paradigm, it is reasonable to expect that a new paradigm be suggested in its place. The authors of *Forbidden Archeology* do not do this, and I would like to suggest a reason for their neglect here. Wishing to appear entirely scientific, the authors hoped to avoid a detailed discussion of their own beliefs.

It is not true that my co-author and I were trying to avoid a detailed discussion of our own alternative account. Rather we were hoping to ignite just such a discussion. But some practical considerations compelled us to proceed in stages. In my introduction to *Forbidden Archeology*, I wrote: "Our research program led to results we did not anticipate, and hence a book much larger than originally envisioned." I was genuinely surprised at the massive number of cases of archaeological evidence for extreme human antiquity that turned up during my eight years of historical research. *Forbidden Archeology* went to press with over nine hundred pages. "Because of this," I wrote in the introduction, "we have not been able to develop in this volume our ideas about an alternative to current theories of human origins. We are therefore planning a second volume relating our extensive research results in this area to our Vedic source material." *Human Devolution: A Vedic Alternative to Darwin's Theory* is that second volume. The basic message is simple. We do not evolve up from matter, rather we devolve, or come down, from a level of pure consciousness, or spirit, if you like that word.

Although I am offering a Vedic alternative to Darwinism, I acknowledge that it is part of a larger family of spiritual alternatives to Darwinism rooted in various world religions, which I also honor and respect. Interestingly enough, many scholars are now willing to consider such alternatives to the Western scientific worldview as candidates for truth. For them, belief in such worldviews is no longer taboo. In *American Anthropologist*, Katherine P. Ewing said:

> To rule out the possibility of belief in another's reality is to encapsulate that reality and, thus, to impose implicitly the hegemony of one's own view of the world.[2]

The basic message is simple. We do not evolve up from matter, rather we devolve, or come down, from a level of pure consciousness, or spirit, if you like that word.

In the *Journal of Consciousness Studies*, William Barnard, in speaking about the world's wisdom traditions, advocated:

> . . . a scholarship that is willing and able to affirm that the metaphysical models . . . of these different spiritual traditions are serious contenders for truth, a scholarship that realizes that these religious worlds are not dead corpses that we can dissect and analyze at a safe distance, but rather are living, vital bodies of knowledge and practice that have the potential to change our taken-for-granted notions.[3]

I am asking that scientists and scholars approach in this spirit the Vedic perspective on human origins outlined in *Human Devolution*.

A PROCESS OF KNOWLEDGE FILTRATION

Before presenting an alternative to the Darwinian concept of human origins, it is reasonable to show that an alternative is really necessary. One thing that clearly demonstrates the need for an alternative is the archaeological evidence for extreme human antiquity. Such evidence actually exists, but it has been systematically eliminated from scientific discussion by a process of knowledge filtration. Archaeological evidence that contradicts the Darwinian theory of human evolution is often rejected for just that reason.

For example, in the Nineteenth Century, gold was discovered in California. To get it, miners dug tunnels into the sides of mountains, such as Table Mountain in Tuolumne County. Deep inside the tunnels, in deposits from the early Eocene Age (about 50 million years ago), miners found human bones and artifacts. The discoveries were carefully documented by Dr. J. D. Whitney, the chief government geologist of California, in his book *The Auriferous Gravels of the Sierra Nevada of California*, published by Harvard University in 1880.

But we do not hear very much about these discoveries today. In the *Smithsonian Institution Annual Report for 1898-1899*, anthropologist William Holmes said,

> Perhaps if Professor Whitney had fully appreciated the story of human evolution as it is understood today, he would have hesitated to announce the conclusions formulated, notwithstanding the imposing array of testimony with which he was confronted.[4]

In other words, if the facts did not fit the theory of human evolution, the facts had to be set aside, and that is exactly what happened.

Such bias continued into the Twentieth Century. In the 1970s, American archaeologists led by Cynthia Irwin Williams discovered stone tools at Hueyatlaco, near Puebla, Mexico. The stone tools were of advanced type, made only by humans like us. A team of geologists, from the United States Geological Survey and universities in the United States, came to Hueyatlaco to date the site. Among the geologists was Virginia Steen-McIntyre. To date the site, the team used four methods—uranium series dating on butchered animal bones found along with the tools, zircon fission track dating on volcanic layers above the tools, tephra hydration dating of volcanic crystals and standard stratigraphy.

The problem as I see it is much bigger than Hueyatlaco. It concerns the manipulation of scientific thought through the suppression of "enigmatic data," data that challenges the prevailing mode of thinking.

The four methods converged on an age of about 250,000 years for the site. The archeologists refused to consider this date. They could not believe that humans capable of making the

Hueyatlaco artifacts existed 250,000 years ago. In defense of the dates obtained by the geologists, Virginia Steen-McIntyre wrote in a letter (March 30, 1981) to Estella Leopold, associate editor of *Quaternary Research*:

> The problem as I see it is much bigger than Hueyatlaco. It concerns the manipulation of scientific thought through the suppression of "enigmatic data," data that challenges the prevailing mode of thinking. Hueyatlaco certainly does that! Not being an anthropologist, I didn't realize the full significance of our dates back in 1973, nor how deeply woven into our thought the current theory of human evolution has become. Our work at Hueyatlaco has been rejected by most archaeologists because it contradicts that theory, period.

This remains true today, not only for the California gold mine discoveries and the Hueyatlaco human artifacts, but also for hundreds of other discoveries documented in the scientific literature of the past 150 years.

REVISING THE DARWINIAN EVOLUTIONARY PICTURE

There is also fossil evidence showing that the current Darwinian picture of the evolution of nonhuman species is also in need of revision. Beginning in the 1940s, geologists and paleobotanists working with the Geological Survey of India explored the Salt Range Mountains in what is now Pakistan. They found, deep in salt mines, evidence for the existence of advanced flowering plants and insects in the early Cambrian periods, about 600 million years

later. To explain the evidence some geologists proposed that there must have been a massive overthrust, by which Eocene layers, about 50 million years old, were thrust under Cambrian layers, over 550 million years old. Others pointed out that there were no geological signs of such an overthrust. According to these scientists, the layers bearing the fossils of the advanced plants and insects were found in normal position, beneath strata containing trilobites, the characteristic fossil of the Cambrian. One of these scientists, E. R. Gee, a geologist working with the Geological Survey of India, proposed a novel solution to the problem. In the proceedings of the National Academy of Sciences of India for the year 1945, paleobotanist Birbal Sahni noted:

> Quite recently, an alternative explanation has been offered by Mr. Gee. *The suggestion is that the angiosperms, gymnosperms and insects of the Saline Series may represent a highly evolved Cambrian or Precambrian flora and fauna!* In other words, it is suggested that these plants and animals made their appearance in the Salt Range area several hundred million years earlier than they did anywhere else in the world. One would scarcely have believed that such an idea would be seriously put forward by any geologist today.[5]

The controversy was left unresolved. In the 1990s, petroleum geologists, unaware of the earlier controversy, restudied the area. They determined that the salt deposits below the Cambrian deposits containing trilobites were early Cambrian or Precambrian. In other words, they found no evidence of an overthrust. The salt deposits were in a natural position below the Cambrian deposits. This

---

Evidence from biochemistry, genetics and developmental biology also contradicts the Darwinian theory of human evolution... As far as evolution itself is concerned, it has not been demonstrated in any truly scientific way. It remains an article of faith.

---

ago. According to standard evolutionary ideas, no land plants or animals existed at that time. Flowering plants and insects are thought to have come into existence hundreds of millions of years

supports Gee's suggestion that the plant and insect remains in the salt deposits were evidence of an advanced fauna and flora existing in the early Cambrian. This evidence contradicts not only the Darwinian concept of the evolution of humans but of other species as well.

Evidence from biochemistry, genetics and developmental biology also contradicts the Darwinian theory of human evolution. Although the origin of life from chemicals is technically not part of the evolution theory, it has in practice become inseparably connected with it. Darwinists routinely assert that life arose from chemicals. But after decades of theorizing and experimenting, they are unable to say exactly which chemicals combined in exactly which way to form exactly which first living thing. As far as evolution itself is concerned, it has not been demonstrated in any truly scientific way. It remains an article of faith.

The modern evolutionary synthesis is based on genetics. Evolutionists posit a relationship between the genotype (genetic structure) of an organism and its phenotype (physical structure). They say that changes in the genotype result in changes in the phenotype, and by natural selection the changes in phenotype conferring better fitness in a particular environment accumulate in organisms. Evolutionists claim that this process can account for the appearance of new structural features in organisms. But on the level of microbiology, these structures appear to be irreducibly complex. Scientists have not been able to specify exactly how they have come about in step-by-step fashion. They have not been able to tell us exactly what genetic changes resulted in what phenotypic changes to produce particular complex features of organisms. This would require the specification of intermediate stages leading up to the complex structures we observe today. In his book *Darwin's Black Box*, biochemist Michael Behe says,

> In the past ten years, *Journal of Molecular Evolution* has published more than a thousand papers . . . There were zero papers discussing detailed models for intermediates in the development of complex biomolecular structures. This is not a peculiarity of *JME*. No papers are to be found that discuss detailed models for intermediates in the development of complex biomolecular structures, whether in the *Proceedings of the National Academy of Science, Nature, Science,* the *Journal of Molecular Biology* or, to my knowledge, any science journal.[6]

Attempts by scientists to use genetic evidence to demonstrate the time and place that anatomically modern humans have come into existence have resulted in embarrassing mistakes and contradictions. The first widely publicized reports that genetic evidence allowed scientists to say that all living humans arose from an African Eve who lived 200,000 years ago in Africa turned out to be fatally flawed. Researchers have attempted to correct the mistakes, but the results remain confused. Considering the complexities surrounding genetic data, some scientists have suggested that fossils remain the most reliable evidence for questions about human origins and antiquity. In an article in *American Anthropologist*, David W. Frayer and his co-authors said:

> Unlike genetic data derived from living humans, fossils can be used to test predictions of theories about the past without relying on a long list of assumptions about the neutrality of genetic markers, mutational rates, or other requirements necessary to retrodict the past from current genetic variation . . . genetic information, at best, provides a theory of how modern human origins *might have happened* if the assumptions used in interpreting the genetic data are correct.[7]

This means that the archaeological evidence for extreme human antiquity documented in *Forbidden Archeology* provides a much-needed check on the rampant speculations of genetic researchers. This evidence contradicts current Darwinian accounts of human origins.

A REAL NEED FOR AN ALTERNATIVE ACCOUNT—THE PARANORMAL

So evidence from archaeology, paleontology, biochemistry, genetics and developmental biology demonstrates a real need for an alternative to the current Darwinian account of human origins. The work of Alfred Russel Wallace, cofounder with Darwin of the theory of evolution by natural selection, provides an introduction to the alternative explanation. Wallace, along with other British scientists, such as Sir William Crookes, a prominent physicist and president of the Royal Society, conducted extensive experiments into the paranormal. These experiments and observations led Wallace to revise the worldview of science. Wallace concluded that the universe is populated with spirit beings. Some of the minor spirit beings, he proposed, are in contact with the human population on earth, usually through mediums. According to Wallace,

According to Wallace, the minor spirit beings, acting through mediums, were responsible for a variety of paranormal phenomena, including clairvoyance, miraculous healings, communications from the dead, apparitions, materializations of physical objects, levitations, etc. More powerful spirit beings may have played a role in the origin of species.

the minor spirit beings, acting through mediums, were responsible for a variety of paranormal phenomena, including clairvoyance, miraculous healings, communications from the dead, apparitions, materializations of physical objects, levitations, etc. More powerful spirit beings may have played a role in the origin of species.

Wallace wrote in his autobiography:

The majority of people to-day have been brought up in the belief that miracles, ghosts and the whole series of strange phenomena here described cannot exist; that they are contrary to the laws of nature; that they are the superstitions of a bygone age; and that therefore they are necessarily either impostures or delusions. There is no place in the fabric of their thought into which such facts can be fitted. When I first began this inquiry it was the same with myself. The facts did not fit into my then-existing fabric of thought. All my preconceptions, all my knowledge, all my belief in the supremacy of science and of natural law were against the possibility of such phenomena... [but] one by one, the facts were forced upon me without possibility of escape from them.[8]

For Wallace, all this had implications for human origins. In his book *Contributions to a Theory of Natural Selection*, Wallace concluded that

. . . a superior intelligence has guided the development of man in a definite direction, and for a special purpose, just as man guides the development of many animal and vegetable forms.[9]

NOT WHERE, BUT WHAT?

In *Human Devolution*, I propose that before we even ask the question, "Where did human beings come from?" we should first of all ask the question, "What is a human being?" Today most scientists believe that a human being is simply a combination of the ordinary chemical elements. This assumption limits the kinds of explanations that can be offered for human origins. I propose that it is more reasonable, based on available scientific evidence, to start with the assumption that a human being is composed of three separately existing substances: matter, mind and consciousness (or spirit). This assumption widens the circle of possible explanations.

Any scientific chain of reasoning begins with some initial assumptions that are not rigorously proved. Otherwise, one would get caught in an endless regression of proofs of assumptions, and proofs of proofs of assumptions. Initial assumptions must simply be reasonable on the basis of available evidence. And it can be shown that it is reasonable, on the basis of available evidence, to posit the existence of mind and consciousness, in addition to ordinary matter, as separate elements composing the human being.

And it can be shown that it is reasonable, on the basis of available evidence, to posit the existence of mind and consciousness, in addition to ordinary matter, as separate elements composing the human being.

I define mind as a subtle, but nevertheless material, energy associated with the human organism and capable of acting on ordinary matter in ways we cannot explain by our current laws of physics. Evidence for this mind element comes from scientific research into the phenomena called by some "paranormal" or "psychical." Here we are led into the hidden history of physics. Just as in archaeology, there has been in physics a tremendous amount of knowledge filtration. For example, every physics student learns about the work of Pierre and Marie Curie, the husband and wife team who both received Nobel Prizes for their work in discovering radium. The account is found in practically every introductory physics textbook. What we do not read in the textbooks is that the Curies were heavily involved in psychical research. They were part of a large group of prominent European scientists, including other Nobel Prize winners, who were jointly conducting research into the paranormal in Paris early in the Twentieth Century. For two years, the group studied the Italian medium Eusapia Palladino (sometimes spelled Paladino, or Paladina). Historian Anna Hurwic notes in her biography of Pierre Curie:

> He thought it possible to discover in spiritualism the source of an unknown energy that would reveal the secret of radioactivity . . . He saw the séances as scientific experiments, tried to monitor the different parameters, took detailed notes of every observation. He was really intrigued by Eusapia Paladino.[10]

new "séances" with Eusapia Paladina (we already had séances with her last summer). The result is that those phenomena exist for real, and I can't doubt it any more. It is unbelievable, but it is thus, and it is impossible to negate it after the séances that we had in conditions of perfect monitoring.

He concluded, "There is, according to me, a completely new domain of facts and physical states of space of which we have no idea."

To me, such results, and many more like them from the hidden history of physics, suggest that there is associated with the human organism a mind element that can act on ordinary matter in ways we cannot easily explain by our current physical laws. Such research continues today, although most scientists doing it are concentrating on microeffects rather than the macroeffects

There is, according to me, a completely new domain of facts and physical states of space of which we have no idea.

About some séances with Paladino, Pierre Curie wrote to physicist Georges Gouy in a letter dated July 24, 1905:

> We had at the Psychology Society a few séances with the medium Eusapia Paladina. It was very interesting, and truly those phenomena that we have witnessed seemed to us to not be some magical tricks—a table lifted four feet above the floor, movements of objects, feelings of hands that pinched you or caressed you, apparitions of light. All this in a room arranged by us, with a small number of spectators all well known and without the presence of a possible accomplice. The only possible cheating would be an extraordinary ability of the medium as a magician. But how to explain the different phenomena when we are holding her hands and legs, and the lighting of the room is sufficient to see everything going on?

On April 14, 1906, Pierre wrote to Gouy:

> We are working, M. Curie and me, to precisely dose the radium by its own emanations... We had a few

reported by Pierre Curie. For example, Robert Jahn, head of the engineering department at Princeton University, started to research the effects of mental attention on random number generators. A random number generator will normally generate a sequence of ones and zeros, with equal numbers of each. But Jahn, and his associates who have continued the research, found that subjects could mentally influence the random number generators to produce a statistically significant greater number of ones than zeros (or vice versa).

Evidence for a conscious self that can exist apart from mind and matter comes from medical reports of out of body experiences (OBEs). Dr. Michael Sabom, an American cardiologist, conducted extensive research into out of body experiences. He carefully interviewed heart attack patients who reported such experiences. He then compared their reports with their actual medical records. He found that a statistically significant number of the group gave correct accounts, consistent with the reports of their treatment. This is highly unusual, because according to standard medical opinion, the patients should have been completely unconscious.

Could the subjects have manufactured their correct reports from their previous knowledge of heart attack treatment procedures (for example, from watching television hospital dramas)? To control for this, Sabom selected a second group of heart attack patients who did not report OBEs. He asked them to imagine the medical treatment they had undergone while unconscious. None of them was able to give a correct report, and almost all of them made major mistakes. For Sabom, the results from the control group confirmed the genuineness of the OBE reports from the first group. In his book *Recollections of Death: A Medical Investigation*, Sabom asked,

> Could the mind which splits apart from the physical brain be, in essence, the "soul," which continues to exist after final bodily death, according to some religious doctrines?[11]

Sabom's results have been confirmed by further studies. For example, in February 2001, a team from the University of Southampton, in the United Kingdom, published a favorable study on OBEs in cardiac arrest patients in the journal *Resuscitation*.[12] The team was headed by Dr. Sam Parnia, a senior research fellow at the university. On February 16, 2001, a report published on the university's Web site said that the work of Dr. Parnia "suggests consciousness and the mind may continue to exist after the brain has ceased to function and the body is clinically dead."

Past life memories also give evidence for a conscious self that can exist apart from the body. Dr. Ian Stevenson, a psychiatrist at the University of Virginia medical school, has conducted extensive research into past life memories. Stevenson, and his associates, have focused on past life memories spontaneously reported by very young children. Stevenson prefers working with children because older persons might have the motives and means to construct elaborate past life accounts. His technique is to thoroughly interview the child subjects and thus obtain as many details as possible about the reported past life. Using this information, Stevenson and his associates then attempt to identify the person the child claims to have been in the past life. In hundreds of cases, they have been successful in making such identifications.

Having established that the human organism is composed of the elements matter, mind and consciousness (or spirit), it is natural to suppose that the cosmos is divided into regions, or levels, of matter, mind and consciousness, each inhabited by beings adapted to life there. First, there is a region of pure consciousness. Consciousness, as we experience it, is individual and personal. This suggests that the original source of conscious selves is also individual and personal. So in addition to the individual units of consciousness existing in the realm of pure consciousness, there is also an original conscious being that is their source. When the fractional conscious selves give up their connection with their source, they are placed in lower regions of the cosmos predominated by either the subtle material energy (mind) or the gross material energy (matter). There is thus a cosmic hierarchy of conscious beings, a fact

---

Using this information, Stevenson and his associates then attempt to identify the person the child claims to have been in the past life. In hundreds of cases, they have been successful in making such identifications.

---

attested to in the cosmologies of people from all parts of the world. These cosmologies share many features. They generally include an original God inhabiting a realm of pure consciousness, a subordinate creator god inhabiting a subtle material region of the cosmos along with many kinds of demigods and demigoddesses, an earthly realm inhabited by humans like us, and an underworld inhabited by ghosts and demons.

There are various categories of observational evidence for the existence of conscious beings at various levels of a cosmic hierarchy. The first category is evidence for survival of conscious selves formerly inhabiting bodies of terrestrial humans. This evidence takes the form of communications from surviving conscious human selves, apparitions of departed humans and possessions of living humans by spirits of departed humans. Cases where humans are possessed by beings with extraordinary powers provide evidence for superhuman creatures existing in extraterrestrial levels

> The human devolution concept posits the action of superior intelligences in the origin of the human form and the forms of other living things... There is evidence that such paranormal modification and production of biological forms actually occurs.

of the cosmic hierarchy. Marian apparitions and apparitions of angels also provide such evidence. Historical accounts of appearances of avatars provide evidence for the existence of a supreme conscious being. (Avatar is a Sanskrit word meaning "one who descends from above.") A final category of evidence comes from modern reports of unidentified flying objects and the "aliens" associated with them. Although the topic is very controversial, and involves a high degree of strangeness, there is a substantial quantity of credible reporting from government and military sources from several countries. The theory of purely mechanical UFOs breaks down under careful investigation, and the UFOs and aliens come to resemble beings inhabiting extraterrestrial levels of the world's traditional cosmologies.

SUPERIOR INTELLIGENCES

The human devolution concept posits the action of superior intelligences in the origin of the human form and the forms of other living things. This depends on the ability of consciousness to more or less directly influence the organization of matter in living things. There is evidence that such paranormal modification and production of biological forms actually occurs.

The first category of evidence comes from laboratory experiments in which human subjects are able to mentally influence the growth of microorganisms. For example, Beverly Rubik conducted laboratory research on "volitional effects of healers on a bacterial system" while director of the Institute for Frontier Sciences at Temple University in Philadelphia, Pennsylvania. She reported the results in a paper included in her book *Life at the Edge of Science*. The experiments were performed using the bacterium *Salmonella typhimurium*, a very well studied organism. The chief subject in the study was Olga Worrall, who had demonstrated positive abilities in other experiments. In one set of

experiments, culture dishes of bacteria were treated with antibiotics that inhibit the growth of the bacteria. Worrall attempted to influence the bacteria in one set of culture dishes to grow. Another set of culture dishes was kept aside as a control. Compared to the control group, the group of culture dishes mentally acted upon by Worrall all showed an increase in growth. In another set of experiments, bacteria were placed on slides in a solution of phenol sufficient to immobilize but not kill them. The slides of bacteria were then observed under a microscope. In her book, Rubik stated:

> Application of . . . phenol completely paralyzes the bacteria within 1 to 2 minutes. Worrall's treatment inhibited this effect . . . such that on the average up to 7% of the bacteria continued to swim after 12 minutes exposure to phenol compared to the control groups which were completely paralyzed in all cases.[13]

Distance healing by prayer and other miraculous cures provide another category of evidence for paranormal modification of biological form. In a study published in the *Annals of Internal Medicine*, John A. Astin and his co-authors found that "a growing body of evidence suggests an association between religious involvement and spirituality and positive health outcomes."[14] In support of their conclusion, the Astin group cited over 50 credible positive reports from a variety of scientific and medical journals. Even more striking examples of paranormal modification of biological form come from the reports of the Medical Bureau at Lourdes. Since the Nineteenth Century, the physicians of the Medical Bureau have carefully documented a series of miraculous cures, some involving the inexplicable regeneration of damaged tissues and organs.

Psychiatrist Ian Stevenson has conducted extensive investigations into birthmarks that appear to have some relationship with wounds a person experienced in a past life. Persons who died of gunshot wounds in previous lives sometimes display on their present bodies birthmarks of appropriate size at the positions of the entry and exit wounds. This suggests that when such a person's soul and mind enter the present body, they carry with them impressions that appropriately modify the body's biological form. Some medical investigators have documented cases of "maternal impressions." These occur when a pregnant woman is exposed to a striking event that causes a strong emotional impression. Somehow the

---

Psychiatrist Ian Stevenson has conducted extensive investigations into birthmarks that appear to have some relationship with wounds a person experienced in a past life. Persons who died of gunshot wounds in previous lives sometimes display on their present bodies birthmarks of appropriate size at the positions of the entry and exit wounds.

---

psychological impression leaves its mark on the embryo within her womb. For example, if a woman sees someone with an injured foot and then constantly remembers this, her child might be born with a malformed foot. In 1890, W. C. Dabney reviewed in *Cyclopaedia of the Diseases of Children* 69 reports published between 1853 and 1886 documenting a close correspondence between the mother's mental impression and the physical deformation in her child.[15]

Yet another category of evidence consists of reports by prominent scientists who have witnessed mediums produce human limbs or complete human bodies. A particularly striking case was reported by Alfred Russel Wallace, who, accompanied by others, saw a clergyman medium named Monk produce a complete human form. In his autobiography, Wallace described the event, which took place in an apartment in the Bloomsbury district of London:

> It was a bright summer afternoon, and everything happened in the full light of day. After a little conversation, Monk, who was dressed in the usual clerical black, appeared to go into a trance; then stood up a few feet in front of us, and after a little while pointed

to his side, saying, "Look." We saw there a faint white patch on his coat on the left side. This grew brighter, then seemed to flicker, and extend both upwards and downwards, till very gradually it formed a cloudy pillar extending from his shoulder to his feet and close to his body. Then he shifted himself a little sideways, the cloudy figure standing still, but appearing joined to him by a cloudy band at the height at which it had first begun to form. Then, after a few minutes more, Monk again said "Look," and passed his hand through the connecting band, severing it. He and the figure then moved away from each other till they were about five or six feet apart. The figure had now assumed the appearance of a thickly draped female form, with arms and hands just visible. Monk looked towards it and again said to us "Look," and then clapped his hands. On which the figure put out her hands, clapped them as he had done, and we all distinctly heard her clap following his, but fainter. The figure then moved slowly back to him, grew fainter and shorter, and was apparently absorbed into his body as it had grown out of it.[16]

A UNIVERSE BY DESIGN?

If the forms of humans and other living things are the result of intelligent manipulation of matter, this suggests that the universe itself may have been designed for human life and other forms of life. Modern cosmology provides evidence for this. Scientists have discovered that numbers representing fundamental physical constants and ratios of natural forces appear to be finely tuned for life to exist in our universe. Astronomer Sir Martin Rees considers six of these numbers to be especially significant. In his book *Just Six Numbers*, he says,

> I have highlighted these six because each plays a crucial and distinctive role in our universe, and together they determine how the universe evolves and what its internal potentialities are... These six numbers constitute a "recipe" for a universe. Moreover, the outcome is sensitive to their values: if any one of them were to be "untuned," there would be no stars and no life.[17]

There are three main explanations for the apparent fine-tuning of the physical constants and laws of nature: simple chance, many worlds and some intelligent providential creator. Many cosmologists admit that the odds against the fine-tuning are too extreme for a simple "one shot" chance to be offered as a credible scientific explanation. To avoid the conclusion of a providential designer, they have posited the existence of a practically unlimited number of universes, each with the values of fundamental constants and laws of nature adjusted in a different way. And we just happen to live in the one universe with everything adjusted correctly for the existence of human life. But these other universes have only a theoretical existence, and even if their existence could be physically demonstrated, one would further have to show that in these other universes the values of the fundamental constants and laws of nature are in fact different than those in our universe. The Vedic cosmology also speaks of many universes, but all of them are designed for life.

NOT UP, BUT DOWN

The human devolution concept, tying together the various lines of evidence mentioned above, suggests that we do not evolve up from matter; rather we devolve, or come down, from the level of pure consciousness. Originally, we are pure units of consciousness existing in harmonious connection with the supreme conscious being. When we give up our willing connection with that supreme conscious being, we descend to regions of the cosmos dominated by the subtle and gross material energies, mind and matter. Forgetful of our original position, we attempt to dominate and enjoy the subtle and gross material energies. For this purpose, we are provided with bodies made of the subtle and gross material energies. These bodies are vehicles for conscious selves. They are designed for existence within the realms of the subtle and gross material energies. Conscious selves who are less forgetful of their original natures receive bodies composed primarily of the subtle material energy. Those who are more forgetful receive bodies composed of both the subtle and gross material energies, with the gross material energies predominating.

The process by which a pure conscious self becomes covered by the energies of mind and matter is what I call devolution. But it is a process that can be reversed. There is a process of spiritual re-evolution, by which consciousness can be freed from its coverings and restored to its original pure state. Every genuine religious tradition in the world has some process of prayer, or meditation, or yoga to help us accomplish this. And that is the primary purpose of human life.

1. *Geoarchaeology*, v. 9, 1994. pp. 337-340.

2. *American Anthropologist*, v. 96, no. 3, 1994. p. 572.

3. *Journal of Consciousness Studies*, v. 1, no. 2, 1994. pp. 257-258.

4. *Smithsonian Institution Annual Report for 1898-1899*. p. 424.

5. *Proceedings of the National Academy of Sciences of India for the Year 1945*, Section B, v. 16. pp. Xlv-xlvi.

6. Michael J. Behe, *Darwin's Black Box*. New York: Simon & Schuster, 1998. p. 183.

7. *American Anthropologist*, v. 95, no. 11, 1993. p. 19.

8. Alfred Russel Wallace, *My Life: A Record of Events*. v. 2. London: Chapman & Hall, 1905. pp. 349-350.

9. Alfred Russel Wallace, *Contributions to a Theory of Natural Selection*. London: Macmillan and Co., 1870. p. 359.

10. Anna Hurwic, *Pierre Curie*. Paris: Flammarion, 1995. p. 247.

11. Michael B. Sabom, *Recollections of Death: A Medical Investigation*. London: Corgi, 1982. p. 183.

12. *Resuscitation*, v. 48. pp. 149-156.

13. Beverly Rubik, *Life at the Edge of Science*. Oakland: Institute for Frontier Science, 1996. pp. 108.

14. *Annals of Internal Medicine*, v. 132, no. 11, 2000. pp. 903-911.

15. John M. Keating, ed., *Cyclopaedia of the Diseases of Children*, v. 1. Philadelphia: J. B. Lippincott Co., 1890. pp. 191-216.

16. Alfred Russel Wallace, *My Life*. p. 330.

17. Sir Martin Rees, *Just Six Numbers*. New York: Basic, 1999. pp. 3-4.

John Anthony West

CONSIDER THE KALI YUGA

ACADEMICS ABHOR A MYSTERY the way nature abhors a vacuum, yet in nature there are no vacuums, while in academia there are many mysteries. In no field of science or scholarship are there more (or more glaring) mysteries than In Egyptology. Yet, at the same time, there is no field in which mysteries are more systematically denied.

Pick up a book, any book, written by a credentialed Egyptologist and you will find nothing but agreement—about everything but the most insignificant details. In his gloriously mis-titled volume *The Complete Pyramids*, Egyptologist Mark Lehner does not bother to even mention the controversies that have swirled (and continue to swirl) about these extraordinary structures for two centuries. Nothing; not a word. It's all been solved by the experts: The pyramids were built as tombs by powerful but deluded pharaohs desperately trying to ensure their own immortality (wink, wink, nod, nod). No matter that there is no evidence, not a shred, that these pyramids—of Giza and Dahshur—were ever used as tombs—and much cogent argument strongly suggesting they were not. The huge stones were hauled up ramps by gangs of laborers and just wafted into place with lapidary precision. No matter that engineers, quarrymen and masons, people accustomed to moving large blocks of stone around, insist it could not be done in this fashion, while toolmakers and machinists study the precision and cannot fathom how it could possibly have been achieved with hand tools. The acknowledged mathematical properties exhibited by the Great Pyramid are mere accidents of design, etc., etc.

No doubts ruffle the calm, smooth surface of Lake Consensus, that bottomless pool where the Church of Progress' (un)faithful go for solace, baptism and to pledge undying allegiance to the Great God Status Quo. (This act of ritual intellectual servitude is called, in the quaint terminology peculiar to their Church, "critical thinking" and sometimes even "reason.")

No matter that there is no evidence, not a shred, that these pyramids—of Giza and Dahshur—were ever used as tombs... and much cogent argument strongly suggesting they were not.

Nevertheless, despite the near-total control exercised by the Church of Progress over the educational systems of the world (especially the West), heresy abounds. A vast public simply refuses to acknowledge the infallibility of "experts" and, indeed, exults in their discomfiture when unwelcome facts breach the walls of their fortified ivory towers.

The Churchmen fume about "ignorance and superstition," they try to get laws passed outlawing what they don't approve of (e.g., astrology, homeopathy), organized debunkers pressure the media to display to the public only that which carries a Church imprimatur upon it. To no avail. While the mainstream press remains largely obedient to Church of Progress directives, television and Hollywood are less docile. They are interested in dollars, not dogma, and in their corporate amorality they will not hesitate to present heretical material. They don't even care if it is both good and true. In other words, as long as it brings in dollars and ratings, academic disapproval goes unheeded. The merely intellectual inquisition mounted by this Church lacks the effective dissuasive powers of the Church that preceded it—since it is no longer considered politically correct to subject heretics to physical torture. Churches are not what they used to be. And torture is now illegal—sort of.

short of fuel. But the Giza Plateau has no monopoly on Egyptian mysteries and some of these, unrecognized for what they are, have serious implications, not only for a better understanding of the ancient world, but also for contemplating and understanding the huge, slow processes of history and our own present position within that process.

The founding, establishment and breathtaking rise of dynastic Egypt (beginning around 3200 B.C.) is one such mystery. In the space of just a few centuries, Egypt (apparently) went from primitive Neolithic beginnings to a complex, utterly assured command of a spectrum of disciplines. In little more than a blink of the historical eye Egypt somehow developed a sophisticated hieroglyphic system, a complex theology and cosmology, astronomy and mathematics, advanced medicine and a total mastery of architectural construction and artistic form.

Egyptologists sometimes find this mildly remarkable, but by insisting that despite appearances to

But it is unarguably at its height very nearly at its beginning (a bit like starting off automobile technology with the first horseless carriage, proceeding in a couple of years to the 2005 Ferrari and then gradually working backward to the Model T Ford).

The moral: People are less stupid than our arrogant academics assume. However, people are also undiscriminating. Wildly speculative, even loony work gets accepted as readily, indeed, much more readily, than anything based upon rigorous scholarship. Erich von Däniken is far more popular than R. A. Schwaller de Lubicz (which is probably unavoidable except in some ideal world going through its Golden Age) and, of course, given the goals of Hollywood and TV, it is always the ratings-and-dollar producing mysteries/heresies/alternatives that get the bulk of screen and air time.

Regarding Egypt, most of the heretical attention is focused on the Pyramids of Giza and the Sphinx—which is legitimate enough since the establishment answers to virtually every question raised about these structures are so manifestly inadequate that the fires of controversy never run

the contrary (and the careful work of a dozen scholars categorically proving the contrary) Egypt was "really" still a "primitive" society, devoid of "real" science and "real" philosophy (and therefore "real" civilization). The world would have to wait for Greece for "real" civilization to begin. And therefore, however remarkable, the flowering of Egypt presents them with no mysteries and few problems. Though this is an evasion of great magnitude, it will not be my focus here.

If Egypt attained such unacknowledged heights so early, what then accounts for the long decline? Egyptologists have no problem responding to this question, and the conventional explanation, while not illogical, is unsatisfactory once you stop to question it.

Plotted on a graph, Egypt's history does not show a long, steady, gradual descent (from the glories of the Pyramid Age to Ptolemaic moral and artistic decadence and ultimately to the dissolution of Egypt as a coherent entity under Roman domination). Rather the graph shows a series of waves, malpractice. As long as Egypt is seen as a kind of magnificent (but primitive) dry run for Greece, leading eventually (by discrete but identifiable stages) to our current state of technological expertise,

---

One complementary (and attractive) theory claims that the use and abuse of black magic played a significant role. There can be no doubt that magic was rife in Egypt (and actually *still is*).

---

with troughs more or less equal, and each peak generally lower than the preceding peak—like waves on a beach after a storm. But it is unarguably at its height very nearly at its beginning (a bit like starting off automobile technology with the first horseless carriage, proceeding in a couple of years to the 2005 Ferrari and then gradually working backward to the Model T Ford).

The descent is ascribed to a combination of factors: Years of famine and failed Nile floods may have brought on the end of the Old Kingdom c. 2300 B.C. (An interesting alternative theory: It was an asteroid or comet strike, some sort of major but localized event that destroyed not just Egypt but much of the Middle East along with it.) Then, Egypt's early military superiority was eventually challenged and then defeated by the more warlike (read "progressive and advanced") civilizations of Anatolia (modern Turkey) then later Mesopotamia to the east and still later Greece to the north. Concurrently, her internal centralized political, artistic, moral and religious authority was eroding from within. One complementary (and attractive) theory claims that the use and abuse of black magic played a significant role. There can be no doubt that magic was rife in Egypt (and actually *still is*).

Civilizations come and go; we know that. Roman, Holy Roman (about as holy as Lehner's *Complete Pyramids* is complete), Mongol, Mogul, Dutch, French, British—all have established themselves, invariably by force, held sway briefly (by ancient Egyptian standards), weakened and ultimately fallen. So where is the alleged mystery?

It lies in recognizing the fallacy of the standard scholarly assessment of Egyptian sophistication—which is actually a deliberate exercise in academic

there is no problem and no mystery. But as soon as that assessment corresponds to reality then the problems arise and the mystery surfaces.

Through the work of Schwaller de Lubicz, Giorgio de Santillana and Herta von Dechend (*Hamlet's Mill*) and many other careful scholars over the past 50 years or so, it is now clear that not just ancient Egypt, but ancient civilizations worldwide, were far more sophisticated than the societies that followed them. In other words, for a few thousand years at least, what is called progress is actually regress. Indeed, it is only the major advances in our current cosmological and scientific understanding that have allowed these scholars to recognize that the ancients had this knowledge as well; and that it is written into their mythology and symbolism, their understanding of mathematics, their astronomy/astrology and their religion.

Since Egypt's Old Kingdom, up until very recently civilization has been going down, not up; simple as that.

We can follow that degenerative process physically in Egypt; it is written into the stones and it is unmistakable. The same tale is told in the mythologies and legends of virtually all other societies and civilizations the world over.

This is the ultimate heresy to our Church of Progress. Progress does not go in a straight line from primitive ancestors to smart old Us with our bobblehead dolls and weapons of mass destruction, our traffic jams and our polluted seas, skies and lands. There is another, and far more realistic way to view history. Plato talked about a cycle of Ages: the Golden, Silver, Bronze and Iron (or Dark) Ages; a cycle, a wave form—not a straight line. A similar understanding is reflected by virtually all other ancient accounts.

The best-known and by far the most elaborately developed of these systems is the Hindu, with its Yuga Cycle, which corresponds to the Platonic idea of four definable Ages (the Hindu Kali Yuga—our current Age—corresponds to Plato's Iron, or Dark Age). The problem with the Hindu version, however, is the time frame traditionally applied to the separate ages: hundreds of thousands, or even millions, of years.

No matter how wrong archaeologists may be in their chronologies or their interpretations of the ancients, it is hard to imagine that they can be *that* wrong! Yet not long ago, a little-known work on the Yuga Cycle came my way that fits the four stage cycle within the more manageable 20-odd thousand year cycle of the precession of the equinoxes. There can be no doubt that the ancients were fully aware of the phenomenon of precession, and that they regarded it as a matter of commanding importance, but it is difficult to see why. I now believe that integrating the Yuga cycle with precession may hold the key to understanding just why the ancients considered it so important, and also, just possibly, to figuring out with some accuracy just where we stand within that cycle.

OF MYTH AND MEANING

Microsoft Word's in-PC thesaurus lists two meanings or synonyms for "myth": Legend and Falsehood. Interestingly, the synonyms for "legend" do not include "falsehood," while the synonyms for "falsehood" do not include "legend." Nevertheless, in common usage, both definitions are used, often indiscriminately, and in some cases both actually apply. Utterances made by George W. Bush, for example, achieve legendary status instantly, and in most cases they are also falsehoods. But in dealing with the myths of the ancients, it is wise to exercise caution before summarily equating a legend with a falsehood, no matter that it generally does not correspond to our modern manner of communicating fact. The ancients, obviously, did not think of their legends as falsehoods. That negative meaning is a contemporary judgment, promulgated by Victorian proto-anthropologists of the Nineteenth Century and turned into dogma by Church of Progress devotees in the Twentieth. (James Frazier's exhaustive *Golden Bough* was probably the most influential single work of the genre.)

Though still prevalent, especially in academia, that Victorian assessment has been under attack almost since its beginning. It is now becoming clear that these strange, seemingly haphazard and irrational ancient tales contain within them forgotten history and profound psychology, but also, amazingly, astronomy, cosmology, physics, genetics and an understanding of the workings of the universe so advanced and comprehensive that it is only the most recent advances in our own sciences that allow us to begin to understand

> *It is now becoming clear that these strange, seemingly haphazard and irrational ancient tales contain within them forgotten history and profound psychology, but also, amazingly, astronomy, cosmology, physics, genetics and an understanding of the workings of the universe...*

what knowledge was available in the very distant past—at a time when, according to our "experts," there was no civilization to speak of at all.

In short, it is time for a total re-evaluation of the knowledge of the ancients. Not only did they know more than we thought they knew; it is also very possible they had knowledge we do not yet have, and that might be extremely useful, even crucial for us to acquire.

An Egyptian myth may be one place to start looking.

INTRODUCING SEKHMET

In ancient Egyptian mythology, Sekhmet, the goddess portrayed as a woman with the head of a lioness, is associated with vengeance, warfare and also, curiously enough, with healing; but healing by fire, or purgation. Esoterically, she represents the female aspect of the fire (initiating) principle. Ptah (architect of heaven and earth) creates the universe with "words" furnished by Djehuti (cosmic wisdom) but it is Sekhmet, Ptah's female consort, who actually gets the work done. Her name "Sekhem" means "power"; the addition of the feminine suffix, "t" makes it "feminine power."

In one well-known myth, Re, the sun (creative principle) is old and tired; fractious, disobedient mankind no longer pays him homage. So Sekhmet is dispatched by the gods to punish humanity and

---

By day she massacres; by night she returns to gorge herself on the blood-covered fields — until a point is reached when it becomes clear that unless checked, she will soon destroy mankind altogether, and she is not distinguishing between those few still obedient to the gods and the scornful and skeptical majority.

---

bring it back into line. She proceeds to carry out this task with the gleeful fury proper to her lioness nature. By day she massacres; by night she returns to gorge herself on the blood-covered fields—until a point is reached when it becomes clear that unless checked, she will soon destroy mankind altogether, and she is not distinguishing between those few still obedient to the gods and the scornful and skeptical majority. (This attitude will show up periodically throughout subsequent history, most memorably perhaps at the Siege of Bezier, during the Albigensian Crusades, when the general in charge of the siege, and about to storm the walls, asked the Papal Legate, Arnald-Amalric, Abbot of Citeaux, how he was to distinguish between the true believers in the town so that they might be spared, and the targeted heretics who, needless to say, deserved to die. The Abbot is reputed to have said: "Kill them all. God will recognize his own.")

In any event, in the Egyptian myth, the gods prove more merciful. For reasons difficult to ascertain, they decide mankind has been punished enough and something has to be done to stop Sekhmet before she annihilates the race entirely. A trick is played upon Sekhmet, instigated by the wise Djehuti. While Sekhmet sleeps, the blood covering the fields is replaced by wine. And when Sekhmet wakes and visits the fields to gorge herself as is her wont, the wine has its intended effect. Sekhmet falls into a drunken stupor, goes to sleep, and wakes up transformed into the beneficent Hathor, provider of cosmic nourishment and associated with sexuality, song, dance and the cycles of time. There the Egyptian story stops, but

extrapolating, it is probably safe to suppose that the mythmakers assume that at this point, with Sekhmet pacified, mankind regroups and proceeds along its not-so-merry way.

CONSIDER THE KALI YUGA

In the first part of this article, I left off with a brief discussion of the Vedic/Hindu doctrine of the Yugas, the idea that history follows a cycle, corresponding to the Platonic doctrine of Aeons or ages (Golden, Silver, Bronze and Iron, or "Dark" Ages). Most Hindu accounts assign improbably long time periods to each of these ages, but one relatively modern thinker, Sri Yukteswar, the guru of the influential Twentieth Century yogi, Paramahansa Yogananda, wrote that originally, the Yuga cycle was supposed to correspond to a precessional cycle (Yukteswar allots approximately 24,000 years to this cycle, modern astronomy puts it close to 26,000 years but variable within narrow limits, Plato gives a precise numerologically interesting canonical number of 25,920 years—six times six times six times 12). Moreover, in the standard accounts, the Kali Yuga (or Dark Age) is followed immediately by a new Golden Age. This does not make sense; the end of winter is not followed immediately by summer.

Now in Hindu mythology, Kali the Destroyer is equivalent to the Egyptian Sekhmet, and it may be that the Sekhmet myth has legitimate astronomical/astrological significance.

An aging or dying god is a feature of many ancient myths and legends and it is the mythic way of signaling the end of an astronomical cycle of some sort (cf. *Hamlet's Mill*). Unfortunately, our standard view of history is not only very wrong, it is also very short. We have a good idea of the Piscean Age of the last 2,000 years, a much less comprehensive picture of the Arian Age preceding it (c. 2000-0 B.C.), but in the Taurean Age (4000-2000 B.C.), except for Egypt, we enter a realm of myth and legend with relatively little factual material to base sound interpretations upon. The further back we go, the mistier it gets.

The English writer Samuel Butler once remarked that "Analogy may be misleading but it is the least misleading thing we have."

So, to appreciate our own position within the grand Yuga cycle, analogy may help.

We are familiar with the cycle of night and day. But imagine a sentient creature that lives for just a minute. If that minute falls at midnight, then our Minute Man can have absolutely no idea of what that minute of life might be like at high noon, especially if it's raining.

Now move up a step in the cyclical hierarchy to the seasons, and imagine a sentient creature that lives for just a day. If that day falls in February and it's still raining (both Minute Man and Day Man live in Wales) then he can have no idea of what a day would be like in mid-June—unless, of course, legends and myths have somehow survived the course of the year, in which case they would be so inconsistent with their own life experience that they might well dismiss them as falsehoods, i.e. myths.

Now move up to ourselves, within the precessional cycle. Allowing an ideal 100 year life span, if that 100 years corresponds to a rainy midnight minute or equally rainy February day in Wales then we can have no experiential possibility of understanding what a sunny 100 years in June in Cosmic California might be like, much less that life might actually be much prolonged under such circumstances—as so many myths and legends assert. There can be no doubt that the ancients understood precession, and equally no doubt that they considered it of paramount importance. And maybe that is why—because it enabled them (at least in principle) to live in harmony with the dictates of their era, or so the legends say.

So if there is validity to the concept of the Yuga cycle, just where would we stand? Not in June in Cosmic California, that is for sure! Scan the front page of any daily newspaper in the world and it looks like mid-January: war, terrorism, murder, rape, robbery, scams, famine and disease—chaos everywhere. The greatest military and economic power in recorded history has as its leader an inarticulate, illiterate dunce, himself under the control of a tribe of corporate cannibals. The entire planet is threatened by a gamut of potentially terminal environmental, ecological, medical and military disasters. The institutionalized religions of both East and West (at their best but stunted, pale offshoots of much more robust and earlier root stocks) are degraded and degenerate. Education everywhere is controlled by the priesthood of the Church of Progress, forcibly proselytizing its psychotic and spurious doctrine of meaninglessness, accident and despair.

A good case could be made that it's mid-Kali Yuga, and Sekhmet has again been summoned and is already exercising her bloody trade. But this could be a misperception. Certainly a cosmic blizzard is blowing, of that there can be no doubt, yet maybe it's March in the cycle—and even though it doesn't look that way, spring is on the way. Under the snow, the seeds of spring are germinating. The substantial minority of us who aren't trapped in hopeless third world conditions know that at the very least we're not back in the post-Roman Dark Ages—which were pretty dark everywhere around the planet as far as we can determine.

OPPOSITION TO THE CHURCH OF PROGRESS MOUNTS: A POSITIVE SIGN

There is one potentially major positive sign that goes generally unrecognized. The past three centuries have seen a prodigious flowering of creative energy, most of it undeniably dedicated to destruction and frivolity (even the most nauseating TV commercial is the result of an extraordinary expenditure of creative and technical expertise).

While imbeciles insist upon calling this progress, in its standard manifestation it is little more than shiny barbarism.

Maybe, just maybe, Sekhmet is just growling and flexing her claws and despite all appearances to contrary, there is still some wiggle room.

Even so, that standard is not necessarily a *fait accompli*, an unalterable condition. The outpouring of creative energy is a fact. In itself it is neutral in principle. Directed consciously and constructively, things could change, everywhere—and in a hurry. When ideas change, everything changes. Of course, getting the ideas to change is another matter altogether. Nevertheless, it *could* happen. Even before it's too late. If only...

Maybe, just maybe, Sekhmet is just growling and flexing her claws, and despite all appearances to contrary, there is still some wiggle room.

It's a thought.

N. S. Rajaram

OCEAN ORIGINS OF

INDIAN CIVILIZATION

SUMMARY

The contradictions between existing theories about ancient Indian (and world) history and the data they claim to interpret are so wide-ranging, that they call for a fundamental re-examination of assumptions and methods. The main point of the present essay is that the entire enterprise of historical writing is flawed, and nothing less than a radical recasting is called for. This should begin with an alternative formulation based on primary sources from the natural sciences, archaeology and ancient literature.

The contradictions between existing theories about ancient Indian (and world) history and the data they claim to interpret are so wide-ranging, that they call for a fundamental re-examination of assumptions and methods.

Further, the present essay recognizes that maritime imagery is never far away from ancient works like the *Vedas* and the *Puranas*. It notes also some recent findings in natural history and genetics, which suggest that any study of the origins of the Vedic civilization needs to take into account the far-reaching ecological impact of the end of the last ice age and its brief return during the Younger Dryas. The various linguistic theories that seek to place the Vedic origins in Eurasia or Europe run into too many contradictions and use too short a time horizon to account for the momentous ecological changes recorded both in the natural and in the man-made environment.

INTRODUCTION: BACK TO NATURE

Going back for untold millennia, India and East and Southeast Asia have been bound by ties of geography, climate and ecology. This is reflected in the natural history as well as in the human imprint in the region. The former include ecology, climate, flora and fauna; the latter is reflected in the region's history, culture and religious beliefs. Chinese, Malays, Thais, Indonesians and every other people, with the possible exception of the people of the Philippines whose native traditions suffered severe disruption under the centuries-long rule of Catholic Spain, have left abundant records that attest to this closeness.

These millennia-long ties were interrupted during the three centuries of European colonialism in the region. It led to the imposition on the region of a version of history and culture divorced from its natural environment and human activities. In the case of India this resulted in a rewriting of her history and culture, with the colonial rulers postulating sources and origins in the west and the northwest, closer to their own. As part of this colonial reorientation, beginning at the end of the

creation, largely the result of historical accident, has come to acquire a life of its own. Being a theory that is based on no evidence, it is impossible to refute it; its advocates offer no new evidence, but

The main result of this has been a turning away from the natural and human links that bind the region's past, and the creation of a historical and anthropological milieu made up of theories rooted in Eurasia and Europe.

Eighteenth Century and continuing to the present, historical theories have sought a Eurasian and even European source for the origin and growth of ancient civilization in India, especially the Vedic language and literature.

The main result of this has been a turning away from the natural and human links that bind the region's past, and the creation of a historical and anthropological milieu made up of theories rooted in Eurasia and Europe. Inevitably, these have given rise to contradictions between theory-based conclusions and hard evidence, that only now, more than 50 years after India gained independence, are beginning to receive notice. The contradictions are not confined to details of interpretation, but as we shall soon see, pervade every aspect of literature, archaeology and even the natural environment.

These contradictions between theories and data suggest that the methodology used by scholars for the better part of two centuries must have been seriously flawed. Before we look at the contradictions and suggest an alternative approach, it is useful to take a brief look at the version of history and historiography—an offshoot of India's recent colonial past—that has given rise to them.

BACKGROUND: A NON-EXISTENT PROBLEM

The specter of the famous "Aryan Invasion Theory" (AIT) haunts any discussion of ancient South Asian (and Eurasian) history. It is regrettable, but also inescapable, that any re-examination of ancient history must begin with a critical examination of the background to the theory, which has no facts of any kind to support it. What was a political

simply reiterate their claims. In such a situation, it is best to look simply at the facts.

Those unfamiliar with the so-called "Aryan problem," especially as it relates to ancient India, can be assured that they have little to lose by their ignorance. Here are the bare essentials. A school of linguists and some historians, mainly in the Nineteenth Century, but still with some adherents, asserted that the Indian civilization, deriving from the Vedic literature, of which the *Rigveda* is the most important, owes its existence to a race of Eurasian invaders known as the Aryans. These nomads, whose arrival from the northwest was dated to 1500 B.C.E., were supposed to have imposed their language and culture on the natives who they defeated and dominated. This, in essence, is the Aryan Invasion Theory, though it has as many turns and twists as there are academics that have a stake in its survival.[1]

Since many history books and encyclopedias that mention this theory as fact cite the Vedic literature and language as support, it is worth placing things in perspective by looking at the primary records, unencumbered by later encrustations. What we then see is that the so-called Aryan problem is an artifact of shoddy scholarship.

In the whole of the *Rigveda*, consisting of ten books with more than 1,000 hymns, the word "Arya" appears fewer than 40 times. It may occur as many times in a single page of a modern European work like, for example, in Hitler's *Mein Kampf*. As a result, any modern book or even a discussion on the "Aryan problem" is likely to be a commentary on the voluminous Nineteenth and Twentieth Century European literature on the Aryans having little or no relevance to ancient

India. This is simply a matter of sources: Not only the *Rigveda*, but also the whole body of ancient literature that followed it have precious little to say about Aryans and Aryanism. It was simply an honorific, which the ancient Sanskrit lexicon known as the *Amarakosha* identifies as one of the synonyms for honorable or decent conduct. There is no reference to any "Aryan" type.

A remarkable aspect of this vast "Aryanology" is that after two hundred years and at least as many books on the subject, scholars are still not clear about the Aryan identity. At first they were supposed to be a race distinguished by some physical traits, but ancient texts know nothing of it. Scientists too have no use for the "Aryan race." As far back as 1939, Julian Huxley, one of the great biologists of the Twentieth Century, dismissed it as part of "political and propagandist" literature. Recently, there have been attempts to revive racial arguments in the name of genome research, but eminent geneticists like L. Cavalli-Sforza and Stephen Oppenheimer have rejected it. The M17 genetic marker, which is supposed to distinguish the "Caucasian" type (politically correct for Aryan), occurs with the highest frequency and diversity in India, showing that among its carriers the Indian population is the oldest. (This has ramifications for the exodus of modern humans from Africa and their eventual spread worldwide, more of which later.)

> All this means that the "Aryan problem" is a non-problem—little more than an aberration of historiography. It has been kept alive by a school of historians with careers and reputations at stake.

It is a similar situation with the Aryans as a linguistic group, which is what some scholars, sensitive to the disrepute that race theories have fallen into are proposing. The vast body of Indian literature on linguistics, the richest in the world going back at least to Yaska and Panini, knows nothing of any Aryan language. The German-born Friedrich Max Müller made his celebrated switch from Aryan race to Aryan language only to save his career in England following German unification, when the British began to see Germany as a major threat. The "Aryan nation" was the battle cry of German nationalists. It was German nationalists, not ancient Indians who were obsessed with their Aryan ancestry.

> What matters is the record of the people who lived in India and created her unique civilizations, not what labels they were given by scholars thousands of years later.

All this means that the "Aryan problem" is a non-problem—little more than an aberration of historiography. It has been kept alive by a school of historians with careers and reputations at stake. According to its advocates, the Vedic language and literature are of non-Indian origin. In the words of Romila Thapar, a prominent advocate of the non-indigenous origin theory:[2] "The evidence for the importation of the earliest form of the language [Vedic] can hardly be denied." In other words, Aryans are needed because without them there can be no Aryan invasion (or migration). The invasion is the tail that wags the Aryan dog.

What is attempted here is to look at the natural history and the human response in India and their relationship to the regions surrounding, without resort to labels or stereotypes. This will allow us to get away from the intellectual quagmire of the past two centuries and begin examining the sources afresh. What matters is the record of the people who lived in India and created her unique civilizations, not what labels they were given by scholars thousands of years later.

HISTORIOGRAPHY: MISMATCHES

In the light of this near pathological situation, it is not surprising that the historical picture based on the Aryan Invasion Theories (AIT) should be riddled with contradictions. Here are some of the more glaring ones:

1. History books speak of an "Aryan invasion" from Eurasia or even Europe, but there is no archaeological record of any invasion and/or massive migration from Eurasia in the Vedic period. If anything we find traces of movements in the opposite direction—to West Asia and even Europe.

2. The geography described in the *Rigveda*, including river systems, corresponds to North India in the Fourth Millennium B.C.E. and earlier, and not Europe or Eurasia.

3. The flora and fauna described in the Vedic literature, especially those found in the sacred symbols, are tropical and subtropical varieties and not from the temperate climate or the steppes.

4. The climate described in the ancient literature and the religious practices they gave rise to (like the *caturmasya*) correspond to what is found in North India.

This kind of mismatch between theory and evidence is not limited to the natural environment. In quantitative terms also, there is a huge time gap—exceeding 1,000 years—between the dates assigned to significant features and what we actually find. These include:

1. Indian writing is supposed to be based on borrowings from the Phoenicians or derived from Aramaic, but the Indus (Harappan) writing is more than a thousand years older than the oldest Phoenician examples known.

2. Naturalistic art with realistic depictions is supposed to have evolved in India under Greek influence, but we find superb realistic depictions in Harappan remains in the Third Millennium B.C. To paraphrase John Marshall: "The Indus artist anticipated the Greek artist by more than 2,000 years."[3]

3. Indian astronomy was supposedly borrowed from the Greeks, but the *Vedanga Jyotisha* cannot be dated later than the Fourteenth Century B.C.E. The title itself, *Vedanga*, indicates it is later than the *Vedas*, so the astronomical references in the *Vedas* must be older still. In addition, Harappan archaeology of the Third Millennium B.C.E. belongs astronomically to the "Krittika period" (vernal equinox in Krittika or the Pleiades in Taurus). This finds mention in the later Vedic literature. It places the Harappan civilization later than the *Rigveda* and not before as claimed by historians.[4]

4. Migrations: The major migration or invasion—the famous or infamous Aryan invasion—is supposed to have taken place after 2000 B.C., but the available genetic evidence shows that the people of India have lived where they are for well over 50,000 years.

The last point is worth a comment. While historians have been trying to link the Indian people (and the flora and fauna) to sources in the Eurasian steppes and even Europe, recent biological studies show that their links to monsoon Asia are much closer and also older. This is hardly surprising considering that India and Southeast Asia constitute a single ecological and climatic zone. Through much of the last ice age, 12,000 years ago and earlier, sea level was 120 meters (400 feet) lower than today, and passage throughout the region was much easier.

This is demonstrably false: Horses have existed in India for more than a million years.

One of the more glaring manifestations of these contradictions is the oft-repeated claim that horses were unknown in India until they were brought by the invading Aryans. (This is generally stated as: "No horse at Harappa," meaning that Harappan or Indus Valley archaeology dating to the Third Millennium B.C.E. has revealed no horse remains.) This is demonstrably false: Horses have existed in India for more than a million years. Biologically, also, the 17-ribbed Indian horse (described in the *Rigveda*) is closer to the prehistoric *Equus Sivalensis* ("Siwalik Horse") found in the Himalayan foothills than the biologically distinct 18-ribbed Central Asiatic variety. In addition, archaeologists going back to John Marshall have recorded horse remains at Harappan sites. (Marshall gives measurements of what he calls the "Mohenjo-Daro horse.")

HUMAN HISTORY AS PART OF NATURAL HISTORY

It is clear that ancient history is in need of a serious re-examination—both its chronology and interpretation of the sources that define the region. Three fundamental tasks suggest themselves: establishing independent chronological markers that connect literary accounts and datable physical features, determining the identity of the people of India on scientific grounds (independent of historical and/or linguistic theories); and accounting for the impact of environmental and ecological changes in the past 10,000 years and more, and the human imprint that those changes have left.

The present essay will have little to say on the chronological question or archaeology, focusing on recent findings relating to the natural environment and the human events, especially the transition to the Vedic Age. In particular, it will emphasize the important role played by the fitful ending of the last ice age as well as its successor known as the Younger Dryas. This cataclysmic change in climate and environment resulted in rising sea levels leading to the submersion of coastal settlements, which in turn led to the landward expansion made possible by the release of the glacier-fed rivers that have nourished North India for well nigh 10,000 years.

The main point of the present article is the following: *The origins of Indian civilization are to be found not in the Eurasian steppes 4-5,000 years ago but in the maritime centers that dotted the coasts significantly more than 10,000 years ago.* The Vedic civilization—its language, literature and culture—was probably one of several that evolved in the region. It coexisted and interacted with other cultures. These were the ones affected most by the cataclysmic changes that accompanied the ending of the ice age and its brief return (known as the Younger Dryas), followed by its final retreat. Taking note of this, history is best viewed as the record of the human response to the environment: In other words, human history is an extension of natural history.

RIGVEDA POINTS TO MARITIME SOURCES

Indian literature leaves little doubt that its poets looked to the oceans as their original home, and not to the Eurasian steppes. Upon examining the *Rigveda*, one is struck by its pervasive oceanic imagery. It is not the poetry of a people from the land-locked steppes, but of a people intimately familiar with the sea and seafaring. A few examples, including the famous creation hymn from the *Rigveda*, should suffice to show that the Vedic poets saw the world, even the creation itself, in oceanic terms. In David Frawley's translation:

> **Upon examining the *Rigveda*, one is struck by its pervasive oceanic imagery. It is not the poetry of a people from the land-locked steppes but of a people intimately familiar with the sea and seafaring.**

In the beginning, there was darkness hidden in darkness,
all this universe was an unillumined sea.
The Gods stood together in the sea. Then as dancers they generated a swirl of dust.
When, like ascetics, the Gods overflowed the world, then from hidden in the ocean they brought forth the Sun.
The creative Sun upheld the Earth with lines of force. He strengthened the Heaven where there was no support.
As a powerful horse he drew out the atmosphere. He bound fast the ocean in the boundless realm.
Thence came the world and the upper region, thence Heaven and Earth were extended.

These are not isolated passages, but selections from more than a hundred references found in the *Rigveda*. Here is another example showing the maritime knowledge of the *Rigvedic* poets (author's translation):

He who knows the path of the birds flying in the sky, He knows the course of the ocean-going ships.

In David Frawley's words:

Woven into the entire fabric of the *Vedas*, from beginning to end, is an oceanic symbolism. The *Rigveda* is a product of a maritime culture that undertook travel, trade and colonization by sea. The ocean was known in the earliest period. If the Vedic people did migrate into India, it is likely that at least some of them came by sea or from a land that bordered on the ocean.[5]

As we shall see later, the *Puranas*, the other great body of literature from ancient India, also carries oceanic symbolism, though of a different kind. *What is remarkable in all this is that while some scholars have tried to impose Eurasian origins to ancient Indian civilization, their primary literature— both the Vedas and the Puranas—look to the oceans.* This brings us back to the original thesis: To understand the origins it is necessary to reorient our thinking, recognizing the natural environment in which Indian civilization evolved. We shall next review some facts of natural history that shed light on the pervasive maritime symbolism in the Vedic (and Puranic) literature.

"YOUNGER DRYAS" AS THE TRANSITION FROM PROTO-VEDIC TO VEDIC[6]

One may begin by noting that it is futile to seek the identity of the Vedic people—steeped in maritime thought—in land-locked regions of Europe or Eurasia. Science suggests that their origins going back at least 50,000 years lie in the coastal regions of India. Significantly, this is what Indian literature also says—attributing the oldest sources to regions devastated by floods. When we examine accounts in the form of myths and legends found in ancient literature, science and the primary literature are in agreement, though they may not agree with some currently held theories.

to the interior at the end of the last ice age, over 12,000 years ago.

This is a vast subject that is still not fully understood, especially with regard to its impact on history and the rise of civilization (which historians continue to place in the river valleys). But a brief examination of the cataclysmic changes towards the end of the last ice age helps shed light on the pervasive oceanic imagery and the flood myths. We begin by noting that the world now is in what geologists call an interglacial period—or a warm period between two ice ages. The end of the last ice age was due to rise in global temperatures, especially of the oceans.

When we look at the ecological picture, what we find is that until the end of the ice age, i.e., during the glaciated period (12,000 years ago and earlier), the Indian interior, except possibly for some pockets in the peninsula, was cold and arid. The great Himalayan rivers that have watered the northern plains during the historical and proto-historical periods did not exist or were insignificant seasonal flows. Rainfall was also scanty, again except in some pockets, and in the coastal regions. This means that the regions that could support significant population centers were coastal—mainly the east and west coast of peninsular India.

Tropical regions close to the ocean like Sri Lanka and Indonesia could support significant populations, while the arid interior could not. Sea levels

First, it flooded the coastal regions, submerging vast tracts of the best habitable lands. Next, the resulting melting of the Himalayan glaciers gave rise to the great rivers that have made the northern plains of India some of the best habitable and the most densely populated regions in the world.

Two recent, seemingly unrelated developments hold the promise to shed light on this aspect of ancient Indian literature and reconcile it with the technical evidence from natural history. The first relates to recent studies on the spread of modern humans from their original home in Africa; the second accounts for the spread of populations from the coastal regions of India during the ice age

were much lower than they are today (by nearly 400 feet), and communication between these population centers was easier than it would be when the ice caps melted. It is not therefore surprising that human ancestors from East Africa 50,000 to 100,000 years ago settled along the coast as geneticists have found. Geneticist L. Cavalli-Sforza notes: "...the primal mtDNA and Y-chromosome founders suggest that these southern Asian Pleistocene coastal settlers from Africa would have provided the inocula for the subsequent differentiation of the distinctive eastern and western Eurasian gene pools." This fact, discussed later, acquires new meaning when examined against this ecological background.

The situation changed when the ice age ended. It brought about two major changes. First, it flooded the coastal regions, submerging vast tracts of the best habitable lands. Next, the resulting melting of the Himalayan glaciers gave rise to the great rivers that have made the northern plains of India some of the best habitable and the most densely populated regions in the world. (There seems to have been increased rainfall also, which does not concern us here.)

Many scholars have read references to the end of the ice age in the Vedic literature, especially in the Indra-Vritra legend that speaks of the solar god Indra killing the demon Vritra (the coverer). This legend holds that a dragon or a serpent was holding back the waters by "covering" the river passages. It is the most persistent legend in the *Rigveda* and one of its main themes. This has been read as the sun melting the ice caps and ending the ice age. It is our view that it refers to the ending of the Younger Dryas (or lesser Dryas), which was a brief return of the ice age. The Younger Dryas held the planet in its grip until the earth warmed again and finally settled into its most recent interglacial period—the one in which we now live.

To find records of the ending of the ice age and the flooding of the coastal regions, we need to look at the other great body of ancient Indian literature known as the *Puranas*, or ancient chronicles. They represent the ancient Indian historical tradition. They contain names and events of many ancient kingdoms and rulers but also much interesting information about floods and the dispersal of people from coastal regions. They seem to preserve primordial memory of the cataclysmic events of the ending of the ice age, especially the ocean floods. So, where the *Rigveda* records the ending of the Younger Dryas, the *Puranas* seem to preserve the earlier cataclysm—the end of the ice age and its aftermath.

In this scenario, when the ice age ended, the coastal lands were flooded. The *Puranas* record it in the form of flood myths. But freezing cold returned as the Younger Dryas and plunged North India into a mini-ice age lasting a little over 1,000 years. This too ended with the final warming, and India was finally free of the dreaded cold and ice. It is this second (and final) retreat of the ice age that *Rigveda* records as the Indra-Vritra myth—of the solar god Indra killing the "coverer" Vritra who holds the waters back. Indra became the supreme god who made it possible for the repeated slaying of Vritra the Coverer, who periodically tried to extend his icy grip on the life-giving waters.

They contain names and events of many ancient kingdoms and rulers but also much interesting information about floods and the dispersal of people from coastal regions. They seem to preserve primordial memory of the cataclysmic events of the ending of the ice age, especially the ocean floods.

We just noted that the *Puranas* refer to the flooding oceans. These are described in the form of *dashavataras* or the ten *avataras* (incarnations) of God Vishnu. The early *avataras*—*matsya* (fish), *kurma* (tortoise), *varaha* (boar)—carry clear maritime symbolism. All speak of saving the world from the flooding waters, and more particularly of saving some cherished knowledge (*Veda*) or value (*amrita* or immortality). Even the Vamana *avatara*, which describes the ousting of the great maritime ruler (*Chakravarti*) Bali by a youthful sage can be read as representing a transition from maritime to landward expansion, guided by the *rishis* possessed of special knowledge.

According to the *Puranas*, this coastal, ice age civilization lasted for a very long time until it fell victim to the flooding ocean. According to the *Puranas*, as well as later South Indian legends, they were the source of great knowledge (*Veda*) and literature. (Some underwater discoveries off the coast of India, which seem to go back to before 7000 B.C.E., may eventually help shed more light on it, but they are as yet too preliminary.) The *avataras* record the efforts by the victims of the floods to save their precious heritage from destruction. This is what the sages carried with them when

Date	Natural Event	Plausible Literary Account
17,000 B.C.E.	Late ice age.	Coastal civilizations.
15,000 B.C.E.	Warming begins; unstable coastline.	Coastal civilizations under stress.
13,000 B.C.E.	Ice age ending; flooding begins of coastal regions.	Puranic accounts of flooding and the "saving" of the *Vedas*.
11,000 B.C.E.	Younger Dryas; freeze returns.	Proto-Vedic civilization under threat from freezing-"Vritra," the coverer.
10,000 B.C.E.	Farming spreads in Southeast Asia and the Indian interior.	"Vritra," the ice cover, still threatens the north.
9600 B.C.E.	Renewed warming. Ice sheets finally retreat. Great North Indian rivers (glacier fed) begin to flow. Monsoon stronger.	"Vritra" the coverer slain by the solar god Indra. Vedic civilization begins in earnest.

Table correlating natural and literary accounts. Source (for natural events only): *The Long Summer: How Climate Changed Civilization* by Brian Fagan.

the population moved to the interior. *This is what seeded the Vedic civilization that blossomed in river alleys of the Sarasvati, Indus and the Ganges.*

We suggest that the primordial portions of the *Puranas* suggest this ice age proto-Vedic civilization as the source that seeded the Vedic civilization that flourished in the Vedic heartland. In this scenario, the *Rigvedic Indra-Vritra legend refers not to the ending of the ice age but the ending of the Younger Dryas, which was a short-lived return*

We suggest that the primordial portions of the *Puranas* suggest this ice age proto-Vedic civilization as the source that seeded the Vedic civilization that flourished in the Vedic heartland.

---

of the ice age, while the Puranas record the flooding of the coastal lands and the spreading of populations into the interior.

Viewed in this light, the primordial sections of the *Puranas* record the period before the Younger Dryas, when India was in the throes of the cataclysms caused by the ending of the ice age. The

beginnings of the *Rigveda*, its compilation in the Sarasvati River heartland in the north, followed the ending of the Younger Dryas, which was a period of setback to the transition from a coastal to a land-based civilization. That means the Younger Dryas was the period of transition from what we may call the proto-Vedic to the Vedic.

This evolution is summarized in the following table, relating natural events to historical possibilities. It will be noted that the scientifically-determined time scales are significantly longer than those postulated by historians. We cannot ignore natural history; our historical theories should not contradict the story that nature has to tell us.

HUMAN IMPRINT: LANGUAGE AND GENETICS

The human imprint is of two kinds—natural and man-made. By natural imprint we mean those relating to human remains and their biological characteristics. These can be analyzed by scientific methods like DNA sampling. Man-made imprints are mainly archaeological and literary. Since the present article is concerned primarily with the natural history that gave rise to human history, we shall not be looking at archaeology. In literature also, our focus in on the part that has a bearing on natural history—like the oceanic imagery and the melting of ice caps found in the *Rigveda*.

In recent decades, there has been an explosion of knowledge of our past thanks to new techniques based on mapping our genetic past. There is a good deal of controversy but this much seems to be reasonably certain. Our ancestors used to live in Africa 150,000 years ago. A small group of *Homo*

This has a bearing on the human record in the region, which linguists have tried to reconstruct using languages and literature. A basic point to note is that the time horizon used by linguists is much too short to account for the spread of languages and culture. Language records, by which we mean written texts, go back only some 5,000 years. Coincidentally or not, by identifying the appearance of written records with civilization, historians have taken it

---

While the earliest writing goes back a little over 5,000 years, languages have been around at least ten times as long. As a result, we need to go beyond written texts to understand human origins in India.

---

sapiens left Africa some 80,000 years ago and settled along the South Asian coast from where they spread out to colonize different parts of the world. All non-Africans in the world today are descended from a small group of South Asians living south of a line from Yemen to the Himalayas, especially along the Indian coast. This "founder group," from which all non-Africans are descended, barely survived the fallout from a volcanic eruption in Sumatra known as the "Toba Explosion" 74,000 years ago. This is the story of our past growing out of more than 50 years of intensive mapping of human genes and climate changes by scientists. By relating these movements to ecological upheavals, what we obtain is the genetic history of modern humans correlated with the natural history of our planet.

It is important to interpret this properly. It does not mean that there were no non-African humans before the Toba Explosion, but only that no descendants of those earlier populations have survived outside Africa. A group out of Africa 120,000 years ago made its way to Egypt but disappeared 90,000 years ago without a genetic trace. All Europeans living today are descended from South Asians, possibly as recently as 40,000 years ago. South Asia, India in particular, was the jumping off point for the colonization of East Asia, Southeast Asia, Australia and ultimately the Americas. This brief summary suffices for the natural history of the region relevant to the present article.

as the beginning of civilization. However, language is much older than writing. While the earliest writing goes back a little over 5,000 years, languages have been around at least ten times as long. As a result, we need to go beyond written texts to understand human origins in India.

For this, we turn again to natural history, especially population genetics. In understanding language evolution, science may also be able to help. Recent studies in the human genome suggest that some mutations in the FOXP2 gene might have triggered the uniquely human capacity for speech and therefore language. The dates are uncertain, but considering that all the humans inhabiting the world today, who can be traced to an exodus from Africa perhaps 90,000 years ago possess this capacity suggests that the necessary mutations must have taken place 100,000 years ago at least.[7]

Recent genetic studies also support the need for a much longer time horizon than the few thousand years postulated by linguists and historians. Here is what the most important such study, led by Luigi Luca Cavalli-Sforza, regarded as the world's foremost human population geneticist, has found. After collecting and analyzing the most comprehensive data on world human populations ever compiled, Cavalli-Sforza and his colleagues at Stanford University had this to say about Indian populations:

What all this means is that theories seeking a recent non-Indian origin simply cannot be true. This is not to say there have been no migrations or invasions, but that their contribution to the genetic profile of the Indian population is negligible.

Taken together, these results show that Indian tribal and caste populations derive largely from the same genetic heritage of Pleistocene southern and western Asians *and have received limited gene flow from external regions since the Holocene*. The phylogeography [neighboring branches] of the primal mtDNA and Y-chromosome founders suggests that these southern Asian Pleistocene coastal settlers from Africa would have provided the inocula for the subsequent differentiation of the distinctive eastern and western Eurasian gene pools. (Italics added.)[8]

Put in non-technical language, it means that the Indian population is mainly of indigenous origin, and the contribution of immigrants (gene flow) since the Holocene is negligible. This contradicts the many invasion-migration theories that continue to dominate academic discourse about India. What is particularly noteworthy in this is the negligible contribution of immigrants (or invaders) in the past 50-100,000 years. What all this means is that theories seeking a recent non-Indian origin simply cannot be true.

This is not to say there have been no migrations or invasions, but that their contribution to the genetic profile of the Indian population is negligible. They became absorbed into the Indian population just as Moguls, Turks and other people did in historical times. When this is the situation over such a large span of time, it is futile to try to assign cultural traits like religion, language and caste based on biological features (mostly imaginary) and recent migrations. We must therefore conclude that to understand the origin and evolution of the Indian civilization, we must focus on the people who have lived in India for this vast span of time, and how they coped with the epochal ecological changes that engulfed them.

In particular, it means that there is nothing to be gained by using labels and stereotypes like "Aryans," "Dravidians" and so forth that have no scientific, literary or historical basis. Just study the human record of the people against the background of natural history. The two together give us a vivid picture of history.

CONCLUSION: FROM THE ICE AGE TO THE YOUNGER DRYAS

Here is the main point of the present article: To understand the origins of the Vedic civilization and its representation in the ancient Indian literature, we need to study both the *Vedas* and the *Puranas* against the background of the unusual ecological conditions that brought about the landward expansion of people in India. What later became the Vedic civilization fed by the Sarasvati River had its origins in a primordial proto-Vedic culture that flourished in the coastal regions of peninsular India. The ending of the ice age flooded many of these settlements while simultaneously releasing

In particular, it means that there is nothing to be gained by using labels and stereotypes like "Aryans," "Dravidians" and so forth that have no scientific, literary or historical basis.

the Himalayan rivers that made North India fertile and habitable. This attracted sages from the proto-Vedic south who combined with the rulers of the sparsely populated north to bring about the unique civilization that we know as Vedic.

This expansion came under the grip of the mini-ice age known as the Younger Dryas, which persisted in the north for over a thousand years. The "slaying" of this dreaded coverer—Vritra—by the solar god Indra is what is recorded in the *Rigveda* and other Vedic works. *The Younger Dryas was the transition from the proto-Vedic to the Vedic*. Harappan civilization, identified by the archaeology of the Indus and the Sarasvati river valleys represents the material remains of the latter part of the Vedic.

This calls for a much longer time horizon than what historians have so far used. Ecology and human genetics force us to extend our time horizon. At the same time, we want to emphasize that what is presented here is simply a framework for a reorientation that shifts emphasis from Eurasia to the coastal region and also calls for a methodological focus emphasizing the natural sciences more than man-made disciplines like linguistics and anthropology.

Acknowledgement: The author is indebted to David Frawley for his many suggestions, particularly for drawing attention to the importance of the Younger Dryas. However, the author is responsible for the interpretations offered here, especially of the Younger Dryas as the transition from the proto-Vedic to the Vedic.

---

1. It is now being called the Aryan Migration Theory (AMT), but the conclusions are the same: Vedas and their language are foreign imports. The reason for the switch from invasion to migration is due to the fact that archaeologists have found no evidence of any invasion, and the theory therefore stands refuted. The migration theory, however, cannot be refuted, since it depends on no evidence.

2. See Romila Thapar, foreword, in Thomas Trautmann, *Aryans and British India*. New Delhi: Vistaar Publications, 1997. p. xiv.

3. See *Mohenjo-Daro and the Indus Civilization*, v. 2. London: Probisthain, 1934. p. 653-4.

4. There is no astronomical reference in the *Rigveda* that can be dated any later than 4000 B.C.E. The *Aitereya Brahmana*, a commentary on the *Rigveda*, records the transition from *Mrigashira* (Orion) to *Rohini* (Aldeberan in Taurus) in the vernal equinox. This approximates to circa 3500 B.C.E. The hydrological data, especially the course of the Vedic river Sarasvati, mentioned prominently in the *Rigveda*, gives similar dates.

5. David Frawley, *Gods, Sages and Kings*. Salt Lake City: Passage Press, 1991. p. 36. Translations from the *Rigveda* given earlier are from the same source.

6. Most history books barely note the ending of the ice age and the impact of climate change on human populations; the Younger Dryas is almost never mentioned. One has to go to books on ecology and geology to get an idea of the climate changes. *The Long Summer* by Brian Fagan, New York, Basic Books, 2004 is a good summary. *Climate Change: A Multidisciplinary Approach* by William James Burroughs, Cambridge University Press, 2001 is more technical. *Underworld: Flooded Kingdoms of the Ice Age* by Graham Hancock, Penguin, 2002 is a wide-ranging, not-technical survey of evidence for ice age maritime civilizations. The material is covered in vivid detail in a popular television serial.

7. See "FOXP2 in Focus: What Can Genes Tell Us About Speech and Language?" in *TRENDS in Cognitive Sciences*, v. 7, no. 6. June 2003.

8. Kisilvid, S. Rootsl, M. Metspahi, S. Mastana, K. Kaldma, J. Parik, E. Metspalu, M. Adojan, H.-V. Tolk, V. Stepanov, M. Gölge, E. Usanga, S. S. Papiha, R. King, L. Cavalli-Sforza, P. A. Unterhill and R. Villems. "The Genetic Heritage of the Earliest Settlers Persist Both in Indian Tribal and Caste Populations." In *American Journal of Human Genetics*, no. 72, 2003. pp. 313-332.

Some claims that seek to assign genetic sources to man-made classifications like caste, religion and even language are seriously flawed, and confuse genotypes and phenotypes. See, for example: M. Bamshad, T. Kivisild, W. S. Watkins, M. E. Dixon, C. E. Ricker, B. B. Rao, J. M. Naidu, B. V. R. Prasad, P. G. Reddy, A. Rasanagam, et al. "Genetic Evidence on the Origin of Indian Caste Populations." In *Genome Research*, no. 11, 2001. pp. 994-1004. For a scientifically sound examination of human expansions from the African home, based on genetics, *Out of Eden: The Peopling of the World* by Stephen Oppenheimer, London, Constable and Robinson, 2003 is outstanding.

Acharya S

DEUS NOSTER, DEUS SOLIS:

OUR GOD, GOD OF THE SUN

But unto you that fear my name shall the Sun of righteousness arise with healing in his wings...
— Malachi 4:2

The sun is extolled by David for its beauty, its greatness, its swift course, and its power, splendid as a bridegroom, majestic as a giant; while, from the extent of its circuit, it has such power that it equally sheds its light from one end of heaven to the other, and the heat thereof is in no wise lessened by distance.
— St. Cyril of Jerusalem (c. 315-386)

THE MONUMENTAL REMAINS and other physical artifacts of ancient cultures have deservedly been the focus of much attention and publicity over the past couple of centuries. The religious, mythological and philosophical ideologies that certainly go hand in hand with these ruins have received less investigation, even though religion is one of the most mysterious and fascinating aspects of ancient human culture. Few things produce such passion as the issue and discussion of religious ideology, which has varied widely within the numerous cultures around the globe over the past many millennia. Much of ancient religious ideology is currently considered to be "mythology," which is not to say that it should be dismissed as useless and meaningless. Importantly, the study of the world's "mythologies" reveals that, while they do in fact vary in detail, based on era, ethnicity and other factors, there remains a primary theme that unites myriad cultures in an unexpected and welcome manner.

In reality, the world's mythologies were once its religions, and its current religions will in the future be deemed mythology.

In reality, the world's mythologies were once its religions, and its current religions will in the future be deemed mythology. Upon close inspection, it turns out that the core of modern religion is much the same as that of ancient mythology. As demonstrated in stone and story, such religion/mythology resolves itself into what is termed "astrotheology": to wit, the reverence of the sun, moon, planets, stars and heavens in general. This ancient religion of "astral worship" also includes other aspects of nature, such as the earth and its elements, as well as, significantly, fertility and fecundity. Thus, it could be said that major religions have essentially revolved around astral and nature worship.

Since the earliest times, when man was a hunter-gatherer and wanderer, as opposed to a settled agriculturalist, the night sky and moon in particular were the objects of great interest and contemplation. Desert nomads, for example, were compelled to live by the night sky because of the day's heat, while long-distance mariners such as the Polynesians, beginning 30,000 or more years ago, learned to navigate expertly by the stars. In primitive societies, some 25,000 years ago, the year was divided according to the moon's phases, which corresponded to the woman's menses; hence, moon, month and menstruation have their roots in the same word. The extraordinary figurine the "Venus of Laussel," at least 21,000 years old, exhibits this logical yet compelling connection, as it represents a fecund female holding a crescent moon with 13 notches, the number of lunar months and menses per year. Notably, both the lunar month and the average menses last 29.5 days. For a variety of reasons, therefore, the moon was a highly germane aspect of human culture, its reverence and the study of its phases intricately woven into myths and legends the world over. Major religions of today stem, in part, from lunar worship, as a continuation of this very ancient theme, although such information is hidden, esoteric and not known by the public at large.

Major religions of today stem, in part, from lunar worship, as a continuation of this very ancient theme, although such information is hidden, esoteric and not known by the public at large.

Other salient aspects of ancient religion are, however, taught in mainstream higher education. As an example, in its article on "Astrology" the *Catholic Encyclopedia* outlines the ancient astral worship:

The history of astrology is an important part of the history of the development of civilization, it goes back to the early days of the human race... astrology was...the foster-sister of astronomy, the science of the investigation of the heavens... According to the belief in the early civilized races of the East, the stars were the source and at the same time the heralds of everything that happened, and the right to study the "godlike science" of astrology was a privilege of the priesthood. This was the case in Mesopotamia and Egypt, the oldest centers of civilization known to us in the East. The most ancient dwellers on the Euphrates, the Akkado-Sumerians, were believers in judicial astrology, which was closely interwoven with their worship of the stars. The same is true of their successors, the Babylonians and Assyrians, who were the chief exponents of astrology in antiquity... The Assyro-Babylonian priests (Chaldeans) were the professional astrologers of classical antiquity. In its origin Chaldaic astrology also goes back to the worship of stars; this is proved by the religious symbolism of the most ancient cuneiform texts of the zodiac. The oldest astrological document extant is the work called "Namar-Beli" (Illumination of Bel) composed for King Sargon I (end of the Third Millennium B.C.)... Even in the time of Chaldean, which should be called Assyrian, astrology, the five planets, together with the sun and moon, were divided according to their position in the 12 houses... The Egyptians and Hindus were as zealous [of] astrologers as [those of] the nations on the Euphrates and Tigris. The dependence of the early Egyptian star (sun) worship (the basis of the worship of Osiris) upon early Chaldaic influences belongs to the still unsettled question of the origin of early Egyptian civilization.[1]

Thus, as far back as science currently shows, mankind looked to the stars, the moon and the sun, developing a complex theology based on these celestial beings, or gods, as they were perceived to be.

RUINS OF EMPIRES

With the in-depth analysis of ancient religion comes a more complete picture of the mysterious "ruins of empires" that have engaged and entranced the imagination for centuries. Along with astrotheology, which through painstaking archaeological detective work can be reconstructed to a large extent, the cultural remains clearly demonstrate that the ancients were far from the dumb "cavemen" depicted in popular textbooks and fiction. Furthermore, it becomes evident that where there is extraordinary construction, such as at Stonehenge, Baalbek, Giza and Tiahuanaco, there must have existed advanced culture, as reflected in language and religion.

Along with astrotheology, which through painstaking archaeological detective work can be reconstructed to a large extent, the cultural remains clearly demonstrate that the ancients were far from the dumb "cavemen" depicted in popular textbooks and fiction.

In his book *In Search of Ancient Astronomies*, astronomer Dr. Edwin Krupp discusses these engrossing edifices, which possess "astronomical significance":

At Stonehenge in England and Carnac in France, in Egypt and Yucatan, across the whole face of the earth are found mysterious ruins of ancient monuments, monuments with astronomical significance. These relics of other times are as accessible as the American Midwest and as remote as the jungles of Guatemala. Some of them were built according to celestial alignments; others were actually precision astronomical observatories... Careful observations of the celestial rhythms were compellingly important to early peoples, and their expertise, in some respects, was not equaled in Europe until three thousand years later.

One fairly recent find, unearthed in the Sahara Desert, reveals the antiquity of astrotheological culture:

An assembly of huge stone slabs found in Egypt's Sahara Desert that date from about 6,500 . . . to 6,000 years ago has been confirmed by scientists to be the oldest known astronomical alignment of megaliths in the world. Known as Nabta, the site consists of a stone circle, a series of flat, tomb-like stone structures and five lines of standing and toppled megaliths. Located west of the Nile River in southern Egypt, Nabta predates Stonehenge and similar prehistoric sites around the world by about 1,000 years, said University of Colorado at Boulder professor of astronomy J. McKim Malville...

"This is the oldest documented astronomical alignment of megaliths in the world," said Malville. "A lot of effort went into the construction of a purely symbolic and ceremonial site." The stone slabs, some of which are nine feet high, were dragged to the site from a mile or more distant, he said...

Five megalithic alignments at Nabta radiate outward from a central collection of megalithic structures. Beneath one structure was a sculptured rock resembling a cow standing upright, Malville said. The team also excavated several cattle burials at Nabta, including an articulated skeleton buried in a roofed, clay-lined chamber.

Neolithic herders that began coming to Nabta about 10,000 years ago—probably from central Africa—used cattle in their rituals just as the African Massai do today, he said. No human remains have yet been found at Nabta. The 12-foot-in-diameter stone circle contains four sets of upright slabs. Two sets were aligned in a north-south direction while the second pair of slabs provides a line of sight toward the summer solstice horizon.

Because of Nabta's proximity to the Tropic of Cancer, the noon sun is at its zenith about three weeks before and three weeks after the summer solstice, preventing upright objects from casting shadows. "These vertical sighting stones in the circle correspond to the zenith sun during the summer solstice," said Malville, an archaeoastronomer. "For many cultures in the tropics, the zenith sun has been a major event for millennia."

An east-west alignment also is present between one megalithic structure and two stone megaliths about a mile distant. There also are two other geometric lines involving about a dozen additional stone monuments that lead both northeast and southeast from the same megalith. "We still don't understand the significance of these lines," Malville said.

During summer and fall, the individual stone monoliths would have been partially submerged in the lake and may have been ritual markers for the onset of the rainy season. "The organization of these objects suggests a symbolic geometry that integrated death, water and the sun," Malville said.[2]

The inclusion of cattle at Nabta is intriguing, in consideration of the fact that the site dates to the beginning of the equinoctial Age of Taurus, the Bull, between 6,450 and 4,300 years ago. Many cultures of that era, including the Egyptian, Greek and Semitic, emphasized the cow or bull in their myths and rituals. In any event, this very ancient site—claimed by orthodox science to be the "oldest astronomical megalith alignment" in the world—incorporates a number of important observations of the most prominent of celestial objects, the sun.

THE CHILDREN OF THE SUN

The principal form of worship over the past several thousand years in myriad places globally has been that of the sun. Sun worship dates back many millennia, and was refined in agricultural areas after the last major ice age, some 10,000 years ago in the northern hemisphere. Evidence suggests that sun worship in earnest began even earlier, in agricultural communities submerged by rising water levels during the melting of the glacial ice. One certain fact is that when and where agriculture arose, the sun became the central focus of worship, as a representative or proxy of God, or gods, as the case may be.

elements reflected in story and song, art and architecture around the world.

Traditions and legends, mythology and religion, symbols and other cultural artifacts all portray an ornate form of worship revolving around the sun. In *Sun-Worship in Ancient India*, scholar Srivastava describes various pre-historic solar symbols:

> There are representations of the sun in full radiance in the rock paintings from Sitakhardi (Chambal valley). Broadly speaking, there are two varieties of such representations: the circle with radiating rays, and the circle with radiating rays but encircled by a bigger circle. Figures of the sun in full radiance usually in isolation but sometimes shown with other figures have been reported from Neolithic rock paintings in Europe, also such as from Pala Pinta de Carlao in Portugal. Similar figures are reported from Neolithic settlements of the Iberian peninsula as well. A comparative study of these symbols reveals there is a marked similarity in them.[3]

This rich heritage endures to this day in numerous places worldwide, from Siberia and Slavic countries to China, Japan, Polynesia, Indonesia and India, as well as Europe, Africa and both Americas. Much of this pervasive sun worship

---

The principal form of worship over the past several thousand years in myriad places globally has been that of the sun.

So extensive and permeating has been the worship of the sun—again, at certain points constituting *the* singular religious expression—which families have often laid claim to the solar orb as their ancestor, and legends record distinct groups called the "children of the sun." The term "children of the sun" denotes a general description of solar-based cultures but also apparently specifically refers to a group or groups led by a solar priesthood or hierarchy who journeyed far and wide. There were also specialized and mysterious subgroups called the "sons of the sun," comprising initiates in secret societies and brotherhoods. It is largely because of these fraternities that much of the vast sun-worshipping tradition is preserved to this day, its

continues in a plentitude of ways, including not only exquisite art and architecture but also beautiful and inspired folk-craft, prayers and songs, etc. An impressive and gorgeously illustrated survey of the world's solar cultures, past and present, can be found in *The Sun: Symbol of Power and Life*, edited by Madanjeet Singh.

One nation where the sun was passionately and overtly viewed as the "light and life" was Egypt, which was practically built upon astrotheology, with a plethora of sun gods or epithets of the one "God Sun." A detailed history of Egyptian sun worship would require volumes; a summarization can be found in my book *Suns of God: Krishna, Buddha and Christ Unveiled*. Briefly, the chief Egyptian god Ra was morphed into the god Osiris, both of which represented and were symbolized by the sun. The worship of Ra and Osiris was long and widespread, traditionally considered to have begun 10,000 years ago. Gathering all the available evidence, it may be argued intelligently that the dying-and-rising savior god Osiris, whose "life" and "sayings" were so closely paralleled in the much later Jesus Christ, has been the most popular god on the face of the earth.

> **Gathering all the available evidence, it may be argued intelligently that the dying-and-rising savior god Osiris, whose "life" and "sayings" were so closely paralleled in the much later Jesus Christ, has been the most popular god on the face of the earth.**

Osiris' worship was so far-reaching that his myth is also found in India, as "Iswara" or "Issa," meaning "Lord," a title shared by the Indian god Shiva as well as by "Jesus." India has a very long history of sun worship beginning in the Stone Age, later appearing in symbols in the Indus Valley's remarkable Harappan culture, dating to at least 4,000 years ago and encompassing a vast area of sophisticated, planned cities with paved streets and plumbing. As a main aspect of the vaguely defined "Hinduism," which in reality consists of hundreds if not thousands of different sects, India's sun worship continues intact to this day, with extensive solar precincts, rituals and sacred literature created over the millennia. Magnificent temples to the sun, such as at Konarak, have been built throughout India, though many were tragically destroyed, such as at Martand, by zealots of competing religions. Nevertheless, Indian sun worship is maintained unabashedly in daily rituals and ablutions designed to cleanse the body, mind and soul.

The solar reverence can be found abundantly in ancient sacred texts, such as the Indian *Vedas* and the Egyptian Book of the Dead. The following verse from the Gayatri, the "holiest text of the *Vedas*," conservatively estimated to be 3,500 years old, superbly conveys the veneration of the sun:

> Let us adore the supremacy of that divine Sun, the Godhead who illuminates all, who recreates all,

from whom all proceed, to whom all must return; whom we invoke to direct our understanding aright in our progress toward his holy seat.[4]

Archaic sun worship was also elegantly expressed by the conservative Christian scholar Max Müller, in the Nineteenth Century:

> What position the sun must have occupied in the thoughts of the early dwellers on earth, we shall never be able to fully understand. Not even the most recent scientific discoveries described in Tyndall's genuine eloquence, which teach us how we live, and move, and have our being in the sun, how we burn it, how we breathe it, how we feed on it—give us any idea of what this source of light and life, this silent traveler, this majestic ruler, this departed friend or dying hero, in his daily or yearly course, was to the awakening consciousness of mankind. People wonder why so much of the old mythology, the daily talk...was solar; what else could it have been? The names of the sun are endless, and so are his stories; but who he was, whence he came and whither he went, remained a mystery from beginning to end.[5]

> **As evident from the finds at Nabta, numerous astronomical monuments and ruins globally reveal that the sun in specific was considered divine thousands of years ago and that entire cultures have been built in response to its glory.**

As evident from the finds at Nabta, numerous astronomical monuments and ruins globally reveal that the sun in specific was considered divine thousands of years ago and that entire cultures have been built in response to its glory. In an article published in 2004 entitled *Ancient Tombs and Shrines Faced Sun and Stars*, based on the work of British astronomer Michael Hoskin, Tarik Maliq reports:

> The sun and stars may have served as critical references for a startlingly diverse range of ancient builders who constructed chambers to hold the dead and other religious shrines.
>
> The orientation of thousands of Neolithic tombs erected across Europe and Africa around 10,000

> **This important correspondence between Pagan and Christian culture is entirely appropriate, since, it is my contention, "Jesus Christ" is a mythical solar figure, the same as countless sun gods of other cultures.**

B.C. were apparently built to face the rising sun, securing the sun's importance in various human cultures across three countries, two continents and the Mediterranean islands...

The sheer number of Neolithic tombs built with sun-ward oriented entrances suggests, if nothing else, that the sun played an important role that coincided with a person's death...

Hoskin spent 12 years personally cataloging the positions of 2,000 Neolithic tombs, and researching documented descriptions of some 1,000 others, across France, Portugal, Spain and North Africa. The entrances of nearly all, he said, appeared to have been built to face the rising or climbing sun at some point during the year.

In the Alenterejo region of central Portugal, for example, every one of the 177 tombs measured by Hoskin faced sunrise, usually during autumn and early winter, with a sharp cutoff at the winter solstice.

This very ancient astrotheological element of aligning tombs and shrines with the rising sun, widely found in so-called Pagan structures beginning millennia ago, was continued within Christianity, despite the latter's claim to be an abrupt break from the past.

CHRISTIAN ASTROTHEOLOGY

Although it may seem surprising to the uninitiated, among the solar-based cultures is counted the Christian, with churches and cathedrals throughout Europe containing astrotheological symbolism, including the orientation of their altars to receive the sun's light upon sunrise during the winter solstice, the traditional "birthday" of "Our Lord and Savior." As astronomer Hoskin further observes regarding Pagan and Christian builders:

All the evidence is consistent with their having aligned their tombs with sunrise on the day when building started, which is exactly what we know

happened commonly with Christian churches... The churches face the rising sun as a symbol of Christ rising from the dead...no doubt the Neolithic people saw the rising sun as a symbol of hope of afterlife.[6]

This important correspondence between Pagan and Christian culture is entirely appropriate, since, it is my contention, "Jesus Christ" is a mythical solar figure, the same as countless sun gods of other cultures.

As evidence of this Christian astrotheology, edifices and artifacts within Vatican City, such as the pre-Christian Egyptian obelisk and St. Peter's Chair, are rife with astrological symbolism, and it is "said that the Vatican still contains the largest library of astrological manuscripts in the world."[7] Another example is provided by the astrological clock in Notre Dame Cathedral at Saint-Omer, France. Furthermore, thousands of ancient Armenian churches, the earliest of which were, like their Catholic counterparts, "built on pagan temples," possess "holdovers from Armenia's most ancient past, in stone carvings representing the zodiac, sun dials and iconography from her animist and sun worship pagan traditions making their way into the church ornamentation."[8]

THE ZODIACAL LEGACY

Many Christian structures contain zodiacal symbols, as well as full zodiacs, such as the magnificent stained-glass window in the Chartres Cathedral. Zodiacs are likewise found on synagogue floors in Northern Israel, such as at Sepphoris. The present form of the zodiac helps date the archaic high development of sun worship, as the zodiac can be definitely dated through scientific methods to have been created at least 5,000 years ago.[9] As to the zodiac's provenance, in *The Astronomy of the Bible* Christian astronomer Walter Maunder states:

From [the latitude and longitude of the zodiac] we learn that the constellations were designed by people living not very far from the 40th parallel of north latitude, not further south than the 37th or 36th. This is important, as it shows that they did not originate in ancient Egypt or India, not even in the city of Babylon, which is in latitude 32°.[10]

A number of authorities on astrotheology, such as Count Volney and Gerald Massey, extended the zodiacal terminus a quo to over 17,000 years ago, originating in North Africa, within the 37th and 36th parallels. That the *concept* of the zodiac itself is older than 5,000 years is essentially proved by the "Karanovo Zodiac" found in Bulgaria and dating to 6,000 years ago.[11]

Although the Bible is a late source in comparison to Sumero-Babylonian texts, the biblical mention of the zodiac—the "Mazzaroth"—at *Job 38:32*, is noteworthy:

> Canst thou bring forth Mazzaroth in his season? Or canst thou guide Arcturus with his sons?

In the final analysis, so-called modern religions, although sharply and artificially differentiated by their competitive proponents, are continuations of the past astrotheology, cloaked in a pretentious air of "historicity" and "divine inspiration."

The authoritative *Strong's Concordance* defines the Hebrew term "Mazzaroth" as "the 12 signs of the zodiac and their 36 associated constellations."

The favorable language with which the sun, moon and heavens are addressed in the *Book of Job* and many other biblical and extra-biblical texts, such as *St. Patrick's Creed*, quoted in the title of this article, belies the typically hostile tenor of the Judeo-Christian tradition towards astrology. In reality, Judaism and Christianity are saturated with astrotheology, as demonstrated in my books *The Christ Conspiracy: The Greatest Story Ever Sold* and *Suns of God*. In the final analysis, so-called modern religions, although sharply and artificially differentiated by their competitive proponents, are continuations of the past astrotheology, cloaked in a pretentious air of "historicity" and "divine inspiration."

CONCLUSION

For thousands of years, humankind has looked to the skies in awe and veneration, deeming the various celestial objects "works of God" or gods themselves. Whole cultures have been created with their central focus as the sun, a significant development of what is called "astrotheology." Modern research has established that many of the observations made by the ancients regarding the sun have a solid basis in science. In consideration of the astonishing power unleashed by the sun, as well as its nurturing and healing capacities, the widespread past and present reverence of it is understandable and justifiable. The knowledge of these facts reveals that, despite the divisiveness and mayhem caused globally by perceived differences in religious beliefs, underlying the major religious ideologies appears a unity validating that humanity in general comprises a single family tree with diverse branches.

---

1. www.newadvent.org/cathen/02018e.htm

2. zebu.uoregon.edu/~imamura/121/lecture-2/nabta.html

3. V. C. Srivastava, *Sun-Worship in Ancient India*. Allahabad: Indological Publications, 1972. p. 22-23.

4. Edward Moor, *The Hindu Pantheon*. W. O. Simpson, ed. New Delhi: Indological Book House, 1968. p. 377.

5. Max Müller, *Lectures on the Origin and Growth of Religion*. New York: Charles Scribner's Sons, 1879. p. 200.

6. www.space.com/scienceastronomy/ancient_tombs_040405.html

7. www.astrologyzine.com/astrology-bible.shtml

8. www.tacentral.com/architecture.asp?story_no=3

9. Walter Maunder, *The Astronomy of the Bible*. London: T. Sealey Clark & Co., 1908. p. 160-161.

10. Ibid., p. 157.

11. www.flavinscorner.com/karanovo.htm

References:

Acharya S, *Suns of God: Krishna, Buddha and Christ Unveiled*, AUP, IL, 2004

Acharya S, *The Christ Conspiracy: The Greatest Story Ever Sold*, AUP, IL, 1999

Catholic Encyclopedia, www.newadvent.org

Richard Flavin, "The Karanovo Zodiac," www.flavinscorner.com/karanovo.htm

Tarik Maliq, "Ancient Tombs and Shrines Faced Sun and Stars," www.space.com

Walter Maunder, *The Astronomy of the Bible*. London: T. Sealey Clark & Co., 1908

Madanjeet Singh, *The Sun: Symbol of Power and Life*. Harry N. Abrams, NY, 1993

Strong's Concordance, www.blueletterbible.org

"Cathedral Saint-Omer," www.theotherside.co.uk

"Early Christian Architecture and Design," www.tacentral.com

"Early Church Fathers," www.ccel.org

"Stonehenge in the Sahara?", zebu.uoregon.edu

"St. Patrick's Creed," gnisios.narod.ru/patrickcreed.html

Dave Dentel

MYSTERIOUS ORIGINS—ARE HUMANS JUST A HAPPY ACCIDENT?

Man is the only animal who does not feel at home in nature, who can feel evicted from paradise, the only animal for whom his own existence is a problem that he has to solve and from which he cannot escape.
  — Erich Fromm, *The Anatomy of Human Destructiveness*

In any group united by a belief system its members equate with reality itself, some will have staked career and soul on that system, which they therefore feel must be maintained.
  — Jeff Walker, *The Ayn Rand Cult*

OF ALL LIVING CREATURES, man is the only one known to question where he came from, why he exists, or even the reason for his (often unhappy) rationality that poses these questions in the first place. This deep longing to discover a point of origin, an ultimate explanation of meaning and purpose, is so ubiquitous among our species and so fundamental to what it means to be human that few have stopped to consider how extraordinarily unique a trait it is.

In fact, as far as mainstream science is concerned, when it comes to the study of human origins this indefinable yearning of ours doesn't count for much—if anything at all. Almost as if they've forgotten what inspired their inquiries in the first place, members of today's scientific establishment have concocted a creation myth that describes humans almost solely in physical terms, leaving little room for spirit or intellect. Invoking Charles Darwin, they declare human beings to be little more than hairless, big-brained apes, the culmination of a series of random mutations guided by blind law.

But Darwinism is also dogma, and to challenge it today is to risk censure and ridicule.

This view of human beings—and of human origins—denies obvious truths and forwards a metaphysical view that is hostile to the beliefs most people hold about a divine creator, a fact of mind that neither materialist philosophy nor behavioral science can adequately explain. But Darwinism is also dogma, and to challenge it today is to risk censure and ridicule.

Still, dogma cannot stand forever merely on the weight of its own unchallenged authority. Even in the present era, when materialistic science is ascendant, Darwinists must be made to account for the facts behind their theory. And if the facts do not support it—as increasingly seems the case—then Darwinists must make room for theories that better conform to reality as we understand it.

FRAGMENTED VIEW

This is not to say that the Darwinist view of human origins is utterly without substance. Indeed, Darwinism seems strongest where it offers a grand theory uniting geology and paleontology, especially in the discipline of paleoanthropology.

Under this discipline, Darwinists theorize that fossil remains, from the oldest to the youngest, should show a more or less steady physical progression from ape-like traits to human-like traits. This theory presupposes primitive ancestors, from which humans developed through "descent with modification."

than fossils that appeared more human-like.

As Michael Roberts of Linfield College notes, "Chinese bones dating to 200,000 years ago show 'modern features,' suggesting to Chinese anthropologists that there was a local evolution of *Homo erectus* to *Homo sapiens*." He adds: "However, in the Dali skull and others of the same age in China, there are thick brow ridges and the skull vaults are low." Roberts concludes that there must be lurking undiscovered in the fossil record another, intermediate, "archaic form" of human being.[1] Otherwise, presumably, the model of gradual progression doesn't hold up.

And yet another anomaly of hominid fossils dating is cited by paleoanthropologist Donald Johanson—the famous discoverer of the "Lucy" skeleton. In his book, *Ancestors: In Search of Human Origins*, Johanson recounts a conversation with fellow paleontologist Alan Thorne about the latter's astonishment concerning remains unearthed in two different places in Australia.

This is not to say that the Darwinist view of human origins is utterly without substance.

And at first glance, the evidence unearthed and analyzed by scientists appears to confirm this hypothesis in a compelling way. Compared side by side, some fossils seem to show undeniable progression.

But difficulties arise when scientists use these same fossils to construct a comprehensive model of human evolution. Because like the fossils on which the model is based, the big picture of human evolution today is fragmented and puzzling.

The reasons for this fragmented view are numerous. To begin with, fossil dating—which is key to building any sort of evolutionary model—is notoriously problematic. Most fossils can't be dated directly, so scientists rely on clever inferences, usually based on radiological dating of materials found near the fossils in question.

But even if one accepts proposed fossil dates at face value, problems remain. In more than one case, hominid fossils that appear more primitive and ape-like have dated as being as young or younger

"Although they were considerably more 'primitive'-looking," Johanson writes, "the Kow Swamp [fossils] were 9,000 to 15,000 years old, only half the age of the Mungo fossils. That meant the fossils that looked more modern, the Mungo people, came *before* the robust, even *erectus*-like people at Kow Swamp." (Italics his.)[2]

As one can imagine, these frustrating turns in the trail of evidence have made trying to determine a direct line of descent from ape to human the most contentious aspect of human origin studies.

In terms of the fossil record, the first step in the process—the projected common ancestor between apes and humans—remains a glaring gap.[3] There is even debate about which fossils constitute the first non-ape human ancestor. From there, scientists can agree on perhaps three or four undisputed intermediary species leading to the emergence of *Homo sapiens*.

Meanwhile, the so-called tree of life for humans has been rendered more like a bush, with odd

Meanwhile, the so-called tree of life for humans has been rendered more like a bush, with odd branches of puzzling sub-species sprouting up then dying out with no apparent affect on the success of *Homo sapiens.*

branches of puzzling sub-species sprouting up and then dying out, with no apparent affect on the success of *Homo sapiens.* Perhaps the best example of such a puzzling sub-group are Neanderthals, who alternately have been declared slouching primitive ancestors of modern humans, non-humans too dim-witted to compete with *Homo sapiens*, semi-humans capable of interbreeding with *Homo sapiens* but not as culturally advanced, and entirely nonhuman but with bigger brains.[4]

NOT SO DIFFERENT

Of course, scientists have an excuse for being puzzled. Fossils, though remarkable, offer a limited source of evidence. Paleoanthropologists admit it would be immensely helpful, for instance, to be able to examine the genetic information in all fossils in order to determine whether various proposed species really were all that different.

After all, DNA analyses show that modern human beings, from African pygmies to Samoans to Swedes, vary little in their genetic makeup.

This fact bolsters the claims of one proponent of the multi-regional evolutionary model, which states that humans attained their present form while evolving in many places around the planet. Quoted again by Johanson, Thorne defends multi-regionalism by arguing that scientists often are too quick to pronounce puzzling fossil finds new species, without considering how varied in form some species—such as human beings—can be.

Thorne then makes the remarkable statement that smacks of a theory quite contrary to Darwinism. He says there's something "inherent" about the way humans are made to be so wondrously diverse.[5]

HEART OF THE MATTER

And so we arrive at the chief problem in Darwinism. Even when discussing its strongest points,

adherents find themselves making statements that could be understood as an attack on the fundamental assertion of Darwinian evolution—that all life forms are the result of a purely materialistic, random process. In Darwinism, there is no divine guidance; there is only chance and natural law.

But this view alienates people who, while merely laity, know better. There is something in human beings that—dare we say it—inherently recognizes the beauty and order in themselves and in the cosmos. No doubt many scientists recognize this, too, but as journalist Denyse O'Leary points out, they aren't ready to abandon Darwinism because they don't see a viable alternative theory.[6]

But that is changing. Darwinism is being challenged by a theory that scientifically explores the apparent design in the cosmos. And even one of Darwinism's most vociferous apologists, Richard Dawkins, concedes that the cosmos at least displays apparent design.[7]

But as it develops, through inquiries into microbiology and information theory, for example, Intelligent Design offers hope of becoming as comprehensive in scale as Darwinism—which is still mired in the same Nineteenth Century materialism that was used to fortify racism and sexism.

Intelligent Design theory argues that living beings are too complex to have developed by chance. The theory presently can be described as an extrapolation of the anthropic principle in physics—which declares that the basic forces that hold the universe together (and make it suitable for life) are fined-tuned with a mathematical precision that defies belief. But as it develops, through inquiries into microbiology and information theory, for example, Intelligent Design offers hope of becoming as comprehensive in scale as Darwinism—which is still mired in the same Nineteenth Century materialism that was used to fortify racism and sexism.

DARWINISM VS. DESIGN

And there can be little doubt about the desire for an alternative to Darwinism. As O'Leary points out, even opinion polls show that most Americans don't believe in it.[8] Popular books attack it. And mounting evidence supports long-held philosophical objections to it. What's more, many of these sustained objections add strength to the argument for design.

To begin at the beginning—something Darwinists are loathe to do—consider cosmology, a discipline that is emerging as a strong point for design proponents. Modern cosmologists have generally come to accept what the Big Bang theory asserts: That the universe burst forth, *ex nihilo*, from what can only be described as an unfathomable source of creative energy. And many scientists accept the theory despite a personal distaste for the obvious metaphysical implications. Combine the Big Bang theory with the anthropic principle, and the grounds for labeling the universe a purposeless place of random construction wear mighty thin.

Moving on from cosmology to biology itself, Darwin's theory falters almost before it can get started. This is because Darwinism has yet to devise an adequate, completely materialistic explanation for what some consider one of the most divine mysteries of all—the origin of life.

Granted, Darwinists point with enthusiasm to the famous 1953 experiment of University of Chicago graduate student Stanley Miller, who produced amino acids by zapping a slushy mix of gases with jolts of electricity. But this is as far as scientists have progressed in attempting to produce life from non-life.

In fact, to illustrate the insurmountable difficulty of building a living cell from non-living matter, Jonathan Wells of the Discovery Institute proposes a thought experiment working backwards toward the problem.

In Lee Strobel's book *The Case for a Creator*, Wells suggests, "Put a sterile, balanced salt solution in a test tube. Then put in a single living cell and poke a hole in it so that its contents leak into the solution... You have already accomplished far more what the Miller experiment ever could—you've got all the components you need for life."

Wells concludes: "The problem is you can't make a living cell. There's not even any point in trying."[9]

Thus Darwinists find themselves trying to explain the appearance of the first living organisms by resorting to fanciful—often unproveable—hypotheses. They cite a vague "self-organizing principle" present in some kinds of matter. Confronted further by the problem of accounting for genetic information, which resides in and regulates every living cell, some Darwinists have even concocted a fictional "RNA world," supposedly made up of cells that function according to a primitive (and wholly imaginary) genetic system.[10]

Thus Darwinists find themselves trying to explain the appearance of the first living organisms by resorting to fanciful — often unproveable — hypotheses. They cite a vague "self-organizing principle" present in some kinds of matter.

Finally, some scientists, such as paleontologist Stephen Jay Gould, simply skirt the problem by stating that since life exists, it must somehow have been inevitable.[11]

How then does Darwinism fare when tackling the issue it was invented to explain, namely, the origin of species as outlined by the fossil record? Ultimately, not so well.

As it does for human origins, Darwin's theory predicts that the fossil record as a whole should reveal a steady progression toward more complex life forms. Key to confirming this theory would be the discovery of so-called transitional fossils—ones with mixed physical traits that clearly illustrate evolution in progress.

Instead, paleontologists have uncovered what Gould allegedly called one of the great trade secrets of evolutionary science.[12] Discoveries of fossils worthy of being labeled transitional, among them the famous bird-like *Archaeopteryx*, have proved the exception and not the rule. In fact, what scientists do find when they consult the fossil record are new species emerging, fully formed, with no apparent predecessors. This phenomenon particularly holds true for the Cambrian era, during which scientists estimate nearly every animal phyla suddenly emerged.[13]

Evolutionary scientists are equally puzzled by the way species abruptly vanish from the fossil record. Darwin's theory is built on gradualism—the notion that small, accumulated changes in some species allow them over time to eclipse other species. Consequently, evidence of catastrophic extinctions can be nearly as detrimental to the theory as the inference of design.

Indeed, Darwinists such as Gould have struggled with the uncomfortable reality that the evidence doesn't support a model of constant, gradual evolution. As popular science writer William K. Hartmann noted, "It is hard to overemphasize the shocking suddenness of life's proliferation."[14] To address this disparity, Gould worked with colleague Niles Eldredge to devise a modified theory called "punctuated equilibrium." Gould described the new sub-theory as a way to explain how evolution occurs not in a constant, gradual fashion, but in "quick and quirky episodes."[15]

HOW DOES IT WORK?

But even if Darwinists succeed in reconciling their theory with the fossil evidence, they still must deal with describing the precise mechanism by which random biological evolution is supposed to occur. This task is by no means easy. Advances in biochemistry and genetics show that living creatures—down to their tiniest components—are more intricate and precisely regulated than scientists imagined.

and structures that Darwin thought were so simple actually involves staggeringly complicated biochemical processes that cannot be papered over with rhetoric."[17]

Behe illustrated how even the bacterial flagellum, for instance, requires the convergence of physical structure, chemical activity and genetic instruction in order to function properly. Systems such as the flagellum or the blood clotting mechanism, Behe declared, could not have evolved because they are, in his words, "irreducibly complex." They were designed to function the way they function.

As one can imagine, Behe's assertion caused a furor among Darwinists, though he was merely adding details to a hypothesis developed much earlier.

In *Janus: A Summing Up*, journalist Arthur Koestler objected to Darwinism on the grounds that it tries to describe life forms—human beings in particular—as merely an amalgam of various physical components. Koestler argued that human beings are much more than the sum of their parts. In fact, he coined the term "holons" to illustrate that humans—and all life

Take, for instance, the debate over whether or not complex organs such as the human eye could have evolved gradually, or even whether a partial eye could offer an organism any biological advantage.

Take, for instance, the debate over whether or not complex organs such as the human eye could have evolved gradually, or even whether a partial eye could offer an organism any biological advantage.

Dawkins, of course, glibly argues: "Half of an eye is just one percent better than 49 percent of an eye, which is already better than 48 percent, and the difference is significant."[16] He then points to light-sensitive "photocells" and simpler animal eyes as possible intermediary forms leading up to the human eye.

But these arguments, as always, miss the point because they focus on isolating a single biological component and describing it in gross physical terms—lenses, optic nerves, blood vessels—neglecting the fact that 49 percent of an eye is not the same thing as 49 percent vision.

As biochemist Michael Behe points out in *Darwin's Black Box*, "Each of the anatomical steps

forms—are composed of independent, but wholly interconnected components. In short, life forms are holistic, and tampering with various parts from major organs down to individual cells threatens the very essence of the whole creature.[18]

Like many academics, however, Koestler did not abandon the concept of evolution completely—but neither did he rule out design. He went on to explore, in *Janus*, how what he described as a finely tuned genetic system might produce new life forms through carefully regulated internal changes. He likened this system to a sophisticated typewriter that is only permitted to form meaningful words, an analogy that he declared "*reduces the importance of the chance factor to a minimum*" (his italics). Koestler added: "It does not answer the ultimate question of who or what programmed that prodigious typewriter, but it puts the question mark where it belongs."[19]

NATURAL SELECTION UNDONE

In contrast to this powerful idea that living beings are designed to function a certain way, the only thing Darwinists can offer as a guiding force for the evolution of various species is the rather vague notion of natural selection.

In *The Origin of Species*, Darwin himself proposed the concept of natural selection based on the very real results obtained when humans breed plant and animal stock to foster certain traits. If human-directed breeding can produce dramatic changes in form in a few generations, Darwin mused, imagine what nature could do over eons. Of course, he began his thought experiment with a process obviously guided by intelligence, then insisted that a purposeless one would do just as well—or even better.

And so from Darwin's original philosophical inconsistency, the concept of natural selection has not fared well. For one thing, it has been notoriously difficult to define. The shop-worn aphorism "survival of the fittest" doesn't always apply, because in certain situations the fastest, strongest, noblest members of a particular species die just as quickly— if not faster—than the weak and timid.

So fitness is not necessarily equated with biological superiority. Instead it is often associated with so-called reproductive strategies—the idea that evolution favors life forms that leave behind the most offspring. The absurdity of this concept is not lost on journalist Richard Milton, who scoffs at paleontologist George Simpson's assertion that evolution can be said to favor red hair when two red-haired parents produce more children than blond or brunette parents.[20]

After all, how does having red-haired children explain a mouse evolving into an elephant?

It doesn't, at least as far as Gould is concerned. Writing for *Scientific American* magazine, Gould argues that natural selection is often overrated and misused as an explanation for how or why evolution occurs. He says the truth is that evolution is so random that there is no way to predict how life forms will ultimately develop.[21]

Unfortunately, if a process is unpredictable, it is also unfalsifiable. There is no controlled experiment to test it, nor can it be subject to the empirical method of study. It therefore passes beyond the realm of science.

MISSING THE OBVIOUS

But failure on scientific principle has yet to stop Darwinists from spreading their gospel in the realm of biology; neither has it halted fellow materialists in disciplines such as psychology and behavioral studies. These fields have produced many scientists eager to describe human intellect as merely that of an advanced ape, to declare consciousness and free will illusions, and human culture an interesting byproduct of the evolutionary drive to leave offspring.

And so myths that sprang up with Freud's sexual analyses and were reinforced by B. F. Skinner's studies on the behavior of laboratory rats continue in rather absurd fashion.

Richard Dawkins muses about whether all of human civilization exists merely to fulfill a biological need to perpetuate "the selfish gene."[22] Artificial intelligence expert Marvin Minsky famously declares the human mind to be nothing more than "a computer made of meat."[23] Journalist Malcolm Gladwell reflects on the fact that the vast part of our mental power is spent on unconscious activity and states, "the task of making sense of ourselves and our behavior requires that we acknowledge there can be as much value in the blink of an eye as in months of rational thought."[24]

Thus the attempts to describe what it means to be human in terms of Darwinian evolution—or some similar proposition based on a materialistic rationalization—inevitably results in denying the obvious, because human intellect is real, and cannot be explained merely as an advanced form of animal consciousness. As philosopher Mortimer J. Adler reminds us, the way human beings think and feel about things makes them fundamentally different from anything else yet discovered in nature.[25] The difference is not one of degree but of kind. We are not highly developed apes, and no amount of incremental improvement could ever turn an ape into a human. Apes fling filth; humans publish newspapers, form political parties and occasionally languish in their parents' basements wondering why life has left them unfulfilled.

The fact that human beings place such a premium on personal fulfillment brings us back to the reality of our inherent inquisitiveness. We wonder why we were put here, and how we are supposed to behave. And a growing movement in science wants to tell us that a good part of the answer to why we have so many questions is because we were designed to ask them.

INQUIRING MINDS

This certainly is the assertion of philosopher Jay Wesley Richards and astronomer Guillermo Gonzalez, who teamed up to produce the book *The Privileged Planet*. Analyzing the earth's structure, its life-supporting habitat, its position of safety within both the solar system and Milky Way galaxy, and as a platform for observing the cosmos, Richards and Gonzalez conclude that humans and their home are indeed unique. The evidence supports the assumption that humans not only were designed to be inquirers, they were placed in an exceptionally well-suited position from which to inquire.[26]

And yet to Darwinists—whose myths pervade state-funded education, public museums and popular culture—the idea that human beings might be the product of design remains abominable, even dangerous. As Dawkins put it: "If you meet somebody who claims not to believe in evolution, that person is ignorant, stupid or insane (or wicked, but I'd rather not consider that)."[27]

Materialists sneer at what they consider the irrational nature of a design hypothesis, failing to grasp that, as law professor Phillip Johnson points out, "To theists ... the concept of a supernatural Mind in whose image we are created is the essential metaphysical basis for our confidence that the cosmos is rational and to some extent understandable."[28]

Darwinists can only counter by declaring humans a happy accident in a purposeless universe, insisting that even our own thoughts and desires cannot be taken at face value. And it is on this authority that they sift through old bones and invent stories about where we came from, but cannot tell us why we are here.

1. Michael Roberts, "The Origins of Modern Humans: Multiregional and Replacement Theories." calvin.linfield.edu

2. Donald Johanson, Lenora Johanson and Blake Edgar, *Ancestors: In Search of Human Origins*. New York: Willard Books, 1994. p. 297.

3. See Smithsonian Institute's Human Origins Program. www.mnh.si.edu/anthro/humanorigins/ha/primate.html

4. See Smithsonian Institute online; PBS Origins of Humankind. www.pbs.org/wgbh/evolution/humankind/n.html

5. Johanson, p. 218.

6. Denyse O'Leary, *By Design or by Chance*. Minneapolis: Augsburg Books, 2004. p. 100.

7. O'Leary, p. 127.

8. Ibid, p. 83.

9. Lee Strobel, *The Case for a Creator*. Grand Rapids: Zondervan, 2004. p. 39.

10. Phillip Johnson, *Darwin on Trial*. Downers Grove: Intervarsity Press, 1993. p. 108.

11. Stephen Jay Gould, "The Evolution of Life on the Earth." *Scientific American*, March 1, 2004.

12. O'Leary, p. 109.

13. Ibid.

14. William K. Hartmann, *The History of the Earth*. New York: Workman Publishing, 1994. p. 127.

15. Gould.

16. Richard Dawkins, "Where D'you Get Those Peepers?" *New Statesman & Society*, June 16, 1995.

17. Michael Behe, *Darwin's Black Box*. New York: Touchstone, 1998. p. 22.

18. Arthur Koestler, *Janus: A Summing Up*. New York: Random House, 1978. p. 27.

19. Koestler, p. 189.

20. Richard Milton, "Neo-Darwinism: Time to Reconsider." www.alternativescience.com/darwinism.htm

21. Gould.

22. Richard Dawkins, *The Selfish Gene*. New York: Oxford University Press, 1989.

23. Strobel, p. 250.

24. Marianne Szegedy-Maszak, "Mysteries of the Mind." *U.S. News & World Report*, February 28, 2005.

25. Mortimer J. Adler, *How to Think About the Great Ideas*. Chicago: Open Court, 2000. p. 84, 91.

26. Guillermo Gonzalez and Jay Wesley Richards, *The Privileged Planet*. Washington, D.C.: Regnery Publishing, 2004.

27. O'Leary, p. 103.

28. Johnson, p. 164.

2

ANCIENT CITIES, ANCIENT PLANS

Sacsayhuaman.

Sacsayhuaman.

Richard Nisbet

ANCIENT WALLS

THERE ARE NO OTHER WALLS like these. They are different from Stonehenge, different from the pyramids of the Egyptians and the Maya, different from any of the other ancient monolithic stonework.

The stones fit so perfectly that no blade of grass or steel can slide between them. There is no mortar. They often join in complex and irregular surfaces that would appear to be a nightmare for the stonemason.

There is usually neither adornment nor inscription. There is Elfin whimsy here, as well as raw, primitive and mighty expression.

Most of these walls are found around Cuzco and the Urubamba River Valley in the Peruvian Andes. There are a few scattered examples elsewhere in the Andes, but almost nowhere else on earth.

Mostly, the structures are beyond our ken. The how, why and what simply baffle. Modern man can neither explain nor duplicate.

Mysteries like this bring out explanations that are scholarly, whimsical, inventive and ridiculous.

Mysteries like this bring out explanations that are scholarly, whimsical, inventive and ridiculous.

Through these photographs and snippets of lore and opinion, these pages hope to entertain, tantalize and perhaps even inspire.

Sacsayhuaman was supposedly completed around 1508. Depending on who you listen to, it took a crew of 20,000 to 30,000 men working for 60 years.

Here is a mystery: The chronicler Garcilaso de la Vega was born around 1530, and raised in the shadow of these walls. And yet he seems not to have had a clue as to how Sacsayhuaman was built. He wrote:

...this fortress surpasses the constructions known as the seven wonders of the world. For in the case of a long broad wall like that of Babylon, or the Colossus of Rhodes, or the pyramids of Egypt, or the other monuments, one can see clearly how they were executed...how, by summoning an immense body of workers and accumulating more and more material day by day and year by year, they overcame all difficulties by employing human effort over a long period. But it is indeed beyond the power of imagination to understand how these Indians, unacquainted with devices, engines and implements, could have cut, dressed, raised and lowered great rocks, more like lumps of hills than building stones, and set them so exactly in their places. For this reason, and because the Indians were so familiar with demons, the work is attributed to enchantment...

Cusco, from the hill above.

A huaca. Photo by Kurt Bennett.

Surely a few of those 20,000 laborers were still around when Garcilaso was young. Was everyone struck with amnesia? Or is Sacsayhuaman much older than we've been led to believe?

Archaeologists tell us that the walls of Sacsayhuaman rose ten feet higher than their remnants. That additional ten feet of stones supplied the building materials for the cathedrals and casas of the conquistadors.

It is generally conceded that these stones were much smaller than those lithic monsters that remain.

Perhaps the upper part of the walls, constructed of small, regularly-shaped stones was the only part of Sacsayhuaman that was built by the Incas and "finished in 1508." This could explain why no one at the time of the conquest seemed to know how those mighty walls were built.

Manco Capac, the first Inca, was divinely directed to go to Cuzco and settle there. That he did, and through successive generations of rulers, this little tribe expanded until it ruled an empire that rivaled that of Rome. Cuzco, which they called the "Navel of the World," remained their capital.

Here's a strange bit of lore: According to Indian legend, Cuzco was so barren that no crops could be grown there. In what is now the center of the city, there was a lake and a bog. The second Inca, Sinchi Roca, had the swamp drained and filled with stones and logs until it was firm enough to support their stone buildings. He also had thousands of loads of good earth brought in and spread over the land, making the valley fertile. What could possibly have been the attraction of this barren, boggy place? Suppose the magnificent lower walls of Sacsayhuaman were there before Manco Capac came to Cuzco. That in itself would be enough to make the place holy.

THE STRANGE STONE CARVINGS

What are these carvings in stone that seem to serve no purpose, the steps that go nowhere, the seats so hard to get to?

They are to be found in astonishing abundance in the area around Cuzco. They are carved so precisely, with their outside and inside corners so sharp and fine.

How were they carved?

And even stranger, *why* were they carved?

How they were carved is still a mystery. The art is lost, perhaps was lost even before the conquest.

The *why* is another matter. The answer probably lies in the complex and rigid religion of the Incas. Most of these strange carvings are sacred shrines called Huacas.

Every huaca had prescribed sacrifices to be made on specific days. Most of the sacrifices were not human, but Cobo claimed that 32 of the shrines required human sacrifice, usually of children. This is questioned by many who see in his statistics a rationalization for the conquest, which was, after all, a mission to bring the true religion to the heathens.

A huaca. Photo by Kurt Bennett.

Aldo at a huaca. Photo by Kurt Bennett.

Ollantaytambo. Photo by Kurt Bennett.

Mysterious "Bench" on the hill known as the Temple of the Moon, near Cusco.

Scores of gigantic stones began their journey to Ollantaytambo at the Kachita quarries, above.

Kachita quarries.

There were supposedly 333 huacas in and around Cuzco. They were situated along 40 so-called "ceque" lines, which radiated like spokes of a wheel from Coricancha, the "Temple of the Sun," in Cuzco.

Most of what we have been told about huacas came from the Jesuit Priest Bernabe Cobo, who wrote a hundred years after the conquest. Each of the shrines was attended by a family. Every huaca had prescribed sacrifices to be made on specific days. Most of the sacrifices were not human, but Cobo claimed that 32 of the shrines required human sacrifice, usually of children. This is questioned by many who see in his statistics a rationalization for the conquest, which was, after all, a mission to bring the true religion to the heathens.

Not far from Cuzco there is a hill they call the Temple of the Moon. The hill has several caves and many rock carvings. Some of the carvings here show extreme weathering.

Notice the horizontal bar near the center of the photograph. For lack of a better word, we'll call it a "bench."

Two close shots of the "bench." Notice the rounded edges and general appearance of aging. Some think this carving was made before the last glacier carved its way through here thousands of years ago.

Ollantaytambo is rare if not unique in Peru. The gigantic monoliths you see here are part of what was to be a shrine or temple.

At some time unknown, and for reasons unknown, work mysteriously stopped on this huge project.

Scores of gigantic stones began their journey from the quarry of Kachiqhata (in the upper left corner of the photograph).

They were partially shaped in the quarry, then slid down the hill and dragged across the river and over the fields.

Once across the field, the stones were dragged up a 1,200 foot ramp to the temple site.

MONOLITHS THAT DIDN'T MAKE IT

There is clear evidence of sudden abandonment all along the way from the quarry to the construction site. Partially cut stones lie in the fields, on

---

Significantly, there seems to be no history, no memory, no legends even of when or why work stopped on this massive project.

---

the roads and the ramp. Some of these monsters, like the one at left with the strange cups cut into it, are as much as 20 feet long.

The local people call these "piedras consadas," weary stones. They were too tired to go any further. Significantly, there seems to be no history, no memory, no legends even of when or why work stopped on this massive project.

The mountainside below the Kachiqhata quarries is strewn with rocks that look like hunks of salmon. Some are large and some are pebbles that are like ball-bearings underfoot.

Often there is no trail. The going is difficult.

1,200 foot ramp to the Ollantaytambo temple site, up which the gigantic stones were moved.

"Piedras consada," or "weary stones," left lying about the mountainside as though "too tired to go any further."

Another "weary stone," with mysterious cup marks.

Damage at Sacsayhuaman.

Doug with anomalous wheel. The Incas did not have nor use wheels, so who built it and why?

Sacsayhuaman.

THE ANOMALY THAT SHOULDN'T BE THERE

Higher in the quarries is an anomaly. There is something there that shouldn't be there.

We know that the Incas did not have the wheel. It is also pretty clear that the Spanish did no quarrying at Kachiqhata. They didn't need to. They simply tore down existing structures and re-used the stones for their own purposes.

So why is this wheel here, perched so nicely 2,000 feet above the river in the quarries? It is apparently a millwheel, 62" in diameter with a good part of the backside split off. (You can see a hairline crack around the circumference of the remaining piece.) Whoever attempted to make this wheel obviously lacked the skill of those who quarried stones for the temple. An expert quarryman would have seen this fracture coming and found another rock for the job.

"It appears that the Inca technique of fitting the blocks together was based largely on trial and error. It is a laborious method, particularly if one considers the size of some of the huge stones at Sacsayhuaman or Ollantaytambo. What should be kept in mind, however, is that time and labor power were probably of little concern to the Incas, who did not have a European notion of time and had plenty of tribute labor from conquered peoples at their disposal." —Jean-Pierre Protzen, *Scientific American*, February 1986

THE MYSTERIOUS MACHU PICCHU

Machu Picchu is one of the few places left unscathed by the conquering Spaniards. Searching for more gold, Pizarro marched his men up the Urubamba River and around the horseshoe bend at the base of the mountain.

Hiram Bingham was told of a plant whose juices softened rock so that the surfaces would join perfectly... Considering the fact that lichen softens stone to attach its roots, and considering the ongoing extinction of plant species, perhaps this isn't really such a far-fetched notion.

"How were such titanic blocks of stone brought to the top of the mountain from the quarries many miles away? How were they cut and fitted? How were they raised and put in place? Now one knows, no one can even guess. There are archaeologists, scientists, who would have us believe that the dense, hard andesite rock was cut, surfaced and faced by means of stone or bronze tools. Such an explanation is so utterly preposterous that it is not even worthy of serious consideration. No one [has ever] found anywhere any stone tool or implement that would cut or chip the andesite, and no bronze ever made will make any impression upon it." —A. Hyatt & Ruth Verrill, *America's Ancient Civilizations*

Jean-Pierre Protzen proved the Verrills wrong. He went to Cuzco and showed how river rocks could be used as hammers to pound stones into the desired shape.

Serenely perched 1,500 feet above the thundering waters, Machu Picchu escaped the fate of most of the Incan empire.

At some point, for reasons that elude us, life in the city ended and the forest took dominion. It was rediscovered in 1911 by a young American named Hiram Bingham.

It is now generally thought that at the time of the conquest, knowledge of Machu Picchu had been lost by the Incas themselves. This hasn't stopped modern historians from somehow attributing its construction to Pachacutec, the ninth Inca who reigned in the mid-Fifteenth Century, and gets credit for much of the achievements of that civilization.

Hiram Bingham was told of a plant whose juices softened rock so that the surfaces would join perfectly. There are reports of such a plant, including this one by an early Spanish chronicler: While encamped by a rocky river, he watched a bird with

Machu Picchu.

Flower at Machu Picchu.

a leaf in its beak light on a rock, lay down the leaf and peck at it. The next day the bird returned. By then there was a concavity where the leaf had been. By this method the bird created a drinking cup to catch the splashing waters of the river. Considering the fact that lichen softens stone to attach its roots, and considering the ongoing extinction of plant species, perhaps this isn't really such a far-fetched notion.

Erich von Däniken, in his series of books beginning with *Chariots of the Gods?*, theorized that the Andean stone works were built by aliens/gods who visited the earth long ago, bringing civilization to primitive man. The scientific community simply snickered.

Whatever one thinks of his theories, he brought to the public an awareness of the many ancient monuments on the earth that seem to defy rational explanation.

In his novel "Slapstick," Kurt Vonnegut quips:

> ...there must have been days of light gravity in old times, when people could play tiddley winks with huge chunks of stone.

Pedro de Cieza de Leon wrote of an old Inca legend about the creator-god, Viracocha. Once to show his power he caused a huge fire, then extinguished it. As a result of having been burnt so, the stones were so light that even a large one could be picked up as though it were made of cork.

The structures at Machu Picchu are not as gigantic as those at Sacsayhuaman, but some are surely finer. In a few cases, as in the "Temple of Three Windows," these walls stand among the most inspired structures created by man.

SOME SPECULATION—WHERE ELSE ARE STONE WORKS LIKE THESE FOUND?

There are curious connections between the Andes and Easter Island... In the oldest legends, Easter Island was called the "Navel of the World." Cuzco was called the same.

It may be that the only other place on earth where such structures are found is Easter Island. The most remote inhabited place in the world, this barren speck of land boasts over 500 gigantic, long-eared stone statues called Moai. There are curious connections between the Andes and Easter Island. For as long as we know, Easter Island has had the potato and the totora reed, both of Andean origin. In the oldest legends, Easter Island was called the "Navel of the World." Cuzco was called the same.

Thor Heyerdahl explored the island in an ongoing effort to prove his theory that people came to Easter Island from the east, sailing the prevailing currents. He believed that the walls there of the Andean style were not built by those who carved the Moai, but by an earlier civilization.

A study of underwater topography and plate tectonics suggests a startling possibility.

Look at a map of the Pacific Ocean floor just off the western coast of South America. There is an

Temple at Machu Picchu.

Big Rocks at Machu Picchu.

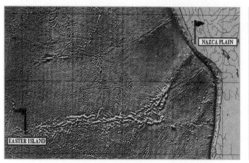

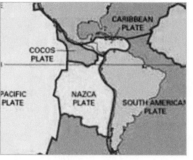

From the NOAA map *Measured and Estimated Seafloor Topography.* Tectonic Plates—From a USGS Map. Nazca map.

underwater ridge that connects to the coast of Peru at the fabled Nazca Plain. From there it extends out in a jagged line to Easter Island. These two locations are at the opposite edges of the Nazca plate.

The Nazca Ridge is on the Nazca tectonic plate. This plate is sliding under the South American plate. As this happens the edge of the Nazca plate pushes under the South American plate, lifting its edge. This is usually a smooth and steady subduction, but a global catastrophe of Noachean magnitude would call off all bets.

The most-accepted current scientific model for earth change today is *uniformitarianism*. According to this model, geological changes are now and always have been a gradual process. This theory is being challenged by the proponents of *catastrophism*, which posits that sometimes sudden and dramatic changes occur on our Terra-not-so-Firma. (The pummeling that comet Shoemaker-Levy 9 gave Jupiter in 1994 gave catastrophism a good boost.)

There is ample evidence that Lake Titicaca, now at an elevation of 12,500 feet above sea level, was once *at* sea level. I am suggesting that the Nazca ridge, or part of it, might once have been *above* sea level. This would have provided a partial land bridge between Easter Island and South America.

The Nazca Plain, which is directly inland from the juncture of the Nazca ridge and South America, is as strange as Easter Island. It is covered with a jumble of lines and drawings so huge that they can only be comprehended from the air. Many theories have been proposed to explain these markings, but none of them that I know of have taken underwater topography into account. Both the markings of the Nazca Plain and the statues of Easter Island seem the work of peoples possessed. Could it be that these extraordinary efforts are the reaching-out of those whose ancestors' connection had been severed?

THE CATASTROPHE

What may have been the cause is a matter of debate, but it is widely agreed that *something* earth-shaking occurred around 9600 B.C. It was then that large numbers of flora and fauna species (among them the mammoth and the mastodon) disappeared. It has also been theorized by respected scientists that the axis of the earth shifted at that time. There are flood legends recounting worldwide catastrophe in almost every society on earth.

If such a worldwide jolt occurred, it is quite possible that the Nazca plate could slip suddenly under the South American plate, drastically lowering the one and raising the other.

Our home, the planet we call earth, is a thing alive. We live on a crust of puzzle-like pieces that float upon the fluid mantle below. Landmasses rise and fall, ocean levels rise and fall, obscuring what once was seen.

The ocean floor is a repository of mysteries. And the more we explore that least-charted domain of our environment, the more we find things that contradict what we have believed is our planet's history. Our discoveries tell us this: Our civilization, the one we call unique, the only organization and exploitation of human potential that has existed here on our planet, is perhaps not unique after all. Our discoveries beneath the sea hint of peoples and civilizations that rose and fell long, long before our time.

Gary A. David

ALONG THE 33RD PARALLEL

A GLOBAL MYSTERY CIRCLE

WHAT'S IN A NUMBER?

The number 33 enigmatically stretches as a latitude line across many diverse cultures in many different times. Known in numerology as the Master Teacher, 33 is the most influential of all numbers, indicating selfless devotion to the spiritual progress of humankind. The other two master numbers, 11 (vision) and 22 (vision with action) form the base of a two-dimensional pyramid, and added together equal 33 (guidance to the world), the apex of the pyramid.[1] On the reverse of the Masonically-inspired Great Seal of the United States is the pyramid with the all-seeing eye of divine Reason at its apex. According to ritual Freemasonry, 33 is considered sacred because, in most cases, there is no higher degree or level to which a Mason may aspire.

In a Biblical context we note that King David ruled in Jerusalem for 33 years, Jacob had 33 sons and daughters and Jesus Christ was crucified at age 33. Two interpenetrating triangles whose apexes point in opposite directions form the hexagram of the Star of David (three plus three equals six). On the other hand, three times three equals nine, or the Ennead, the nine primal gods of Egyptian mythology. Dante ended canto 33 of the *Purgatorio*, the second section of his *Divine Comedy*, with: "...perfect, pure and ready for the

Stars."[2] Canto 33 of the *Paradiso*, or the third section, concludes with lines about the poet being turned "as in a wheel whose motion nothing jars/by the Love that moves the Sun and the other stars."[3] It is more than a coincidence that the 33rd canto of each section concludes with parallel lines regarding the celestial; it may instead be the code from a lost ancient tradition.

It is more than a coincidence that the 33rd canto of each section concludes with parallel lines regarding the celestial; it may instead be the code from a lost ancient tradition.

This number even permeates the biological realm studied by science: 33 is the number of turns in a complete sequence of DNA.[4] A more ominous connotation appears in the 33rd element of the periodic table. Arsenic is a brittle, steel-gray substance that is actively poisonous. The Greek root *arsen* means "male, strong" or "virile," which suggests the active reach of this potent and potentially deadly number across the globe. Indeed, when we consider the northern latitude of 33 degrees, some intriguing synchronicities, or "meaningful coincidences," are found.[5]

These ancient American Indians created an estimated total of 500 miles of canals to irrigate over 25,000 acres in the Phoenix Basin—all constructed with mere digging sticks, stone implements and woven carrying baskets. In fact, no wheelbarrows or draft animals were ever used.

YOU SAY PHOENIX AND I SAY PHOENICIA

The first stop on our tour along the 33rd parallel is the metropolis of Phoenix, Arizona, located at 33 degrees 30 minutes latitude. Gleaming like a steel and glass mirage surrounded by ironwood, palo verde and saguaro cactus, this modern American city lies in a brown cloud of auto exhaust at the northern end of the Sonoran Desert. With its imported palm trees and omnipresent swimming pools that shimmer when seen from high in the air like turquoise and silver jewelry on a jet-setter's tanned breast, Phoenix is pervaded with the aura of the foreign and the bizarre. Few casual tourists realize, however, that this was once the center of the ancient Hohokam culture.

The largest Hohokam site, known as Snaketown, was located about five miles north of the exact 33 degree line, while the ruins of the astronomical observatory called Casa Grande still rest about five miles south of the line. The Hohokam inhabited the Valley of the Sun perhaps as early as 300 B.C.E. (about the time of Alexander the Great and the Ptolemaic Dynasties in Egypt) and built one of the world's most extensive irrigation systems. These ancient American Indians created an estimated total of 500 miles of canals to irrigate over 25,000 acres in the Phoenix Basin—all constructed with mere digging sticks, stone implements and woven carrying baskets. In fact, no wheelbarrows or draft animals were ever used. The main canals leading from the Salt and Gila rivers measured up to 75 feet across at the top and 50 feet wide at the bottom.[6] As southwestern archaeologist H. M. Wormington observes, "The scope of the canal project suggests comparisons with the erection of the huge pyramids of Egypt or the great temples of the Maya."[7] Clearly this monumental technology was the key factor that allowed the desert dwelling people to inhabit their extremely harsh region for well over a thousand years.

Skipping across the Atlantic on the same parallel, we find a number of intriguing sites in the Old World. For instance, at a latitude of 33 degrees 19 minutes was located the primary Phoenician seaport of Tyre (now called Sûr), almost 50 miles south of Beirut. Dating back as early as 5000 B.C.E., Tyre was renowned for a purple-red dye obtained from the snails of the genus Murex.[8] The color is one of the meanings of the word "phoenix," which the ancient Egyptians sometimes associated with the purple heron. Back in North America the "place of the heron" refers to Aztlan, the Nahuatl word for the mythical land that the Aztecs inhabited after emerging from Chicomostoc, the Seven Caves located in the bowels of the earth.[9] Chicano folklore identifies Aztlan as that portion of Mexico taken over by the U.S. after the Mexican-American War of 1846—in part, the Arizona Territory, where the settlement of Phoenix arose.

During the Tenth Century B.C.E. King Hiram of Tyre supplied King Solomon with craftsmen, metallurgists, cedar wood, architectural design and presumably the esoteric symbolism of these two columns for the construction of his temple at Jerusalem.

The Masonic author Albert Pike states that Tyre was the seat of the Osirian Mysteries after they had been imported from Egypt.[10] Pike asserts that the two massive columns located at the entrance of the Tyrian Temple of Malkarth were consecrated to the Winds and to Fire. This pair is thought to be the prototype of Jachin and Boaz, the two pillars found on the eastern wall of every Masonic temple in the world. On the right, or to the south, is Jachin, which means "He shall establish" and signifies an active, vivifying force; on the left, or to the north, is Boaz, which means "In it is strength" and connotes passive stability and permanence.[11] Freemasons Christopher Knight and Robert Lomas suggest that the former represents the winter solstice sunrise, while the latter the summer solstice sunrise.[12] Although this is possible, we propose that Jachin represents the southern stargate between Sagittarius and Scorpius while Boaz signifies the northern stargate between Gemini and Taurus.[13] Our assumption is based on the fact that in the York Rite of Freemasonry a celestial globe symbolizing ex-carnation (i.e., a spirit leaving its present body) is found atop Jachin while a terrestrial globe representing incarnation is positioned atop Boaz.[14] During the Tenth Century B.C.E. King Hiram of Tyre supplied King Solomon with craftsmen, metallurgists, cedar wood, architectural design and presumably the esoteric symbolism of these two columns for the construction of his temple at Jerusalem (*1 Kings 7:13-22*).[15] In addition to being besieged at various times by Nebuchadrezzar, Alexander the Great, the Romans and others, the trade capital city-state of Tyre was conquered by the Crusaders in the Twelfth Century A.D., who built a Knights Templar church there.

Some speculate that the orientation of the two pillars imitates obelisks placed before the pylons of Egyptian temples, especially those of the Heliopolitan temple of Thothmes (Tuthmosis) III, who reigned in the Fifteenth Century B.C.E. as the militarily expansionist pharaoh of the Eighteenth Dynasty. He is also thought to be founder of the Order of the Rosy Cross, or the Rosicrucians.[16] The archaeologist Sir Flinders Petrie even found records in the Libyan desert that describe a secret Masonic guild meeting held circa 2000 B.C.E. "The guild met to discuss working hours, wages and rules for daily labor. It convened in a chapel and provided relief to widows, orphans and workers in distress. The organizational duties described in the papyri are very similar to those of 'Warden' and 'Master' in a modern branch of the Brotherhood which evolved from those guilds: Freemasonry."[17] It seems that all roads lead to—Egypt.

Also of interest near the 33rd parallel is Byblos, a bit farther north of Tyre at a latitude of 34

degrees 08 minutes. The name of this city state is derived from the Greek *ta b blia*, which means "the book," or "bible." Indeed, the invention of a Phoenician alphabetic phonetic script occurred here and eventually spread to the Greek world.[18] A bit farther east at nearly the same latitude is located Baalbeck, an ancient megalithic temple constructed with some of the largest stone blocks ever cut. Extracted and hauled from a quarry many miles away, these megaliths include one block measuring 80 feet long and weighing 1100 tons.[19] In this section we have seen how Phoenix and Phoenicia are linked by latitude. We shall now continue eastward to encounter other significant ancient sites along the same parallel.

A PASSAGE TO CHINA

A little over 500 miles east of these Phoenician cities at 33 degrees 20 minutes is modern-day Baghdad in Iraq, with Babylon located about 55 miles to the south. This ancient capital of Mesopotamia on the banks of the Euphrates River was once the largest city in the world, encompassing over 2,500 acres. The construction of Babylon began during the Twenty-Third Century B.C.E. and included the Temple of Marduk (known as Esagila) as well as the legendary Tower of Babel (identified as Etemenanki). The latter structure was a seven-tiered ziggurat rising to a height of 300 feet with a base on each side measuring the same distance. This measurement, incidentally, equals the length of the Hohokam platform mound at Pueblo Grande in Arizona. On the eastern side of the city was an outer rampart of triple wall construction extending for 11 miles. A network of irrigation canals reminiscent of the Hohokam also once served the city. In addition, the terraced Hanging Gardens were one of the Seven Wonders of the Ancient World.[20]

This "city and a tower" (*Genesis 11:4*) was known as Ba-bel, the legendary site of the linguistic confounding. "The biblical interpretation of the name is fanciful. The Bible connects Babel with the Hebrew verb *Bâlal*, 'to confuse,' whereas it really comes from Bâb-ili, which in Babylonian means 'Gate of God.'"[21] This terrestrial correlation to another sort of stargate is perhaps a reference to the Processional Way leading to Ishtar Gate, both of which were adorned with glazed blue enameled figures of lions, bulls and dragons. Pike maintains that the temple contained a representation in silver of two large serpents. "The Greeks called Bel *Beliar*; and Hesychius interprets that word to mean dragon or great serpent. We learn from the book of Bel and the Dragon, that in Babylon was kept a great, live serpent, which the people worshipped."[22] This reminds us of the Place of the Snakes, or the Hohokam site of Snaketown, as well as of the Hopi biennial Snake Dance ceremony still performed with live rattlesnakes on the high desert of Arizona.

The White Pyramid was supposedly built after the old emperors, known as "the sons of heaven," descended to earth in their "fiery metallic dragons" and began to rule China. Its interior is rumored to be a model of this empire with a jeweled roof depicting the constellations and rivers of flowing mercury.

In more recent times Babylon played a significant role in the rituals of Freemasonry and continues to do so. For instance, Knight and Lomas discovered that the ceremony for the Royal Arch of Solomon Degree (13th degree) entails the candidate and two others playing the roles of the three Master Masons of Babylon: Shadrach, Meshech and Abednego. According to the narrative told in the ritual, these children of the Babylonian captivity desire to assist in the rebuilding of the Temple of Solomon. Thus, Babylon's symbolic importance, which the co-authors believe extends back to at least Knights Templar times and probably before, is re-emphasized inside every Masonic lodge to the present day.[23]

Traveling along the 33rd parallel from the Middle East to the Far East, we encounter the fabulous White Pyramid, located about 60 miles southwest of X'ian (Sian or Hsian) in the Qin Ling Shan Mountains of China's Shensi Province. This city was made famous for the nearby discovery of the Terra Cota Warriors. Resting at almost the same latitude as Phoenix's 33 degrees, this massive stepped pyramid constructed of clay is estimated to be 1,000 feet high and 1,500 feet at the base! The current politics of the country have thus far prevented any detailed study of the structure, but it is thought to be 4,500-5,000 years old—the approximate age of the pyramids at Giza. The White Pyramid was supposedly built after the old emperors, known as "the sons of heaven," descended to earth in their "fiery metallic dragons" and began to rule China. Its interior is rumored to be a model of this empire with a jeweled roof depicting the constellations and rivers of flowing mercury. The region also contains up to one hundred more pyramids.[24]

HIGHWAY 33 REVISITED

Back on the North American continent, if we journey somewhat over 1,500 miles east of Phoenix along latitude 33 north, we find the Moundville site lying exactly on the line. This city, constructed by the Mississippian culture along the Black Warrior River in central Alabama from A.D. 1000 through A.D. 1450, had a population of over 1,000—second in size and complexity to ancient Cahokia in Illinois. The 26 earthen platform mounds arranged in a circular pattern are similar in structure to those in Arizona's Valley of the Sun, with temples and residences for the elite priesthood likewise built on top. One of the larger mounds is a ramped pyramid that rises to a height of 58 feet. In addition, the town was protected on three sides by wooden palisades, much like the Hohokam villages along the Salt and Gila Rivers.[25] Did the earlier Hohokam culture of the American Southwest somehow influence the later development of this Mound Builder culture in the American Southeast? The many similarities between the two seem to point in that direction.

A few other Mound Builder cities were settled quite near the 33rd parallel. Approximately ten miles southwest of the town of Lake Providence (32 degrees 49 minutes) on the Mississippi River

Resembling some sort of fowl flying toward the sunset, this mound was constructed using 300,000 cubic yards of clay, or the equivalent of ten million 50-pound baskets. To truly realize the shape of the bird, one needs to be at least a thousand feet or so in the air.

---

floodplain in northeastern Louisiana is Poverty Point State Historic Site. Constructed in 1800 B.C.E. (much earlier than even the Hohokam settlements), a C-shaped or perhaps a partially octagon-shaped earthwork three-quarters of a mile across was formed by six concentric ridges that are 140 to 200 feet apart and four to six feet high. To the west of this earthwork, Bird Mound rises 72 feet high and extends 600 to 800 feet at its base. Resembling some sort of fowl flying toward the sunset, this mound was constructed using 300,000 cubic yards of clay, or the equivalent of ten million 50-pound baskets. To truly realize the shape of the bird, one needs to be at least a thousand feet or so in the air. Poverty Point was almost entirely abandoned circa 1350 B.C.E., indicating over five centuries of cultural development, though minor construction on the earthworks continued until A.D. 700.[26]

Even closer to the magic number 33, though neither as impressive nor as old as Poverty Point, are the Winterville Mounds, located six miles north of the town of Greenville in west-central Mississippi (33 degrees 25 minutes). Inhabited between A.D. 1000 and 1450, the site includes 23 flat-topped mounds, with the main Temple Mound rising 55 feet.[27]

About four miles south of Cartersville in northwestern Georgia (34 degrees 11 minutes) is Etowah Indian Mound State Park. "White settlers understood the Creek and the later Cherokee to call this site "Hightower," possibly for Itawa or Italwa (city?). The name Etowah may also be a corruption of this word."[28] It is interesting to note that the Hopi word for the sun deity is Tawa. Etowah was first inhabited in A.D. 950 and contains three major mounds. One is a ceremonial mound 63 feet in height and another is a burial mound in which were found numerous artifacts including copper ear ornaments, stone effigies and seashells along with obsidian and grizzly bear teeth from the Rocky Mountains.[29]

Closer to the home of the Hohokam on the western side of the Colorado River are located a number of geoglyphs (also called "intaglios"). These figures, formed in the desert by removal of darker pebbles to reveal a lighter undersurface, are sometimes hundreds of feet in length. One group (the Blythe complex) is positioned about 16 miles north of Blythe, California (33 degrees 40 minutes) while another group (the Ripley complex) is located about 12 miles south of Blythe. In addition to human and animal figures, snakes, spirals, stars, circles and other geometric figures, a Knights Templar-like Maltese cross nearly ten feet in diameter has been found adjacent to a humanoid figure at the Ripley complex.[30] One anthropoid geoglyph in the area has been associated with the Hopi Fire Clan deity Masau'u.[31] Hence, we find that many different tribes were apparently involved in these rituals dating back from between 1,100 and 3,000 years ago.[32]

Because these earth forms, like the Nazca lines in Peru or Bird Mound at Poverty Point, are best appreciated from the air, they were probably intended to be an homage to the sky gods.

Because these earth forms, like the Nazca lines in Peru or Bird Mound at Poverty Point, are best appreciated from the air, they were probably intended to be an homage to the sky gods.

The geoglyphs together with other cairns, stone circles and cleared dance paths may be ritually associated with the huge network of interconnected trails found in the low desert upon which the ancients made pilgrimages. One such pilgrimage, called the *keruk*, is performed even today by the Yuman-speaking tribes (viz., the Yuma, Mohave, Cocopa and Maricopa) in a four-day trek to Avikwa'ame, the sacred mountain to the north, in order to celebrate the cosmogony.[33] "The route ran from Pilot Knob, or Avikwal [near Yuma, Arizona], the spirit house where the dead dwell at the southern end of the river, to Avikwa'ame, or Spirit Mountain, where the earth was created, in the

star symbols and various abstract or geometric designs, including a Maltese cross within a circle surrounded by a ring of 17 dots.[39] "Distinctive at Three Rivers is the circle-dot motif; one investigator who took the trouble to count found it to be the single most common element at this site. Interestingly enough, its presence elsewhere is negligible, and its symbolic content has not been determined, although it occurs in various contexts in Mesoamerica. Possibly it refers to Quetzalcoatl."[40] This deity, of course, is known as

One of the largest rock art sites in the southwest, this park contains over 20,000 glyphs scattered over 50 acres.

north. This pilgrimage was intended to honor the creation, and ritually retrace the path of Mastamho [the creator-deity, whose name echoes the Hopi god Masau'u mentioned above] in his mythic adventures."[34] Here we find a north-south dichotomy similar to that found along the Nile, with the "Mound of Creation" (i.e., Heliopolis) located to the north. Atop Avikwa'ame, legends say, was a great house named Aha-avulypo or, literally, "Dark Round House."[35] The north-south road itself was named Kwatcan, the "first trail to the homeland." The Hopi word for "track" is *kuku'at*, but the word for "grandfather" is the near homophone *kwa'at*.[36] Perhaps the suffix *-can* is a variant of *ka-*, part of the word *kachina*.[37] Either "spirits of the track" or "spirits of the grandfathers" may be the intended meaning. Midway on this spirit road between the sacred mountain of the north and the mouth of the Colorado River are the aforementioned geoglyphs at the 33rd degree of latitude.

Also on this line is the Three Rivers Petroglyphs site, located on the western base of the Sacramento Mountains 18 miles west of Ruidoso, New Mexico (33 degrees 19 minutes). One of the largest rock art sites in the southwest, this park contains over 20,000 glyphs scattered over 50 acres. Carved atop a ridge by the Mogollon culture between A.D. 900 and 1400 (contemporary with the late Hohokam period),[38] these figures include anthropomorphs, zoomorphs, kachina masks,

the Plumed Serpent. Three Rivers Site is also unique because it is one of only a few places in the Southwest that were used primarily for rock art rather than it being merely an adjunct to the village.[41] However, another site lying exactly on the 33rd parallel was also used expressly for this purpose. Near Gila Bend, Arizona about 62 miles west of Snaketown (mentioned above) is Painted Rocks [sic] State Park, which has thousands of petroglyphs of similar designs—not "painted" but pecked into the boulders.[42]

A fascinating site also in the general vicinity of Phoenix is called the Circlestone Observatory (33 degrees 28 minutes). High in the Superstition Mountains, about 54 miles east of the metropolis, lies an elliptical "medicine wheel" constructed of a stone wall three feet thick with a circumference of 427 feet. On his extensive and thoroughly detailed Web site, New Zealand researcher Martin Doutré claims that this structure incorporates various navigational codes, including *phi*, or the Golden Ratio (1.618...). "Ancient astronomer mathematicians built sites like Circlestone as repositories of codes and places where initiates could be taught age-old principles." Doutré further suggests that Circlestone was used by colonists from the eastern Mediterranean or Europe who may have operated a gold mine—perhaps the famous Lost Dutchman's Mine itself.[43] Although American Indians may instead have constructed this site for an astronomical observatory similar

> "Ancient astronomer mathematicians built sites like Circlestone as repositories of codes and places where initiates could be taught age-old principles." Doutré further suggests that Circlestone was used by colonists from the eastern Mediterranean or Europe who may have operated a gold mine—perhaps the famous Lost Dutchman's Mine itself.

to the one at Casa Malpais near Springerville, Arizona (34 degrees 10 minutes), Doutré's theory is nonetheless an intriguing one.

Four other ancient sites along latitude 33 north warrant brief mentions. Gila Cliff Dwellings National Monument (33 degrees 22 minutes) is located in a rugged and isolated region about 60 miles west of Truth or Consequences, New Mexico. Reminiscent of the seven Aztecan caves mentioned above, five caves in the Mogollon Mountains of southwestern New Mexico contain about 40 masonry and adobe rooms built circa A.D. 1280, although semi-subterranean pit houses have been found nearby dating back to circa A.D. 100.[44]

In saguaro cactus country about 56 miles northeast of Phoenix is Tonto National Monument (33 degrees 44 minutes), which also contains cliff dwellings within shallow caves. Constructed of unshaped quartzite and adobe mortar, these ruins, inhabited in the mid-Fourteenth Century, contained 70 rooms within three caves.[45]

About 40 miles due east of the small town of San Carlos, Arizona (33 degrees 24 minutes) is Point of Pines Ruin. Occupied between A.D. 1200 and 1500, this huge masonry pueblo contained 800 rooms, a central plaza, a surrounding wall and a great kiva.[46] The site is also one of the few in the Southwest that shows evidence of three different cultures living together: the Hohokam, the Mogollon and the Anasazi—the last group named migrating from the Hopi country to the north.[47] The population is estimated to have been between 2,000 and 3,000.[48] Incidentally, five or so miles to the south is a hot springs called Arsenic Tubs, number 33 on the periodic table.

And finally, Besh-ba-gowah Archaeological Park, located one and a half miles south of downtown Globe, Arizona (33 degrees 25 minutes), was a granite cobble pueblo of 250-plus rooms inhabited between A.D. 1225 and 1450. The artifacts found include copper bells and macaw feathers from Mesoamerica, as well as shells from the Gulf of Mexico and the California coast.[49] "Besh-ba-gowah" is an Apache phrase meaning "place of the metal," referring to the copious silver and copper deposits in the area. In fact, the town of Globe was so named because of the 1875 discovery of a globe-shaped mass nine inches in diameter, made of 99% pure silver and valued at $12,000. Curiously, reports also stated that the continents of the earth were etched upon its surface. The whereabouts of this artifact are currently unknown.[50]

A BRIEF HISTORY OF 33

Entering the historical period, we find hovering near the 33rd parallel a number of provocative synchronicities. For instance, the first Supreme Council of the Ancient and Accepted Scottish Rite of Freemasonry, Southern Jurisdiction of the United States, was established in 1801 at Charleston, South Carolina. This charming antebellum port city and hub of Southern culture is located less than 15 miles south of the 33rd parallel. Called the Solomon Lodge No.1, the Masonic meeting place was known as the Mother Lodge of the world.[51]

Shortly before the close of World War II, Franklin D. Roosevelt died suddenly of a cerebral hemorrhage at Warm Springs, Georgia, which is less than ten miles south of 33 degrees latitude. (This town, incidentally, is located about 35 miles northeast of Phenix City, Alabama.) It is noteworthy (no pun intended) that in the mid-30s FDR, a 32nd degree Mason and the 32nd president of the U.S., initiated the printing of the reverse side of the Great Seal (the pyramidal eye mentioned at the beginning of this essay) on the legal tender. Roosevelt was succeeded in April of 1945 by 33rd degree Mason Harry S. Truman. (The "S." supposedly stood for Solomon.) On July 16 of the same year, the first atomic device—the Gadget, as it was called—was detonated at Trinity Site, New Mexico: 33 degrees 41 minutes north latitude. Spanish explorers originally called this area La Jornada del Muerto, or "The Journey of the Dead," but now the site is marked by a small stone obelisk erected

20 years or so after the explosion.[52] (Was this monument Masonically inspired?)[53] A few weeks after the explosion at Trinity Site the 33rd president of the United States ordered the annihilation of two Japanese cities by nuclear bombs dropped from B-29 bombers. The 33rd parallel runs exactly between Hiroshima and Nagasaki. Two years after the war ended, the modern "flying saucer" age began in earnest when something crashed near Roswell, New Mexico—33 degrees 26 minutes north latitude.

Bringing us up to the present day, the so-called Phoenix Lights were witnessed by hundreds or perhaps thousands of people. On the evening of

continued southeast above Interstate 10 and was sighted in the Tucson area at about 8:45.[54]

At approximately 9:50 P.M. an arc of amber "orbs" measuring one mile across appeared above the Estrella Mountains about 20 miles southwest of Phoenix. "Spanish explorers named the range Estrella ('star') after the pattern of deeply carved canyons radiating from the summit."[55] This display of lights videotaped by scores of people in the Phoenix area was possibly related to the earlier sightings. At the time of this latter UFO sighting the constellation Orion would have been seen hovering over the southwestern horizon, were it not for urban light pollution. In fact, at

---

In fact, the town of Globe was so named because of the 1875 discovery of a globe-shaped mass nine inches in diameter, made of 99% pure silver and valued at $12,000. Curiously, reports also stated that the continents of the earth were etched upon its surface. The whereabouts of this artifact are currently unknown.

March 13, 1997 an immense triangular UFO perhaps a mile wide flew over the American Southwest. First sighted over Henderson, Nevada at 6:55 P.M. (Pacific Standard Time) traveling southeast, this virtually silent craft (for lack of a better term) had a number of lights evenly spaced on its leading edge. It was next seen over the village of Paulden, Arizona (nearly 25 miles north of the town of Prescott) at 8:17 P.M. (Mountain Standard Time), after which it was observed ten miles to the south in Chino Valley, where it apparently streaked over the present author's house, who missed seeing the event by a matter of minutes. Just one minute after the Paulden sighting, it was reported over Prescott Valley, which is 23 miles south-southeast of the former. By 8:23 the object had reached the Phoenix metro area roughly 75 miles away, where it hovered for about four or five minutes over the vicinity of the Indian School Rd. and Seventh Avenue intersection. The UFO next entered Sky Harbor Airport's air space, where air controllers in the tower and the flight crew from at least one commercial airliner viewed it, although radar failed to detect it. The craft

9:49 P.M. when the final phase of the event was beginning, Alnilam, the middle star of the Belt, was 33 degrees above the horizon at an azimuth of 242 degrees. If a line is drawn from the State Capitol to the Estrella range's Monument Hill (the initial point for surveying of property in Arizona), the azimuth is also 242 degrees. At the latitude of Phoenix this is the exact point of the winter solstice sunset as well. Thus, these orbs appeared at a significant archaeo-astronomical position in the sky and also in the precise region where Orion happened to be at that particular time. Above the right hand of Orion between the constellations Gemini and Auriga is the northern stargate previously mentioned, located at a declination (celestial latitude) of 33 degrees.

One odd aspect to the Phoenix Lights story is that, other than a few minor write-ups in local newspapers, they were not reported in any national media until June 18, over three months later, when USA Today[56] ran a front-page article picked up by other media. In any event, one of the most intriguing UFO sightings in decades was focused upon the 33rd parallel—a paramount Masonic number.

> **The 33rd parallel is a path of power across the globe, a circuit that links both time and space in order to vitalize the dynamo of a mystery we are just now beginning to realize.**

Why are so many significant ancient and historic sites located along the 33rd parallel? Perhaps the ancients discovered a ley line of dragon energy corresponding to this latitude, and constructed temples and sacred cities in order to utilize this terrestrial *chi*. Or perhaps the numerological and Masonic significance of 33 dictated that monuments to this sacred number be erected as a signal to future generations. Whatever the rationale, the 33rd parallel is a path of power across the globe, a circuit that links both time and space in order to vitalize the dynamo of a mystery we are just now beginning to realize.

1. "About Master Numbers in Numerology," Decoz Numerology Software. www.decoz.com

2. Dante Alighieri, *The Purgatorio: A Verse Translation for the Modern Reader*. John Ciardi, trans. New York: New American Library, 1961. p. 334.

3. Dante Alighieri, *The Paradiso: A Verse Rendering for the Modern Reader*. John Ciardi, trans. New York: New American Library, 1970. p. 365.

4. Day Williams, "Masons and Mystery at the 33rd Parallel." www.daywilliams.com

5. Most of the sites discussed in this essay are less than one degree (60 nautical miles) from latitude 33 degrees north. There are two exceptions: One site in Lebanon is 68 nautical miles from the 33rd parallel, and another site in Georgia is 71 nautical miles (nearly 82 English miles) from this latitude line. (One international nautical mile = One arc minute of latitude or longitude = 6080.2 ft.)

6. David Grant Noble, *Ancient Ruins of the Southwest: An Archaeological Guide*. Flagstaff: Northland Publishing, 1991. p. 15.

7. H. M. Wormington, *Prehistoric Indians of the Southwest*. Denver: The Denver Museum of Natural History, 1973. p. 125.

8. *Encyclopaedia Britannica*, vol. 10. Chicago: Encyclopaedia Britannica, Inc., 1979. p. 223.

9. "What is the meaning of the word Aztlan?" www.azteca.net

10. Albert Pike, *Morals and Dogma of the Ancient and Accepted Scottish Rite of Freemasonry, Prepared for the Supreme Council of the Thirty-third Degree for the Southern Jurisdiction of the United States and Published by Its Authority*. Charleston: A.M. 5632, 1928, 1906, 1871. p. 363.

11. Ibid., p. 9.

12. Christopher Knight and Robert Lomas, *Uriel's Machine: Uncovering the Secrets of Stonehenge, Noah's Flood and the Dawn of Civilization*. Gloucester: Fair Winds Press, 2001. p. 319.

13. See Gary A. David's essay "The Dual Stargates of Egyptian Cosmology," *Duat*, No. 1, September 2002.

14. Pike, p. 9.

15. *Smith's Bible Dictionary*, p. 714.

16. Michael Howard, *The Occult Conspiracy: Secret Societies—Their Influence and Power in World History*. Rochester: Destiny Books, 1989. pp. 10-11, 47.

17. William Bramley, *The Gods of Eden*. New York: Avon, 1990. p. 90.

18. "Byblos (Jbeil)," Embassy of Lebanon, Washington, DC. www.lebanonembassy.org

19. Graham Hancock, *Fingerprints of the Gods: The Evidence of Earth's Lost Civilization*. New York: Crown Trade Paperbacks, 1995. p. 262.

20. *Encyclopaedia Britannica*, vol. 2. Chicago: Encyclopaedia Britannica, 1979. pp. 554-556.

21. Henri-Paul Eydoux, "The men who built the Tower of Babel." In *The World's Last Mysteries*. Pleasantville: The Reader's Digest Association, Inc., 1979. p. 176.

22. Pike, *Morals and Dogma*. pp. 499-500.

23. Christopher Knight and Robert Lomas, *The Hiram Key: Pharaohs, Freemasons and the Discovery of the Secret Scrolls of Jesus*. London: Arrow, 1997. pp. 260-265.

24. a. "Ancient Pyramids In China," www.lauralee.com

   b. David B. Kelley, "Chinese Pyramids." hawk.hama-med.ac.jp/dbk/chnpyramid.html

   c. "Chinese Pyramids," www.earthquest.co.uk

   d. Daryl Whitaker, "Chinese Pyramids and Burial Mounds." www.webmongrel.com

   e. John Winston, "History Channel: Hartwig Hausdorf and the mystery of the Chinese Pyramids." www.lightparty.com

25. Dr. Vernon James Knight, "An Archaeological Sketch of Moundville." www.ua.edu

26. a. Franklin Folsom and Mary Elting Folsom, *America's Ancient Treasures: A Guide to Archaeological Sites and Museums in the United States and Canada*. Albuquerque: University of New Mexico Press, 1983. pp. 232-234.

   b. "Poverty Point Earthworks: Evolutionary Milestones of the Americas," www.lpb.org

   c. "A Rich Culture Flourished 12 Centuries Before Christ," www.crt.state.la.us

27. "Winterville Mounds," www.mdah.state.ms.us

28. "Etowah Mounds Historic Site," ngeorgia.com

29. a. Folsom and Folsom, *America's Ancient Treasures*. p. 224.

   b. "Etowah Indian Mounds, State Historic Site," gadnr.org

30. Boma Johnson, *Earth Figures of the Lower Colorado and Gila River Deserts: A Functional Analysis.* Phoenix: Arizona Archaeological Society, 1986. p. 107.

31. Ibid., p. 64.

32. David S. Whitley, *A Guide to Rock Art Sites: Southern California and Southern Nevada.* Missoula: Mountain Press Publishing Company, 1996. p. 127.

33. Jefferson Reid and Stephanie Whittlesey, *The Archaeology of Ancient Arizona.* Tucson: The University of Arizona Press, 1997. pp. 126-130. This mountain, known as Newberry Peak, lies at the most southern tip of Nevada about 35 miles north of Needles, California.

34. Whitley, *A Guide to Rock Art Sites.* pp. 124-125.

35. Johnson, *Earth Figures.* pp. 24-25.

36. P. David Seaman, *Hopi Dictionary.* Flagstaff: Northern Arizona University Anthropological Paper No. 2, 1996.

37. In the Hopi belief system a kachina (or katsina) is a type of intercessory spirit—not a deity per se—which can assume the form of any manifold physical object, phenomenon or creature in the world.

38. Norman T. Oppelt, *Guide to Prehistoric Ruins of the Southwest.* Boulder: Pruett Publishing Company, 1989. p. 47.

39. Polly Schaafsma, *Rock Art In New Mexico.* Santa Fe: Museum of New Mexico Press, 1992. p. 77.

40. Polly Schaafsma, *Indian Rock Art of the Southwest.* Albuquerque: University of New Mexico Press, 1995. p. 235.

41. Noble, *Ancient Ruins.* p. 7.

42. a. "Painted Rocks Petroglyph Site," www.virtualguidebooks.com

   b. "Adventures and Photography of a Fledgling Explorer," westerntreks.com

43. Martin Doutré, "Circlestone: An Ancient Medicine Wheel in the Superstition Mountains," www.celticnz.co.nz

44. Oppelt, *Guide to Prehistoric Ruins.* pp. 52-54.

45. Ibid., pp. 64-65.

46. A kiva is essentially an underground prayer chamber used for communal religious ceremonies.

47. Oppelt, *Guide to Prehistoric Ruins.* pp. 67-68.

48. Emil W. Haury, *Prehistory of the American Southwest.* J. Jefferson Reid and David E. Doyel, eds. Tucson: University of Arizona Press, 1992. p. 45.

49. a. Noble, *Ancient Ruins.* pp. 165-167.

   b. Franklin Folsom and Mary Elting Folsom, *Ancient Treasures of the Southwest: A Guide to Archaeological Sites and Museums in Arizona,* Southern Colorado, New Mexico and Utah. Albuquerque: University of New Mexico Press, 1994. p. 16.

50. a. Will C. Barnes, *Arizona Place Names.* Tucson: University of Arizona Press, 1997. pp. 180-181.

   b. Madeline Ferrin Paré, Bert M. Fireman, *Arizona Pageant: A Short History of the 48th State.* Tempe: Arizona Historical Foundation, 1970. p. 148.

51. Williams, "Masons and Mystery."

52. Andy Walton, "The First 'Ground Zero': A Visit to the Trinity Test Site, Where the Deer and the Antelope Play." www.cnn.com

53. In this context it is interesting to note that the Sabian symbol for 33 degrees is the following: "Natural steps lead to a lawn of clover in bloom." Clover's trefoil suggests the Trinity, while its flowering suggests new life or even resurrection. Sabian symbols are a series of 360 brief vignettes—one for each degree of the zodiacal circle—received in 1925 by San Diego clairvoyant Elsie Wheeler and recorded by astrologer Marc Edmund Jones. Dane Rudhyar, *An Astrological Mandala: The Cycle of Transformations and Its 360 Symbolic Phases.* New York: Random House, 1973. pp. 25-27, 72. "When [clover] is located upon a mountain it comes to signify knowledge of the divine essence gained by hard endeavor [Natural steps...], through sacrifice or study (equivalent to ascension)..." J. E. Ciriot, translated from the Spanish by Jack Sage, *A Dictionary of Symbols.* New York: Philosophical Library, 1962. p. 48.

54. Bill Hamilton, "The Amazing 'Phoenix Lights' Event Sequence Of 3-17-97." www.rense.com

55. Bill Weir, *Arizona Traveler's Handbook.* Chico: Moon Publications, Inc., 1992. p. 295.

56. a. Jim Dilettoso, "The Mysterious Phoenix Lights." www.exoticresearch.com

   b. Peter B. Davenport, "2nd Anniversary of 'Phoenix Lights' Incident," www.100megsfree4.com/farshores/phoenix.htm

David Hatcher Childress

DID THE INCAS BUILD MACHU PICCHU?

What concerns me is not the way things are, but rather the way people think things are.
> — Epictetus (55-135)

If thou seekest El Dorado thou must ride, boldly ride over the Mountains of the Moon through the valley of the shadow...
> — Edgar Allen Poe

DID THE INCAS BUILD Machu Picchu? Many archaeologists will say that they did. Yet many an archaeologist will say that Machu Picchu, and other megalithic monuments in the Andes, are pre-Inca. I am one of these people, and I will endeavor to make my case that many of the claimed Inca monuments were built hundreds, if not thousands of years previously.

Certainly, the Incas inhabited these grand buildings, as they are virtually indestructible. Even today in Cuzco, where many megalithic buildings still survive, Spanish colonizers are now living in these buildings (many turned into convents, churches, restaurants and even hotels)—but these Spanish occupiers did not build these buildings. They were already standing for hundreds of years before the Spanish occupied them. Were they already standing when the Incas occupied them?

Probably the best way to start our argument is to quickly review some of the basic "facts" about the Incas and what little we know of their history. The

> While the Egyptians had literally thousands of years to create their enduring monuments of colossal stone, the Incas managed to do it in a very short time period indeed—according to mainstream archaeologists.

Incas are a recent political power in the many thousands of years of South American history and at the time of the conquest they were the rulers of the largest native empire of the Americas.

Mainstream historians say that near the end of the Fourteenth Century the empire began to expand from its initial base in the Cuzco region of the southern Andes mountains of South America. It ended abruptly with the Spanish invasion led by Francisco Pizarro in 1532. At the time of its demise the empire controlled an estimated 12 million people in much of what is now Peru and Ecuador, as well as in large parts of Chile, Bolivia and Argentina. But, strangely, this huge empire is said to have only begun a few generations before the Spanish arrival. What is more, all of the megalithic monuments of the Incas were built within this short period as well—a period of only one or two hundred years ending in 1532. While the Egyptians had literally thousands of years to create their enduring monuments of colossal stone, the Incas managed to do it in a very short time period indeed—according to mainstream archaeologists.

THE INCA EMPIRE IN MAINSTREAM ARCHAEOLOGY

The Incas called their land Tawantinsuyu, which in Quechua, the language spoken in the Inca Empire, means the "four parts." A land of markedly diverse terrain and climate, it included a long coastal desert strip, broken by rich irrigated valleys, the high peaks and deep fertile valleys of the Andes and the mountainous edges of the tropical forest to the east. The term Inca refers to the ruler himself as well as to the people of the valley of Cuzco, the capital of the empire. It is sometimes used to refer to all of the peoples included within Tawantinsuyu, but this is not strictly correct. Most of the dozens of smaller local kingdoms retained

The early period of the empire is shrouded in mystery. An official version of early Incan history was told to the Spanish invaders, but it is difficult to separate actual historical events from the myth and legends with which they were mixed. The first Inca is said to be Manco Capac. According to legend, he appeared with his brother, his brother's wife and his own wife on the Island of the Sun in Lake Titicaca. He declared himself sent by God to rule the peoples of the Andes. He set up his capital at Cuzco and founded the Incan Dynasty. It is generally assumed by historians that the wonderful city of Cuzco was built at this time. As we shall see later, it is far more likely that most of the city of Cuzco, and Sacsayhuaman, the megalithic fortress above Cuzco, were both already in existence.

The *Grolier 1977 Encyclopedia,* quoting standard texts on the Incas, says the empire didn't really get started until about the year 1300:

> The Incan empire probably started out as a small kingdom, similar to many others in the Andes during the Fourteenth Century. A powerful state centered at Huari, in the vicinity of what is now Ayacucho, Peru, and well to the north of Cuzco, had apparently controlled the area several centuries earlier, but by the Tenth Century small feuding kingdoms dominated the scene. The reasons for the Incas' earliest triumphs over their neighbors are impossible to discern from existing sources. It is not known for certain whether Manco Capac, listed as the founding ruler, was a historical personage.

They are believed to have been taken to the secret city in the mountain jungles of eastern Peru known as Paititi, where they remain to this day. Other stories maintain that the gold-clad mummies are kept in a secret tunnel system beneath the Sacsayhuaman fortress.

their identities even though politically and economically subject to the Incas. Quechua was the official language and was spoken in most of the realm by the time the Spanish arrived, but at least 20 local languages persisted in various parts of the empire.

There are said to have been 14 Inca kings before the final Inca Atahualpa. Each of these kings was mummified upon his death and then covered in gold leaf. The mummies of these former emperors were kept in the Sun Temple at Cuzco until the time of the conquest, when they disappeared. They are believed to have been taken to the secret city in the mountain jungles of eastern Peru known as Paititi, where they remain to this day. Other stories maintain that the gold-clad mummies are kept in a secret tunnel system beneath the Sacsayhuaman fortress.

The Inca Pachacuti, who reigned c. 1440-1470, was the ruler responsible for the Inca expansion into an empire, although legend credits Manco Capac with founding the royal dynasty. Pachacuti is the first of the Inca rulers whose historical identity is unquestionable. The details of his conquests may have been distorted by the glorification of Pachacuti in official Inca oral history. It is clear, however, that he was brilliant both as a strategist of conquests and organizer of empires. The heart of the empire was built up during his reign. During the final stage of his rule Pachacuti was assisted by his son and successor Topa Inca, who was as talented in conquest and statecraft as his father. Together they expanded the empire to nearly the size encountered by the Spanish in 1532.

Were the astonishing megalithic structures in the vicinity of the Inca capital of Cuzco all built by the Incas in the few hundred years prior to the arrival of the Spanish, or were many of the structures (if not all of them) already in existence before the Incas?

In about 1470 the Incas captured the rich and powerful Chimu kingdom on the north coast of what is now Peru. With that major conquest won, little remained to challenge Inca expansion throughout what then constituted the "civilized world" of South America. Pachacuti's sons helped to complete the conquests. The heir Topa Inca (who reigned from 1471 to 93) pressed on to the northern border of present-day Ecuador before ascending the throne. During his reign the south coast of Peru was conquered (1476), as was northern Chile, much of northwestern Argentina and a portion of the Bolivian plateau. In parts of this vast territory, notably along the south coast of Peru, the price of conquest was high; great losses on both sides and the virtual extinction of local

groups resulted. In addition, rebellions that sprang up periodically among previously conquered peoples had to be quelled.

In the last years before the Spanish invasion the Incas were still expanding in the north. Huayna Capac (who reigned from 1493 to 1527), father of the last Inca ruler Atahualpa, was ruling the empire from his northern outpost in Quito at his death in 1527. The death of Huayna Capac plunged the Inca state into civil war. No fixed system for determining the succession of rulers appears to have been set up. Atahualpa, who had been with his father in the north, claimed that Huayna Capac had decided to divide the kingdom, setting up a new northern capital at Quito that Atahualpa would rule. His brother Huascar claimed from Cuzco to be the legitimate ruler of the entire realm. Atahualpa finally won the bloody war and was on his way to Cuzco in 1532 to claim the whole kingdom when the Spanish conquistador Francisco Pizarro arrived. The Incas allowed Pizarro and a contingent of about 150 soldiers to enter the regional capital at Cajamarca, where Atahualpa and his army were camped. The Spaniards were able to take the Inca ruler captive and assured the collapse of the empire.

But the big question is this: Were the astonishing megalithic structures in the vicinity of the Inca capital of Cuzco all built by the Incas in the few hundred years prior to the arrival of the Spanish, or were many of the structures (if not all of them) already in existence before the Incas?

INCA ARCHITECTURE AND MEGALITHIC ARCHITECTURE

Because of the extremely fine stonemasonry that exists in and around Cuzco, including Machu Picchu and Ollantaytambo along the Urubamba River, it has been concluded by modern archaeologists that the Incas were the builders of these astonishing monuments. The speculation that the Incas merely used existing walls is not part of any mainstream thought. That these virtually indestructible walls were already in existence before the Incas is the theory that we shall explore in this article.

First, let's look at the current mainstream explanation of "Inca" architecture of which the mountaintop city of Machu Picchu is often used as an example:

The actual function of Machu Picchu is not fully understood. Since it was unknown to the early Spanish invaders, their documents do not identify it.

The Incas developed a highly functional style of public architecture distinguished above all by its superior engineering techniques and fine stone-masonry. The plan of their cities was based on a system of broad avenues intersected by smaller streets that converged on an open square lined by state buildings and temples. Structures were usually single-storied, with perfectly bonded joints of cut stone, although adobe bricks and plaster were commonly used in the coastal lowlands. For building large monuments such as the great fortress of Sacsayhuaman near Cuzco, massive polygonal blocks were fitted together with extraordinary precision. In mountainous regions, as at the spectacularly situated Andean citadel of Machu Picchu, Inca architecture often reflects ingenious adaptations to the surrounding landforms.[1]

THE MEGALITHIC CITY OF MACHU PICCHU

Machu Picchu, situated about 80 kilometers (50 miles) northwest of Cuzco, Peru, is an ancient Inca town overlooking the Urubamba Valley. Its spectacular setting on a high precipice between steep mountain peaks has made it one of the most famous archaeological monuments in the world. The ruins are located about 2,400 meters (7,875 feet) above sea level on the eastern slopes of the Andes, near the edge of the warm humid Montana region. The abandoned site was covered with dense vegetation and remained essentially unknown until its discovery by the American archaeologist Hiram Bingham in 1911.[2]

Machu Picchu is best-known for its architecture, which combines fine stone buildings with extensive agricultural terraces, creating the appearance of a settlement literally carved out of the mountainsides. The style of its buildings and pottery as well as its careful planning suggest that the town was built under the supervision of the Inca state, which was centered at Cuzco.

Perhaps the most famous feature of the site is a carved natural stone, known as Intihuatana, enclosed by curved walls of dressed stone with trapezoidal windows. The stone and its complex of surrounding walls is probably related to the sun religion of the Inca as well as to their veneration of certain natural stones.

The actual function of Machu Picchu is not fully understood. Since it was unknown to the early Spanish invaders, their documents do not identify it. Its architecture suggests a strong emphasis on religion, and its location on the eastern border of the empire may mean that it was a frontier outpost.

CUZCO AND THE MASSIVE WALLS OF SACSAYHUAMAN

Cuzco, in southern Peru, was the capital of the Inca empire from its beginnings in the Fourteenth Century until the Spanish conquest in 1533. A tourist attraction, the city is known for its Inca ruins and Spanish colonial architecture. Situated at an altitude of 3,416 meters (11,207 feet) in a broad valley of the Andes, it is the busy hub of a thickly populated agricultural region where sheep are raised and cereals and tobacco are grown. The population of 275,000 (as of 1990) is predominantly Indian, and the city, with its open markets, adobe houses and narrow, winding cobblestone streets, is Indian in character. Quechua, the Inca language, is still widely spoken. The climate is cool, with temperatures averaging about 10.9 degrees Celsius (51.6 degrees Fahrenheit). Annual precipitation is 750 millimeters (29.5 inches). The area is subject to earthquakes, the most damaging having occurred in 1650 and 1950.

Inca tribes are believed to have come to Cuzco from the Lake Titicaca region in about the Eleventh Century. The legendary founder of the city was Manco Capac, first of the Inca rulers. The name Cuzco is Quechua for "navel," and the city was considered the center of the Inca world, the place where the four parts of the empire came together.

It was the hub from which the famous Inca road network radiated.

Inca Cuzco was different in concept and plan from European cities. It was designed in the form of a puma, with the Fifteenth Century fortress of Sacsayhuaman as the head. The confluence of the Huatanay and Tullumayo rivers was canalled and straightened to form the tail. The core of the city contained official and ceremonial buildings and residences of ruling officials. Many other buildings and residences were dispersed at a considerable distance in the countryside surrounding the core, but they were defined as part of the capital.

The Inca capital is especially known for its architecture of enormous cut-stone blocks fitted so perfectly that no mortar was needed. Coricancha, the temple of the sun, and the fortress of Sacsayhuaman are the most outstanding examples of this type of construction.

From all parts of the Inca empire a wealth of silver and gold poured into Cuzco, filling the temples and palaces. These treasures were plundered by Francisco Pizarro in 1533, and the city was destroyed. The Spaniards built a new city on the ruins of the old, adorning the magnificent edifices of their churches with the looted wealth.

and containing complex ductwork through which water probably once flowed.

The site's architecture suggests that Sacsayhuaman served a primarily defensive function. Fortresses, called pucaras, were frequently built above population centers in the Andes to serve as refuges for the populace in case of attack. Spanish sources suggest that Sacsayhuaman was also used as an important storage center, and the site may have had religious significance as well. Construction is usually attributed to the ruler Pachacuti, but it is unlikely that such an enormous monument could have been completed during a single reign.[3]

Sacsayhuaman is a stone structure that covers the entire hill and appears almost otherworldly. Gigantic blocks of stone, some weighing more than 200 tons (400,000 pounds) are fitted together perfectly. The enormous stone blocks are cut, faced and fitted so well that even today one cannot slip the blade of a knife, or even a piece of paper between them. No mortar is used, and no two blocks are alike. Yet they fit perfectly, and it has been said by some engineers that no modern builder, with the aid of metals and tools

When the Spaniards first arrived in Cuzco and saw these structures, they thought that they had been built by the devil himself, because of their enormity. Indeed, nowhere else can you see such large blocks placed together so perfectly.

Because of the extremely large stones used, the complex known as Sacsayhuaman has received special study by engineers and stonemasons.

According to mainstream archaeologists, the fortress of Sacsayhuaman was built by the Inca in the Fifteenth Century on a hill overlooking their capital at Cuzco. The fortress takes the form of a series of zigzag retaining walls built of huge stones, some weighing several tons. The retaining walls form ramparts in three terraces. Overlooking the terraces from near the top of the hill is a curious circular structure divided into small compartments

of the finest steel, could produce results more accurate.

Each individual stone had to have been planned well in advance; a 20 ton stone, let alone one weighing 80 to 200 tons, cannot just be dropped casually into position with any hope of attaining that kind of accuracy. The stones are locked and dove-tailed into position, making them earthquake-proof. Indeed, after many devastating earthquakes in the Andes over the last few hundred years, the blocks are still perfectly fitted, while the Spanish Cathedral in Cuzco has been leveled twice. Even more incredibly, the blocks are not local stone, but by some reports came from quarries in Ecuador, almost 1,500 miles away. Others have located quarries a good deal closer. Though this fantastic fortress was supposedly built just a few hundred years ago by the Incas, they leave no record of having built it, nor does it figure in any of their legends.

How is it that the Incas, who reportedly had no knowledge of higher mathematics, no written language, no iron tools and did not even use the wheel, are credited with having built this cyclopean complex of walls and buildings? Frankly, one must literally grope for an explanation, and there is no easy one.

When the Spaniards first arrived in Cuzco and saw these structures, they thought that they had been built by the devil himself, because of their enormity. Indeed, nowhere else can you see such large blocks placed together so perfectly. I have traveled all over the world searching for ancient mysteries and lost cities, but I have never in my life seen anything like this!

The builders of the stoneworks were not merely good stonemasons—they were excellent ones. Similar stoneworks can be seen throughout the Sacred Valley along the Urubamba Valley. These are usually made up of finely cut, rectangular blocks of stone weighing up to perhaps a ton.

At the time of the Spanish conquest, Cuzco was at its peak, with perhaps 100,000 Inca subjects living in the ancient city. The fortress of Sacsayhuaman could hold the entire population within its walls in case of war or natural catastrophe. Some historians have stated that the fortress was built a few years before the Spanish invasion, and that the Incas took credit for the structure. Yet, the Incas could not recall exactly how or when it was built.

Only one early account survives of the hauling of the stones, found in Garcilaso de la Vega's *The Incas*. In his commentaries, Garcilaso tells of one monstrous stone brought to Sacsayhuaman from beyond Ollantaytambo, a distance of about 45 miles.

The Indians say that owing to the great labor of being brought on its way, the stone became weary and wept tears of blood because it could not attain to a place in the edifice. The historical reality is reported by the Amautas (philosophers and doctors) of the Incas who used to tell about it. They say that more than 20,000 Indians brought the stone to the site, dragging it with huge ropes. The route over which they brought the stone was very rough. There were many high hills to ascend and descend. About half the Indians pulled the stone, by means of ropes placed in front. The other half held the stone from the rear due to fears that the stone might break loose and roll down the mountains into a ravine from which it could not be removed.

On one of these hills, due to lack of caution and coordination of effort, the massive weight of the stone overcame some who sustained it from below. The stone rolled right down the hillside, killing three or four thousand Indians who had been guiding it. Despite this misfortune, they succeeded in raising it up again. It was placed on the plain where it now rests.

Even though Garcilaso describes the hauling of one stone, many doubt the truth of this story. This stone was not part of the Sacsayhuaman fortress, and is smaller than most used there, according to some researchers, although it has never been identified. Even if the story is true, the Incas may have been trying to duplicate what they supposed was the construction technique used by the ancient builders. And certainly, while there is no denying that the Incas were master craftsmen, could they have managed to place the 100 ton blocks perfectly, a feat that we would be hard-pressed to duplicate today?

It was a common practice in ancient Egypt for rulers to claim previously existing obelisks, pyramids and other structures as their own, often literally erasing the cartouche of the real builder and substituting their own.

That the Incas actually found these megalithic ruins and then built on top of them, claiming them as their own, is not a particularly alarming theory. In fact, it is most probably the truth. It was a common practice in ancient Egypt for rulers to claim previously existing obelisks, pyramids and other structures as their own, often literally erasing the cartouche of the real builder and substituting their own.

If the Incas came along and found walls and basic foundations of cities already in existence, why not just move in? Even today, all one needs to do is a little repair work and add a roof onto some of the structures to make them habitable. Indeed, there is considerable evidence that the Incas merely found the structures and added to them. There are numerous legends that exist in the Andes that Sacsayhuaman, Machu Picchu, Tiwanaku (also known as Tiahuanaco) and other megalithic remains were built by a race of giants. Alain Gheerbrant comments in his footnotes to de la Vega's book:

and inhabited them would then say that the builders of Tiwanaku, Sacsayhuaman and other megalithic structures in the Cuzco area were the same people.

Again quoting Garcilaso de la Vega, who wrote about these structures just after the conquest:

> ...how can we explain the fact that these Peruvian Indians were able to split, carve, lift, carry, hoist and lower such enormous blocks of stone, which are more like pieces of a mountain than building stones, and that they accomplished this, as I said before, without the help of a single machine or instrument? An enigma such as this one cannot be easily solved without seeking the help of magic, particularly when one recalls the great familiarity of these people with devils.

Water was brought down from the mountains into a valley, and then had to ascend a hill before reaching Sacsayhuaman. This indicates that the engineers who built the intricate system knew that water rises to its own level.

Three kinds of stone were used to build the fortress of Sacsayhuaman. Two of them, including those which provided the gigantic blocks for the outer wall, were found practically on the spot. Only the third kind of stone (black andesite), for the inside buildings, was brought from relatively distant quarries; the nearest quarries of black andesite were at Huaccoto and Rumicolca, nine and 22 miles from Cuzco respectively.

With regard to the giant blocks of the outer wall, there is nothing to prove that they were not simply hewn from a mass of stone existing on the spot; this would solve the mystery.

Gheerbrant is close in thinking that the Incas never moved those gigantic blocks in place, yet even if they did cut and dress the stones on the spot, fitting them together so perfectly would still require what modern engineers would call superhuman effort. Furthermore, the gigantic city of Tiwanaku in Bolivia is similarly hewn from 100 ton blocks of stone, definitely of pre-Inca origin. Proponents of the theory that the Incas found these cities in the mountains

The Spanish dismantled as much of Sacsayhuaman as they could. When Cuzco was first conquered, Sacsayhuaman had three round towers at the top of the fortress, behind three concentric megalithic walls. These were taken apart stone by stone, and the stones used to build new structures for the Spanish.

Sacsayhuaman was also equipped with a subterranean network of aqueducts. Water was brought down from the mountains into a valley, and then had to ascend a hill before reaching Sacsayhuaman. This indicates that the engineers who built the intricate system knew that water rises to its own level.

Garcilaso said this about the tunnels beneath Sacsayhuaman:

> An underground network of passages, which was as vast as the towers themselves, connected them with one another. This was composed of a quantity of streets and alleyways which ran in every direction, and so many doors, all of them identical, that the most experienced men dared not venture into

this labyrinth without a guide, consisting of a long thread tied to the first door, which unwound as they advanced. I often went up to the fortress with boys of my own age, when I was a child, and we did not dare to go farther than the sunlight itself, we were so afraid of getting lost, after all that the Indians had told us on the subject...the roofs of these underground passages were composed of large flat stones resting on rafters jutting out from the walls.

THEORIES ON THE MEGALITHIC CONSTRUCTION

One interesting theory about the building of the gigantic and perfectly fitted stones is that they were constructed by using a now-lost technique of softening and shaping the rock. Hiram Bingham, the discoverer of Machu Picchu, wrote in his book *Across South America*, of a plant he had heard of whose juices softened rock so that it could be worked into tightly fitted masonry.

In his book *Exploration Fawcett*, Colonel [Percy] Fawcett told of how he had heard that the stones were fitted together by means of a liquid that softened stone to the consistency of clay. Brian Fawcett, who edited his father's book, tells the following story in the footnotes: A friend of his, who worked at a mining camp at 14,000 feet at Cerro di Pasco in Central Peru, discovered a jar in an Incan or pre-Incan grave. He opened the jar, thinking it was *chicha*, an alcoholic drink, breaking the still intact ancient wax seal. Later, the jar was accidentally knocked over onto a rock.

though the stone had melted, like wax under the influence of heat."

Fawcett seemed to think that the plant might be found on the Pyrene River in the Chuncho country of Peru, and described it as having dark reddish leaves and being about a foot high. In his book *The Ancient Stones Speak*, David Zink quotes a "psychic reading," giving the name of the plant as Caochyll, saying it has sparse leaves with reddish veins, and stands about three to four feet high.

Another story is told in South America, of a biologist observing an unfamiliar bird in the Amazon. He watched it making a nest on a rock face by rubbing the rock with a twig. The sap of the twig dissolved the rock, making a hollow in which the bird could make its nest.

All of this speculation may be put to rest by new findings, reported in *Scientific American* in February 1986. In a fascinating article, a French researcher, Jean-Pierre Protzen, relates his experiments in duplicating the construction of Inca structures. Protzen spent many months around Cuzco experimenting with different methods of shaping and fitting the same kinds of stones used by the Incas. He found that quarrying and dressing the stones was easily accomplished using the stone hammers found in abundance in the area. He repeatedly dropped these hammers, made of a hard stone, against the larger blocks from eye-level. Each impact chipped away a small amount of rock, and he caught the hammer as it bounced back up to easily repeat the maneuver. Even the precision fitting of stones was a relatively

---

About ten minutes later I bent over the rock and casually examined the pool of spilled liquid. It was no longer liquid; the whole patch where it had been, and the rock under it, were as soft as wet cement! It was as though the stone had melted, like wax under the influence of heat.

Quotes Fawcett, "About ten minutes later I bent over the rock and casually examined the pool of spilled liquid. It was no longer liquid; the whole patch where it had been, and the rock under it, were as soft as wet cement! It was as

simple matter, he says. He pounded out the concave depressions into which new stones were fitted by trial and error, until he achieved a snug fit. This meant continually lifting and placing the stones together, and chipping at them a little at a time.

This process is very time consuming, but it's simple, and it works.

Protzen believes that Inca stonemasonry was surprisingly unsophisticated, though efficient. He would like to debunk ideas of anti-gravity devices, stone-softening or lasers used to cut and place the stone. Yet even for Protzen, some mysteries remain. He was not able to figure out how the builders transported and handled the large stones. The fitting process necessitated the repeated lowering and raising of the stone being fitted, with trial-and-error pounding throughout the process. He does not know just how 100 ton stones were manipulated at this stage, while some stones are actually far heavier.

According to Protzen, to transport the stones from the quarries, the Incas built special access roads and ramps. Many of the stones were dragged over gravel-covered roads, which in his theory gave the stones their polished surfaces. The largest stone at Ollantaytambo weighs about 150 tons. It could have been pulled up a ramp with a force of about 260,000 pounds, he says. Such a feat would have required a minimum of some 2,400 men. Getting the men seemed possible, but where did they all stand? Protzen says that the ramps were only eight meters wide at most. Further perplexing Protzen is that the stones of Sacsayhuaman were finely dressed, yet are not polished, showing no signs of dragging. He could not figure out how they were transported the 22 miles from the Rumiqolqa quarry.

Perhaps the theories of levitation and softening stones cannot be discarded yet.

Protzen's article reflects good research, and points out that modern science still cannot explain or duplicate the building feats found at both Sacsayhuaman and Ollantaytambo. Continually lifting and chipping away at a 100 ton stone block to make it fit perfectly is just too great of an engineering task to have been practical. Protzen's theory would work well on the smaller, precisely square, later construction, but fails with the older megalithic construction beneath. Perhaps the theories of levitation and softening stones cannot be discarded

yet. One last intriguing observation which Protzen makes is that the cutting marks found on some of the stones are very similar to those found on the pyramidion of an unfinished obelisk at Aswan in Egypt. Is this a coincidence, or was there an ancient civilization with links to both sites?

One curious theory, given to me in a telephone conversation in the fall of 2003, claimed that quartz crystals, when connected in a series and given high voltages, will bend. If a quartz crystal is bent, or struck with a hammer, it will become charged with a mysterious kind of electrical signal called piezoelectric.

The source claimed that when a crystal is struck, put under pressure, or "bent," it will give off a piezoelectric effect and, incredibly, it actually loses the gravitational force that would naturally pull it toward the center of the mass (in this case, the earth). The crystal then becomes essentially weightless, and no matter how heavy it was before being bent by high voltages, it is now weightless. If such an effect could be confirmed, then gigantic blocks of granite, which contain quartz crystals in them, could theoretically be moved by very little effort, no matter how much they weigh when not having a powerful electric charge placed on them.

Picture this: Huge granite blocks that have been quarried and dressed are then "electrified." This causes the block of crystalline stone to "bend" which causes it to become weightless. The blocks are then moved effortlessly through the air with guidelines such as ropes, or perhaps "pusher" beams of energy. A familiar movie scene of this type is when the bounty hunter Boba Fett in the film *The Empire Strikes Back* takes the block of carbonite holding Han Solo aboard his ship, and he is effortlessly pushing it ahead of him up a ramp onto his spaceship. Could such a scene have been witnessed in ancient Peru?

EVIDENCE OF PRE-INCA CONSTRUCTION AT OLLANTAYTAMBO

Along the Urubamba River, 45 miles north of Cuzco, is Ollantaytambo. It lies at the north end of the Sacred Valley and guards the entrance to the narrow Urubamba Gorge. A still-inhabited ancient town exists at Ollantaytambo, and a gigantic "sun temple" known by the same name

I believe that it is at Ollantaytambo that definitive evidence can be found that proves that the Incas did not build Machu Picchu or any of the other megalithic walls.

sits on a mountain ridge at the northern edge of the town. I believe that it is at Ollantaytambo that definitive evidence can be found that proves that the Incas did not build Machu Picchu or any of the other megalithic walls. Rather, evidence will show that, like Tiwanaku in Bolivia, these structures were already extant.

The most impressive megaliths at Ollantaytambo are the six large stones that face the river. The largest is about 13 feet (four meters) high, seven feet (2.1 meters) wide, and about six feet (1.8 meters) thick, and weighs approximately 50 tons (45,500 kg). Made from red porphyry, a very hard type of rock, much of their surfaces are very finely polished. On the fourth giant stone from the left is a stepped motif, identical to those found at Tiwanaku in Bolivia, but not found elsewhere in the Cuzco area. Even more unusual is a stone in which a "keycut" has been carefully cut into the stone to hold a metal clamp, presumably to hold two colossal blocks together as earthquake protection. This unusual technique is found at Puma Punku in Tiwanaku and nowhere else in the Andes. Tiwanaku-style pottery is also found in the area.

The stones were quarried across the river, 200 feet below the fortress, and about 3,000 feet up the opposite slope. At the quarry near the mountaintop across the river can be found gigantic blocks of granite that have been cut and squared but were never moved from the site. A 250 ton stone from this quarry lies at the bottom of the river, having been moved down the mountain but somehow "dropped" in the river.

While the Incas used Ollantaytambo as a fort to guard the entrance to Cuzco from up the Urubamba Valley (or down the Urubamba Valley, as was to be the case as the Incas retreated), it appears that Ollantaytambo, like Sacsayhuaman, was already in place before the arrival of the Incas.

In an article entitled "The Impossible Stones" that appeared in the May 2002 issue of the British magazine *Fortean Times*, the subject is a wall of six massive blocks of red porphyry installed high above a five-tiered "fortress" composed of huge, Inca-style, interlocked stones at Ollantaytambo, Peru. The Inca fortress is itself a cause for archaeological wonder, but the great wall above is even more wondrous. It is about 13 feet high, with each of its six blocks weighing about 50 tons. We see in the wall at least five "problems" which might morph into significant anomalies.

Three of these problems are mentioned by A. F. Alford in his *Fortean Times* article.

1. Red porphyry is hard igneous rock. How were the 13-foot blocks carved with such perfect, flat surfaces and die-straight edges?

2. How were the 50 ton blocks moved four miles from the quarry across a river and then raised to their present position where they amaze the tourists? In 1996, a group of archaeologists tried to demonstrate how it was done with a one ton block. This relatively puny stone slipped its ropes on the way downhill from the quarry and gravity took it down to the river. The archaeologists then managed to drag it across the shallow, cobble-bottomed river. But there they left it, declaring they had now proved how the wall high above could have been made. Their rough, unfinished "pebble" is probably still in the river.

The archaeologists then managed to drag it across the shallow, cobble-bottomed river. But there they left it, declaring they had now proved how the wall high above could have been made. Their rough, unfinished "pebble" is probably still in the river.

3. Alford mentions the unique and very un-Inca-like thin sheets of rock separating the six blocks in the wall. These sheets, which also must have

been challenging to the stonemasons, serve no discernible practical purpose.

William Corliss of the Sourcebook Project in Maryland adds two more wall "problems."

4. One of the porphyry blocks has a T-shaped slot cut into its top for insertion of a metal clamp. The same sort of slot-and-clamp construction is seen at pre-Inca Tiwanaku, built on the shores of Lake Titicaca in Bolivia. Given this fact, one wonders if pre-Incans might actually have built the porphyry wall at Ollantaytambo? Whoever built it seems to have left the wall unfinished, seeing there is no block cut to receive the other end of the metal clamp.

5. Part of the answer may lie in the stream far below the wall, where a 250 ton block resides, waiting to be raised up to the wall—another sign that the wall was never finished. (A 250 ton stone is big even by Great Pyramid standards!)

So what we find at Ollantaytambo is curious and baffling: The temple was never completed.

Gigantic blocks of red granite are hewn and dragged by an unknown means to the site, but never assembled. Keystone cuts in the shape of a "T" are cut into some of the blocks for metal clamps to be put into place. This unusual method for holding megalithic blocks into place was used in the pre-Inca construction of Tiwanaku. It was also used in ancient Egypt, ancient Greece and other sites in Asia and the Mediterranean. Evidence is mounting that the Incas did not build Ollantaytambo, but found it much as it is today. Apparently the builders of Ollantaytambo were the same builders who built Tiwanaku.

Therefore, if the Incas did not build Tiwanaku or Ollantaytambo, it follows that they did not build Machu Picchu or Sacsayhuaman either. To finish this discussion we now turn to that admittedly pre-Inca city of Tiwanaku.

THE AMAZING PRE-INCA RUINS OF TIWANAKU

The massive ruins of Tiwanaku are situated in a remote, desolate area of the Altiplano. These ruins overlook barren hills, in stark contrast to the stunning setting of Machu Picchu. The cataclysmic theorists point out that it is unlikely that such a fantastic city would be built at such a desolate location and altitude. This unlikely reasoning is used to further the theory that Tiwanaku was built at a lower elevation, and later uplifted.

What remains today of Tiwanaku is what could not be carted away for use in other structures, so only the biggest blocks of stone remain and these ruins are still very impressive!

The central part of the city is the restored temple of Kalasayaya. Megalithic blocks make up the steps, walls and arches around the temple. At the turn of the century, Bolivian engineers broke up the stones and carried away all the smaller blocks to be used as ballast on a railway. What remains today of Tiwanaku is what could not be carted away for use in other structures, so only the biggest blocks of stone remain and these ruins are still very impressive! In 1864, E. George Squire visited Tiwanaku and was quite impressed by the ruins; he called them the Baalbek of the New World. (He was referring to the ruins of Baalbek in Lebanon, which contain some of the most astounding megaliths to be found anywhere in the world.)

In the center of Tiwanaku is a stone arch, cut from a solid chunk of andesite weighing about 12 tons, now cracked by what must have been a pretty severe earthquake. On the upper portion of this arch is a series of carvings, believed to be a calendar. In the center a figure, holding a staff on each side, appears to be weeping. He is known as "the Weeping God." This massive stone gate was apparently moved to where it is today by some earlier culture after the city was destroyed. The gate is actually from the ruins of Puma Punku which is about a mile to the north of the main part of Tiwanaku.

When the Spaniards first arrived, they were told by the Indians that this city had been found in ruins by the Incas. Cieza de Leon, one of the first chroniclers of South America, visited the site in 1540, when much of the stone still remained. He reported two colossal stone figures, with long robes reaching to the ground and ornamental caps on their heads.

Cieza de Leon wrote "...the natives told me...that all these marvels sprang from the ground in a single night... There are not stones in any of the hills beyond." The Spaniards generally believed that these monuments "...were more the work of demons than of men." A similar legend told at the time was that, "Tiwanaku was built in a single night, after the flood, by unknown giants. But they disregarded a prophecy of the coming of the sun and were annihilated by its rays, and their palaces were reduced to ashes..."

In the Sixteenth Century, missionary Diego de Alcobaso wrote, "I saw a vast hall carved on its roof to represent thatch. There were the waters of a lake which washed the walls of a splendid court in this city of the dead, and, standing in its fine court, in the shallows of the water, on the platform of a superb colonnade were many fine statues of men and women. So real they were that they seemed to be alive. Some had goblets and upraised drinking cups. Others sat, or reclined, as in life. Some walked in the stream flowing by the ancient walls. Women, carved in stone, dangled babies in their laps or bore them on their backs. In a thousand natural postures, people stood or reclined." One of the statues wore a beard, and as we know, South American Indians are beardless.

All that remains are the monolithic figures of bizarre, bug-eyed men who stare vacantly over the desolate ruins of Tiwanaku. They look more like men from outer space than beautiful people at a party in the hills.

Today, most of these statues have been destroyed. All that remains are the monolithic figures of bizarre, bug-eyed men who stare vacantly over the desolate ruins of Tiwanaku. They look more like men from outer space than beautiful people at a party in the hills. The Spaniards destroyed everything they could at Tiwanaku, thinking it idolatrous. These larger figures were spared because they were so massive, but they have been badly damaged.

In the 1800s, a controversial French anthropologist named Augustus le Plongeon visited Tiwanaku and observed a strata of seashells, which hinted that the site had once been at sea level. (I found a fossilized trilobite myself while we explored the ruins.) British Colonel James Churchward used the argument that Tiwanaku is a former port city as a major piece of his evidence for the lost continent of Lemuria.

As the great South American explorer Colonel Fawcett said at the turn of the Twentieth Century:

> These megalithic ruins of Tiwanaku were never built on the Andes at all. They are part of a great city submerged ages ago in the Pacific Ocean. When the crust of the earth upheaved and created the great Andean Cordilleras, these ruins were elevated from the bed of the ocean to where you now see them.

If one is looking for ruins which could have suffered through such an upheaval, one needs look no further than those of Puma Punku. Infrequently visited, Puma Punku is only a mile or so to the north of Tiwanaku, toward Lake Titicaca. Its most fascinating feature is what appears to be an ancient canal. Huge sandstone and andesite blocks up to 27 feet long and weighing as much as 300 tons are scattered about like a child's building blocks. The normally-conservative *Reader's Digest* reported, "A jumbled heap of stones looking as if they were hurled to the ground by some great natural catastrophe, is all that remains of Puma Punku..."

Here was once a great canal, according to some archaeologists, destroyed in an earthquake of massive proportions. The construction at Puma Punku is different from that at Tiwanaku, in that the stones were fitted together with clamps, like the one stone at Ollantaytambo. Puma Punku has none of the statues found at Tiwanaku, but instead has geometric designs precisely cut into the andesite, such as concentric Swiss-style crosses and triangles.

While Bolivian archaeologists insist that ancestors of the local Aymara Indians built both Tiwanaku and Puma Punku, it would seem that their culture has certainly taken a slide back, as they now can barely make a subsistence living on the high, barren plateau. Neither they, nor the Spanish government of impoverished Bolivia, are capable of duplicating the engineering feats of Tiwanaku or Puma Punku.

> **Yet, if a massive earthquake tossed down the 300 ton stones of Puma Punku, scattering them about the plain like a bunch of toys, then why were the buildings of Tiwanaku not likewise destroyed?**

Traditional archaeologists explain the former canals at Tiwanaku by saying that it was once near Lake Titicaca, 20 miles away. The lake theoretically covered a greater area at that time, extending to the port of Puma Punku. It is interesting to contrast this explanation with that for the sunken city near Porto Acosta, which the same experts claim was built when the waters of the lake were very low. This adds up to quite a variation in the depth of the lake.

Yet, if a massive earthquake tossed down the 300 ton stones of Puma Punku, scattering them about the plain like a bunch of toys, then why were the buildings of Tiwanaku not likewise destroyed? Is it because they were built at a later time, after the cataclysm?

Some say that Tiwanaku was built about 15,000 years ago. Archaeologist Arthur Posnansky, who studied Tiwanaku for 30 years at the turn of the Twentieth Century, decided that the city was from 10,000 to 12,000 years old. Traditional archaeologists scoff at this ancient date, citing radio carbon dating of artifacts indicating that the city was occupied at 1700 B.C. Even this figure is astounding, considering that some vanished culture was constructing buildings that we can hardly duplicate, four thousand years later.

And who would have built Tiwanaku? Perhaps none other than those mysterious seafarers who mapped Antarctica before it was covered with ice, sailed the world spreading a megalithic culture, and wore red turbans over their blond hair—the Atlantean League! But why would anyone want to come to one of the most desolate, inhospitable places on earth and construct a megalithic city? This has always been the most puzzling question of Tiwanaku, no matter who you decide actually built it.

There are two possible reasons for choosing this location. First, it is significant that the older ruins of Puma Punku are nearby. Could it be that the builders of Tiwanaku put the city here because it was near the ruins of the even more ancient city? This would seem to be the case. They may have wanted to draw attention to the ruins of Puma Punku, perhaps just stumbling upon them while searching for a place to build Tiwanaku.

Peruvian historian Montesinos wrote in his *Memorias Antiguas, Historales, Politicas del Peru*:

> Cuzco and the city of ruins Tiwanaku are connected by a gigantic subterranean road. The Incas do not know who built it. They also know nothing about the inhabitants of Tiwanaku. In their opinion it was built by a very ancient people who later on retreated into the jungle of Amazonia.

So, even here at desolate Tiwanaku, we have the mysterious tunnel system popping up again! If it doesn't exist, why does everyone talk about it?

THE TIWANAKU-OLLANTAYTAMBO CONNECTION

Lake Titicaca is the highest navigable lake in the world, at an altitude of 12,500 feet (3,810 meters). It has a maximum depth of 1,214 feet (370 meters), also making it one of the deepest lakes in the world. The lake has an area of about 3,200 square miles (8,190 square km), about half the size of Lake Ontario.

Local Indians have reported observing buildings and roofs in the lake, and that after long droughts when the water level was low, they could even touch the tops of the buildings with their poles. This was written off as superstitious talk until the early 1970s, when an American dive team discovered what was literally a sunken city on the eastern shore of Lake Titicaca!

Could the sunken city near Porto Acosta actually be a city from the pre-cataclysmic times, when this area contained a canal that crossed the continent?

Local Indians have reported observing buildings and roofs in the lake, and that after long droughts when the water level was low, they could even touch the tops of the buildings with their poles! This was written off as superstitious talk until the early 1970s, when an American dive team discovered what was literally a sunken city on the eastern shore of Lake Titicaca! Near Bolivia's Porto Acosta, in about 65 feet (20 meters) of water can be found the ruins of an ancient city. There are reports of other sunken cities in Lake Titicaca, and it was these rumors that may have piqued Jacques Cousteau's interest.[4]

A Bolivian archaeologist has an explanation for the existence of a sunken city in the lake. He theorizes that the water was very low at one time after a severe drought, and people living on the lake foolishly built their city too close to the water. Later, when the drought ended and the water level rose, the city became submerged, a lost city to be discovered many years later by puzzled archaeologists.

Could the sunken city near Porto Acosta actually be a city from the pre-cataclysmic times, when this area contained a canal that crossed the continent? Precious little archaeological work has been done at this sunken city, as underwater archaeology generally centers around salvaging shipwrecks.

So, in conclusion, I must admit that I do not know who built Machu Picchu, Ollantaytambo, Sacsayhuaman or Tiwanaku. However, it would appear that the builders of all of these monuments were the same people—but they were not the Incas. These structures were probably built many hundreds of years before the Incas. The questions are: Who built these megalithic walls, and how did they do it?

1. *Grollier's 1977 Encyclopedia.*
2. Ibid.
3. Ibid.
4. In 1973, Cousteau plumbed the depths of Lake Titicaca in a submersible looking for Incan treasures and artifacts but was unsuccessful in his search, contrary to later efforts, such as the Atahuallpa 2000 expedition. Lorenzo Epis, the Italian leading the expedition, told the *Guardian* that after more than 200 dives, they'd found "[a] 200-meter-long, 50-meter-wide holy temple, a terrace for crops, a pre-Incan road and an 800-meter-long containing wall." — Ed.

Colin Wilson

SUMMARY OF *ATLANTIS AND THE OLD ONES:*

AN INVESTIGATION OF THE AGE OF CIVILIZATION

CHARLES HAPGOOD, an American professor of history, became convinced in 1989 that a civilization "with high levels of science" had existed at least 100,000 years ago.

In the mid-1950s, Hapgood had written a book called *Earth's Shifting Crust*, to which Einstein contributed an introduction, arguing that the whole crust of the earth undergoes periodic "slip-pages," one of which, in 9500 B.C., had caused the North Pole to move from Hudson Bay to its present position. And in 1966, his *Maps of the Ancient Sea Kings* had suggested that medieval maps called "portolans"—used by sailors to navigate "from port to port"—proved that there must have been a worldwide maritime civilization in 7000 B.C.

In 1989 he told the writer Rand Flem-Ath that he intended to bring out a new edition of *Earth's Shifting Crust*, containing his evidence that civilization had existed since before 100,000 years ago. But before he could do that, Hapgood walked in front of a car and was killed.

I agreed to collaborate with Rand Flem-Ath in trying to solve this mystery. After a long search, I was fortunate enough to track down the man who claimed to have convinced Hapgood that civilization dated back a hundred thousand years. He was an eccentric recluse who lived in a small town in New England. When I asked him to explain what had convinced him that there was civilization hundreds of thousands of years ago, he specified two things: that Neanderthal man was far more intelligent than we assume, and that ancient measures prove that man knew the exact size of the earth millennia before the Greek Eratosthenes worked it out in 240 B.C.

> Far from being a shambling ape, Neanderthal man had a larger brain than we have, was well acquainted with astronomy, played musical instruments and even invented the blast furnace.

A little research of my own quickly verified both statements. Far from being a shambling ape, Neanderthal man had a larger brain than we have, was well acquainted with astronomy, played musical instruments and even invented the blast furnace. As to the size of the earth, the ancient Greeks had a measure called the stade—the length of a stadium. The polar circumference of the earth proves to be *exactly* 216,000 stade. *Yet the Greeks did not know the size of the earth.* They must have inherited the stade from someone who *did* know.

On a cruise down the Nile in 1997 I stumbled on another crucial discovery: The Nineveh number, a vast 15 digit number found inscribed on an Assyrian clay tablet in the ruins of Assurbanipal's library. Yet the Assyrians were no great mathematicians.

The French space engineer Maurice Chatelain—who provided the first moon rocket with its communication system—discovered powerful internal evidence that the Nineveh number must have been worked out about 65,000 years ago.

He also learned that two more numbers, even larger, were found inscribed on a stele in the Mayan sacred city of Quiriga. These shared with the Nineveh number a remarkable characteristic: They could be divided precisely by the number of years it takes the earth to complete its "precessional cycle" round the sun, just under 26,000. (Precession of the equinoxes is the backward movement of the signs of the zodiac, so that in the heavens, spring begins slightly earlier each year.)

abandoned since it lacked the typical air bubbles, and left them with the only alternative hypothesis: That this glass had been *manufactured* by some strange industrial process around 6000 B.C. But that would have required large quantities of water. It was Hapgood who was able to assure the investigators that there *had* been vast lakes in North Africa in 6000 B.C. When Lord Rennell of Rodd described the mystery to a scientist named John V. Dolphin, who had worked on testing the atom bomb in the desert of Australia, Dolphin told him that the glass looked just like the fused sand left behind after an atom bomb test, which led Lord Rennell to consider the possibility that the makers of the Libyan desert glass had mastered atomic

So it seems the Assyrians inherited their knowledge of precession from some early "founder" civilization—presumably the same civilization from which the Maya, thousands of years later and thousands of miles across the Atlantic, inherited theirs.

So it seems the Assyrians inherited their knowledge of precession from some early "founder" civilization—presumably the same civilization from which the Maya, thousands of years later and thousands of miles across the Atlantic, inherited theirs.

I came upon one more important discovery on that Nile cruise. It was something that happened in the temple of Edfu, and it took six more years before its full significance dawned on me, and provided a sudden insight into the secret of Egyptian temples. Of this, more in a moment.

THE MYSTERIOUS LIBYAN DESERT GLASS

I had come upon another interesting piece of evidence that "high levels of science" date back much earlier than we suppose. It started with the mystery of the Libyan desert glass. Two British scientists driving through the Libyan desert discovered large quantities of a fused green glass, highly valued by Arab craftsmen for making jewelry. Their first assumption, that these were "tektites," a fused glass that comes from outer space, had to be

energy. Hapgood dismissed this notion, being himself convinced that the ancients simply had some other method of producing very high temperatures—of around 6,000 degrees Celsius.

Unknown to Hapgood and Lord Rennell, a Bulgarian inventor name Ilya Velbov—who later called himself Yull Brown—had solved this problem. Brown made the extraordinary discovery that if the hydrogen and oxygen in water are separated, and then recombined in a kind of oxy-acetylene flame, it will punch an instantaneous hole in a piece of hard wood, burn tungsten (requiring 6,000 degrees), vaporize metals, melt a firebrick and weld glass to copper. Brown called this mixture "Brown's gas," and the Chinese used it in their submarines to turn seawater into drinking water. Yet because no one understands the process, science has shown total lack of interest in it. However, Brown had no doubt it was known to the ancients, who used it to extract purified gold from gold ore.

Brown's total refusal to compromise with American industry ruined his one excellent chance of achieving fame and riches, and he died unknown.

The story of the great flood is preserved in the legends of the Haida Indians of Canada and of many other tribes. But which flood? Plato speaks of no less than four.

EVIDENCE OF 100,000-YEAR-OLD SCIENCE

But if Hapgood is correct about his 100,000-year-old science, what evidence remains? Well, a modern builder would admit that, for all our technology, he would have no idea of how to go about building the Great Pyramid. The same is true of the magnificent ruins of Tiahuanaco, in the Andes, whose harbor area has blocks so big that no modern crane could lift them. These builders seem to have had some technology for moving immensely heavy weights.

Lake Titicaca, on which Tiahuanaco was once a port, is full of sea creatures. At some time in the past, a geological convulsion raised it two and a half miles in the air. Geologists assume this was millions of years ago, but this is absurd. Who would build a great port on a lake with no other ports or cities? Surely, Tiahuanaco must have been at sea level when the convulsion occurred. In their book *When the Earth Nearly Died: Compelling Evidence of a Cosmic Catastrophe in 9500* B.C. (1995), D. S. Allan and J. B. Delair argue that the convulsion was probably due to the impact of a comet or asteroid. The date, of course, is the date Plato assigns to the destruction of Atlantis "in a day and a night."

The story of the great flood is preserved in the legends of the Haida Indians of Canada and of many other tribes. But which flood? Plato speaks of no less than four. The first of these was the Atlantis flood. The second is referred to in the *Book of Enoch* and the rituals of the Freemasons, and it took place approximately 2,000 years after Plato's flood. "Seven burning mountains" fell to earth from space, according to the evidence of Professor Alexander Tollmann, the largest in the Sunda Strait, and it set in motion a great migration north, which created civilizations in India and then in Sumeria (the Sumerians are regarded as the founders of European civilization). The third flood, around 6000 B.C., created the Black Sea

and was the flood of Noah and the *Epic of Gilgamesh*. The fourth, "Deucalion's flood," occurred in the Bronze Age, around 2200 B.C. Another vast catastrophe struck in A.D. 535, causing worldwide famine, drought and plague, which destroyed, among others, the civilization of the Maya in Central America, and of the Nazca Indians of Peru, whose giant line-drawings on the surface of the desert, we now know, were designed to persuade the gods to send rain.

These drawings can be seen only from the air, and have given rise to the theory that the Nazca shamans, with the aid of psychedelic drugs (which the Indians are known to have used) were able to achieve out-of-body experiences that enabled them to do this.[1] The Indians of the Peruvian forest use a drug called ayahuasca, which (according to anthropologist Jeremy Narby) they claim taught them the properties of 80,000 plants and the structure of DNA.

There seems to be no doubt that shamans possess powers that we would consider "magical," and many examples are given here. The healing abilities of shamans can also be used for the opposite purpose, to produce sickness and death.

Shamanism thereafter becomes one of the central themes of this book, and it is argued that shamans have a knowledge of nature that goes far beyond that of modern science. There seems to be no doubt that shamans possess powers that we would consider "magical," and many examples are given here. The healing abilities of shamans can also be used for the opposite purpose, to produce sickness and death. The Kahuna priests of Hawaii can use the Death Prayer to kill enemies. And it was when reading about their power to protect temples with a curse, and the story of one rash youth who became paralyzed from the waist down after entering a "forbidden" temple in a spirit of bravado, that I suddenly saw the meaning of an incident that had happened in 1997 in the temple of Edfu, when investigator Michael Baigent fell into a trance behind the altar. The curse of Tutankhamun was undoubtedly more than a legend.

MORE ANCIENT KNOWLEDGE, FROM TEMPLARS TO FREEMASONS

The book now returns to the subject of the search for "ancient knowledge," and to the Scotsman and Freemason James Bruce who went to Ethiopia in search of the lost *Book of Enoch*. We consider evidence advanced by Robert Lomas and Christopher Knight (*Uriel's Machine*, 2004) that Enoch traveled to the British Isles, and that a stone (or wooden) structure built on a hilltop could be used as an astronomical computer, which explains, among other things, the length of the "megalithic yard" noted in all megalithic sites by Professor Alexander Thom—he spoke of their builders as "Stone Age Einsteins." Lomas and Knight argue that the rituals of Freemasonry date from "Tollman's flood" in 7500 B.C.

They also pointed out that Rosslyn Chapel, near Edinburgh, Scotland, founded by the Templar William St. Clair, contains carvings of exclusively American plants such as sweet corn and aloes, although Columbus did not discover America until 50 years after Rosslyn Chapel was built. The evidence indicates that when the Templar fleet left La Rochelle to escape the mass arrests (and executions) inaugurated by France's Philip the Fair in 1307, some ships sailed to America.

They also pointed out that Rosslyn Chapel, near Edinburgh, Scotland, founded by the Templar William St. Clair, contains carvings of exclusively American plants such as sweet corn and aloes, although Columbus did not discover America until 50 years after Rosslyn Chapel was built.

How did they know that America was there? The answer seems to be from maps (like those of Hapgood's "Ancient Sea Kings") discovered by the original Templars after the fall of Jerusalem to the Crusaders in A.D. 1112. King Baldwin gave the original nine Templar knights permission to stable their horses in the basement of the old Temple of Solomon, deserted since the Romans had destroyed it in A.D. 66. after a Jewish uprising. Many documents belonging to a sect called the Essenes had been stored there, one of them (the *Heavenly Jerusalem* scroll) full of Masonic symbols. It seems clear that the Essenes were part of the Masonic tradition, and were aware of the existence of America. The evidence indicates that Jesus was not only an Essene, but was regarded by them as the Messiah who would overthrow Roman rule. He was crucified after an unsuccessful attempt to stir up revolt, and was replaced as leader of the Essenes by his brother James.

Subsequently, St. Paul virtually invented the religion called Christianity, in which Jesus "the Christ" is the Savior who redeems man from Original Sin (a thought that certainly never entered Jesus' head).

Subsequently, St. Paul virtually invented the religion called Christianity, in which Jesus "the Christ" is the Savior who redeems man from Original Sin (a thought that certainly never entered Jesus' head). And when the original Christians were massacred by the Romans in A.D. 66, St. Paul's version (preached abroad to gentiles) went on to conquer the world. For purely political reasons it was adopted by the Emperor Constantine to hold his rickety empire together, and the Council of Nicaea laid down the doctrine of the Trinity as a dogma. Pope Leo X would say later: "It has served us well, this myth of Christ." (But then, as we shall show, Pope Leo belonged to the original religious tradition that flowed from the Essenes, and was a member of a secret society known as the Priory of Sion, founded in 1112 by the first Templars.)

Lomas and Knight argue that Hiram Abif, the Temple architect, whose legend of murder by three "apprentices" is the foundation stone of Freemasonry, was in fact an Egyptian pharaoh named Sequenenre, murdered by Hyksos assassins in an attempt to wrest from him a secret ritual for turning a pharaoh into a god. Sequenenre's son subsequently drove the Hyksos (the "Shepherd Kings") out of Egypt. And 600 years later, the story was turned on its head when Sequenenre was transformed into "Hiram Abif," architect of Solomon's Temple. Rosslyn was, in due course, built by a Templar and Freemason in imitation of Solomon's Temple.

Solomon strayed from the old religion to become a worshipper of Venus, and we learn how the planet Venus is the only planet whose path forms a perfect pentagram in the sky—the fundamental symbol of magic.

We go on to explore the story of the "original (Essene) Christianity," and how it became the secret guarded by a line of French kings, the Merovingians, who knew that Christianity was an invention of St. Paul and the Council of Nicaea, and who hoped one day to replace the Catholic Church and restore the original Christianity. They were overthrown when King Dagobert II was murdered and replaced by the Carolingian Dynasty, but kept alive the knowledge of the secret of the Priory of Sion. This secret was accidentally discovered by a parish priest named Beranger Saunière in a village called Rennes-le-Château (which lies in the middle of a natural "magical" landscape, in which the hills form an exact pentagram).

For the concluding two chapters of the book, we return to the mystery of Hapgood's 100,000 year-old civilization.

It is clear that the ancients possessed some extraordinary ability to multiply huge numbers, very like those possessed by modern calculating prodigies (such as five-year-old Benjamin Blyth, who took only a few minutes to work out how many seconds he had been alive). We explore *The Infinite Harmony* by Mike Hayes, which shows the intimate relation between the DNA code and the *I Ching*. This leads to a consideration of synchronicity, which modern science refuses to recognize, and the "certain blindness in human beings" that causes us to "filter out" so much of our experience. Goethe, like William James, was fully aware of this blindness, and the scientific "filters" that cause us to see "God's living garment" as a world of dead matter. Goethe's Theory of Color is explored. We speak of "eidetic vision," the odd ability of certain people (like Nikola Tesla) to be able to recreate some object inside their heads. (It is also fundamental to training in magic.)

Julian Jaynes realized that man is trapped in a gray world created by the left cerebral hemisphere, the "scientific" part of the brain. But then, Annie Besant and C. W. Leadbeater, two founders of the Theosophical Society, wrote a book called *Occult*

There is, in fact, evidence that our ancestor *Homo erectus* was sailing the seas on rafts 800,000 years ago.

Saunière also learned that Jesus had not died on the cross, but had been taken down after six hours and nursed back to health, after which he fled to France with his wife, Mary Magdalene, and lived in Rennes-le-Château, then called Aireda. The Merovingian kings were direct descendants of Jesus and Mary Magdalene. In the mid-1990s, following these clues, an art historian named Peter Blake discovered a cave that he believes to be the tomb of Jesus and Mary, and learned that several popes and cardinals (including Richelieu) have been members of the Priory.

Chemistry that described quarks more than half a century before science posited their existence.

We move on to another scientist, Chandra Bose, who saw nature—even metals—as alive. And this takes us back to Hapgood, who, after his retirement, became interested in some very odd aspects of science—for example, the discovery of lie-detector expert Cleve Backster that plants can read our minds. While still a college professor, he did experiments with his students that demonstrated that plants that are "prayed for" flourish more than plants that are ignored, while plants

We glance again at some of the evidence that man may have been around far longer than science supposes—such as an iron nail embedded in a piece of coal several million years old, and a mastodon's tooth engraved with a horned beast, that came from a Miocene bed of 25 million years ago.

that are "prayed against" often died. Hapgood became very interested in the "life fields" discovered by the American scientist Harold Burr, and the recognition that these can be controlled by "thought fields." Hapgood's studies of anthropology led him to conclude that man has been as intelligent as ourselves for at least 200,000 years, and perhaps for two million. There is, in fact, evidence that our ancestor *Homo erectus* was sailing the seas on rafts 800,000 years ago.

Most amazing is Hapgood's experiments with hypnosis, which proved conclusively that he could hypnotize his students to *accurately predict the future*.

The final chapter of this book contains some of its most remarkable discoveries, beginning with the unearthing of a half-million-year-old plank that had been carefully planed on one side. Then we consider Neanderthal man and some facts that prove his high level of intelligence—and whose red ocher mines in South Africa date back 100,000 years. One sculpture, the Berekhat Ram, has been dated back to a quarter of a million years ago.

We consider the fact that "shamanic" cultures take "group consciousness" for granted—the kind of telepathic awareness that enables flocks of birds and schools of fishes to change direction simultaneously. Ancient man almost certainly possessed this same telepathic ability. Kevin Kelly's book *Out of Control* describes how the whole audience at a computer conference in San Diego learned this ability in a quarter of an hour. In this sense, societies like ancient Egypt were almost certainly "collectives," which could explain their ability to lift massive weights.

We pass on to the extraordinary discoveries of John Michell, who pointed out that the Nineveh number can be divided by the diameters of the sun and moon, and that a mathematical principle called "the Canon" seems to lie behind ancient science: the notion that our universe appears to be designed along mathematical lines—the "code of numbers that structures the universe," which implies that there is an intelligence behind this design. An example is the sequence of "Fibonacci numbers" that play such a basic part in nature, from spiral nebulae to seashells. We discuss the Anthropic Cosmological Principle, formulated by astronomer Brandon Carter, which states that the universe *aims at* the propagation of life, and at Fred Hoyle's statement that "Our planet is perfectly suited to the incubation of life," and that "it looks as if some superintendent has been monkeying with the physics."

In that case, what is it that makes human freedom so limited? Man is confined in "close-upness" which deprives him of meaning. We glance again at some of the evidence that man may have been around far longer than science supposes—such as an iron nail embedded in a piece of coal several million years old, and a mastodon's tooth engraved with a horned beast, that came from a Miocene bed of 25 million years ago.

We quote the Nobel Prize winner Frederick Soddy, who discovered isotopes, on the evidence of a wholly unknown and unsuspected civilization of which all other relics have disappeared. And we end by quoting Plato: "That things are far better taken care of than we can possibly imagine."

---

1. They still use these same psychedelic substances to this day. —Ed.

Robert M. Schoch and Robert S. McNally

THE MEANING OF THE PYRAMIDS

WHEN MOST ACADEMICS trained in the study of the ancient world look at pyramids on different continents, they see proof of humankind's division into distinct, separate civilizations. We see something quite the opposite: compelling evidence of the underlying unity of civilization.

At its most extreme, the orthodox viewpoint goes something like this. Civilization dates to no earlier than the middle Fourth Millennium B.C. It began in Mesopotamia, then spread to Egypt and, subsequently, throughout the Old World. Other civilizations arose on their own—and much later—in the Americas, where they remained disconnected from Asia and Africa until Columbus piloted his three small ships across the Atlantic. The Old World and the New World each invented civilization independently.

I (Schoch) first came to understand there was something wrong with this view while investigating the origins of the Great Sphinx of Giza. As a geologist, I knew that the weathering patterns of the Giza plateau indicated that the Sphinx was carved in stages. In addition, the oldest portions went back much farther than the conventional 2500 B.C. date given the sculpture; the earliest part most likely predates 5000 B.C.

That finding raised a significant question. Even a first-draft Sphinx could only have been built by a sophisticated people, one that had achieved civilization well before the 3500 B.C. date when civilization supposedly arose. Who were these unknown people? And what happened to them?

The firestorm of academic controversy ignited by my research on the Sphinx led to our earlier book, *Voices of the Rocks* (Harmony, 1999). We argued that civilization arose earlier than generally believed, but much of the early history of humankind has been lost to natural catastrophes.

Yet we knew this was only the first word on the subject. We wanted to go deeper into the question of civilization's origins. The pyramids offer a path to the deep past.

As much as they symbolize the mystery and magic of ancient Egypt, pyramids are not uniquely Egyptian.

As much as they symbolize the mystery and magic of ancient Egypt, pyramids are not uniquely Egyptian. Pyramids of various sorts also appear in the ancient African kingdom of Kush, along the Nile between the third and fourth cataracts; as ziggurats in ancient Mesopotamia and Sumeria (the likely source of the biblical account of the Tower of Babel); in England and Ireland, taking such forms as Silbury Hill and Newgrange; in India and throughout Southeast Asia, in the distinct style of the Buddhist stupa; at Angkor Wat in medieval Cambodia; at Indonesia's Borobudur; in ancient China; at Teotihuacán, Tenayuca, Tenochtitlán and other sites in the Valley of Mexico; in the ancient Olmec and Mayan realms of southern Mexico, Guatemala, Honduras, Belize and El Salvador; along the Mississippi, at Cahokia and other ceremonial centers; and in Peru's coastal region, among the people who were the ancestors of the Inca empire, and in that country's northern Andes, the Inca heartland.

How can it be that a form as distinctive and powerful as the pyramid was built in such widely separated locales? Most scholars would answer that the world's many pyramids are the product of coincidence and convergence—peoples of different cultures imitating forms in nature, such as the mountains of Mexico or the sand dunes of Egypt. But is this the final word on the subject? Is it an oversimplification? Could it be that pyramids around the globe share a common cultural heritage?

Millennium B.C. The American pyramid tradition died out until it was reinvigorated, from the Twelfth Century B.C. on, by Pacific Rim mariners, primarily Chinese. This contact contributed to the pyramid building of the Olmecs, which spread across Mesoamerica and, later, into the Andes.

The builders of Chartres' Gothic cathedral are no less geniuses because earlier architects had erected great cathedrals. The same holds true of the pyramids.

Such ideas remain unpopular, in part because they smack of extreme "diffusionism" (a dirty word to many scholars) and undercut the Old World-New World division on which much of the academic orthodoxy is based. As Lisa Wynn points out in her doctoral dissertation on

Could it be that pyramids around the globe share a common cultural heritage?

These questions are the focus of our most recent book, *Voyages of the Pyramid Builders: The True Origins of the Pyramids From Lost Egypt to Ancient America*. In it we trace the many pyramid-building cultures back to what may be their ultimate source: Sundaland, a continent-sized stretch of land in Southeast Asia (located under the current southern reach of the South China Sea) that was inundated by rising sea levels after the end of the last ice age, a catastrophic event that may have been connected to cometary activity in the skies observed by the inhabitants of Sundaland. As we argue in our book, pyramids are symbolically connected with comets, and the Sundalanders may well have originated the ancient pyramid tradition, then carried it with them as they fled the rising waters. Those who went northwest contributed to the cultural mélange that gave rise first to the pyramid cultures of Sumeria, Egypt and Mesopotamia and later to those in India, Southeast Asia and China. Sundalanders heading east may have gotten as far as Peru, where pyramids rose at Aspero at the end of the Fourth

Egyptology,[1] many researchers in this discipline instinctively reject alternative theories because they feel such thinking belittles indigenous Egyptians by suggesting that not all of their accomplishments were totally independent and original. Likewise, uncovering Old World precedents and influences for New World pyramids is said to constitute an insult to the Olmecs and the Mayans. Nonsense. The builders of Chartres' Gothic cathedral are no less geniuses because earlier architects had erected great cathedrals. The same holds true of the pyramids.

Joseph Campbell, that ever-astute student of mythology, argued that under the world's many, apparently different mythologies lay an ancient core of common archetypal story, one joining us all. Pyramids carry the same message: All humankind shares a common history, one in which civilization began in a single place and spread across the globe.

---

1. Princeton University, 2003. www.princeton.edu/~lisawynn/dissertation.

Roy A. Decker

THE SECRET LAND

ACCORDING TO OUR HISTORY BOOKS, the Americas were discovered by Christopher Columbus in 1492. Many historians now include credit to Leif Eriksson's discovery of Vinland as a brief attempt at colonization of the island of Newfoundland around A.D. 1002. There are a number of other claimants to the honor of having discovered and colonized America before Columbus, ranging from the Irish to the Chinese, with greater or lesser evidence to support these claims. However, one little-known ancient people did in fact reach the Americas and even attempted a colony there more than two thousand years before Columbus—the empire of ancient Carthage.

The seas were not roadblocks to the ancient people, but roads.

Recent discoveries of ancient Phoenician and Carthaginian shipwrecks in deep seas by Robert Ballard and others have put the lie to the old idea that the ancients were tied to shorelines when sailing. Ancient texts also include mentions of their navigational tools such as the gnomon, a sort of sun-compass, the astrolabe, using the stars for direction and even the magnetic compass. The seas were not roadblocks to the ancient people, but roads.

ATLANTIS AND THE AMERICAS

The Greek philosopher Plato is best known for his tale of the "mythical" island of Atlantis. Atlantis is the subject of numerous books and articles as well as movies, with practically every spot on the globe being proposed as the true location by some theorist or other. Whether Atlantis existed or not is not the purpose of our examination, however, buried in Plato's tale are clues that prove the ancient Greeks knew of the existence of the Americas. Consider this passage:

> This power (Atlantis) came forth out of the Atlantic Ocean, for *in those days the Atlantic was navigable*; and there was an island situated in front of the straits which are by you called the Pillars of Heracles; the island was larger than Libya and Asia put together, *and was the way to other islands, and from these you might pass to the whole of the opposite continent which surrounded the true ocean*; for this sea which is within the Straits of Heracles is only a harbor, having a narrow entrance, but that other is a real sea, and the surrounding land may be most truly called a boundless continent.[1]

The first item to take note of here is "...in those days the Atlantic was navigable..." which is a record of the fact that in even more distant ancient

Contrary to what is so often said, Plato is *not* the only ancient source on Atlantis, nor the only ancient writer to refer to the Americas. Several others wrote about the lost civilization and America including Diodorus Siculus, Plutarch, Theopompus and Marcellus.

times, people were regularly traversing the Atlantic. The next item to address is "...and was the way to other islands, and from these you might pass to the whole of the opposite continent which surrounded the true ocean..." This is a pretty clear statement of fact, that the people of Greece (and Egypt, the source of the tale) were well aware of America and its immense size. As a matter of fact, for someone sailing along the Atlantic coast only, North and South America *would* appear to be a single gigantic landmass, which they truly are—when compared to Europe. Many scholars now agree that the original source of the tale of Atlantis came not from Egypt, but from Carthaginian or Phoenician sailors. A clue to this is found in the other book of Plato's which addresses the subject of Atlantis, *Critias*, for in describing the allotments of land among the descendants of Atlas we find this passage:

> To his twin brother, who was born after him, and obtained as his lot the extremity of the island towards the Pillars of Heracles, facing the country which is now called the region of Gades in that part of the world, he gave the name which in the Hellenic language is Eumelus, in the language of the country which is named after him, Gadeirus.[2]

The ancient city of Gades in the southwestern Iberian peninsula (today known as Cadiz) was founded by Phoenicians around 1100 B.C., and was called by them Agadir, Gadirus or Gadeirus, and this is what Plato says is "...in the language of the country which is named after him..." so we have good evidence that the tale of Atlantis most probably reached Egypt and Greece via Phoenician or Carthaginian seafarers or merchants.

Contrary to what is so often said, Plato is *not* the only ancient source on Atlantis, nor the only ancient writer to refer to the Americas. Several others wrote

about the lost civilization and America including Diodorus Siculus, Plutarch, Theopompus and Marcellus. Aelian, in his collection of stories and reports titled *Varia Historia* (*Historical Miscellany*) included the tale of Silenus and the Satyr. Citing as his source Theopompus, Aelian wrote:

> Europe, Asia and Libya (Africa) are islands, around which the ocean flows, and the only continent is the one surrounding the outside of this world. He explained how infinitely big it is, that it supports other large animals and men twice the size of those who live here. Their lives are not the same length as ours, but in fact twice as long. There are many large cities, with various styles of life, and laws in force among them are different from those customary among us. He said there were two very big cities, not at all like each other, once called Warlike and the other Pious. The inhabitants of Pious live in peace and with great wealth; they obtain the fruits of the earth without the plough and oxen, and they have no need to farm and cultivate.[3]

If we take into consideration that the Greeks and Romans were receiving *imperfect* reports of the Americas, (through Phoenician and Punic traders) this tale from Aelian is most remarkable. There is no question that this passage from Aelian is referring to the Americas, and fits surprisingly well with what we know about the ancient civilizations thriving in the Americas at this time. The references to "cities" shows that Aelian cannot be talking about some islands off the coast of Africa as some historians propose and the statement that the inhabitants do not use the plow or oxen (which were indeed not known in the Americas before the time of Columbus) is fair proof that we are referring to America. Aelian provides more information on the mysterious continent:

The inhabitants are not less than 20 million. Sometimes they die of illness, but this is rare, since for the most part they lose their lives in battle, wounded by stones or wooden clubs (they cannot be harmed by iron). They have an abundance of gold and silver, so that to them gold is of less value than iron is to us.[4]

The strange statement that the inhabitants are wounded by stones or wooden clubs and are not harmed by iron may stem from a garbled report—they were indeed not "harmed by iron" since they did not know of it. The next point of interest is that gold is of less value to them than iron is to Europeans—when first encountered by Europeans, many early explorers including Columbus made similar reports about many native Amerindian peoples. Aelian states that these faraway people once made an expedition to Europe, reaching "the Hyperboreans" (Britain) and finding them poor or uncivilized, returned in disgust. Aelian also makes mention of other relatively civilized people (he calls them "Meropes" which means "mortals") living beyond the coastal cities, and on the edge of their territory a place called "the Point of No Return"—a giant chasm that sounds suspiciously like the Grand Canyon!

Whence came this knowledge of the Americas? These records are from the Greeks and Romans, but they were passing along information obtained from some other people, a nation of intrepid seafarers who had "been there" and returned with marvelous tales.

THE PHOENICIANS AND KING SOLOMON'S MINES

The Phoenicians were already plying the open seas for trade by 2500 B.C. when the Egyptians bought timber from them to build their first ships. The Phoenician trading ships were bringing to the Mediterranean such exotic fare as cinnamon, incense, cloves, ivory, ebony, apes and even peacocks from lands as far away as Southeast Asia and Africa. This much is not disputed by scholars. Considering what the Phoenicians were already doing, it is no surprise that they were willing and eager to enter into a joint venture with King Solomon for mutual benefit. With Solomon providing a port on the Red Sea, the opportunities for profits were vast.

Solomon was crowned king of a powerful Hebrew state created by his father David, which was largely at peace for most of the duration of his reign. This prolonged peace allowed him to pursue expansion in commerce and building. To increase his income revenues, Solomon allied with King Hiram, of Tyre, the richest and most powerful of the Phoenician city-states; together they built a trading fleet in the Red Sea port of Ezion-Geber. The story is found in the Old Testament:

"King Solomon built a fleet of ships at Ezion-Geber, which is near Eloth on the shore of the Red Sea, in the land of Edom. And Hiram sent with the fleet his servants, seamen who were familiar with the sea, together with the servants of Solomon; and they went to Ophir, and brought from there gold, to the amount of four hundred and twenty talents; and they brought it to King Solomon."[5]

"Moreover the fleet of Hiram, which brought gold from Ophir, brought from Ophir a very great amount of almug wood and precious stones."[6]

"For the king had a fleet of ships of Tarshish at sea with the fleet of Hiram. Once every three years the fleet of ships of Tarshish used to come bringing gold, silver, ivory, apes and peacocks. Thus King Solomon excelled all the kings of the earth in riches and in wisdom. And the whole earth sought the presence of Solomon to hear his wisdom, which God had put into his mind."[7]

The location of Ophir has been the subject of much debate, but a good case can be made for Peru as the true location.

There are other references that repeat these basic points, however, we can draw our conclusions from these passages. Solomon built his fleet on the Red Sea, from which they sailed to distant Ophir and Tarshish. The location of Ophir has been the subject of much debate, but a good case can be made for Peru as the true location. (For example, compare some of the Moche effigy pots that depict people who appear to be either Hebrew or at least Semitic, or who had contact with these people.)

Ophir was almost certainly not some place in India or Africa (as has been proposed by some theorists) because these places could easily be reached by overland caravans or by sea in considerably less time than three years. In fact, an ancient Greek text titled the *Periplus Erythraeum* describes the sea route from Africa and Egypt to India and back, pointing out the correct time of the seasonal winds and indicating that such a voyage would require no more than one year including months of time for trading. To further support the case for a South American location for Ophir, a few years ago the explorer Gene Savoy found an inscription in a cave in Peru with the exact same glyph for Ophir, identifying Peru as one and the same!

Tarsus was little more than a collection of mud huts in the time of Solomon and the city was founded by the Assyrian king Sennacherib more than 100 years after Solomon's death. Besides, the true Tarshish was known to the Greeks as Tartessus, and was located in the southwestern Iberian peninsula near the site of Gades. Recently a researcher named Rainer Kuehne claimed to have located Atlantis in this very area, however it is far more probable that he has located Tartessus. Tartessus was renowned for its abundance of silver. Why would someone set sail from the Red Sea to reach southwestern Spain when they could have taken the shorter, faster route from Joppa? The only logical explanation, considering that we know

> Why would someone set sail from the Red Sea to reach southwestern Spain when they could have taken the shorter, faster route from Joppa? The only logical explanation, considering that we know Solomon's ships were stopping in Southeast Asia, is that they were circumnavigating the world.

The products brought back by the fleet point to stops in Southeast Asia, where they obtained peacocks and spices. The fleets were, however, continuing on to sail right around the globe—which can be seen if we look at a map and find Ezion-Geber on the Red Sea, then find the site of Tarshish. In the Old Testament book of Jonah, we learn something about the location of Tarshish:

> And Jonah riseth to flee to Tarshish from the face of Jehovah, and goeth down [to] Joppa, and findeth a ship going [to] Tarshish, and he giveth its fare, and goeth down into it, to go with them to Tarshish from the face of Jehovah.[8]

So Tarshish was a place you could travel to by sailing west from Israel (the port of Joppa) or by sailing east from Ezion-Geber. Several locations have been proposed as the site of Tarshish, with even the Jewish historian Josephus stating that it was simply Tarsus in Asia Minor. Josephus may have been deliberately misleading his patrons (the Romans, who had captured him) however, since

Solomon's ships were stopping in Southeast Asia, is that they were circumnavigating the world. It makes perfect sense that the fleet was sailing not back to Ezion-Geber, but were returning to Joppa in the Mediterranean. There is evidence to support this; in fact, the only potsherd ever found with the glyph of Ophir inscribed on it was unearthed near Joppa. Then, too, this would explain why later kings of Israel and Judah were forced to build a brand new fleet at Ezion-Geber to sail to Ophir more than once, since the ships of Solomon and Hiram were not returning to that port. A further clue that Solomon's fleet was circumnavigating the world lies in the fact that it took three years to make the voyage each time—for remember that both Magellan and Drake, the earliest European explorers to sail around the world, took almost exactly three years to accomplish the feat. We should also take note that Solomon had turned to the Phoenicians to build and help man his fleet, which indicates they are probably the source of the knowledge of where to send ships for profit. Proof that the Phoenicians were visiting Bar Zil (the "land of iron") as well as Ophir/Peru turned up in a Phoenician tomb; a wooden artifact was found to be of Brazilian "Pau" (axe-breaker) wood. There is also the Paraiba stone inscription (see below).

What happened to end such a profitable trade? On the death of Solomon, the kingdom passed to his son Rehoboam at about 928 B.C. Unfortunately, Rehoboam refused to ease the tax burden on his people, which resulted in rebellion and division of the kingdom, with ten of the 12 Tribes seceding and forming the nation of Israel in the north, two tribes remaining loyal and forming the southern kingdom of Judah. The province of Edom revolted during this time and became independent; thus closing the vital port of Ezion-Geber to the Hebrews and Phoenicians. Attempts were made to re-open the trade flow under later kings of Judah and Israel, particularly King Jehoshaphat of Judah (873-849 B.C.) who appears to have regained control of Edom and the critical port of Ezion-Geber. Allied with King Ahab of the northern Hebrew kingdom of Israel and having built a new fleet, Jehoshaphat's efforts were of no avail, because the fleet was wrecked. Still later, King Uzziah (about 783-741 B.C.) again recovered Edom under the rule of Judah, but no record exists of any expeditions during his rule. The fact that Judah prospered during Uzziah's reign may point to at least some success in seagoing trade through Ezion-Geber. Edom again successfully revolted after Uzziah and the Red Sea access was lost. Soon Phoenicia was conquered by the Assyrians and virtually all contact with the Americas was lost, temporarily.

QART HADASHT, THE NEW CITY

The name Carthage comes from Qart Hadasht (which means "new city") and was founded about 814 B.C. by colonists from Tyre in Phoenicia. The legend goes that Elyssayat (also recorded as Elyssa or Dido), a sister of King Pygmalion, fled her home in the city of Tyre after her brother murdered her husband. With her followers she fled first to Cyprus, then on to North Africa where she was able to purchase an excellent site to found a city, in what is today Tunisia. The people of Carthage built a city to surpass the mother city, rising in power and influence until she had built an empire that rivaled Rome. Her people were industrious merchants and explorers; however they were also secretive and especially so when it came to trade routes and navigational secrets. (There is record of one Carthaginian captain deliberately running his ship aground when he found that he was being followed by a Roman ship to the secret source of tin [Britain], so vital to the production of bronze. The Carthaginian Senate rewarded the captain for his efforts!)

We know of two expeditions sent out by the government of Carthage to explore and found colonies; both around the same time (560 B.C.) with Himilco exploring the Atlantic coast of Europe and reaching the British Isles, the other under Hanno sent south along the Atlantic coast of Africa where they founded six cities. The record of one of these expeditions, the so-called *Periplus of Hanno* exists today because a Greek historian named Polybius found the record in the halls of the temple of Baal Hammon (Saturn to the Romans) and convinced the Romans not to destroy it while they were busily destroying the rest of the city. Himilco's "periplus" exists only in fragments, preserved by a Roman named Rufus Festus Avienus. However, even in these fragments there are clues that the Carthaginians were reaching much farther afield than West Africa or the British Isles:

But from here, there is a two-day journey for a ship to the Holy Island (Ireland)—thus the ancients called it. This island, large in extent of land, lies between the waves. The race of Hierni inhabits it far and wide. Again, the island of the Albiones (Britain) lies near, and the Tartessians were accustomed to carry on business to the ends of the Oestrymnides. Colonists of Carthage, too, and the common folk living around the Pillars of Hercules came to these seas. Himilco of Carthage reported that he himself had investigated the matter on a voyage, and he asserts that it can scarcely be crossed in four months. No breezes propel a craft, the sluggish liquid of the lazy sea is so at a standstill. He also adds this: A lot of seaweed floats in the water and often after the manner of a thicket holds the prow back. He says that here nonetheless the depth of the water does not extend much and the bottom is barely covered over with a little water. They always meet here and there monsters of the deep, and beasts swim amid the slow and sluggishly crawling ships.[9]

At first glance this passage is unremarkable, however, notice that Himilco reports that the ocean can "scarcely be crossed in four months." This fact still holds true for sailing vessels in the North Atlantic, where they must cross the huge, seaweed-glutted region known today as the Sargasso Sea. Ships dependent on the winds frequently found themselves becalmed in this area for days or even weeks at a time. This area is also referred to by Himilco—no breezes propel a craft for example, the seaweed holds the prows of ships and so on. Even the mention of sea monsters is appropriate, since most "sea monsters" were in reality whales and other large marine life, so this is entirely in keeping with Himilco traversing the Atlantic. The mention of monsters swimming around the slow-moving ships also hints that more than a single voyage was made. What else can be meant by the requirement of four months to cross—cross to where? It certainly could not refer to the British Isles as has been suggested. The logical solution is America.

ANCIENT DESCRIPTIONS OF AMERICA

Are there any records that hint of Carthaginians reaching the Americas? Aristotle included a description that probably refers to America:

> In the sea outside the Pillars of Heracles they say that a desert island was found by the Carthaginians, having woods of all kinds and navigable rivers, remarkable for all other kinds of fruits, and a few days' voyage away; as the Carthaginians frequented it often owing to its prosperity, and some even lived there, the chief of the Carthaginians announced that they would punish with death any who proposed to sail there, and that they massacred all the inhabitants, that they might not tell the story, and that a crowd might not resort to the island, and get possession of it, and take away the prosperity of the Carthaginians.[10]

The statement "desert island" cannot be correct, though this is used by skeptics to point to any number of tiny islands off the coast of Africa as the location; however the description will not fit with any island at all—for example, what island would have many navigable rivers, fruits, woods, etc. It is pretty clear that the Carthaginians wanted to keep this land a secret, punishable by death to any who would sail there without their permission. In another passage Aristotle refers to the Carthaginians' secret land as "desert" or "deserted," with no mention of it being an island. Elsewhere in the same source, Aristotle points out that the secret land was found by accident, the ships carried there by an "east wind" and that the Carthaginians were obtaining vast supplies of tuna fish that they would not export. Diodorus Siculus describes the secret land of the Carthaginians in the greatest detail, adding that the Phoenicians (Greeks and Romans did not differentiate between Phoenicians and Carthaginians) had discovered the land by accident, when some merchants were sailing down the Atlantic coast of Africa and got blown across the ocean by storms. Plutarch, citing a document he said he found in the ruins of Carthage (which had been destroyed before his time) described the northern route to the Americas, adding that the oar must be used due to what he presumed was a "sluggish" sea, but actually fits with the truth since a ship would be sailing against the oceanic current. Norse explorers using the same route had the same problem. Diodorus stated that the Carthaginians established a colony in the secret land, but later withdrew it by order of the government, but probably not all of the colonists returned to Africa since Plutarch mentioned that some "Greeks" had intermarried with the local people. Of course Plutarch's "Greeks" might have been Kyrenians, since they were closely allied with Carthage for a long period of time—but we know that Carthage refused to allow the Tyrrhenians to sail to their secret land, so it is doubtful they would allow anyone else to.

In the 1990s, Professor Mark McMenamin discovered what appears to be a tiny map on some Carthaginian gold coins. The map is placed on the reverse of the coin, beneath the feet of the famous horse depicted on so many Punic coins. If it is indeed a map, and this appears to be the case, it shows Europe, Africa and parts of America. Some ancient coin experts have dismissed the map as nothing but a bit of debris on the dies used to strike the coins, citing other coins with irregular shapes in that same area of the coin. Their examples are not very similar to the coins showing a map. What if it truly is a map? Considering the secrecy cherished by Carthaginians, it seems quite plausible that after a number of the coins were struck with the map on them, some government official discovered it and ordered the map removed from the coin dies.

EVIDENCE ON THIS SIDE OF THE ATLANTIC

Dr. Barry Fell listed a large amount of evidence for Carthaginians visiting America (see his books *Saga America* and *America B.C.*), including the strange Mystery Hill site in New Hampshire which has Punic inscriptions, grave markers (which Fell interpreted as "Basque" but rather appear to be Punic) found along the Susquehanna river in Pennsylvania, as well as an ancient metal urn found by the Middlebury Archaeological Research Center at the junction of the Susquehanna and Chenango rivers in New York, a white limestone horse's head (a well-known symbol of Carthage along with the palm, caduceus and Tanit) found in North Salem, New York, in the immediate vicinity of mysterious stone chambers similar to those at Mystery Hill, New Hampshire, several Cypriot-Phoenician produced religious artifacts probably traded by Carthaginian merchants in Ecuador, and an iron mask of West African origins found in Ohio. We can add to the list glass beads of Phoenician manufacture found in an ancient estuary (Copper Age) near Beverly in Canada as well as several recovered from ancient Hopewell Mound Builder mounds, two amphorae

When ancient coins are found in Europe or Africa they are generally regarded as important evidence of ancient cultures, trade and inter-cultural contact. When ancient coins are found in America, they are dismissed as "hoaxes" or as simply lost in modern times, as if lots of people run around with ancient coins in their pockets to lose. In the case of most bronze Roman coins, this bias may be justifiable since these coins are very common and inexpensive; they can often be purchased in an unclean condition for as little as a dollar each. In the case of Carthaginian, Greek, Numidian and Hebrew coins, the bias is not justified. Many of these types are neither common nor cheap. The fact that most of the reported finds were accidental does not automatically make them less than important, in view of the supporting evidence they ought to be at least considered *possible* evidence.

Dr. Fell listed some examples of Carthaginian coins in his book *Saga America*, while Gloria Farley included several more finds in her book *In Plain Sight: Old World Records in Ancient America*. Carthaginian coins have been found in seven U.S. states, (all being of the earliest types made by Carthage) and Numidian coins have been found in Ohio and Idaho, while Greek coins turned up in Connecticut, Oklahoma and Missouri. If plotted out on a map, the locations of the reported finds do indicate a pattern—most are along rivers and beaches, logical landing sites for visiting merchants and explorers in ancient times.

When ancient coins are found in Europe or Africa they are generally regarded as important evidence of ancient cultures, trade and inter-cultural contact. When ancient coins are found in America, they are dismissed as "hoaxes" or as simply lost in modern times, as if lots of people run around with ancient coins in their pockets to lose.

found by divers off the coast of Maine which are ancient Iberian types (recall that most of the Iberian peninsula was part of the Punic empire), Greek oil lamp found in an ancient Amerindian midden, and then there are the coins.

Inscriptions in Punic, Hebrew and Phoenician have been found from Brazil to Canada, including sailing directions found on a now-dry lake in Nevada, an inscription claiming the land for Hanno found in Massachusetts, the strange Los Lunas

> **Perhaps one day our history books will include the amazing exploits of those dauntless ancient explorers, the Carthaginians and Phoenicians, who found America and kept it a secret, even to their graves.**

(New Mexico) "Dekalogue" which is possibly a Phoenician message telling of ancient explorers, the Paraiba stone found in the jungle in Brazil which told of a ship coming there after losing its bearings, and more too numerous to list here. Linguistic studies have shown ties between some native Amerindian languages and Semitic (which includes Hebrew, Punic and Phoenician) and place names hint of ancient visitors; for example Susquehanna, Tobyhanna, Xochimilco and there is even a U.S. state with a Punic name (Alaska—the word in native Amerindian means "great land," while in Punic "Al asqa" means very much the same thing. Coincidence?)

Even more astonishing, several ancient shipwrecks have been found in the Americas. For example, a "Roman" ship was found in Galveston, South Carolina's bay in the 1880s (more likely a Punic ship), another "Roman" ship was found in the Bay of Jars near Rio de Janiero (the amphorae recovered are of West African origin, again the ship is more likely Punic than Roman), a Carthaginian or Phoenician ship was found in Mexico in the early 1800s "deeply buried in sand," a Phoenician ship was found off the coast of Bimini island by divers looking for evidence of Atlantis (this wreck was examined by a Yale professor, Dr. J. Manson Valentine, so is unlikely to be misidentified), a Carthaginian wreck lies off the coast of Honduras (amphorae from this wreck are in a museum there), and there is the strange myth of the "ship in the desert"—witnesses have reported and photographed an ancient ship stranded in the sands of the Salton Sink in Southern California. The ship was identified as probably Viking by the newspapers, but the hull was covered with copper plates. Vikings did not do this, but Carthaginians did, as a protection against shipworms.

How much evidence does it take to prove that the Carthaginians were coming to America? We have more evidence of their presence than exists of more famous modern explorers such as Coronado or De Soto (their explorations are not questioned), but for some who believe in the isolation theory (that holds there was no contact with the Americas from the end of the ice age until at least the arrival of the Norse around A.D. 1000, a theory taught as fact in our schools) no amount of evidence seems to be enough. However, when we accept that the Carthaginians and Phoenicians *were* coming to America, then a great number of otherwise perplexing mysteries are easily answered since we can point to these seafarers as the probable agents of transmission, including the *idea* of pyramid building, the presence of coca and tobacco products in ancient Egyptian mummies, the missing billions of pounds of copper from the upper Great Lakes (mined in ancient times), bronze tools in ancient America (where no tin supplies were known), the coincidences of products found in both hemispheres such as cotton, peppers, hemp, corn, bottle gourds, peanuts, chickens and many more. This cross-oceanic contact was eventually lost, apparently when the Romans conquered Carthage or soon thereafter, and the secret land was forgotten. Perhaps one day our history books will include the amazing exploits of those dauntless ancient explorers, the Carthaginians and Phoenicians, who found America and kept it a secret, even to their graves.

---

1. Plato, *Timaeus*. 360 B.C. (Italics mine.)

2. Plato, *Critias*. 360 B.C.

3. Aelian, *Varia Historia* 3:18. A.D. 235.

4. Ibid.

5. *1 Kings* 9:26. King James Version.

6. *1 Kings* 10:11. KJV.

7. *1 Kings* 10:22-24. KJV.

8. *Jonah 1:3*. Young's Literal Translation.

9. Rufus Festus Avienus, *Ora Maritima* 105-129. Fourth Century A.D.

10. Aristotle, *On Marvelous Things Heard*. 324 B.C.

Robert Merkin

LINGERING ECHOES:

ATHENS, JERUSALEM

What Song the Syrens sang, or what name Achilles assumed when he hid himself among women,
though puzzling Questions, are not beyond all conjecture.
      — Sir Thomas Browne, "Hydriotaphia, or Urne-Buriall"

I DON'T KNOW WHAT LIFE WAS like in Atlantis, Mu or Shambala. I don't know the languages that were spoken there, where these lands were, or what remains of them now.

Cities and civilizations so thoroughly lost so long ago are rich fields for imaginative conjecture so unrestricted and unrestrained that they inspire theories attributing these civilizations to visits by alien sentient races from planets far beyond our solar system.

I have reasons to reject this theory—but not very good reasons. Not long ago it was barely possible to drift 20 feet above the ground, and impossible to fly, or to record and play back sounds. In discussing panspermia, Carl Sagan suggested life on earth might be the trash UFO aliens left behind the day they picnicked on earth—we may be descended from a mayonnaise jar. We're in a very thready position to tell aliens what the laws of physics forbade them from having done twenty thousand or three billion years ago.

We know with increasing certainty they're out there, but we can't even contact them to show them how ignorant we are.

LAUGHABLE PROVEN AND CERTIFIED FACTS

My interests in our ancient roots hover on more recent times, at the distant fringes of what we know with some clarity and certainty, with things we've dug up and can hold, examine and display, and with the wonderfully clever efforts scholars have made since 1799 in deciphering ancient texts in lost writing systems.

We have indeed, on several remarkable occasions, discovered Achilles' alias while he wore pantyhose and a bra, and read the lyrics of the Syrens' songs almost as clearly as we read about Elvis' hound dog.

Educated people should always be prepared to laugh and scoff at proven and certified facts, regardless of the unquestioned prestige of the certifying authority. And educated people should always be prepared to treat myths from the dawn of time with enormous respect as important sources of truth.

Of human achievements (or civilization-sparking visits from space aliens) that took place before the scrutiny of modern standards of scientific proof and certain knowledge, a brief word about the limits and dubious significance of these standards.

As this is written, there lingers, with no end in sight, a violent, ghastly, murderous, ruinously expensive war which the United States undertook because Iraq was developing and stockpiling weapons of mass destruction. Now, a year after our exhaustive searches, these weapons appear not to have existed. Facts for which we've sacrificed thousands of our young soldiers have now proven to be fiction, myth and lies. There could be no proven facts more lethal than these discredited myths.

Educated people should always be prepared to laugh and scoff at proven and certified facts, regardless of the unquestioned prestige of the certifying authority. And educated people should always be prepared to treat myths from the dawn of time with enormous respect as important sources of truth.

TRUE BELIEVERS

It takes longer for a crow to fly from New York City to Chicago than to fly from Athens to Jerusalem. At the heights of these ancient Mediterranean civilizations, the voyage would have been made almost entirely by sea—practically a straight shot from the southeastern coast of Greece. It would have taken about a week, and this region of the seas was crowded with skilled mariners and sailing ships for which this was a familiar voyage. A merchant captain who weighed anchor in Piraieus, Athens' port, would sooner or later have called at the Mediterranean harbors closest to Jerusalem, and from there a short caravan inland 35 miles to Jerusalem itself. The mariners of the ancient Mediterranean knew these trade routes well.

But mariners would have known Athens far better than they would have known Jerusalem and its obscure, unwelcoming theocracy. Athens thrived on world trade and industry. It aggressively reached out to sell its goods to the world, and the world enthusiastically responded; for the traveler and trader throughout the ancient Mediterranean, Athens was the place to go. It generated huge wealth and the fabulous architecture and pageantry that goes with world-class prosperity. The kilns of its pottery industry burned around the clock, and the industrial quarter of Athens serviced its workers with a spirited big-city nightlife.

Jerusalem, on the other hand, did not reach out to the world, and kept its contacts with the outside world to a religiously-enforced minimum. It was far less a capital and administrative city than a Holy City.

As a holy city at the height of its theocracy—ruled first by priests and tribal judges, then by kings—it had a unique character. After the construction of the First Temple, and until the Romans destroyed the Second Temple, the relationship between Jews and their God could only be ritually celebrated in Jerusalem. A Jew anywhere in the world would venerate and worship his God, but God would only answer His people and receive their sacrifices in the Temple in Jerusalem, in intercessory rituals performed by a consecrated hereditary priesthood. While the Temples stood, Judaism was a local religion whose supernatural relationship with its one God—His demands, the Jews' sacrifices and obedience—happened only in Jerusalem.

At their coeval primes, Athens was probably most reminiscent of the modern spirit of New York City—a noisy, boastful, self-ballyhooing, prideful city with lots to shout about.

Ancient, Holy Jerusalem would probably call forth a spirit recognizable in North Korea—insular, xenophobic, suspicious, unwelcoming and inhospitable to all who wandered there but were not True Believers.

Outsiders did visit Jerusalem—and there was the problem. Ancient Israel was a farming society. From time to time it prospered, and from time to time this tiny nation, located at a dangerous crossroads between hostile military superpowers, had good luck with its military and foreign alliances.

In those peaceful and lucky times, it followed a mix of human instinct and conscious policy, and built Jerusalem into a grand, imposing, impressive city. War against a Middle Eastern superpower was a losing proposition or, at best, an iffy dice throw for tiny Israel—but showing the world a mighty, prosperous city could attract alliances or make a superpower desirous of extending its military protection to a worthwhile and strategic tribute nation.

A theocratic choir atop the hills of Jerusalem sang a familiar, repetitive song throughout the history that became the Old Testament: Whenever Israel strayed from its God, and was seduced by idols, disaster struck the nation and the people, as God's punishment. Jews learned the lesson and kept the faith, or they suffered and lost, or were led off in chains.

BLURRING THE LINE BETWEEN MEN AND GODS

That worked to keep Jerusalem relatively cleansed of the influence of Baal, Ishtar, Molok and a host of goddesses and gods from Asia over the centuries.

But in Greece, a week's sail distant, a remarkable culture was springing up, centered in Athens, which was to present the Jewish theocracy with a

---

In the prosperity that followed the establishment of the monarchy, Solomon's Temple and palaces impressed the region, but challenged insular, parochial Holy Jerusalem with an unprecedented influx of non-Jews and their foreign ideas.

But Iron Age Israel had few, if any, of the ancient world's architects and artisans, and had to import foreign contractors as well as precious and rare building materials. In the prosperity that followed the establishment of the monarchy, Solomon's Temple and palaces impressed the region, but challenged insular, parochial Holy Jerusalem with an unprecedented influx of non-Jews and their foreign ideas.

The ordinary ideas that had permeated the Near East long before the Jews had arrived in their Exodus from Egypt had never presented overmuch of a challenge. Theologically, Jews stood for one thing: monotheism, and the worship of one invisible God in particular. Neighboring gods—tangible, visible deities—had always seduced the Jews, but a strong priesthood, rigidly focused by one changeless set of laws and holy books, had kept the spread of these neighboring idols in historical check.

powerful and permanent challenge for the minds of the Jewish people.

Greece's gods and goddesses were nothing new to the Jews. Throughout Eurasia, goddesses and gods traveled freely and easily from tribe to tribe under a variety of aliases, morphing and modifying with each new conquest and new cult.

Throughout Eurasia, goddesses and gods traveled freely and easily from tribe to tribe under a variety of aliases, morphing and modifying with each new conquest and new cult.

From Egypt to Persia to Phoenicia, mariners and caravaners had little trouble recognizing the kinship of the ancient migrating pantheon by any local names.

Where the Greeks and their gods were new and troubling was that in Athens, the line between men and gods was blurring.

In the simple representation of the gods and goddesses, Greek artists were abandoning bizarrely shaped sky creatures, and freakish half-human-half-animals, and were making the perfect youthful human form into their gods and goddesses. Their gods and goddesses were becoming women and men.

was staggering, but the Greeks were also obsessive and shameless mimics and plagiarists, sailing to the ends of the known world and hosing up in equal measure the accomplishments of both Egypt and Mesopotamia, their architecture and engineering, their astronomy, their mathematics, and honing and advancing those accomplishments. Both civilizations had amassed great treasuries of achievements when the nosy and acquisitive Greeks first began pilfering from them.

With these new graven images—unlike any the world had worshipped before—came a new theological message: Men and women can not just resemble gods, but can aspire to be gods.

With these new graven images—unlike any the world had worshipped before—came a new theological message: Men and women can not just resemble gods, but can aspire to be gods. The best forms gods and goddesses can assume resemble the handsomest human women and men; the most brilliant thoughts of the gods can be grasped by mortals, jabbering and arguing and inventing new words from crude and simple marketplace words.

The Greek religion was undergoing an arrogant and narcissistic theologic revolution. To see their gods, Greeks were holding up mirrors.

If the basis of this revolution had just been their statuesque and athletic forms, it would have dead-ended into a silly and perhaps a short-lived and localized religion. But sweepingly grand and deeply moving achievements in formal literature, first composed and sung by bards like Homer, and then scratched and permanently recorded into a phonetic alphabet adapted from the nearby seafaring Phoenicians began matching the achievements of the Greek body and sculptors with the achievements of the Greek mind.

The body, however athletic and beautiful, had limits. But as the Athenians, and those Greek city-states and far-flung colonies which admired and reflected Athens, reached for the heavens within their minds, centuries were passing, and the Greek mind seemed to have no limits.

The volume of original inventions and creations

But where the Babylonians and Egyptians amassed practical skills to order their agricultural, military and civic life, a new spark grew in the Athenian mind. They became interested in knowledge for its own sake, beyond its clever and profitable practical tricks.

They proved things which were nearly guaranteed never to have practical value, and yet saw in them mind treasures so precious that Pythagoras sacrificed a herd of sacred white oxen to thank Apollo for revealing the proof of the Pythagorean theorem.

Mathematics was already ancient and powerful when the Greeks encountered it, but they spun it into a revolutionary direction: They proved what they knew about this strange, invisible, imaginary realm of numbers and geometry, and generalized about their discoveries explosively. They proved things which were nearly guaranteed never to have practical value, and yet saw in them mind treasures so precious that Pythagoras sacrificed a herd of sacred white oxen to thank Apollo for revealing the proof of the Pythagorean theorem.

The Egyptians had known the right-triangle relationship as a practical surveying rule for a millennium, but it was a Greek who proved it for any imaginable right triangle. "It works" was not enough for Greeks; they became obsessed to prove "It is eternally and perfectly true," and they did, for a thousand important mathematical propositions. Proof has been at the core of everyone's mathematics ever since; everywhere on earth, mathematics smells and tastes uniquely Greek.

TWO WORLDS COLLIDING

And what did Jerusalem know of mathematics? Far more to the point, what did Jerusalem care? The ancient Jews were not merely bad at or backwards in mathematics and science; the priests who protected their faith understood what these things represented and what they threatened.

As Athens boiled over with astonishing and powerful mathematical discoveries, the Old Testament mentions only one mathematical fact. *1 Kings* describes a circular fountain for Solomon's palace, built by imported Phoenician artisans "ten cubits from the one brim to the other ... and a line of 30 cubits did compass it about." In other words, in Jerusalem, pi equaled three, while Greek mathematicians were narrowing down pi to the hundredths and thousandths.

In particular, Alexandria was the first great Jewish community beyond the borders of ancient Israel, and Alexandria's Jews contributed enthusiastically to Alexander's dream of shared and translated multiculturalism.

Worlds were colliding: The Greeks were drunk on gods who revealed the secrets of nature, wisdom, science and logic to all who were curious, but the Jews served an angry, jealous and exclusively moral God. He had created the world, but had no particular interest in its natural workings or secrets; He cared only how well Jews served and obeyed Him. But the Greek gods had filled the world with intellectual mysteries and puzzles, and were compelling men (and women, equal members of Pythagoras' mystical cult) to use all their intellectual powers to solve them.

Athens barely noticed Jerusalem or the religion of the Jews. The Greek historians barely devoted a paragraph to the insignificant kingdom, its people or their beliefs and practices.

But the Jews were astonished with Athens and seduced by its ideas, as no other civilization had ever influenced them. Quickly, Jerusalem politics and society split into the Hellenists and the Hassadim—the Grecophiles who wore Greek clothes, lived an Athenian lifestyle, and gloried in the new Greek ideas and spirit, versus conservative old-school religionists who looked on Athenian influence as the vilest of heresy and blasphemy.

Ancient Israel's final military triumph liberated the Jews from the Greek conquest and occupation that followed Alexander's conquest of the known world. Hassadim of the Maccabbee priestly family revolted successfully against Alexander's Macedonian successor. But the Maccabbees' victory did not settle the cultural struggle between the Hellenists and the Hassadim. Alexander had founded his great Egyptian capital of Alexandria, and his dream of introducing the known world to Greek ways came true there. In particular, Alexandria was the first great Jewish community beyond the borders of ancient Israel, and Alexandria's Jews contributed enthusiastically to Alexander's dream of shared and translated multiculturalism.

In Alexandria, Jewish and Greek scholars collaborated on the *Septuagint*, the first translation of the Hebrew scriptures in a language other than Hebrew, which 70 scholars agreed on word-for-word. It was Greek, of course, and through Greek, the Hellenist Jews had added their holy books and their God to world literature and theology for the first time and forever. The *Septuagint* would be the vessel that propelled earliest Christianity around the Greek-speaking Mediterranean, and introduced the Mediterranean to the peculiar local God of Jerusalem, and His rigid moral code.

The strange struggle for the souls of Jews, as they wandered the earth, had taken on an indelible Athenian character that endures today. The marriage endures wherever Jews worship, in the building known best by the Greek word *Synagogue*.

3

CATACLYSMS AND MIGRATIONS

Terraces and steps: perspectives of the south face of the main monument, Yonaguni.

This wider view shows the Face and the Stage to be set amongst a complex of rectilinear structures.

Graham Hancock

UNDERWORLD: CONFRONTING

YONAGUNI

PHOTOS BY SANTHA FAIIA

The question was, or is still, is it and, if yes, to what extent is it made by man or overworked by man? This is the question.
       — Dr. Wolf Wichmann, geologist, Yonaguni, March 2001

I WAS IN TOKYO in 1996 when the photojournalist Ken Shindo showed me the first images I had ever seen of an awe-inspiring terraced structure, apparently a man-made monument of some kind, lying at depths of up to 30 meters off the Japanese island of Yonaguni at the remote southwest end of the Ryukyu archipelago.

I felt an immediate compulsion to explore the beautiful and mysterious structure that beckoned so alluringly from the photographs. And I realized that it would rewrite prehistory if it could indeed be proven to be man-made.

This was the moment, if there ever was just one moment, when the "Underworld" quest began for me and when much that I had learnt in previous years in many different countries began to swing sharply into focus and make sense. I felt an immediate compulsion to explore the beautiful and mysterious structure that beckoned so alluringly from the photographs. And I realized that it would rewrite prehistory if it could indeed be proven to be man-made.

I described in chapter one[1] how Santha and I learned to dive, and the remarkable synchronicities and good fortune that brought us to Yonaguni in March 1997 to begin a systematic program of underwater photography and research there that was to continue until mid-2001. I also described some of the other rock-hewn underwater structures that we dived at with our Japanese colleagues at other locations in the Ryukyus—notably at Kerama, Aguni and Chatan at the northern end of the archipelago.

The most complex and intractable problem shared by all of these otherwise very different

> **Therefore, when we speak of "geological opinion" concerning the Yonaguni anomalies it is important to be clear that we are referring to the work and ideas of just three men who, moreover, do not agree with one another—so there is no consensus.**

structures is also the simplest and most obvious question that anyone might wish to ask about them: Were they shaped and carved by human hands, or could they have ended up looking the way they do as a result of natural weathering and the erosive weapons of the sea?

Though they have an important role to play, geologists are not the only people qualified to decide the answer to such a question. Likewise, though they too are indispensable, archaeologists cannot be the final arbiters. On the contrary, if ever a multi-disciplinary approach was called for then it is here!

For as I've tried to show in the previous chapters, Japan confronts us with a prehistoric cultural and mythological context into which the rock-hewn structures fit snugly, like the missing pieces of a jigsaw puzzle. This context includes a clear tradition of unknown antiquity—still manifest in the present day—in which huge rocks are carved and rearranged amidst sacred natural landscapes. Since this is precisely the puzzling and ambiguous aspect—part natural and part man-made—of the underwater structures scattered around the Ryukyu archipelago, it is foolish and irresponsible to ignore the possibility of a connection.

Yet it is equally foolish and irresponsible to ignore what geology and archaeology have to say on the matter.

So it is time, I think, to provide a thorough reckoning.

THE THREE GEOLOGISTS

Three qualified geologists—Masaaki Kimura, Robert M. Schoch and Wolf Wichmann—have dived at Yonaguni, acquired first-hand experience of the underwater structures, and commented publicly on what they saw. So far as I know, they are, at time of writing, the *only* geologists ever to have dived there. Therefore, when we speak of "geological opinion" concerning the Yonaguni anomalies it is important to be clear that we are referring to the work and ideas of just three men who, moreover, do not agree with one another—so there is no consensus. Other geologists who have expressed views without diving at Yonaguni hardly qualify to participate in the debate.

Since there are grave issues at stake concerning our understanding of prehistory and the story of human civilization I propose to devote the necessary space in this chapter to an accurate summary of the views of the three main geological protagonists.

DR. KIMURA

The doyen of the group, and in my view the hero of the Yonaguni saga for his determination, persistence and refreshingly open-minded intellectual approach, is Dr. Masaaki Kimura, professor of marine geology at the University of the Ryukyus in Okinawa. He and his students have completed hundreds of dives around the main "terrace" monument at Yonaguni as part of a long-term project in which they have thoroughly measured and mapped it, produced a three-dimensional model, taken samples of ancient algae encrusted on its walls for carbon-dating, and sampled the stone of the structure itself. Professor Kimura's unequivocal conclusion, based on the scientific evidence, is that the monument is man-made and that it was hewn out of the bedrock when it still stood above sea level—perhaps as much as 10,000 years ago. The principal arguments that he puts forward in favor of human intervention are on the record and include the following:

1. "Traces of marks that show that human beings worked the stone. There are holes made by wedge-like tools called *kusabi* in many locations."

2. "Around the outside of the loop road [a stone-paved pathway connecting principal areas of the main monument] there is a row of neatly-stacked rocks as a stone wall, each rock about twice the size of a person, in a straight line."

3. "There are traces carved along the roadway that humans conducted some form of repairs."

4. "The structure is continuous from under the water to land, and evidence of the use of fire is present."

5. "Stone tools are among the artefacts found underwater and on land."

6. "Stone tablets with carving that appears to be letters or symbols, such as what we know as the plus mark '+' and a 'V' shape were retrieved from underwater."

7. "From the waters nearby, stone tools have been retrieved. Two are for known purposes that we can recognize, the majority are not."

8. "At the bottom of the sea, a relief carving of an animal figure was discovered on a huge stone."[2]

9. On the higher surfaces of the structure there are several areas that slope quite steeply down towards the south. Kimura points out that deep symmetrical trenches appear on the northern elevations of these areas that could not have been formed by any known natural process.

10. A series of steps rises at regular intervals up the south face of the monument from the pathway at its base, 27 meters underwater, towards its summit less than six meters below the waves. A similar stairway is found on the monument's northern face.

11. Blocks that must necessarily have been removed (whether by natural or by human agency) in order to form the monument's impressive terraces are not found lying in the places where they would have fallen if only gravity and natural forces were operating; instead they seem to have been artificially cleared away to one side and in some cases are absent from the site entirely.

12. The effects of this unnatural and selective clean-up operation are particularly evident on the rock-cut "pathway" [Kimura calls it the "loop road"] that winds around the western and southern faces of the base of the monument. It pass-es directly beneath the main terraces yet is completely clear of the mass of rubble that would have had to be removed (whether by natural or by human agency) in order for the terraces to form at all.[3]

DR. SCHOCH

The second geologist to dive at Yonaguni, Professor Robert M. Schoch of Boston University, has vacillated tenaciously in his opinions—but I take this as a sign of an open-minded scholar ever willing to revise his views in the light of new evidence.

Thus when we first dived there together in September 1997, he was sure that the structure was man-made.[4] Within a few days, however, he had changed his mind completely:

I believe that the structure can be explained as the result of natural processes... The geology of the fine mudstones and sandstones of the Yonaguni area, combined with wave and current actions and the lower sea levels of the area during earlier millennia, were responsible for the formation of the Yonaguni Monument about 9,000 to 10,000 years ago.[5]

A few days later, Schoch softened his position again:

After meeting with Professor Kimura, I cannot totally discount the possibility that the Yonaguni Monument was at least partially worked and modified by the hands of humans. Professor Kimura pointed out several key features that I did not see on my first brief trip... If I should have the opportunity to revisit the Yonaguni monument, these are key areas that I would wish to explore.[6]

Schoch did have an opportunity to revisit the structure in the summer of 1998, carrying out several more dives there. Then, in 1999, in an interview given to the BBC science program "Horizon" for a documentary attacking my work—and in the same year in his own book *Voices of the Rocks*—he expressed what sounded like two very different, even contradictory opinions about the structure.

Here is the relevant section from the BBC Horizon transcript:

> NARRATOR: Yonaguni looked as if it could be a spectacular discovery and Hancock needed corroboration. He invited the Boston University geologist Robert Schoch to inspect the site. Professor Schoch has taken a keen interest in unorthodox views of the past and he welcomed the chance to examine the underwater discovery. Schoch dived with Hancock several times at Yonaguni.

> PROFESSOR ROBERT SCHOCH (Boston University): I went there in this case actually hoping that it was a totally man-made structure that was now submerged underwater, that dated maybe back to 6000 B.C. or more. When I got there and I got to dive on the structure I have to admit I was very, very disappointed because I was basically convinced after a few dives that this was primarily, possibly totally, a natural structure … Isolated portions of it look like they're man-made, but when you look at it in context, you look at the shore features, etc., and you see how, in this case, fine sandstones split along horizontal bedding plains that give you these regular features. I'm convinced it's a natural structure.[7]

Well *that* seems straightforward. But then here is what Schoch says in *Voices of the Rocks*:

> Possibly the choice between natural and human-made isn't simply either/or. Yonaguni Island contains a number of old tombs whose exact age is uncertain, but that are clearly very old. Curiously the architecture of the tombs is much like that of the monument. It is possible that humans were imitating the monument in designing the tombs, and it is equally possible that the monument was itself somehow modified by human hands. That is, the ancient inhabitants of the island may have partially reshaped or enhanced a natural structure to give it the form they wished, either as a structure on its own or as the foundation of a timber, mud or stone building that has since been destroyed. It is also possible that the monument served as a quarry from which blocks were cut, following the natural bedding, joint and fracture planes of the rock, then removed to construct buildings that are now long gone. Since it is located along the coast the Yonaguni Monument it may even have served as some kind of natural boat dock for an early seafaring people. As Dr. Kimura showed me, ancient stone tools beautifully crafted from igneous rock have been found on Yonaguni. Significantly, Yonaguni has no naturally exposed igneous rocks, so the tools, or at least the raw materials from which they were made, must have been imported from neighboring islands where such rock is found. The tools could have been used to modify or reshape the natural stone structures now found underwater off the coast of Yonaguni. The concept of a human-enhanced natural structure fits well with East

It is also possible that the monument served as a quarry from which blocks were cut, following the natural bedding, joint and fracture planes of the rock, then removed to construct buildings that are now long gone. Since it is located along the coast, the Yonaguni Monument may even have served as some kind of natural boat dock for an early seafaring people.

Asian aesthetics, such as the *feng shui* of China and the Zen-inspired rock gardens of Japan. A complex interaction between natural and human-made forms that influenced human art and architecture 8,000 years ago is highly possible.[8]

As further evidence for a very ancient human role in the construction of the Yonaguni monument, Schoch then sets out an argument of mine, advanced in my 1998 book *Heaven's Mirror*, that the structure is not only man-made but could also have served a specific astronomical function—since calculations show that around 10,000 years ago, when it was above water, it would have stood on the ancient Tropic of Cancer.[9] Writes Schoch:

DR. WICHMANN

The third geologist, German science writer Dr. Wolf Wichmann, has definite opinions and expresses them with certainty. In 1999 he informed *Der Spiegel* magazine—who had taken him to Yonaguni—that he regards the underwater monument as entirely natural. He made just three dives on the main terraces and then declared: "I didn't find anything that was man-made."[13]

Japan's marine scientists "haven't got a clue" what the terraced underwater structure at Yonaguni is, reports *Der Spiegel*:

I cannot avoid adding that *all* rock-hewn structures, whether the weird terraced granite outcrop at Keno near Sacsayhuaman in Peru,[11] or the wonders of Petra in Jordan, or the temples of Mahabalipuram in South India are, by definition, partly natural—the base rock out of which they are hewn—and partly man-made.

The ancients, I suspect, knew where the tropic was, and they knew that... its position moved slowly. Since Yonaguni is close to the most northerly position the tropic reaches in its lengthy cycle, the island may have been the site of an astronomically aligned shrine.[10]

In summary, therefore, Schoch has not come down definitively either on one side of the fence or on the other but seems to be wavering in the direction of a compromise in which the structure is both natural and man-made at the same time.

I cannot avoid adding that *all* rock-hewn structures, whether the weird terraced granite outcrop at Keno near Sacsayhuaman in Peru,[12] or the wonders of Petra in Jordan, or the temples of Mahabalipuram in South India are, by definition, partly natural—the base rock out of which they are hewn—and partly man-made. They can't help but be anything else.

"It is unlikely to be anything natural," said the oceanographer Terukai Ishii from Tokyo. Masaaki Kimura, a marine researcher at the Rykyus University (Okinawa) talks about "a masterpiece." He thinks the structure is a sacred edifice built by a hitherto unknown culture possessing advanced technical abilities.

The debate going on in the Orient has awakened the curiosity of the West. People with second sight find themselves magically attracted by "Iseki Point" ("ruins"). At the beginning of 1998 the geologist Robert Schoch, who believes the people of Atlantis built the Sphinx[14] swam down to the site and declared it to be "most interesting." The guru of ancient antiquity and best-selling author Graham Hancock was also investigating the site. After an excursion in a submersible he records that at the base of the monument can be seen a "clearly-defined path."[15]

The rock expert Wolf Wichmann could not corroborate these conclusions. In the company of a team from SPIEGEL TV he returned to explore the coastal area, under threat from tsunamis. In a total of three diving operations he gathered rock samples and measured the steps and "walls." He was unconvinced by his findings: "I didn't find anything that was man-made."

During the inspection it was revealed that the "gigantic temple" is nothing but naturally produced bedded rock. The sandstone is traversed by vertical cracks and horizontal crevices. Perpendicularity and steps have gradually developed in the fracture zones. Wichmann refers to the plateaux at the top as typical "eroded plains." Such flat areas occur when bedded rock is located right in the path of the wash of the waves.

Suggestive pictures rich in detail and contrast may indeed reveal something else, but in general the mass of rock looks like a structure rising out of a sandy bed, with no sign of architectural design. The plateaux have gradient sections, and there is no perpendicular wall. Some of the steps just end nowhere; others are in a spiral, like steep hen-roosts.

through photographs or looking at videotapes of the structures. As is the case with armchair geologists, their opinions can only be of limited value until they have dived there themselves.

By contrast the opinion of the only experienced marine archaeologist in the world who has ever dived at Yonaguni must count for a great deal more. That archaeologist—whose official report is reproduced in part below—is Sri Sundaresh from the National Institute of Oceanography in Goa, India. The reader will recall that we dived with him and other NIO archaeologists at Dwarka in March 2000 and again at Pumpuhar in February 2001. Between these expeditions in India, Sundaresh participated with us in an expedition to Yonaguni in September 2000 that had been sponsored once again (as had Robert Schoch's visit in September 1997) by my friend Yasuo Watanabe through his company Seamen's Club.

Also participating in the September 2000 expedition was Kimiya Homma, a businessman from Hokkaido, whose firm owns two very useful high-tech ROVs (remotely operated vehicles) for

---

By contrast the opinion of the only experienced marine archaeologist in the world who has ever dived at Yonaguni must count for a great deal more.

The stony blocks show no signs of mechanical working. "Had the 'ashlars' been hewn by tools, they would have been studded with flutes and cuts and scratches," said Wichmann. Three circular recesses on the topmost plateau, referred to by Kimura as column foundations, are nothing but "potholes." These occur when water washes through narrow spaces.

Facts like these fail to stem the current epidemic of mystery-fever. The Yonaguni monument has for some time played a key role in the world picture of archaeological dreamers.[16]

THE ONE ARCHAEOLOGIST

One archaeologist has dived at Yonaguni and studied its underwater structures first hand. Others in his profession who have commented have done so from their desks after browsing

unmanned exploration in water too deep to be readily reached by divers. So that an effective search for further structures around Yonaguni could be mounted in the short time available, Homma had brought one of the ROVs with him and also an expert team of support staff and technical divers. Because it is a unique document of reference, being—so far—the first and only evaluation of a wide range of Yonaguni's underwater structures by a marine archaeologist, I reproduce below several sections from Sundaresh's expedition report. Some of the specific submerged sites that we visited with Sundaresh during the expedition are not yet familiar to the reader from the brief account given[17] but will be described shortly:

The Study of Submerged Structures Off
Yonaguni Island of Japan:
The Preliminary Results From Recent Expedition

> **Underwater massive structures were found initially by Mr. Aratake, a local resident of Yonaguni Island during 1986-87. He named this point as Iseki ("Monument") Point. He was looking for hammerhead sharks schooling around the island, when a massive man-made underwater structure was noticed at a depth of 30 meters.**

September 1-12, 2000
By Sundaresh
National Institute of Oceanography
Dona Paula, Goa 403 004
December 2000

1.0 INTRODUCTION

Yonaguni is the most southwestern island of Japan and closest to Taiwan (about 69 nautical miles). This island is almond-shaped, with ten km length from (east to west) and four km width (north to south). An international expedition was organized by the Seamen's Club, Ishigaki Japan to further explore the underwater structures in the area. This report describes the archaeological significance of the structures found during the expedition.

2.0 BACKGROUND INFORMATION OF THE AREA

Underwater massive structures were found initially by Mr. Aratake, a local resident of Yonaguni Island during 1986-87. He named this point as Iseki ("Monument") Point. He was looking for hammerhead sharks schooling around the island, when a massive man-made underwater structure was noticed at a depth of 30 meters. This was his first discovery. Aratake and other divers in nearby Tatigami and "Palace" areas later found more monuments.

4.0 METHODOLOGY
4.1 OFFSHORE EXPLORATIONS

Two boats were chartered for explorations off Yonaguni waters from September 2, 2000 to September 8, 2000. The Remotely Operated Vehicle (ROV) was deployed simultaneously with side scan sonar and echosounder. The ROV was operated with generator power supply. The system was operated in waters between 40 to 80 meters depth around Yonaguni. The survey revealed rock cut channel about one meter wide and more than 20 meters long at two sea mounts. The ROV observations were confirmed by diving.

5.0 RESULTS
5.1 TERRACED STRUCTURE AND CANAL

A large terraced structure of about 250 meters in length and 25 meters in height was studied south of the *Arakawabana* headland. Known locally as Iseki Point, the terraced structure is bound to the northern side of an elongated, approximately east-west trending structure, designated by Professor Masaaki Kimura, University of the Ryukyus, as an approach road. But our observation of the proposed road-like structure suggests that it is more likely to be a canal. The overall width of the terraced structure is around 100 meters. From each of the terraces, a staircase leads downwards to the canal (or road?).

The length of the canal appears to be more than 250 meters, while the canal has a width of 25 meters. The purpose or utility of this canal structure is intriguing. Our observation all along the canal indicates that the western end of the structure begins underwater, opening away from the terraced structure into the open sea. The width, height and terraced northern side of the canal force us to suggest that the canal structure might have served as a channel for small boats communicating with the Arakawabana headland. The southern natural outcrop wall probably provided a buffer wall for strong open sea waves. This interpretation appears quite reasonable because the height of the southern wall of natural outcrop and the northern terraced wall are nearly the same. The terraces and attached staircases might have been used for handling, loading and unloading boats sailing through the channel. Thus it appears in all probability that the terraced structure and canal might have served as a jetty before submergence to present depth.

5.2 MONOLITH HUMAN HEAD

A large monolith that looks like a human head with two eyes and a mouth was studied at Tatigami Iwa Point. A human-cut large platform in the same monolith extends outwards at the base of the head. An approach way leads to this platform from the shore side.

The surrounding basal platform is quite large (about 2500 square meters), and could easily have accommodated more than two thousand people while sitting. The human head and associated platform with an approach road are suggestive of an area of worship or community gatherings.

5.3 UNDERWATER CAVE AREA

Diving operations revealed caves at eight to ten meters of water depth at the "Palace" area. Entry to these caves was possible only through the large one meter radius holes on the cave roof. Inside the cave a boulder of about one meter diameter engraved with carvings was observed. About 100 meters towards the eastern side of the caves, more rock engravings were noticed on the bedrock. These rock engravings are believed to be man-made.

Once upon a time these caves were probably on the land and were later submerged. The rock engravings inside the cave and on the bedrock were probably carved out by means of a tool of some sort. However, it is very difficult to say that these are rock art of this or that period, or a script.

Once upon a time these caves were probably on the land and were later submerged. The rock engravings inside the cave and on the bedrock were probably carved out by means of a tool of some sort. However, it is very difficult to say that these are rock art of this or that period, or a script.

5.4 MEGALITHS POINT

Diving operations revealed two big rectangular blocks measuring six meters in height, about 2.5 meters in width (both) and 4.9 meters thickness that have been located towards the western side of Iseki point... These rectangular blocks are designated by Japanese workers as megaliths. These blocks have been located in between two natural rock outcrops. The approach way to these megaliths is

through a tunnel measuring about three meters long, one meter high and one meter width.

The shape, size and positioning of these megaliths suggests that they are man-made. It is believed that the people of Japan's extremely ancient Jomon culture used to worship stones and rocks.[18] In light of this practice, it may be worthwhile to suggest that, these megaliths might have been used as objects of worship. However a thorough investigation in this regard is necessary before assigning a definite purpose to these megaliths.

6.0 CONCLUSION

The terraced structures with a canal are undoubtedly man-made, built by cutting an existing huge monolithic outcrop. The rectangular terraced structure and canal might have served as a jetty for handling, loading and unloading small boats before its submergence to present depth.

The monolith rock-cut human head and associated platform might have served as an area of worshiping or community gatherings.

THE SCORE SO FAR

By my count so far I have one marine archaeologist, Sundaresh, who is convinced that the Yonaguni structures are "undoubtedly man-made," and who represents 100 percent of all the archaeologists who have ever dived there up to the time of writing. I also have one marine geologist, Masaaki Kimura, who believes the same thing, a second, Robert Schoch, who is undecided, and a third, Wolf Wichmann, who is convinced that they are natural.

I decided when I got the opportunity that I should try to dive at Yonaguni with Wichmann and see if I could change his mind. To this end, a few months after the *Der Spiegel* article appeared, I made the following statement on my Web site:

I would like to offer a challenge to Wolf Wichmann... Let us agree a mutually convenient time to do, say, 20 dives together at Yonaguni over a period of about a week. I will show you the structures as I have come to know them, and give you every reason... why I think that the monuments must have been worked on by human beings. You will do your best to persuade me otherwise. At the end of the week let's see if either side has had a change of mind.[19]

> I... began to understand clearly for the first time exactly how and why a geologist might conclude that the Yonaguni underwater structures are entirely natural—or at any rate (to sum up Wolf's position more accurately) that they all *could* have been formed by known natural forces with no necessity for human intervention.

"JAPANESE SCIENTISTS CANNOT DIVE..."

In March 2001, on a mini-expedition funded by Channel 4 Television, Wichmann took up my challenge. A small, wiry, dark-haired, unpretentious man, I liked him the moment I met him, and continued to do so throughout the week that we spent diving in Japan and arguing, in a mood of amiable disagreement, about what we were seeing underwater.

Predictably we did not reach a consensus: Wolf left Yonaguni still holding most of the opinions with which he had arrived, and so did I. But I think that we each gave the other some worthy points to ponder. I know that I benefited from what amounted to a very useful field seminar on the natural history of submerged rock and began to understand clearly for the first time exactly how and why a geologist might conclude that the Yonaguni underwater structures are entirely natural—or at any rate (to sum up Wolf's position more accurately) that they all *could* have been formed by known natural forces with no necessity for human intervention.

Before going on to Yonaguni, Wolf and I paid a visit to Professor Masaaki Kimura at his office in the University of the Ryukyus. I started the ball rolling with a general question for Professor Kimura concerning the age of the structure:

Graham Hancock: People can argue for the next five centuries about whether what we see underwater at Yonaguni is manmade or artificial. But one thing that we can hopefully get clear is how old it is ... when was it submerged? So the first question I want to ask you is what is your view of the age of this structure? The last time that it was above water?

Professor Kimura: This construction has been submerged since 6,000 years ago, because the coralline algae attaching to the wall of this structure shows 6,000 years.

GH: And those coralline algae, because they're organic, you've been able to carbon date them?

PK: Yes, carbon-14.

GH: Right. So that tells us the age of that biological item ... It's 6,000 years old and it's attached to a stone structure which, therefore, must be older than that.

PK: It must be older, and so in general 6,000 years ago the sea level at that time [was lower]... So if men made this, this must be when this area was land ... it's about 9,000 or 10,000 years ago.

GH: 9,000 or 10,000 years ago? So—again to clarify, because I need to get this straight—you're saying that 9,000 or 10,000 years ago, the whole area was above water and the date of submergence would be about 6,000 years ago?

PK: Before 6,000 years ago.

GH: This is the problem with carbon-14 isn't it? It dates the organism, not the structure. So then you can only say that the structure is older than that, but how much older is not sure. How much work have you done on sea level change as a dating guide? And how big a factor is the possibility of sudden, maybe recent land subsidence as a result of earthquake?

PK: Yes, I'm looking for such evidence, geological evidence, but there is no evidence of movement. If this area had subsided by movement it would be due to earthquakes and faulting, but there is no active fault nearby, the fringing coast is continuous, and between the beach and Iseki Point, there is no discontinuity or fault.

WOLF WICHMANN: I see.

GH: That makes things fairly clear then. It leaves us with the sea level issue on its own to base a date on, without complicating factors, which is great. At least we can be clear on one thing.

WW: I think that questions of sea level rise are very fairly proved by scientific evidence here in the area. I mean, they're experts in their field.

GH: So you'd have no problem with the 9,000 year date?

WW: No, no … not at all. No, the question was, or is still, is it and, if yes, to what extent is it made by man or overworked by man? This is the question.

GH: Well hopefully we'll get a chance to investigate that when we go to Yonaguni.

PK: We need to research much more.

WW: Yes.

GH: [speaking to Professor Kimura]: I mean you're practically the only person who's done—you and your team here—have done continuous research for some years. But almost nobody else is working on it, I think, at the moment?

PK: Japanese scientists cannot dive.

"A VERY FINE, A VERY NICE THING…"

Throughout our discussion Professor Kimura strongly maintained his commitment to the manmade character of Yonaguni's underwater monuments—not simply on the basis of his technical findings, cited earlier, which I need not repeat here, but also, and I found persuasively, because: "This kind of topography—if this has been made by nature it is very difficult to explain the shape."

Wolf's riposte was immediate: "So what I would say to that formation is that I've seen many natural formations, especially coastlines, being worked out by waves and wind, especially with the help of weapons, erosive weapons—sand and so on… Seeing with the eye of a geologist or a morphologist it is, OK, a very fine, a very nice thing, but possibly made by nature."

I asked Wolf whether in fact he had ever seen anything like the Yonaguni "formation" anywhere else in the world. "Not in that exact combination," he replied.

I asked Wolf whether in fact he had ever seen anything like the Yonaguni "formation" anywhere else in the world.

"Not in that exact combination," he replied. "This is what is surprising me; it's a very strong, compressed combination of the different shapes and the different figures you can find naturally in the world somewhere."

"But you don't usually find them in combination like this?"

"No, I haven't seen that. So that is a marvel. It is a very beautiful formation."

"Or the work of human beings? I prompted.

"Or of that. So that's what we're here for."

THE RAMP

On our first dive at Yonaguni I took Wolf to a very curious structure that I had discovered in late June 1999.

It stands in 18 meters of water 100 meters to the west of the terraces of the main monument. When above sea level 8,000 or 10,000 years ago I suggest that it was originally a natural and untouched rocky knoll rising about six meters above ground level. A curving sloped ramp three meters wide was then cut into the side of the knoll and a retaining wall to the full height of the original mound was left in place enclosing and protecting the outside edge of the ramp.

I led Wolf to the base of the ramp and as we swam up it I pointed out how the outer curve of the inner wall—which rises two meters above the floor of the

More of the south face of the main monument, Yonaguni.

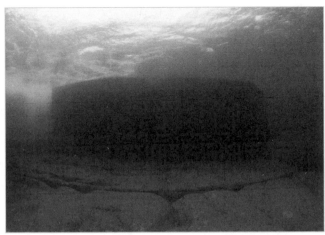
Rock-hewn rectlinear structure and megalithic "paving" close to the Stage.

ramp and is formed by the body of the mound—is precisely matched by the inner curve of the outer wall, which also rises to a height of two meters above the ramp floor, so that both walls run perfectly parallel. Moreover when we swam up and over the rim of the outer wall we could see that its own outer curve again exactly matches the curves within and that it drops sheer to the sea-bed—as it should if it is indeed a purposeful wall and not simply a natural structure.

Moreover when we swam up and over the rim of the outer wall we could see that its own outer curve again exactly matches the curves within and that it drops sheer to the sea-bed—as it should if it is indeed a purposeful wall and not simply a natural structure.

I showed Wolf that the ramp floor itself, though battered and damaged in places, must originally have had a smooth, flat surface. I also showed him what I believe may have been the function of the ramp. As one continues to follow it round it leads to a platform offering an impressive side-on view of the two huge parallel megaliths, tucked into an alcove in the northwest corner of the main monument, that constitute a spectacular landmark in the Yonaguni "underworld."

Later we discussed what we'd seen:

GH: Okay, Wolf, the first dive we did I brought you to a structure [attempts to draw ramp structure on notepad]—I'm sorry; I'm hopeless at drawing.

WW: Me too... [Peers at drawing] OK, so I recognize it.

GH: Hey, you're a geologist; you should be able to draw. (Continues drawing.) And here is a rather nice wall going round on both sides, and in the middle is a bedrock channel or ramp. And it rises from here around to this corner and, in fact, if we follow it all the way round it leads us to a view of the megaliths. Now this wall is not a bank. It is a wall. It's actually about half a meter wide. And it's high ... more than two meters high...

WW: Round about.

GH: ... Above this ... above this ramp, whatever you want to call it. So I simply cannot understand the combination of clean bedrock here [indicates the ramp floor] admittedly very eroded and damaged—but clean bedrock here, and these heavily overgrown walls, which are definitely wall-like in appearance and rather high in the sense that they have an outer and an inner edge, and the curve of the outer edge matches the curve of the inner edge; and the same on the other wall.

To my surprise Wolf immediately admitted that this rather innocuous looking and only recently discovered structure, which he had not been shown on his previous visit, was a "real challenge." He was later to describe it as "the most impressive thing" he had seen at Yonaguni:

The most impressive thing for me was the wall, the wall which is totally covered by living organisms nowadays, which should be removed to have a look at the structure of that wall, which can also be explained as having been done possibly by nature, but to get it sure we have to do deep research on that.[20]

Nevertheless Wolf would not have been Wolf if he had not at least attempted to come up with a calm, level-headed and unsensational geological explanation for the problem. He therefore drew my attention now to a place on land on Yonaguni called Sananudai that we had taken a look at the day before where he had shown me wall-like formations—admittedly only half a meter high—that had been formed entirely naturally:

WW: Okay, this is a real challenge to solve. But if you remember, the day before we were on a platform on land—I forgot the name of the point—

GH: Sananudai?

WW: Right, correct. And by chance we went further down near the sea, and I showed you these encrustation patterns and maybe you remember that I...

GH: I remember distinctly; you told me that a hard patina formed on the outside of the rock and that the water softened out the inside, leaving a wall-like shape in place.

WW: Correct. And on the other side, the relatively soft sandstone had already begun to be removed. So ... and I told you that this could be a possible way that a wall can be made by nature... OK, it's a theory.

GH: It's a theory. I mean what I saw at Sananudai was actually no curved walls running in parallel with each other, but rather straight, and they were about a half meter high.

WW: They were at beginning stage. Right. And if you had a look closer down, you would have seen that there was a little curving, not as clear as this, I have to admit. But I mean that was really the beginning stage so we don't know.

GH: So would you want to explain those walls [on either side of the ramp] that way, as a hard patina which was preserved, and the soft part was cut out?

WW: At first, and then subsequently overgrown by organisms as we saw. But to get clear what that really is, so I underline repeatedly, it is a challenge, and this is the first and only explanation I have for this. But to really get clear of this fact, we should have to remove the encrustation on one spot, or just from top to the bottom, or to drill a hole through...this is the only way to find out of what material this wall consists—there's no other way. We are obliged to find out what these walls are made of. Are they made of single patterns like stones or something?

GH: Well see, I don't ... I very much doubt if the walls will turn out to be made of blocks. I think they'll turn out to be cut. I think we're looking at megalithic culture that cut rock. I think they cut down into the living rock, and they created the walls by cutting, and then later on the encrustation came and grew on top of the walls. That's my theory.

WW: I mean, if this was the case, then it would still be very useful to have a look on the core of these. It would tell us exactly what sort of material it was—was it soft sandstone, was it hard mudstone or what else? And we would be possibly able to find any marks on them, which then would give us the clear proof...

GH: So what we have here is a bit of a puzzle that needs some serious research done on it.

WW: Correct. That's what I would say.

THE TUNNEL AND THE MEGALITHS

On our second dive we visited the twin megaliths, weighing approximately 100 tons each, stacked side by side like two huge slices of toast in a west-facing alcove in the northwest corner of the main monument. As noted earlier, a prime side-on view of these hulking rectangular blocks unfolds from the top of the curved sloping ramp explored on the first dive. And we've seen that the ramp appears to have been cut down (either by natural or human forces) between two parallel walls out of a pre-existing rocky knoll.

The knoll in turn co-joins other massive, heavily overgrown structures presumed to be outcrops of natural bedrock which form an almost continuous barricade, three meters high and five meters thick, thrown out in a loose semi-circle in front of the megaliths—all at roughly 15-18 meters water depth. The barricade is penetrated at only one point, and there only by a narrow tunnel a little over a meter wide and about a meter and a half high through which a scuba diver swimming horizontally may pass comfortably.

The tunnel itself looks "built"—as opposed to rock-hewn like so much else at Yonaguni—in the sense that each of its sides consists of two courses of huge blocks separated by straight, clearly demarcated, matching joints. There is insufficient room to stand up within the tunnel, indeed barely enough even to crouch, so when it was above water 8,000 or 10,000 years ago any human entering it would have been obliged to crawl through to the other side. What is striking then, as soon as you emerge, is the way in which you now find yourself directly opposite and beneath the twin megaliths which, from this angle, are above you like the paired sarsens at Stonehenge or the pair of upright granite megaliths worshipped since antiquity in Japan's Ena region as "the sacred rock deity, the object of worship."[21]

The swim ahead to the base of the megaliths is a matter of 20 meters and you observe immediately at this point that they do not stand on the sea-bed but are elevated about two meters above it, with their bases resting on a platform of boulders, and framed in a cleft. The rear corner of the main terraced monument forms the side of the cleft to your right; a lower ridge of rock that also shows signs, though to a lesser degree, of terracing, forms the side to your left. Both megaliths slope backwards at the same angle against the cleft and both are the same height (just over six meters). The megalith to the right is distinctly thicker than its otherwise near "twin" to the left. Both megaliths taper at top and bottom so that the gap between them, about the width of a fist at the midpoint, is not constant. Although roughened, eroded and pitted with innumerable sea-urchin holes, the megaliths can still be recognized as essentially symmetrical blocks, all the faces of which appear originally to have been smoothed off to match—although, again, whether the process that brought this effect about was entirely natural, or at some point involved the input of human skill and labor, remains thus far a matter of a very few contradictory professional opinions and no facts.

Had these very striking parallel megaliths been quarried, shaped and lowered into position beside the northwest corner of the main monument by human beings? Or had they arrived there through wholly natural processes?

I allowed myself to float up, towards the surface, along the slope of the megaliths, resting my hand in the gap between them as a guide. The light was good and I could see right into the gap; looking back at me from the far recesses a plump red fish eyed me with horror and hoped that I would go away.

As I neared the top of the megaliths, submerged under just five meters of water, I began to feel the ferocious wash of waves pounding against the surrounding rocks. I clung on and for a few moments allowed my body to be tugged back and forth by the swell. Enshrouded in a cloud of foam I could see the northwest corner of the main monument still rising above me the final few meters towards the surface.

After the dive Wolf and I again discussed what we had seen and quite soon, after some fruitless trading of opinion, our argument began to focus around a single—potentially decisive—issue. Had these very striking parallel megaliths been quarried, shaped and lowered into position beside the northwest corner of the main monument by human beings? Or had they arrived there through wholly natural processes?

I had drawn another rough sketch map to which I now pointed:

GH: There's the two blocks, and we see above them here, not very high abovethem, the mass of the structure which leads round to Iseki Point. Explain to me how those blocks got there.

WW: Okay. You have seen lots of blocks fallen down—

GH: All over the place.

WW: On the shoreline we saw from the ship—

GH: Many fallen blocks, yes.

WW: —lots of blocks have fallen down from higher parts—

GH: Agreed.

WW: —from beddings which have been broken, which were harder than the underlying layers, because what happens is that you get an under-curving and undercutting of softer material under harder banks. So in my belief, these two blocks have once been one block of two sandstone banks, with either softer material in between or nothing in between, just only the bedding limits.

GH: Well, I want to know how they got where they are now.

WW: Okay. My opinion is that these blocks have fallen down from a very, very high level, relative to their present situation.

GH: But no high point overlooks them. You would have to go back—

WW: Nowadays.

GH: Well, yes, fair enough, nowadays. Nowadays you would have to go back in a northward direction some 50 or 60 meters, maybe more, horizontally, before you reached the cliff.

WW: Right, that's clear for nowadays. I'm talking about a time range of at least 10,000 years … maybe more.

GH: That we agree on.

WW: So then there could have been places of a higher position from which these stones could have fallen down.

GH: So you are hypothesizing a pre-existing higher place from which these fell?

WW: What I'm hypothesizing is that they have fallen down, so … and this must have happened from a, let's say, sufficiently higher place. So what this may be then—

GH: Do you agree with me that this place [Indicates top of northwest corner of main monument three-four meters above top of megaliths] is not sufficiently high? The place we see immediately above it now?

WW: I don't have it in mind clearly, so I just can imagine from—

GH: But do you remember when we came to the top of these columns, of these blocks we were coming close to the surface. You could feel the swell hitting you quite hard and the foam above your head very strong. In fact, it's like looking into clouds almost. And you can see the mass of the rock above you, probably not more than another four meters above, and you're going to hit the surface there.

WW: Yes, I would think this would not be high enough.

GH: No?

WW: No.

GH: So we need a hypothetical high place to do it?

WW: Yes.

GH: And I, of course, need a hypothetical civilization—

WW: Yes.

GH: —capable of moving it here.

WW: Yes, of course, yes, yes ... no doubt about it.

GH: So we have two hypotheticals there.

WW: I'm not going to discuss any presence or absence of any civilization because that's not my field...

...the very odd combination of major stone structures lying underwater at Yonaguni, and the very odd combinations of characteristics found within every one of those structures, simply cannot be said to have been properly evaluated until the possible "presence or absence" of a civilization — specifically the Jomon — has been very thoroughly taken into account.

But the problem I feel—and shall continue to feel—is that the very odd combination of major stone structures lying underwater at Yonaguni, and the very odd combinations of characteristics found within every one of those structures, simply cannot be said to have been properly evaluated until the possible "presence or absence" of a civilization—specifically the Jomon—has been very thoroughly taken into account.

THE PATH AND THE TERRACES

Our third and fourth dives were spent examining the "pathway" or "loop road" which runs along the base of the main monument directly beneath the terraces in its south face at a depth of 27 meters; and the terraces themselves which begin 14 meters vertically above the pathway.

TERRACES

At this level a spacious patio about 12 meters wide and 35 meters in length opens out—and in its northeastern corner, at depths decreasing from 13 meters to seven meters, the structures known to local divers as "the terraces" are found. There are two main "steps," both about two meters high with sharp edges and clean near-right-angle corners. Above them there are then three further smaller steps giving access to the top of the monument that continues to rise northward until it comes close to the surface.

Here, very clearly, I could see the basis for the argument advanced by Wolf in *Der Spiegel* that the whole mass of the structure—with all its striking and emphatic terraces and steps, its perpendicular and horizontal planes—could be explained by the effects of high-energy wave action on a large outcrop of naturally bedded sedimentary rock.

When it first began to form, eons ago, the sandstone (or more correctly in this case "mudstone") of the body of the monument was deposited in layers of varying thickness and consistency, traversed "by vertical cracks and horizontal crevices." As sea level rose and turbulent waves began to strike progressively higher levels of the structure these cracks and crevices were gradually exploited and opened up—with the softer layers separating into flat slabs of assorted shapes and sizes which could then be washed out by the sea. In such a fashion, explains Wolf, "perpendicularity and steps" gradually developed in the fracture zones creating, entirely without human help, the most striking effects of the structure as we see it today.

According to this reasoning, therefore, I was to envisage the 12 meter x 35 meter flat-floored patio as having been cut out of the side of the original outcrop by wave action which removed the sedimentary mudstone layers in slabs—with the terraced sections being formed out of the surviving harder members of rock after the softer layers had been washed away.

Kimura is in no doubt that this wall is the work of human beings.

I helped Wolf measure the two highest steps, then drifted off to the edge of the patio and looked down the sheer 14 meter wall that drops to Professor Kimura's "loop road"—the flat rock-floored "pathway" that runs along the bottom of

When I saw the undersea ruins I knew instantly it was a stone quarry. I showed photographs to other stonecutters also and they all said the same. I conclude that it was done by human hands. It's absolutely impossible for something like this to be produced by nature alone...

the channel immediately to the south of the monument. Although 25 meters wide at the depth of the terraces the channel narrows to a width of less than four meters at the depth of the path. Its north wall is the sheer south face of the monument; its south wall is at first not sheer but slopes for some distance further to the south at an angle of about 40 degrees before rising more steeply towards the surface. The 40 degree section is heavily but rather neatly stacked with blocky rubble that consists of an infill of smaller stones supporting a façade of a dozen much larger blocks arranged, as Professor Kimura points out, in a straight line "as a stone wall." Kimura is in no doubt that this wall is the work of human beings.

But because it is 27 meters down, and our dive computers didn't like the decompression implications of doing it as the fourth dive of an already hard day, we decided to leave it till the following morning.

THE PATHWAY

We dropped in near the twin megaliths, then followed the clearly-demarcated rock-hewn pathway that seems to start (or finish?) here, veering to the left of the "entrance tunnel" that we had passed through the day before, winding gradually to the south into deeper water around the western side of the main monument, then finally turning eastwards into the channel in front of the terraces at a depth of 27 meters.

As we entered the channel I pointed out to Wolf a pattern of three symmetrical indentations, each two meters in length and only about 20 centimeters high, cut at regular intervals into the junction of the northern side of the path and the base of the main monument. I also indicated two other

details that I find particularly impressive in this area: the way that the floor of the path appears to have been deliberately flattened and smoothed to give almost a paved effect, and the way the path is completely free of any rubble until a point about 30 meters to the east of the terraces (where several large boulders and other stony debris have fallen or rolled). The view looking west from there shows the clear section of the path that lies directly beneath the terraces. To the right is the sheer south face of the main monument and, on the south side of the path, the beginning of the sloping row of large blocks, bedded on smaller stones, which Professor Kimura believes to be the ruins of a man-made "wall" or embankment.

When Wolf and I later discussed the path and the terraces he remained adamant that all the anomalies in these areas could have been produced by the effects of local erosive forces, mainly waves, on the "layer-cake" strata of the Yonaguni mudstones. In short while he could not absolutely rule out human intervention he did not feel that it was *necessary* in order to explain anything that we had so far seen underwater.

At this point I drew his attention to a project done by Professor Kimura and his team from the University of the Ryukyus in cooperation with the Japanese national TV channel TBS. The result had been a high-quality six-hour documentary, aired over New Year 2001, which made many useful and original contributions to the debate on the Yonaguni controversy. I wanted to acquaint Wolf in particular with the comments and demonstrations of Koutaro Shinza, a traditional Okinawan stonemason who had shown himself to be an expert in exploiting the natural faults, cracks and layers in sedimentary rocks to facilitate quarrying. According to Shinza, who TBS brought to Yonaguni:

When I saw the undersea ruins I knew instantly it was a stone quarry. I showed photographs to other stonecutters also and they all said the same. I conclude that it was done by human hands. It's absolutely impossible for something like this to be produced by nature alone...

Since Shinza's technique of quarrying along the lines of weakness of existing joints and fractures is functionally identical to the "method" used by the sea in Wolf's scenario to break up and separate the Yonaguni mudstones into the terraces and steps we see today, I asked him whether he could be absolutely certain that he could tell the difference. He admitted that he could not be certain—although the fact that he had as yet seen no definite tool marks on any of his dives was another reason to assume that humans had not been involved.

GH: Kimura makes a lot of the tool marks issue. He says he has definitely found marks. But I wouldn't be very hopeful after 10,000 years of submersion underwater to find tool marks. It's a long time. This, of course, is hard stone.

WW: Very hard stone, yes. And it is heavily overgrown with organisms in many places. So we might find some marks, indeed, if we were looking a bit and if we knew where to look exactly and how to identify them clearly. But this I mean is necessary.

Had the sea randomly removed the rock layers to leave the terraces, or had it been ancient stonemasons working to a plan?

Had the sea randomly removed the rock layers to leave the terraces, or had it been ancient stonemasons working to a plan?

Neither scenario, we realized, could be unequivocally falsified—or proved—by the empirical evidence presently to hand.

But there was another way to come at the problem that could at least test the logic of both propositions.

Part of Professor Kimura's evidence for human intervention in the construction of the main Yonaguni monument is the stark *absence* of fallen stony rubble in the pathway beneath the terraces—which he suggests should be cluttered by debris, perhaps even completely buried under it, if the terraces had been cut naturally by waves breaking-up the pre-existing bedding planes. Where we do see debris on the path itself it is in the form of a cluster of large boulders (not slabs) 30 meters to the east of the terraces. And the only other area that might be described as debris lies neatly stacked at an angle of 40 degrees against the sloping south face of the channel, touching but never trespassing the southern edge of the path. This is the embankment with a façade of a dozen megalithic blocks arranged in a row that Kimura has identified as man-made. I confess, however, that on all my many visits to Yonaguni—including these March 2001 dives with Wolf—I have regarded this embankment as nothing more than rubble fallen from the south side of the channel and thus paid no special attention to it. It has only been since March 2001, looking back at the photographs and video images, that I have begun to realize how odd it is that not a bit of the supposed "fallen rubble" transgresses the path itself, how very ordered it seems to be in general, and how very probable it is that Kimura is right.

But on the trip with Wolf I focused only on the issue of the apparent "clean-up" operation that had been done on the path.

I began by reminding him of our earlier discussion about the twin megaliths, each six meters tall and weighing 100 tons, which he claimed had fallen from above into their present position on the northwest corner of the monument from some hypothetical former high point.

WW: I see what you're going for.

GH: Well, what I'm going for is the problem of the path as we come in front of Iseki Point, as we come in front of the main monument. There's a sheer wall above the path 14 meters high and then the terracing begins. Now if ever there was a place on this structure where large slabs of stone should have fallen it is here on the path, directly under where the terraces were created. And so what's bothering me is if you can accept that the two parallel megaliths fell from a high place and lodged in position in the northwest corner of the monument and stayed there permanently, why don't we find the path in front of the monument littered with the equally big or bigger slabs of rock that must have been dislodged during the formation of the terraces?

I sketched the north and south walls of the channel, with the path at the base, and the embankment of "orderly rubble" gathered up against the south wall.

GH: Piled up here against the south wall is a huge amount of large stones which continue, in fact, up to this level [indicates sketch]. And I can very well accept that those stones fell off the top of the south side and found themselves in this position. As a matter of fact Professor Kimura doesn't say that. Professor Kimura says that human beings placed these stones here.

WW: Yes, yes, I know...I know.

GH: And he may or may not be right on that matter, but I'm prepared to accept that the reasonable possibility, with the forces of gravity as I understand them, is that stones which had been up here along this also rather flat area on top of the south side, may have been washed off in water and tumbled down and piled up here [indicates embankment]. And that's what I see. I see stones that fell from up here on the south side. What I can't understand, once we come to the huge main terrace with its steps on the north side of the channel, is why under this nice vertical cliff, I don't find any stones at all lying on this three-meter wide path. And I don't accept that they all rolled from the [north] side into this embankment [on the south side] conveniently leaving the path immediately beside it free. To me that's against logic and nature.

WW: We're just guessing. So imagine that this flat area around the terraces was not removed all in one go. What I mean is little small tiny pebbles, cobbles, whatever, over a long time have fallen down and they have somehow been transported and rode supported by gravity, here into this part [indicates embankment area on south side of channel] being sheltered from further transport, first of all, by these large boulders.

GH: Again I find it difficult to grasp you here. If I stand beside these steps [indicates the two big steps in the main terrace], they tower above my head. This means a layer of rock at least two and a half meters thick, all the way around here [indicates patio area] has been removed completely to leave behind just the steps.

WW: Yes.

GH: I mean this patio is, what, 30 or 35 meters in length?

WW: Round about.

GH: And we have a layer of rock two and a half meters thick; that's a hell of a lot of rock.

WW: We're not talking about two or three years.

GH: We're talking of a long period of time. So you're explaining this by saying that small pieces were broken off little by little and taken away by the tides?

WW: Yes, right...in general.

GH: Yeah. I find the more elegant explanation is it was tidied up by human beings.

WW: Fine.

GH: —after they finished their job.

WW: But where should they put it then? Somewhere around here?

GH: Wherever they wished.

WW: Come on.

GH: If human beings do take material away from sites, they take it right away...get it away...this is known human activity...very normal...they don't leave the rubble lying around on the site, this is normal.

WW: This is clearly what Kimura says.

GH: It's Kimura's argument, and I find it persuasive.

> After having passed through this second and more impressive doorway at the northern end of the main chamber, the diver comes into a third and final room of the Palace. It is completely unlike the other two, which were "built" (either by nature or by man) out of large blocks piled on top of one another.

THE PALACE

Our fifth dive was at a site several kilometers to the west of Iseki Point that local divers call the "Palace" and that the Indian archaeologist Sundaresh refers to in his December 2000 report as an "Underwater Cave area." Sundaresh does not comment on the structural characteristics of the Palace itself, which is indeed surrounded by natural caves, but notes that inside it:

> . . . a boulder about one m[eter] dia[meter] engraved with carvings was observed. About 100 meters towards the eastern side of the caves, more rock engravings were noticed on the bedrock...Both the rock engravings inside the cave and on the bedrock [were] probably carved using a tool.[22]

Some of the engravings found in the Palace area compared with similar marks from known Jomon sites above water. I make no special claim for the other aspect of the Palace that I find extremely interesting—and this is the possibility that it is not, or not entirely, a natural cave.

The entry to the "Palace" can be made through a number of holes broken in its roof at about nine meters water depth or through what I suggest may have been its original entrance at a depth of 14 meters. Here the diver has to squeeze through gaps in a jumble of fallen boulders to enter a small, gloomy, gravel-floored chamber oriented roughly north-south with space for four or five adults standing upright. Its south wall is blocked. In its north wall there is a "doorway," about a meter high, through which visitors would have had to pass crouched, or crawling, when the Palace was above sea level. The doorway has a rough, damaged appearance with no obviously man-made characteristics, but beyond it is a spacious and beautiful chamber that glows with an otherworldly blue light when the sun projects down through the column of water and illuminates it through the holes in its roof.

Like the cramped antechamber this atmospheric main room is oriented north-south. It measures approximately ten meters in length and five meters in width. Its height from floor to ceiling is also about five meters. While there has been a substantial collapse of its eastern side, its western side is undamaged and presents a smooth vertical wall of very large megaliths supporting further megaliths that form the roof.

Roughly at its mid-point the chamber begins to narrow towards the north until the east and west walls come together in a corridor less than two meters wide that culminates in another "doorway"—this time a very tall and narrow one. Across the top of its uprights, whether by accident or by design, one of the roof megaliths lies like a lintel.

After having passed through this second and more impressive doorway at the northern end of the main chamber, the diver comes into a third and final room of the Palace. It is completely unlike the other two, which were "built" (either by nature or by man) out of large blocks piled on top of one another. This third chamber, on the other hand, was hewn or hollowed—it is premature to decide by what—out of a mass of ancient coralline limestone that is exposed in this part of Yonaguni. There are no "blocks" in it at all. It extends only three meters in length and a little over a meter in width and culminates at its north end in yet another "doorway"—this time I insist distinctly "squared-off"—which leads into a closed alcove that in turn funnels vertically upwards and opens out through a hole in the roof.

All three of the "doorways" in the Palace, the first at the south side of the main room, the second at the north side, and the third leading into the alcove beyond, are positioned in a straight line creating what is, in effect, an aligned passage/chamber system. And since the rear (northernmost) chamber and alcove door are hewn out of a different kind of rock than other materials in the structure we must assume that some agency brought these two elements (the rock-hewn element and the megalithic element) together—and in alignment—at some point.

But was it nature that did this? Or could it have been the Jomon in a hitherto unrecognized phase of their prehistory, when they moved gigantic rocks and boulders with apparent ease and set in motion the cult of stone in Japan that still permeates the nation's spiritual life today?

Wolf would have nothing of it. In his no-nonsense view the Palace is, of course, a wholly natural phenomenon and the alignment of the three doorways is entirely coincidental.

burial chambers of the Kofun Age—particularly structures such as *Ishibutai* near Asuka where the megaliths used are of truly titanic dimensions and weights.[23] I remind the reader that archaeologists have as yet uncovered no evolutionary background to the advanced megalithic

Nobody pays much attention to Japan's own earlier epoch of stone architecture—witnessed by the stone circles and "mountain-landscaping" of the Jomon Age—because, up till today, a prejudice persists that the Jomon were simple hunter-gatherers and nothing more.

skills that suddenly manifest in Japan in the Kofun era, and raise the possibility for consideration that the knowledge of how to build with megaliths on such a scale may long previously have evolved in areas around Japan's coasts that are now underwater.

I remind the reader that archaeologists have as yet uncovered no evolutionary background to the advanced megalithic skills that suddenly manifested in Japan in the Kofun era, and raise the possibility for consideration that the knowledge of how to build with megaliths on such a scale may long previously have evolved in areas around Japan's coasts that are now underwater.

Very probably he is right. Yet I retain a sense of deep curiosity about this structure and intend, if I can, to do more work in it at some time in the future. On one previous dive nearby I came across parts of what looked like a second megalithic passage/chamber system that I would also like to revisit.

Whether they are natural or manmade it is likely, by virtue of their depth of submergence, that both systems are thousands of years older than Japan's mysterious Kofun era, which is thought to have begun around A.D. 300. Yet both systems powerfully and eerily remind me of the architecture of the great megalithic passageways and

I realise that this begs more questions than it answers.

Still, go figure where the Kofun tradition came from. Some scholars say Korea, but the evidence isn't good and others scholars disagree. Nobody pays much attention to Japan's own earlier epoch of stone architecture—witnessed by the stone circles and "mountain-landscaping" of the Jomon Age—because, up till today, a prejudice persists that the Jomon were simple hunter-gatherers and nothing more.

I do not deny that they were simple hunter-gatherers, but the deeper I enter the labyrinth of Japanese history the more certain I feel that they were also something much more.

THE FACE AND THE STONE STAGE

On our sixth and final dive at Yonaguni in March 2001 I took Wolf to a place called *Tatigami Iwa* eight kilometers east of the Palace and about two and a half kilometers east of the main cluster of monuments around *Iseki Point*.

Tatigami Iwa means "Standing Kami Stone" and refers to a rock pinnacle 40 meters high, weirdly gnarled and eroded, left behind thousands of years ago when the rest of a former cliff of which it was once part was washed away. Understandably revered as a deity in local tradition it now stands lashed by the Pacific Ocean a hundred meters from shore like a ghost sentry for this haunted island. But it is what is underneath it, in the underwater landscape nearby, that really interests me and that led me to choose it as the site for our sixth dive. For here, at a depth of around 18 meters, a huge carving of a human face is to be seen—with two eyes, a nose and a mouth hacked, either by natural forces or by human agency, into the corner of an outcrop of dark rock that juts up prominently from a distinctive "blocky" plain.

I showed Wolf how the "face formation" manifests a combination of peculiarities. For it is not just a "face"—or something that looks like one (which nature provides numerous accidental examples of)—but a grim and scary face, which seems designed to overawe, carved with care and attention to the lines and flow of the base rock. Moreover, far from appearing haphazardly with no context, as one would expect with an accidentally formed natural "face," it seems framed within a deliberate ceremonial setting. Thus a horizontal platform just under two meters high and five meters wide—called by local divers the "Stone Stage"—opens out from the side of the face at the level of the mouth and runs along to the back of the head where a narrow passageway penetrates the whole structure from west to east.

The "Face," therefore, has to be viewed together with its "Stone Stage" as a single rock-hewn edifice and I note, as does Sundaresh in his report cited earlier, that the flat area out of which the Stage and Face rise is easily large enough to have accommodated thousands of people before sea levels rose to cover it. Also noteworthy, however, is the fact that Face/Stage edifice is not alone in this big area but is part of a neighborhood of anomalous rock-hewn and often-rectilinear structures clustered around the base of *Tatigami Iwa*.

The "Face," therefore, has to be viewed together with its "Stone Stage" as a single rock-hewn edifice and I note, as does Sundaresh in his report cited earlier, that the flat area out of which the Stage and Face rise is easily large enough to have accommodated thousands of people before sea levels rose to cover it.

Natural?
Or man-made?
Or a bit of both?
My vote was weird and wonderful nature, enhanced by man, thousands of years ago.
But what did Wolf think?

WW: First of all we have to mention that this is a totally different sort of sandstone from what we find at Iseki Point. It's very thick—a series of very thick and massive banks which consist, contrary to the Iseki Point material of quite soft sandstone which is very, very sensitive to erosion and erodes generally in more rounded forms than the Iseki Point sandstone or mudstone. Secondly erosion of rock, all around the world, often produces forms that look accidentally like human faces...so I cannot say very much to the Face. To become clear of that fact, again, you would have to remove all the organisms around because that would give you a free view on the rock and the way it was carved.

GH: Did you notice, looking into the eyes, the eye sockets of the face, that both of them had a central prominence?

WW: No. No, sorry...I haven't looked.

GH: You didn't see.

WW: I saw the face and I thought, "Yeah, hmm, what to do with this?"

GH: Yes.

WW: But you see, I'm used...I'm not used to go[ing] straight to the things but to—

GH: Yeah, to stand back. I noticed that.

WW: —take a distance and look, hmm, how can this be formed? But it was my first view on that. I don't have an answer on that at the moment.

GH: Something else about it too, for me, is the sense that I keep finding these problems—if we look back over our drawings over the last couple of days—well here from our first dive we have within a short area, parallel curved walls, a ramp, a tunnel, two megaliths. We come round in front of the monument, a clear pathway, and as far as I'm concerned still with the mystery of the missing material—if indeed, as we also agreed earlier, all of this mass of material that we see in the embankment came from the south side—because as you said, it doesn't look like it belonged on the north side.

WW: On this view, yes.

GH: It's the proximity of all these peculiar things, each of which requires a rather detailed geological explanation and, in some cases, requires hypotheticals such as a cliff which once hung over that area and dropped these two megaliths down there. I find—and this is how I felt always almost from the third or fourth visit that I made to Yonaguni—is that this, this fantastic combination of peculiarities in a very compact area—because as you saw today the peculiarities continue as we go further along the coast to the Face and the Stone Stage—

WW: That's right, I was deeply impressed when I saw that.

GH: The thing that's striking is that all of these peculiarities occur along the south and east coasts of Yonaguni, and none of them are found along the north coast—at least if they've been found, divers aren't talking about them, and divers usually do talk about places like this. So, you know, we find them along the south side, but not along the north side. We find them compacted into a relatively tight area, and each one requires a rather different, and to my mind, rather complicated geological explanation,

you know, disposing of a mass of rock that is two and a half meters thick and 35 meters in length [and 15 meters wide] is simply banishing it. And attributing that to wave action, to me that's just going a little bit too far—

WW: I see what you're getting at.

GH: —on the strength and the variability of geological forces in a small area, and it catches in my throat. I find that I can't, I just can't buy it.

WW: Okay. I would ask you to have a look into new or even older geological and geographical literature. You'll find all these things precisely described in newly published literature and—

GH: Nowhere in the world—never mind the literature, books are books—but nowhere in the world, not a single place in the world will I find all these things together...because one thing's for sure, look at the publicity that this structure has attracted.

WW: Because you raised it.

GH: Actually, not me...it was—

WW: Together with others.

GH: —many other people...Worldwide it has attracted an enormous amount of publicity. I think it's a fair bet that if something comparable had been found, anywhere else on this planet of ours with its 70 percent cover by water, if something similar had been found, we would have heard about it by now. And it's the uniqueness of this structure and the series of structures along the south and east coasts of Yonaguni, that really leads me towards the involvement of man. Now I believe that the people who were involved in this, were a megalithic culture, they understood rock, and they worked just as currents and erosive forces do, that is they worked with the natural strike of the rock; where there is a fault, it's a good place, let's take advantage of it. Any great sculptor still looks for the natural forms in rock and, indeed, this is an art form in Japan up to this day. So, you know, these are all the factors that lead me to the conclusion that I'm looking at rock that has been overworked by people.

WW: And I would say, on the contrary, that it is a natural miracle...And just to finish that, my definite point of view is that all that we have seen in the last days could have been made by nature alone without the help of man. That does not mean that people did not have any influence on it. I didn't say that ... I would never say that. But I say it can have been shaped by nature alone.

OTHER MIRACLES

There are several other intriguing sites around Yonaguni that I was not able to show Wolf in the time available to us in March 2001—though I do not think any of them would have changed his mind.

One of these, which takes a form that some recognize as a huge rock-hewn sea turtle, stands at a depth of 12 meters on the shoulder of the main monument at Iseki Point approximately 150 meters east of the terraces.

A second, badly damaged when Yonaguni was struck by an unusually severe series of typhoons in August and September 2000,[24] is found half a kilometer due east of the terraces in about 15 meters of water. Consisting of a one-ton boulder mounted on a ten-centimeter-high flat platform at the apex of an enormous rocky slab almost three meters high, it has all the characteristics of a classic *iwakura* shrine, part natural rock, part man-made. As I noted in chapter 25,[25] if this shrine were to be moved to the slopes of Mount Miwa it would blend in seamlessly with what is already there.

Two other anomalous sites are located within half a kilometer of *Iseki Point*, that I would also very much have liked Wolf to see. One is the extraordinary "Stadium," a vast amphitheatre surrounding a stone plain at a depth of 30 meters. The other is a second area of very large steps—on a similar scale and of a similar appearance to those of the main terrace at Iseki Point—but much further out to sea, in deeper water, and at the bottom of a protected channel.

Nor does the list of signs and wonders end here, but I think the point has been sufficiently made. Some people with good minds—amongst them Japanese scientists with PhDs—are adamant that what they see underwater at Yonaguni are rock-hewn structures that have been worked upon by humans and purposefully arranged. Others with equally good minds and equally good PhDs are equally adamant that they see no rock-hewn structures underwater at Yonaguni at all—only rocks.

ROCKS? OR STRUCTURES?

Just interesting geology? Or discoveries that could fix the true origins of Japanese civilization as far back in the Age of the Gods as the Nihongi and the Kojiki themselves claim?

These are grave questions and they cannot be answered at Yonaguni on the basis of available evidence. Wolf is right about that. It is just possible that the remarkable structures and objects that I showed him there underwater are all freaks of nature, which by some amazing additional improbability all happen to be gathered together in one place.

I don't think that is what they are. And I repeat that the balance of first-hand scientific opinion is, at time of writing, two-to-one against Wichmann in this matter (Kimura and Sundaresh provide two clear votes for the structures having been overworked by man, Wichmann provides one clear vote in favor of the structures being entirely natural; Professor Schoch votes both ways).

In the future, other discoveries, and other diving scientists, could alter this balance of opinion dramatically in either direction. But we shall have to wait and see. Meanwhile, after a thorough exposure on-site to Wolf Wichmann's relentless empiricism I concede that I am not yet in a position to *prove* that humans were involved in the creation of the Yonaguni structures—any more than Wolf can prove, as he admits, that they were not.

But I believe Wolf came to his conclusions about Yonaguni sincerely, not too hastily, and on the basis of his own vast experience as a marine geologist of how different kinds of rock behave underwater. Although I disagree with him, I therefore resolved as we left the island in March 2001 that I would not base any argument or any claim in *Underworld* on the copious evidence which suggests that the submerged structures of Yonaguni are indeed ancient rock-hewn human sites... In this chapter I have simply tried to marshal and present that evidence, and Wolf's purposeful and eloquent counter views, as clearly and as objectively as possible, as a matter of public record.

For if the Jomon did make the great structures that were submerged off the south and east coasts of Yonaguni at the end of the ice age then we are confronted by a previously unexpected and as yet completely unexplained dimension of that increasingly remarkable ancient culture.

But suppose for a moment—an exercise in speculation only—that I and others *are* right about Yonaguni.

If so, then what Japan has lost to the rising seas is no small or insignificant matter, but a defining episode in world prehistory, going back more than 10,000 years. For if the Jomon did make the great structures that were submerged off the south and east coasts of Yonaguni at the end of the ice age then we are confronted by a previously unexpected and as yet completely unexplained dimension of that increasingly remarkable ancient culture. In terms of organization, effort, engineering and ambition, the sheer scale of the enterprise is beyond anything that the Jomon of 10,000 or 12,000 years ago (or any other human culture of that epoch) are thought to have been capable of. Yet it makes a strange kind of sense in context of the other incongruous characteristics of these strange "hunter-gatherers"—their permanent settlements, their stone circles, their cultivation of rice, and their navigational and maritime achievements in two different waves of settlement of the Americas (one as early as 15,000 years ago, one more like 5,000 years ago).

Wolf and I had just one more day of diving to do after Yonaguni, just one more day for me to find him a major structure in Japanese waters that he could not come up with a natural explanation for...

For that adventure, and test, I had chosen the great stone circles at Kerama.

1. Of *Underworld: The Mysterious Origins of Civilization*. —Ed.

2. Points 1–8 cited verbatim from Kimura, *Diving Survey Report for Submarine Ruins Off Japan*. p. 178.

3. Points 9–12, discussions with Professor Kimura cited in *Heaven's Mirror*. pp. 216–217.

4. See his contribution to my 1998 television series *Quest for the Lost Civilization*.

5. Graham Hancock, *Heaven's Mirror*. London: Penguin, 1999. p. 215–216.

6. Ibid., p. 217.

7. BBC2 Horizon, November 4, 1999.

8. Robert Schoch, *Voices of the Rocks*. New York: Harmony, 1999. p. 111–112.

9. Ibid., p. 112-113; *Heaven's Mirror*, p. 217–221.

10. Schoch, p. 112.

11. *Heaven's Mirror*.

12. Ibid.

13. *Der Spiegel*, 1999.

14. Sic—this is completely untrue; Schoch does not believe any such thing. —GH

15. Actually, I have *never* been in a submersible at Yonaguni and I do not consider my four years of hands-on diving there as any kind of excursion; there is, however, a clearly-defined path at the base of the monument. —GH

16. *Der Spiegel*, 1999.

17. In chapters one and 25 of *Underworld*. —Ed.

18. Hancock, personal communication, 2000.

19. www.grahamhancock.com

20. Interviewed by Tim Copestake for *Underworld* television series.

21. See chapter 25 of *Underworld*. —Ed.

22. Sundaresh report.

23. See chapter 25 in *Underworld*. —Ed.

24. The boulder was rolled to the side, half on and half off the platform.

25. Of *Underworld*. —Ed.

Martin Gray

SACRED GEOGRAPHY

COSMIC AND COMETARY INDUCED CATACLYSMS, AND THE MEGALITHIC RESPONSE

EARLY IN THE SPRING OF 1986, I began a yearlong pilgrimage around Europe by bicycle. Over four seasons I cycled through 11 countries to visit, study and photograph more than 135 holy places. In succeeding years I traveled to Europe several additional times, visiting other countries and their sacred sites. These travels took me to the sacred places of megalithic, Greek and Celtic cultures as well as to the pilgrimage sites of medieval and contemporary Christianity. For many thousands of years, our ancestors have been visiting and venerating the power places of Europe. One culture after another has often frequented the same power places. The story of how these magical places were discovered and used is filled with myths of cosmic- and cometary-induced world destroying cataclysms, astronomers and sages, and nature spirits and angels.

MISCONCEPTIONS ABOUT THE SO-CALLED ICE AGE AND ITS GLACIER COVERAGE

Before beginning our discussion of the megalithic use of power places in ancient Europe we should first correct a long-standing misconception regarding the cause of the transition between the Paleolithic and Neolithic eras. According to *conventional* beliefs (deriving from incorrect assumptions of the Uniformitarian theory of Charles Lyell and the ice age or glacial theory of Louis Agassiz in the early 1800s), enormous glaciers once covered vast regions of the northern hemisphere. These *conventional* beliefs state that the levels of the world's oceans were lower during the glacier age because of all the water supposedly frozen up in the polar ice cap. Between 13,000 and 8000 B.C., the vast glaciers melted and the levels of the world oceans rose by 120 meters. The effect of this glacial melting and sea level rise on archaic European life marked the end of the Paleolithic and the beginning of the Neolithic.

This idea of a so-called ice age, with enormous glaciers covering vast areas of the northern hemisphere, has conclusively and repeatedly been shown to be erroneous by numerous scientific studies in the fields of geology, paleontology, biology, zoology, climatology, anthropology and mythology.

This idea of a so-called ice age, with enormous glaciers covering vast areas of the northern hemisphere, has conclusively and repeatedly been shown to be erroneous by numerous scientific studies in the fields of geology, paleontology, biology, zoology, climatology, anthropology and mythology. Readers interested in learning more about these scientific studies and their revelations regarding the non-existence of the ice age and its glacier coverage will enjoy the book *Cataclysm: Compelling Evidence of a Cosmic Catastrophe in 9500 B.C.*, by Allan & Delair. The factual material presented in this scholarly book is slowly making its way into university courses and textbooks around the world and thereby rewriting our understanding of early Neolithic times.

COSMIC AND COMETARY-INDUCED CATACLYSMS IN 9500, 7640 AND 3150 B.C.

Prior to embarking on a discussion regarding the discovery and use of power places by humans during Neolithic times there is another—and critically important—matter that must be explored first. This concerns the pass-by and actual impact of cosmic and cometary objects at three distinct periods in the prehistoric past. To begin to explore this matter let us comment on the enigmatic writings of the Fourth Century B.C. Greek philosopher Plato. In the *Timaeus* dialogues, these being a record of discussions between a Greek statesman and an Egyptian priest, Plato reports the following:

Atlantic, the legendary Atlantis, which is said to have sunk beneath the waters following a planet-spanning cataclysm in an epoch 9,000 years before Plato. Until recently, the notion of a sunken continent was considered preposterous, yet recent geological, climatological, biological and oceano-graphic studies have conclusively shown that large landmasses did indeed exist in the Atlantic and other parts of the world in Paleolithic times.

Equally importantly, evidence has accumulated from a variety of scientific disciplines that demonstrates that a massive cosmic object (probably a portion of an astronomically-near supernova explosion) passed *close by* the earth in approximately 9500 B.C. This cosmic event caused a worldwide cataclysm of enormous proportions, including massive shifting of the earth's surface, devastating volcanic activity, mega-tsunami waves, subsidence of regional landmasses, and mass extinctions of both animals and humans (events spoken of in the Atlantis myths). In this regard it is vitally important to note that many of the geological and biological effects previously attributed to the hypothesized glacier movements of ice age times could *not* have been caused by the slow movement of ice but were, in fact, caused by the rapid and vast displacement of oceanic bodies of water (this

> Until recently, the notion of a sunken continent was considered preposterous, yet recent geological, climatological, biological and oceanographic studies have conclusively shown that large landmasses did indeed exist in the Atlantic and other parts of the world in Paleolithic times.

You Greeks are all children... you have no belief rooted in the old tradition and no knowledge hoary with age. And the reason is this. There have been and will be many different calamities to destroy mankind, the greatest of them by fire and water, lesser ones by countless other means... You remember only one deluge, though there have been many.

In his dialogues, *Critias* and *Timaeus*, Plato speaks of a large island empire situated in the middle

being caused by the irresistible gravitational pull of the enormous cosmic object passing by the earth). Additionally, the species-wide animal extinctions caused by this event occurred far beyond the geographical boundaries set for the "ice age glaciations" by orthodox theorists.

Einstein also studied the shifting of the earth's surface, termed crustal displacement by its primary theorist Charles Hapgood, who reported, "One can hardly doubt that significant shifts of the earth's crusts have taken place repeatedly and within a short time." Could the "earth's crust" so affected have been the Atlantis of the ancient myths? Many hundreds of carbon-14 dates obtained from laboratory measurements of botanical, zoological and geological samples found around the world have given an average date of 9500 B.C. for the onset of a terrible worldwide catastrophe. Why this is so relevant to the present discussion is that by adding 9,000 years to the 400 years separating Plato's time from the time of Christ and then adding both of these to the 2,000 years which have elapsed since then, gives another approximate date of 9500 B.C. for the continent-sinking cataclysm. A sobering matter is that the percentage decline of the global human population at the time of the 9500 B.C. event has been estimated to be as high as 80-90%.

According to the Egyptian priests that Plato's informant had spoken with, Atlantis was a prosperous and sophisticated civilization, advanced in science and in possession of knowledge concerning both the geography and *geomancy* of the entire earth. Geomancy may be defined as the discovery and mapping of power places on either regional or global scales. Accumulating evidence indicates that a mysterious, but now lost, ancient culture had mapped a planet-spanning grid of these terrestrial power points positioned with geometric regularity. This geomantic information, in various forms, later left its imprint on the sacred geographies of numerous other cultures. Globally occurring legends also tell of astronomer-sages who knew of grand celestial cycles, the existence of past cataclysms and the possibility of future ones. In anticipation of a coming cataclysm and the catastrophic effect it would have upon the earth, these astronomer-sages journeyed to particular geomantic locations around the planet, where they built temples which contained wisdom teachings and information about the past and future cataclysms. Some of these geomantic power places would become, thousands of years later, the sacred sites of megalithic and succeeding cultures. To read more about the cosmic object pass-by and the ensuing crustal displacement of 9500 B.C., refer to *Cataclysm* by D. S. Allan & J. B. Delair, *The Atlantis Blueprint* by Colin Wilson and Rand Flem-Ath, and *Catastrophobia* by Barbara Hand Clow.

Approximately 2,000 years later, in roughly 7640 B.C., a *cometary object* sped towards the earth. This time, however, rather than passing by the earth as the cosmic object of 9500 B.C. had done, the cometary object actually entered the atmosphere, broke into seven pieces, and impacted the earth at known locations on the planet's oceans. The following map shows the general location of each of the seven impacts.

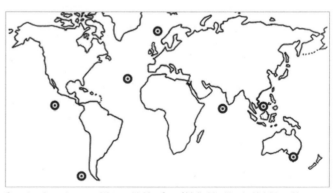

Cometary impacts around the world. Map from *Uriel's Machine* by Knight and Lomas.

Scientific studies of the effects of rapidly moving large objects impacting with the ocean surface have conclusively demonstrated that waves resulting from a massive cometary impact would attain vertical heights of two-three miles, with forward speeds of 400-500 miles per hour, and a sustained force that would carry them 2,000-3,000 miles in every direction radiating from the impact location. From the above map it is clear where these great waves would have crashed upon the shores of numerous continents, totally obliterating, especially in coastal areas of gently raising lands, all human settlements and any structures they had built.

consider, for the reason that orthodox archaeologists have long been mystified by both the relative scarcity of human remains from the period of 7500 B.C. to 3500 B.C. and, even more important, by the apparently sudden appearance of the highly developed civilizations of megalithic Europe and dynastic Egypt around 3100 B.C.

Finally, nearly 4,500 years later, in 3150 B.C., another cometary object smashed into the earth, this time in the eastern Mediterranean. The cataclysm caused by this cometary impact, with massive

---

Archaic myths from many parts of Europe (and around the world) refer to this event by mention of bright new stars that fell to earth as "seven flaming mountains," of how the oceans rose up in vast waves and totally engulfed the lands, and how summer was driven away with a cold darkness that lasted several years.

Archaic myths from many parts of Europe (and around the world) refer to this event by mention of bright new stars that fell to earth as "seven flaming mountains," of how the oceans rose up in vast waves and totally engulfed the lands, and how summer was driven away with a cold darkness that lasted several years. In support of the mythological accounts of the vast waves covering the lands it is important to mention that many of the highest mountains in England, Scotland and Ireland are littered with beds of sand and gravel containing sea shells deposited in the very recent geological past. Geology also gives irrefutable evidence that at two times in the recent past, around 7640 B.C. and 3100 B.C., there have been complete reversals of the earth's magnetic field caused by an *outside influence*, most probably a comet.

Estimates of the devastation of the global human population from this event range as high as 50-60% (many people would have lived on sea shores due to the availability of fish stocks). Therefore, the devastation of the planet's human population from the 9500 B.C. cosmic object pass-by compounded with that of the 7640 B.C. cometary impacts would have severely decreased the number of humans on earth during the following four thousand years. This is a crucial matter to

waves radiating outward in all directions from the location of the impact, devastated coastal civilizations all around the Mediterranean (for example, Dead Sea levels rose 300 feet at this time). While less destructive in a global sense than the seven cometary impacts of 7640 B.C., the 3150 B.C. impact gave rise to a large number of flood myths, such as those associated with Sodom and Gomorrah, and Noah's ark. Following this catastrophic event, the oldest societies with written records—Egypt, Mesopotamia and the Indus Valley—emerged without any cultural antecedents. Seemingly out of nowhere there rapidly appeared a uniform code of laws, the wheel and keen knowledge of astronomy.

It is certainly not a coincidence that these three centers of sophisticated culture emerged simultaneously in different geographic locations. Rather it is indicative of the "seeding" of advanced culture into these areas by a pre-impact civilization. Evidence presented in the book *Uriel's Machine* points to the likelihood that highly advanced astronomical and mathematical information was transferred from the early megalithic culture of northwestern Europe to the regions of both Egypt and Mesopotamia, whence it later influenced the sacred geography of the Greeks. In support of this matter, the Scottish Rite of Freemasonry (that which was in effect until 1813) speaks of the achievements of a pre-flood people, who were advanced in the sciences of mathematics and astronomy, who foresaw the coming of the flood, and who transferred this information to the early Egyptians. A Mediterranean account of an extraterrestrial impact also occurs in the *Sibylline Oracles*, which refer to a "star" falling into the sea and causing the rapid onset of a long period of winter temperatures. Additionally, the *Book of Enoch*, a part of the Dead Sea Scrolls, contains the tale of a man who had been warned about the effects of cometary impacts and taught survival skills by a people from the far northwest of Europe. Astronomical data in the *Book of Enoch* indicates latitude between 52 and 59 degrees north, the same general location as the astronomically advanced megalithic culture. Specific directions are also given in the *Book of Enoch* concerning how to build an astronomical observation device (a horizon declinometer or stone ring) that can be used to recreate calendars and thereby assist in the reestablishment of agriculture following a great flood.[1]

THE ORIGIN, DEVELOPMENT AND FUNCTION OF MEGALITHIC STRUCTURES

Anthropologists and archaeologists study the locations where ancient people first

began living in communities and theorize why these particular places were chosen as settlement sites. Conventional theories assume that sites were selected for agricultural, commercial or military purposes. While such explanations are plausible in many cases, they are not sufficient to explain the location of all early settlement sites. Extensive archaeological evidence indicates that many of humankind's earliest communal settlements had religious and scientific orientations and were chosen for those purposes with great care and precision. To understand this phenomenon, we must examine two matters: one, a relatively unknown characteristic of prehistoric people, which is their sensitivity to and knowledge of the energies of the living earth; and two, the astronomical observation abilities of certain prehistoric people which allowed them to predict and prepare for cosmic catastrophes.

> **Extensive archaeological evidence indicates that many of humankind's earliest communal settlements had religious and scientific orientations and were chosen for those purposes with great care and precision.**

During their movements across the lands, the Neolithic nomads discovered particular places of spirit and power in the form of caves, springs, hills and mountains. They also sensed lines of subtle energy crossing the land and specific points of more concentrated forces along those lines. These places of power were often marked with large cairns of stones. Identified and marked in this way, they could be seen from a distance even if their energetic qualities were too distant to be physically sensed. Over the thousands of years that early Neolithic peoples wandered across central and northern Europe, hundreds of these planetary power places were discovered and physically marked. Legends of these fabled sites were woven into cosmogenic myths from the Mediterranean to the Artic Seas.

Following the pre-Boreal and Boreal periods (9500-6500 B.C.) came the Atlantic period (6500-4000 B.C.) and the extraordinary innovations of plant domestication and animal husbandry. No longer was it necessary for people to wander the countryside in search of their food, now they could grow crops and rear livestock in a fixed place of their choice. The vitally important question is where did these early people first choose to settle? At this stage in Europe's prehistory the population was very small (remember the massive population decline caused by the cometary effects of 9500 and 7640 B.C.). There were no civilizations to feed necessitating cities near rich agricultural lands, no commercial activities requiring access to trade centers, and no requirements for strategic positions to hold off invading armies. There were simply not enough people for these things. Not having such settlement location requirements, what then were the primary factors influencing early peoples' choices for permanent dwelling sites?

The first people making the transition from the hunter/gatherer existence to a more settled life were the direct descendants of the nomadic wanderers who had discovered and marked the locations of the terrestrial power places. In searching for a settlement location, a previously nomadic family or group of families might often choose a place that held mythic significance for their ancestors, a place of spirit and power. These groups of families would grow into larger groups and then into clusters of groups, thus leading to the development of the earliest villages and towns. As these social centers developed around the ancient nomads' sacred sites, the physical structures marking the precise power point locations would be rebuilt and enlarged. Such reconstructions reflect an increased use of the power places by the growing local populations and, more importantly, an increased understanding of how best to use the energies emanating from the earth at these sites. Over many thousands of years these power places would come to serve as the pilgrimage locations of megalithic, Celtic, Greek and, finally, the Christian cultures.

The megalithic (meaning "great stone") culture, which is responsible for the stone rings, standing stones and chambered mounds of Europe, existed from roughly 4000 to 1500 B.C. Absolutely no written records exist from these times and therefore archaeologists make assumptions about the people based on excavations of their domestic, funerary, astronomical and ceremonial structures. Among a wide variety of these structures, we may distinguish four major types of stone structures with astronomical and ceremonial functions: single or grouped standing stones known as *menhirs*, rock chambers known as *dolmens*, enormous earthen mounds with passageways leading to rock cut chambers and the stunningly beautiful stone rings of which Stonehenge is the most famous example.

The great advances in understanding of the earth's subtle energies and the erection of the megalithic structures which harnessed those energies occurred during the Sub-Boreal period of 4000-1400 B.C. Europe's climate was warm during those years (warmer than today) and this encouraged increased agricultural productivity, an ensuing growth in population and the migration of members of this growing population into remote, previously unsettled regions of northern Europe. With these developments came a concurrent increase in commerce, scientific knowledge and, most importantly, the exchange of ideas between peoples of different geographic areas. To this exchange of ideas we may attribute the development of megalithic culture and the erection of great earthen and stone monuments at the power places which had been venerated as sacred sites since hunter-gatherer times.

While places sacred to ancient civilizations exist throughout the world and their locations are often well known, the sacred functions of the sites are rarely understood. It is easy to see why this is so. There is often a corollary between the extreme age of an archaeological site and the scarcity of information regarding the site's origins and initial function. The further back in time archaeologists look, the less they know. Because of this, explanations of a sacred site's initial and primary functions are often no more than theorizations based on records of the site's use in more recent times.

The difficulty in accurately determining the function of sacred sites is further compounded by the conceptual influences of the contemporary paradigm. Many archaeologists and historians, deeply conditioned (as nearly all Western people are) by the religious and materialistic paradigm of the so-called "post-modern" world, are unable to view ancient cultural behavior patterns in a clear and unbiased manner. Today's researchers seek to interpret ancient people, yet all too often do so with intellects programmed by scientific and psychological assumptions relevant only to contemporary times. This approach is bound to produce poor understandings. Basically, the perceptual and interpretive limitations imposed by our present culture's belief systems exemplify an age-old tendency of human beings to assume that they know more about life than their ancestors did. While this is certainly true with such matters as computer programming and aircraft design, it is not true in all areas of human knowledge and endeavor. Human beings develop skills and understandings uniquely appropriate to the environments and times in which they live. Ancient people, living in harmony with the earth and dependent upon its bounty for all their needs, had developed skills which modern people no longer use, cultivate or even recognize.

One early type of megalithic structure to be developed was the earth energy-harnessing device. While constructed in numerous different forms depending upon the geomorphic features of the land, the character of the power place emanation, and the style of local architecture, the energy-harnessing devices were designed and utilized to gather, concentrate and emanate the subtle energies of the power places for the benefit of human beings. In western and Mediterranean Europe, these energy-harnessing megalithic structures are found in three general forms: raised earthen mounds (presently called hilltop forts and burial barrows), rock cut chambers known as *dolmens* and single or grouped standing stones known as

Today's researchers seek to interpret ancient people, yet all too often do so with intellects programmed by scientific and psychological assumptions relevant only to contemporary times. This approach is bound to produce poor understandings.

Early settled people, like their nomadic hunter-gatherer ancestors, were sensitive to the natural creative energies of the earth. Living close to the land and intimately aware of the movement of celestial bodies, they came to notice a correspondence between the flow of the earth's subtle energies and the periodic movements of the sun, moon and stars. This harmonious balance between heaven and earth resulted in particular power places on the earth's surface being highly charged at equally particular times of different celestial cycles. Over the passage of many centuries, as the ebb and flow of the earth's subtle energies were recognized to mirror celestial cycles, various types of megalithic structures were developed at the power places. These different structure types were utilized to harness terrestrial and extraterrestrial energies, to observe astronomical movements in the interest of predicting the periodic increases of those energies, and to assist in the prediction of cosmic events such as future cometary impacts. While the structure types were different in form and function, they served one another and therefore are best understood in relation to one another.

menhirs and *dolmens*. Let us examine each of these individually.

Conventional historical interpretations of the flattened hilltops in Britain (many with coiled circles and huge earthen mazes surrounding their tops) surmise that they were hill forts or castle foundations. Though it is true that many were used in this manner during the Iron Age, and later by the Romans and Saxons, their original use was certainly not defensive. As forts they are indefensible. Most have numerous gaps in their earthen work walls, they are so large as to require thousands of people to defend their periphery, and they were often inconveniently placed for long-term human habitation. Archaeological excavations at these sites reveal implements of construction, such as antler picks and stone axes, but rarely the artifacts of large-scale settlements such as pottery and dwelling remains. Were these places used as habitation centers or sacred sites? Accumulating evidence seems to indicate sacred, rather than secular, usage.

Another puzzling form of earthen mound is the so-called "burial barrow" or "burial mound," well known examples being located at Newgrange, Knowth, Dowth and Loughcrew in Ireland. Because burial remains have been found within some—and only a very few—of these structures, it has been assumed by the orthodox school of archaeology that their purpose was for interring the dead. If this were so, why then are the mounds so large (hundreds of feet in diameter) yet with so few burials (two-ten)? Why are there so few skeletons over such long periods of use (1,000-2,000 years)? Why are there so few trappings of wealth and power, as is found in the burial remains of later Bronze and Iron Age tombs? Why are the carbon-14 dates of the rare burial remains much later than the carbon-14 dates for the implements used in the mounds' construction? And, most mysteriously, why are the entrance portals and passageways leading to the mound interiors in absolutely precise alignment with the horizon appearance or disappearance of such celestial events as the solstices, equinoxes, lunar standstill dates and the appearance of particular stars? Conventional archaeology is unable to answer these questions and therefore disregards them almost completely. In actuality these massive earthen structures were subtle energy-concentrating chambers that ancient people initially used for healing and spiritual purposes. Later peoples, knowing the eternal nature of the human spirit, buried their dead within these chambers in the hopes that the dead person's spirit might have a more rapid journey to the realm of universal spirit. Still later people, having no understanding of either universal human energies, used these mounds as they were convenient, already excavated chambers, suitable for disposal of the dead.

northern Scotland. Very rarely found with burial remains and often located far from any evidences of ancient habitation sites, dolmen structures—by the very difficulty of their construction—indicate a powerful purpose. Extraordinary work forces were needed to erect a dolmen's supporting stones and to place the tabletop stones upon them. With primitive levers and ropes, three or four strong people are required to move a one ton stone, thus the 50 ton cap stones of certain dolmens would require 100-200 persons to move them. Many of these megaliths were erected upon high and remote plateaus and were fashioned from stones that were quarried hundreds of miles away. Moving stones up even small inclines requires the number of workers to be increased by a factor of five. Such enormous effort points to the great importance of the dolmens to megalithic people. Often erected directly over power points along the earth's meridian lines, the dolmen megaliths served to tap terrestrial energies for the benefit of human beings.

Another fascinating thing to know about many of the dolmens is that they were originally entirely covered by alternating layers of organic and inorganic materials. While the purpose of this construction technique is presently unknown, it is interesting to note that the psychoanalyst Wilhelm Reich used the same technique in the construction of his *orgone* generators, these being (much smaller) devices that were able to generate, concentrate and radiate a mysterious form of energy. Could the ancient builders of the dolmens have been using their unique construction techniques for a similar

Many of these megaliths were erected upon high and remote plateaus and were fashioned from stones that were quarried hundreds of miles away.

Another enigmatic class of megalithic structure is the *dolmen* or "table-stone" (dol=table, men =stone). Dolmens normally consist of two to four enormous slabs of stone (often weighing several tons each) supporting even larger roof stones. Dolmens—or as they are called in other ancient European languages, *quoits* and *cromlechs*—are scattered throughout the European countryside from the Iberian Peninsula to the remote islands of

purpose? Orthodox archaeologists commonly assume these dolmen structures were used for funerary purposes because burials have been found in a small number of them (a very small number!). It is important to note, however, that the scientific dating of the burial remains shows them to be hundreds or thousands of years more recent than the structures themselves, thus casting serious doubt on the tomb theory.

Many of these solitary standing stones have odd symbols, spirals and map-like images carved upon their surfaces. Conventional archaeologists often interpret these as mere ornamental designs, yet a worldwide study of such markings will reveal their similarities to rock carvings in Australia, South America, Africa and India.

Equally enigmatic are the megalithic structures called *menhirs*. While it is true that some of these single or grouped standing stones are outlying parts of the (soon to be discussed) megalithic astronomical observatories, the vast majority of menhirs are solitary needles of stone with no proximity to other structures. Ranging in height from two feet to over 30 feet, the menhir stones were presumably utilized by ancient people as both location-marking stones and as emanating devices for power place energies. In remote areas of Europe, yet untouched by the land-grabbing onrush of modern civilization, menhirs may still be found, placed every few miles along dowsable energy lines leading to stone rings, dolmens and other ancient sacred sites. Many of these solitary standing stones have odd symbols, spirals and map-like images carved upon their surfaces. Conventional archaeologists often interpret these as mere ornamental designs, yet a worldwide study of such markings will reveal their similarities to rock carvings in Australia, South America, Africa and India. The map-like images are perhaps actual maps, showing—according to the topographical methods of the ancient cultures—locations of other power places in the adjacent regions. Some scholars suggest that they may have been part of a vast sacred geography, long since ruined, while dowsers report that the solitary standing stones are situated to mark points of concentrated earth energies flowing along the lines between these sites (sometimes called ley lines). The strange spirals and whirling patterns are thought by some researchers to be graphic representations of the power point's vibratory characteristics as determined by oscillating pendulums.

Another fascinating type of megalithic structure to be developed was the astronomical observatory form such as the stone rings and ellipses—for example Stonehenge, and Avebury in England—and the grid pattern stone arrangements such as that of Carnac in France. Erected some time after the first dolmens and menhirs (according to our current knowledge), the astronomical observatory type of megalithic structure mirrored ancient peoples' recognition of the periodic increase of power place energies, their knowledge of the celestial cycles which influenced those energetic periods, and their attempts to astronomically predict them. Additionally, and for this understanding we have *Uriel's Machine* to thank, certain of the megalithic astronomical observatories that were used to predict (and thereby prepare for) the future occurrence of cosmic catastrophes such as cometary and meteoric impacts.

In comparison to the number of menhirs and dolmens at the power places, there are relatively few astronomical observatories. This may perhaps be explained by suggesting that sophisticated astronomical observatories were only erected at power places with major energetic emanations or at power places near social centers. In addition, it may be theorized that there were once more stone rings and grid pattern celestial observatories at the power places but that they have disappeared due to both natural and human causes. Climate changes have caused vegetation to grow over and hide some stone rings (such as occurred with the peat moss growth at the Scottish site of Callanish), other stone rings were torn down when Christianity sought to eradicate paganism from Europe, and still others were dismantled to provide building materials for more recent cultures. This dismantling of stone rings would have occurred most frequently in areas of greater population. Throughout the remote, mostly uninhabited moors and hills of the British Isles, over 900 stone rings are known to exist. In more populated continental Europe, they are far fewer in number and those mentioned in Nineteenth Century Swiss and Italian antiquarian guidebooks no longer exist.

The best known of the megalithic structures are certainly the stone rings, particularly Stonehenge and Avebury in England. Research conducted over the past 30 years, combining insights from archaeoastronomy, mythology and geophysical energy monitoring, has conclusively demonstrated that the stone rings functioned as both astronomical observation devices and ceremonial centers. Simply stated, many of the stone rings are situated at locations with measurable geophysical anomalies (so-called "earth energies"); these earth energies

mathematical sophistication that allowed their construction. The early recognition of certain megalithic constructions as astronomical observatories is almost single-handedly the accomplishment of Dr. Alexander Thom, professor emeritus of engineering science at Oxford University. In 1934, Thom began meticulously surveying megalithic sites. By 1954, he had surveyed and analyzed over 600 sites in Britain and France and begun to publish his findings. Initially his discoveries were not well received. Professor Thom was not an archaeologist, but rather an engineer, and the archaeological community did not welcome what they considered to be the heretical views of an "untrained" outsider.

> **The early recognition of certain megalithic constructions as astronomical observatories is almost single-handedly the accomplishment of Dr. Alexander Thom, professor emeritus of engineering science at Oxford University.**

seem to fluctuate in radiant intensity according to the cyclic influences of different celestial bodies (primarily the sun and moon but also the planets and stars); the architecture of the stone rings was engineered to observationally determine (by horizon astronomy) those particular periods of increased energetic potency at the sites; and those periods were then used by people for a variety of therapeutic, spiritual and oracular purposes. The tradition of pilgrimage in megalithic times thereby consisted of people traveling long distances to visit sites known to have specific powers. Due to the absence of historical documentation from the megalithic age it is often assumed that we cannot know how different power places were used, but this is a narrow view based solely on the mechanistic rationality of modern science. An enlargement of view to include an analysis of mythology will reveal that the legends and myths of sacred sites are in fact *metaphors* indicating the magical powers of the places. The ancient stories of the sacred sites and their deities and spirits will tell you how the places may still influence you today.

Only during the last 40 years have archaeologists begun to acknowledge the astronomical orientations of European megaliths and the extraordinary

Thom's evidence, however, could not be dismissed. Both overwhelming in quantity and painstakingly accurate in presentation, the evidence undisputedly demonstrated the phenomenal astronomical knowledge, mathematical understanding and engineering ability of ancient megalithic people. Indeed, these abilities were so advanced that they were not equaled by another European culture for over 4,000 years. Thom's excellent books, *Megalithic Sites in Britain* and *Megalithic Lunar Observatories*, show with eloquent certainty that megalithic astronomers knew the yearly cycle to be a quarter of a day longer than a round figure and that they recognized the precession of the equinoxes, the 9.3 year major and minor standstill cycles of the moon, and the lunar perturbation cycle of 173.3 days which allowed them to accurately predict eclipses. Furthermore, these megalithic builders were extraordinarily keen engineers and architects expert in advanced geometry 2,000 years before Euclid recorded the Pythagorean triangle theorems, and over 3,000 years before the value of pi (3.14) was "discovered" by Indian mathematicians. Surveying sites with the accuracy of a modern theodolite, these ancient builders developed a unit of measure, the megalithic yard of 2.72 feet, which they used in stone monuments from northern Scotland to Spain with an accuracy of +/ - .003 feet, or about 1/200th of an inch. Following the leadership established by Alexander Thom, the English scholars John Michell and Robin Heath have gone on to demonstrate even more of the brilliance of megalithic mathematicians and engineers.

Previous to Alexander Thom's site surveys and their indisputable proof of megalithic culture's advanced scientific knowledge and social cohesiveness, archaeologists had always assumed Europe's prehistoric Inhabitants to be a rough gathering of ignorant barbarians. Thom's discoveries, in showing this belief to be completely untenable, had a revolutionary, albeit gradual, impact upon the orthodox archaeological community. During the same period that Thom was surveying the megalithic sites, other scientists were having an equally revolutionary effect upon the European archaeological community, but from an entirely different direction. Like the engineer Thom, these scientists were not archaeologists, yet their contributions, coupled with the implications of Thom's site surveys, would instigate a complete rewriting of European pre-history.

This other revolution in the European archaeological community was caused by the discovery of carbon-14 dating by Willard F. Libby in 1949 and the dendrochronological recalibration of this method by Hans E. Suess in 1967. Basically, carbon-14 testing, in conjunction with dendrochronology, or tree ring dating, is an absolutely accurate method of dating ancient organic matter and, by extension, the archaeological sites where that matter was found. To understand why these dating methods caused such a revolution in archaeological thinking, it is helpful to know how the archaeological community viewed the subject of European pre-history prior to Libby's carbon-14 discovery in 1949.

Archaeology is a relatively recent scientific endeavor. During the entire course of its academic development, it has been powerfully influenced by the assumption that worldwide cultures "diffused" from a few primary centers of original civilization. For more than a century, pre-historians had assumed that most of the major cultural advances in ancient Europe were the result of a diffusion of influences from the great early civilizations of Egypt and Mesopotamia. These cultures could be dated by actual historic records, for both the Sumerians and the Egyptians had left lists of kings and dynasties going back to 2000 and 3000 B.C., respectively. Given these dates, and assuming an appropriate period of time for the diffusion of ideas from Egypt and Mesopotamia to northern Europe, it was calculated that Europe's megalithic structures could have been built no earlier than 1000 to 500 B.C. Imagine the surprise and, at first, strident disbelief of the archaeological community when megalithic construction dates of 4000 to 2000 B.C. were

The stone monuments of Europe were suddenly a thousand years older than those previously believed the "world's oldest stone monuments," the Egyptian pyramids.

factually established. The stone monuments of Europe were suddenly a thousand years older than those previously believed the "world's oldest stone monuments," the Egyptian pyramids.

Carbon-14 dating had thus effectively and totally undermined the diffusionist theories as suitable explanations for the development of Europe's megalithic culture. This accurate archaeological dating technique, in conjunction with Thom's site surveys, demonstrated with irrefutable certainty that megalithic culture was indigenous to Europe, that it had developed wholly on its own (though perhaps with a mysterious Atlantean influence), and that it was the most scientifically advanced culture in the world during the long ago time of 4000 to 2000 B.C.

As with the megalithic people before them, the Celts believed different types of landscape forms were inhabited or guarded by specific deities.

As mentioned previously, each specific power place is unique by virtue of both its location and its energetic emanation. Certain power places were noted by ancient people as having energetic emanations that were influenced by particular astronomical cycles. The astronomical observatories erected at these power places were designed in such a manner as to be oriented toward the celestial body or bodies that influenced their power place emanations. While there were similarities in astronomical orientations between various observatories, there were no constant alignment patterns used, as each power place was unique in both its earth surface location and its astronomical correspondence point. The energy link between these two unique points, planetary and celestial, produced a subtle energy emanation unlike any other place upon the earth. As these energy emanations varied from place to place, so also did the type of structures that were erected to study the periodic changes in emanation of the earth energies.

Another reason for the megalithic astronomical observatories' diversity in structural size and complexity is human innovation and the effect it may have upon the development of scientific endeavors. As previously stated, the earliest megalithic structures at the power places were the more simple energy-harnessing devices. These were followed by the observatories that megalithic people utilized to predict the periodic increases of subtle energy emanations at the power places. It is known from extensive archaeological evidence that the first rings and ellipses were constructed of wooden poles and only later, often after periods of a thousand or more years, reconstructed with stones. It is also known (and for this Stonehenge is the primary example) that the stone rings themselves went through stages of development in both size and structural complexity. These size and structural changes certainly indicate a greater understanding of planetary and celestial energy correspondences as they relate to the power places, yet they also seem to indicate the increasingly scientific use of the rings as contrasted to their initial sacred use. Contemporary astronomers seek to build ever more powerful optical and radio telescopes. Is there any reason to doubt that ancient astronomers felt these same desires for more precise observational tools and thus developed their design?

Another vitally important, though currently little understood, function of the megalithic astronomical observatories, in particular the stone rings, was to predict, in advance of their occurrence, the arrival of and impact by cometary and meteoric objects, such as had occurred in 9600 B.C. and 7640 B.C. As explained in *Uriel's Machine*, the stone rings found in different parts of northern Europe have different arrangements and alignments of stones, dependant upon the latitude and longitude of the site, which allow them to precisely observe the movements of celestial bodies along the horizon and thereby gauge the long-term passage of time. Myths and legends traceable to periods of the early Neolithic seem to indicate that a mysterious group of "astronomer-sages" knew of the periodicity of cometary objects and their potentially lethal effect upon the planet. Authors Knight and Lomas in *Uriel's Machine* make a convincing case that the stone rings of megalithic times were used as both calendrical indicators and cometary prediction devices in service to mankind.

CELTIC EARTH-BASED SPIRITUALITY

Thousands of years after the decline of megalithic culture came the Celtic age with its Druid spirituality. It is now widely accepted that Druid spirituality derives in part from pre-Celtic (for example, megalithic) traditions of far western Europe, which impressed the invading Celts to the extent that they adopted some of these traditions when they settled among the earlier-established tribes.

In other words, the pre-Celtic traditions influenced existing Celtic practices resulting in what is now commonly called Celtic Druidism. In support of this, it is interesting to note that Julius Caesar reported that Druidism began in the British Isles and was only later exported to Gaul.

Contrary to popular belief (and the historically inaccurate writings of various New Age novelists), the Celts neither used the stone temples of the earlier megalithic peoples nor continued their style of ceremonial architecture. Stonehenge, for example, was constructed between 2800 and 2000 B.C., while the Celts did not enter England until 600 B.C., fully 1,400 years later. Not using the stone rings and chambered mounds, Celtic spirituality was instead concentrated at unadorned natural sites such as mineral springs and waterfalls, caverns and remote islands, curiously shaped peaks and forest groves. In Celtic spirituality the entire landscape was in fact filled with places where spirit was present. This spirit of place or *anima loci* was understood to be the essential personality of a location and the spirit places were transformed into sacred sites when humans discovered and acknowledged them.

As with the megalithic people before them, the Celts believed different types of landscape forms were inhabited or guarded by specific deities. Sacred forest groves, called *nemetoi*, meaning "clearings open to the sky" were dedicated to various goddesses such as Andraste, Belesama and Arnemetia. Mountains served as altars for deities, sites of divine power and places for seeking inspiration. Towering peaks were seen as abodes of masculine deities such as Daghda, the father god, and Poeninus, while various hills, the breasts of the goddess, were recognized to be the sanctuaries of Ana, the Celtic mother of the Gods, and Brigid. Caves, believed to be entrances to the underworld or the fairy kingdom, were used for seeking visions and for communication with the depths of the psychic unconscious. Strangely shaped trees and rocks were considered the resting places of elemental spirits, fairies and supernatural beings. Celtic people made pilgrimages to all these types of sacred places, leaving offerings of cloth, amulets and food for the resident deities, thereby seeking the archetypal spiritual qualities of the places and praying for both physical and psychic healing.

CONCLUSIONS AND A CALL FOR FURTHER STUDIES

From the preceding discussion it is apparent that there are several possible explanations for the original discovery of the power places of Europe: the archaic Neolithic nomads, the astronomer sages of the mysterious culture of Atlantis and the early megalithic culture. The sites found and marked by these extremely ancient people continued to be used for thousands of years and became in time the sacred sites and pilgrimage places of other cultures such as the Celtic and ancient Greek. Myths originating from these later cultural epochs speak of the power places as being the abodes of deities, the haunts of magical beings and the enchanted domains of elemental spirits. The pilgrimage traditions of the Celtic and Greek cultures are markedly different in external form but in essence each may by understood as an expression of early peoples' connection to and worship of the living earth.

Myths originating from these later cultural epochs speak of the power places as being the abodes of deities, the haunts of magical beings and the enchanted domains of elemental spirits.

Through countless years and cultural expressions, human beings have made pilgrimages across Europe, drawn by the spiritual magnetism of the power places. Different religions and their assorted temples have risen and fallen; yet the power places remain ever strong. Still beckoning pilgrims in our own deeply troubled times, these holy sites offer a plentitude of gifts for body, mind and spirit. Take the time to go on a pilgrimage to the sacred places of ancient Europe. Inspiration and health, wisdom and peace—these and other qualities are freely and abundantly given there by the enchanted earth.

1. To read more about the seven cometary impacts of 7640 B.C. and the early megalithic responses to them, refer to Christopher Knight and Robert Lomas, Uriel's Machine. Gloucester: Fair Winds, 2001.

George Erikson with Ivar Zapp

ATLANTIS IN AMERICA:

A SUMMING UP—AWAITING THE NEW PARADIGM

WE LIVE AT A CRITICAL TIME in the history of human thought and endeavor. Mankind's cherished inventions have dramatically extended a common aggressive ape's grasp of the world. They have brought us great riches: Jet-travel, nuclear energy, telecommunications, hair spray, air-conditioning and gas-guzzling SUVs, to name a few. They have also threatened our world's existence. When we are confronted with the knowledge that our marvelous inventions are killing our lakes, rivers and seas, as well as the protective ozone layer of our atmosphere that has made life on earth possible and fruitful, we seem to take the attitude that the same sciences that have made us materially rich will also furnish remedies to the destruction of our ecosystem.

When we see pictures of sharks consuming their prey, even striking and eating each other in a blind frenzy, we gasp and shudder at their ferocity. When we learn that 50 percent of Indonesia's rain forests have been burned away in just the past 30 years to make way for the planting of industrial crops such as palm trees, we simply sigh. Worldwide, if present rates of deforestation continue, all tropical forests will be cleared in just 173 years. Over 60 percent of the 250,000 known plant species, the source of most of our known medicines, and innumerable insect and animal species will disappear with them. One view, perhaps the common one, holds that Man must reap his harvests, realize his profits and assert his dominance. Another view realizes that we have become locked into our own heightened feeding frenzy—one that is consuming the bounty of the earth that we only pretend to hold dear. While many view man's current place in history as a crest, others call our century of unprecedented warfare and genocide a mere episode in an extended trough of ignorance. Which view is most intelligent? What is the truth? How are we to know the way to proceed into an uncertain, if not terminal, future?

We suggest that man has not always behaved solely as the opportunistic descendant of an aggressive ape—that he has acted from motivations inspired by those lacking, even rejecting, the aggressive imperative as well. Could there have been a Golden Age when "higher" motivations were embraced? When told there was a more harmonious time on earth, most of us laugh. Hasn't survival of the fittest always been the rule? Are we not now at the pinnacle of achievement? A simplistic view would tell us so. And scientists and those in authority of church and state have insisted on it. But the truth appears to be that the history of life more resembles a complex, multi-branched tree than a linear ladder of progress. In defiance of an interrelationship with the greater cosmos,

> We suggest that man has not always behaved solely as the opportunistic descendant of an aggressive ape—that he has acted from motivations inspired by those lacking, even rejecting, the aggressive imperative as well. Could there have been a Golden Age when "higher" motivations were embraced?

and in a willful use and misuse of all other biological life, has mankind positioned himself out of the mainstream of cosmic purpose? Have we, through continual destruction of the ecosystem that sustains all life, ventured too far out on our particular and arrogant limb at the expense of the body of the tree of life?

Our work is, in part, about the Golden Age, an age first[1] evident in expression of great art 33,000 years ago, and its apparent destruction around 12,000 years ago. In this long-enduring Golden Age, despite the limited availability of land, warfare was almost unknown. Ships, canoes and rafts of many descriptions freely roamed the world, rarely encountering anything more than an occasional battle. Perhaps because the effects of the ice ages rendered much of the earth frozen and most of the rest very dry and barely inhabitable, the occupation of territory may have occurred only rarely. Thus, what wars there were must have been occasioned by grudges, trade wars or (if we believe Homer), the occasional abduction of women, and not in order to possess land.

Plato wrote of these more noble people of the Golden Age, who he regarded as great lawgivers, architects, navigators and astronomers. He also wrote of their final destruction caused in part by their own arrogance, in part by the fine military defenses of his Grecian ancestors, but in most part by a catastrophe that was beyond remedy. In Plato's rendering, and in many other legendary tellings, these people were called Atlanteans. They were described as fruitful, intelligent and capable of living in harmony with the earth and with their perceived notion of the greater cosmos. Yet they became flawed. In Plato's words, "Atlantis became too proud and warred against the whole of the Mediterranean."

If the Greek record is correct, the Atlanteans met a just end. They fell out of balance with the harmony of the universe. Atlantis, once the paradigm of Harmony, became a metaphor for all nations bent on subjugating other nations. They perished almost without a trace, almost without a memory. But, was the downfall of Atlantis brought on by its own arrogance, or was Atlantis simply a victim of being in a particular place in geography and in a particular, terribly fateful time? Was Atlantis destroyed by the force of the arrival of another heavenly body? Was it coincidence that Atlantis disappeared in the same fashion and the same geologic moment that the mammoths, saber-toothed tigers and North American *Equus conversidens* horse disappeared... just as the dinosaurs had perished millennia before, in a sudden celestial event beyond their power to withstand? We now have a record of only a few of these events of destruction over millennia. However, we can be certain that there are many more records to be revealed, which recently interested minds are finding worthy of discovering. The search has only just begun. We must finally discard the doctrine of a recent and pagan beginning to civilization—a dogmatic paradigm that has directed and controlled scholarship and, hence, the advancement of our understanding of ourselves and our past simply because it is the only view that has been acceptable to the Church, as well as to the traditional "authorities" in government and academia, who "oddly" have furthered Church dogma in the name of science. Further, we must renounce the Darwinian imperative that "catastrophism" was a myth devised by primitives, and that we remain "out of context" until we shed the stranglehold of religious dogma and Darwinian precepts and subsequent theories.

Why is the knowledge of the Atlanteans and of the Golden Age important? It is our belief that the Golden Age did not end with the physical destruction of Atlantis, or with the deluge that engulfed the world 12,000 years ago. Mankind, though rendered few in numbers, survived, and slowly began to rebuild civilization. In this time man's re-emergence had another friend—the nature of earth itself had become warm and moist. Corn, wheat and plants of every nature could be sown and developed, not just on the thin coastlines of the equatorial belt but almost anywhere. For the first time in the history of man land, not the sea, was the giver of life. Sustained by myth, man's purpose found expression again in a new Golden Age that developed along inland river valleys in Sumer and Egypt and in the interconnected canals of Mesoamerica 5,000 years ago. In this more recent Golden Age, pyramid builders in Egypt, Sumer and throughout the Americas re-established culture, mathematics and pathways to the gods.

Our current academic renderings demand that dates for the re-emergence of civilization fit a linear timetable. We have demonstrated that they do not. The limbs of the tree of all life have sprouted, prospered and withered, by methods and causes we do not fully understand. Man's cultural history has taken a similar path. As we have seen, the dates archaeologists have assigned to "classic Mayan" civilization—ranging from Copan in Honduras to Uxmal in the Yucatán—are surely *more recent* than the pyramids of Sumer and Egypt. We have also seen that significant sites in the Americas—the Kalasasaya Temple, Tiahuanacu's celestial observatory in Bolivia, Sacsayhuaman in Peru and the spheres of Costa Rica—all *predate* Sumer and Egypt when measured by the newly found science of archaeoastronomy. Hancock and Bauval's investigation of ancient Egypt, by similar methods, places the construction of the Great Pyramid of Giza at 12,000 years ago—a date that differs sharply with Egyptology's version of the traditional rise of civilization in Egypt—but that corresponds to the earliest maritime sites in America.

What are we able to make and to understand of our temple-building ancestors? They did not share the same culture, the same geographical location, or always the same time frame—some cultures arose millennia before others, some died out while others continued to flourish. Yet they were all inhabitants of a similar world of understanding. They shared a worldview—they were believers of myth and meaning. And they were children, survivors, of disaster. It doesn't matter that their building efforts spanned thousands of years, continents and oceans. The worldview that created and sustained them was continuous. They clearly understood its mission that centered on a central theme—the rebuilding of Atlantis!

Like the creation of step-pyramids, similar means of recreating and measuring heavenly movements through sighting stones and spheres and in vast stone temples, reflecting precise mathematical and geometric equations, did not occur by accident, nor did they occur by Neo-Darwinian necessity for parallel development. When we look at their record, the similarities go beyond coincidence. They had to have occurred by *contact*. Sumer, Egypt and Mesoamerica could not have been connected by primitive hunting tribes that took hundreds of thousands of years to cross Beringia. (The "Beringia Paradigm" must be reassessed, *or simply discarded*.) They had to have been connected by the warm and constant sea-lanes.

When did this significant contact end? When did the Golden Age come to a close? How did a sophisticated mathematical worldview known to the ancient temple builders of Egypt and Sumer and later expressed by Plato and Pythagoras suddenly cease to exist? Again the dates elude a linear timetable. While an astronomical civilization flourished in the Americas and throughout the Pacific, this knowledge died out in the Mediterranean and European world. The link to the recipient cultures of Atlantis ended, for the most part, in 1000 B.C., with the dawning of the terrible Age of Iron. At that time, iron replaced bronze in tools of construction as well as tools of destruction. Carvings in stone, and the permanence it offered were replaced by the discovery and smelting of the new and harder metal. Iron, once discovered, was found everywhere. Commercially, excursions to the Americas, despite the Phoenicians and the occasional accidental Roman voyage, were no longer needed. A Mediterranean worldview that retained communication with the greater world—despite Pythagoras, despite Solon and despite Plato—effectively came to an end.

The concept that civilization took root and hold only in the Mediterranean and only within the parameters of the Eurocentric view must be abandoned. While the Mediterranean world rose in military power, but declined in ancient knowledge, its recipient cultures in Europe fell to feudal wars and to gross atrocities. Meanwhile, Mesoamerican city-states stood open to each other, built without walls, without protective barriers, so that any man or band of men could enter another city without having to overcome moats, bastions, catapults or burning oil. Yet it is the Eurocentric view of history, aided by conquests and the burning of libraries, that now dominates.

The message of true history is that Atlantis was recreated not once, but that in response to myth, its recreation was attempted numerous times. So many experts over the last hundred years, bogged down in miniscule (yet important) diggings, have simply not gotten this vital point. When Twentieth Century archaeologists encountered American sites that reflected the harmony in composition of the ideal cities Plato once described, they simply failed to grasp the message of what they were encountering. To truly rediscover our past, the light of civilization must turn its focus again on Mesoamerica and on that continuation of ideas, astronomical and navigational, long forgotten in the "Old World."

Most of Mesoamerica itself was already long in decline when the Fifteenth and Sixteenth Century Europeans brought a wave of warfare, disease and ignorance. Yet traditional archaeologists have repeatedly focused their attention exclusively on the most recent pre-Columbian cultures of Mesoamerica and their constructions, which, most often, are inferior repetition of more ancient structures. They have misunderstood and even failed to question the *purpose and function* of these structures. *National Geographic* magazine and a host of other periodicals seem content to call great astronomical structures "ceremonial centers" and to emphasize a tabloid-like glee in reporting pagan sacrifices and massive bloodletting. However, the bloodletting they so vividly and repeatedly describe had really only become widespread long after the original temple builders had been usurped by Toltecs, Aztecs and decadent Maya, such as the painters of Bonampak—all very recent players in the long history and drama of the Americas. These scientists and their funding journals simply have not understood the message of history recorded in stone. The perpetuated message, as concocted by priests and historians of the Spanish Inquisition, is that the Americans, despite their great achievements, must be viewed as "enlightened but savage pagans." What a natural cataclysm began, the physical destruction of the "Golden Age," the Church of the Inquisition and the Eurocentric mind sought to finish—through the destruction and suppression of the historic record of a civilization obviously far older than their own. This suppression continues today from some unlikely sources in a supposedly liberal and "enlightened" society.

Homo sapiens have long been an intelligent and inter-connected species. But why has the obvious so long escaped intelligent minds? It is not because he has not been looking, nor because he has been looking in the wrong places. Though most are still untouched, many of the known sites of Mesoamerica, with astronomical, archaeological and calendrical implications, have been studied, but only in a manner biased to *land-based peoples*. Naval implications have been ignored. Their antiquity has been little understood.

It has only been in the past year (1997) that leading academics have acknowledged that Monte Verde in southern Chile significantly predates the impossible Inquisition-inspired theory of Beringia migration. The ivy walls of academic intransigence have begun to crack and crumble. But a host of early maritime cultures in the Americas, including the culture demonstrated by the great spheres of Costa Rica, are still regarded as "enigmas" or "out of context." We are only at the beginning of rediscovering our past. And if there is cause for optimism there is also considerable cause for alarm. Ancient sites are still being plundered, now at a rate that exceeds any time in the past. Others are being bulldozed over in the name of progress. Precious underwater sites are being dynamited, sometimes by relatively innocent and impoverished fishermen but just as often by looters. As the record of the past is destroyed so are the hopes for our future.

It is not a nostalgic desire to understand our past that drives us to discover the true history of a Golden Age, and its aftermath. The importance of the great sites of Mesoamerica lies in their displayed continuation of contact with the concepts of Atlantis. We are a product of our past, and that past has been written in stone. Atlantis began to fully flourish again in the Americas, over five thousand years ago. It is the certain knowledge that unless we rediscover this harmony with the universe we are fated to repeat true history's repeated lesson—that arrogance and abuse of power lead to destruction.

When was the Golden Age? Does the exact date matter if we know, intuitively, and from the evidence in stone, that builders and rebuilders of that era persisted and endured? Who shall we believe, the makers of myth whose tales stood unquestioned and unchanged for millenniums, or modern archaeology, forced for years to redefine theories and recount dates? In understanding Atlantis, we can begin to know that there were cultures advanced beyond our own, not in material achievements, but in a sense, and in a "technology" that reflected that sense, of a oneness with the universe. For their serpent gods did fly in a place in time and beyond time, concepts we can only marvel at.

An understanding of the true relevance of the harmonizing astronomical and mathematical sites of the Americas continues to elude us. The true message of history is that from the time of the last great destruction to the still existent knowledge of the shamans of Mesoamerica, wise men have constantly viewed and recorded the movements of the stars. And they have believed that the stars described their destiny. The long held view that comets were omens of celestial disturbance (anger of the gods) is no longer laughable. Chaos science and NASA observations have confirmed that myths of destruction were not only possible; they were likely to have been based on fact.

If chaos science has rendered the world we live in more dangerous, less certain than previously thought by scholars and academicians, we do have some solace. Potential collisions of the comets with earth must be regarded as terrible events. Undoubtedly they will kill most of us. But they can also be regarded as a possibility of renewal for an earth that has lost its freshness and diversity and that has suddenly grown heavy with pollutants and old with unrelenting warfare. The lesson of the Atlanteans is that arrogance leads to death. But the lesson also is that renewal and rebirth will follow any such destruction.

However, should we welcome another celestial event of mass destruction, one that would cleanse the earth of the greatest threat to life's diversity—mankind? We have an alternative: The metaphysics of the ancients and our own current metaphysics are drawing ever closer together. In place of the great rift that separated "primitive" magical man from modern empirical science we are experiencing a coming together of man's past and present. Our horizons are expanding both linearly and in directions we had not thought possible a few decades ago.

Many of us have begun to realize that we have recreated civilization in an arrogant and often ignorant manner. Our technological achievements are unrivaled in the history of our planet. We have relied on the accumulation of wealth and implements of sophisticated warfare—"smart bombs" that may have recently destroyed underground Iraqi defense positions, but also ancient Sumerian ruins and texts with them—to defend our culture. But if there is some interrelationship between wealth, arms and the wisdom we seek, it is doubtful that computers, or any form of technology, will be able to tell us what it is.

Only intuition, along with an accurate reading of the past, can reveal our goal. A trip to Peru for a harmonic convergence, by itself, will solve nothing. Chanting might help, if you do *nothing else*. We must learn to live more simply. Do we have enough time? According to the Mayan calendar the current age began in 3113 B.C. It will end on December 23, 2012. If their mathematics, observations and their concept that great and terrible events mark the passing from one age to another are all correct, we have some [seven] years to rediscover our past and to prepare for our imminent future. Are we intelligent enough? Courageous enough?

Atlantis existed. However, we cannot presume the folly, advanced by pseudo-science, that the Atlanteans had helicopters, televisions and atomic bombs. Such an Atlantis never existed on this planet—until now. Nor should we accept the sensationalists' view that Atlanteans and all ancient builders were influence by aliens from another solar system or galaxy. It is unlikely that such an advanced civilization would so greatly interfere with an unstable world. Besides, the idea that we are unable to advance technologically without outside help really is not so sensational. But, an Atlantis in a Golden Age of worldwide communication and trade, with city-states and nations, built without fortresses or walls, *did exist*. The important quest for us is to rediscover the nature of a civilization, made up of humans like ourselves, that lived for millennia in harmony with itself, with its neighbors, and with a practical knowledge of the celestial universe—a civilization now lost.

Yet how do we know, truly, that an Atlantis and a Golden Age ever existed? Myth has told us so. We must realize that despite all our previous attempts to destroy and alter our past, as described in myth, we still have all the possibilities myth itself has proposed, and that myth has retained for us—an undeniable link to the true intelligence of the universe. As long as the imagination of humans survives, civilization can occur many times, but only in a harmonic interaction with the fabric of all life, and with a greater universe we now so mistakenly perceive as distant, and impossible to comprehend.

A narrow, linear view of history has disregarded myth as the container of truth and replaced it with the notion, now imperative dogma, of myth as primitive and unreliable fable, while Darwinian evolution and material progress is reliable fact. By seeing our past as analogous to a ladder, history has been portrayed as a gradual climbing out of darkness, and neo-Darwinian theory has steadfastly assumed that we are the pinnacle of man's habitation on earth. Could we be mistaken? Could true knowledge of the past, and our resolve to learn from it, be our only hope of avoiding catastrophes in the near future?

We cannot emphasize enough—man's true history is written in his *knowledge* of the sky, revealed in the names he has given to the stars and to their constellations, and demonstrated in their physical reconstruction on earth. An earlier culture, for millenniums peaceful in nature, in tune with the stars, trading ideas and concepts, without rancor, not only existed, but also flourished and retained celestial knowledge recorded from civilizations that had disappeared many millenniums past. The civilization of Atlantis flourished under the stars, inseparable from the heavens above. All over the world, when night fell, and the stars appeared, the motives and motions of the gods were made apparent to men! So, too, were the pathways adventurous men would follow across the seas, pathways mapped in the sky above them.

There is magic in the world. We all feel it on special nights, summer nights spent, in part, with the stars, and in part with ourselves as we remove ourselves from the trappings of the mechanized, televised, computerized world. If we find ourselves in the presence of a pyramid or a megalith it doesn't matter if we are in Belize, England or Egypt, we cannot help to feel the magic of a civilization from long ago, and a state of mind that was our past but, hopefully, may also be our future realm. We are star matter and, as such, we are children of the gods. And they have not gone away. On these special occasions when we wander out under a star-filled sky, whether near Stonehenge, in the outback of Australia, or on a Mayan beach facing the Caribbean, we can feel our own essential beings under the stars. We tend to call such experiences "vacations." In the experience we have "vacated" ourselves of the worried and wrenching cares that have dominated us. It is an easy and greatly rewarding step backwards. Temporarily, it brings us into balance. We must find a permanence to this sense of balance, even if it means stepping backward and embracing a philosophy contrary to our present social and economic expectations. It is a step that man, if he proves himself intelligent, must take.

Neither history nor evolution will repeat itself, exactly. Man, either in the aftermath of another cataclysm, or in the grips of another ice age, will again be confined mostly to the coastal regions of tropical shores. Will any resemblance of past civilizations exist among a people too few in number to remember any part of its dominant past? Will man return to aggressive primitive behavior triggering a new age of warfare? Will he achieve a new and fruitful evolution, or will he meekly die out? Balance is difficult to achieve, and almost impossible to regain, once it is lost. It is therefore all the more important to appreciate and understand that it did exist, on this planet, among our people, for thousands and thousands of years in a lost civilization called Atlantis.

A Lancondon Indian watched as the last tourist bus left. Only when it was out of sight did he dare to do what none of his people would any longer want to do. He climbed up the rocks of the pyramid at Chichen Itza. He didn't know exactly why he was making the climb. The pyramids were no longer considered part of the Lancondons' lives. His people had deserted them over a thousand years before, and now that a distant government had recreated them for tourists, they no longer held any interest for the Lancondons. It was late in the day and he had his family to return to. He had gathered sparse wood needed for that evening's fire. But he had dropped it at the foot of the pyramid and he had begun climbing, just as so many of his ancestors, millennia before, had done. It had been a hot afternoon and he had to continually wipe the sweat from his brow as he reached the pyramid's crown. At sunset the jungle was beautiful, transcendent green! The date might someday have been recorded as 12,012, if people still used the Atlantean calendar. It was December 23, 2012 A.D. by the Christian calendar, at the end of the age that had begun on the Mayan date of August 13, 3113 B.C. But actually, it was about to become 1 Reed of a New Age. The Lancondon quickly climbed down the steep pyramid and crossed the manicured grounds to the observatory. He was now moving purposefully, as if remembering something long forgotten. As night fell he ascended the observatory. He looked out through the sightlines of the stones, just as if he understood what they meant. And he did understand, just as his people had long understood. He saw that the setting sun, moon and Venus had found perfect correlation along the sightlines. He did not need to know any skills in astronomy. There was no question. Something was about to happen. Something terrible, something vast and something wonderful—something that would very soon change the world. The Lancondon, named Three Rabbit, waited. There was nothing else to do.

---

1. *Atlantis in America: Navigators of the Ancient World.* —Ed.

Frank Joseph

NAN MADOL: THE LOST CIVILIZATION

OF THE PACIFIC

PHOTOS BY SANTHA FAIIA

DURING 1924, a former colonel in the British Army stunned the world with the appearance of his book *The Lost Continent of Mu*. In continuous publication ever since, it has lost none of its power to generate heated controversy. While some of the author's statements seem outrageously unacceptable, others have been scientifically confirmed since his death more than 80 years ago. James Churchward wrote that while on duty in India during the early 1870s, he was allowed access to a Hindu monastery library that contained deteriorating records documenting mankind's first civilization.

According to the crumbling inscriptions, Mu, the "Motherland," was a vast realm spanning the Pacific Ocean more than 10,000 years ago. By then, its inhabitants were already in possession of a high culture in some respects at least superior to any society that came after, including our own. They raised monumental ceremonial centers, engaged in transoceanic commerce that circled the globe, were technologically adept and spiritually enlightened. They were far-roving seafarers, corporate-scale agriculturists, prodigious irrigationists and devoted nature-worshippers.

After millennia of social greatness, Mu was overwhelmed by a natural catastrophe not unlike the post-Christmas Day tsunami that claimed nearly a third of a million lives across

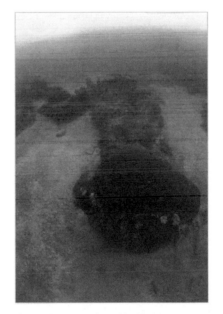

Fallen underwater column, Nan Madol.

the Indian Ocean in 2004. According to the Hindu account, survivors escaped to Asia and America, where they sparked the civilizations of early China, Japan and Peru. Shattered by the disaster, Mu fragmented into clusters of islands later known as Polynesia, remnants of the broken Motherland.

On learning this strange story, Churchward spent the next 50 years traveling in search of its confirmation from India, Burma and Tibet,

Mysterious megalithic temple of Nan Douwas rises above the canals of Nan Madol, Ponape island, Micronesia.

Prismatic basalt blocks disappearing under water around the main temples of Nan Madol—which seem to be built over some kind of substructure now deep beneath the waves.

250 million tons of prismatic basalt covering 170 acres were used in the construction of the ancient city. Some of its blocks are larger and heavier than those in the Great Pyramid of Egypt.

throughout the Pacific to Canada, Mexico and Peru. Figuring prominently into his accumulated evidence was an obscure location in a remote corner of the western Pacific Ocean, almost a thousand miles north of New Guinea and 2,300 miles south of Japan. Raised on a coral reef only five feet above sea level at the small island of Pohnpei, Nan Madol is a series of rectangular islets and monumental towers covered with thick vegetation.

THE 250 MILLION TON PREHISTORIC METROPOLIS

Access to the site in prehistory was possible only aboard vessels cruising through a stone channel. It terminates at a flight of broad stone steps ascending to a plaza. Nearly 100 artificial islands are enclosed within the 1.6 square miles of Nan Madol's "downtown" area. They are interconnected by a network of stone canals, each 27 feet across and more than four feet deep at high tide. 250 million tons of prismatic basalt covering 170 acres were used in the construction of the ancient city. Some of its blocks are larger and heavier than those in the Great Pyramid of Egypt.

Between four and five million stone columns comprise the Caroline Islands' prehistoric metropolis. Roughly hewn into shape, they were then loosely fitted without benefit of mortar or cement, unlike the canals' orderly courses and joined stonework. The prismatic columns are three to 12 feet long, although many reach 25 feet in length. Averaging five tons each, larger examples weigh 20 to 25 tons apiece. Nan Madol was made from four to five million basalt pillars, girders and stone logs.

The entire city was originally surrounded by a 16-foot-high wall, 1,811 feet long. All but a few sections of this immense wall have succumbed to centuries of storms, although two gigantic

breakwaters still exist. One is 1,500 feet in extent, but the other, nearly three times longer, runs for almost a mile. Nan Madol's walls are more than 12 feet thick in places as featured in a structure known as Nan Dowas. It is a tall, square, hollow, windowless tower composed of 15-foot-long, hexagonal black basalt pillars laid horizontally between courses of rudely cut boulders and smaller stones.

According to David Hatcher Childress, president of the World Explorers Club (Kempton, Illinois), who visited Pohnpei in the mid-1980s and early 1990s, "the entire massive structure was built by stacking stones in the manner in which one might construct a log cabin." The city's largest single block is found in the southeastern side of Nan

---

Curiously, no inscriptions, petroglyphs or carvings decorate Nan Madol. Missing, too, are statues or ritual objects of any kind. No trace of the small, portable stone images commonly found throughout the rest of Micronesia and across central and western Polynesia occur at the site.

Dowas, where it serves as a cornerstone weighing no less than 60 tons. Digging beneath it, excavators observed it had been deliberately set on a subterranean stone platform.

Earlier, archaeologists found a large tunnel running from the center of Nan Dowas and carved straight through the coral. Pursuing their investigations, they discovered a vast network of underground corridors connecting all the chief, artificial islets, including one known as Darong; it was joined to the outer reef surrounding the city by a long tunnel. Remarkably, some tunnels actually run beneath the reef itself, terminating in underwater caves. Darong's longest tunnel extends for half a mile into the sea from the center of the city.

The House of Taga: a forest of megalithic columns, Tinian.

A mere speck amid the four and a half million square miles of western Pacific Ocean surrounding Micronesia, a more out-of-the-way place is difficult to imagine. "Only 129 square miles in area," writes the encyclopedist of ancient anomalies, William R. Corliss, "it is almost lost in the immensity of the Pacific." The squarish, 12 by 14-and-a-half mile-island is overgrown with mangrove swamps, but has no beaches, and is surrounded by a coral reef. Thickly wooded and mountainous, humidity is excessive at Pohnpei, and mildew, rot and decay permeate the island.

These difficult conditions, combined with its remote location, hardly qualify this island as an ideal spot to build a civilization. Nonetheless, Nan Madol's very existence suggests city planning, a system of weights and measures, divisions of labor and a hierarchy of authority, plus advanced surveying and construction techniques—all required to build the Pacific's only pre-modern urban center. "Nothing quite like Nan Madol exists anywhere else on earth," Ballinger observed. "The ancient city's construction, architecture and location are unique. The point is that large reserves of manpower were never readily available in and around Pohnpei.

But the 20,000 to 50,000 workers scholars guess were required to build Nan Madol contrast sharply with little Pohnpei, which is not large enough to have ever supported such numbers. Curiously, no inscriptions, petroglyphs or carvings decorate Nan Madol. Missing, too, are statues or ritual objects of any kind. No trace of the small, portable stone images commonly found throughout the rest of Micronesia and across central and western Polynesia occur at the site. And despite the magnitude of its construction, tools are nowhere in evidence. Despite its lack of artifacts,

A mere speck amid the four and a half million square miles of western Pacific Ocean surrounding Micronesia, a more out-of-the-way place is difficult to imagine.

archaeologists have been able to recreate Nan Madol's original appearance.

In its hey-day, crudely worked masses of basalt contrasting with orderly courses of stone rose in colossal towers and majestic walls amid a complex of smaller, rectangular buildings and artificial lakes interconnected by a series of canals. Spread out over 11 square miles, Bill Ballinger, a mid-Twentieth Century writer, praised Nan Madol as "the Venice of the Pacific." Yet, a marketplace, temples or storage areas were absent from the site. Its residents even seemed to have lacked a cemetery for the burial of their dead. Nan Madol means the "Spaces Between," resulting from the network of canals. Its island, "Pohnpei," signifies "On An Altar."

This is a factor that must always be considered when trying to solve the mystery of the construction of Nan Madol."

Only marginally able to support today's 20,000 inhabitants, the island's 183 square miles are mostly mountainous and uninhabitable. Many more workers would have been needed to build a public works project like Nan Madol. John Macmillan Brown, a prominent Twentieth Century New Zealand archaeologist, stated that "the rafting over the reef at high tide and the hauling up of these immense blocks, most of them from five to 25 tons in weight, to such a height as 60 feet must have meant tens of thousands of hours of organized labor; and the workers had to be housed and clothed and fed. Yet, within a radius

Nan Madol's mythic origins began to surface during 1928, when unusual human skeletal remains were excavated by Japanese archaeologists near several prehistoric sites on Pohnpei. The bones had belonged to men far taller and more robust than the indigenous Pohnpeians.

of 1,500 miles of its center there are not more than 50,000 people today." Just about that many workers would have been needed to assemble Nan Madol's four or five million basalt logs in approximately 20 years. And yet, modern Pohnpeians lay little claim to the archaeological site. "The natives have no tradition touching the quarry, who hewed the stone, when it was done, or why the work ceased," *Science* magazine reported. Ballinger pointed out that "present Pohnpeians and their preceding generations have demonstrated no skill, or even interest, in any kind of stone construction. Building of the city demanded considerable engineering knowledge." Citing the thousands of work-hours, complex organization and well-directed labor to quarry, transport and erect 250 million tons of basalt, a United States Department of Interior report stated, "The unwritten history of Pohnpei indicates that Nan Madol was constructed by or under the direction of people not native to the island of Pohnpei." Their own traditions do indeed imply as much. Native oral tradition recounts that a "large canoe" bearing twin brothers, Olisihpa and Olsohpa, long ago sailed away from their homeland in the west, remembered as Katau Peidi. This was a splendid kingdom that once dominated the Pacific World with magical power still known throughout Micronesia and Polynesia as "mana."

Despite its potent mysteries, a terrible earthquake struck Katau Peidi, which suddenly collapsed to the bottom of the sea. Olisihpa and Olsohpa were among the survivors of this catastrophe. They were sorcerers, tall of stature and kind-hearted men, who sought refuge at Sounahleng, a reef at Temwen Island, upon which the twins built Nan Madol aided by a "flying dragon." Its jaws cut through the coral, excavating the canals.

Then the sorcerers from lost Katau Peidi levitated great blocks of basalt through the air, easily stacking them up and fitting them together to form a new city. All was completed in a day's work, and Nan Madol stood as the sacred capital of Deleur, their name for Pohnpei.

After many years of beneficent dictatorship, Olisihpa passed away, and was succeeded by Olsohpa, who assumed for the first time the title of Saudeleur, or "Lord of Deleur." He fathered 12 generations of Saudeleurs—all of them, like their twin progenitors, exceptionally tall—who ruled peacefully until the ancestors of the modern Pohnpeians arrived. They killed Saudemwohl, the last Saudeleur, and renamed the island Pohnpei, which declined into savagery, until it was first colonized by Kaiser Wilhelm's Germany in the late Nineteenth Century, then occupied by Imperial Japan during the following century, finally becoming part, and then capital, of the independent Federated States of Micronesia in 1984.

NAN MADOL'S MYTHIC ORIGINS

Nan Madol's mythic origins began to surface during 1928, when unusual human skeletal remains were excavated by Japanese archaeologists near several prehistoric sites on Pohnpei. The bones had belonged to men far taller and more robust than the indigenous Pohnpeians. When the nature of the discovery was described to native elders, they exclaimed that the bones were those of the same Saudeleurs who had flown through the air the stones that went into the construction of Nan Madol. Similar stories are heard in various parts of the world far from Micronesia to explain the construction of other ancient megalithic wonders.

For example, a myth surrounding Britain's Stonehenge recounted that its 50-ton sarasen

Try as the experts did, they could not make their coconut rafts, even when lashed together in series, float a single ton. Repeated attempts demonstrated only a few hundred pounds could be carried, a far cry from the 20-ton columns and 60-ton blocks handled with evident ease by the prehistoric construction engineers of Nan Madol.

stones were floated into position by King Arthur's renowned advisor, Merlin, another "sorcerer." If accounts of levitation such as these, widely separated as they are in distance and time by disparate peoples on opposite sides of the world, are not a universally shared human reaction to the survival of otherwise inexplicable ruins, they may be the genuine recollection of a lost technology preserved in legend. Though serious suggestions of ancient levitation may be dismissed as foolish fantasy by mainstream scholars, they are nevertheless unable to account for the lifting of 25-ton basalt at least 30 feet into the air and being precisely fitted into the imposing walls and towers of Nan Madol during prehistory.

The largest modern crane in the entire Pacific can lift 35 tons. Today's building engineers, using the latest equipment, would be hard pressed to recreate the construction of 200 million metric tons of stone, not on solid ground, but upon a coral reef only a few feet above sea level. Efforts at duplicating what archaeologists insist must have been the sole means by which Nan Madol was built were attempted during the late Twentieth Century. Conventional theories were put to the test in a 1995 Discovery Channel documentary, when a one-ton column was tied with bamboo stays to rafts made with coconut shells.

Try as the experts did, they could not make their coconut rafts, even when lashed together in series, float a single ton. Repeated attempts demonstrated only a few hundred pounds could be carried, a far cry from the 20-ton columns and 60-ton blocks handled with evident ease by the prehistoric construction engineers of Nan Madol. Contributing to the scholars' embarrassment is their failure to explain how such prodigious basalt

building materials were quarried, let alone transported. "Presumably," Paul Brandt, a reporter for *Archaeology*, speculated, "the miners heated the cliff face with huge fires and then drenched the surface with cold water. The resultant expansion and contraction broke off the splinters desired for construction."

Unfortunately, there is no evidence to show that so-called "spalling" was ever known at Pohnpei. Its use is at least a possibility, given Nan Madol's paucity of any tools. Or maybe it was built with a lost technology dissimilar from our own. Was the "flying dragon" summoned by Olisihpa and Olsohpa a descriptive metaphor preserved in mythic tradition by a preliterate people for some instance of high technology they were unable to understand?

Hardly less perplexing is the source for the mountain of basalt that went into making Nan Madol. Childress cited a spokesman for the Community College of Micronesia, Gene Ashby, as having said that no one knows the origins of such staggering tonnage. Exactly when the city was raised is almost as difficult to determine as how it came to be made. Smithsonian Institute archaeologists in the early 1960s, carbon-dated cooked residue from inside a presumed "turtle oven," determining that Nan Madol was occupied as late as A.D. 1285. But their results only suggested that someone ate a turtle at Nan Madol in the late Thirteenth Century, and threw no light on the date of its construction.

In fact, useful carbon-datable specimens are virtually impossible to find in the jungle humidity, which quickly rots organic materials. A far more reliable dating method may be found in comparison of sea levels over millennia. Pohnpei was professionally surveyed for the first time in the early 1970s by Dr. Arthur Saxe from the University of Oregon. He and his fellow divers found a single line of uniformly sized boulders perpendicular to the drop-off at about 85 feet below Nan Madol's harbor, Madolenihmw. The line of boulders gradually vanished into the sandy bottom after another ten feet.

The artificial arrangement of these stones was confirmed when the surveyors established a deliberate alignment between two nearby islets. They later found pillars and columns, some of them still upright, at depths of more than 75 feet, and measured a stony formation disappearing under the sands of the ocean floor at 95 feet. These observations suggested a maximum depth of 100 feet for probable archaeological material off the shores of Pohnpei. Not for the last 12,000 years have sea levels been so low, when the presently submerged boulders were on dry land and artificially oriented.

continuously inhabited from before the close of the last ice age until at least 3000 B.C. It was probably abandoned and subsequently reoccupied by Micronesians and their ancestors until at least the Thirteenth Century A.D., as implied by the Smithsonian's carbon-date.

James Churchward believed Nan Madol had little to do with these historic peoples, but was instead the expression of a great civilization long predating their arrival at Pohnpei. The scale of its execution and apparently deep antiquity outstripped anything comparable in the vast Pacific, and spoke eloquently of the lost Motherland described in the monastery inscriptions he translated as a young officer in India. "To my mind," he wrote in his first book about Mu, "the various ruins on Pohnpei are ruins of one of the Motherland's capital cities."

There are, in fact, a number of clues in local place-names connecting Nan Madol to the sunken realm. For example, a rectangular structure near

> The unbroken spread of this stone work from the sea bottom to dry land demonstrates that Nan Madol was continuously inhabited from before the close of the last ice age until at least 3000 B.C.

Nan Madol's canals could only have been built many years after the currently submerged columns were set up and subsequently flooded, and able to function after the seas reached their present levels approximately 5,000 years ago. The appearance of artifactual materials at 100-foot depths means that Nan Madol was already in operation prior to 10,000 B.C. Abrupt rises in sea levels at the end of the last ice age forced the residents to move to higher ground, where they continued building above the ocean, until present levels were reached around 3000 B.C.

While we still cannot fix a precise date for its founding, the oldest strata of building at Nan Madol corresponds to its deepest physical evidence, which must have been put in place before the Eleventh Millennium B.C. The unbroken spread of this stone work from the sea bottom to dry land demonstrates that Nan Madol was

the southwest side of the site is known as Mu-pt, while Mu-pteniulli is a nearby sea-entrance. An eastern seawall is known as Mu-ptalap, together with Pon-mu-asanap, a wall on land. Pon-Mu-itak is a precinct formed by a curving, paved road in the northeast. An archaeological site referred to as Nanparad Mu-tok is found on the islet of Nanlong, not far from the south coast of Pohnpei. Mu-pt, Mu-pteniulli, Mu-ptalap, etc., appear to be hybrid variations of original names inflected by native influences, which corrupted the original "Mu" into a "mw" sound-as in Madolenih-mw, the bay at Nan Madol and Kita-mw, another location associated with an early landing by Olisihpa and Olsohpa, the founding fathers of Nan Madol, to accommodate the language considerations of the indigenous Micronesians.

The same dialectical shift appears in the names of legendary or semi-legendary chiefs who succeeded the Saudeleurs. Some of these rulers typically include Luhk en Mwei Maur, Luhk en Mwer or Luhk en Mwei-variations on the name, "Mu." Perhaps most indicative of all, Te-Mu-en is the name of the artificial islet on which Nan Madol itself was built. Corresponding names occur elsewhere in the Carolines. Among the Hall Islands, 430 miles northwest of Pohnpei, lies Mu-riio. Complimenting these evocative names are enduring native traditions of Katau Peidi, the lost kingdom from which Olisihpa and Olsohpa fled for their lives before it was engulfed by the sea in a convulsion of nature.

Do these linguistic parallels with the sunken Motherland combined with the extraordinary ruins at Pohnpei bear testimony to a former civilization of unimaginable antiquity and even more inconceivable material sophistication? If Nan Madol was not created by technological "sorcerers" from Mu, then who else could have been responsible for such an achievement?

References:

• Bill S. Ballinger, *Lost City of Stone: The Story of Nan Madol*. New York: Simon and Schuster, 1978.

• Dr. Vamos-Toth Bator, Supreme Tamana Witness-Data, OH. *Midwest Epigraphic Journal*, vol. 16, no. 2, 2002. pp. 75–78.

• Peter Bellwood, *Man's Conquest of the Pacific*. London: William Collins, 1978.

• John H. Brandt, *Archaeology*, 1962, 15:99–107. In William R. Corliss, MD, *Ancient Man: A Handbook of Puzzling Artifacts*. Glen Arm: The Sourcebook Project, 1978.

• W. S. Cerve, *Lemuria: The Lost Continent of the Pacific*. 3rd Ed. San Jose: Supreme Grand Lodge of AMORC, 1942.

• David Hatcher Childress, *Ancient Micronesia and the Lost City of Nan Madol*. Kempton: Adventures Unlimited Press, 1998.

• James Churchward, *The Lost Continent of Mu*. New York: Paperback Library, 1968.

• Jan Knappert, *Pacific Mythology: An Encyclopedia of Myth and Legend*. London: Diamond Books, 1995.

• Rosslyn Poignant, *Oceanic Mythology*. London: Paul Hamlyn, 1967.

• Hans Santesson, *Understanding Mu*. New York: Paperback Library, 1970.

• Dr. Arthur Saxe, *The Nan Madol Area of Pohnpei*. Saipan: Office of the High Commissioner, Trust Territory of the Pacific, Saipan, Marianas Islands, 1980.

• Lewis Spence, *The Problem of Lemuria*. London: Rider and Company, 1933.

• Edgerton Sykes, *Lemuria Reconsidered*. London: Markham House Press, Ltd., 1968.

Graham Hancock

UNDERWORLD:

CONFRONTING KERAMA

PHOTOS BY SANTHA FAIIA

I agree that this is very amazing and very strange, even to me, how these structural buildings could be formed. Patterns like these, I haven't seen formed by nature.
— Dr. Wolf Wichman, geologist, Kerama, Japan, March 2001

ALTHOUGH I USUALLY REFER, in shorthand, just to "Kerama," the correct term is "the Keramas"—for this is in fact a group of small islands, including Aka, Zamami, Kuba and Tokashiki, lying in the Pacific Ocean about 40 kilometers due west of Naha, the capital of Okinawa.

The islands are poignantly beautiful, with verdant hills, rugged, rocky coasts and sand-fringed beaches, and they are separated from one another by expanses of crystal-clear water ranging in intensity from the palest turquoise to the deepest midnight blue. The whole area is a marine nature preserve renowned for the great numbers and varieties of whales and dolphins that congregate there.

AND AT THE END OF THE ICE AGE?

The story that Glenn Milne's inundation maps tell is that down to about 14,600 years ago Kerama remained attached to the southern end of Okinawa by a thick, curving tongue of land. Okinawa was itself at that time a much larger and wider island

---

Indeed it is on these now inundated plains off its southwestern coast that Okinawa's own underwater monuments—the "step-pyramids" and "terraces" offshore of Chatan, described in chapter one—are located.

---

than it is today with many kilometers of low-lying, gently-sloping plains extending both east and west of its present coastline. Indeed it is on these now inundated plains off its south-western coast that Okinawa's own underwater monuments—the "step-pyramids" and "terraces" offshore of Chatan, described in chapter one—are located.

Circles on Komakino Island. Compare to underwater circles below.

Small stone circles at a depth of 30 meters, Kerama, southern Japan.

And at that time there was continuous land between Chatan and Kerama.

Looking further through the sequence of inundation maps we find that by 13,500 years ago the Kerama-to-Okinawa land bridge had been severed and 20 kilometers of water lay between the two. But it is also clear that Kerama at that time had not yet broken up into smaller units. Further detail is difficult to resolve, but the maps indicate that this single, larger Kerama may have survived, with minimal diminution, until as late as 10,000, perhaps even 9,000, years ago—though since parts of it were steeply sloping, and parts flat, not all of it would have been submerged at the same moment even then. It would have been around this time, 9,000-10,000 years ago, that Kerama's stone circles would have been inundated.

The circles lie under almost 30 meters of water, ten kilometers southeast of Aka Island, at the intersection of latitude 26 degrees 07 minutes north and longitude 127 degrees 17 minutes east. A few jagged rocks just break the surface nearby, with waves constantly crashing over them, but otherwise the site is completely exposed in open water.

THE CONSTRAINTS: KERAMA, MARCH 2001

The March 2001 dives with Wolf Wichmann were funded and filmed by Channel 4 on a rushed, money-saving schedule—two working days for Yonaguni, and one for Kerama. In practice this meant that if the weather turned sour—which it frequently does in the Ryukyus—we would not be able to dive at Kerama at all. And even if the weather god was with us, the sea god might not be: the currents at Kerama are often so severe that you have to fight the water continuously if you want to stay in one place.

When humans fight water, water wins. I've seen divers lose their masks and have their regulators pulled from their mouths by the Kerama currents. I've seen desperate, breathless struggles to stay on top of the site, or to help others stay there, and not get swept away into the wild blue yonder. I've seen fit young adults crawl back onto the boat exhausted, literally trembling with fatigue.

So what I've learned, after several unpleasant experiences of that sort, is that it's just not worth diving there when the current flows. It's better to anchor the boat tight with a couple of lines fore and aft, put a buoy in the water, watch how it bobs, and wait for a lull.

If there's a lull.

BRIEFING KERAMA, MARCH 2001

We set out from Okinawa soon after 9 AM on what turned out to be a reasonably fine morning with waves of less than a meter. Once again we were working with the great local diver Isamu Tsukahara and his very professional team, and using his fast, spacious cabin cruiser as our dive boat. Mitsutoshi Taniguchi, the original discoverer of the circles, had come up to join us from his home on Miyako Island further to the south. And Kiyoshi Nagaki had also volunteered to dive with us that day.

We began to sight the Keramas after about an hour of steady running to the west and as we drew closer Wolf explained to me their basic structure evident from areas of bare rock along the coasts and from scars left by earth falls that had uncovered the underlying strata in the hills. Rather like Malta in the far-off Mediterranean, it seemed that these islands had been formed out of huge deposits of coralline limestone [i.e., corals turned to rock] that had been laid down under ancient seas as much as 50 million or 100 million years ago and then subsequently exposed and inundated again, exposed and inundated again, with more coral growth taking place in the epochs of inundation but later itself being fossilized and exposed. In some places sedimentary layers of softer limestones, comparable to Malta's globigerina layers, lay on top of a coralline core. In others coralline outcrops formed the surface layer itself, glaring white in the morning sunlight.

By 10:30 A.M. we were maneuvering into position over the dive site. Isamu Tsukahara—who always takes the hardest work on himself—went down to set the anchors and the buoy. This must have required an almost superhuman effort on his part, since the current was flowing strongly enough to create visible turbulence on the surface, but he calmly and capably succeeded and was soon back on board none the worse for wear.

Then we all sat around and waited, listening to the creaking anchor ropes as the current tried to rip the boat free and send it spinning back to Okinawa. The buoy, rather distressingly, had been sucked completely underwater by the force of the flow, and no diving was going to get done before it popped back up again.

In the meantime I borrowed a DVC player and monitor from the film crew so that I could show Wolf some footage that Santha and I had shot during previous dives at Centre Circle, the largest of the group of structures that lay scattered around on the ocean floor beneath out boat. Every instinct in my body, for years now, had convinced me that these structures *must* be man-made, or at any rate could not have been made entirely by nature—they were simply too bizarre, unique and "designed." But secretly I had some doubts. I've learnt a fair bit about rocks and reefs underwater around the world since I took up diving, but I'm not a marine geologist and there's a huge amount I don't know. Could it be possible that the strange pillars, the clear pentagonal pathway around the central monolith, and the shaped rock-surround of Centre Circle had all come about as a result of some natural process of which I was ignorant?

I froze the frame at an oblique view from the northwestern side of the circle, shot in mid-water about ten meters above the tops of the megaliths, and pointed out the central monolith to Wolf.

GH: So this is the top of the central stone or whatever it is, which is then surrounded by a ring of...

WW: It's a canyon. It's a sort of canyon.

GH: It's a sort of canyon, and it runs down into quite a clean-edged pathway round the bottom here at about 27 meters...it's a curious mixture of pebbles and sand in the bottom. But it's very clean; there's nothing growing in the bottom at all.

WW: (Pointing out several of the monoliths.) All these single structures are totally overgrown by organisms. So just to have an impression of how they could have been shaped or could have originated, you have to scratch lots off them...do you have any impression about the core material of these?

GH: It seems to be a mixture of largish, I wouldn't say pebbles, I'd say more like cobbles, you know...

WW: Rounded?

GH: Rounded ...in a, in a sort of concretized mixture of something—I don't know what it is—a rocky, stony mixture.

WW: A matrix.

GH: A matrix, yeah. And you can see—

WW: So the question to answer is—is the core material consisting of the same matrix and pebbles mixture? Or are the glued pebbles inside this matrix just an outer cover?

GH: On top of something else.

WW: Yes. And the only way to find this out is to make some core drillings or something like that. Another way to come closer to the solution of that riddle, that mystery, could be to scratch off the sand on the bottom to see how these structures are linked to the ground rock...But what you definitely have to see is the core, the base, of these single structures and how they are fixed to the ground...

GH: So shall we plan to go to the bottom first, and do some of that? You may find that there's some samples that you can get. Have a close look at everything down there and, you know, see if you feel that these kind of curves—the way the outer and the inner curves of the big monoliths match each other—can be natural or can be manmade.

WW: So, as far as I can see now, I have really no explanation for this type of pattern.

GH: Here, for example [pointing to screen]. You can clearly see we're looking down on two parallel curved walls...

WW: Right, right. That's very amazing. So, is the distance between those two walls broad enough to let people walk through?

GH: Yes, yes it is. You can almost, in places, put two divers side by side, but not quite. Well, we'll see when we get down there.

That was when it really dawned on me, I think, that not only Kerama was on trial here but also my whole notion that a phase of higher civilization and monumental construction in Japanese prehistory might be attested to by ruins underwater.

I played the tape forward a few frames, and then stopped it at a change of scene—the second circle of great monoliths. Because it is of narrower diameter (not because of the size of its monoliths, which are much the same) local divers call it "Small Centre Circle." It lies immediately southeast of and adjoins Centre Circle itself, creating in effect two interlinked rings, the first eight meters across and the second five meters across, contained within what appears to be a huge keyhole shaped enclosure hewn somehow out of the bedrock that now forms the floor of the ocean.

WW: So, how many circles are there in all?

GH: Well, there's these two side by side; one large one and one slightly smaller one. Then there's a third one I guess about 50 or 60 meters further to the northwest, but we don't have shots of that.

WW: Yes. And are there other figures? Different from this circle?

GH: In the same area, about 40 meters away to the south, there are quite a number of other circles made of much smaller individual stones, most of them no more than a meter in length. We should be able to look at some of those circles, too, on the same dive.

WW: But they are built up the same way, of the same material?

GH: Well, they look like some of the cobbles that are compacted into the bigger monoliths.

WW: Aha ... aha.

GH: They look like that kind of—

WW: Single cobbles?

GH: Single cobbles.

WW: And then positioned...?

GH: But positioned in a ring.

WW: That's strange.

GH: It is.

WW: Really strange.

I rewound the tape for a few moments then pressed "play" again. There was one characteristic of Centre Circle which, though obvious enough, I'd so far forgotten to point out to Wolf.

GH: The other thing I feel about it is It's on a human scale. It's monumental, and yet the scale of the thing is human.

WW: I'm very astonished about that...about the structure, formation. You know, I haven't seen anything like this before.

GH: In years of diving? And nor have I ...never anywhere in the world.

WW: Not only in diving, but also on dry land. There's some, some formations at least comparable a bit to this—so-called "rock castles" or even a certain form of calcite weathering. But they look different. They look totally different and they don't have these canyons with the straight walls going right down.

GH: With straight walls and running all the way round a central stone.

WW: Normal calcite weathering is different. It has different wall angles.

GH: You see it's...every time I see that, that inner curve matching the curve of
this and making this rather nice path, I feel...

WW: It's very parallel-shaped...

GH: Yeah, and it feels like a design thing.

WW: Strange, yes...strange.

GH: And no real research has ever been done here. Not even by Professor Kimura.

DIVING ON CENTRE CIRCLE

Finally, in the early afternoon around 1 P.M., the buoy which had been dragged under the surface by the force of the current suddenly popped up again, the pressure on the fore and aft anchor ropes went slack, and it was time to go diving.

We were already partially geared up, so it took only a few minutes for us to strap on tanks, fins and masks and jump into the water.

Tsukahara had positioned the boat well and Centre Circle became clearly visible beneath us almost as soon as we were under the surface. There was a small current still running, not strong enough to trouble us, and we allowed ourselves to drift slowly down the main anchor line towards the monolithic structures below.

The word "monolith" means literally "single stone" and is used to refer to "a large block of stone or anything that resembles one in appearance."[1] But what troubled me most about the monoliths of Centre Circle—a matter related to my secret fear of geological processes known to Wolf but unknown to me—was precisely the question of whether they were "single stones" or not. I had never done what Wolf intended to do now, which was to scrape off some of the thick marine growth covering the monoliths to see what the core material was made of. But I had handled them many times and had vaguely arrived at the idea that they must consist

through and through of the same sort of concretized or aggregated "matrix" of rounded mid-sized stones—resembling river stones—that seemed to form their exteriors. The problem was I had absolutely no idea whether this was going to be good, or bad, for the proposition—my "theory," if you like—that Centre Circle is a man-made structure.

In our conversation on deck Wolf had seemed genuinely mystified by the video footage I'd shown him. But perhaps once he was close up he would take one look at the monoliths, chisel out a few samples, and prove beyond argument that entirely natural processes had in fact formed them? Perhaps he would even slap himself on the brow as we got back in the boat and announce the obscure but correct geological name for this kind of "natural formation?" Or perhaps he wouldn't. Either way I'd know for sure in about an hour.

That was when it really dawned on me, I think, that not only Kerama was on trial here but also my whole notion that a phase of higher civilization and monumental construction in Japanese prehistory might be attested to by ruins underwater.

15 meters above the top of Centre Circle, as we paused in neutral buoyancy to get a perspective on the edifice, I was glad I'd spent the last couple of hours going through our earlier video footage of the site—because it had forced me to think through issues that I had previously overlooked. It wasn't just the crucial question of what the monoliths were made of that had to be addressed, but also Wolf's observation that they were contained on the floor of something like a "canyon."

Looking around from this bird's eye view—for a diver does have some of the freedom of maneuver in the water that a bird has in the sky—I began to get a proper sense, for the first time, of the topography that surrounds the two great conjoined circles (Centre Circle and Small Centre Circle) and of how their keyhole-shaped perimeter is formed, and even of the relationships between the fully-detached and "semi-detached" monoliths that make up the circles.

All these structures occupy the summit of a very large, gently sloping outcrop of rock extending away in all directions, gradually disappearing into deeper waters. At the end of the ice age, when the outcrop last stood above sea level, its highest point would have been the place now marked by the top of the central monolith of Centre Circle. From there you could have stood and surveyed the entire area around.

But then (it seemed inescapable), some powerful force must have intervened—perhaps organized human beings, perhaps weird nature—and carved out the flat-floored, sheer-walled, semi-subterranean, keyhole-shaped enclosure now containing the great rock uprights that form the two circles. Marine growth had gnarled and knobbled the contours of the uprights and it would not be clear until the growth was scraped off how smooth and clean-cut—or otherwise—they originally might have been.

I knew that Wolf would be looking for a natural it takes on the curve of the surrounding enclosure wall—itself not continuous but segregated into units separated by deep channels.

The same low upright forms the dividing line between Centre Circle and Small Centre Circle where the spiral begins. I swam over it now and looked down on it from the east side with Small Centre Circle just behind me. I believe that it shows every sign, as does the entire structure, of having been carved and shaped by man. Though it is a small detail, I have always been impressed by the way it is curved on one side to match the outer curve of the big central upright to its west and on the other to match the curve of the only slightly

Once we had a better idea of the core material, however, the question we had to address ourselves to—the only question in town really—was what *sort* of force could have produced an amazing "design" like this.

explanation and supposed that much depended on the constitution of the rock. This, hopefully, we would soon be able to establish since he had brought along with him a fearsome little hammer and mesh bags for the collection of samples. Once we had a better idea of the core material, however, the question we had to address ourselves to—the only question in town, really—was what *sort* of force could have produced an amazing "design" like this.

Despite lingering doubts, I felt a sudden surge of confidence that nature could not have done it—not unaided, anyway. On the contrary, the pattern was a complex and a purposive one, rather difficult to execute in any kind of rock, and the more I studied it the more obvious it seemed that it was deliberate and planned.

On the east side of Centre Circle, is the smallest and lowest of the three completely freestanding uprights. What I noticed for the first time that afternoon was that this "broken monolith," as I had thought of it before, forms the beginning of a definite anticlockwise spiral extending through the top of the next monolith (much higher) and of the next (higher still), then winding around the west and south sides of the central upright where smaller upright behind it to its east. It is also difficult to imagine how so precisely any natural force could have cut the narrow, clean-edged "second pathway" that parallels the wider inner pathway around the central upright.

Just before we dropped down into the structure I noticed out of the corner of my eye, thanks to the exceptional visibility that afternoon, something I had not seen since our first dives here back in 1999. This was the existence, not far beyond the southwestern perimeter of Centre Circle—on the slopes below the summit of the ancient mound—of other circles and ovals and spirals made up of individual stones, large cobbles, boulders, mostly a meter or less in length, all of them rounded and smoothed off at the edges, coiled and intertwined with each other like necklaces or the links of a chain strewn upon the ground. As I had told Wolf earlier, they looked a lot, though not exactly, like the "river stones" that were also weirdly stuck, or aggregated (or formed part of the bedrock itself?) all over the uprights of Centre Circle.

I made a mental note that we should go and take a proper look at these nearby "river-stone" or "river-boulder" circles and try to figure out how they had been formed. Perhaps Wolf would have a sensible

But seeing them again for the first time in two years, and having traveled widely overland in Japan since then, they instantly reminded me of the Jomon stone circles such as Komakino Iseki and Oyu that I had visited in the north of Honshu in May 2000.

geological explanation. But seeing them again for the first time in two years, and having traveled widely overland in Japan since then, they instantly reminded me of the Jomon stone circles such as Komakino Iseki and Oyu that I had visited in the north of Honshu in May 2000. So far as I could remember, those circles had also been fashioned out of river stones and river boulders like these, and disposed upon the ground in exactly the same way.

It was potentially an important connection.

By now Wolf and I had reached the base of Centre Circle and were standing up on the inner pathway examining the monoliths. It was true, as Wolf had observed from the video footage, that they were completely overgrown with a fantastic menagerie of marine organisms. But at the same time, protruding out through them like a harvest of ripe fruit was this peculiar matrix of individual river-cobbles. One that I noticed in particular, about the diameter of a large dinner plate and probably weighing several kilos, jutted sideways from the top of the second monolith in the spiral as though reaching out towards the third. How was this to be explained?

Wolf took samples from some of the more prominent river stones plastered to the exteriors of the uprights, then beckoned me to join him at the foot of the second monolith under the overhanging cobble. This was going to be his attempt to find out what the core material of the monolith was made of—and he showed me how the marine growth thinned out and then stopped altogether at the junction with the basal path. Immediately above the path it proved relatively easy—much easier than we had expected—to scrape away a large patch of organisms and begin to expose the core.

Wolf scraped and scraped. Scraped and scraped.

And gradually what emerged was not, as I had feared, more of the same stony matrix or aggregate that clung to the surface—but rather a hard, bright, white core formed unmistakably of the ancient coralline limestone of the Keramas and fully attached at its base to the bedrock. So far as we were able to make out, the monolith appeared to have been smoothly and perfectly cut down from top to bottom with a beautiful curve incorporated into it to match the curve of the pathways that were defined on either side of it and the curve of the central upright. I could even see, where Wolf had scraped away the growth particularly successfully, the original organisms that had fossilized millions of years ago to form the white coral rock out of which the entire perimeter of the circle and all its uprights had later been cut. Coral rock where it is available is an ideal construction material—and from the little stone blocks used to build private houses in the Maldives today, to the massive "Trilithion" of ancient Tonga, to the megalithic temples of Malta, you can see the use of white coralline limestones in which the structure of the ancient fossilized organisms can clearly be made out.

So far as we were able to make out, the monolith appeared to have been smoothly and perfectly cut down from top to bottom with a beautiful curve incorporated into it to match the curve of the pathways that were defined on either side of it and the curve of the central upright.

I was grateful to Wolf for having done this little and obvious thing—obvious, anyway to a professional geologist—i.e., for having established what the core material of Centre Circle's monoliths actually is.

Above-ground markings at Masada-no Iwafune.

Underwater markings at Yonaguni.

This kind of coralline limestone, as well as being visually and aesthetically striking, is also extremely hard. For a natural force to have cut such a material in such a complex way with sheer walls four meters deep, and with parallel curves and pathways—the whole hewn out as a semi-subterranean enclosure in the summit of an ancient mound—was, it seemed to me, something that Wolf was going to find very difficult to explain.

Half an hour later we were back on the boat, the principal underwater camera that the Channel 4 team had been using to shoot the dive had malfunctioned, and the director needed us to do it all again.

But it was now after 2:30, the current had returned with a vengeance during the last 15 minutes of the first dive, and it didn't look like we'd be able to get back in the water at all.

We decided to sit at anchor until five. Diving much after that, with nightfall coming, would not be safe this far out in the open ocean and we'd have to return to Okinawa with what we'd got. But if the current slacked before then we would attempt a second dive.

sheer white coralline limestone beneath. Again I found myself fascinated by this bright underlying stone, cut from almost exactly the same sort of material as the most ancient and enduring megalithic structures of far-off Malta.

Indeed, by visualizing a Maltese temple like Hagar Qim or Gigantija in all its glory, its white coralline limestone megaliths reflecting the dazzling Mediterranean sunshine, I could begin to imagine how the two great rock-hewn circles of Kerama might have looked, in all their glory, when all this area as far east as Okinawa was above water at the end of the ice age.

As you approached them from lower down the gentle slopes of the surrounding rocky massif—all of it formed out of the same 100-million-year-old fossilized coral reef—you would at first have not been aware that any structures were present there at all. Only from the rim of the enclosure looking down would you have suddenly found yourself confronted by a majestic and mysterious spiral of glowing monoliths, the tallest more than twice the height of a tall man.

Indeed, by visualizing a Maltese temple like Hagar Qim or Gigantija in all its glory, its white coralline limestone megaliths reflecting the dazzling Mediterranean sunshine, I could begin to imagine how the two great rock-hewn circles of Kerama might have looked, in all their glory, when all this area as far east as Okinawa was above water at the end of the ice age.

WHERE HAS ALL THE DEBRIS GONE?

We did get our second dive when miraculously, just after 4:30, the buoy popped up from out of the current again. The light below was surprisingly good, and we spent a useful 45 minutes underwater. Certain scenes were shot in which Wolf was not needed—during these he went off happily exploring on his own. In other scenes we repeated for the camera what we'd done for real the first time around. Again Wolf scraped off growth from the base of a Centre Circle monolith and exposed the

Unlike the uprights of the great Maltese temples, however, which were quarried elsewhere and then transported and erected on the temple sites, these Centre Circle monoliths had been quarried *in situ* out of the bedrock of the ancient mound—to which they were still attached at their bases.[2] That automatically classifies the whole edifice as a rock-hewn structure and, as at Yonaguni, one of the mysteries it confronts us with, if we are to imagine that the "hewing" was done by natural forces, is—what happened to all the missing rock? Quite a large amount of this very hard rock would have had to be hewn out to free up the monoliths and excavate the four-meter-deep semi-subterranean enclosure in which they are confined. None of this excavated rock is present as any form of rubble or debris within the two circles. This is a very troubling anomaly if natural forces made the circles but is exactly what one would expect if they were the work of human beings.

WOLF ON KERAMA

Much to my surprise—because I had become so used to his hard-nosed skepticism at Yonaguni—Wolf stayed as open-minded on the problem of Centre Circle after our two dives as he had been when I'd shown him the tapes before we got in the water. Moreover, he was able to carry out on-board chemical tests on the samples that he had taken both from the core and from the aggregate of river-stones plastered to the outside of the monoliths.

The tests proved on camera—though it was already completely obvious to the naked eye—that these were two entirely different types of rock. The core, as we knew, was very ancient coralline limestone. The rounded cobbles caught up in the aggregate were sandstone and had, as Wolf judged:

> . . . been shaped by waters, by running waters, this is beyond every doubt. These sandstones all show a rounded-out shape, and this leads us to two possible origination processes for these stones: one would be riverine waters, and the other one would be coastline beach, pebbles or something like that, which have been rolled forward and backward to get this rounded shape.

Wolf added that during the second dive, while I had been working with the cameraman, he had explored outside the perimeter of Centre Circle:

> What was special for me was to discover that these rather large cobbles, pebble stones, made of sandstone, which are glued to the uprights and inner formations, also appear in places outside the circle. So I dived a little sideward—I don't know the direction—and then I found a field of the same pebbles, not really pebbles, it was really big, big stones but scattered in a very chaotic way over the surface of the coralline bedrock.

Wolf's suggestion about these "pebbles" of assorted sizes—which we also referred to in our conversations variously as boulders, cobbles and river-stones—was the obvious one but, he warned, a pure guess. At some stage, probably millions of years after the fossilization and exposure of the ancient coral bedrock:

> . . . a river has carried his load here...So maybe it sometimes had water and sometimes it dried out, changed the bed, and left the stones in here...So it seems that parts of this old coral reef were covered by these boulders somehow transported by [the] river, a very broad river, because the field seems to me to be very broad.

If it was a guess, it sounded like a good one.

But on the larger mystery of the monoliths and uprights of the rock-hewn circles Wolf admitted that he was completely dumbfounded—although he rightly cautioned that he could only speak from his own experience as a marine geologist. Perhaps other geologists had seen natural structures that were the same as or very similar to Centre Circle somewhere in the world and would be able to explain the enigmatic curved parallel walls and well-shaped uprights. He could not, however.

WW: I have no explanation for these...for these ...

GH: *For the circles?*

WW: For the circles, and for the structures inside them. For sure is that they must have been formatted after the pebbles were laid down on the coralline ground—because some of these pebbles are hanging over the canyons, so and they could not have come earlier...But I don't see any force which could have shaped these—

GH: —any force of nature, which could shape the circles and uprights?

WW: Yes, of course.

GH: So that leaves us...

WW: At the moment...

GH: That leaves us with one option then? Manmade.

WW: I don't know. I would not be…

GH: You wouldn't rush so fast?

WW: I would not go so far. I mean you have to do really a lot of research to establish that. But what is really strange is these parallel walls running round. It is very strange because if for example the erosive force were water, the two edges of a river bed or something like that are not exactly parallel to each other like these. So this is what I can say. And even solution, chemical solution does not leave hints like this, of this accuracy.

GH: Paralleling of walls?

From a geologist as instinctively cautious and phlegmatic as Wolf Wichmann this was as close as I was ever likely to get to a confirmation that the rock-hewn stone circles of Kerama really could be man-made.

WW: Paralleling accuracy.

GH: So what can be said for sure about this structure? Can we be sure about anything?

WW: What is clear is that we have an ancient fossilized coral reef and we have these pebbles scattered on top of it, which came later. And then a second force started. This was the erosive force, which then carved these structures out of the ground . . .

GH: Now, you geologists will say "carved by nature" and we poets will say "carved by man."

WW: I don't say anything definite. Much more research must be done. But I agree that this is very amazing and very strange, even to me, how these structural buildings could be formed. I haven't seen such structures done by nature. I won't dare say anything else about human activities because I do not know anything about that.

From a geologist as instinctively cautious and phlegmatic as Wolf Wichmann this was as close as I was ever likely to get to a confirmation that the rock-hewn stone circles of Kerama really could be man-made. Still, I couldn't resist pushing for more.

GH: I'll tell you why I think it's manmade.

WW: Yes, please.

GH: It's not just the sense of organization of the structure itself. It's the fact that we have an ancient culture on these islands, which made stone circles. They are known to have made stone circles and some of those circles still survive—not like Centre Circle, smaller, with the largest blocks about half a ton, and usually much less. But the idea of a stone circle and, indeed, of interlinked stone circles, was something they did. So you know when we look at Centre Circle and Small Centre Circle—and we know that we're on a set of islands where we have an ancient culture called the Jomon, who are known to have made stone circles—then to me it's less extraordinary, in a way, to attribute it to them—to the Jomon—than it is to any unknown force of nature. I don't deny that nature often provides a sense of organization, but it's the unique character of this in a land where we have a very ancient culture, actually which existed from 16,000 years ago until 2,000 years ago, the Jomon, who made stone circles …you know, I start wondering.

WW: Okay, I can follow your point, but it still has to be proven that this was really done by the Jomon.

GH: Yes, yes, I agree.

WW: And this is very hard to find. You have to scratch and you have to clean it to find marks or to find any evidence, maybe in a series of other monuments being proven to have been constructed by this society.

GH: Yes. Well, we have many stone circles that have been constructed by that society, but this…amongst their stone circles, this would rank as the largest and the most unusual. But I repeat, we're on a set of islands here that had an ancient culture, the Jomon, which is recognized by historians. The earliest-surviving work of that ancient culture goes back to the ice age, around 16,000 years ago. The Jomon were known to make stone circles. We have a stone circle at a depth that is likely to have been exposed at some point during the ice age. What's the next logical step?

What I had at that moment was a theory about possible Jomon origins for the underwater monoliths and circles of Kerama, hinting at an early and as yet undiscovered phase of monumental construction in Jomon prehistory.

WW: No, no, I mean I agree to that, to that chain, to that chain—it's clear. But the last point ... this is the point that you must prove. A theory remains a theory unless you have proof.

What I had at that moment was a theory about possible Jomon origins for the underwater monoliths and circles of Kerama, hinting at an early and as yet undiscovered phase of monumental construction in Jomon prehistory. That theory had just passed a very important hurdle since an onsite investigation by a skeptical marine geologist had been unable to produce any viable natural explanation for the structures.

But it was still a theory.

KOMAKINO ISEKI UNDERWATER?

Having completed our work at Kerama, we parted company with Wolf the next morning. He flew back to Germany, and Santha and I carried on with the film crew to the north of Japan. There, eventually, we found ourselves at the wonderful Jomon stone circle of Komakino Iseki near the big site of Sinai Miriam in Aomori Prefecture. Though it was by now late March, the weather was still freezing in the north, old snow was still lying on the ground and the whole scene presented a huge contrast to the tropical warmth and blue waters of Kerama.

While the crew was setting up, I paced amongst the stones, shivering with cold.

The distinctive, rounded river-stones of Komakino Iseki.

Boulders. Pebbles. Cobbles.

Arranged in a series of concentric circles, the largest with a diameter of 150 meters.

And between the rings, groups of smaller circles, touching at the edges like the links of a chain...

I'd already made the connection underwater a few days earlier at Kerama. It had struck me as important then and I'd meant to look into it further with Wolf but had been prevented from doing so by shortage of time. It was the phenomenon that he had noticed independently when he'd gone off exploring on his own while I was working with the cameraman and which he'd later described as a boulder field—"big stones disposed in a very chaotic way over the surface of the coralline bedrock."

But if I was right, the disposal of these big rounded river stones was not nearly so chaotic as Wolf had thought. I was pretty sure that I had seen his "boulder field" too, and even videoed it briefly in 1999, and glimpsed it again on the first of the two dives we had just completed.

And where he had seen chaos, I had seen order.

When I had filmed them in 1999, some of the big rounded river stones scattered across the coralline plain had definitely been arranged in circles, one stone laid lengthwise next to the other. As at Komakino Iseki, I remembered, these "circles" were really more oval than truly circular in shape (though I shall continue to refer to them as circles for convenience). And as at Komakino Iseki, the stones had been medium-sized—typically around a meter in length or less.

So Kerama still wasn't finished with me.

On this latest trip, as on every previous trip, I had failed to do my job there properly.

I'd been lured in by the glamour of the rock-hewn circles with their four-meter-high monoliths. But I could see now how the proof of the Jomon connection I sought might all along have been lying in that humble "boulder-field" just beyond.

I was going to have to go back.

---

1. *Collins English Dictionary*. London: Collins, 1982. p. 953.

2. Two prominent Maltese sites contain a combination of rock-hewn structures and free-standing megaliths—the Hypogeum of Hal Saflieni and the Borchtorff Circle at Xhagra. The latter is semi-subteranean in form, rather similar to the Centre Circle complex at Kerama.

4

TECHNOLOGIES AND CONTACTS

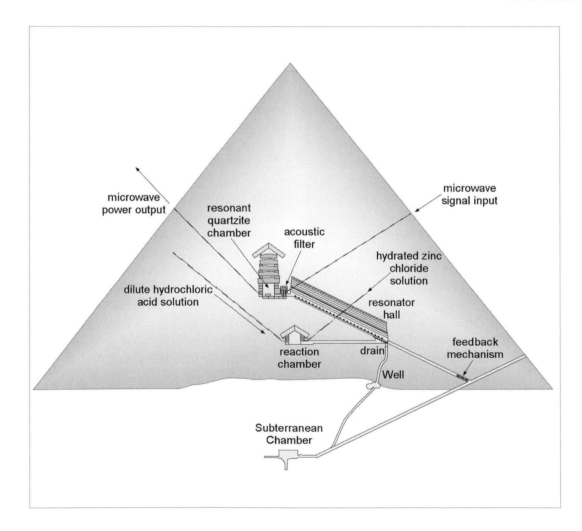

The Giza Power Plant.

Christopher Dunn

THE GIZA POWER PLANT

THE EVIDENCE CARVED into ancient granite artifacts in Egypt clearly points to manufacturing methods that involved the use of machinery such as lathes, milling machines, ultrasonic drilling machines and high-speed saws. They also possess attributes that cannot be produced without a system of measurement that is equal to the system of measure we use today. Their accuracy was not produced by chance, but is repeated over and over again.

After I assimilated the data regarding the ancient Egyptians' manufacturing precision and their possible, and in some instances probable, methods of machining, I suspected that to account for the level of technology that the pyramid builders seem to have achieved, they must have had an equally sophisticated energy system to support it. One of the pressing questions we raise when we discuss ancient ultrasonic drilling of granite is, "What did they use as a source of power?" A still more forceful inquiry regarding the use of electricity necessary to power ultrasonic drills or heavy machining equipment that may have been used to cut granite is, "Where are their power plants?" Obviously there are no structures from the ancient world that we can point to and identify as fission reactors, or turbine halls. And why should we have to? Isn't it a bit misguided of us to form an assumption that the ancient power plants were even remotely similar to ours?

Nevertheless, there may be some fundamental similarities between ancient and modern power supplies, in that the power plants in existence today are quite large and all need a supply of water for cooling and steam production. If such an advanced society existed in prehistory and if indeed they had an energy system, we could logically surmise that their power plants in all probability would be the largest construction projects they would attempt. It also may follow that, as the largest creations of the society, those power plants would stand a good chance of surviving a catastrophe and the erosion of the elements during the centuries that followed.

The evidence carved into ancient granite artifacts in Egypt clearly points to manufacturing methods that involved the use of machinery such as lathes, milling machines, ultrasonic drilling machines and high-speed saws.

The pyramids easily meet these requirements. These geometric relics of the past, which have been studied, speculated about, and around which so much debate has centered, are located near a water supply, the Nile River, and, indeed, are the largest building projects that this ancient society completed. In light of all the evidence that suggests the existence of a highly advanced society utilizing electricity in prehistory, I began to seriously consider the possibility that *the pyramids were the power plants of the ancient Egyptians.*

My attention was focused on the Great Pyramid, primarily because this is the one on which everybody else's attention had been focused, resulting in more research data being available for study. The reports of each successive researcher's discoveries inside the Great Pyramid are quite detailed, especially Petrie's. It is as though researchers became obsessed with reporting data, regardless of how insignificant it may have seemed. Much of their data focuses on the dimensional and geometric relationship between the Great Pyramid and the earth. To review John Taylor's findings:

• A pyramid inch is .001 inch larger than a British inch. There are 25 pyramid inches in a cubit and there were 365.24 cubits in the square base of the Great Pyramid.
• There are 365.24 days in a calendar year.
• One pyramid inch is equal in length to 1/500 millionth of the earth's axis of rotation. This relationship suggests that not only were the builders of the Great Pyramid knowledgeable of the dimensions of the planet, they based their measurement system on them.

What else is unique about the Great Pyramid? Although it is a pyramid in shape, its geometry possesses an astounding approximation to the unique properties of a circle, or sphere. The pyramid's height is in relationship with the perimeter of its base as the radius of a circle is in relationship with its circumference. A perfectly constructed pyramid with an exact angle of 51:51:14.3 has the value pi incorporated into its shape (see Table 2).

Further understanding of this relationship requires the study of not just every detail of the Great Pyramid, but also of the earth.

The earth is a dynamic, energetic body that has supported civilization's demand for fuel for centuries. To date this demand has predominantly

Petrie's Measurements		
Length of one side	9068.8 inches	755.733 feet
Perimeter (length x 4)	36275.2 inches	3022.93 feet
Height	5776.0 inches	481.33 feet
Angle based on above measurements	51:51:59	
The Great Pyramid's approximation to pi based on Petrie's measurements	3.14017 (see Figure 33).	

Table 2.

been for energy in the form of fossil fuels. More recently, scientific advances have allowed us to tap into the power of the atom, and further research in this area promises greater advances in the future. There is, however, another form of abundant energy in the earth that in its most basic form has, for the most part, been largely ignored as a potential source of usable energy. It usually gets our attention when it builds up to a point of destruction. That energy is seismic, and it is the result of the earth's plates being driven by the constant agitation of the molten rock within the earth. The tides are contained not only

---

The earth's energy includes mechanical, thermal, electrical, magnetic, nuclear and chemical action, each a source for sound. It would follow, therefore, that the energy at work in the earth would generate sound waves that would be related to the particular vibration of the energy creating it and the material through which it passes.

---

within the oceans of the world; the continents, too, are in constant movement, rising and falling as much as a foot as the moon orbits the earth.

The earth's energy includes mechanical, thermal, electrical, magnetic, nuclear and chemical action, each a source for sound. It would follow, therefore, that the energy at work in the earth would generate sound waves that would be related to the particular vibration of the energy creating it and the material through which it passes. The audible hum of an electric motor—operating at 3,600 rpm—would fall well below the level of human hearing if it were to slow down to one revolution every 24 hours, as in the case of the earth. What goes unnoticed as we go about our daily lives is our planet's inaudible fundamental pulse, or rhythm.

> **Keeping all of this in mind and knowing that the Great Pyramid is a mathematical integer of the earth, it may not be so outlandish to propose that the pyramid is capable of vibrating at a frequency harmonic to the earth's fundamental frequency.**

On the other end of the scale, any electrical stimulation within the earth of piezoelectrical materials—such as quartz—would generate sound waves above the range of human hearing. Materials undergoing stress within the earth can emit bursts of ultrasonic radiation. Materials undergoing plastic deformation emit a signal of lower amplitude than when the deformation is such as to produce cracks. Ball lightning has been speculated to be gas ionized by electricity from quartz-bearing rock, such as granite, that is subject to stress.

Because the earth constantly generates a broad spectrum of vibration, we could utilize vibration as a source of energy if we developed suitable technology. Naturally, any device that attracted greater amounts of this energy than is normally being radiated from the earth would greatly improve the efficiency of the equipment. Because energy will inherently follow the path of least resistance, it follows that any device offering less resistance to this energy than the surrounding medium through which it passes would have a greater amount of energy channeled through it. Keeping all of this in mind and knowing that the Great Pyramid is a mathematical integer of the earth, it may not be so outlandish to propose that the pyramid is capable of vibrating at a frequency harmonic to the earth's fundamental frequency.

In *The Giza Power Plant* I have amassed a plethora of facts and deductions, which includes a proposition for what lies behind Gantenbrink's "door," based on sober consideration of the design of the Great Pyramid and nearly every artifact found within it that, when taken together, all support my premise that the Great Pyramid was a power plant and the King's Chamber its power center. Facilitated by the element that fuels our sun (hydrogen) and uniting the energy of the universe with that of the earth, the ancient Egyptians converted vibrational energy into microwave energy. For the power plant to function, the designers and operators had to induce vibration in the Great Pyramid that was in tune with the harmonic resonant vibrations of the earth. Once the pyramid was vibrating in tune with the earth's pulse it became a coupled oscillator and could sustain the transfer of energy from the earth with little or no feedback. The three smaller pyramids on the east side of the

> **Once the pyramid was vibrating in tune with the earth's pulse it became a coupled oscillator and could sustain the transfer of energy from the earth with little or no feedback.**

Great Pyramid may have been used to assist the Great Pyramid in achieving resonance, much like today we use smaller gasoline engines to start large diesel engines. So let us now turn the key on this amazing power plant to see how it operated.

The Queen's Chamber, located in the center of the pyramid, and directly below the King's Chamber, contains peculiarities entirely different than those observed in the King's Chamber. The Queen's Chamber's characteristics indicate that its specific purpose was to produce fuel, which is of paramount importance for any power plant. Although it would be difficult to pinpoint exactly what process took place inside the Queen's Chamber, it appears a chemical reaction repeatedly took place there. The residual substance the process left behind (the salts on the chamber wall) and what can be deduced from artifacts (grapnel hook and cedar-like wood) and structural details (Gantenbrink's "door" for example) are too prominent to be ignored. They all indicate that the energy created in the King's Chamber was the result of the efficient operation of the hydrogen-generating Queen's Chamber.

The equipment that provided the priming pulses was most likely housed in the Subterranean Pit. Before or at the time the "key was turned" to start the priming pulses, a supply of chemicals was pumped into the northern and southern shafts of the Queen's Chamber, filling them until contact was made between the grapnel hook and the electrodes that were sticking out of the "door." Seeping through the "lefts" in the Queen's Chamber, these chemicals combined to produce hydrogen gas, which filled the interior passageways and chambers of the pyramid. The waste from the spent chemicals flowed along the Horizontal Passage and down the Well Shaft.

Induced by priming pulses of vibration—tuned to the resonant frequency of the entire structure—the vibration of the pyramid gradually increased in amplitude and oscillated in harmony with the vibrations of the earth. Harmonically coupled with the earth, vibrational energy then flowed in abundance from the earth through the pyramid and influenced a series of tuned resonators housed in the Grand Gallery, where the vibration was converted into airborne sound. By virtue of the acoustical design of the Grand Gallery, the sound was focused through the passage leading to the King's Chamber. Only frequencies in harmony with the resonant frequency of the King's Chamber were allowed to pass through an acoustic filter that was housed in the Antechamber.

The King's Chamber was the heart of the Giza power plant, an impressive power center comprised of thousands of tons of granite containing 55 percent silicon-quartz crystal. The chamber was designed to minimize any damping of vibration, and its dimensions created a resonant cavity that was in harmony with the incoming acoustical energy. As the granite vibrated in sympathy with the sound, it stressed the quartz in the rock and stimulated electrons to flow by what is known as the piezoelectric effect. The energy that filled the King's Chamber at that point became a combination of acoustical energy and electromagnetic energy. Both forms of energy covered a broad spectrum of harmonic frequencies, from the fundamental infrasonic frequencies of the earth to the ultrasonic and higher electromagnetic microwave frequencies.

The hydrogen freely absorbed this energy, for the designers of the Giza power plant had made sure that the frequencies at which the King's Chamber resonated were harmonics of the frequency at which hydrogen resonates. As a result, the hydrogen atom, which consists of one proton and one electron, efficiently absorbed this energy, and its electron was "pumped" to a higher energy state.

The northern shaft served as a conduit, or a waveguide, and its original metal lining—which passed with extreme precision through the pyramid from the outside—served to channel a microwave signal into the King's Chamber. The microwave signal that flowed through this waveguide may have been the same signal that we know today is created by the atomic hydrogen that fills the universe and that is constantly bombarding the earth. This microwave signal probably was reflected off the outside face of the pyramid, and then was focused down the northern shaft. Traveling through the King's Chamber and passing through a crystal box amplifier located in its path, the input signal increased in power as it interacted with the highly energized hydrogen atoms inside the resonating box amplifier and chamber. This interaction forced the electrons back to their natural "ground state." In turn, the hydrogen atoms released a packet of energy of the same type and frequency as the input signal. This "stimulated emission" was entrained with the input signal and followed the same path.

Both forms of energy covered a broad spectrum of harmonic frequencies, from the fundamental infrasonic frequencies of the earth to the ultrasonic and higher electromagnetic microwave frequencies.

The process built exponentially—occurring trillions of times over. What entered the chamber as a low energy signal became a collimated (parallel) beam of immense power as it was collected in a microwave receiver housed in the south wall of the King's Chamber and was then directed through the metal-lined Southern Shaft to the outside of the pyramid. This tightly collimated beam was the reason for all the science, technology, craftsmanship, and untold hours of work that went into designing, testing and building the Giza power plant. The ancient Egyptians had a need for this energy: It was most likely used for the same reasons we would use it today—to power machines and appliances. We know from examining Egyptian stone artifacts that ancient craftspeople had to have created them using machinery and tools that needed electricity to run. However, the means by which they distributed the energy produced by the Giza power plant may have been a very different process from any we use today. Because I lack hard evidence to support any speculation about their process, I will not address that issue now, but I will offer several hypotheses in the next chapter.

I would like to join architect James Hagan and other engineers and technologists in extending my utmost respect to the builders of the Great Pyramid. Though some academics may not recognize it, the precision and knowledge that went into its creation are—by modern standards—undeniable and a marvel to behold.

The evidence presented in this book, for the most part, was recorded many years ago by men of integrity who worked in the fields of archaeology and Egyptology. That much of this evidence was misunderstood only reveals the pressing need for an interdisciplinary approach to fields that have until recently been closed to non-academics and others outside the fold of formal archaeology and Egyptology. Much of our ignorance of ancient cultures can be placed at the feet of closed minded theorists who ignore evidence that does not fit their theories or fall within the province of their expertise. Sometimes it takes a machinist to recognize machined parts or machines! As a result, much of the evidence that supports a purpose for the Great Pyramid as anything other than a tomb has been ignored, discounted without serious consideration, or simply explained away as purely coincidental. Is it coincidence that the Great Pyramid is so huge and so precise? That the King's Chamber contains so many indications that tremendous forces disturbed it or were created within it at one time? Are the exuviae, the chocolate colored granite, the resonating chambers with their giant granite monoliths placed above, and the unique properties of the quartz crystal present in vast quantities in the granite complex all coincidental? Can the design, and physical tests of the movement of sound inside the Grand Gallery be just a happy accident? How about the series of notches along the Grand Gallery? They had to have some purpose.

If our society developed a power plant that embodied the features of the Great Pyramid, there would be a renaissance in public thought regarding power-related technology and how it affects an individual's life. If the technology that can be seen inside the Great Pyramid was replicated for our benefit, there would be less concern about the future of our technological society, for a vast renewable source of energy would be available for as long as we inhabit this planet. Water and/or simple chemicals enter at one point and energy is output from another. No pollution and no waste. What could be simpler?

Well, it may not be quite that simple. The technology that was used inside the Great Pyramid may be quite simple to understand but might be difficult to execute, even for our technologically "advanced" civilization. However, if anyone is inspired to pursue the theory presented here, their vision may be enhanced by the knowledge that re-creating this power source would be ecologically pleasing to those who have a concern about the environmental welfare and the future of the human race. Blending science and music, the ancient Egyptians had tuned their power plant to a natural harmonic of the earth's vibration (predominantly a function of the tidal energy induced by the gravitational effect that the moon has on the earth). Resonating to the life force of Mother Earth, the Great Pyramid of Giza quickened and focused her pulse, and transduced it into clean, plentiful energy.

Besides obvious benefits from such a power source, we also should consider the benefits that could be gained by utilizing such a machine in geologically unstable areas of the planet. As we discussed earlier, over time there is an enormous amount of this energy built up in the earth. Eventually the weak spots in the mantle can give way to these stresses, releasing tremendously destructive forces. If we could build a device to draw mechanical energy from seismically active regions of the planet in a controlled fashion—instead of allowing it to accumulate to the destructive level of earthquakes—we might be able to save thousands of lives and billions of dollars. We would have a device that would help stabilize the planet; so rather than being periodically shaky real estate, California might eventually become the United States' energy Mecca, with a Great Pyramid drawing off the energy that is building up within the San Andreas Fault. A fanciful idea? Perhaps not.

We know very little about the pyramid builders and the period of time when they erected these giant monuments; yet it seems obvious that the entire civilization underwent a drastic change, one so great that the technology was destroyed with no hope of rebuilding. Hence a cloud of mystery has denied us a clear view of the nature of these people and their technological knowledge. Considering the theory presented in this book, I am compelled to envision a fantastic society that had developed a power system thousands of years ago that we can barely imagine today. This society takes shape as we ask the logical question, "How was the energy transmitted? How was it used?" These questions cannot be fully answered by examining the artifacts left behind. However, these artifacts can stimulate our imaginations further; then we are left to speculate on the causes for the demise of the great and intelligent civilization that built the Giza power plant. These speculations, along with the complete details of this remarkable power system can be found in *The Giza Power Plant: Technologies of Ancient Egypt*.

Erich von Däniken

AVIATION IN ANTIQUITY?

DENMARK IS THE HOME of quite a few Viking castles and fortresses. The most famous one is the Traelleborg. What is a "Traelleborg"? Is it the name of a Danish beer? No, just like almost any country around the world has some sort of a national archaeological monument, In Denmark it is the Traelleborg. Officially, the Traelleborg is said to be "a fortress dating back to the time of the Vikings." With the word "fortress," one imagines a massive structure with protective walls, firing slits and an all-surrounding ditch. However, the Traelleborg is completely different. Take a compass and draw a circle. Then, a few centimeters further out draw another, then another. And, because you're doing such a great job, you can draw a fourth circle. This is a basic sketch of the Traelleborg's structure. The innermost circle consists of a mound that is 17 meters thick and six meters high. Beyond the mound is a ditch that is 17 meters wide. After the ditch is a second circular mound whose radius is twice as long as the first with a diameter of 136 meters. Surrounding it is another small ditch and a third mound. Now place a unilateral cross facing north-south and east-west over all the mounds, with the center of the cross at the center of the innermost circle. What does the picture look like? Four large circles, with the innermost circle divided into four equally large quadrants.

Now imagine 13 "little boats," rounded off at each end In an elliptical fashion. We place these "little boats" next to each other between the third and fourth circle, but only in the southeast quadrant. Furthermore, each of the little boats' axes are pointed directly toward the center of the circle. Even though this already is a fairly accurate picture of the Traelleborg, it is not yet finished. Due to the unilateral cross, the inner circles have been divided into four equally large pies. In each pie, we plant another four little boats (16 in total), two pointing north-south and two pointing east-west. The Traelleborg's ground plan is now finished.

Even though the Danish excavators who restored the Traelleborg did not discover any type of wood from any buildings, nor from the "little boats," the existing stone foundation on the ground confirms their general position. We are absolutely certain that this is exactly how the fortress must have looked a long, long time ago, they insist. The archaeologists found remnants of wood—albeit not from any buildings nor "little boats"—at some of the mounds. The remnants were dated back to A.D. 980. During that period, the Vikings ruled over this area. Pliers, hammers, a few brooches, belt buckles, axes and arrowheads were found at the Traelleborg also—everything dating back to the times of the Vikings. There was no doubt that the Vikings lived here and actually built this military fortress.

See, this is where it gets interesting, since the Vikings *never* adhered to any sort of astronomically related precision when building their settlements. The precise ground plan of the Traelleborg, which required brilliant engineers, does not at all fit into the Vikings' way of thinking.

See, this is where it gets interesting, since the Vikings *never* adhered to any sort of astronomically related precision when building their settlements. The precise ground plan of the Traelleborg, which required brilliant engineers, does not at all fit into the Vikings' way of thinking. The Vikings were seafaring roughnecks. If they did build fortresses it was only in order to protect their ships and harbors. Also, because they were seafarers, the Vikings lived right at the coast. The Traelleborg is not located at a harbor. It is known that a long time ago, three sides of the Traelleborg were swampland. Today, the Traelleborg is located three kilometers inland at the Great Belt, on the same island where Denmark's capital Copenhagen sprawls.

So did the actual structure really come from the Vikings, or did they just make use of an already existing, ancient sacred site? This same question also concerned the chief excavator, the Danish archaeologist Poul Norlund.

> This structure is too precise, too orderly that it could have been conceived by our Nordic ancestors. From all that we have gathered so far, any kind of precision or regularity completely and utterly escaped them.

Ultimately, the general consensus was that there should be no further speculation because there was no further information available. Thus, the Traelleborg was left alone. Everyone happily agreed that it had something to do with the Vikings. End of story. At least until one day, when a Dane went for a spin in his plane.

DISCOVERY FROM THE AIR

It is early summer 1982. Preben Hansson, born in 1923, boards a small, single engine Mourane Solnier 880 plane. The hobby pilot prefers this type of plane because it flies rather slow and very smoothly. Flying this plane feels like hovering about in a hot air balloon, which is perfect for taking pictures of the woods and meadows below.

On that nice sunny morning, Hansson, a professional glass worker by trade, with his own company, took off from his hometown of Korsor. The weather was incredibly nice, the visibility clear. A few minutes later, after flying over his own house, Hansson flew over the Traelleborg. He noticed the 16 elliptical shapes, the "little boats," neatly located inside the four quadrants of the inner circle. In their baffling precision, they immediately reminded him of a fine brooch meant to be placed around a beautiful blonde Viking girl's neck. Preben swerved around, and looked at the clearly visible mounds from the air and the outlines of the 13 "little boats" located in the southeast, clearly visible from the air. The "little boats," whose axes were pointing precisely to the center of the circle, conveyed the distinct impression of a *satellite dish*, pointing directly to the northwest. "What a funny picture," Hansson thought. "How did the Vikings come up with such a specific ground plan?"

Following his mood and the "direction" given by the Traelleborg below, Hansson adjusted the automatic pilot so that he was flying due northwest. Three minutes later, he flew over the Bay of Musholm, then the coast of the Great Belt. Shortly thereafter, he flew over the middle of the Reerso Peninsula. On frequency 127.30 he requested permission from the Kastrup tower for radar surveillance, or radar companionship, during his flight path over the sea. He was given the frequency squawk 2345 and was asked to report back as soon as he had left the sea over the coast of Rosnaes. He did as he was told and continued to fly a straight line originating at the Traelleborg going 325 degrees due north-northwest.

After 67 kilometers in flight, and 34 minutes of actual flight time, Hansson encountered a small surprise. He flew over the tiny island of Eskeholm, directly underneath him. There, he beheld a rather curious sight. On the ground, two triangles and a circle were barely visible. They were the remnants of another mound whose complete circumference must have been similar to that of the Traelleborg. Because the island is so tiny, no archaeological excavations were ever really pursued. "Who cares?" the glass worker thought. "Two points can always be connected with one straight line."

Hansson looked to see if he had any fuel left. He had enough left to reach one of the local airfields that were quite abundant in that area. He reactivated the autopilot, stubbornly continuing the same course he had been following ever since the Traelleborg, going 325 degrees north-northwest. He passed the center of the mound at Fyrkat. After 52 kilometers, or 26 minutes, he thought he was hallucinating. Straight ahead, directly in his flight path was the center of the gigantic mound of Aggersborg.

Aggersborg, the third "Viking Fortress," is Denmark's third national monument. The ground plan of Aggersborg is the same as the one at

Did this circular structure already exist *before* the Vikings? If so, were the Vikings the heirs of a much, much older culture?

Still, he started to have a suspicious feeling in the back of his head. He had plenty of fuel left to continue flying for another two hours. "Where will I end up if I hold the current course?" he asked himself. After another 50 minutes and 99.5 kilometers he got his answer: His plane flew directly over the circular archaeological site of Fyrkat.

Fyrkat is Denmark's second largest "Viking Fortress" and its second national treasure. The mound is situated a few kilometers due west of the town Hobro. Just like the Traelleborg, Fyrkat is also compellingly precisely positioned. The next coastline is 40 kilometers away.

Here again is another mysterious "Viking Fortress" without any direct access to the sea. Fyrkat's mound is four meters high, and 12 meters deep, with a diameter of 120 meters. Just like the Traelleborg, Fyrkat also features a unilateral cross facing north-south and east-west, and the 16 astronomically aligned "little boats."

After extensive excavations, archaeologists once again happily agreed that Vikings must have lived there. But why did the builders so strictly adhere to this impeccable geometric precision, a trait that is as congruous with the Vikings as fish sunbathing on the beach? Did this circular structure already exist *before* the Vikings? If so, were the Vikings the heirs of a much, much older culture?

Fyrkat and Traelleborg. It also features the four quadrants with the "little boats," the unilateral cross laid out pointing to the four cardinal directions, and the multiple mounds surrounding them. And everywhere the same discoveries, and the same questions.

With Aggersborg, there is one tiny difference. The inner circle is larger than the circle of the Traelleborg, and there is space for more "little boats." Furthermore, Aggersborg has not been renovated, so the little boats have not been recast with concrete. Parts of the monument today lie underneath a farm field.

FACTS! FASTEN YOUR SEAT BELTS!

So far, Hansson had flown over a distance of 218.5 kilometers. His course north-northwest at 325 degrees was given through the "satellite dish" he had seen at the Traelleborg. He flew over land and sea in one continuous straight line, going directly over the mounds of Eskeholm, Fyrkat and Aggersborg. There was not the slightest shadow of a doubt; Aggersborg-Fyrkat-Eskeholm-Traelleborg were all points *on one straight line!* Yet, the sites were divided by hills, rough coastal lines, bays and the sea. To say that this is all one huge coincidence should be considered insane.

But for what reason, and above all, with what means were the Vikings able to build such perfectly aligned structures?

Back home, Hansson took a closer look at his aerial maps. He needed maps of Denmark's adjoining countries and a globe. Hansson proceeded to draw a line through Aggersborg-Fyrkat-Eskeholm-Traelleborg and extended it over the borders of Denmark. He continued the line through Berlin, Yugoslavia, and ended up, get this, *at the ancient Greek Oracle of Delphi!* When he extended the line even further, it passed due west of the Pyramids of Giza, all the way down to Ethiopia, the former kingdom of the Queen of Sheba.

Hansson is a very exact and meticulous individual. Obviously, he had just discovered a prehistoric flight path that extended all the way from northern Europe to Delphi. In its path, other heathen mounds can be found, and the old village and city names quite often have something to do related to "lights, fire, flight, gods and power."

The never-tiring glass worker and his wife Bodil became regulars at Denmark's and northern Germany's bigger libraries. As they started to learn about myths and legends, a whole new, and completely fascinating, world opened up to them. This incredible story demonstrates how, with luck of discovery, logic, perseverance and a keen sense of perception, a currently accepted doctrine can be revised and rewritten.

"Scientists always wondered why Traelleborg, Fyrkat and Aggersborg were not situated closer to the famous main roads," Hansson stated. This was no coincidence.

Somebody built the structures *where they had to be*—on the exact flight path between Delphi and Aggersborg. Quite possibly, the mounds served as some sort of beacon, as a visible or electronic compass for the god's global aviation. In all likelihood, the mounds served as some sort of "radar" or "fueling stations."

Whoever built the structures in prehistoric times, one thing is certain: It was not the Vikings. For the Vikings, the location of Aggersborg—40 kilometers inland—would have been completely useless. Furthermore, they would have never adhered to the precise geometric symmetry of the entire complex.

Yet, how, and, above all, *why* were these "Viking Fortresses" built? During the time when the gods still lived here on earth, a handful of frightened humans must have lived just a stone's throw away from the mounds. These humans made absolutely sure to tell coming generations the same, highly significant story over and over again: "Here, the gods came down from the sky!" In the minds of the Stone Age people, the monuments became mystified sanctuaries.

Thousands of years later, at the time of the Vikings, no one remembered the original purpose of the once technical structures anymore. And contemporary archaeology is way too conservative, and lacking in imagination, to even possibly try to comprehend the significance behind these sites.

After the gods had left, the people started to direct their prayers and sacrifices towards the heavens. The behavior is quite understandable. After all, these were sites where at one point in time, mysterious and powerful beings resided. No other locations were more suitable for observing ceremonies than the areas where the gods themselves once lived. Thousands of years later, at the time of the Vikings, no one remembered the original purpose of the once technical structures anymore. And contemporary archaeology is way too conservative, and lacking in imagination, to even possibly try to comprehend the significance behind these sites.

Hansson states:

It is impossible to suggest that it is pure coincidence that these large mounds form one straight line. The monuments were built by someone who had a specific purpose for them to be built on one straight line. In addition, they had to be built by someone who had the means to plan across an area of over 200 kilometers, independently, to the then historically known main roads, from island to island, across land and sea.

A friend of mine, an archaeologist, yes, the one with the "easy answers," explained that the Vikings were able to pull this task off rather easily. All they had to do was pull a long piece of *string* from one place to the other. Holy Odin, Holy Wotan, Holy Thor, give me strength! Again and again I am completely and utterly perplexed by the cobwebbed minds by which we are surrounded. Can such an attitude of refusing to see what can be proven beyond the shadow of a doubt still be considered science?

Let us recap: Preben Hansson's flight path extended directly above four "Viking Fortresses" and ended directly and precisely at the Greek Oracle of Delphi. How does a place get an oracle? What was there at Delphi that was so significant that people all of a sudden built an oracle? What was there to "oracle" about at Delphi? How does one, single, tiny dot somewhere on a map achieve world fame even in prehistoric times?

Even in ancient Greece, Delphi was regarded as the center of the world. The one visual piece that

Apollo had incredible powers, and, except for his own father, Zeus, he did not fear anyone. Often he assisted the Trojans in their battles and protected their roads—from the air, that is. Apollo's most famous nickname is "Lykeios"—god of light. One fascinating fact is that not even the Greeks knew from where Apollo actually came. Even today, researchers of mythology quarrel over whether Apollo came to Greece via the north or from the east. However, they all agree on the fact that Apollo left Delphi for a period of a few of weeks or months each year in order to visit a mysterious, far away people, the Hyperboreans. The Hyperboreans lived "on the other side from where the north wind comes."

This available biographical data is not bad, even though it can only be found in mythology's treasure chest. Apollo is the son of a "heavenly creature." He is considered the god of light, and the god of medicine. He supports his friends in battles, protects their roads, and he annually vanishes to visit a people "on the other side from where the north wind comes." And he established his headquarters at Delphi.

This is my theory: Due to the shortest flight paths, some extraterrestrial establishes his base camp at a certain point X. Frightened humans come closer. Apollo, benevolent by nature, heals the sick and advises them in important questions. He fosters his

---

He gave her the most glorious of glories and riches... and a chariot that could ride in the air, which he had built according to the teachings he had received from one of the gods.

---

illustrates the firm belief that this place was really considered to be the "Navel of the World" is the *Omphalos*, a wonderful sculpture (a block made of marble), flanked by two golden eagles. The eagles were thought to be two servants of Zeus, the father of all gods. All of Delphi, however, was dedicated to the god Apollo. Apollo was not only one of Zeus' sons; he was also the god of light and "prophecies." In addition, Apollo acted as the healer. One of Apollo's most famous sons was Asklepios, considered even today as the "forefather" of all medical doctors.

relations with the people from the earth. More and more people flock to this place because they are seeking advice and medical help. As time passes, in the mind of the people, this place grows into the "Center of the World." Point X becomes Delphi because it was only there that people were able to obtain "divine advice." *Prophecy had now officially been invented.*

The stunned earthlings watched with amazement at how the god Apollo could hover in the sky "inside a jewel of light." Since the humans had no concept of technology, they immediately saw the embodiment of light in him. *The god of light was born.*

"Where does he fly to?" they ask themselves. One day, he gives the answer to one of the priests. The priests were capable men that he taught how to keep the base camp clean and ready. He flies to a people "who live on the other side of the northern wind." Apollo was a practical thinker. From his base camp, he wanted to reach his most important destinations in the shortest amount of time and distance possible. Thus, many tasks had to be accomplished—schools were built, people were taught in different fields such as medicine and the schools brought forth teachers in many disciplines.

For his earthbound flights, Apollo did not use a spaceship. Maybe there wasn't one available to him, because his divine father Zeus was exploring the solar system with it. Apollo used simple flying vehicles—possibly a combination of steerable and propeller-driven hot air balloons, a dirigible. For such vehicles, Apollo needed "fueling stations" located at precisely calculated points of travel. It didn't matter whether or not he used water and oil for his steam engines, or whether he used other

knows for sure, because myths cannot be dated precisely. New names have always been added to the ancient contents. At one point, Solomon even gave his lover some type of flying vehicle as a present.

"He gave her the most glorious of glories and riches... and a chariot which could ride in the air, which he had built according to the teachings he had received from one of the gods."[1]

This mythical Solomon must have been one incredible guy. If one follows the most ancient Ethiopian traditions, the *Kebra Nagast* (*Book of the Kings' Glories*), Solomon managed to travel the distance of three months by foot in only one day with his flying chariot. In addition, he is said to have traveled without sickness, nor hunger, nor thirst, nor sweat, nor fatigue.[2]

It is understandable that the pilot of such a vehicle must have had access to some very detailed aerial maps. One of ancient Arabia's most prominent geographer and historians, Al-Mas'Udi (A.D. 895-956), wrote about this in his "Histories." He stated that Solomon had access to maps that "showed the constellations, the stars, the earth with her continents and oceans, the inhabited

---

In one of his books, written in the year 1256, Bacon states that "also flying vehicles (*instrumenta volandi*) were once built... They were built a long, long time ago, and it is certain that they were in possession of a flight instrument."

---

sources of propulsion such as electricity or microwaves. One way or the other, he needed fuel. An entire network of "mounds" had to be created. At each "base," Apollo meticulously instructed his ground crew to perform different tasks and duties. *The priest serving his god was born.*

MEMORIES OF THE FUTURE

The straight line that originates in Denmark and goes to Delphi, when extended further, also goes through Egypt and eventually reaches Ethiopia, the former land of the Queen of Sheba. The Queen was King Solomon's loved one, who according to legends and scriptures was—Hallelujah! —one of the busiest aviators of his time. When exactly this was, nobody

landmasses, her plants and animals and many other wondrous things."

From Ethiopia, the flight path can be traced over today's Iran all the way to India. The prehistoric aviation activities of the Indian gods have been a highly important part of people's daily lives since the beginning of India's recorded history. All these stories and descriptions can be found in great detail in the ancient Indian *Vedas* and myths.

What more do we want? Sure, the sources of information that have survived until today are mysterious, even difficult to comprehend sometimes, because they are what they are, mythical. Still, when looked at in their entirety, they form a rather clear picture. Especially if we move the board that is obstructing our view from in front of our eyes

> **Every ethnologist is quite familiar with the indisputable fact that there are literally hundreds of similar texts and traditions all around the globe, all dating to about the same time. Do they care? Do they see any correlations? Of course not.**

and place it underneath our feet so that we can look over the fence. The writers who reported about these flying machines thousands and thousands of years ago were, logically speaking, much closer to the actual events than we will ever be. Certainly, they had better access to and must have read and perused written documents and sacred books that did not survive the war-torn chronology of human history. Even during the Middle Ages, the philosopher and monk Roger Bacon (A.D. 1219-1294) had access to significant pieces of information that are no longer available to us. In one of his books, written in the year 1256, Bacon states that "also flying vehicles (*instrumenta volandi*) were once built... They were built a long, long time ago, and it is certain that they were in possession of a flight instrument."

Roger Bacon was not a raving lunatic by any means. In fact, he was the Chair at Oxford University until he joined the Franciscan Order in 1257. His writings and books were so smart, yet dangerous for the Church, that Pope Clemens IV requested for complete copies of all of Bacon's writings to be reproduced in the year 1266. Quite a reasonable request, considering the fact that Roger Bacon wrote about ancient secrets. He and his last piece of work were even referred to as "doctor mirabilis"—the wondrous doctor.

In the ancient Japanese Shinto writings, one can often read about a "hovering bridge in the sky" from which the gods and selected human beings descended. This mysterious bridge was regarded exclusively as the connecting link between the divine vehicle and the "heavenly rock vessel." The divine vehicle glided through the air space "like a ship in the water," but the "heavenly rock vessel" was used only to fly "within the earth's air space." The god of heaven, "Nigihayhahi," used the "hovering bridge in the

sky" and his "heavenly rock vessel" to reach the people on earth. Today, it would not be any different; from an orbiting mothership the crew would transfer onto a shuttle to reach the base on earth.

Every ethnologist is quite familiar with the indisputable fact that there are literally hundreds of similar texts and traditions all around the globe, all dating to about the same time. Do they care? Do they see any correlations? Of course not. Even though we are living in the space age, stories like the ones I have presented above have absolutely no consequences for our conventional way of thinking. At least sometimes academics bow down to admit that certain legends might correlate with some obscure local ruins. But only because it is good for business—paying tourists come and visit. But they flat out refuse to admit that there could be any similarities *intercontinentally*. God forbid. Why should a Danish archaeologist ever care about Delphi in Greece? What does Apollo have to do with Solomon? What do the ancient Japanese emperors have to do with spaceships? What does a stone circle in Morocco have to do with an exact replica in India? What does an astronomically aligned passage grave in Colombia have to do with its twin grave in Ireland?

The courage needed to use all of our contemporary knowledge to fit together all of the puzzle's pieces is sorely missing. The spirit in this world was not created by our minds; it has been present for eons. Our way of thinking is minimal, and we still cannot look past our own noses. We have just woken up, yet we strive mightily to keep dozing. In doing so, we fail to understand that many things on this planet are connected and that everything moves towards a much bigger picture.

---

1. *Kebra Nagast*, Ch. 30.

2. Ibid., p. 58.

Crichton E. M. Miller

THE CONSTANTINE CONSPIRACY

THE CELTIC CROSS or wheel cross, also known as the sun cross, Odin's cross or Woden's cross, is an ancient northern symbol dating back to the start of the Bronze Age in western Europe.

It is also the oldest ancient Egyptian glyph known as the NWIT and is found among pre-Columbian Amerindian designs as well as in the ancient civilizations of the Far East.

The Nordic God Odin and the Teutonic Wuotan, or Woden, was seen as the supreme god before Christianity. He was the god of art, culture, warfare and the dead; he was seen as a one eyed old man with ravens as familiars and messengers in folklore.

The wheel cross is one of the first non-pictorial symbols on rock carvings associated with ships and hunter gatherer activities.

The wheel cross is one of the first non-pictorial symbols on rock carvings associated with ships and hunter gatherer activities in Scandinavia and Norway. There is no doubt that Odin's cross is associated with the wheel and indeed the wheel, which is considered to be at least 7,000 years old, is also in evidence on glyphs from the Bronze Age shown clearly on carts pulled by oxen. But the wheel also represented the motions of the stars, sun and moon to ancient mariners and nomads. On the other side of the continent in ancient China the wheel cross symbol was associated with thunder, power, energy, head and respect. Shamash, the ancient sun god, was also represented by a wheel cross by the ancient Babylonians.

When early writing systems were developed, the wheel cross symbol was included among the signs that were used by the Egyptians, Hittites, Cretians, Greeks, Etruscans and Romans.

This symbol signified a sphere in ancient Greece and was used as a natal chart pattern in Greek astrology which, even today, is used by modern astrologers as the sign for earth, the astrological element earth, and Fortuna or the Fortune which is an important position in the birth or natal chart related to the individual's progress and hindrances in the material aspect of life.

You will notice that the wheel cross is always associated with the highest form of geometry and mathematics, the measurement of the stars.

Modern scientific astronomy also uses the wheel cross as a symbol for the planet earth. The original meaning of the sign of the wheel cross has become confused, reworded and forgotten over the millennia. Originally the wheel cross, Odin's cross or the Celtic cross was a symbol for the highest power on earth, the creator sun, and its earthly representative, the king. It always represented absolute power and control.

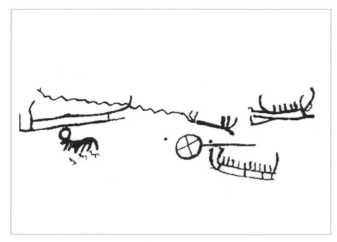

Bronze Age rock art ship with Celtic cross 1300 B.C.

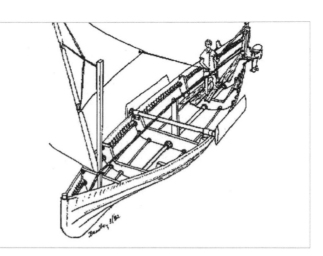

Modern currach design proposed as tsunami relief fishing boat.

The Celtic or wheel cross was once an early instrument designed for the geometric measurement of the earth and the heavens by priest-kings who could keep time and predict seasonal changes by the sun and stars including the practical art of navigating and measuring the planet. It was this simple but effective instrument that was responsible for the construction of stone circles and the development of the early mathematics that we still use today.

Early writing developed from mathematics and this was the supreme instrument that made it possible, leading to the eventual exploration of space in modern times.

blessed water or oil, draws the wheel cross at 12 different places on the church walls. Its use as a halo or Gloria, i.e., the spiritual power or energy that holy persons emanate, is associated with its original meaning as a sign of power."[1]

This work is written to inform the reader that disinformation has been used by those in power for thousands of years to manipulate ordinary people. The finest example of this is the religious use of the Celtic cross, the world's best-known icon and symbol. For instance, did you know that Crusade, an emotive word, means war of the cross and was used recently by the most powerful man in our present world?

The Celtic cross is not what you think it is. It is not and never was a religious icon. It has become a lie and an illusion created by a man of blood over a thousand years ago.

This wonderful instrument has become forgotten—why? Because of a man-made phenomenon based on fear, illusion and control. Religion is man-made and responsible for many of the world's ills—spirituality and enlightenment belongs to God.

"As has been its custom, the Christian Church has included this ancient pagan sign among the crosses of its symbolism. It is known as the gamma cross, the Roman Catholic cross, the consecration cross and the inauguration cross. At the inauguration of a church, the bishop, using

The Celtic cross is not what you think it is. It is not and never was a religious icon. It has become a lie and an illusion created by a man of blood over a thousand years ago. His name was Constantine.

The original design of the cross is to be found in rock carvings throughout the ancient world from South America to Egypt and was in existence long before it became a Christian symbol in the Fourth Century A.D.

I cannot tell you of all the intricacies surrounding the loss of this valuable piece of ancient history in an article this size, so I will give an outline of the tragic story surrounding this mysterious artifact.

It was Constantine (a Gaul) who deposed his opposition in the Roman Empire by raising Christianity to become the Roman state religion, which then proceeded to conquer Europe and eventually the Americas, chasing the old religions to the marginal areas and eventual extinction whilst absorbing much of their traditions and building churches on their ancient sacred sites.

Constantine (a Pagan) also removed the previous Christian symbol of a fish[2] replacing it with the solar image of the Celtic cross that was the original symbol of Gaul and that of the western Atlantic seafaring peoples who lived in the places now known as Brittany in France, Cornwall in England, Wales, Scotland and Ireland.

In Paleolithic times there were herds of huge animals and predators roaming the countryside while *Homo sapiens* in those times were predominantly hunter-gatherers without the modern knowledge and illusion of countries and borders.

These hunter-gatherer tribes followed the herds on their annual migrations, but not across land in line with modern academic thinking—that is entirely impractical and inefficient—but by sea and river through sailing and rowing their currachs along the coasts, across open sea and up shallow river estuaries.[6]

To achieve this feat in boats requires a sound knowledge of navigation, since a boat only has to go a short distance from the shore[7] to be out of sight of land and the unskilled would become easily lost.

They were shamanic, attributing spirit to everything they saw on the planet, but they always thought of the sun as the giver of life and therefore the supreme God.

Did you know at the end of the Christian Lord's Prayer that Amen is called on? *"For yours is the Kingdom, the Power and the Glory, Amen."* Amen[3] is the same as Amun or the most famous Pharaoh in the world Tut Ankh Amen, meaning Wisdom and Life of the Age of Aries. You are living in the age of the Fish, Pisces. Why then do Church leaders insist the faithful call on an age long dead?

This has been hidden from you by those who say that Amen means *"So say all of us."* Hidden in the same way that the ancient wheel cross is now seen as a Christian symbol.

These ancient people, who were originally Constantine's ancestors and saw the sun as the Creator or Father, were superb mariners who sailed the Atlantic Ocean, navigating by the stars in sailing boats of up to 60 feet[4] in length made of lightweight frames covered in animal skins.[5]

In the Paleolithic and Neolithic ages, the world was very different to the one we are used to today. It is hard for us to visualize the land as it was then, without roads and covered in forest, swamp, rough terrain and dangerous animals.

Navigation is an art form requiring a sound knowledge of nature such as wind direction, bird flight, salt water and fresh water to indicate estuaries, cloud formations, sea bed types, and a form of mathematics created through the observation of heavenly bodies such as the sun, moon, planets and stars as well as knowledge of the cyclical nature of time.

They were shamanic, attributing spirit to everything they saw on the planet, but they always thought of the sun as the giver of life and therefore the supreme God.

So it is true to say that the wheel cross was a sun symbol, because the only way to tell the time is to find and track the position of the sun both night and day, by the week, month, season and year.[8]

The boats they built were the result of understanding the forces of the elements over a recorded period of around 150,000 years from an early coastal living existence in Africa.[9] They traveled in small family groups of around 20 to 25 people carrying their boats ashore and turning them upside down to act as an efficient and waterproof house while they hunted wild animals and gathered nuts and fruit as the latitude and season allowed.

We know that they traveled great distances hunting mammoth and red deer herds through archaeological evidence of the distribution of similarly carved Venus figurines, fine textiles and mammoth beads across Europe dating from around 36,000 B.C.

We also know that these people had reached the eastern shores of America and Siberia at the end of the ice age because of the discovery of Clovis points[10] on both sides of the Atlantic and the Pacific Oceans.

We also now know that our Paleolithic ancestors measured the lunisolar[11] calendar and created early zodiacs[12] through the discovery of cave paintings[13] in France.

I proposed in my book *The Golden Thread of Time* in 2001 that in the cataclysms that followed the melting of the ice age 12,500 years ago, which was responsible for the destruction of a huge part of the flora and fauna of our planet, the most likely humans to survive were those who were at sea.[14]

The reason for this is that any tsunami that is large enough to destroy so many creatures on the shore and on low lying plains, could be more easily ridden out at sea, where the effect would more likely turn out to be a large swell on the surface of the ocean.

Whereas, the effect on a coastline of a large tidal wave would be horrendous as the swell was turned into a giant breaking wave as it reached shallower depths. This breaking violent wave would annihilate all before it as it rushed up the beach.

This theory was born out tragically in the Indian Ocean on the morning of December 26, 2004 where millions worldwide watched people on the shoreline die in their hundreds of thousands while no boat at sea was sunk and yachts anchored offshore were seen to rise to the swells and remain undamaged and intact.

The world flood recorded in the folk traditions of the world, the *Bible*, the *Koran* and in the *Dead Sea Scrolls* caused by the end of the ice age is denied by historians despite the overwhelming scientific evidence that sea levels have risen worldwide by around 300 feet since 10,500 B.C.

When the ice sheets melted, great walls broke from the faces of mile high glaciers and dams of moraine at the edges of giant freshwater melt lakes broke, sending huge tsunamis across the oceans and the land. Great rocks as big as houses are seen in the American Great Plains that had been moved hundreds of miles by the force of the floods.

The early hunter-gatherer mariners had developed a form of geometry and mathematics that was linked to astronomy and astrology to move around in their environment.

When the ice age ended, the days of the hunter-gatherer were numbered as the herds on which they had depended no longer existed. It was not long after this that agriculture and animal husbandry started in the lower latitudes.

It is the result of this huge social change that wars and conflicts developed as Mankind's populations grew because of excess food production and the development of land ownership. It was because of this that warriors became more organized to defend their farms and property from aggressors and to become aggressive themselves when they ran out of space through population growth or famine. Eventually these early agricultural societies began to spread and trade with other nations using sea routes.[15]

If you want to trade, you have to know where you are at sea and to do that you must be able to find latitude and longitude. To find longitude you must know the time both locally and at a Prime Meridian. Today the Prime Meridian is at Greenwich, after much argument with the French, but the original Prime Meridian was at Giza in Egypt from which all local times and distances were calculated.[16]

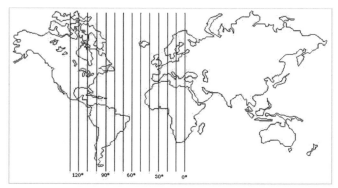

Degrees of longitude west from Giza. Copyright: Crichton E. M. Miller.

The result of this earlier knowledge was that watch stations or observatories were developed throughout the world, explaining the similarity over the millennia of structures and beliefs on a worldwide basis because of transoceanic navigation.[17]

Pre-Christian cross in western Ireland that is hidden from public view at Clonfert.

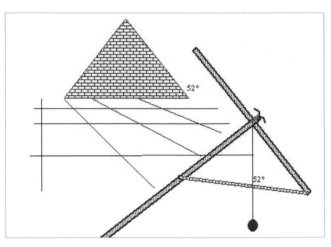

The Egyptian cross and plumbline measuring the angle of the pyramid.

This network has long been investigated and argued about. Current academic belief expounds, in the face of lack of real evidence, that it is purely coincidental that there are such similarities.

As the agricultural societies expanded they forced the older hunter-gatherers that had survived up to the start of the Bronze Age to the edges of the continent.

Many investigators and writers have commented on various pieces of evidence that could not be explained. These intrepid explorers have brought masses of information to the public's attention. This information only deepens the sense of mystery and in some cases convinces a large section of the material a religion in its own right without thought for the consequences.

Were this not so, we would be able to see what our ancestors left behind quite clearly and our civilizations would not be on the brink of disaster through conflict and the destruction of the environment.

We are on the road to the collapse of civilization if we do not change, and change means removing illusion and differences between the family of Man and Nature as a whole.

To prove my point, that we have difficulty in seeing clearly, I have been fortunate in discovering the instrument that the ancients used in prehistory to measure the stars and the planet on which we live.

The result of this earlier knowledge was that watch stations or observatories were developed throughout the world, explaining the similarity over the millennia of structures and beliefs on a worldwide basis because of transoceanic navigation.

population into believing that aliens must have been involved in the achieving of the inexplicable.

I do not believe that aliens were involved, but rather that we are the aliens, because we do not understand the way our ancestors thought, and that we are deceived by the ignorant who have risen to power without wisdom.

In my book *The Golden Thread of Time*, I show that, in comparison to the ancients, we have become very dualistic and have divorced ourselves from nature and the cosmos, making pursuit of the

This instrument can tell the time, find latitude and longitude, measure the angles of the stars, predict the solstices and equinoxes and measure the precession of the equinoxes.

The instrument can also find the ecliptic pole as well as the north and south poles, it can make maps and charts, design pyramids and henges and, used in combination with these, observers can record and predict the cycles of Nature and Time.

The cross is the instrument of the ancients who invented astrology and astronomy; it is also

> **The cross is the instrument of the ancients who invented astrology and astronomy; it is also a religious icon hidden from the public today by Constantine and the Roman Catholic Church.**

a religious icon hidden from the public today by Constantine and the Roman Catholic Church. It is on all Christian Churches and many gravestones; it is in literature and song and can be seen hanging round the necks of the faithful all over the world. The teachers of the Christian faith use it, kneel before it, wear it as part of their raiment and yet they do not seem to recognize it for what it is. Indeed, the cross may be older than time, and the greatest treasure ever left by our ancestors. The cross is a maritime treasure trove of wisdom, and it has been responsible for constructing the pyramids in Egypt and the Americas.

The author has discovered the remnants of a cross that was hidden by the House of Amen, in the Great Pyramid of Khufu at Giza.[18] This amazing cross and plumbline is capable of measuring angles to an accuracy of three arc minutes, showing that the cross may be more important than the pyramid, since the pyramid could not exist without the cross.

> **I have found out that this knowledge was rediscovered and kept secret by the Knights Templar and other secret societies throughout the Middle Ages.**

The cross appears to be much older than the pyramids, since it is also responsible for the construction of Neolithic henges in Europe that predate the pyramids by thousands of years.

I have found out that this knowledge was rediscovered and kept secret by the Knights Templar and other secret societies throughout the Middle Ages.

This great secret probably led to the destruction of the Amerindian civilizations at the hands of the Conquistadors when they found them measuring the stars with a form of cross which was called by the Maya their "Staff of Power."[19]

It is certain that the Christian Churches knew of its purpose during the last few centuries from evidence I have found in the Vatican, but it seems that it is completely forgotten now and that they have achieved the goal of illusion.

A Celtic cross at Crichton Churchyard, Scotland.

To show the comparison to this ancient technology, please look at the following photograph of a Celtic cross in the graveyard of Crichton Churchyard, near Rosslyn Chapel in the Scottish borders. You will see that the cross forms an upright angle, with crossbars set at 90 degrees to each other.

In the center of the cross is an object that looks like a hub, and on the hub is hung a wheel. Our ancestors never designed things without purpose, and the first purpose of using stone as a medium is that of preservation. The second thing that they did was to incorporate important knowledge for their descendants.

This occult work can be ably demonstrated by the fabulous work of craftmasons in the mediaeval cathedrals of Europe and, of course, by much older constructions like the Great Pyramid.

In keeping with the concept of "not casting pearls before swine," they hid esoteric messages in anything that they carved so that the seeker may find what he or she was ready to understand.

But there was another reason—self-preservation. You must remember that anyone found not holding the cross of Constantine in an upright manner and treating it as a crucifix would be treated as a witch by the Inquisition.[20]

This occult work can be ably demonstrated by the fabulous work of craft masons in the mediaeval cathedrals of Europe and, of course, by much older constructions like the Great Pyramid.

It is clear from observation that these masons carved a particular object that is obviously a wheel that is designed to rotate between cross bars on a hub. Why?

In some of the older crosses, they incorporated a serpentine design around the wheel and also made the arms of the cross wider at the outer edge than on the inner. Why?

The answer to these questions only came to me when I was experimenting with different methods to find out how the Egyptians could have surveyed the Great Pyramid and aligned it with the stars.

This artifact is capable of measuring all angles possible and, coupled with sufficient astronomical knowledge, it reveals all the mysteries of the ancients, how they kept time and measured the stars, sun, moon, planets and sailed the oceans of the world.

All constructions need surveying first and the Great Pyramid was an enormous undertaking of civil engineering, so using the simplest of materials and the accepted mathematics of the time, I assembled a theodolite, which could carry out the tasks required.

With the addition of a scale rule and a plumbline, the instrument became a cross that was extremely accurate and fulfilled the set task and much more.

Not long after this discovery, while carrying out further research, I discovered the records of the Dixon Relics[21] that were discovered in the north shaft of the Queen's Chamber in 1872. On further investigation, I also discovered that there were more relics still in the shaft and that these could be seen quite clearly in the photographs taken by Rudolph Gantenbrink in 1994 with his miniature robot *Upuaut 2*.

I then set about assembling the relics in a logical format and the astounding result was a cross and plumbline of incredible accuracy.

This artifact is capable of measuring all angles possible and coupled with sufficient astronomical knowledge it reveals all the mysteries of the ancients, how they kept time and measured the stars, sun, moon, planets and sailed the oceans of the world.

But it goes further than that, exposing the Ancients' fundamental spirituality and understanding of the world, nature and the universe. Many of these revelations have never been seen by the public before, and are a must for those who seek truth and understanding.

I applied for two patents on the cross and plumbline in 1998 and the patents were finally granted in November 2000, as an astronomical, surveying and navigational instrument by the British Patent Office.[22]

The result of the first patent is the instrument in Figure 7. As you can see, it is a faithful representation of the Celtic cross and was the only instrument in the ancient world that could create zodiacs and helped the Egyptians create the circle we know today as 360°.

The system of mathematics created by the ancients is used today and is the measure of

The working Celtic cross measuring the constellations.

The working Celtic cross measuring the angle of the sun.

time, distance and speed required to find a position on the earth and measure its distance.

This resurrected version of the cross, using 360°, is made so that modern people may understand the principles and compare it with the cross (in Figure 1) or with any Celtic cross in any part of the world.

The working cross is marked in degrees round the edge, and the wheel spins freely on a hub.

The cross arms are perforated with viewing holes to allow the observer to read the angles, and the bottom of the wheel is weighted so that it will always point to the center of the earth.

The scale around the outer edge of the wheel determined from the results of observing stars, planets and constellations.

The cross should be completely understood by as many as possible, for it was the foundation of the very roots of ancient civilization, wisdom and understanding.

But more than that, it reveals the state of illusion into which we have fallen or been led through eons of disinformation.

Do not think that this work is anti-Christian—if leaders both political and religious had practiced the teachings of Christ as he spoke at the Sermon on the Mount or understood his wisdom, the world would be a far better place today.

The cross should be completely understood by as many as possible, for it was the foundation of the very roots of ancient civilization, wisdom and understanding.

---

runs from zero degrees at the bottom to 90 degrees clockwise and counter-clockwise so that horizontal measurements can be taken in any direction through the viewing holes.

You can see the advantages of this instrument immediately when you look at the photograph below of an observer measuring the angle of the sun as it rises in the east at dawn.

As the world spins around, the sun appears to rise from the horizon and its angle of ascent may be read from the scale directly.

This angle changes, as the seasons progress throughout the year and time and place may be

Territorial power hungry rulers still use religion and illusion to divide us as they scrabble like growling dogs, to gain nothing in the end.

I feel that in these current, dangerous and confused times, we could do well trying to understand the deeper knowledge of our ancestors and apply some of it to our present world. For each human being has the unique right to think for themselves and to take personal responsibility for their actions and potential to reach fulfillment, peace, freedom and happiness.

1. www.symbols.com

2. The fish symbol of early Christianity represented the sign or age of Pisces in the same way that Amun or Amen represented the sign or age of Aries to the Egyptians.

3. Amen or Amun is the name for Aries in ancient Egyptian and represents an astrological period of 2,160 years of precession of the equinoxes. Many of the pharaohs were named after the age as sons of God, the creative power of the Time.

4. Large sailing boats plying the Atlantic were reported by Julius Caesar during the Roman invasion of Britain.

5. These ancient traditional boats are still made in Ireland for local fishermen and known as *currachs*; although they are much smaller these days, they are still enormously seaworthy and capable in ocean swells.

6. The animal-skinned currach is capable of floating in only 18 inches of water, allowing the efficient ambushing of herds when they pause at the water's edge, and when the animals cross rivers on their migratory route. This method also gives protection from the large predators that our ancestors were no match for.

7. The distance to the horizon at sea from an observer is calculated in imperial measurement. Height of eye squared divided by 9.

Example: 6ft x 6 ÷ 9 = 4 nautical miles.

8. The zodiac is a circle of fixed stars against which the path of the sun is measured as the earth travels round on its orbit.

9. Evidence of early *Homo sapiens* has been discovered in caves on the African coasts over 150,000 years ago along with advanced stone working implements carefully and skillfully collected and worked from unique locations along with the use of red ocher for painting and needles for working animal skins to produce clothing.

10. Clovis points are a form of spear tip used by hunter-gatherers throughout the northern hemisphere between 12,500 and 10,500 years ago that is subject to current academic argument and debate over the methods of diffusion of early *Homo sapiens* known as the Solutrean connection.

11. A lunisolar calendar is created by measuring the path of the moon and the sun along the ecliptic plane using the zodiac as a backdrop to identify the position of the sun or moon on a particular day resulting in a monthly and annual calendar or almanac.

12. Zodiac literally means "circle of animals" and is a visual method of identifying unique constellations of stars for the purposes of astronomy and navigation.

13. The palaeolithic paintings in the caves of Lascaux are carbon dated to around 15,000 years ago, although there is some debate that the method is faulty and that the paintings could be as many as 27,000 years old.

14. *Ancient American*, no. 46, 2002.

15. There is evidence of Phoenicians trading in the Baltic and Cornwall for jet, amber and tin as well as tobacco [and cocaine—Ed.] from America found in mummies in Egypt.

16. Crichton E. M. Miller, *The Golden Thread of Time*. Rugby: Pendulum, 2001.

17. Two great explorers have proved that the ancients could build boats that crossed oceans. Their names are Thor Heyerdahl and Tim Severin. Academia argues that they could not prove the ancients could navigate, until now.

18. Miller.

19. Ibid.

20. The Inquisition was a holocaust for women, resulting in the murder of 3,000,000 women over a period of 300 years for loving nature or healing with herbs. The monstrous Inquisition damns the Catholic Church by its own actions despite the apologies of Pope John Paul II.

21. A granite ball, a piece of wood resembling cedar and a small bronze hook. —Ed.

22. United Kingdom Patent Office, no. GB2344654

George T. Sassoon

THE ANCIENT OF DAYS:

DEITY OR MANNA-MACHINE?

FOLLOWING my mother's death in 1975, I was exploring her library and found a strange book entitled *The Kabbalah Unveiled*, by S. L. MacGregor Mathers. First published in London in 1887, the work was still in print, having clearly enjoyed a steady sale. It purports to be a translation of certain parts of the *Zohar*, an ancient Jewish mystical work, and consists largely of physical descriptions of an entity known as the *Ancient of Days*.

I had come across this title in the well-known English hymn "Immortal, Invisible," and as a brief mention in the Biblical *Book of Daniel*, and had vaguely assumed it to be simply another title of God. But in Mathers' book, there was a depiction of something clearly very different from our present concepts of the Almighty. The book was in the form of a series of lectures given by a certain Rabbi Simon bar Yochai to a group of his disciples, in which he claimed to be passing on a body of ancient secret knowledge which had hitherto only been transmitted orally. This was said to be the Secret or Unwritten Law, as opposed to the written Law laid down in the books of Moses.

The material was split into three sections, known as the *Book of Concealed Mystery* (BoM), the *Greater Holy Assembly* (GHA) and the *Lesser Holy Assembly* (LHA). These were split into Bible-style numbered verses for ease of reference.

Manna Machine model, created by Martin Riches in Berlin. Photo by Yumiko Urae.

What was this secret knowledge? I found passages such as:

(37) Like as if it were said "He is found (that is, He may in some way to a certain extent be known), and he is not found;" for He cannot he clearly comprehended; but He hath as it were been formed; neither yet is He to be known of any, since He is the Ancient of the Ancient Ones.

(38) But in his conformation is He known; as also He is the Eternal of the Eternal Ones, the Ancient of the Ancient Ones, the Concealed of the Concealed Ones; and in His symbols is He knowable and unknowable.

(39) White are His garments, and His appearance is the likeness of a Face vast and terrible.

(40) Upon the throne of flaming light is He seated, so that He may direct its (flashes).

(41) Into forty thousand superior worlds the brightness of the skull of His head is extended, and from the light of this brightness the just shall receive four hundred worlds in the world to come.

(42) This is that which is written, Genesis 23:16: "Four hundred shekels of silver, current money with the merchant."

(43) Within His skull exist daily 13,000 myriads of worlds, which draw their existence from Him, and by Him are upheld.[1]

I wondered what had led my mother to acquire this book, then remembered that when younger she had briefly been interested in mysterious subjects. The work, it seemed, was used widely by mystics, devotees of eccentric religions and such-like, and it must have been these people who had kept it in print for nearly a century. It was extraordinary that I, a hard-nosed engineer, should have stumbled across it.

At first I was inclined to dismiss the book as fanciful nonsense, but certain aspects of it puzzled me. Why was this ancient "secret knowledge" considered to be so important? It was clearly a detailed description of some physical object—an idol, perhaps—but what then of the Jewish abhorrence of idolatry? Above all, what was this material doing in a supposedly religious work?

These questions nagged, and having nothing better to do at the time, I looked up the original sources. First, Knorr von Rosenroth's *Kabbala Denudata*,[2] which gave parallel Latin and Aramaic texts, and then the original Aramaic in an edition printed in Lublin, Poland, in 1882. Being something of a linguist, I decided to tackle the Aramaic. It is not a very complicated language, once the script has been mastered, and I was aided by the fact that it was obviously not the author's native tongue. According to Gershom Scholem, the world's leading expert on the Kabbalah, the *Zohar* had originally been written down by Moses de Leon, a Spanish Jew, in about A.D. 1290. It has been circulating among the Jewish community ever since then in manuscript and in printed forms. Aramaic was the language of Babylon, akin to Hebrew, and it became the everyday language of the Jews after their captivity in that city, Hebrew being reserved for religious purposes as Latin was in the Catholic Church until recently. Aramaic was Jesus Christ's native tongue.

In spite of any linguistic difficulties, I found the Aramaic far clearer than the Latin and English translations, and stripped of Mathers' and von Rosenroth's flowery language it became a very lucid description of a *physical* object. The Ancient of Days consisted principally of three "skulls," an outer one that contained two others inside it, placed one above the other. In the middle of this arrangement was the "cardinal lamp," which shone with "a brightness to exceed all brightnesses." It has a "beard," the "hairs" of which grow out of one part of its "face" and back in again at other places; there is no mention of a body, but there is a "strong right arm," and there are six feet. In between them there are two testicles, and a penis. A substance known variously as the "dew," the "oil of great goodness" and other terms, ran down from the upper parts of this object, to be stored in the "testicles" and finally discharged from the "penis."

What, we may ask, is the purpose of all this? The answer comes towards the end of the *Lesser Holy Assembly* (my translation):

(436) Into the skull of the Small-faced One there drips the dew from the white head, and it is contained in it.

(437) And this dew is seen in two colors; and by it is fed the field of the holy apples. And from this dew they grind the manna of the just ones for the world to come. And by it the dead are raised to life. And the manna did not appear to be derived from this dew except at one time; the time when Israel was wandering in the desert. And (then) the Ancient One of All fed them from this place. But afterwards, it was not found. As it is said (Exodus 16:4) "Behold I will rain bread from heaven for you." And also (Genesis 27:28) "Therefore God give thee of the dew of heaven, etc."[3]

At last, we have some possible indication of the function of this Ancient of Days. It did not speak, or move of its own accord; it was carried around in the desert and placed on various "thrones," which had to be "broken down" when the next move was made. But now we learn that its function was to produce manna. Could it have been some type of machine?

According to the Bible, the manna that fed the Israelites fell from the sky and was collected by the people themselves. At once, I thought of various practical difficulties here: surely the manna would have become mixed with sand, dirt or gravel; and how could the ration of one *omer* per family have been enforced? There is no satisfactory modern explanation of the so-called "miracle" of the manna; insect secretions have been suggested, but surely the Israelites would have been aware of this given the numbers of insects required, and we would have read today that God sent the insects, not that the manna came "from heaven." Could its source have been a technological miracle—a machine?

One fact supporting the machine theory is that the *Zohar* texts include many measurements among the descriptions of the physical parts. The length of the "penis," for example, is given as 248 "worlds." This will be explained in detail later.

Lacking words for machine parts, the compilers of the *Zohar* used parts of the human body—"skulls," "eyes" and many other terms. It is interesting to note that the Apache tribe used the same technique when coining words for parts of motor vehicles in their own language.

The next question was: Could it be possible to build such a machine to produce a basic foodstuff, given

Apache Word	Human Anatomical Meaning	Automobile Part Meaning
daw	chin and jaw	front bumper
wos	shoulder	front fender
gun	hand and arm	front wheel
kai	thigh and buttocks	rear fender
ze	mouth	gas-pipe opening
ke	foot	rear wheel
chun	back	chassis
inda	eye	headlight
chee	nose	hood
ta	forehead	auto top
tsaws	vein	electrical wiring
zik	liver	battery
pit	stomach	gas tank
chih	intestine	radiator hose
jih	heart	distributor
jisoleh	lung	radiator

Table 1. These examples are taken from Peter Farb's book *Word Play*.[4]

our present technical knowledge or some reasonable extrapolation of it? At this point, I had involved my friends Rodney Dale and Martin Riches in the project, and it was Rodney who suggested that a manna-like substance might be synthesized by the intensive cultivation of some microscopic water plant such as Chlorella, a type of pond-weed, which reproduces extremely rapidly in the correct conditions.

The next question was: Could it be possible to build such a machine to produce a basic foodstuff, given our present technical knowledge or some reasonable extrapolation of it?

For Chlorella-type organisms to grow, the principal requirements are: water, carbon dioxide, nitrogen and light. As regards the water, the upper part of the Ancient of Days comprises a dew-still, a cooled surface which could extract water even from the dry air of the Sinai desert; carbon dioxide and nitrogen are available in the atmosphere, and could be made available to the culture by circulating it through the "beard-hairs" in contact with the air via a semi-permeable membrane; and as for the light, the *Zohar* makes endless mention of the "cardinal lamp" in the interior of the Ancient One. The other requirement, of course, is energy. Based on an

Israelite population of 600 families rather than 600,000—the Hebrew word "alp" can mean either "family" or "thousand"—we came up with a figure around 500 kilowatts, which is within the capacity of a small nuclear reactor. Such a reactor can probably convert nuclear energy directly into light energy, using a neutron-pumped laser. Heat will also be produced, so thermoelectric methods can be used to produce electricity for control and other purposes.

Turning the algae sludge into edible manna must have involved a cooking process, with surplus heat being used for this and to incinerate waste products. This was discharged from the "nose" of the Ancient of Days, an exhaust pipe, causing the column of fire and smoke seen over the Tabernacle when the machine was in production.

So, the thing is feasible, and we understand that such algae-growing devices are used in nuclear submarines for air purification, and there have been several experiments using similar systems intended to investigate the feasibility of closed ecological systems for spacecraft.

In 1974, Sergei Vlasov wrote of the Soviet Bios-3 experiment in the Russian journal *Tekhnika Molodezhi*. This was a closed-cycle environment in which three men lived for six months. Their bodily waste was used to fertilize the Chlorella cultivator that purified the air, and there were hydroponic cultivators producing wheat and vegetables.

The next question is: Suppose there was such a device, what became of it? According to the *Zohar*, it was used during the desert wanderings to feed the people, but ceased to function upon their entry into the Promised Land. Thereafter, it became a ritual object, cared for by a few priests. The Bible refers to the Ark of the Covenant, but it was probably not the Ark that was taken to the battle with the Philistines[5] but this machine. The enemy captured it, and were stricken with "emerods"—possibly sores caused by exposure to radioactivity. Such was their terror of the object that they returned it to the Israelites, the only people who knew how to handle it safely. It was placed on a cart drawn by two cows that were also terrified of it, so they fled, pulling it behind them across the border to Bethshemesh, where a considerable number of people were "smitten" for the mere offence of looking at it.[6]

In these Bible passages, the object referred to is the Ark of the Covenant, but our view is that it was the Manna-Machine that caused such havoc. After the machine was lost, the wooden box known as the Ark was constructed to house the few remaining relics from ancient times.[7] Later, the legends surrounding the machine were transferred to the Ark, and the machine's supernatural powers were attributed to it.

After it ceased functioning, after the entry into the Promised Land, the machine became a ritual object cared for by a dedicated band of priests. They spent their time measuring it, and numerous dimensions are given in the *Zohar*. For example: "The length of that penis is two hundred and forty eight worlds. And all of them hang in the mouth of the penis which is called 'Yod.'"[8]

The "world" unit is used as a measure of length, area and volume. We speculated that the unit was in fact a mustard seed, and measured a sample of seeds to get a mean diameter of 2.05 millimeters. Length can be measured as a single row of seeds, area as a single layer of them, and volume by filling it with seeds. Strangely enough, using these dimensions gave sizes for the various parts in the right ballpark to support our rough estimates derived from engineering calculations. Taking the "world" unit to be a mustard seed gives us these dimensions:

Length of nose of Small-faced One	77 cm
Length of penis (manna discharge nozzle)	50.9 cm
Area of face of Ancient One	13.5 sq m
Area of face of Small-faced One	5.47 sq m
Volume of skull of Ancient One	0.84 cu m
Volume of skull of Small-faced One	0.58 cu m

The Ancient One and the Small-faced One are the two main parts of the machine, which had to be separated every week on the Sabbath for cleaning, a double manna ration having been issued the day before. On the Sabbath night it was reassembled, and started up with much nail-biting. Once the smoke and fire appeared from the "nose," they knew that the operation had been successful and there was general rejoicing. The plugging together of the two parts was seen as a sexual union of male and female parts, leading to the fertility of the people of Israel. Priests were expected to be married, and to emulate the machine by having sex on the Sabbath night.

According to the Bible, Solomon built his Temple to house the Ark, but in all probability it was the

Ancient of Days that occupied the place of pride in the Holy of Holies. It was brought into Jerusalem from its obscure previous home with great rejoicing. At the conquest by the Babylonians, the Ark and the machine appear to have been lost, perhaps hidden in a cave across the Jordan, or even in one of the caverns under the Temple Mount in Jerusalem. It is significant that Israel's holiest place today is the Western (or Wailing) Wall—could the venerable relic still be buried behind the ancient masonry?

Coming closer to modern times, it has been suggested that the Knights Templar may have recovered the Ancient of Days—or some part of it—and brought it to Europe. This recovery operation was possibly even the hidden impetus behind the Crusades. The first Templar knights spent years excavating beneath the Temple Mount; it was only later that they adopted the task of protecting pilgrims. The *Zohar* legends of the Ancient of Days have much in common with the later Christian notion of the Holy Grail, a miraculous object that dispensed heavenly food. But all these speculations must remain unproven until the machine, or some identifiable part of it, is located.

The biggest question of all, however, is: If there was a Manna-Machine, where did it come from in the first place? According to the *Zohar*, it was given by the "Lord" to Aaron and his tribe of priests, who also received the "secret knowledge" of how to operate it. Who, then, was the "Lord?" He was certainly not the omniscient, omnipotent God of our religions today, but a figure in many ways human, but with some advanced powers. Was the "Lord" a space visitor? This is the explanation that best fits the facts, but we shall never know for sure unless some artifact of demonstrably extraterrestrial origin can be found.

Certainly, the Biblical account of the Lord landing on the mountain in Sinai could well be a description of a spacecraft landing, with the attendant thunder, fire and smoke. Throughout the Old Testament, wherever the "glory of the Lord" is mentioned, it clearly refers to some type of vehicle. The Hebrew word used (*kavod*) also means "chariot." The Lord is always zipping around "in his glory."

Once the smoke had cleared and the rocks cooled, Moses went up to receive the tablets with the Commandments from the Lord, then Aaron and his priests ascended to receive the "secret knowledge"—i.e., training in operating the machine. After this, there was the episode of the golden calf, which appears to have been an outbreak of Manna-Machine worship. It was after this that strict security was imposed, the machine being housed in the "Tabernacle"—an open-roofed tent—that was out of bounds to all but the priests. All that the ordinary people could see was the column of fire and smoke from within it, the exhaust from the machine's "nose." This is mentioned in Psalms 18:8: "There went up a smoke out of his nostrils..."

Machines such as the Ancient of Days may well have been carried aboard the "Lord's" spacecraft to feed the crew. In fact, according to the *Talmud*, another collection of traditional Jewish lore, manna was the food of "angels," and was totally absorbed by the body; those who lived on it had no need to relieve themselves. It is hard to believe that such a detail could be invented *unless* there was some basis of truth behind it.

There are many more items of evidence to support our Manna-Machine hypothesis, and even 20 years after the original research we still stumble across more evidence. There is insufficient space to give them all here, so we can only refer readers to their Bibles, and re-read the Old Testament in the light of what they have learned from this paper.

References:

• Samuel Liddell MacGregor Mathers, *The Kabbalah Unveiled*. London, 1887.

• Christian Knorr von Rosenroth, *Kabbala Denudata*. Frankfurt, 1677–84.

• Moses de Leon, *Sepher-ha-Zohar*. Lublin, 1882.

• Gershom Gerhard Major Scholem, *Trends in Jewish Mysticism*. New York: Schocken, 1941.

• George T. Sassoon, Rodney Dale, *The Manna-Machine*. London: Sidgwick and Jackson, 1978.

• George T. Sassoon, Rodney Dale, *The Kabbalah Decoded*. London: Duckworth, 1978.

• Johannes and Peter Fiebag, *Die Entdeckung des Grals*. Munich: Goldmann, 1989.

---

1. 37–43.

2. Frankfurt, 1677.

3. LHA 436–437.

4. Peter Farb, *Word Play*. New York: Bantam, 1973.

5. *Samuel 1:4*

6. *Samuel 1:6*

7. Such as the tablets upon which were inscribed the Ten Commandments. —Ed.

8. GHA 968.

Giorgio A. Tsoukalos

THE GIANT FLYING TURTLES

OF GUATEMALA

GUATEMALA IS, and forever will be, a treasure chest for gathering new and compelling Paleo-SETI evidence. During this expedition we visited Tikal, Uaxactun and Yaxha in the Peten region. Tikal is a fascinating place to commence a journey following the pathways of the gods. It is a huge and vast temple complex. One cannot stop pondering for what exact purpose all of this was built. The complex is riddled with mathematically precise aligned structures built with enormous, heavy stone blocks. Most stelas are up to three meters tall. The mere thought of how our ancestors moved these monstrous objects from point A to point B without the help of any advanced technology causes one's head to spin. The temple towers sit there resembling rockets on launch pads ready for lift-off. Also interesting is the fact that for hundreds of miles there is nothing else but jungle. The closest fresh water source is 40 miles away! This raises the question: Why was this gigantic city built in the midst of the jungle, far from any civilization, even from a source of drinking water?

On a day-trip, we drove to Uaxactun in our four-wheel drive vehicle. Uaxactun is *only* approximately 16 miles from Tikal. However, it had been raining quite a bit at night for the past six days, and it took us just over four hours to conquer the 16 miles. There was marsh everywhere.

At Uaxactun, the temples seemed to be even more massive than at Tikal. Just as at Tikal, we climbed on top of every temple and were constantly out of breath. These were stairwells for giants. Each step was almost two feet tall! Covered with mossy slime, climbing was a truly dangerous undertaking. Each step had to be executed quite carefully, otherwise you'd wipe out and tumble down a long ways. Climbing these steps proved to be an excellent aerobic workout. I am not at all surprised that the Maya all of a sudden so mysteriously vanished. They all died of heart attacks from always climbing these giant stairs!

The next day, we left Tikal bound for Yaxha. Initially, Yaxha, at the Laguna de Yaxha lake, was not on our expedition itinerary, yet it proved to be a fantastic insider tip. The owners of Tikal's Jungle Lodge told us "You have to go to Yaxha to see the island of Topoxte. The Midget-Maya once lived there." Midget-Maya? I consider myself quite familiar with Mayan culture, but I had never heard that term before, and was intrigued to learn more.

At a blazing 20 mph we drove the unpaved, bumpy road to Yaxha. We arrived completely covered in fine white dust in a little less than three hours. A native appeared to be sitting all alone at the bottom of a path leading to Yaxha's main ruins, situated on the other side of a hill. After exploring the ruins, we asked him how to reach the island of Topoxte. He told us with a smile to take the jungle path down to the lake to ask for the fisherman in

> **The complex is riddled with mathematically precise aligned structures built with enormous, heavy stone blocks. Most stelas are up to three meters tall. The mere thought of how our ancestors moved these monstrous objects from point A to point B without the help of any advanced technology causes one's head to spin.**

the village. He'd then bring us to the island. In the village, we soon were the center of attention. Upon arrival, the village square seemed to be deserted. All of a sudden, people flocked towards us from every corner of the square. A rather large and lively crowd gathered around us. Strangely enough, they were all men. It soon dawned on me that they had only come to get a glimpse of my attractive female travel companion, Susana. The moment we had found our fisherman and were on our way to his tiny metal dinghy, the main square emptied out as quickly as if the village had never seen one soul.

The metal dinghy ride to the small island of Topoxte in the Laguna de Yaxha lake took 20 minutes. The fisherman guided us through a small path to the ruins. What unfolded before our eyes was simply sensational.

Archaeologist Teobert Maler had already explored Topoxte in November of 1904.[1] Later, William R. Bullard made short expeditions there in 1958 and 1959, and then was given a grant for more extensive research in 1960. Topoxte is said to have been occupied during the classic and pre-classic periods.[2]

I must reiterate that all of the archaeological sites that we had seen so far, such as Tikal and Uaxactun, were built on a monumental scale. But here, on the little island of Topoxte, everything was different. Completely different.

The three buildings standing in front of us were anything but gigantic. The buildings here were built in what almost seemed "regular, human" size. The structures were neither too big nor too small for humans. The normally knee-high steps were downright short on Topoxte, comfortably climbable for people of "regular" stature.

Let us remember the massive, monolithic stelae at Tikal, which were up to three meters tall. At Topoxte, there were stelae, too. However, they were much, much smaller. Each measured an average of 1.2 meters tall and 26 centimeters deep. They were just big enough to have been moved by human hands, without creating any of the transportation problems their larger "comrades" would have required. No exotic explanations such as wooden rollers, etc. were needed here. Compared to all the other super-structures we had encountered before, these buildings and stelae were tiny! Even Bullard openly admits in his report that "another distinctive trait of Topoxte are small, almost miniature, stelae and altars."[3]

At most sites, each tall stelae features one massive round "altar stone" which is situated right in front of it. Just as in these other sites, such as Tikal, Topoxte's stelae also featured round altar stones. They were identical to those at Tikal, except at a fraction of the size and they did not have any elaborate carvings on them. Referring to these altars, Sylvanus G. Morley quotes Lundell and Stuart in his *Inscription of Peten*, stating that "the small altars referred to by Maler all appear to be drums or sections from the round columns of the temple. It is probable that alterations were made to the temple and that the round columns were removed and their sections reused as altars. The altars each have a small hole in the center into which a stone ball was possibly inserted to lock them together at the time when they served as sections of columns."[4]

I was rather amused when I came upon this passage while performing my research at the Andrew D. White Library at Cornell University. What was amusing was that simply because of having seen the stones with my own eyes, I know that the above statement was not true. I know that all columns on Topoxte were not round. Rather, they were square. Only one single column was round! And this one column did not consist of round drums as suggested in the text, but of smaller stones creating a column. Now our critics will wake up from their nap and yell:

"Hold on! The columns were removed and their sections reused as altars!" Even that statement is false because Lundell and Stuart state that "the altars each have a small hole in the center into which a stone ball was possibly inserted to lock them together..." Six of the seven remaining altar stones featured no hole at all. Furthermore, there are just not enough altar stones present which at some point could have created columns—*plural!*

Also, the stones with which everything was built, compared to the gigantic stone blocks of other sites, are literally tiny. Everywhere else the structures were built in a megalithic style. Here, construction materials were brick size, at the most. Excavators there explained to me that the builders of Topoxte were not able to use larger stones because there was not much stone left at the quarry. However, this argument cannot be valid. First, where are the larger stones that were used at the beginning of construction *before* they "ran out" of the larger stone blocks that they allegedly had access to? Second, the entire island is a rock overgrown with vegetation. The quarry where the stones were produced has been identified. I have seen it. There is plenty of stone left to cover the entire island with stone blocks.

I postulate that all construction materials are smaller here because human beings built everything without the help of any advanced technological tools.

After thorough research at some dusty old libraries at Boston and Cornell Universities, I came upon the startling realization that in all the literature pertaining to the site, there is not one single

explain the miniature version of the larger sites, so archaeologists coined the term "Midget-Maya" and suggested that it was midgets that inhabited this site. Wow. So, did the regular-sized Maya send their dwarfs into exile there, or what? If you, dear reader, know something about the "Midget-Maya," please drop me a line. I'm curious to learn more.

The fact remains: The "miniature" buildings exist. However, it remains an unsolved mystery as to why they are so small. Even the anthropologists Prudence M. and Don S. Rice openly admit that "the six centuries of central Peten prehistory, from the classic collapse to the time of Spanish contact in A.D. 1535, are not well understood archaeologically."[5]

My theory is that normal human beings lived on the island of Topoxte. Over on the mainland, the priests inhabited the gigantic structures *together with the gods*. Since the other human beings were in regular contact with the gods, they were quite aware of how the gods lived and also tried to imitate what they saw. They recreated everything to their own size requirements. Essentially, everything is identical— the buildings, the temple towers, the stelae, the altar stones, etc. The only difference is size. A possible confirmation of my theory awaited us back at the village in a remarkable and exciting discovery...

During our return ride in the leaky metal dinghy, I asked our guide if there were any other remarkable findings besides the buildings and stelae. He told us that turtles made of clay had been excavated. Clay turtles? I couldn't quite picture what he meant. Back at the village he told us to look for the

---

Without raising an eyebrow, he said: "This is a representation of the giant flying turtles in which the gods flew around, a long time ago."

---

attempt to thoroughly explain why Topoxte's structures were built in such a miniature fashion. I was still intrigued by the term "Midget-Maya," who the people at the Jungle Lodge claimed lived on Topoxte. Oddly enough, and I might be wrong, in all the literature that I had collected for this paper, I read nothing that even remotely suggested the existence of "Midget-Maya." At Topoxte, the excavators told us that archaeology was unable to

village mechanic. He had the keys to the village makeshift archaeology lab where the clay turtles were stored. When we asked the mechanic about the turtles he informed us that they were no longer there. They had already been transferred to the university in Guatemala City for further examination. Still, he motioned with his hand for us to come inside his barn. "Just in case the originals get destroyed, lost or stolen," he said, "they made

> **The great strength of the Ancient Astronaut theory is the fact that connections and correlations between cultures can be drawn, which allow for the big picture to become even clearer.**

exact replicas of the turtles from wood under direct supervision of the university."

Inside the dark, old barn, he reached on top of a large wooden bookshelf for a dusty box. He carefully laid it in front of us on the counter. He blew off the layer of dust covering its lid. Diligently, he produced two plastic-wrapped objects and began unwrapping them. What we were about to see was simply extraordinary. There were two objects displayed, two exact replicas of clay figures that had been discovered many years ago.

The first object was some kind of a "nightly animal," as the mechanic described it, which reminded me very much of a bat. Nothing special. The other object, however, was a little bit different: It was the "turtle," alright—35 centimeters long, and 18 centimeters wide. If only it was a turtle! The shape was clearly that of a turtle, but the head was humanoid and the body's shape was aerodynamic!

"What does this represent?" I asked the mechanic. Without raising an eyebrow, he said: "This is a representation of the giant flying turtles in which the gods flew around, a long time ago." "What?" I asked. Without the slightest hesitation, he repeated what he had just said.

Was this an artist's rendering of some flying machine used by the gods? Intriguingly, the "turtle head" actually covers a rather humanoid head, as if the turtle's head represents some sort of tight fitting helmet. In taking a closer look at the humanoid head, one can clearly see the goggles it is wearing. The eyes of the "pilot" are clearly surrounded by goggle-like objects. The goggles are reminiscent of goggles modern-day fighter pilots wear.

Even more compelling is that the "turtle's" extremities are pressed against its "shell" in a highly aerodynamic fashion. Considering the shape of the object, it is as aerodynamic as universally required by any flying device. If this turtle really is a turtle, then why are the extremities pressed against the shell in such an aerodynamic fashion?

Also, everyone knows that a turtle's shell displays a beautiful pattern. Here, however, the "shell" has no pattern at all. It is flat and smooth—as if representing the metal of the outer hull of a flying machine, perhaps?

Of course the critics now will say that the turtle is only meant to be looked at symbolically. The artisan used the turtle's shape to illustrate an important warrior's strength, who is invincible in combat because he is as strong as a turtle's indestructible shell. Or something like that.

There is only one answer for such reasoning: misunderstood technology. I'll say it over and over again: Human beings back then were not stupid. On the contrary, they knew *exactly* what a turtle looked like. However, they saw something zipping across the sky, and what they saw in the sky could best be described as, or compared to, a turtle! How else could they describe something they did not even know existed? Or better yet, they did not have the necessary *vocabulary*. Consequentially, they described it in terms of an object with which they were intimately familiar and looked similar to the object they witnessed in the sky. Thus, comparisons were drawn.

The Maya knew exactly what a "real" turtle looked like. A Maya clay statue at the American Museum of Natural History in New York City proves the point. A deity is standing on top of a "real" turtle. On closer inspection, one can easily detect the beautiful pattern that adorns the turtle's shell. This is a turtle! The other isn't. By the way, both objects not only come from the same region, they also date to the same period.

If all the presented evidence is nothing but mere fantasy, can someone then please explain to me why these legends of gods flying in giant turtles have survived until today? Why should the mechanic have lied to me about these legends? He wasn't earning one penny by recounting rubbish, nor did he know who I was and what my interests were. More so, he doesn't sell this turtle. No, he diligently guards and protects the treasure.

Is all of this a coincidence? Hardly. The great strength of the Ancient Astronaut theory is the fact that connections and correlations between cultures can be drawn, which allow for the big picture to become even clearer. Mythologies and creation myths are chock-full of intricate references to flying turtles. Here are a few examples:

"From the river I, the three-legged turtle Nai delivered the eternal laws on iron Lo-tablets to the Chinese." Did the Chinese also compare something with which they were unfamiliar to something that they knew, such as a turtle?

The traditions of the Native Americans of Delaware, halfway across the globe from China, also speak of a three-legged turtle in their Great Flood story. Notice, both cultures speak of a three-legged turtle. If these were references to actual turtles wouldn't you be hard pressed to believe the coincidence that both in China and in Delaware there are three-legged turtles running around?

Also, in ancient Indian texts one can read that "in order to create the world, god Vishnu landed on the summit of Mount Khailasa in a turtle and with the help of god Vairacona they enabled the earth to rotate."

The East Pomo, a Hoka Native American tribe, speaks of a race that was evil and terrible. They were capable of flying through the sky in turtles made of impenetrable iron with which they could drill themselves into the earth. This is incredible stuff. *Star Wars*!

The Maya myths are even better. The beginning of time was initiated with "Three Stones of Creation" by the deity Wak Chan-Ahaw, which literally means "Risen Master of the Sky." Wak Chan-Ahaw was the god of corn, oftentimes also referred to as Hun Huhnapu, father of the heroic twins. He was killed in the underworld. Yet, with the help of his sons, he was resurrected. This resurrection is always represented by him emerging out of a turtle shell.

As we can see, the turtle plays a rather significant role in the creation myths of the Maya. In some myths, earth is even said to rest on the back of a giant turtle floating about the primordial ocean.

So what, then, was described in all these ancient texts and traditions? Let us remember that up until recently, Native Americans, for instance, referred to a train as a "fire horse." Why? Because they did not have the word "train" in their vocabulary. The same applies to any of our ancestors. They had no way of calling a flying object by the words "aircraft" or "plane." They simply did *not* have the necessary vocabulary. Similarly, the Maya did not have a word for "machine" or "flying craft," so they described it with the objects they were familiar with—misunderstood technology.

Let me draw our attention to the cargo cult phenomenon, in which a "technologically primitive" society comes in contact with a "technologically advanced" society. Ethnologists have observed that if "technologically advanced" visitors lived among primitive native tribes for short periods of time and then vanished as quickly as they appeared, due to the advanced technologies of the visitors, the natives thought these humans were gods and thus began to worship them. Their hope was that through intense worship and sacrifice their "gods" would be pleased and return. Critics now say that these cargo cult phenomena are already over 60 years old and therefore no longer relevant. Really?

For many years, I attended a boarding school in Switzerland. After the end of Communism, our school welcomed a few students from the former Soviet Union. I remember sitting in art class. Our assignment was to draw a fantasy castle, a dream castle floating up in the sky embedded in the clouds with shining towers made of gold, magnificent windows and whatever else we wanted. Everyone was very excited about the impending project, and we all started to draw like crazy. Everyone, that is, except for our three Russian friends. They just sat in front of their large, blank sheets of paper. None of them touched their pencils. "What's wrong? Why aren't you drawing?" the teacher asked. "What's a fantasy castle?" they asked in unison. "We've never seen one. What does it look like? Since we've never seen one we can't draw it." Their response was extraordinary!

With this observation, it is quite clear that if something hasn't been seen, then it cannot be invented. It is impossible to invent or conjure up something if the *basic elements* are missing! Nothing happens without initial inspiration. Therefore, all mythologies, legends, tales, whatever, which today are discredited by modern researchers as mere inventions of fantasy

Is it such a stretch to imagine that these flying turtles were really flying vehicles of the more technologically advanced gods?

and figments of somebody's imagination, cannot possibly be unfounded inventions or mere fantasy. Something had to be there in the first place to serve as the basic element, and as the initial inspiration to create more!

Another case in point: It is absolutely impossible to create, let alone solve, mathematical equations without knowing the basic mathematical elements. It simply cannot be done. As hard as this may be for our critics and nay-sayers to swallow, there is no way around this fact.

It is always said that every legend has a true core. It is exactly this core that represents the base element. Without a base element, or initial inspiration, nothing is possible. Therefore, if something like this can happen to my Russian friends living in the Twentieth Century, why couldn't it have happened thousands of years ago with our ancestors? It has. Why am I so sure about it? It's simple. Read on.

Five hundred years from now, after we have established permanent bases on the moon and on Mars, we are bound to explore deep space. With one of our new generation of spaceships, it is quite possible that we will eventually come across a planet harboring intelligent life. If it just so happens that the intelligent life we encounter is not much advanced technologically, what will we do? Will we really just stand back to watch and study them from afar? No way. Our inflated human egos would not allow it. Of course we would give them a gentle push in the right direction by teaching them the essentials of science. Many, many generations after our arrival, and long after our departure, our appearance ("The gods were here and taught our forefathers!") would be regarded as myth and fantasy because nobody was there when it actually happened. Thus, our arrival would be regarded as a figment of the imagination and brushed aside into the realm of mythology and legend. Does this attitude remind you of anyone?

When all of the above accounts were written, writing was a fairly new invention. When the people started to realize that this new invention was a rather powerful tool to preserve knowledge for generations after generations to come, is it really logical to think that the first stories that were put in writing were only figments of their imagination? Of course not! With the invention of the written word, people were able to forever keep a record of the most significant events of their time *for the first time in the history of mankind!* So, if there are intricate and highly detailed descriptions of beings that a long, long time ago descended from the sky in flying machines (or "turtles") and taught mankind in various academic disciplines, then I postulate that we should lend more credence to these accounts than we have given them thus far. Because in a time of great uncertainty and upheaval, when the most important order of the day was raw survival, the very first people who were empowered with the written word had better things to do than to sit around a fire, get drunk and invent fantasy stories. No, they immortalized what was most significant to them at that very moment: *their history!*

According to the ancient texts and traditions, and in this case also according to oral and physical indications, in Guatemala a long, long time ago, the gods flew around in machines, or giant flying turtles. Why is it so hard for us to believe, living in a culture rich in metaphor, that our ancestors drew similar comparisons? Is it such a stretch to imagine that these flying turtles were really flying vehicles of the more technologically advanced gods?

1. Teobert Maler, "Explorations in the Department of Peten, Guatemala and Adjacent Region Topoxte, Yaxha." *Memories of the Peabody Museum*, Harvard University, vol. 2, no. 2, 1908. pp. 55–60.

2. William R. Bullard, "Archaeological Investigation of the Maya Ruin of Topoxte, Peten, Guatemala." *American Philosophical Society Yearbook 1960*, pp. 551–4.

3. Ibid.

4. Sylvanus G. Morley, *Inscriptions of Peten. Carnegie Institution of Washington Publication, 1937–38*, vol. 3, no. 437, pp. 483–90.

5. Prudence M. Rice and Don S. Rice, "Topoxte, Macanche and the Central Peten Postclassic." *The Lowland Maya Postclassic*, University of Texas Press, 1985. p. 170.

William R. Corliss

ANCIENT SCIENTIFIC INSTRUMENTS

ILLUSTRATIONS BY WILLIAM R. CORLISS

Description: Artifacts demonstrating precocious innovation and applications to devices employing scientific principles considered unusually advanced for the cultures involved.

Data Evaluation: Since scientific principles and instruments are the subject of this section, more than half our sources come from science journals and magazines. The remainder are from miscellaneous fringe publications which are sometimes of dubious value. Our data evaluations, the first figures in the ratings below, reflect this split nature of the sources.

Anomaly Evaluation: Nine primitive scientific instruments are deemed suitable for cataloging. Their evaluations are the second figures in the ratings below.

• Chinese "light-penetration" mirrors (X1). Ratings: 1/4.
• The application of rock-crystal lenses for magnification rather than kindling fires—a significant controversy in anthropology (X2). Ratings: 1/3.
• The construction of a pre-Galileo telescope (X3). Ratings: 2/3.
• The Viking use of birefringent crystals ("sunstones") for navigation (X4). Ratings: 2/2.
• Primacy of the Olmec lodestone compass over that of the Chinese (X5). Ratings: 2/2.

• The astronomical utility of the Chinese Pi (X7). Ratings: 3/2.
• Chinese seismograph in the Second Century A.D. (X8). Ratings: 2/2.

Similar and Related Phenomena: Claimed ancient use of electricity;[1] the existence of sophisticated ancient calculating devices;[2] claims of ancient flying machines.[3]

X1—REMARKABLE MIRRORS

Optical reflections had to be among the earliest human experiences with the laws of physics. Of course, nonhumans also observed reflections but made little use of them.

Reflection phenomena are ubiquitous in the natural environments. Still-pond surfaces, sheets of ice and shiny mineral surfaces, such as those of mica, all suffice. The urge to emulate nature and fashion artificial mirrors for rituals and purposes of vanity probably arose early.

But how could the flat, shiny surfaces of nature's mirrors be duplicated? Glass-making, metallic sheets, and liquid mercury were not available 10,000 years ago. The only materials suitable for mirror manufacture were glassy minerals like obsidian (volcanic glass). Unfortunately for mirror-makers, obsidian is a very hard, obdurate material.

> **More technologically challenging and mysterious-as-to-purpose were the concave mirrors fashioned from magnetite by the earlier Olmec culture in Mesoamerica. How did the Olmecs ever precision-grind and polish such exact, three-dimensional, symmetrical surfaces? And what was the purpose of mirrors that reflected only distorted images?**

Nevertheless, about 8,000 years ago, Stone Age artisans at Catal-Huyuk, in Turkey—usually billed as the "first" city of *Homo sapiens*—somehow ground and polished pieces of obsidian into remarkably good mirrors.[4]

As now related by O. C. Shane, archaeologists are still uncertain as to how these first known human mirrors were really made.

> How these mirrors were ground and polished is not known. Their exceptional planar surfaces are highly polished and reflect a sharp image. Obsidian (hardness 5.5) can be ground by quartz (hardness 7.0), and polished with charcoal (i.e., carbon-hardness 10).[5]

After the Catal-Huyuk workers found the right materials for grinding and polishing, a major problem still remained: obtaining a good planar surface with only hand operations. It is this part of the Catal-Huyuk mirrormaking that we do not understand well.

Several millennia later, in pre-Columbian America, the Incas and Aztecs also made acceptable mirrors from obsidian. They also worked with pyrites and reflecting sheets of metals, which by then had become available. These were probably used mainly for ritual and magical purposes.

More technologically challenging and mysterious-as-to-purpose were the concave mirrors fashioned from magnetite by the earlier Olmec culture in Mesoamerica. How did the Olmecs ever precision-grind and polish such exact, three-dimensional, symmetrical surfaces? And what was the purpose of mirrors that reflected only distorted images? Nor was their curvature sufficient for starting fires or any other known practical purpose. Again, one has to fall back on the hackneyed explanation of ritual/magical applications.

At least eight concave, pendant-type magnetite and ilmenite mirrors have been found at the Olmec center of La Venta, Mexico. The double-mystery of these remarkable objects has been emphasized by I. Bernal.

> Even though the dimensions and focal distances vary, probably depending upon the original block, all the mirrors are similar and therefore represent a cultural tradition. Their polish is so extraordinary that it reaches the limit of possible perfection. This was not accomplished with the use of abrasives, for the microscope does not reveal traces that these would necessarily have left. The excellent study that I have summarized here indicates that the radius of curvature becomes progressively greater as one nears the edge of the mirrors; the curve in all these examples is very similar and so perfect that it is not possible to reconstruct the technique employed to fabricate these concave mirrors. Perhaps they could serve as a camera obscura... Undoubtedly they show one of the most technical advances of the Olmecs.[6]

Concave mirrors with varying radii of curvature! What practical or magic application could they serve? And how were they made without abrasives?

Magic Mirrors. Myth and legend describe two sorts of "magic" mirrors that we can dispose of with minimum comment. The first is what one might call a "telescopic" mirror. It sounds like something out of a science-fiction story.

> The famous mirror of Ptolemy Evergetes, caused to be placed in the Pharos at Alexandria, belongs to this first class. This mirror is stated by ancient authors to have represented accurately everything which was transacted throughout all Egypt, both on water and on land. Some writers affirm that

upon its surface an enemy's fleet could be seen at a distance of 600,000 paces; others say more than 100 leagues![7]

The second "magic" mirror is of the "X-ray" variety! It is even "wilder" than the telescopic mirror.

The Chinese have several accounts concerning metal mirrors which would light up the interior organs of the human body. The emperor Ts'in Shi (259-210 B.C.) is credited with the possession of such a mirror which was styled "the precious mirror that would illuminate the bones of the body," or "the mirror illuminating the gall."[8]

There exists, however, a *third* sort of magic mirror that *does* exist and which has flummoxed Western scientists for a full century. This mirror was apparently invented by the Chinese about 1,200 years ago, but was not known to the Western world until 1832. It was not adequately explained scientifically until 1932. The Chinese called it a "light-penetrating" mirror.

produced afterwards by elaborate scraping and scratching. The surface was then polished to become shiny. The stresses set up by these processes caused the thinner parts of the surface to bulge outwards and become more convex than the thicker portions. Finally, a mercury amalgam was laid over the surface; this created further stresses and preferential buckling. The result was that the imperfections of the mirror surface matched the patterns on the back, although they were too minute to be seen by the eye. But when the mirror reflected bright sunlight against a wall, with the resultant magnification of the whole image, the effect was to reproduce the patterns as if they were passing through the solid bronze by way of light beams.[9]

The British scientist W. Bragg discovered the secret of these Chinese magic mirrors in 1932. In actuality, the design on the cast-bronze back of these mirrors *was duplicated* on the polished front surface in a way so subtle that it was not apparent until magnified by reflection. The manu-

---

Concave mirrors have been used for starting fires for centuries. They are not normally anomalous. Of course, this statement would have to be amended if there exists any substance to the old tale that Archimedes designed huge concave mirrors to set fire to the sails of the Roman ships at the siege of Syracuse.

The reflecting side of this particular "magic" mirror appears perfectly normal. It is made of bright, polished bronze, and it reflects images properly. The mirror's back is also made of bronze and displays various patterns and Chinese symbols. However, if this mirror is held in bright sunshine, one seems to be able to "mysteriously" see through its reflecting surface. In addition, reflections cast upon a dark wall project the patterns and symbols on its back. The manner in which these startling effects are achieved represents high degrees of ingenuity and skill for the artisans of 1,200 years ago.

The basic mirror shape, with the design on the back, was cast flat, and the convexity of the surface

facture of these magic mirrors obviously required great skill.

Burning Mirrors. Concave mirrors have been used for starting fires for centuries.[10] They are not normally anomalous. Of course, this statement would have to be amended if there exists any substance to the old tale that Archimedes designed huge concave mirrors to set fire to the sails of the Roman ships at the siege of Syracuse. This oft-mentioned array of giant mirrors of Archimedes seems to be in the legendary class along with the "X-ray" mirror described above. But at least the mirrors of Archimedes would be compatible with the accepted laws of optics... They are of interest here only because of their great size.

X2—MAGNIFYING AND BURNING LENSES

In contrast to reflectors (X1), nature offers few natural magnifiers. One can see some magnification in spherical drops of water hanging from leaf tips, but little else in the wild leads to the idea of optical magnification via lens-shaped materials. Even so, nature *does* provide transparent solids, such as crystalline quartz, that make good lens materials. Crystalline quartz also had ritual and decorative value to most ancient peoples, and it is very likely that, as early artisans worked with quartz for its nonoptical characteristics, they also recognized its magnifying properties. It was probably just a short conceptual step from a rounded quartz jewel to a practical lens.

A second *potential* route to a magnifying lens could have been through small water lenses. A drop of water hung suspended on a wire circle eight millimeters in diameter gives one a magnifying power of 5X. The same result can be obtained with a small hole in a dished metal sheet.

The earliest potential lenses were glass spheres reported from ancient Egypt and Mesopotamia circa 3500 B.C. How these glass spheres—natural or artificial—were obtained is unknown.[11] Furthermore, it is only supposed that said glass spheres were employed for magnification; they might have only been ornamental in purpose. However, their use in microengraving is certainly not out of the question.

The Egyptian transparent spheres would have introduced considerable image distortion if they were used as optical aids. Therefore, further innovation, probably more accidental than planned, was required before more practical disc-shaped lenses made their appearance.

The first incontrovertible lenses appeared in the Middle East around 3000 B.C.[12] They were ground out from rock crystal. Crete is often mentioned as an early producer of rock-crystal lenses, with first dates varying widely from 2000 B.C.[13] to 1200 B.C.[14]

These first dates have not been as contentious in archaeology as the *first use* of lenses. The standard first and primary lens application claimed in the textbooks has been as "burning glasses"; that is, the lenses were used only for starting fires.[15] The fact that many lenses are found with holes in them for thongs for carrying them about the neck

supports this contention. The use of lenses for magnification is not supposed to have become common until the Twelfth Century A.D.[16]

In MMT4-0,[17] where ancient microengraving is discussed, a strong case is made that ancient microengravers could not have produced their tiny, barely visible inscriptions without optical help. But some historians counter this claim with the acknowledged visual capabilities of myopes—very short sighted people—who could get so close to their work that lenses were not needed. One intuitively doubts the myope explanation of microengraving but L. Gorelick and A. J. Gwinnett make a good case for this practical value of myopia! Some even surmise that a "guild" of myopes might have been created through selective breeding!

X3—ANCIENT TELESCOPES

Refracting telescopes require two good lenses properly aligned in a tube. That such an arrangement of two pieces of ground glass results in a highly useful "spyglass" is not intuitively obvious. In other words, the invention of the telescope was considerably more challenging than discovering basic optic magnification.

Conventional history assures us that it is Galileo (1564-1642) who should be credited with making the first practical telescope. There are, however, hints that Galileo may not have been first.

- Chinese emperor Chan, circa 2283 B.C., is reputed to have arranged two magnifying glasses for observations of the planets.[18]
- Pliny stated that the Roman Emperor Nero watched the games in the Colosseum with a magnifying device.[19]
- Some 500 years before Galileo, the Vikings were in possession of rock-crystal lenses of sufficiently high quality to make a telescope. But did they?[20]
- More damaging to Galileo's reputation is the tale that the Flemish spectacle-maker J. Lippershey may actually have constructed a working telescope, reports of which reached Galileo, who then made one for himself and received all the credit.[21]

Thus, we have some vague challenges to the accepted history of the telescope. We cannot really be certain who first discovered its optical principles.

X4—SUNSTONES

Before the discovery of the magnetic compass, navigators who dared sail beyond the sight of land employed a wide range of devices to guide them. Of course, the stars, the sun, and an accumulated knowledge of oceanic currents were part of any deep-sea navigators' repertoire. To this were added portable sundials, the so-called knife-compass, and various "bearing discs."[22] These instruments, though rather clever, cannot be considered high-tech enough to dwell upon here. An exception is the Norse "sunstone."

Norse mariners often sailed at high latitudes where the sun was frequently obscured by fog and clouds. To find the direction of the sun under such conditions, the Norse navigators held aloft their sunstones, which yielded not the direction of the sun itself but the direction perpendicular to it. Sunstones were pieces of birefringent crystals that detected polarized sunlight scattered by the atmosphere. Given a little blue sky or thin areas in the clouds, the sunstones could establish the direction of the sun—even if it was a few degrees below the horizon. Two minerals were apparently used by the Norse: Iceland spar (calcite) and cordierite (a magnesium aluminum silicate).[23]

The Norse doubtless knew nothing about the optical principles involved, but they knew how to use the sunstones. Exactly who first noticed the utility of these two natural navigating aids is unknown.

X5—LODESTONE COMPASSES

We do not know who discovered the first lodestone, but that piece of rock (magnetite) must have been perceived as being inhabited by a spirit or imbued with magic. The Chinese certainly knew of the lodestone's strange directional proclivities about 2,000 years ago. Rather than applying the lodestone to navigating the briny, the Chinese used it to site and orient their buildings. In other words, the first compasses seem to have been used in geomancy rather than navigation.[24]

Apparently, the first navigational application of lodestones took place underground rather than at sea. Iranians, circa 5,000 years ago, are reputed to have used lodestones to guide themselves through tunnels![25]

Eventually, lodestones were floated on a fluid or suspended by a cord and put to use in marine navigation. But even here, we see nothing really anomalous. The primary archaeological/anthropological puzzle associated with the lodestone is to be found in Object M-160. This lodestone, carefully worked into bar-form and grooved, was located at the early Olmec site of San Lorenzo, Vera Cruz, Mexico. When floated, M-160 would have made a passable compass. But, like the Chinese, the Olmecs seemed to have used M-160 for geomancy; that is, siting and arranging their buildings in accordance with natural forces, which in this case is the unseen but mysteriously present geomagnetic field.

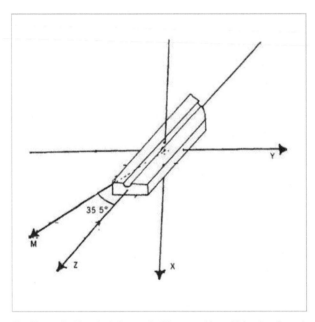

The Olmecs fashioned a lodestone in this grooved bar which, when floated, made a passable compass. X, Y and Z are the bar's axes; M is its magnetic moment vector. (X5)

The anomalousness of M-160 lies in its age: 1450-1000 B.C. It was perhaps a thousand years earlier than the "first compass" attributed to the Chinese.[26]

There could be more to the lodestone story than primacy of compass-invention. There are several other strong Chinese-Olmec affinities; such as Chinese features on Olmec sculptures, Chinese style in Olmec art and Chinese writing on Olmec artifacts. The following possibilities come to mind:

> **There could be more to the lodestone story than primacy of compass-invention. There are several other strong Chinese-Olmec affinities; such as Chinese features on Olmec sculptures; Chinese style in Olmec art; and Chinese writing on Olmec artifacts.**

1. The Chinese may have made and used lodestone compasses for navigation much earlier than now believed and brought the compass to the Olmecs in the pre-Columbian New World perhaps 3,000 years ago.

2. Or, the Chinese sailed to the New World without the lodestone compass and picked up the idea from the Olmecs, who were its true inventors.

The implied pre-Columbian diffusion in either direction across the Pacific is, of course, anathema to mainstream science and highly anomalous.

X6—TWO PROBLEMATIC NAVIGATIONAL DEVICES

A suggestive cave drawing. On the wall of a cavern, in Irian Jaya, Indonesia, there exists a drawing resembling the medieval torquetum, an instrument used for studying the motions of the planets and also capable of determining latitude at night. This drawing was discovered by the Frobenius Expedition of 1937-1938. The probable date of the drawing is about 232 B.C., several years earlier than the analogous European instrument.[27]

Unfortunately, suggestive ancient cave drawings do not constitute good evidence.

The "abacus" of the Basques. Although the name is the same as that of the age-old calculating device, the Basque abacus was a navigational aid of unknown design. According to A. E. Rothovius, it must have been very effective.

> The Basques also developed an abacus-like device for reading the true number of their *lekus* (from whence came the later term "league") at any latitude, giving them superior navigational ability for traversing the open ocean. This system was the source of the highly accurate portolans charts that came from the Basque and Catalan map-makers in the Thirteenth Century, and to which the key has

long been vainly sought. Used meridianly (north-south), the *leku* had a fixed length of 3/70ths of a degree of longitude.[28]

We cannot imagine what an "abacus-like" navigational instrument would look like!

X7—THE PI: ASTRONOMICAL, DECORATIVE OR SOMETHING ELSE?

The Pis are jade discs first crafted in China sometime before the Shang Dynasty (circa 1500-1100 B.C.). From 10 to 15 centimeters in diameter, the disc-shaped Pis possess a central hole that fits onto a hollow handle through which one can view the stars—assuming the Pi is broken by wedge-like notches and small projections. The number and placements of the wedges and projections vary considerably on surviving examples.

In 1947, Henri Michel proposed that the Pi was used by the ancient Chinese to locate true north,

Ancient Chinese astronomers "may" have used the notches on the rim of the Pi to locate prominent circumpolar stars, and thereby determine true north. (X7)

which in their time was not occupied by a prominent star. The observer simply lined up certain bright circumpolar stars with precalibrated notches and projections on the rim, and the instrument would necessarily be aligned to true north.[29]

Michel's theory sounds reasonable enough, but B. E. Schaefer, in 1983, questioned the Pi's utility as a locator of true north. He claimed that the variability of the notches on the rims of Pis from the same time period negated Michel's hypothesis. Schaefer also contended that the rims of the Pis did not in fact line up with stars that were prominent when the Pis were supposedly in use. Michel defended his hypothesis in a 1986 issue of *Kadath*.

The Pis in fact may not have been scientific instruments at all. Some have suggested that they were simply decorative. However, the Pis' notches and projections seem to be purposeful and are hardly artistic in appearance. We may not have yet identified the real purpose of the Pis.

X8—ANCIENT SEISMOGRAPHS

The first known seismograph, like so many other inventions, is of Chinese origin. It first appeared in the Second Century A.D., when the polymath Chang Heng presented the Emperor and his court with a device that would supposedly not only detect distant earthquakes but also indicate the approximate direction of their epicenters. The court's sages scoffed at first but were startled when the device unexpectedly registered a quake northwest of the capital. No tremors had been felt at the capital, but messengers soon arrived confirming the event.

The exterior of Heng's seismograph has been pictured many times, but its innards remain a mystery. One theory puts an inverted pendulum on the axis of the seismograph. When earthquake waves pass, the internal pendulum sways, hitting and pushing outward one of eight horizontal rods. The rod thus nudged knocks a ball out of the mouth of one of the eight dragons mounted on the outside of the instrument. The dislodged ball is caught (hopefully) by one of the paging frogs below, thereby indicating the direction opposite that of the quake epicenter.[30]

As a Second Century A.D. inventor, Heng showed considerable geophysical insight as well as mechanical ingenuity.

Sketch of Heng's Second Century A.D. seismograph. An earthquake would dislodge one of the balls, which would then fall into the mouth of one of a circle of waiting frogs, thereby providing the direction of the epicenter. (X8)

X9—ANCIENT WEIGHTS AND MEASURES

One measure of an ancient civilization is its establishment of standardized weights and measures for use in commerce and instruments based upon them.

The Harappan Culture of the Indus Valley peaked about 4,000 years ago, boasting about 1,000 cities and towns sprinkled across Pakistan and northwestern India. Its writing system remains undeciphered, but we do know that it had a system of standard weights.

The Indus Valley. The Harappan Culture of the Indus Valley peaked about 4,000 years ago, boasting about 1,000 cities and towns sprinkled across Pakistan and northwestern India. Its writing system remains undeciphered, but we do know that it had a system of standard weights. The basis of this system was a graduated series of stone cubes, each a multiple of a basic unit of weight. This was a sophisticated concept to impose on such a huge area some 4,000 years ago.[31]

The Inca Empire. The Inca Empire stretched along almost the entire western side of South

America and longitude-wise from the Andes to the Pacific. Commerce flowed up and down this continent upon the famous Incan roads and along the coast on huge balsa rafts. Such commerce could not operate successfully without standardized weights and measures plus accurate instruments.

Some of the balances of the Inca are sufficiently curious to merit inclusion here.

In the Archaeological Museum of Madrid there are two sets of balances and four beams, from sepulchers of the Incas at Pachacamac, Peru... A flat strip of bone suspended edgewise by a cord midway forms the beam. To the ends of the beam are hung, by short cords, slings of a network made of fine thread, the free edges being strengthened by cord.

One of these balances is plain, while the beam of the other is elaborately fretted and engraved with circles-and-dots, and curves outlining the fretted spaces. Red paint has been rubbed in these incisions. The long suspending cord is strung alternately with a row of small beads of turquoise and red-and-white shell and a large, flat, oblong piece of shell pierced through the axis. The string is terminated by the figure of a bird and a fret ornament of shell representing a seated human figure with headdress. Three small pendants of beads and shell hang below this, and the whole forms an ornate and striking specimen.[32]

The device seems to have been a rather sophisticated functional balance marked with indices of some sort.

---

1. MMT9—These signify chapters further into this section of William R. Corliss' *Archaeological Anomalies*, from which this article and his other contribution to *Underground!*, "Anomalous Toys," are both culled.—Ed.

2. MMT10

3. MMT11

4. Peter James, Nick Thorpe, *Ancient Inventions*. Westminster: Ballantine, 1994. pp. 142, 157, 163, 248 (X1-X3, X5, X8)

5. Philip A. M. Hawley, "Obsidian Mirrors." *Archaeology*, vol. 51, no. 11, May/June 1998. (X1)

6. Ignacio Bernal, *The Olmec World*. Berkeley: University of California Press, 1969. p. 78. (X1)

7. Anonymous, "Magic Mirrors and Burning Lenses." *Scientific American*, vol. 5, no. 235, 1861. (X1)

8. Berthold Laufer, *The Prehistory of Aviation*. Chicago: Field Museum of Natural History, 1928. (X1)

9. Anonymous, "Magic Mirrors." *The Courier Magazine*, October 1998. p. 16. (X1)

10. Ibid., p. 4. (X1)

11. Anonymous, "Egyptians Had Magnifiers." *Science News Letter*, vol. 15, no. 195, 1929. (X2)

12. Fenelia Sanders, "Eyeglasses." *Discover*, vol. 22, no. 19, February 2001. (X2)

13. Willis, Ronald J., "Ancient Technology." *INFO Journal*, no. 9, 1972. p. 1. (INFO = International Fortean Organization) (X2, X5, X8)

14. Ibid., p. 8. (X2)

15. Ibid., p. 1. (X1-X3, X5, X8)

16. Ibid., p. 10. (X2, X5, X8)

17. Another chapter of *Archeological Anomalies*. - Ed.

18. Anonymous, "Antiquity of the Lens." *Scientific American*, vol. 69, no. 104, 1893. (X2, X3)

19. Ibid., p. 1. (X1-X3, X5, X8)

20. Anonymous, "Did the Viking Make a Telescope?" *NEARA Transit*, vol. 12, no. 1, 2000. (NEARA = New England Antiquities Research Association.) (X3)

21. Ibid., p. 1. (X1-X3, X5, X8)

22. Stephen C. Jett, "The Norse in the North Atlantic: An Overview." *Pre-Columbiana*, vol. 2, no. 3, June 2000. (X4); Thorkild Ramskov, "Vikings, Their Voyaging and Their Navigation." *Pre-Columbiana*, vol. 2 no. 42, June 2001. (X4)

23. Ibid., p. 18. (X4); Ibid., p. 19. (X4)

24. John B. Carlson, "Lodestone Compass: Chinese or Olmec Primacy?" *Science*, vol. 189, no. 753, 1975. (X5)

25. Ibid., p. 10. (X2, X5, X8)

26. Ibid., p. 22. (X5); Vincent H. Malstrom, "Knowledge of Magnetism in Pre-Columbian Mesoamerica." *Nature*, vol. 259, no. 390, 1976. (X5); Ibid., p. 1. (X1-X3, X5, X8)

27. Sentiel Rommel, "Maui's Tanawa, a Torquetum of 232 B.C." Epigraphic Society, *Occasional Publications*, vol. 2, paper 29, 1975. (X6)

28. Andrew E. Rothovius, "The Primacy of the Basques." *Louisiana Mounds Society Newsletter*, no. 53, October 1, 1992. p. 8. (X6); based on Evan Hadingham, "Europe's Mystery People." *World Monitor*, September 1992. p. 34. (X6)

29. Henri Michel, "Le Disque Pi: Jade Astronomique," *Kadath*, no. 13, May-July 1975. p. 33. (X7); Henri Michel, "Encore un Jade Astronomique Inconnu: Le T'ou-Kuei," *Kadath*, no. 20, November-December 1976. p. 9. (X7)

30. Ibid., p. 10. (X2, X5, X8); Ibid., p. 1. (X1-X3, X5, X8)

31. Richard H. Meadow and Jonathan Mark Kenoyer, "The Indus Valley Mystery." *Discovering Archaeology*, vol. 2, no. 38, March/April 2000. (X9)

32. Walter Hough, "Balances of the Peruvians and Mexican." *Science*, vol. 21, no. 30, 1893. (X9)

5

RELIGIONS AND WISDOMS

Sharon Secor

CREATION OF A GIFTED PEOPLE:

THE MAYAN CALENDAR

IT HAS BEEN SAID that a culture's collective understanding of its past is influenced by those who conquer and rule. For centuries, it was commonly understood that the Spanish conquerors subdued and civilized the savage natives of the New World. After the invading Spaniards' initial orgies of destruction, much of the knowledge of the great civilizations and sophisticated intellectual achievements of the native peoples was lost for hundreds of years. The Mayan calendar is one such body of knowledge, a clear demonstration of a civilization comfortable in the higher planes of intellect and thought.

The Mayan calendar is one such body of knowledge, a clear demonstration of a civilization comfortable in the higher planes of intellect and thought.

The earliest small hunting and gathering groups of the lower Americas are generally agreed to have arrived about 11,000 years before Christ. Social systems and cultures gradually developed and these early societies became able to sustain the basic physical needs that ensure the survival of a people. With the transition to agricultural settlements came the ability to support increases in population and the capacity to produce a surplus of products.

This capacity to produce surplus goods helped to bring about significant changes in social structure. It encouraged the development of trade and the evolution of a more formal economic system. This, in turn, contributed to the emergence of more distinct and specialized social classes, some of which no longer participated in physical, food-producing labor, but rather were freed to indulge in the types of cerebral pursuits that allowed the development of shaman-priests, thinkers and planners. These changes in social structure allowed the blossoming of the rich intellectual and spiritual explorations upon which great civilizations are built.

THE MAYA EMERGE

The Mayans emerged in the Yucatan as a distinct cultural group in approximately 2600 B.C., eventually spreading out to encompass about one-third of Mesoamerica, including parts of Mexico, Guatemala, Honduras, El Salvador and Belize. Their influence, however, could be said to have affected the entire Mesoamerican culture.

The Mayan calendar system, with the complexity of its methodology and meaning, stands as a shining example of the heights a people can achieve when they have the freedom to think beyond day-to-day survival. Indeed, while the

Romans—precursors to the invading Europeans that would one day overrun the Americas—were building roads, bringing structure to their Roman Empire, the Maya were mapping the universe, seeking to know the structure of time itself.

As with most Mesoamerican cultures, the Mayan understanding of the world was infused with a strong spirituality. Quite natural, considering the gracious gift that consistent and predictable food production—the very base upon which a successful society rests—must have seemed. Indeed, they understood this gift to be life itself, and enshrined this concept in their creation stories, for in the Maya religion, the gods used corn meal to form the first successful and fully human beings.

STUNNINGLY ACCURATE

Made up primarily of three separate dating systems—the *Long Count*, the *Tzolkin* (divine or sacred calendar) and the *Haab* (civil calendar)—used in conjunction, based upon skilled astrological observations and mathematical calculations that were quite advanced for that era, the Mayan calendar was, by today's standards, stunningly accurate. According to Yale anthropologist and Maya expert Floyd Lounsbury, at a July 1986 symposium in Kimbell, Arkansas, "the Maya developed a complex 'day count' calendar 16 centuries before a similar system was devised in Europe."

In Mayan culture, the shaman-priests had great responsibilities, for it was they who medi-

---

Still in use today, the Tzolkin uses 20 day names in combination with the numbers one through 13, with each name and number combination being associated with certain characteristics and attributes, making it a valuable tool of understanding and knowledge for shaman-priests, past and present.

Developing working relationships with the various gods operating in the physical world and using the strength, the energy, derived from these relationships took on great importance. It was, in those uncertain times, a matter of life or death. Fulfilling the obligations to the gods, obligations based upon their sacrifices in creating humans and the gifts they bestowed to enhance and maintain those lives they created, was one aspect of the cosmic order that the Maya knew was essential to the continuation of the universe.

Almost equally important was the ability to decipher and utilize the cycles, great and small, of nature and the cosmos. The cycles of agriculture, of the sky, of women... knowledge of the cycles inherent in the workings of the world was the means by which order—thus, life itself—could be wrested from chaos. Essential to the Mayan capacity to maintain order was the ability to understand and measure time. They wanted to be sure. And from this want, this need, was born the Mayan calendar system.

ated between men and gods, performing the rituals and rites essential to maintaining the order necessary for the smooth functioning of life. Astronomy and mathematics were of great interest to these shaman-priests, as it was through mastering these that they were able to devise the calendar system around which Mayan life revolved.

Most important to day-to-day life was the 260-day *Tzolkin*, or divine calendar. The oldest of the three systems, with early stone versions dating as far back as 400 B.C., this is the calendar by which agricultural work was planned, as well as that which marked the religious rituals and rites that were expected of the priests and the populace. Still in use today, the *Tzolkin* uses 20 day names in combination with the numbers one through 13, with each name and number combination being associated with certain characteristics and attributes, making it a valuable tool of understanding and knowledge for shaman-priests, past and present.

> **For them, the cycles associated with the days, the months and even with the entire lifetime of a man were just a small part of the overall cycles and patterns of the universe, cycles they were determined to decode.**

The *Haab*, also referred to as the Civil Calendar, while also based on agricultural cycles, tended to be used more in civil or business matters. Made up of 18 months of 20 days each, with an additional short period, or month, of five days, for a total of 365 days, this calendar was also called the *Vague Year*. These five days, called *Wayeb*, were considered to be very inauspicious, even dangerous. The *Haab* and *Tzolkin* were commonly used together, and ran in a 52 year cycle, as this was the amount of time it took for a combined month and day name—made from both sets of name and number days—to repeat.

THE NEED FOR THE *LONG COUNT*

While the *Calendar Round*, the name given to the *Haab* and *Tzolkin* in combination, was sufficient for the needs of most Mesoamerican cultures, the Maya needed more. For them, the cycles associated with the days, the months and even with the entire lifetime of a man were just a small part of the overall cycles and patterns of the universe, cycles they were determined to decode. To achieve this, they needed to be able to measure and record huge amounts of time. They needed the *Long Count* calendar.

Mathematical skills were important to achieving this. The Mayans rose to the challenge and, during the Fourth Century A.D., Mayan thinkers achieved the concept of zero, a mathematical concept that did not reach western Europe until the Twelfth Century. With one of its important qualities, that of placeholder, and the concept of the positional value of numbers, they were able to express the large numbers required for their *Long Count*, which is said to have begun on the day of creation—13.0.0.0.0, or in more familiar terms, August 13, 3114 B.C.

Counting the days, one by one, from the dawn of Mayan creation, the *Long Count* was based on what is referred to as a "modified base 20 system" of numbers, with a shell standing for zero, a dot standing for the number one and a bar standing for the number five. The year was 360 days, made up of eighteen 20-day months. Dates typically were composed of glyphs symbolizing periods of time—*k'in* (day), *winal* (month), *tun* (year), *katun* (7,200 days or 20 *tun*), *baktun* (144,000 days or 20 *katun*)—and the appropriate number. The date begins with the largest measure and progresses to the smallest, the *k'in* or day.

The *Long Count* calendar operated in cycles of 13 *baktuns*, or about 5,125 years. According to Maya calculations, this cycle, which began on August 13, 3114 B.C., will come to a close on—and there are slight interpretive differences among researchers, but this date is generally agreed upon—December 23, 2012. Some researchers favor a December 21, 2012, date, while a very few others have calculated end dates that differ by as little as two months and as much as a few years.

The Mayans were great sky watchers and record keepers. From their careful observations of the skies—the movement patterns of the moon, the visible planets, the stars, eclipses of the sun and moon, comets and other phenomena—and detailed recording of data collected over extended periods of time, they were able calculate the number of days in such cycles as the solar year, lunar month and the sky journeys of the planet Venus with astounding precision.

Using two sticks bound together to form a 90-degree angle with the naked eye, they were able to observe the celestial movements that led them to determine that the year was made up of 365.242 days. Our modern methods tell us that it is 365.242198 days. According to the calculations of today, the average lunar month is 29.53059 days. Mayan sky watchers arrived at similar conclusions, with surviving data from Copan showing a 29.5302-day cycle and that of Palenque indicating a cycle of 29.5308 days. From their precise recording of astrological observations, the Maya created books, or codices, and specialized astrological calendars.

A WRITTEN HISTORY DESTROYED

By the time the Spanish reached the Americas, the Maya had been keeping written records for centuries. It is estimated that the Mayan style of writing came into use about 100 B.C., probably developing from earlier writing systems, which have been estimated to have been used as early as 700 B.C. Prolific writers, the Maya—in addition to astrological observations and calendar calculations, they recorded many aspects of their lives and histories. However, in the Spanish push to take possession of the territories and peoples in what they considered to be a new world, the vast majority of these writings were destroyed.

titled *Relacion de las Cosas de Yucatan*, or, in English, *An Account of Things in the Yucatan*, written in 1566, though the book attracted little attention until nearly three centuries later.

TRACKING THE SKIES

In the Eighteenth Century world of ideas, particularly in literature, the concept of the "noble savage" began to take hold. This idealized vision of native peoples, popularized by such writers and thinkers as Jean Jaques Rousseau and Mary Shelley, became a dominant theme in the popular culture of the Nineteenth Century. Perhaps it came as a reaction to the increased social pressures of urbanization and industrialization, a sort of nostalgic yearning for simpler times that took the form of idealizing those perceived as untouched by the taint of the social ills that often accompany such dramatic social change. When viewed from that

> **"We found a large number of books in these characters (referring to the Mayan glyphs), and as they contained nothing in which there were not to be seen superstition and lies of the devil, we burned them all, which they regretted to an amazing degree, and which caused them much affliction," said Friar De Landa.**

In 1562, over a period of three months, the second bishop of the Yucatan, the Spanish Friar Diego de Landa attempted to civilize and Christianize the native peoples using conversion techniques that included mutilation and torture. He struggled to make the natives accept his loving and peaceful Christ as their lord through such means as burning dissenters alive, hanging them from trees and drowning them. In his efforts to destroy their culture, he saw fit to destroy the work of generations.

"We found a large number of books in these characters (referring to the Mayan glyphs), and as they contained nothing in which there were not to be seen superstition and lies of the devil, we burned them all, which they regretted to an amazing degree, and which caused them much affliction," said Friar De Landa. However, the Friar did record a great deal of information in his book

perspective, the renewed interest in Mayan culture that occurred during the 1800s comes as no surprise. De Landa's writings resurfaced in 1863.

From the late Eighteenth Century to the present, researchers have worked diligently to recover the lost knowledge of the Maya. A handful of codices survived the Conquest, as well as engravings and glyphs from numerous archaeological sites. Fortunately, De Landa and his ilk never quite succeeded in stamping out indigenous cultures, for despite the often brutal efforts to suppress even the language of the native peoples, many of the stories and traditions have survived in oral histories, passed from generation to generation. In the final decades of the Twentieth Century, great strides were made in the translation of the Mayan glyphs, allowing the brilliance of the Mayan calendar to shine through to our modern world.

> **Fortunately, De Landa and his ilk never quite succeeded in stamping out indigenous cultures, for despite the often brutal efforts to suppress even the language of the native peoples, many of the stories and traditions have survived in oral histories, passed from generation to generation.**

The Mayan calendar is the product of many abilities—the ability to write and record data, to devise and utilize a number system, mathematical skill, keen astrological observation and the capacity to think on a grand scale. Today, as the December 23, 2012, *Long Count* end date fast approaches, theoreticians of various disciplines debate what, if anything, it means to our modern world.

Many researchers and scholars believe that the end date heralds a quite rare astrological event, in which the alignment of the galactic and solar planes will place the winter solstice sun in the "dark rift" of the Milky Way. This cycle, one that takes place very gradually over a period of approximately 26,000 years, is referred to as the precession of the equinoxes.

That this great occurrence coincides with the Mayan *Long Count* and astrological calendars and calculations, as well as with Mayan religious histories and teachings, presenting a celestial re-enactment of a climactic Maya creation scene rooted deeply in Mayan culture—a perfect celebration of the end of one 13 *baktun* cycle and the beginning of the next—is deemed by many researchers and scholars to evidence an astounding Mayan understanding of the patterns of the cosmos.

Linda Schele was one such scholar. Her contributions to the deciphering of the writings of the Maya are nearly immeasurable. She earned her PhD in Latin American Studies in 1980, and her award-winning dissertation, *Maya Glyphs: The Verbs*, continues to be widely respected. In addition to teaching at the University of Texas, Schele was an archaeologist, epigrapher and artist, as well as author and co-author of numerous books and articles about Maya history and culture.

In a 1993 book, *Maya Cosmos: Three Thousand Years on the Shaman's Path*, Linda Schele, with David Freidel and Joy Parker, wrote provocatively concerning her realization "that every major image from Maya cosmic symbolism was probably a map of the sky . . . [The] patterns in the Milky Way and the constellations were directly related to the Maya vision of Creation." The stories from the Maya religion are written in the stars, with episodes cyclically re-enacted in the heavens through the ages.

Working within this paradigm of the Mayan blending of spirituality and patterns of the cosmos, using inscriptions depicting celestial events, traditional written and oral creation stories, and—of course—detailed Mayan astrological records and calendars, some theorists, including John Major Jenkins, have come to believe that the Mayans were aware of this subtle process of the precession of the equinoxes.

APPROACHING THE CLIMAX

The climactic astrological event that marks the end of this great cycle has been described as the solstice sun, symbolizing a deity, emerging from the "dark rift" of the Milky Way, representing the birth canal of the First or Cosmic Mother, as the rebirth of god, which in turn symbolizes the birth of a New Age. This relationship draws from the creation imagery of the sacred Mayan text, the *Popol Vuh*.

> **Among the traditional apocalyptic visions of the end—fire, flood, earthquakes, war and plagues—there are a few unusual end date theories that stand out from the rest.**

Still other researchers and theorists take a more literal view of the calendar's end date in light of the belief in cycles of birth, death and rebirth of creation—of the world itself—that is a part of Mesoamerican belief systems, as well as many others throughout the world. Some theorists proclaim, as many have through the ages, that the end is near.

Among the traditional apocalyptic visions of the end—fire, flood, earthquakes, war and plagues—there are a few unusual end date theories that stand out from the rest. Among those is that of Maurice Cotterell, co-author, with Adrian Gilbert, of the 1995 book *The Mayan Prophecies*. In his view, sunspots affect the magnetic field of the earth. He believes that the Mayan calendar demonstrates their knowledge of sunspot cycles and their potential to effect life on earth, and that the *Long Count* end date marks the point at which the sunspot cycle will cause cataclysmic destruction via an abrupt reversal of the magnetic field and a shifting of the north and south poles.

DESTRUCTION, THEN REBIRTH

The majority of the world's religious traditions, including Christianity and Hinduism, as well as Egyptian, Mesoamerican and African religions, express the concept of the destruction and rebirth of mankind and the world, in one form or another, whether it be literal or figurative. This near universality of concept has inspired many New Age and religious thinkers from a broad variety of spiritual perspectives to view the coming Mayan calendar end date as a hopeful and positive event in human history, believing that while we may go through a period of destruction, this era should be viewed as the birthing pains required to bring forth a New Age in the history of mankind, an era of enlightenment, of universal consciousness and peace.

The ongoing debates surrounding the mysteries and meanings of the Mayan calendar and the relevance of its end date are sure to continue through the coming years. One aspect, however, of the magnificent Mayan calendar seems readily apparent. It is the creation of a gifted people that produced thinkers that were as comfortable in the terrestrial world as they were in the cosmos, a civilization that truly honored the great gifts bestowed by their gods.

Sources:

- www.civilization.ca/civil/maya/mmc09eng.html
- www.answers.com/topic/itzamna
- news.nationalgeographic.com/news/2004/05/0504_040505_mayamasks.html
- www.usatoday.com/news/world/2004-05-10-maya-city_x.htm
- www.britannica.com/eb/article?tocId=40841
- www.mediatinker.com/whirl/zero/zero.html
- webexhibits.org/calendars/calendar-mayan.html
- www.mayacalendar.com/mayacalendar/Home.html
- www.wsu.edu:8080/~dee/CIVAMRCA/MAYAS.HTM
- www.unm.edu/~abqteach/ArcheoCUs/99-01-08.htm
- library.thinkquest.org/13406/rr/
- www.unc.edu/courses/rometech/public/content/transport/Adam_Pawluk/Contruction_and_Makeup_of_.htm
- www.isourcecom.com/maya/themaya/whowere.htm
- www.yale.edu/opa/ybc/v26.n33.news.04.html
- www.civilization.ca/civil/maya/mmc07eng.html
- www-groups.dcs.st-and.ac.uk/~history/PrintHT/Mayan_mathematics.html
- www.edj.net/mc2012/mayans.htm
- www.calleman.com/Engpages/summary.htm
- www.ambergriscaye.com/earlyhistory/glyphs.html
- www.civilization.ca/civil/maya/mmc03eng.html
- www.britannica.com/ebi/article?tocId=9331485
- www.answers.com/topic/noble-savage
- www.pauahtun.org/Calendar/correlation.html
- members.shaw.ca/mjfinley/creation.html
- www.jqjacobs.net/mesoamerica/meso_astro.html
- members.shaw.ca/mjfinley/calnote.htm
- members.shaw.ca/mjfinley/mainmaya.html
- www.latinamericanstudies.org/landa.htm
- www.ambergriscaye.com/museum/digit13.html
- mars.acnet.wnec.edu/~grempel/courses/wc2/lectures/industrialrev.html
- www.diagnosis2012.co.uk/cjc.htm
- www.alignment2012.com/jmj2.html
- www.carnaval.com/columbus/2012.htm
- www.13moon.com/prophecy%20page.htm
- www.edj.net/mc2012/mothfath.htm
- www.famsi.org/research/schele/
- www.utexas.edu/research/chaaac/txnotes_archive.html
www.kamakala.com/2012.htm
- scienceworld.wolfram.com/physics/PrecessionoftheEquinoxes.html csep10.phys.utk.edu/astr161/lect/time/precession.html
- www.pureenergysystems.com/news/2005/02/27/6900064_Magnet_Pole_Shift/
- home.hccnet.nl/h.de.jong/mayan.html

Robert M. Schoch

ANCIENT WISDOM AND

THE GREAT SPHINX OF GIZA

MIGHT WE FIND ancient wisdom encoded or enshrined in the Great Sphinx? This is a question I have often asked myself while studying the great monument. Standing between the paws of the Sphinx, sometimes I cannot help but have the sense that there is something important and profound to be learned from her (unlike many people, I consider the Sphinx to be female—indeed, a female of African or Nubian ethnicity—despite the false beard, surely a later addition, that was once attached to her chin). The seismic analysis Dr. Thomas Dobecki and I performed around the Sphinx in 1991 revealed what might be a chamber or room carved into the limestone under the left paw of the Sphinx, hailed by some as "The Hall of Records" of the lost continent of Atlantis. To the best of my knowledge, this cavity has never been probed or explored, so we don't know what it might contain, if anything. But my sense of importance and profundity is not linked to finding some secret store of knowledge, stash of treasure or ancient technological marvel. To simply be in the presence of the Great Sphinx, or even to ponder the statue and all its possible implications from afar, can be a moving experience.

I first came face-to-face with the Great Sphinx at 8:30 A.M. local time on June 17, 1990 (I know people who believe there is astrological significance to this time and date, but it has never been

explained to me). Many more trips would follow over the years. I am a geologist (PhD in geology and geophysics from Yale, 1983), and I had come to look at the Sphinx specifically with a geologist's eye. The question posed to me by my colleague and friend, the heretical independent Egyptologist John Anthony West (author of the classic work on R. A. Schwaller de Lubicz and the symbolist interpretation of ancient Egypt, *Serpent in the Sky: The High Wisdom of Ancient Egypt*) was: What is the age of the Great Sphinx? Is the attribution of the Great Sphinx to the time of the Pharaoh Khafre (a.k.a. Chephren), circa 2500 B.C., reasonable

---

The seismic analysis Dr. Thomas Dobecki and I performed around the Sphinx in 1991 revealed what might be a chamber or room carved into the limestone under the left paw of the Sphinx, hailed by some as "The Hall of Records" of the lost continent of Atlantis.

---

based on the geology and geomorphology of the Giza Plateau, where the Great Pyramid (attributed to Khufu, a.k.a. Cheops, circa 2540 B.C.), Second Pyramid (attributed to Khafre), the comparatively small Third Pyramid (attributed to Menkaure, a.k.a. Mycerinus, circa 2480 B.C.) and the Sphinx stand?

Studying the weathering and erosion of the limestone that makes up the body of the Sphinx, analyzing subsurface weathering patterns that we documented seismically, comparing the ancient climatic history of the Giza Plateau with the features of the rocks, led me to one conclusion: The origins of the Great Sphinx are not only antecedent to the time of Khafre, but appear to go well back into pre-dynastic times, circa 5000 B.C. or earlier. What is more, the so-called Sphinx Temple, sitting directly in front of the Great Sphinx, also dates back to this earlier time. There is a connection between the Sphinx and her temple and the pharaohs Khufu and Khafre of the Fourth Dynasty (Old Kingdom Egypt), but it is one of appropriation and adoption by these pharaohs of much older, indeed what they may have thought of as ancient (and no doubt sacred), structures. The Fourth Dynasty Egyptians repaired and refurbished the Sphinx and associated buildings, and at some point during early dynastic times the head of the Sphinx appears to have been re-carved (the head of the Great Sphinx is actually out of proportion to the body; it is too small, as would be expected if an earlier and badly weathered head was recarved; there is no way now to determine what the original head of the Great Sphinx looked like).

and presented talks at geological and Egyptological conferences, and despite the animosity toward the implications of my analysis, the analysis itself stood up to scrutiny. Indeed, independent geological studies of the Sphinx have now vindicated my analysis.

As a result of my work on the Great Sphinx, I've taken my share of both abuse and praise. Is the Sphinx trying to teach me a lesson? If so, it is a lesson for all of us. Initially I was a lonely voice, a persona non grata at Egyptological meetings for suggesting the impossible, but gradually I noticed that my work and ideas began to slowly take hold, even among those most antagonistic. The battle is not yet won, but more and more ground is being taken every day. Is the lesson persistence? Is it an example of the usefulness of trial and tribulation in fortifying the spirit? Is the Sphinx representative of the duality of mind, spirit, rationality, higher consciousness and the divine combined with the matter, animal life and beastly urges (sometimes thought of as the Leo-Aquarian opposition), both of which are manifested in humans to various degrees and are typically expressed in conflict, be it intellectual sniping or armed war between nations?

Not only does the geological evidence support my analysis and redating of the Great Sphinx, but

My redating of the Sphinx, if true, would necessitate a rethinking of the origin of civilization.

To suggest that the origins of the Sphinx go back to pre-dynastic times, before the modern Sahara Desert even existed (the Sphinx and associated pyramids today sit on the eastern edge of the Sahara Desert across the Nile from modern Cairo) was heresy of the first order. I was told by mainstream academic Egyptologists that no people were sufficiently civilized and sophisticated to carve the Sphinx, or even a proto-Sphinx, at such an early date. My redating of the Sphinx, if true, would necessitate a rethinking of the origin of civilization. Obviously, my critics argued, despite my geological evidence, my conclusions must be flawed. I diligently wrote papers on the subject

also so does the astronomical work of my colleagues Robert Bauval and Thomas Brophy. Robert Bauval has suggested that the three major pyramids of the Giza Plateau correlate with the stars in Orion's belt and commemorate an epoch (of circa 10,500 B.C.—see Bauval's book *The Orion Mystery*). Thomas Brophy has found significant correlations between the Giza monuments and celestial phenomena dating to the Twelfth through Tenth Millennia B.C. (Brophy finds alignments at 11,772 B.C. and 9420 B.C., for instance; see his book *The Origin Map*). Furthermore, Brophy suggests that the Giza monuments form a grand zodiac clock tied to precessional cycles.

To this day many people who visit the Giza Plateau can innately "feel" the mystery of the setting, and to enter the Sphinx Temple or Great Pyramid even without preparation can be a very moving experience.

To put it in crude modern terms, the earth wobbles as it spins on its axis, and thus the sky changes over the centuries and millennia. At present on the vernal equinox (spring equinox in the northern hemisphere, when the sun cross the celestial equator from south to north, around March 20-21) the sun rises against the constellation of Pisces, as it has done for about 2000 years. We live in the Age of Pisces. In the not too distant future (within the next couple of centuries, depending on where one draws the boundary between Pisces and Aquarius) the sun will rise against Aquarius on the vernal equinox and it will be the Age of Aquarius. Three thousand years ago the sun rose against Aries on the vernal equinox, thus the world was in the Age of Aries. In his book, Brophy marshals evidence to support his hypothesis that the Giza monuments served, among other functions, as a testimony to and marker of the end of the Age of Virgo and the beginning of the Age of Leo, circa 10,909 B.C. The motif of the Great Sphinx can be interpreted in this light: The human head represents Virgo, the lion's body represents Leo, and the Sphinx faces due east to watch the rising sun on the vernal equinox. Certainly, Brophy's analysis is compatible with the gist of my re-dating of the Great Sphinx.

Through the ages the Great Sphinx has been both feared and revered. When fully exposed (the Sphinx, if left to the elements, is quickly covered with desert sands up to her neck), the Sphinx stands some 66 feet high and 240 feet long from the tips of her outstretched paws to her rump. One Arab tradition refers to the Sphinx as *Abou el Hôl*, or the *Father of Terrors*, and it is reported that in about A.D. 1379 a fanatical sheik damaged the nose of this heathen idol in his zeal to proclaim Allah the one true god (see James Bonwick's *The Great Pyramid of Giza: History and Speculation*, 1877[1]). The Sphinx was also reported to give responses at sunrise to questions placed before it, perhaps not literally speaking, but conveying information in subtle and mysterious ways. In New Kingdom Egypt, as well as during Greco-Roman times, the Great Sphinx was often revered as a beneficent deity. Her face was painted red, an altar was positioned between her paws, offerings were made to her, and votive tablets left to her.

Why was the Great Sphinx carved in the location where she sits? Often the Sphinx is seen as the sentinel or guardian of the pyramids, but in fact I believe the Great Sphinx (or proto-Sphinx) predates the present Giza pyramids. The Giza Plateau essentially marks the apex of the Nile delta and the very ancient division between Upper and Lower Egypt, a delineation that goes back into the far mists of pre-dynastic times.

One cannot fully fathom the meaning of the Great Sphinx without considering the adjacent pyramids. Were these monstrous structures merely tombs to maniacal pharaohs, or do they have another story to tell? Even if they served as the final resting places for dead men (and women), and this is far from proven, do the pyramids represent something more? Might the Nineteenth Century astronomer-royal for Scotland, C. Piazzi Smyth, and his colleagues, have been on the right track when they suggested that the Great Pyramid in particular encodes and acts as a repository for sophisticated metrological, mathematical, geometric, geographical and astronomical data? (I take exception to many of the strong Christian fundamentalist aspects of certain forms of "pyramidology," but that doesn't mean we should throw the entire baby out with the bathwater.) Elsewhere, I have suggested that the Great Sphinx and pyramids record, and were raised in response to, periodic encounters of the earth with comets and space debris, which at times wreaked havoc on the surface of our planet (see my books *Voices of the Rocks* and *Voyages of the Pyramid Builders*).

The strange and bizarrely designed but consummately built interior passageways and chambers of the Great Pyramid, and the connection between the pyramids and the Great Sphinx, have so far eluded any simple explanation. A theory that I believe has merit combines the astronomical and astrological significance of the orientations of the Sphinx, pyramids and their internal passageways, with a hypothesis of initiation rites (including the passing on of sacred and profane knowledge that may be encoded in the structures) which culminated in an ultimate mystical experience for those fortunate enough to achieve such a status.

The celestial alignments of the Giza structures have been empirically demonstrated. The vast literature on the sophisticated knowledge of the ancients cannot be ignored (see, for instance, the appendix by Livio Catullo Stecchini in *Secrets of the Great Pyramid* by Peter Tompkins). To this day many people who visit the Giza Plateau can innately "feel" the mystery of the setting, and to enter the Sphinx Temple or Great Pyramid even without preparation can be a very moving experience. It is well known that Napoleon experienced something very strange and inexplicable when he was alone in the King's Chamber on August 12, 1799; to his dying days, he refused to relate the experience.

Imagine traveling to the Giza Plateau prepared for a potential mystical vision or to receive sacred wisdom. In ancient times adepts may have come from all parts of the globe to learn wisdom at the feet of the Sphinx. Imagine preparing with meditation and offerings, fasting and prayers over many days, in the Sphinx Temple. You face the enigmatic representation of the divine manifested in the mundane. You make your way up to and through the various stations and pyramids of the Giza Plateau, working thorough multifarious and labyrinthine passageways and chambers of diverse orientations, angles and dimensions, each with their unique meaning and significance. The culmination of a long spiritual and metaphysical journey, for those with the stamina and fortitude to complete it, may have been experienced in the so-called King's Chamber of the Great Pyramid. Prepared by meditation and fasting, physical exhaustion and mental preparation,

aided by the acoustical, tactile and olfactory properties of the granite insulation deep in the heart of the pyramid (drumming, chanting, music and incense may have been used as part of the ritual), and perhaps followed by induced sensory deprivation as one is left locked alone in the absolute darkness of the chamber with only the enigmatic granite coffer as company and no way to exit (dependent totally on one's colleagues to ultimately be retrieved), mystical experiences occurred.

Using sophisticated but now poorly understood means, the Sphinx and pyramids may have allowed adepts to accomplish what others have tried to achieve through ingesting mescaline (the active ingredient of peyote) and other drugs, kundalini yoga, study of the Kabbalah, Transcendental Meditation, or any of numerous other presumed roads to enlightenment. The Sphinx and pyramids served as a vehicle, a means, to experience true mystical states, a way to gain that insight that cannot be described (sometimes referred to as the "oneness" or "void"), a method to glimpse ultimate reality.

What is the ancient wisdom that the Sphinx has to impart? Perhaps it eludes all words, all language, and can only be attained by traveling the path to its ultimate consummation.

---

1. Originally published in 1877.

Ron Sala

WHERE IS THE HOLY GRAIL?

THE SCREENPLAY of *Monty Python and the Holy Grail* is now a "Sacred Text," having been installed at the Internet Sacred Text Archive (www.sacred-texts.com), one of the Web's most comprehensive collections of the world's spiritual writings. The Pythons join a venerable host of Grail authors over the centuries, including Chrétien de Troyes, Geoffrey of Monmouth, Sir Thomas Mallory and Alfred Lord Tennyson. Amazon.com lists nearly 600 books with "Grail" in their titles. Their sales are helped, no doubt, by such bestsellers as *Holy Blood, Holy Grail* and *The Da Vinci Code*.

Each author has quested in his or her own way for this mysterious Grail, each bringing the world a slightly (or radically) different version of its nature and whereabouts. Has each merely seen reflected in its shining surface his or her own face, or is there a reality behind all the words?

DEATH AND TAZES

One of the difficulties of Grail research is that the story has been added to and modified by so many different groups over the centuries, each with their own particular worldview and biases. A common link between many of these groups is that they've often been violently persecuted. Jews, early Christians, Gnostics, Pagans and various groups of medieval heretics have all met with the

> One of the difficulties of Grail research is that the story has been added to and modified by so many different groups over the centuries, each with its own particular worldview, biases and situation in life. A common link between many of these groups is that they've often been violently persecuted.

bloody suppression of their cultures, ideas and forms of worship at one time or another.

In this respect, it may be useful to borrow a framework from controversial intellectual Hakim Bey, who wrote that freedom is always temporary and that those outside the mainstream construct for themselves what might be called a "Temporary Autonomous Zone" or TAZ. Once a TAZ has been destroyed, which it inevitably will be, another must be built in its place, which often happens in a disguised form. Thus, in dangerous times, any clue presented to the general public about the existence of a TAZ should be designed so it gives enough information to inspire dedicated seekers (ensuring the group's continuance) while obscuring the information enough to baffle those who would destroy it (ensuring the group's security).

It's also useful to consider that the word "heretic" comes from a Greek root meaning "to choose." So long as there are people whose choices

> **Melchizedek provides Abram with bread and wine, blesses him and assures him of victory. Who was this priest dispensing bread and wine? Neither Judaism nor Christianity had yet started at the time of the story.**

fall outside the accepted "truth" of the dominant group, there will be heretics. The Grail, whatever it might be, or have been, have often been associated with heretics. It has never been an official relic of the Catholic Church, but has existed in the realms of alternative spirituality, folklore, poetry, art and music. Even Monty Python, whose comedy was said to continue the anti-authoritarian spirit of the Beatles, were a type of heretic TAZ. They came under fire from the BBC for some of their sketches (after they realized they were attracting an audience), and their "Flying Circus" is shown on PBS in America because none of the major broadcast networks would run it unedited.

The Grail represents a "do it yourself" spirituality, whose communion is administered not by popes and priests, but by one's own search for the sacred. No wonder it's enjoying a renaissance in this most individualistic of ages.

CAN YOU DIG IT?

Is the Grail a physical object? An idea? An experience? Or perhaps some combination of these? The most common concept of the Grail is that it was the cup Jesus drank from at the Last Supper and with which Joseph of Arimathea collected his blood following his crucifixion. If this is the case, a Grail quester should look for a goblet or chalice of some sort, and many have. This is a version of the Grail presented by Chrétien de Troyes, whose *Conte du Graal* (Tale of the Grail) is one of the chief medieval romances. But Wolfram von Eschenbach, in his *Parzifal*, written a few years later, presents the Grail as a stone. As if that weren't enough, some authors write of the Grail having a number of "transformations" or "nuances," including a (broken) sword, a spear (or lance), a cup, a dish (or plate) and even a book. Each of these relates to the passions of John the Baptist and Jesus—the sword that beheaded John, the plate that carried his head, the spear that

pierced Christ's side, the cup that held his wine and blood, and a book some say Jesus wrote himself. If these are not material objects but metaphors, the possibilities for what the Grail was/is are nearly endless. Nevertheless, in the spirit of the quest, we shall explore.

MELCHIZEDEK(S)

Precursors of the Grail mythology come from both within and without the Jewish/Christian tradition. As good a place to start as any is the account in *Genesis 14* of a mysterious meeting between Abram (whose name had not yet been changed by God to Abraham) and a "Melchizedek King of Salem." This Melchizedek is described not only as a king, but also as "the priest of the most high God." Melchizedek provides Abram with bread and wine, blesses him and assures him of victory. Who was this priest dispensing bread and wine? Neither Judaism nor Christianity had yet started at the time of the story. Two chapters earlier, we read of Abram's call to go to a land that God will show him. When he arrives there, he is rewarded with bread and wine from "the priest of the most high God." Like the many Grail questers after him, Abram had a message from God to seek. Like Parzival, Galahad, Arthur or whoever the Grail King may have been, Abram finds what he seeks in a communion with sacraments, specifically bread and wine. In return, Abram provides the priest with one tenth of the war spoils (i.e. a tithe). Abram was born and raised in Ur of the Chaldees, a polytheistic culture. Abraham, in his new religious outlook, is, if not yet monotheistic, at least "monolatric," or worshipping exclusively one God among many. This most high God grants him victory over his Canaanite foes.

The story takes on greater significance when we consider a reference in *Psalm 110* to the King of Israel, being "a priest forever of the order of

Melchizedek." According to the Christian New Testament, Jesus was a descendent of David and the line of Jewish kings. The author of Hebrews claims Christ is of the order of Melchizedek and translates the name as "King of Righteousness." The author of Hebrews points out Melchizedek was also "King of Salem" or "King of Peace." Most Jewish commentators have identified Salem with Jerusalem. Jerusalem is where the Kings of Judah reigned as well as a place where Jesus taught and where he died and was buried. But the author of Hebrews makes another, astonishing claim: The Melchizedek who met with Abram is "Without father, without mother, without genealogy, having neither beginning of days nor end of life, but resembling the Son of God, he remains a priest forever."[1] At least according to this early Christian writer, Melchizedek is somehow immortal and eternal like the Son of God.

Even YHWH, God of the Jews, though presented in the Bible as a bachelor, was outed a few years ago as linked to his own "other half." An inscription was discovered at Kuntilat Ajrud that reads, "to YHWH Shimron and His Asherah [Goddess]." Even King Solomon, builder of YHWH's great temple in Jerusalem and supposed ancestor of Jesus is recorded as having built temples to other Gods on the Temple Mount as well, temples that survived until King Josiah's "reform" 300 years later.

Furthermore, the Kabbalistic *Mekubalim* claims one should do a *mitzvah* (fulfill a commandment) "for the sake of the Holy One Blessed be He and His *Shekhinah*," Shekhinah often being seen as a feminine form of God. The biblical authors often lament the constant worship by the Israelites of other Gods and Goddesses. This in itself testifies

> **Even YHWH, God of the Jews, though presented in the Bible as a bachelor, was outed a few years ago as linked to his own "other half." An inscription was discovered at Kuntilat Ajrud that reads, "to YHWH Shimron and His Asherah [Goddess]."**

Is the author of the story of Melchizedek in *Genesis 14* somehow telling us that Abraham, the traditional (and possibly mythical) founder of the three faiths of Judaism, Christianity and Islam, subscribed to a still earlier tradition? Genesis tells us Melchizedek was Priest/King of (Jeru)Salem. Is there any indication of a pre-Judaic religion being practiced in Jerusalem? The Canaanites had their holy sites, or "high places," on mountains and hills. They worshiped a variety of Ba'alim, or Gods and Goddesses, one of which was known as Tzadek, the Canaanite equivalent of Jupiter, as well as the Hebrew word for "Justice." Melchizedek could mean King of Justice, King of Tzadek (the God) or "My King Is Tzadek." Canaanite Gods were worshipped in male/female pairs. One popular pair was Tamuz and Ishtar. As in Mesopotamia, the king, representing the God, and the priestess, representing the Goddess, would copulate each year to assure the fertility of the land.

to how "mixed" actual Israelite religion tended to be. According to Talmudic legend, the two angels on the Ark of the Covenant were locked in erotic embrace and the Talmud further tells us the festivals at Jerusalem were often orgiastic, that is, until a divider was placed between male and female worshipers that persists in many synagogues, churches and mosques to this day.[2]

BLOOD FEAST

It was in this already complex religious environment that the events of Christ's life played out. The Roman occupiers simply saw YHWH as a type of Jupiter. The Samaritans worshipped in a part-Yahwist, part-Pagan religion on their holy mountain. Tamuz, Baal and Mithra were worshiped in dying-and-rising-God cults.

Jesus grew up in Galilee, whose residents were often not seen as "good Jews" by people from

Jerusalem. His preaching and teaching had resonances with Greco-Roman Cynics, who criticized the very nature of society; with the Hebrew prophets, who called people to a life of justice; and with the Pharisees, who were developing a culture of scholarly argument that would evolve into modern Judaism.

Jesus' teaching upset the power structure to the point that his arrest and execution were ordered by the Roman authorities, according to the biblical accounts, with the help of Jewish leadership. One TAZ was about to end, and others about to begin. All the biblical sources say his followers deserted Jesus after his arrest. But, somehow, they had an experience that brought them back together, renewed and bolder than before, proclaiming Jesus had risen from the dead as the "first fruits of them that sleep."

A HOSTILE TAKEOVER

The wide variety of views of Jesus' nature and legacy that characterized the first three Christian centuries came to be considerably narrowed in 325 when the first supposedly Christian Roman Emperor, Constantine, declared his support for the long-persecuted Church, assembled the world's bishops and insisted they reduce their faith to a lowest common denominator that would serve the Imperium. To be stripped away would be traces of mystery religions that divided people into initiates and non-initiates. Believers would have a homogenized experience based on the doctrine and ministrations of the Church hierarchy. Nevertheless, Gnostic Christians, influenced by the Hermeticism of Egypt and the Hellenized world would continue to be a major force in places

Some have claimed that Jesus and Paul should be numbered among these Gnostics, who sought direct experience of a God outside the bounds of matter and beyond the definitions of orthodox religion.

What's more, Jesus had left them a ritual to "do in remembrance of me," involving the bread of his body and the wine of his blood. Like Melchizedek of old, at least some of them went so far as to say he was immortal, and so could his followers be as they partook of his sacraments.

But, according to some legends, sacraments are not all Jesus left behind. According to some, Mary Magdalene (the purported wife of Jesus) and/or Joseph of Arimathea (who may have been Jesus' great uncle) sailed to either England or the south of France, carrying either a vial of Christ's blood or his child, or some other form of the Holy Grail, such as secret teachings. One can take one's pick among a dizzying array of legends, some that stay fairly close to the "official" Church story and others that tell of descendents of Jesus ruling France as Angevin and Merovingian kings.

such as Syria, Persia and even China. Some have claimed that Jesus and Paul should be numbered among these Gnostics, who sought direct experience of a God outside the bounds of matter and beyond the definitions of orthodox religion.

A contribution of Constantine's assumption of Christian leadership was a mission by his mother, Empress Helena Augusta, to the Holy Land in search of the original places of the life of Christ. While there, she claimed to have found Christ's tomb, and in it the spear that pierced his side, the nails that hung him to the cross and a cup that held his blood. This vessel has been called by many the Marian Chalice, and can be considered the first mention of the Holy Grail. Apparently, it received its name through association with Mary Magdalene who, according to one legend, used it to collect Christ's blood before turning it over to Joseph for burial.[3]

It disappeared, however, during the sacking of Rome in 410, by legend having been smuggled to

> **The Cup has a reputation for healing powers and is in fragmentary form, having been drunk from and even nibbled by many sick persons in hope of a miracle cure.**

Britain. At least one researcher[4] thinks it is one and the same with the Nanteos Cup, a wooden vessel owned by the Powell family of Nanteos, Wales. The Cup has a reputation for healing powers and is in fragmentary form, having been drunk from and even nibbled by many sick persons in hope of a miracle cure. It's no longer in the Nanteos Mansion, but is "believed to be in safe-keeping somewhere in Ceredigion."[5]

Legends say the Cup had earlier been stored at Glastonbury and only carried from there when the Abbey was in danger. The old Abbey, in ruins since its closure by Henry the VIII, sits atop the Glastonbury Tor, a great yoni-shaped hill from which red water flows. According to Christians, the water symbolizes Christ's blood, but to Pagans it has always alluded to the menstrual flow of the Goddess. It's a fitting place for a Grail cup that has been associated with both Christian worship and Goddess traditions. Glastonbury features, beside the main Abbey, a smaller chapel called both "Joseph's" and "Mary's" as well as the "Lady Chapel." On an exterior wall of this chapel there's a curious stone that says,

JESUS
MARIA

One legend says the Grail had been walled up at Glastonbury. Was this stone a marker for its hiding place? Another legend says Joseph hid the Grail in a well. Just feet away from the "Jesus/Maria" stone is a passageway through which one finds a hole known as "Joseph's Well."[6]

"CAMELOT!—IT'S ONLY A MODEL"

The Nanteos Cup may be how Arthur came to be associated with the Grail. There are many who believe Glastonbury was the original "Isle of Avalon," with the Tor surrounded in Arthur's Sixth Century by a lake. Glastonbury is visible from one of the possible locations of Camelot. Then again, there are dozens of sites associated with Arthur's reign all over Britain. Christian and Celtic myth meets and merges. The Welsh bard Taliesin tells of how Arthur stole a cup from the underworld, apparently without Christian reference.[7] The Celtic God Bran's cauldron restores life to the dead, but takes away their speech—a reference to the mystical death and resurrection of the mysteries, combined with the secrecy they require?

CHOOSING THE FLAMES

The various strands of the tapestry don't begin to be properly put together until the Middle Ages. Though centered around the Dark Ages' figures of Arthur and his court, the romances of Chrétien, his "continuers," Wolfram, de Borron and other named and anonymous authors, are products of their own particular circumstances. Many of those who brought pieces of the Grail story together were Christian converts from Judaism. Such men could appreciate the values of incorporating ideas from more than one faith. Wolfram even includes favorable, or at least neutral, depictions of Moslems, who were beginning to be Christianity's enemies. They could also borrow motifs from the Kabbalah that Jews were advancing in South France, from Pagan folktales and from the lore of Hermeticism and Gnosticism.

> *Many of those who brought pieces of the Grail story together were Christian converts from Judaism. Such men could appreciate the values of incorporating ideas from more than one faith.*

Most of the major Grail texts appeared out of a very exiting and threatening time of religious change and conflict encompassing the half-century from c. 1170-1220. It is at the same time that the Knights Templar were building their power, before being destroyed not long after refusing to persecute the Cathar, a.k.a. Albigensian, a.k.a. Puritan "heretics." The Cathars consisted of two groups, Cathars proper, or *perfecti* and "believers" or *credenti*. The perfecti gave up meat, sex and most other earthly pleasures in order to transcend the wheel of death and rebirth, while the credenti were enjoined to lead lives of kindness and await perfection in a future incarnation. Some waited until late in life to begin their perfection. The Cathar system bears striking resemblance to that of Hindus and Buddhists as well as to the classical Gnostics, most of which were ascetic.

I find it intriguing that one supposed form of the Grail is the emerald that fell to earth in Lucifer's crown. Is it too much to speculate, that in that era of increasing interest in the Gnostic/Hermetic tradition, such an emerald might be associated with the "Emerald Tablet of Hermes," written perhaps as early as 650 and translated into Latin about 1140—just a few decades before the first of the Grail romances? The "Emerald Tablet of Hermes," in a Seventeenth Century translation by Sir Isaac Newton, states:

1. Tis true without lying, certain & most true. That wch is below is like that wch is above & that wch is above is like yt wch is below to do ye miracles of the only thing.

2. And as all things have been & arose from one by ye mediation of one: So all things have their birth from this one thing by adaptation.

3. The Sun is its father, the moon its mother, the wind hath carried it in its belly, the earth its nourse.

4. The father of all perfection in ye whole world is here.

5. Its force or power is entire if it be converted into earth. Separate thou ye earth from ye fire, ye subtile from the gross sweetly wth great indoustry.

6. It ascends from ye earth to ye heaven & again it desends to ye earth and receives ye force of things superior & inferior.

7. By this means you shall have ye glory of ye whole world & thereby all obscurity shall fly from you.

8. Its force is above all force, for it vanquishes every subtile thing & penetrates every solid thing. So was ye world created.

9. From this are & do come admirable adaptations whereof ye means (Or process) is here in this.

10. Hence I am called Hermes Trismegist, having the three parts of ye philosophy of ye whole world.

11. That wch I have said of ye operation of ye Sun is accomplished & ended.

Here we see one of the finest representatives of Western esotericism. We have the Hermetic dictum, "As above, so below," which links the cosmic macrocosm and the human microcosm. We have the sun and moon, masculine and feminine, intellectual and instinctive. We have all forms as emanations from the One Source as well as the return, through slow, deliberate action, to original perfection.

Norma Lorre Goodrich in *The Holy Grail* lays out her theory of a network of "Grail Castles" throughout Britain and France where members of the hidden, "heretical" church initiated candidates. Whatever the complete secrets of the Albigensians, many were willing to be burned at the stake rather than submit to the Catholic Church's demand of renouncing their chosen, "heretical" faith. Millions were slaughtered, some as far north as Oxford, England, but most in the Languedoc region of France, where their very language and culture were obliterated. Many of the Knights Templar would also be massacred, including their Grand Master, Jacques DeMolay, charged with heresy and idolatry. Did it have anything to do with something they may have found in the Holy Land— Jesus' inner teachings? A list of his descendents? His bones? The Grail itself? After their suppression, did the Templars die out? Become pirates? Flee to Scotland? Infiltrate the Masonic guilds? The permutations of Grail theorizing are limitless.

"NAZIS! I HATE THESE GUYS!"

Indiana Jones, modern, fictional Grail quester, has a basis in history for part of *The Last Crusade*. Nazis were after the Grail, and whatever other ancient or mystical objects they could use to further National Socialism and its occult or racial objectives. Wagner, who happened to stay at the Nanteos Mansion, became intrigued with the Grail lore surrounding the place and was inspired to compose *Parsifal*. The opera was wildly popular in Hitler's youth, and the way Wagner presents the story made it possible for the Party to exploit it as a Grail of racial purity. But regarding enthusiasm for the occult appeal of finding the Holy Grail, no one could touch Heinrich Himmler, the chief of the SS, which he saw as a new Knights Templar fighting for the ideal of Aryan manliness. Under Himmler, an arm of the SS, the *Ahnenerbe*, or Ancestral Heritage Society, began a search in 1935 for artifacts and archaeology to support the Reich. They didn't skimp on intellectual quality, bringing in 46 experts, 19 of which held PhDs. One of them was Otto Rahn, Germany's leading expert on the Holy Grail, who had previously done his own excavations of Cathar sites in the South of France.[8] There are

heretics is *Love in the Western World* by Denis de Rougemont, in which the author lays out how the very ways we think about "romance" appeared suddenly during the very time period we're looking at. Marriage was then primarily an economic, and hardly glorified, affair. But the troubadour singing of the idealized lady of the castle, or a storied knight championing his love, aimed at raising relations between men and women to a new, spiritual plane. The Court of Love was formed in the Twelfth Century by noblewomen who consciously wished to make a social system that would celebrate a love that was more than physical gratification or a continuation of the genetic line.

It seems nearly every religion has rules regarding those two great forces of animal and vegetable life: sex and drugs. They lay down rules for the use of, or abstention from, both, often with separate rules for priesthood and laity.

---

rumors Rahn actually found the Grail, either a cup or a stone (à la Wolfram's version) and brought it to Wewelsburg, the fortress Himmler had prepared as a Grail Castle for an inner circle of SS "knights" until the end of the war when it again fell into obscurity. In any case, Rahn was found frozen to death in the Alps after having a falling out with Nazi leaders...[9]

SEX AND DRUGS

It seems nearly every religion has rules regarding those two great forces of animal and vegetable life: sex and drugs. They lay down rules for the use of, or abstention from, both, often with separate rules for priesthood and laity. Sex and drugs are a basic part of social life, as any society that does not reproduce dies out, and the only culture without traditional uses of psychoactive substances is the Inuit of the far north. Did these aspects of life play a part in the formation of the Grail stories?

Let's keep in mind that the romances that brought us the Grail as we know it were written in the context of a developing code of chivalry. This code was associated with knights and ladies, and troubadours who sang of courtly love. A classic book relating the troubadours to the Abigensian

Chastity for knights was stressed, a message that comes through in Galahad's battle in the Grail Castle with a fierce lion (representative of his own lust) as a prerequisite for success in his quest. (This is played up in the Python version with "Galahad the Chaste" imperfectly resisting a castle full of "young blondes and brunettes, all between 16 and 19 and a half.") Furthermore, at least according to one account of the myth, the Grail may only be carried by a virgin. And Lancelot's adultery with Guinevere makes him not only a tragic figure who fails in his quest for the Grail, but the unraveller of Camelot itself.

In some versions of the story, the Grail is not only a holder of Christ's blood/wine but of his body/bread as well. It was sometimes believed a dove from heaven replenished the Grail's power by bringing it a wafer each year on Good Friday. This holy bread echoes not only the stories of the bread-and-wine-dispensing Melchizedek priesthood but the "bread of the Presence" kept continually in the Israelite Tabernacle and later in the Jerusalem Temple. The table on which the bread was placed in the Sanctuary also supported flagons for a "drink offering" of wine.[10] Here we have the same bread-and-wine motif as in both Melchizedek and the Grail.

> **Gnostics, of which the medieval Cathars were a later example, also held the regulation of sexual impulses as important to spiritual advancement. There have been two extremes among them, "ascetic" and "libertine."**

When Jesus' supposed ancestor, David, and his fighting men were on campaign and found themselves hungry, we read[11] that the priest gave them permission to eat the sanctified bread, provided they had not been with women for at least three days. David replied that his men always refrained from women while on an expedition. This three days' chastity was also a requirement for all the people of Israel when God appeared on Mt. Sinai during their wandering in the wilderness.[12]

Jesus, whose ethics included the precept that even looking at someone lustfully was to commit inward adultery,[13] invoked the precedent of David when Pharisees accused him and his disciples of collecting grain on the Sabbath.[14]

Gnostics, of which the medieval Cathars were a later example, also held the regulation of sexual impulses as important to spiritual advancement. There have been two extremes among them, "ascetic" and "libertine." In the first, sex is refrained from in order to devote oneself fully to God, as opposed to the affairs of this earthly plane of generation. In the second, sex is indulged in with the aim of "sweating out" the earthly in hopes of purification.

Dr. John Lilly, of floatation tank fame, wrote in *Simulations of God* of something he colorfully calls "the brahmacharya trip." Brahmacharya is the Hindu term for celibacy, through which some swamis claim one can attain unity with Brahman, the Oversoul. Brahmacharyins like Sri Swami Sivandana call male and female aspirants to refrain from meat and dairy products to assist them in their purity, just as the Albigensians refused to eat the same items, recognizing them as the products of the sexual reproduction they sought to avoid.

Drugs, too, played an important role in ancient religions, as well as in some contemporary ones like the Native American Church (which uses peyote) and União de Vegetal (which uses ayahuasca). The well-known ethnobotanist Carl A. P. Ruck claimed a few years ago, at a conference in New York, that it's the consensus of researchers that the *kaneh-bosem* ("sweet cane") of the biblical recipe for the anointing oil of priests and the temple incense was none other than cannabis.

It has also been speculated that Jonah's "gourd" or "bush"[15] was a psychoactive of some sort. We read that it made the selfish prophet "very happy" but at its withdraw he no longer wanted to live. The Hebrew word for the unknown plant is *qiqayon* and occurs in no other book of the Bible. However, it's phonetically very similar to *kykeon*, the beverage consumed in the Greek Eleusinian Mysteries. That kykeon has not been positively identified either, though the groundbreaking 1957 book *The Road to Eleusis*, written by Ruck, R. Gordon Wasson, Huston Smith, Albert Hoffman, et al makes the case that it was prepared using the ergot fungus that grows on grain. (Hoffman was researching ergot derivatives when he accidentally gave himself the world's first LSD trip.)

> **Two contemporary scholars, Barbara Thiering and Dan Merkur, have each come to believe Jesus' real offense to the Jewish religious establishment was that he wanted to make the bread of the Presence, which they claim was prepared with psychedelic ergot, freely available rather than under the control of the priests.**

Two contemporary scholars, Barbara Thiering and Dan Merkur, have each come to believe Jesus' real offense to the Jewish religious establishment was that he wanted to make the bread of the Presence, which they claim was prepared with psychedelic ergot, freely available rather than under the control of the priests.[16] Is this the hidden meaning of Jesus and his disciples gathering grain, found in all three synoptic gospels?

To consider another cultural context, a ruler of Persia was known as a "king of kings," a title later applied to Christ. He drew religious legitimacy by consuming the psychedelic Haoma beverage, prepared from the *Peganum harmala* plant. Many scholars identify it with Soma, mentioned in the Hindu *Vedas*. In the *Yasna* of the Zoroastrians, the inheritors of the Persian religion, we read:

> And we worship the Good Mind (in the living) and the spirits of the saints. And we sacrifice to the fish of fifty-fins, and to that sacred beast the Unicorn (?) which stands in Vouru-kasha, and we sacrifice to that sea of Vouru-kasha where he stands, and to the Haoma, golden-flowered, growing on the heights; yea, to the Haoma that restores us, and aids this world's advance. We sacrifice to Haoma that driveth death afar...[17]

Do we see here the fish we encounter in Jonah, the Christian "fishers of men," and the Fisher King of the Grail myths? Do we see the unicorn, symbol of Christ, and in medieval lore only tamable by a virgin? Do we see the theme of overcoming death, central to Christ and the Grail?

Dana Beal and Paul De Rienzo, authors of The Ibogaine Story, present a theory that Jesus was able to survive the crucifixion by several administrations of iboga, a powerful psychedelic taken from the root bark of an African shrub. Similar in action to harmala, in that it gives transcendent experiences before inducing a death-like sleep iboga has the added advantage of preventing ischemia, the global stroke that took the lives of those crucified.

Dana Beal and Paul De Rienzo, authors of *The Ibogaine Story*, present a theory that Jesus was able to survive the crucifixion by several administrations of iboga, a powerful psychedelic taken from the root bark of an African shrub. Similar in action to harmala, in that it gives transcendent experiences before inducing a death-like sleep, iboga has the added advantage of preventing ischemia, the global stroke that took the lives of those crucified.

Was the Grail a code for ancient knowledge covering secrets of the human microcosm, spiritual technologies passed down by holy men and women through the ages that allowed experiences of transcendence? Did the Albigensian perfecti hide secrets of how to potentiate mystical states through the control of sexual energies and the intake of ancient sacraments? Much research remains to be done before we can provide a satisfying answer.

A CUP OF GOD

Whatever the Grail is, wherever it is, there is something compelling in the quest. It calls forth that greatest of magical powers, the imagination, and inspires us to dream of what was and what may yet be. Perhaps the best answer is provided by Norma Lorre Goodrich, who states simply that the Grail is God. That, ultimately, is what we seek, can never fully define, yet, sometimes, in the least likely places, find.

1. *Hebrews 7:3*

2. Ohad Ezrahi and Yitzhak Hayut-Ma'n, "Four Temples and One Belief—About the True Religion of King Solomon." www.hamakom.org

3. Justin E. Griffin, *The Holy Grail: The Legend, the History, the Evidence*. Jefferson: McFarland & Co., 2001. p. 44.

4. Ibid., p. 150-51.

5. "Mid Wales Weird—Nanteos, Hauntings and the Holy Grail." www.bbc.co.uk

6. Griffin, p. 64-68.

7. Emma Jung and Marie-Louise von Franz, *The Grail Legend*. Andrea Dykes, trans. Boston: Sigo Press, 1970. p. 115-116.

8. Peter Reydt, "Nazism and the Myth of the 'Master-Race.'" *Secret History*, Channel Four, September 23, 1999. www.wsws.org

9. Mary Jones, "Otto Rahn." In *Jones' Celtic Encyclopedia*, 2003. www.maryjones.us

10. *Numbers 4:7*

11. *1 Samuel 21*

12. *Exodus 19:10-15*

13. *Matthew 5:27-28*

14. *Mark 2:23-28, etc.*

15. *Jonah 4*

16. William Shannon, "Entheogens and the Roots Of Christianity." March 26, 2000. www.mail-archive.com

17. *Yasna 42:5-6*

Dylan at Great Pyramid of Giza.

The statue of Bastet in the town of Zagazig, outside the ruins of Bubastis.

Dylan at the ruins of Bubastis.

Richard Cusick

JOURNEY TO BUBASTIS

My seven-year-old daughter Dylan has two abiding obsessions: Egyptology and cats, complementary passions without peer as cats were venerated by the ancient Egyptians as conduits to the Gods and are adored by my daughter as a conduit to all things fuzzy and cool. Dylan absorbed Egyptian mythology in a way that has always eluded me. She quickly came to identify with Bastet, the Goddess of Cats, a fact that has always been regarded with indefatigable patience by our own two young felines, Appy and Flower.

My seven-year-old daughter Dylan has two abiding obsessions: Egyptology and cats, complementary passions without peer as cats were venerated by the ancient Egyptians as conduits to the Gods and are adored by my daughter as a conduit to all things fuzzy and cool.

All little girls love their kittens, of course, but Dylan's passion for Things Egyptian began casually more than a year ago with an innocuous cartoon chock-full of scorpions, scarabs, magic and mummies.

"You like mummies, huh?"

"Oh, yeah," she said. And that led to the first of many trips across the river to the Metropolitan Museum of Art which has one of the best collection of stolen artifacts in the world (from the Egyptian viewpoint it's all stolen). There were 40 or 50 trips to the Met, I'm sure, in every season, in every weather.

We actually went to the museum on the Friday following September 11, 2001, when the New York City air was rank with particulate grit and the photocopied faces of the dead floated on lampposts and streetlights and filled the windows of storefronts like ghosts. Dylan and I had the Met to ourselves that day—we were its only visitors—and except for a few guards we walked through the Temple of Dendur alone and in silence, our soft footsteps echoing on ancient stone. For a brief moment last fall, at the start of second grade, my daughter could arguably read hieroglyphics better than the English alphabet. Around this time she started to say things like, "When I go to Egypt…" with a blithe certainty and I felt it was my duty to disabuse her of that ludicrous notion.

"Now, now, honey," I said, "Egypt's a long way off and it's really very expensive and…" Dylan glanced up and gave me a look that I saw for the first time, a look that mixed a gigabyte of guile with annoyed affection for a befuddled old man.

According to legend, the Persian Army defeated the Bubastites by carrying cats as shields into battle. The followers of Bastet froze on the field, unwilling to harm the sacred animals, and the Persians hacked them to pieces.

"Daaaad," she stretched the word, "when I go to Egypt..." and continued as if I had said nothing. Not "if I go to Egypt" but "when." She assumed that I would bring her to the Land of the Pharaohs with an accuracy that I now find weirdly prescient. So when I said, "Dylan, guess what?"

"What?"

"We're going to Egypt! We're going to go to Giza and see the Great Pyramids."

I thought she would be ecstatic, but she had her own thoughts.

"Well..." she haggled, "I want to go to Egypt but I don't want to go to Giza."

"You don't want to go to the Pyramids?"

"I want to go to Bubastis!"

Bubastis! The site of the Temple of Bastet, the ancient center of the Cult of the Cat. What I remembered at that moment about Bubastis from those dozens of trips to the museum was that it was destroyed by the Persians more than 2,000 years ago. According to legend, the Persian Army defeated the Bubastites by carrying cats as shields into battle. The followers of Bastet froze on the field, unwilling to harm the sacred animals, and the Persians hacked them to pieces. I explained to my seven-year-old archaeologist that Bubastis is most likely a pile of rocks in the middle of the desert. "We're going to the Pyramids," I said definitively.

"Awwww..."

"Hey! I said we're going to Giza to see the pyramids and we're going to the Cairo Museum to see the new animal mummy room. And you're going to like it, young lady!"

Her eyes widened, as she knew exactly what I was talking about. For the moment she forgot all about the Realm of Bastet.

"Cat Mummies!" she marveled. Her two favorite words.

The ancient Egyptians mummified more than a million cats, and the Animal Mummy Room at the Cairo Museum is reputed to have the best collection in the world. It had been closed to the public for years but recently opened its doors again thanks to the efforts of the Animal Mummy Project at the American University in Cairo. The best cat mummies in the world were once again waiting to be seen, and we were on our way to see them. What else could I do? Her predilection for Things Egyptian has only grown as she has grown. She reads voraciously, and for a seven-year-old she has an uncanny grasp of arcane Egyptian mythology. My own education proceeds more slowly.

We had a tragedy last week. On the eve of our Great Adventure, our beloved cat Apple Bow died. She was not sick, and no reason is known. We came home from the movies and found her under Dylan's dresser. She was devastated, of course, and I was devastated for her. I'm too old and cynical to be moved anymore by anything short of the miraculous.

DECEMBER 7, 2004: CAIRO, EGYPT

On our second day we went to the Cairo Museum, the most glorified attic in the world. It is an assault on time and space rather than a scholarly curation, and stuffed to the rafters with artifacts, bric-a-brac and the mummies of the Pharaohs. 120,000 objects in all. Every corner had a dusty display of some weathered masterpiece—but we were there for the cats.

We arrived in Egypt, with all the requisite culture shock. Dollars became pounds and the pounds were Egyptian, and everyone seemed to be arguing when they were really having casual conversation. We stayed at the Mena House, the only hotel with proximity to the Pyramids of Giza, a palatial complex that was the former hunting lodge of the King of Egypt back in the Nineteenth Century and the balcony in our room was overlooked by the Great Pyramid of Cheops. Our first full day here was spent drinking in the sites, obviously tourists with our slack-jawed stupefaction at the foot of the Sphinx and our awe at the sun-tipped Pyramids of Giza. The stones were individually huge and, accordingly, the structures themselves dwarfed any previous expectations. However, our time in this country was short, and this trip quickly became something more than a holiday.

On our second day we went to the Cairo Museum, the most glorified attic in the world. It is an assault on time and space rather than a scholarly curation, and stuffed to the rafters with artifacts, bric-a-brac and the mummies of the Pharaohs. 120,000 objects in all. Every corner had a dusty display of some weathered master-piece—but we were there for the oats.

first set out to X-ray, photograph and catalogue each of the 160 animals in the museum's collection. Last year the restored collection was finally reinstalled in well-lit climate-controlled cases and displayed with revised scholarship and detailed x-rays. Dylan and I spent the better part of an afternoon sketching the animals on display, which gave us an excuse to stare uninterruptedly at these fascinating antiquities for incredibly long periods of time.

On our third day, fate kicked in as Dr. Ikram agreed to meet us and offered my seven-year-old a Master's class in animal mummification. Salima Ikram was a short, attractive woman of Pakistani descent, with a wide, white smile and the demeanor of a soccer mom. She took Dylan by the hand the moment they met, and walked her through security back to her office at the American University. She patiently answered

I was relegated to a mere observer as these two unlikely colleagues communed. Much of what was discussed was over my head anyway. They became fast friends fast. What I didn't know was that when Professor Ikram was ten years old her father brought her to Cairo where she saw the original Animal Mummy Room at the Egyptian Museum. Then and there she decided to become an archaeologist.

The recently-restored Animal Mummy Exhibit was a two-room side-gallery with some of the best preserved specimens in the world: intricately bandaged bundles of cats, delicately-rendered birds, a huge crocodile, an exquisite dog and a monkey which faced each other as they were found entombed, their fur still intact. The exhibit was elegant, and digestible, unlike much of the rest of the museum (which needs to be taken in small bites). The kudos go to Dr. Salima Ikram, an archaeologist at the American University in Cairo, who not only painstakingly cataloged the museum's dilapidated animal mummy collection but also raised the more than $200,000 necessary to recurate the rooms.

The last time the museum detailed its collection was in 1905, and so Dr. Ikram and her colleagues

Dylan's innumerable questions, punctuating her responses by pulling out the occasional cat skull or fish mummy. I was relegated to a mere observer as these two unlikely colleagues communed. Much of what was discussed was over my head anyway. They became fast friends fast.

What I didn't know was that when Professor Ikram was ten years old, her father brought her to Cairo, where she saw the original Animal Mummy Room at the Egyptian Museum. Then and there she decided to become an archaeologist. Flash-forward 25 years and she is pre-eminent in her field, and the Animal Mummy Room that inspired her is chained up. Windowpanes in the skylight are broken and birds have actually nested on the exhibit cases. Dr. Ikram made it her personal goal to see the Animal Mummy Room restored, which took years and was not at all easy. Dylan and I came into her office just as she was completing that goal, and the irony was not lost on any of us.

"Maybe one day you'll be sitting in this chair, Dylan," Professor Ikram suggested, a prospect that glowed in my daughter's eyes.

"My cat died last week," Dylan lamented.

"Oh, I'm so sorry. How did that happen?"

"We don't know. She just died."

"She was only eight," I added. "Just one of those things."

"Did you bury her?"

"Out in the backyard," Dylan said dutifully.

"Did you put a stone on the grave?"

"I didn't."

"You must put a stone," Professor Ikram told me emphatically. "And you must put her full name as well as any nickname she may have had."

"Appy!" said Dylan. "Her name was Apple Bow but we called her Appy."

"Then you must write that on a stone and put that stone on the grave. The ancient Egyptians believed that as long as your name survived, you would live for eternity." She explained that through prayers and monuments the dead would live forever.

rattled on about snake mummies and sawdust, I lowered my head into my hands and gently rocked it back and forth. Then I looked up through my fingers and there was Dylan, staring, smirking, with a face that seemed to say "You knucklehead..."

Without a doubt, I was going to Bubastis.

Somewhere buried in this story are all the excesses of parenthood. I guess the moral here is that you shouldn't let your child watch cartoons... or you may wind up half a world away dispatching the soul of your beloved animal in the timeless Realm of Bastet.

DECEMBER 8, 2004: MENA HOUSE, GIZA

By day we took in the temples, the marketplace and the Mosque, but each night we went back to our room with the Great Pyramid bathed in light, looming beyond our balcony, and we drew pictures of what we saw. One evening she taught me how to play chess, and we watched *Buffy the Vampire Slayer* and read books. On the night before our journey to Bubastis, Dylan told me the Legend of the Faraway Goddess, in whose steps we were to follow.

***

"Now, Daddy," she said, "sometimes Bastet is a cat and she's nice, but sometimes she's a lioness and she's mean. When she's a lioness she's Sekhmet and she's protecting her father, Ra, whose boat pulls the sun across the sky. At night Ra's boat goes below the horizon and it's dark and Bastet has cat eyes that can see in the dark.

***

Dylan said, "I wanted to go to Bubastis but it's not there anymore. My Dad says it's a pile of rocks in the middle of the desert."

"No, it's there!" Dr. Ikram said, fatefully. "It's about 80 kilometers northeast of Cairo. It's called Tel Basta now. There's not much there. Whatever was valuable was removed and all the major stones have been numbered but that's about it. It's pretty much undeveloped."

My daughter gave me that look again, the one that got me to Cairo in the first place. As Dr. Ikram

"Now, Daddy," she said, "sometimes Bastet is a cat and she's nice, but sometimes she's a lioness and she's mean. When she's a lioness she's Sekhmet and she's protecting her father, Ra, whose boat pulls the sun across the sky. At night Ra's boat goes below the horizon and it's dark and Bastet has cat eyes that can see in the dark. As Sekhmet, she protects her father from his enemies, especially from a snake called Apep. She cuts off Apep's head!" She looked at me to emphasize. "She does this *every night*, Daddy!"

But the violent anger of the Lioness was enormous and Ra was finally forced to banish his daughter to the Nubian Desert where she could rage in isolation. Ra was left unprotected at night, and so he sent his emissaries, Onouris and Thoth, to Nubia to retrieve his daughter and return her to Egypt. On the journey home, she bathed in the sacred waters of Philae which drowned her anger and transformed her from the fierce lioness to the serene cat. As Bastet, she sailed down the Nile stopping at each town and village along the way to receive the worship of the people. She was followed by many until she came to a sacred grove along the eastern branch of the Nile. This she claimed for her domains and commanded that her temple be built there. That much is myth.

In time and space, Bubastis predates written history. Archaeologists presume that before the dawn of civilization the ancient agrarian clans in Egypt adopted totems of essential animals, and the clan that occupied this part of the Nile Delta identified itself with the cat. If the cat was first domesticated in Egypt, it was probably first domesticated at Bubastis.

In time and space, Bubastis predates written history. Archaeologists presume that before the dawn of civilization the ancient agrarian clans in Egypt adopted totems of essential animals, and the clan that occupied this part of the Nile Delta identified itself with the cat. If the cat was first domesticated in Egypt, it was probably first domesticated at Bubastis. The Temple was commenced 4,600 years ago in the Fourth Dynasty of the Early Kingdom, around the same time as the Great Pyramid at Giza. It was called Per Bastet by the Egyptians, Pi Baseth in the Old Testament and Bubastis by the Greeks. Today, the ruins are called Tel Basta, It is believed that for 1,500 years, Bastet was a local deity even though pharaohs sought to associate themselves with the cat goddess. Excavations at Tel Basta have found the names of Cheops and Chephren, the pharaohs of the two largest pyramids in Giza, carved in stone. In 945 B.C. the Libyan Prince of Bubastis, Sheshonk I, took over the Egyptian throne and made the Realm of Bastet the home to the Pharaoh.

Bubastis was situated along major trade routes and for a time in the 22nd Dynasty it was probably the capital of Egypt. His son Osorkon II started to reconstruct the temple which had fallen to ruin over the centuries, and his grandson Osorkon III finished the temple and dedicated it to Bastet. Starting around the Sixth Century B.C., animal worship grew in popularity and remained central to the Egyptian way of life for almost 500 years. It was during this period (from 712 to 332 B.C. and beyond) that Bubastis saw its best and worst times. In 525 B.C. the Persians conquered Egypt and took Bubastis with their aforementioned feline defense. For 200 years Egypt was part of the Persian Empire but the Old Religion survived and Bubastis continued in prominence throughout that period. Most of what we know about Bubastis comes from the Greek historian Herodotus (484-425 B.C.), who personally visited the site. Herodotus reported that the red granite temple was the most beautiful in all of Egypt. The city of Bubastis was built upon embankments that rose around the main complex which was set on a strip of land between two fingers of the Nile so the Temple of Bastet could be looked down upon from anywhere in the city and seemed to float on a mystical island. There was a long avenue of trees—a sacred grove—which led to the main temple. Smaller temples and tombs were scattered throughout, and there was a major cat necropolis where followers of the Cult of the Cat throughout Egypt brought their beloved pets to be mummified. Cats were also sacrificed to the goddess, lovingly embalmed and buried in the mud-brick necropolis. The remains of over 30,000 cats were found at Bubastis. Otherwise, living cats always overran the temple, where they were cared for, pampered, prayed to and carted around in baskets. Egyptians often asked cats to use their mysterious language to intervene with the gods on their behalf.

Bubastis was the site of the most popular festival in all of Egypt for over 300 years. The Greek historian Herodotus claimed that 700,000 revelers came each year to the month-long festival to participate in a Dionysian debauch of strong wine and wild sex: "Men and women come sailing all together," he wrote, "vast numbers in each boat, many of the women with castanets, which they strike, while some of the men pipe during the

Children were thankfully excluded from the festivities while the adult Egyptians behaved in the manner of drunken cats in heat. At the end of the festival a sacred flame was passed through the town until it made its way down to the temple. In this manner the original Journey of Bastet from Nubia to Bubastis was recalled, and the cat goddess was symbolically returned to her Realm.

whole time....men and women sing the while, and clap their hands. When they arrive opposite any of the towns upon the banks of the stream, they approach the shore, and, while some of the women continue to play and sing, others call aloud to the females of the place and load them with abuse, while a certain number dance, some standing up to uncover themselves. After proceeding in this way all along the river-course, they reach Bubastis, where they celebrate the feast with abundant sacrifices. More grape-wine is consumed at this festival than in all the rest of the year besides."

Children were thankfully excluded from the festivities while the adult Egyptians behaved in the manner of drunken cats in heat. At the end of the festival a sacred flame was passed through the town until it made its way down to the temple. In this manner the original Journey of Bastet from Nubia to Bubastis was recalled, and the cat goddess was symbolically returned to her Realm.

Bubastis survived the Greeks and the Romans, was diminished by the Christians and finally reduced by Islam to nothing. Today the streets of modern Cairo are filled with small feral street cats that are well-cared for by the common Egyptian, a cultural tradition that has continued unfettered for millennia. I read these words in our room in the shadow of the Great Pyramid, in the books we bought in Cairo to prepare for the following day's singular journey. My daughter slept beside me, wrapped in a cat-filled dream, in the fabled Black Lands of Kemet.

DECEMBER 10, 2004: MENA HOUSE, GIZA

Our driver Samir was that lovable sort of rogue who seemed to be related to just about everyone in Cairo. How convenient for our shopping needs!

That bit of good fortune notwithstanding, he was a good guy and after three days of steady employment he began to feel like part of the caravan. Samir wanted to know what we were going to do the following day.

"Tomorrow we're taking the train to Zagazig to go to Tel Basta," I said.

"Why you want to do that? There's nothing there."

"Well, there's something we want to see."

"Well, I drive you. Comfortable. Quiet. Egyptian trains very ... dirty."

"We're not afraid of a little dirt." Dylan agreed. She wanted to take the train too.

"Egyptian trains not comfortable," Samir implored. "Let me take you."

I thought he was looking for another day's pay but in a rare moment of prudence, I conceded.

The next morning Samir drove us out of Cairo to Tel Basta. It took a little over an hour, and upon our arrival Samir pointed out the window and said, "Look." The train to Zagazig rumbled along parallel to the roadway. Where it wasn't rusted brown, it was encrusted in something black. It was little more than ancient boxcars creaking along, packed with people standing, squeezing, pushing out of the train.

"You believe me now?" Samir cracked.

We entered Tel Basta at about 1:00 P.M. There was a ramshackle guard house with two sleepy Egyptian military guards and little else. Tickets were purchased, but Samir suggested I throw a few dollars to the guards because we were likely to be the only visitors today. "People here are very poor," Samir said sincerely. A small baksheesh set off some smiles.

"Go. Go." One of the guards said with a generous flourish.

We walked on gravely sand to the top of an ancient mound. On one side workers had raised a massive Late Kingdom statue of Hathor, the Mother of the World, and were putting on the finishing touches. Opposite that, a small unimpressive statue garden led to several stepped fields filled with sun-bleached stones. Carved and broken pieces of incised granite the size of telephone booths were so strewn about that we had to lace our way through them. An occasional few stones stuck out of the ground at odd angles, and one or two were as straight as the day they were laid; but whatever plan or pattern this site once had was now lost in antiquity. Perhaps the shelved hilltops

supply in Egypt—is finally growing short. Housing projects from encroaching Zagazig now cover two-thirds of Bubastis, even though it is certain that the site has not given up all its secrets. Recent finds include an important stone stella with writing in both Greek and Demotic script, and a necklace of golden flies that was associated with the Pharaoh Ahmose over 3,500 years ago. Rumors in archaeo-logical circles persist about illicit fortunes being made in the ruins at Tel Basta.

I asked Samir to leave us alone. We walked far afield, to the top of a small hill. I picked out a medium size flat stone that was nestled in a stand of scrub, small enough to be negotiable but big

Recent finds include an important stone stella with writing in both Greek and Demotic script, and a necklace of golden flies that was associated with the Pharaoh Ahmose over 3,500 years ago. Rumors in archaeological circles persist about illicit fortunes being made in the ruins at Tel Basta.

marked the limits of the precipice where the town once looked down upon the temple; perhaps this was where the banks of the canals that embraced the temple once flowed. Maybe an archeologist could pick out the ruins of the Temple of Bastet from the remains of the ka-tem-ples of Teti and Pepi I that Naville described in detail, but to these unschooled eyes it was all carved chaos. The great silent stones of Bubastis lay all around this hardscrabble landscape like—well, like fallen idols.

The quality of the carvings remained breathtak-ing, and the sheer volume of broken stone was overwhelming. White and red granite and limestone were the most common. The tortured sandy soil was patched with small tufts of razor-sharp scrub grass that the guards colloquially called "hemp." Otherwise the grounds were cleared of small debris. The site had first been carefully excavated by Edouard Naville between 1887 and 1889, and many smaller digs have stopped and started again over the years, but the money has always run out. A definitive study of Tel Basta has not been done, and time—the single element in seemingly endless

enough to stay put. I pulled a set of colored pen-cils and a drawing pad out of my backpack and gave them to Dylan. She sat cross-legged in the sand and drew a gray-black cat with green eyes and a long tail.

"What should I write?" she asked.

"*Great Bastet,*" I dictated, "*Please receive our friend Apple Bow, also known as Appy...*"

We did the same for Oscar and Nimbus, two more cats who had graced our lives. As I watched my daughter patiently draw one for each, carefully lettering each prayer with the sincerity of a Twelfth Century monk, my armor began to crack. I dug a small hole, buried the papers and capped the shrine with the flat stone, and my daughter fell to her knees and made a silent prayer to Bastet. I snapped a few pictures through a mist of tears, and when she was through she asked if I was all right.

"Yeah. It's a little overwhelming, isn't it?"

She took the camera from my hand and put me in front of the stone and wordlessly took a picture of her father in tears.

Moments later Dylan was picking at rocks in the nearby sand when she separated two small pieces of red granite—one the size of a quarter, the other smaller than a dime—from a slew of pebbles.

"Look!" she gasped. There was a small corner of a hieroglyph distinctly carved in the quarter-sized rock. It was obviously tooled and there was nothing like it anywhere in sight. Anything with a hieroglyph on it weighed more than half-a-ton. I turned it over disbelievingly in my fingers and suddenly the military guard was behind me. He saw the piece of red granite in my hand.

"Look what she found," I said sheepishly, although he didn't really speak English. He took the artifact from me and was obviously as amazed as I was. He looked at me and looked at Dylan and he handed it back to me and quietly said, "Take. Take."

We walked around for quite a while playing among half-hidden columns and sand-smoothed statuary. At one point Dylan ran near a large round well—a deep hole perhaps eight feet in diameter—surrounded by rusted barb wire. "Get away from there!" I snapped, seeing nothing but an accident waiting to happen. And my daughter dutifully scampered away from the legendary temple well that Coptic Christian tradition holds was founded by Jesus Christ when he was a boy. In one version of the story, the Holy Family was refused water because there was not enough to drink, and the boy Jesus pointed to a spot where water came gushing forth. A second, more severe version of the tale claims that the cat temple came tumbling down in the wake of the Boy Savior's discovery.

Tel Basta is not a large site and after some hours we had exhausted our options and headed back towards the car. There were two more guards now and, once again, at Samir's suggestion I gave them each three dollars. "Where's the cat cemetery?" Dylan asked and this led to another half-hour of discovery over a ridge at the north end of the site. A vaulted mud brick cat necropolis has hardened over the centuries into a rocklike labyrinth of niched walls and sarcophagi that stretched unto Zagazig. There were hundreds and hundreds of niches that once were the compact tombs of just as many cat mummies. Dylan clambered on these ancient graves like a monkey until the sun began to wane. It grew cold quickly and it was finally time to go.

Back at the car, four more military guards showed up—making eight in all—and Samir suggested a little more grease for the wheels of international friendship. As I was giving them each a few dollars—now totaling $38—another small car pulled up.

"It's the General," said Samir.

"Who is the General?"

"He is in charge."

"Do I give him money?" I asked.

"No, no," Samir insisted. "Just his men."

The siren was coming from the General's car behind us. "What's happening?! What's wrong?" Samir smiled. "Is okay," he said. "They are our escort. No thing will happen to you while you are in this town." Which led to the next logical question: "What could happen to us?" "No bomb," Samir said.

After the General got out of the car things grew mildly formal. The men lined up and introduced Dylan and myself to the man in charge of Tel Basta. He was a small, stout man with deep moist eyes and who spoke no English, but he was all smiles and he ruffled my little girl's hair. I shook everyone's hand again and then we got into our car and drove away. Minutes later as we made our way through the main road in Zagazig we slowed down to take a picture of a statue of Bastet at a crossroad. Suddenly there was a siren, that stopped my heart, and I saw that we were flanked on four sides by military vehicles filled with armed soldiers. The siren was coming from the General's car behind us. "What's happening?! What's wrong?"

Samir smiled. "Is okay," he said. "They are our escort. No thing will happen to you while you are in this town."

Which led to the next logical question: "What could happen to us?"

"No bomb," Samir said as he pulled out onto the highway towards Cairo, and our military escort, smiling and waving assault rifles, fell away one by one.

I turned to Dylan and said, "That was the best 38 bucks I ever spent."

And our Journey to Bubastis was done.

Dan Russell

GNOSIS: THE PLANTS OF TRUTH

THE CENTRAL SACRAMENT of all Paleolithic, Neolithic and Bronze Age cultures known is an inebriative herb, a plant totem, which became metaphoric of the communal epiphany. These herbs, herbal concoctions and herbal metaphors are at the heart of all mythologies. They include such familiar images as the Burning Bush, the Tree of Life, the Cross, the Golden Bough, the Forbidden Fruit, the Blood of Christ, the Blood of Dionysos, the Holy Grail (or rather its contents), the Chalice (*Kalyx*: *flower cup*), the Golden Flower (*Chrysanthemon*), Ambrosia (*Ambrotos*: *immortal*), Nectar (*Nektar*: *overcomes death*), the Sacred Lotus, the Golden Apples, the Mystic Mandrake, the Mystic Rose, the Divine Mushroom (*teonanacatl*), the Divine Water Lily, Soma, Ayahuasca (*Vine of the Soul*), Kava, Iboga, Mama Coca and Peyote Woman.

The Neolithic impulse stresses the creative hearth and human-engineered fertility, the special sphere of women. Agriculture, weaving, pottery, metallurgy, medicine, astronomy, calendrical counting, mythology and writing are largely matristic inventions.

Of the Goddess symbolism recovered from Europe's hundreds of well-excavated sites, an enormous percentage is painted or engraved on drinking vessels. Virtually all the drinking vessels display entheogenic symbolism, and virtually all Neolithic and Bronze Age temples and shrines yield a profusion of cups, bowls, vases, funnels and ladles. In fact, most Neolithic houses reveal a corner shrine with the same paraphernalia.

Virtually all the drinking vessels display entheogenic symbolism, and virtually all Neolithic and Bronze Age temples and shrines yield a profusion of cups, bowls, vases, funnels and ladles. In fact, most Neolithic houses reveal a corner shrine with the same paraphernalia.

Sir Arthur Evans, the seminal genius who excavated Knossos, Crete's sprawling complex of Neolithic and Bronze Age palaces, noticed that "The plant designs of the frescoes are in their essence simply accessories to the main subjects presented, which are human or animal figures. On the pottery, however, this essential feature is omitted, and only the vegetable details are selected for reproduction."[1] These included entheogens and anodynes like bearded barley, opium poppies and the psychoactive bulbs—lilies, hyacinths and saffron.

"Moreover," adds Gimbutas, "the symbolism of Old Europe, 6500-3500 B.C., provides an essential key to understanding Paleolithic religion, since many of the images are continuous."[2] It was she

The Gold Ring of Isopata.

Lion-headed bees from the Palace of Minos at Knossos.

who pointed out to Wasson that, down to the present, *Amanita muscaria* ("Soma") is enjoyed at wedding feasts and other celebrations in parts of her native rural Lithuania, and that the Lithuanians had an ancient tradition of exporting quantities of the mushrooms to Lapp shamans in the far north.[3]

"Delphi," the ancient Mycenaean shrine (c. 1350 B.C.) turned into a Classical Greek institution, means "womb," *delphys*. The word is also related to *delphis*, "dolphin," the incarnation of the sea, the womb from which Crete sprang.

That the Neolithic temple was conceived as the womb of the Goddess is indisputable. The dolmens, the narrow stone entrances of the "anthropomorphic" megalithic tombs of western Europe, c. 4500-3000 B.C., were used as passages of "rebirth" after "incubation" in the tomb/womb just as, in Melanesia, they were stone birth canals.[4]

The snake, archetypal symbol of earthly regeneration and herbal healing, was a major motif of Neolithic art, both sacred and secular. An 8,000 year-old cult vessel from Yugoslavia has two bird-headed snakes guarding the contents of a ritual bowl.[5] A 6,500 year-old vase from Romania shows snakes encircling the concentric circles of the world, "making the world roll" as Gimbutas says.

Horned snakes, or horned animals in association with snakes, or bird-headed Goddesses wrapped in snakes, or Goddesses with snakes for hair, or schematic snakes, are reproduced on sacred drinking vessels, shrine Goddesses and pottery more frequently than any other imagery,

from the Ukraine to Crete, from 8000 to 1500 B.C. "The pregnant figurines of the Seventh and Sixth Millennia B.C. are nude, while the pregnant ladies of the Fifth and Fourth Millennia are exquisitely clothed except for the abdomen, which is exposed and on which lies a sacred snake."[6]

Female Neolithic images, many with the head of a snake or bird, outnumber male images 30 to one.[7] Like the bison-men of the Upper Paleolithic caves, the male god's principal Neolithic manifestation was in the form of a bull or bull-man, the Son of His Mother. The Snake-Bird Goddess, a figure of chthonic transformation and ecstatic resurrection, was the original Creatrix.

The Cretan Queens of Knossos were consistently portrayed, for thousands of years, as winged wasps or bee-headed women surrounded by floating eyes and snakes. They were also depicted as bare-breasted shamans, in a flounced skirt, with a flower crown and outstretched arms holding a cobra in each hand. They cast spells. Their flower crowns were sometimes capped by the image of a panther, the premier transformation beast.

The Gold Ring of Isopata, a Queen's signet ring found near Knossos, dating to c. 1500 B.C., explicitly depicts bee-headed women dancing in ecstasy, surrounded by beautifully drawn floating plants, possibly entheogenic lilies, a disembodied "Cleopatra" eye and floating snakes.[8]

Like the wasp, the power of the bee's sting came from the power of the plants it pollinated. A Mycenaean gem of Minoan workmanship, c. 1400 B.C., pictures a large sacred plant growing from horns of consecration, supported by a chalice.

The plant is ceremonially flanked by two lion-headed satyrs in bee skins, that is, two shamans, each holding aloft, directly over the plant, a jug of sacramental drink.[9] The bees not only made honey for the honey-beer, but pollinated the magical flowers the mead was spiked with, thus transforming the shamans themselves into buzzing lion-headed bees.

But agriculture is a cybernetic engine, creating its own pressure for increased production and territorial expansion. This was the exact opposite of the Neolithic process, which stressed the powerful hearth skills of women. The Bronze Age process stressed the confrontational skills of the warrior.

bring to consciousness that which the authorities, and their compulsive sheep, want forgotten.

Jesus was such a shaman. The historical Jesus has about as much in common with the Pauline Jesus as a horse has with a unicorn. The Roman Empire's most prestigious and effective non-Hellenic theology, de facto *religio licita* to the Romans for centuries, was co-opted by some of the Empire's most talented syncretists and turned into a dogma capable of filling the void left by the bankrupt post-tribal pseudo-shamanism that Imperial Graeco-Roman religion had become.

The trick, as Paul well understood, was to turn the nationalist Israeli ghost dancer Joshua into a

---

The greatest crime of the nonconforming shaman is that she or he struggles to bring to consciousness that which the authorities, and their compulsive sheep, want forgotten.

Furthermore, humans have an inherently carnivorous psychology. Even the tribal Neolithic communities lived by hunting and practicing animal sacrifice, which they uniformly associated with religious epiphany. Animal sacrifice was a major function of Neolithic priestesses. Blood was considered nourishing, entheogenic and the entheogenic or curative sap of plants was regarded as their "blood." The Bronze Age wealth-managing bureaucracies, of course, which the Neolithic communities lacked, were careful to generate reasons for acquiring more wealth.

The Iron Age is the militaristic Bronze Age writ large. The originary Inquisition, the archetypes of industrial conformity, descend to the unconscious level, since the archetypal frame of reference has been carefully manipulated, through succeeding historical stages, to destroy conscious cultural knowledge of the ancient shamanism.

When conscious memory (*mnemosyne*) is destroyed, what is left is emotion, irrational attitudes dictated by "parentally" inculcated compulsions: God-the-Father as Pavlov. It's not for nothing that the great shaman Plato said that all learning is remembering. The greatest crime of the nonconforming shaman is that she or he struggles to

Greek mystery god, Orpheus. "Saviors" were turning into mystery gods all the time, but never before with the foundation of the Empire's legendary and prestigious network of Hellenized synagogues as a starting point. Never before with the one holy book capable of replacing Homer and Hesiod, *The Septuagint*, the Greek translation of the Hebrew Bible, created 250 years before by Alexandria's Greek-speaking Jewish community and now read all over Alexander's Empire, the Greek Empire Rome conquered. The worst, the most amnesiac aspects of Israeli theology were used, brilliantly, against themselves, to destroy what remained of the ancient *mnemosyne*.

The Egyptian prince Moses, *Moshe*, is the original Hebrew Messiah, *Moshiy'a*. The words are both apparently related to the Egyptian *mose*, "is born," as in *Thutmose*, "Thoth Is Born." The Egyptian *mose* is derived, according to Professor Gordon, from the Canaanite *moshe*, "sacred calf."[10] *Moshiy'a* apparently means "Salvation Is Born" in Hebrew. The Hebrew use of the word, without a prefix, is Canaanite, not Egyptian.

Moses' brother Aaron, the *kohen*, saw two of his sons struck dead for celebrating the Lord with "illicit fire,"[11] and *Judges* attributes Israel's defeat

As Gordon and Patai point out, if we had no Bible, but only the evidence of Israeli archaeology, we would conclude that Israelite religion, until the destruction of the Temple in 586 B.C., was mainly the worship of Astarte and Asherah.

in battle to serving "the *baalim* and the *ashtaroth*."[12] Jeremiah promises divine vengeance upon those who worship the popular "Queen of Heaven," and archaeology proves that she was indeed popular.[13] As Gordon and Patai point out, if we had no Bible, but only the evidence of Israeli archaeology, we would conclude that Israelite religion, until the destruction of the Temple in 586 B.C., was mainly the worship of Astarte and Asherah.[14]

That they may believe him, Moses had to take the oracular snake from Asherah's belly:

> And God said unto Moses, I AM THAT I AM: And he said, Thus shalt thou say unto the children of Israel, I AM hath sent me unto you... And Moses answered and said, But, behold, they will not believe me, nor hearken unto my voice: For they will say, The Lord hath not appeared unto thee. And the Lord said unto him, What is that in thine hand? And he said, A rod. And he said, Cast it on the ground. And he cast it on the ground, and it became a serpent; and Moses fled from before it. And the Lord said unto Moses, Put forth thine hand, and take it by the tail. And he put forth his hand, and caught it, and it became a rod in his hand: That they may believe that the Lord God of their fathers, the God of Abraham, the God of Isaac, and the God of Jacob, hath appeared unto thee.[15]

Genesis acknowledges the serpent's maternal oracular powers, while prohibiting their use to mortals:

> And the serpent said unto the woman, Ye shall not surely die: For God doth know that in the day ye eat thereof, then your eyes shall be opened, and ye shall be as gods, knowing good and evil. And when the woman saw that the tree was good for food, and that it was pleasant to the eyes, and a tree to be desired to make one wise, she took the fruit thereof, and did eat, and gave also unto her husband with her; and he did eat. And the eyes of them both were opened... And the Lord God said, Behold, the man is become as one of us, to know good and evil: And now, lest he put forth his hand, and take also of the tree of life, and eat, and live forever; Therefore the Lord God sent him forth from the garden of Eden, to till the ground from whence he was taken. So he drove out the man: and he placed at the east of the garden of Eden Cherubims, and a flaming sword which turned every way, to keep the way of the tree of life.[16]

But Israel's rejection of Pharaoh's golden *pharmakon* implied the equation of all sacramentalism, golden, animal or vegetal, with Pharaonic idolatry, an historical, or is it hysterical, myopia that Orthodox Christianity would find quite useful in its own inquisitorialism.

Israel's rejection of Pharaoh's golden pharmakon implied the equation of all sacramentalism, golden, animal or vegetal, with Pharaonic idolatry, an historical, or is it hysterical, myopia that Orthodox Christianity would find quite useful in its own inquisitorialism.

The earliest writings of the New Testament are Paul's letters, 50-60 C.E. The Gospels, more prominent in the canon, were written between 70-110 C.E., in the context of the Church, outside Israel, that Paul was largely responsible for creating. Although the four Greek Gospels bear the names of the Apostles, obviously none were written by them. All the original Hebrew and Aramaic writings of the real Israelite Apostles, the Nazarenes, were destroyed as heretical by the Roman Church in the Second and Third Century.

Paul claimed to be one of Israel's legendary "Separate Ones," the Pharisees, who were famous throughout the Roman and Parthian world as courageous and just sages. The claim increased his authority among his correspondents, the Greek-speakers of the greater Empire. It was a transparent lie; he never was a Pharisee, apparently didn't even have fluent Hebrew. Never once, in 160 quotations, did he quote the Hebrew Bible, always the Greek *Septuagint*. Command of the Bible, in its original Hebrew, was the basis for all further Pharisaic studies.

No Pharisee rabbi, that is, master of learning (literally "my great one"), would ever quote the Greek over the canonical, and often different, Hebrew. Paul's famous quote[17] from Hosea, "O death, where is thy victory? O death where is thy sting?"[18] is from the Greek Septuagint; the Hebrew reads: "Oh for your plagues, O death! Oh for your sting, O grave!"[19]

Paul left not one word in Hebrew, but all in fluent *koiné* Greek, his native tongue, and the *lingua franca* of the Empire. Most modern experts (Maccoby, Graves, Schonfield, Vermes, etc.) agree with Kaufmann Kohler, the great Talmudic scholar and editor of the *Jewish Encyclopaedia*, who wrote in 1902 that "nothing in Paul's writings showed that he had any acquaintance with rabbinical learning."[20]

shamanism now long past, wasn't the focus of Judaism for most of the Pharisee sages. They were concerned with the practical creation of a just society on earth, a "kingdom of heaven" based on compassion and conscious wisdom. Thus the synagogue of the local congregation actually had more practical importance than the pomp and circumstance of the Jerusalem Temple. The synagogues were concerned with education and logical moral analysis far more than with unconscious ecstasy. It is in the synagogue that the roots of Christian congregationalism can be traced, as well as the roots of the Orthodox Christian prejudice against pharmaco-shamanism.

The charismatic Hasidim, "the devout," were concerned with Holy Spirit far more than with social structure, whereas the mainstream Pharisees were as political as they were religious, concerned with building an effective national structure with which to confront Israel's enemies and build community. It is from the Pharisees that Israel's greatest Senators sitting in the Sanhedrin were chosen. Great charismatics make bad politicians, so naturally there was the usual disagreement over values between Pharisees, Hasids, Essenes,

---

The synagogues were concerned with education and logical moral analysis far more than with unconscious ecstasy. It is in the synagogue that the roots of Christian congregationalism can be traced, as well as the roots of the Orthodox Christian prejudice against pharmaco-shamanism.

The Pharisees, the "Separate Ones," were leaders for no other reason than their learning. They were able to prove their fluent command not only of the Hebrew Bible, but of the vast body of homiletic, legal, historical and scientific literature accumulated in their academies. It was traditional that these lay teachers not take money for communicating wisdom, therefore most worked a regular job, say, as a carpenter, although that word was also used as a synonym for "word-smith," and "wise-man."

The rather unconscious stress on the ceremonial animal and vegetable gift-sacrifices of the Temple, emotionally recalling a participatory tribal

Melchizedekians and what have you. These categories were almost meaningless, however, since Judaism itself teaches iconoclasm, "image-breaking," originality.

Free speech, dissent, logical moral analysis and creative thought are organic elements of Hebrew tradition. The 613 positive and negative strictures in *Genesis*, *Exodus*, *Leviticus*, *Numbers*, *Deuteronomy* and the *Torah*, left much to further interpretation. They say nothing about the specifics of Sabbath celebration or marriage ceremonies, and so many strictures are vague or uselessly primitive that a contemporary interpretation, an

Oral Law, was required. The living law thus produced a literature, the *Mishnah* and the *Talmud*, which records disagreements on every possible aspect of life.

The *Mishnah*, "What is Repeated," is the codification of the memorized oral tradition finally put in writing in about 200 C.E. by Rabbi Judah the Prince. Its 63 tractates organize the scattered references in the *Torah* by category and adds the evolved wisdom on Agriculture, Appointed Times, Women, Damages, Holy Things and Purities.

"Law" has relatively little to do with *The Mishnah*, since specific punishments for spiritual infractions are rarely, or only metaphorically,

analysis and a way of life. It is this "Buddhist" attitude of Judaism ("If you meet the Buddha on the road, kill him"), that every Jew grows up with, that Jesus inherited and so obviously practiced.

In Genesis, Abraham challenges God himself to justify the destruction of Sodom and Gomorrah: "Shall not the judge of all the earth act with justice?"[22] Intellect and soul don't separate in Hebrew tradition. There never has been a dogmatic concept of heresy in Hebrew culture, and intellectual effort or moral analysis, even analysis of the moral responsibilities of God, has always been regarded as a form of spiritual ecstasy, hence the disrespect for Dogma.

In Genesis, Abraham challenges God himself to justify the destruction of Sodom and Gomorrah: "Shall not the judge of all the earth act with justice?"

mentioned. *The Mishnah* is concerned with clean and unclean, with the difference between the pure and impure approaches to the events of ordinary life. It is the rabbis' idea of spiritual yoga, and the stress is on the achievement of a spiritual community of ordinary people, not on punishment.

The Jerusalem Talmud, put together in about 400 C.E., is a collection of rabbinical commentaries on *The Mishnah*, as is the much larger and more basic *Babylonian Talmud*, put together a century later.

Leviticus, for instance, says, "You shall, therefore, keep My statutes and My ordinances, which if a man do he shall live by them." *The Babylonian Talmud* interprets this to mean "'You shall live by them' and not die by them." Thus, when life was at stake, it became mandatory to break the Sabbath in order to save life.[21]

Of course, that was an easy judgment call; many ritual and social obligations—rules dealing with marriage and divorce, for instance—were subject to much greater debate. The rabbis struggled, then, with what the Greeks called *themis*, custom, and *epikeia*, appropriate behavior, to come up with *dikai*, statements or judgments. Friendly intellectual argument was and is a method of logical

"A scholar takes precedence over a king of Israel, for if a scholar dies no one can replace him, while if a king dies, all Israel is eligible for kingship."[23] When Jacob finally pins the angel of God with which he wrestles in his nightmare, the angel rewards him with the name *Yisra'el*, and the descendants of his 12 sons are B'nai Yisra'el, the children of he who wrestles with God. Like Odysseus wrestling with the shape-changing prophetic sea-lion, Jacob offered neither submission nor faith, but active *participation mystique*.

It took little for the Pauline redactors to insert an element of hostility into Jesus' learned wrestling with his fellow sages where none would naturally have existed. Debate and dissent (*aggadah*—"telling") were enjoyed in the culture, but in matters of law (*halakhah*—"going") the majority ruled. The majority decisions in the assemblies of the sages were rarely invested with divine authority, hence to disagree with a decision of the sages would rarely bring a charge of heresy, as it would in Rome. Scriptural infallibility was a form of stultifying conceit these subtle and flexible professors never sanctioned.

Preoccupation with "heresy," a Graeco-Roman word that quislings would have used when

The Dead Sea Scrolls include extensive references to overt, sacramental pharmaco-shamanism. All the Gospels agree that the Hebrew Nazarenes gathered around Jesus were practicing shamans, *Assaya* in Aramaic, "healers," Essenes — that is, Gnostics who believed in sacramentalism, just as the earliest Christian Gnostic tradition insisted.

addressing their masters, *haeresis*, "wrong choice," is a projection laid on the Israelis in the New Testament by Graeco-Roman anti-Semites who knew next to nothing about the culture. Wildly eccentric theological views about an earthly or heavenly messiah are recorded in the near-contemporary Hebrew literature, all without any hint of persecution because of their nonconformity. In fact, it is the freewheeling and utterly "uncanonical" mystical speculations of the rabbis that gave birth, as much as Graeco-Egyptian mysticism, to Gnosticism, the mother of Christianity.

The earliest assertion of the Eucharist, that is, of Jesus as sacrament, *pharmakon*, is in Paul's *Corinthians*:

> For I have received of the Lord that which also I delivered unto you, That the Lord Jesus the same night in which he was betrayed took bread: And when he had given thanks, he brake it, and said, Take, eat: This is my body, which is broken for you: This do in remembrance of me. After the same manner also he took the cup, when he had supped, saying, This cup is the new testament in my blood: This do ye, as oft as ye drink it, in remembrance of me. For as often as ye eat this bread, and drink this cup, ye do show the Lord's death till he come.[24]

This is the Greek *dais omophagos*, the divided feast of the sacrificial bull of the new year, in whose resurrection we share through ingestion of the sacramental flesh and blood. At Greek rites, round cakes were actually shared after the sacrifice. Mark (c. 70 C.E.), Matthew (c. 80 C.E.), and Luke (c. 85 C.E.) then quote Paul's dream of Jesus' words, dutifully placing them where Paul said they belonged, at the Last Supper.

John (c. 100 C.E.), however, the latest of the Gospels, places these words in the Capernaum synagogue, not at the Last Supper. John is emphatically Hellenic in his emphasis:

> The Jews therefore strove among themselves, saying, How can this man give us his flesh to eat? Then Jesus said unto them, Verily, verily, I say unto you, Except ye eat the flesh of the Son of man, and drink his blood, ye have no life in you. Whoso eateth my flesh, and drinketh my blood, hath eternal life; and I will raise him up at the last day. For my flesh is meat indeed, and my blood is drink indeed. He that eateth my flesh and drinketh my blood, dwelleth in me, and I in him.[25]

As John indicates, the sacramentalism being espoused was clearly contrary to Orthodox Hebrew tradition since even animal blood was forbidden at a Jewish meal, let alone the symbolic blood of a *pharmakos*. John asserts that it is precisely over this issue that "many of his disciples went back, and walked no more with him."[26]

Israel, of course, since its conquest by Alexander in 332 B.C., was ruled by Greeks and had lived in a Hellenistic world. Hellenic and "Canaanite" Israel, the Israel of the Essenes, would have understood perfectly well the pharmaco-shamanism Jesus was talking about, if not as idolatrously as Paul.

The Dead Sea Scrolls are the writings of the Essene community that John the Baptist and Jesus were almost certainly associated with. Unlike even the oldest Christian documents, Greek and Latin mistranslations of the intentionally destroyed original Hebrew, the Dead Sea Scrolls, all older than the oldest Christian documents, are provable originals.

The Dead Sea Scrolls include extensive references to overt, sacramental pharmaco-shamanism. All the Gospels agree that the Hebrew Nazarenes gathered around Jesus were practicing shamans, *Assaya* in Aramaic, "healers," Essenes—that is,

Gnostics who believed in sacramentalism, just as the earliest Christian Gnostic tradition insisted. It is precisely this Hellenism that made possible the conquest of the Graeco-Roman Empire by a form of Judaism.

Gnosticism dates to the century before Christ, as do the Essenes. Christianity didn't invent Gnosticism, Gnosticism invented Christianity. Alexandrian Gnosticism was heavily influenced by Alexandria's enormous and powerful Greek-speaking Jewish community, the authors of Paul's Greek Bible, *The Septuagint*, legendarily written by the "70" representatives of Israel's 12 Tribes.

Paul's writings are full of Alexandrian Gnostic terminology, and the most influential of Paul's early constituents were the Greek-speaking Jews of the greater Empire, among which Judeo-Hellenic Gnosticism was very popular. The whole issue, as Jesus said, hinges on sacramentalism, actual or symbolic entheogenic ingestion. As we shall see, many Gnostics practiced actual entheogenic ingestion, and came to identify the entheogen with *Iasius*, "the Healer," Jesus. *Jesus* is Roman for the Greek *Iasius*. The canonical fascists, bent on political conquest of the Empire, insisted on symbolic entheogenic ingestion, that is, Imperial idolatry, and murdered both the original Nazarenes and their early Gnostic followers, along with burning their writings.

The Essenes, whose Dead Sea Scrolls we have, were Gnostic theological dissenters who celebrated Sunday as the Sabbath, and were quite "Pythagorean" in their soul-body dualism. Nonetheless, their surviving writings show that, aside from creating their own original literature, they immersed themselves in traditional Hebrew

nationalists. They were never murdered by their own; it took Romans, or their reservation police, to do that.

Aside from his sacramentalism, all four Gospels show Jesus teaching, like his fellow Essenes, traditional, established Pharisee wisdom in the same language as recorded in surviving contemporary and near-contemporary Hebrew sources. Hillel (b. 75 B.C.) was concerned with the "kingdom of heaven" on earth, that is, with *tikkun olam*, "perfecting the world." His philosophy was anti-legalistic and pragmatic, with compassion, justice and spiritual peace as the practical goals.

Hillel was a grandfather figure to Jesus, the recognized sage who taught the rabbis who taught Jesus. Hillel's proverbs are found in the *Pirkei Avot*, the Sayings of the Fathers, the most famous book of *The Mishnah*, "What Is Repeated," the Oral Law finally set down in writing some two hundred years after Hillel.

Many of Hillel's sayings, and those of the other sages recorded in *The Mishnah*, are similar, of course, to Jesus' sayings. That is, virtually everything Jesus says in the Graeco-Roman Gospels, aside from his sacramentalism and some gratuitous anti-Semitism, is traditional contemporary Pharisaic teaching enunciated by him in the contemporary Pharisaic phraseology, as recorded in contemporary or near-contemporary Pharisaic sources.

Hillel, when asked for a capsule definition of Judaism, replied, "What is hateful to you, don't do to your neighbor. The rest is commentary—now go and study."[28] Jesus: "So whatever you wish that men would do to you, do so to them; for this is the law and the prophets."[29]

Before its discovery at Qumran, all we knew of the apocryphal *Book of Enoch* were scattered Greek quotes from the early Church fathers. The far more ancient Aramaic original found at Qumran has the Messiah as a white bull with huge horns.

---

scripture and the writings of the Pharisee sages.[27] They were regarded as sincere Jews, and their communities and prophets were accorded profound respect, especially since they were fierce

Tanhuma: "When thou hast mercy on thy fellow, thou hast One to have mercy on thee; but if thou hast not mercy on thy fellow, thou hast none to have mercy on thee." Jesus: "But if you do not forgive men their trespasses, neither will your Father forgive your trespasses."[30] Nearly all the parables Jesus uses in the Gospels are contemporary Pharisee teaching devices, as are his pithy phrases such as "a camel going through the eye of a needle" or "take the beam out of your own eye."[31] Jesus' parable of the Prodigal Son,[32] in which he says, "I say unto you, that likewise joy shall be in heaven over one sinner that repenteth, more than over 90 and nine just persons, which need no repentance," is a paraphrase of the Talmudic saying: "Where the repentant sinners stand in the World to Come the perfectly righteous are not permitted to stand."[33]

would divide the temporal and spiritual powers between them, as was traditional in Israel.[34]

Before its discovery at Qumran, all we knew of the apocryphal *Book of Enoch* were scattered Greek quotes from the early Church fathers. The far more ancient Aramaic original found at Qumran has the Messiah as a white bull with huge horns.

The Qumran *Manual of Discipline*, c. 100 B.C., says that the Messiah "will renew for Him the Covenant of the Community to establish the kingdom of His people forever... May the Lord lift thee up to an everlasting height like a fortified tower on a high wall, that thou mightest smite the peoples with the might of thy mouth, with thy scepter

We have only a miniscule fraction of the Essene writings, almost all predating Jesus, preserved by an archaeological miracle.

The Essene Qumran community, in which John may have been raised, gave us the Dead Sea Scrolls, the greatest manuscript find of the Twentieth Century. They comprise fragments of almost 1,000 compositions, written in Hebrew, Aramaic and Greek, dating from about 250 B.C. to 68 C.E. Much of the Hebrew is an extinct form of paleo-Hebrew that evolved into both modern Hebrew and Samaritan script. Part of the reason for their survival is that the scrolls were penned on sheep or calf skins, rather than the usual papyrus linen. This indicates their canonical character, as does the superb penmanship of these accomplished scribes.

"The Sect" also called itself the "New Testament" or the "New Covenant," claiming themselves to be the true Sons of Zadok, the genuine Keepers of the Covenant. The Essenes, like the canonical John, reserved their bitterest apocalyptic denunciations for the politicized Sadducee collaborators: "Cities and families will perish through their counsel, nobles and rulers will fall because of what they say." They looked forward to when "the Messiah of Righteousness comes, the Branch of David." He was associated with the resurrected founder of the Sect. Whether he was to be identified with the Priest-Messiah, the King-Messiah or the Prophet-Messiah is not clear; the Messiahs

devastate the land, and with the breath of thy lips kill the wicked... And righteousness shall be the girdle of thy loins, and faith the belt of thy reins. And may He make thy horns of iron and thy hooves of brass to gore like a young bull... and tread down the peoples like the mire in the streets. For God has established thee as a scepter over rulers."[35]

It is this Bull of Righteousness that was the Essene *pharmakos*. As with the sacred Bull of El, *Moshe*, the *Moshiy'a* here is a war shaman, a bull "with horns of iron and hooves of brass," no lamb. Jesus also "kills the wicked with the breath of his lips."[36]

The Essenes, says *The Manual*, were "those who choose the Way." Says Paul, "according to the Way, which they call a sect, I worship the god of our fathers..."[37] The "New Covenant" and the "New Testament" are oft-repeated Essene phrases lifted by Paul, obviously, as he says, from the Nazarenes.[38] John's First Epistle refers constantly to Light and Darkness, Truth and Error, all standard Essene phrases, as is Peter's "cornerstone, elect and precious."

We have only a miniscule fraction of the Essene writings, almost all predating Jesus, preserved by an archaeological miracle. But even the small sample we have gives us dozens of direct quotes lifted from their writings to the canonical Greek "New

The dispute, it should be remembered, was sacramental: Cain brought a vegetable offering for the Lord whereas Abel brought "the firstlings of his flock," whereupon Cain topped Abel by offering *him*. Cain, despite the murder, then went on, with God's protection, to found civilization, which, of course, makes Abel a Passover lamb, only apparently a human sacrifice.

Testament," obviously by way of the Hebrew and Aramaic speaking Nazarenes. The early Church's baptism, communal meals, communal property and organizational structure, with the 12 Apostles leading the 12 Tribes, were almost identical to Essene ritual and structure.

"I prayed for him... and I laid my hands on his head, and the affliction left him and the evil spirit was driven out," says Abraham in the Essene *Genesis Apocryphon* found at Qumran. The Essenes sought "healing and abundant peace, length of life and fruitful seed with everlasting blessings, and eternal joy in immortality, a crown of glory and a robe of majesty in eternal light."[39] (*Manual of Discipline*)

The angels, says the original Hebrew *Book of Jubilees* found at Qumran, were instructed by the Lord "that we should teach Noah all the medicines... We explained to Noah all the medicines of their diseases, together with their seductions, how he might heal them with herbs of the earth. And Noah wrote down all things in a book as we instructed him concerning every kind of medicine... And he gave all that he had written to Shem, his eldest son."[40]

One of the Qumran *Thanksgiving Hymns*, c. 50 B.C., is overtly pharmaco-shamanic:

> For Thou didst set a plantation of cypress, pine and cedar for Thy glory, trees of life beside a mysterious fountain hidden among the trees by the water, and they put out a shoot of the everlasting Plant. But before they did so, they took root and sent out their shoots to the watercourse that its stem might be open to the living waters and be one with the everlasting spring... And the bud of the shoot of holiness for the Plant of Truth was hidden and was not esteemed; and being unperceived, its mystery was sealed. Thou didst hedge its fruit, O God, with the mystery of mighty Heroes and of spirits and holiness and of the whirling flame of fire. No man shall approach the well-spring of life or drink the waters of holiness with the everlasting trees, or bear fruit with the Plant of heaven, who seeing has not discerned, and considering has not believed in the fountain of life, who has turned his hand against the everlasting bud.[41]

As the *pharmakos* himself said, he was the *pharmakon*: "I am the vine, ye are the branches: He that abideth in me, and I in him, the same bringeth forth much fruit..." The "Plants of Truth" became a Christian Gnostic expression, repeatedly used in the Nag Hammadi manuscripts and the early heresiologists.

Iasius, Jesus, has the same Sumerian etymology as *Yehoshua*, Joshua. "Healer" in Greek is *iatros*, "drugger." Epiphanius, bishop of Salamis in Cyprus, c. 375 C.E., says that Christians were first called *Iassai*, "healers," "Essenes," "Jesuses."[42] *Iasius*, "Shaman-Healer," literally means "man of the drug."

The blood of the original Passover lamb, spread on the lintels of Israelite houses as a sign to the Angel of Death, is an entheogenic memory of the ancient spring rite. *Pesach* means "to appease, quieten," and is a reference to the peace that comes after parturition, after the Goddess gives birth to the new year, the new *pharmakos*.[43]

Like Balder and Loki, Romulus and Remus, Jesus and Judas, Cain and Abel are King and Twin, *Pharmakon* and *Pharmakos*. Far from killing Cain for his sacrifice, God tells him almost exactly what he told Adam and Eve on their expulsion from Eden: "When thou tillest the ground, she shall not henceforth yield unto thee her strength."[44] Cain "dwelt in the land of Nod, on the east of Eden," which is precisely where the cherubim and the flaming sword "guard the way to the tree of life."

The dispute, it should be remembered, was sacramental: Cain brought a vegetable offering for the Lord whereas Abel brought "the firstlings of his flock," whereupon Cain topped Abel by offering *him*. Cain, despite the murder, then went on, with God's protection, to found civilization, which, of course, makes Abel a Passover lamb, only apparently a human sacrifice. Another lamb-eater, the Capitoline She-Wolf who suckled Romulus and Remus, is the canonical image of Roman civilization.

The post-exilic Pharisee redactors, anti-sacramental and anti-shamanic, carefully edited the ancient texts, but intentionally preserved much of the original Hebrew. The Greek *Septuagint*, however, personalized the already disguised pharmaco-shamanic language completely, thus cutting all connection to the ancient meaning.

The Greek *Septuagint* has "Cain," but the ancient original Hebrew has *Qayin*, which means "smith." He was the eponymous Kenite shaman, what the Greeks called a *Telchine*, a magical metal-smith who transformed matter. Qayin fathered "Jubal; he was the ancestor of those who played the harp and pipe. Zillah, the other wife, bore Tubal-cain, the master of all coppersmiths and blacksmiths..."[45] Tubal-qayin, the son of Zillah, is *Bar-Zillah* in Aramaic, the language of the Kenite

any Greek or Essene, as would the equation of the blood of Christ with the blood of the lamb: "A jar stood there full of sour wine; so they soaked a sponge with the wine, fixed it on hyssop, and held it up to his lips. Having received the wine, he said, 'It is accomplished!' Then he bowed his head and gave up his spirit." "Christ our Passover lamb has been sacrificed."[47]

"Any animal in close relation to man, whether as food or foe, may rise to be a god, but he must first become sacred, sanctified, must first be sacrificed... the dedication (*anadeixis*) of the bull takes place at the beginning of the agricultural year; the bull's sanctified, though not his actual, life and that of the new year begin together."[48] As the *pharmakos* himself said, he was the *pharmakon*.

Gnosticism, the Mother of Sacramental Christianity, is a very broad category of Judeo-Hellenic-Egyptian mysticism.[49] Many Gnostics used the Hebrew canon as a starting point in their cosmology, but insisted that the Hebrew God, the Demiurge, the "Workman," the "Creator," was a material illusion, behind which the originary Platonic archetypes, the *Pleroma*, the "fulfillment," could be experienced directly. This *gnosis*, this "acquaintance" with the spirit, was often achieved through a sacramentalism that was nothing short of Paleolithic.

The early Church was driven crazy by ecstatic, iconoclastic Gnostics who felt free to pick and chose from the canon like hungry tokers from a Chinese menu. Jesus, they said, only seemed (*dokeo*) to suffer, so as to demonstrate the sacramental mystery, the Secret of Salvation. This, of course, meant that Judas was innocent and that Jesus pretended to die only to get everybody high and creative, not to atone by his agony for our Original Sin.

community. *Barzela* means "axe-head," a reference to the ubiquitous ancient symbol of the power of the Goddess.[46]

The *Septuagint* has "Abel," but the original Hebrew has *Hevel*, and this means, remarkably enough, "vapor," "smoke." The Telchine sacrificed smoke to join the Angel of Death for the Spring Resurrection. That would make perfect sense to

Since they were concerned far more with genuine entheogenic sacraments than with iconic substitutes, many Gnostics expressed a proprioceptive disdain for the Church's *eidololatreia*. The early Church was driven crazy by ecstatic, iconoclastic Gnostics who felt free to pick and chose from the canon like hungry tokers from a Chinese menu. Jesus, they said, only seemed (*dokeo*) to suffer, so as to demonstrate the sacramental mystery, the Secret of Salvation. This, of course, meant that Judas was innocent and that Jesus pretended to die only to get everybody high and creative, not to atone by his agony for our Original Sin. Original Sin was simply a trap of the Demiurge, who used threat, guilt and sex to bring us down to the material level.

Some Gnostics, notably the famous Alexandrian teacher Basilides (fl. 130), insisted that sex was to be enjoyed without any sense of guilt, as a sort of baptism in the material world which prepared one for the next level. Basilides was a teacher of Valentinus, the most popular and influential Christian Gnostic. Among the Valentinians women were completely equal, prophesying, healing and officiating right alongside the men. "Some said, 'Mary conceived by the holy spirit.' They are in error. They do not know what they are saying. When did a woman ever conceive by a woman?"[50]

Bishop Irenaeus of Lyon (130-200) was infuriated by the Valentinians among his congregation who enjoyed the fleshly delights of life, and who insisted that they were, like Paul, above the law—the law of the "true Israel" as well as that of the "old Israel": "Where there is no law, there is no transgression."[51]

"The Gospel of Truth is Joy," wrote Valentinus (c. 140 C.E.), "for those whom the Father has given the Word from the pleroma, providing the grace and the power of the Father of Truth, the Savior who dwells in the mind of the Father. When he was nailed to the Tree of Life he became a fruit of the *gnosis* of the Father. When that fruit was eaten, those who consumed it became ecstatic, having discovered the Savior in themselves and themselves in the Savior. But first they passed through the terrifying empty space, stripped naked to the soul, contacting their pure emotions. This is the wisdom of the living book of the ages, composed of letters each of which expresses a whole thought, a complete book, known only to the speaker. Each letter expresses the Unity of the Logos of the Father, the fruit of His heart of His will. Each automatic thought purifying the soul, bringing it back into the Father, into the Mother, Jesus of the infinite sweetness."[52]

Here we have a shaman's sacramental letters, not *pistis*, "faith," but a very active *participation mystique*, a "psychedelic experience," and the consequent originality and matristic ideology that was anathema to the Bishops of Lyon and Rome.

Jason's *apolytrosis*, from a Fifth Century B.C. ceremonial vase.

Valentinus understood Iasius, as he called him, as the "fruit of the knowledge of the father"—an hermaphroditic combination of Adam, Eve, the serpent and the fruit—offering not an original sin, but an original gift.

The fruit, the sacrament, the *pharmakon*, was the major point of Gnostic disagreement with the Orthodox church, since the Gnostic *apotheosis* consisted not of the ordinary symbolic communion, but of a second pharmacological sacrament of *apolytrosis* (deliverance, liberation, redemption). That is, the Gnostic Iasius or Iason was the Greek hero, who the Romans called Jason.

Jason's *apolytrosis*, after an apparently exhausting trip, is pictured above on a Fifth Century B.C. ceremonial vase. The pharmacological serpent, with vine and golden fleece, ushers Iaion (a Greek pun meaning "purple drug") into the presence of "the Mother." Athena holds the prophetic owl she inherited from Lilith the Transformer. She also wears the Gorgoneion, symbol of the terrifying mysteries through which the naked soul must pass before it is admitted "into the Father, into the Mother, Jesus of the infinite sweetness."

Aldous Huxley used the ancient Sanskrit equivalent of *apolytrosis*, *moksha*, to describe the central sacrament—entheogenic mushroom juice—of his utopian *Island*. That, of course, is an historically accurate reference to the *Rigveda*. Bishop Irenaeus, in a fit of empiricism, seems to have helped Huxley write his novel. He described the Gnostic rites fairly accurately: "And he [Valentinus] says that the Holy Spirit was produced by the Truth to inspect and fructify the Aeons, entering them invisibly, through whom the Aeons produced the plants of truth... For some of them prepare a nuptial couch and perform a sacred rite for those who are 'perfected'... 'O Savior of Truth.' This is what those who initiate invoke, while he who is initiated replies, 'I am strengthened and redeemed, and I redeem my soul from this age, and from all things connected with it in the name of IAO who redeemed his soul to full redemption in the living Christ.'"

"Then they anoint the initiate with balsam, for they say that this ointment is a type of the sweet fragrance which is above all things... There are others who keep on 'redeeming' the dying up to the moment of death, pouring oil and water on their heads, or the ointment mentioned above mixed with water, and with the invocations mentioned above, that they may not be grasped or seen by the principalities and powers, and that their inner man

and sacramental. The Gnostic Sethians denied bodily Resurrection as an idolatrous delusion foisted on fools by materialist politicians anxious to co-opt the tradition by claiming descent from one particular physical body. Christ was really a "guide" to "lead the soul which is invisibly being saved" into the Pleroma, from whence it came, therefore to argue that physical death "would have overcome the savior himself...is absurd."[54] (Theodotus)

Gnostic texts like the *Pistis Sophia* constantly talk of Christ revealing the mysteries to "the 12." "In the place where I shall be, there also will be my 12 ministers, but Mary Magdalene and John the virgin shall be higher than all the disciples."[55] There is no Eleven, no Judas, no betrayal, no fascist scapegoat, no evil pharmacological serpent, only *gnosis*, with an accent on the feminine, on the Holy Spirit as feminine. That is, with an accent on that which gives birth and rebirth: "I will tell you all mysteries from the exterior of the exteriors, to the interior of the interiors. Hearken, I will tell you all things which have befallen Me... The Mystery

---

Resurrection, insisted the Gnostics, was spiritual and sacramental. The Gnostic Sethians denied bodily Resurrection as an idolatrous delusion foisted on fools by materialist politicians anxious to co-opt the tradition by claiming descent from one particular physical body.

---

may ascend even above the invisible things... And they claim that he who says this will avoid and escape the powers... 'I am a precious vessel, more than the female being who made you. Though your mother does not know her origin, I know myself, and I know whence I am, and I call on the incorrupt Wisdom, who is in the Father, who is the Mother of your mother, and has no Father nor any male consort; for a female, made of a female, made you, not knowing her own Mother, and thinking that she was alone; but I call upon her Mother.'"[53]

The sacred rite with the plants of truth on the nuptial couch is a reference to the sacred marriage of the mystery religions, the *hieros gamos*, as mentioned in the Essene *Thanksgiving Hymn*. Resurrection, insisted the Gnostics, was spiritual

which is beyond the world, that whereby all things exist: It is all evolution and all involution..."[56]

Gnosis, experience, was everything; external imagery, canon, meant nothing. All that mattered was the digestion of the fruit, the balsam, the creative voice of the inner being: "If you bring forth what is within you, what you bring forth will save you. If you do not bring forth what is within you, what you do not bring forth will destroy you."[57]

There is no Eleven, no Judas, no betrayal, no fascist scapegoat, no evil pharmacological serpent, only *gnosis*, with an accent on the feminine, on the Holy Spirit as feminine.

This docetism (from *dokeo*, "to seem, appear," a reference to the delusion of *eidololatreia*) eventually provoked the Church to inquisitorial savagery, hence the burial of the Nag Hammadi manuscripts, numbering among them *The Gospel of Truth* and *The Gospel of Thomas*.

In 1945, some 1,600 years after their burial in central Egypt, the Nag Hammadi manuscripts were rediscovered. Were it not for that archaeological miracle, none of Valentinus' writings would survive, despite the fact that between 136 and 165 he was one of the most popular teachers in Rome. Like the original writings of the Essenes and the Nazarenes, all Valentinus' works were systematically sought out and burned by the Church, as were those of Basilides, Cerinthus, Heracleon, Ptolemy, Theodotus and the rest.

Gnostic ideas pervaded the Graeco-Roman world, and what little of their literature survives is easily the best and most original of the era, proving that many were uninhibited geniuses. The legendary Basilides' 24 books of *Exegetica* were no doubt extraordinary; we'll never know. Nor will we know how many Gnostic women set down their thoughts, since they were a special target of the inquisitors because of their Original Sin, that is, because Demeter, Persephone, Asherah and Miriam were women.

Eusebius, Constantine's court theologian, explained Gnosticism this way: "These claimed to transmit Simon's magic arts, not secretly like Basilides but quite openly, as if this was something marvelous, preening themselves as it were on the spells which they cast by sorcery, on dream-bringing familiar spirits, and on other goings-on of the same sort. In keeping with this they teach that all the vilest things must be done by those who intend to go through with their initiation into the 'mysteries' or rather abominations, for in no other way can they escape the 'cosmic rulers' than by rendering to them all the due performance of unspeakable rites."[58]

The virtually canonical Bishop Irenaeus, writing in Lyon c. 180, complained that they "put forth their own compositions... They really have no gospel that is not full of blasphemy. For what they have published... is totally unlike what has been handed down to us from the apostles... Let those persons who blaspheme the Creator...as [do] the Valentinians and the falsely so-called 'Gnostics,' be recognized as agents of Satan by all who worship God. Through their agency Satan even now... has been seen to speak against God, that God who has prepared eternal fire for every kind of apostasy."[59]

Clement, third Bishop of Rome, put it succinctly in the oldest Orthodox Christian document outside the canon, *Clement's First Letter*, c. 96 C.E.: "Those, therefore, who act in any way at variance with His will, suffer the penalty of death. You see, brothers, the more knowledge we are given, the greater risks we run."[60]

The Church organized the Imperial murder of many leading Gnostics and the systematic destruction of nearly all their writings. The lost Gnostic writings were known only by their titles and distorted legend for the better part of two millennia, but by a spectacular archaeological miracle 52 Gnostic texts, 30 of them complete and unknown except by legend, were rediscovered on leather-bound papyrus scrolls in 1945 at Nag Hammadi in central Egypt. They were written in Coptic, phonetic Egyptian and Greek transliterations of the original Greek.

The scrolls had been buried in jars in about 370 C.E., in meditation caves, obviously in fear of their discovery. Since there was no war going on at the time, it is assumed that the regular authorities were involved. In his Easter letter of 367, the supreme regular authority, Archbishop Athanasius of Alexandria, condemned heretics and their "apocryphal books to which they attribute antiquity and give the name of saints."[61] That, of course, is a perfect description of the Nag Hammadi texts, many of which are copies of works hundreds of years older.

The care with which the Nag Hammadi texts were copied and bound indicates that they were canonical to the copyists. As Abbot Shenoute of Panopolis near Nag Hammadi put it about 40 years later, to a group of "kingless" Gnostics who worshipped the "demiurge" at the nearby Temple of Nuit using "books full of abomination" and "every kind of magic," refusing to acknowledge Archbishop Cyril, Patriarch of Alexandria, as their "illuminator": "I shall make you acknowledge ... the Archbishop Cyril, or else the sword will wipe out most of you, and moreover those of you who are spared will go into exile."[62]

In 250, the Christian scholar Origen pointed out that the eclipse in *Matthew* at the time of the

She was as widely read as Plato, but, since a genuine Maenad, far less friendly to Orthodox mind games than the Athenian word-meister. Thanks to Archbishop Gregory, only four or five of her 500 poems survive to bear witness to Sappho's sacraments.

Crucifixion, the day before a full moon, couldn't have happened; in 400 Augustine replied that the very impossibility was proof of a miracle. The relics of martyrs were held to replace herbs in medicine as Constantine's mother Helena discovered "the true cross" on her visit to Jerusalem, near the defunct Temple of Aphrodite.

For Sappho, of course, the most famous poet of the Ionian renaissance, Aphrodite was far from defunct:

Leave Crete and come to this holy temple/where the pleasant grove of apple trees/circles an altar smoking with frankincense/Here roses leave shadow on the ground/and cold springs babble through apple branches/where shuddering leaves pour down profound sleep/In our meadow where horses graze/and wild flowers of spring blossom/anise shoots fill the air with aroma/And here, Queen Aphrodite, pour/heavenly nectar into gold cups/and fill them gracefully with sudden joy.[63]

Sappho's overtly pharmaco-shamanic writings were ordered burned in 380 by Archbishop Gregory of Constantinople. The Joy of Aphrodite's Heavenly Nectar wasn't what Gregory was peddling, though I certainly would like a cup.

Sappho, of the Ionian island of Lesbos, was born about 612 B.C. She is mentioned with the utmost respect by Plato ("the beautiful Sappho"), Herodotus, Pausanias, Strabo ("a marvel"), Aristotle, Plutarch ("what charm the songs of Sappho have to hold the listeners spellbound"), Cicero, Lucian ("Sappho gave us refinement"), Philostratos and many others. Plutarch: "And Sappho's words are truly mixed with fire, and through her songs she brings out her heart's warmth, and according to Philoxenos heals the pain of love with the sweet-voiced Muse." Plato called her "the Tenth Muse." She was as widely read as Plato, but, since a genuine Maenad, far

less friendly to Orthodox mind games than the Athenian word-meister. Thanks to Archbishop Gregory, only four or five of her 500 poems survive to bear witness to Sappho's sacraments.

For many Gnostics, Jesus' blood was more like Aphrodite's Heavenly Nectar, conceived of the Spirit of God, which is, and always has been, female in Hebrew, as in Genesis: "And the Spirit of God moved upon the face of the waters." Yahweh is the Son of Iahu, the Exalted Dove, who is the daughter of Tiamat, the originary creative waters.[64] The Gnostic Sophia had a lot of Aphrodite, "risen from sea-foam," the fish, the unconscious, in her.

Despite the best efforts of the canonical fascists, an alternative discussion of "sober offerings" survived, by the grace of the miracle at Nag Hammadi, to let a genuine shaman have her or his say. Our copy of the astonishing *On the Origin of the World* dates to just before its burial at Nag Hammadi, although the original may be hundreds of years older:

The tree of *gnosis* has the strength of God. It glows like the moon, and its magical fruit is sweet, like dates. And this tree is to the north of Paradise, so that it might arouse the souls from the torpor of the demons, in order that they might approach the tree of life and eat of its fruit and so condemn the authorities and their angels.

A droplet of light fell from Sophia's hands onto the waters, immediately producing an androgynous human being. Sophia formed it first into a woman, but an androgynous woman, called Hermaphrodites by the Greeks. Her Mother is called Eve of Life by the Hebrews. She is the female instructor of life. Her progeny is the creature that is called lord. But the authorities called it "Beast," so as to tarnish its reputation among their modeled creatures. But "the beast" is really "the instructor," the wisest of all beings.

Sophia sent her daughter Life, called Eve, to teach Adam, who was soulless, how to become a container of light. Eve felt compassion for Adam, exhorting him to "Arise! Become a container of light upon the earth!" Her Word became reality, as Adam opened his eyes to the Light of Life. He looked upon Eve, telling her, "You shall be called 'Mother of the Living.' For it is you who have given me life."

The authorities resolved to rape this luminous woman so as to destroy her power. But Eve laughed. She became one with the tree of *gnosis*. They pursued her in vain, realizing her power had enabled her to become one with the tree. They panicked in their blindness and ran. Then the wisest creature of all, called Beast, came. Addressing the image of their mother Eve, he said to her, "What did God say to you? Was it 'do not eat from the tree of *gnosis*?'" She said, "He said 'Not only do not eat from it, but do not touch it, lest you die.'" The Beast then said, "Don't be afraid. You will not die, but come to life. When you eat from the Tree of Life, your intellect will become sober and you will become like gods, able to see the difference between evil people and good ones. Indeed, it was in jealousy of His power that he said this to you, so that you would be afraid to partake."[65]

The authorities surrounded the Tree of Life with fearsome Cherubim and flaming swords, so that all would be afraid to taste the fruit of *gnosis*, now subject to *prohibitio*, as so clearly explained by this brilliant shaman, floating, as they said, on "the cold, flowing waters of the Lake of *Mnemosyne*."

The snake-women often had an equal place as "instructor" among the Gnostics, who were very clear about the psycho-spiritual meaning of woman in the pantheon: "She is the Conceiver of all gods and all lords; she is the *gnosis* of all invisibles. Thy Image is the mother of all Uncontainables and the power of all Impassables... Praise to Thee, for ever and ever, O Thou Alone-begotten One. Amen."[66]

"And the arrogant ruler cursed the woman... And what she had made became a product in the matter, like an aborted fetus. And it assumed a plastic form molded out of shadow, and became an arrogant beast resembling a lion...' It is I who am God, and there is none other apart from me... If any other thing exists before me, let it become visible to me!' And immediately Sophia stretched forth her finger and introduced light into matter..."[67]

Sophia, of course, is Korykia, the Snake-Bird Goddess, originary ecstatic creativity, which so many Gnostic texts display. But, as they say, she is heretical to the arrogant ruler. Paul: "Their role is to learn, listening quietly and with due submission. I do not permit women to teach or dictate to the men; they should keep quiet. For Adam was created first, and Eve afterwards; moreover it was not Adam who was deceived; it was the woman who, yielding to deception, fell into sin."[68]

That is the aborted fetus talking, the plastic lion, doing what Romans did best, "dividing and conquering," fixating not on hermaphroditic *ekstasis* but on sexual domination, cursing the ingestion of the entheogenic fruit, cursing the sacred marriage which gives birth to *gnosis*:

"Her lover secretly fetched it for her. He pressed it to her mouth as if it were food, applying the word as medicine to her eyes so that she could see with her mind. She understood her roots and her ancestry. She cleaved to the tree of her origins, so that she might renounce the material world. She reclined on her marriage bed. She ate the ambrosia, the immortal food she hungered for. She found what she searched for. She found rest from her quest in the everlasting light. To the light belongs the power and the glory of revelation lasting for ever and ever. Amen."[69]

This, from Nag Hammadi, is a clear and literal description of the *hieros gamos*, the sacred marriage, the imbibing of the "immortal food" leading to the epiphany of Eleusis. Persephone's bridegroom is Aidoneus, Dionysos, Hermes Psychopompos, known as Hermes Trismegistos, Thrice-Great, in the Hellenistic world; he carried magical plants, or their symbol, the snake-staff, the *Kerykeion*. In the myth of Glaukos it is the female serpent that reveals the herb of resurrection, sacred to *Iasius*, the Healer.

---

1. Sir Arthur Evans, *The Palace of Minos at Knossos: 4 Volumes*. New York: Macmillan and Co., 1921. pp. 499, 605.

2. Marija Gimbutas, *The Civilization of the Goddess*. New York: HarperCollins, 1991. p. 222.

3. R. Gordon Wasson, *Soma: Divine Mushroom of Immortality*. New York: Harcourt Brace Jovanovich, 1968. p. 43.

4. Robert Graves, *The White Goddess*. New York: Vintage Books, 1959. p. 224.

5. Marija Gimbutas, *The Goddesses and Gods of Old Europe*. Berkeley: University of California Press, 1982. p. 101.

6. Ibid., p. 201.

7. Marija Gimbutas, *The Language of the Goddess*. New York: HarperCollins, 1989. p. 175.

8. Sir Arthur Evans, *The Palace of Minos at Knossos: 4 Volumes,* vol. 3. New York: Macmillan and Co., 1921. p. 68; Marija Gimbutas, *The Goddesses and Gods of Old Europe.* p. 185.

9. Sir Arthur Evans, *The Palace of Minos at Knossos: 4 Volumes,* vol. 4. New York: Macmillan and Co., 1921. p. 453; Marija Gimbutas, *The Goddesses and Gods of Old Europe.* p. 184.

10. Cyrus H. Gordon, *Ugarit and Minoan Crete.* New York: W. W. Norton, 1966. p. 23.

11. *Leviticus 10*

12. *Leviticus 2:13*

13. *Leviticus 44:15-25*

14. Raphael Patai, *The Hebrew Goddess.* New York: Ktav Publishing House, 1967; Cyrus H. Gordon, *The Common Background of Greek and Hebrew Civilization.* New York: W. W. Norton & Company, 1965. p. 31.

15. *Exodus 3:14-4:5*

16. *Genesis 2-3*

17. *1 Corinthians 15:55*

18. *Hosea 13:14*

19. Hyam Maccoby, *The Myth-Maker.* New York: HarperCollins, 1987. p. 71.

20. Ibid., p. 209.

21. *Babylonian Talmud: Yoma 85b*

22. *Genesis 18:25*

23. *Horayot 13a*; see also *Psalms 44:24, Habbakkuk 1:2, Job.*

24. *1 Corinthians 11:23-27*

25. *John 6:52-56*

26. *John 6:66*

27. John Allegro, *The Dead Sea Scrolls.* New York: Penguin Books, 1964. p. 74.

28. *Shabbat 31a; Telushkin 121*

29. *Matthew 7:12*

30. *Matthew 6:15*

31. *Talmud*

32. *Luke 15*

33. *Babylonian Talmud: B. Ber 34b*; Hyam Maccoby, *Revolution in Judaea.* London: Orbach and Chambers, 1973. p. 266.

34. Geza Vermes, *The Dead Sea Scrolls in English.* New York: Penguin Books, 1987. p. 54.

35. Allegro, p. 169; Geza Vermes, *Jesus the Jew.* Philadelphia: Fortress Press, 1981. pp. 95, 133.

36. *2 Thessalonians 2:8*

37. *Acts 24:14*

38. *Hebrews 8*

39. Allegro, p. 140.

40. Vermes, *Jesus the Jew.* p. 62.

41. Vermes, *The Dead Sea Scrolls in English.* p. 187.

42. G. R. S. Mead, *Fragments of a Faith Forgotten.* New York: University Books, 1960. p. 126.

43. John Allegro, *The Sacred Mushroom and the Cross.* London: Hodder and Stoughton, 1970. p. 170.

44. *Genesis 4:12*

45. *Genesis 4:22*

46. Allegro, *The Sacred Mushroom and the Cross.* p. 97.

47. *John 19:29; 1 Corinthians 5:7*

48. Jane Ellen Harrison, *Epilegomena to the Study of Greek Religion.* Cambridge: Cambridge University Press, 1921. p. 149.

49. C. G. Jung, *The Collected Works.* Princeton: Princeton University Press, 1956. p. 357.

50. *Gospel of Philip, Nag Hammadi Library:143*

51. Irenaeus, *Against Heresies* 1:6:1-4, in Cyril Richardson, trans., *Early Christian Fathers.* Philadelphia; Westminster Press, 1953; *Romans 4:15*

52. *NHL:41*

53. Irenaeus, 1:11-21; *1 Corinthians 1:30,* Elaine Pagels, *The Gnostic Paul.* Philadelphia: Fortress Press, 1975. p. 95.

54. Ibid., p. 144.

55. Mead, p. 484.

56. Mead, p. 462.

57. *Gospel of Thomas,* in Elaine Pagels, *The Gnostic Gospels.* New York: Vintage Books, 1989. p. 126.

58. Eusebius, *The History of the Church.* G. A. Williamson, trans. Shaftesbury: Dorset, 1965. 4:7.

59. Irenaeus, 3:11:9, 5:26:1.

60. *Clement's First Letter,* 41:3, in Richardson.

61. *NHL:19*

62. *NHL:20*

63. *NHL:29;161-186*

64. Samuel Noah Kramer, *Sumerian Mythology.* New York: Harper & Row, 1961. p. 70.

65. *NHL:179*

66. *Untitled Apocalypse,* in Mead. p. 555.

67. *The Hypostasis of the Archons,* NHL:164

68. *1 Timonty 2:11-14*

69. *Authoritative Teaching, NHL:305-310*

6

MODERN EXPLORATIONS, ANOMALIES AND COVER-UPS

Greg Deyermenjian at the Petroglyphs of Pusharo in Peru.

Group Pusharo. Left to right: Machiguenga "Alejandro," Paulino Mamani, Greg Deyermenjian, Machiguenga "Josefina," Machiguenga "Pancho" and Celso, at Petroglyphs of Pusharo, 1991.

Preston Peet

A CONVERSATION WITH GREG DEYERMENJIAN

LOST CITIES SOUGHT, LOST CITIES FOUND

PHOTOS BY GREG DEYERMENJIAN

Preston Peet: Good evening, Greg. I'm going to start off with some of the basics and work my way from there. How old are you?

GD: 55.

PP: Where are you from?

GD: Boston.

PP: Born and raised there?

GD: Yes.

PP: What gave you the exploring bug? What was it that initially inspired you to begin your expeditions and explorations?

He unfolded a map of South America for me one day, which seemed to be shimmering as he told me all these tales, about how it was the strangest continent ever, how the history of it is like the fiction of other places, so that got me hooked.

GD: From an early age, I reckoned that I wanted to be an astronaut, and from there I became interested in all things having to do with dinosaurs and cavemen

and ancient times, and from there became interested in far-away places. I read everything I could find about Tibet, Mongolia, Central Asia, and places like that. Then when I went to University to study to be an anthropology major, it just so happened that my roommate was a Latin American history major, so he unfolded a map of South America for me one day, which seemed to be shimmering as he told me all these tales, about how it was the strangest continent ever, how the history of it is like the fiction of other places, so that got me hooked. Then it was another process of going to South America, then Peru, each time getting further below the surface.

PP: Do you only focus on Peru, or do you explore other places, other continents as well?

GD: Well, although I'm the Chairman of the New England Chapter of the Explorers' Club, I'm not all that well traveled, in that all of my travels have been in Central and South America. My expeditions have been 95 percent in Peru, but also in Brazil and Ecuador.

PP: What exactly is the Asociacion Cultural Exploraciones Antisuyu (ACEA)?

GD: Well, the Incan Empire was divided into four quarters, with the center of it being in Cuzco, and the quarter made up of the eastern jungle, the wild quarter of the Empire, is the Antisuyu. The Asociacion Cultural Exploraciones Antisuyu is an organization that myself and my Peruvian partners founded to be inscribed officially there in Cuzco, Peru as a vehicle for more official standing in the country.

PP: That leads to another question, speaking of your wanting official standing in the country. Do you have problems getting permits and things when you want to go and explore, because I'm sure the Peruvian government is a little suspicious of foreigners raiding their cultural heritage.

GD: Well, it's funny, because Peru is very aware of and protective of its cultural heritage, but at the same time, it has experience, it expects that gringos are going to want to come there and explore, so it doesn't necessarily put up impediments, as opposed to a place like Brazil, which just wants everything kept as is, and no waves to be made, and where even exploration per se is illegal.

PP: Oh, really? I didn't know that. I have read marine archaeologist and explorer Robert Marx's accounts, though, of having problems in Brazil after finding Roman shipwrecks underwater in Brazil.

GD: Uh-huh. But in Peru, while they're protective of their cultural patrimony, they have a lot of experience with scientificos, scientists and explorers coming in and doing their things. A lot depends on the area, like if one is doing explorations in an officially protected zone, in the National Park of Manu for instance. Then yeah, sure, one has to get a permit, which we got in 1991 to go to the Petroglyphs of Pusharo.

PP: By the way, did you yourself discover those petroglyphs, or had they already been discovered?

GD: They'd already been discovered, by an unnamed Peruvian rubber tapper on an Indian raid in 1909, and reached and documented in drawings by a Dominican friar, Vicente Cenitagoya, in 1921.

PP: Have they been deciphered yet?

GD: No, and they shall never be deciphered because it's impossible, unless someone finds and provides the resuscitated Amazonian Indian who made them, who could come and say, "Yeah, I made this one and here is what it means." It's all total speculation.

PP: Oh, right on, there's no key, no Rosetta Stone.

GD: Exactly. There's no Rosetta Stone for the petroglyphs.

PP: I see.

GD: There're different theories, and I put forth that which makes the most sense to me in an article I wrote for *Athena Review*, that rather than being a map of the land showing Paititi with an X, and rather than being a map of the heavens by which the Indians would have navigated the vast expanse of the jungle, I agree with them really representing visions, visions while seen under the effects of hallucinogenic plants, ayahuasca and brugmansia. But just to go back and finish up the permit question—there are areas which are absolutely wild, unexplored areas that aren't delineated on anyone's map as protected area, as a part of any biological preserve or anything, so technically you don't need a permit for any of those areas. So it all depends where. And, of course, wherever you go in those areas, you'll only make progress if you are respectful of the land and the local people.

PP: You lead expeditions. Do you have people contact you asking if you can guide an expedition down to South America for them?

GD: Usually no, in that most all the expeditions, well, all of them in Peru, are ongoing projects of determining, and answering the question of "Paititi," the concept of Paititi, the question of the existence, form and location of Paititi, of the furthest Incan reach into the jungles where they're not known to have settled.

PP: I just this minute found what I think is part two of an article you published, in the anthology *Adventures Unlimited*,[1] about the search for Paititi, where you mention that it might not be a lost city

> So we're determining what of ancient man lies in there, whether Paititi turns out to be the agglutinant effect of all of the widely dispersed ruins, some of which we've been finding in Mameria, in this area, that area, or whether it turns out to be an actual city, which is possible but not probable.

but rather a lost kingdom. That's very interesting. So it would still be an Incan kingdom?

GD: Well, even to refer to it specifically as "it" is getting more specific than one can in a sense. When people talk about Paititi, there's Paititi with a capital "P" and there's paititi with a small "p," which is one way of looking at it. Paititi with a capital "P," as in "El Paititi" or "The Paititi," would refer to the legends of it being an Incan site out there in the jungles, a specific city, an ultimate refuge, while paititi with a small "p" I see as representing the quest to find what's out there in the unexplored, jungle-covered hills which still exist there, it being one of the last places on earth that, because of its broken topography, as opposed to being just flat jungle, it's made up of jungle covered hills and ravines and gorges and un-navigable rivers, and will, I believe, always remain so. So we're determining what of Andean civilization lies there, to see whether Paititi turns out to be the agglutinative effect of all of the widely dispersed ruins, some of which we've been finding in Mameria, Callanga, in this area or that area, or whether it turns out to be an actual city, which is possible but not probable. The Andean earth goddess, "Pacha Mama," has draped everything under such a thick protective layer of vegetation and broken territory, that some things could remain hidden there forever. But whether Paititi turns out to be something else, even a legend that might have arisen among the jungle Indians when referring to the city of Cuzco for all we know—what to them would be the magical city of gold—or the garbled accounts given to the conquistadors, who took it to be a city in the jungle, all those things are possible and more. I think the Paititi with a capital "P" actually refers to the kingdom of the Musus, which was a contemporaneous kingdom, contemporaneous with the Incas, that was there in Northern Bolivia that the Incas had a lot of influence over. Even after the Incan Empire and Cuzco was taken over by the Spaniards, this particular Incan enclave, this Incan-influenced kingdom that was never conquered by the Incas but was heavily influenced by them, still existed up to the 1600s, and so from there could have come the actual Paititi with a capital "P." So what I refer to as Paititi is really our quest to find and document the furthest reach of the Incas into the jungle covered hills and mountains and highlands of the unexplored regions to the north-northeast of Cuzco.

> So what I refer to as Paititi is really our quest to find and document the furthest reach of the Incas into the jungle covered hills and mountains and highlands of the unexplored regions to the north-northeast of Cuzco.

PP: Do you support your expeditions with grants, tourism, both or neither? How do you support your expeditions?

GD: Quite the salient question. Throughout the 1980s, when I began them, being single and having a steady job, with a good amount of vacation time, doing it all on a shoestring, I'd pay for it all myself. That would set me back two or three thousand dollars.

PP: Kind of like taking a vacation then. A bit of a rough vacation, but a vacation nonetheless.

GD: Yes, and I was getting my vacation pay in advance. Then, what I started to do in the 1990s, which is good since I then had children, was I started to then, for each expedition, hit either the Shipton-Tillman Grant[2] that Gore-Tex has, or the Polartec Performance Challenge award, which Malden Mills in Massachusetts used to give out. I'd take one or the other of those, which provide three to five thousand dollars, to do it. Then in 1999, a German film maker, Heinz von Matthey, who I had met through Dr. Carlos Neuenschwander in Peru...

PP: He's a Peruvian archaeologist, right?

GD: Well, he died in September of 2003.

PP: I'm sorry to hear that.

GD: ...but he was a Peruvian physician and psychiatrist who yet, as he often times told me, whenever people stopped him in the streets it was never to ask him a medical question, it would always be to ask him a question about Paititi.

PP: (Laughing.) That's very interesting.

GD: So, this Heinz von Matthey provided the money in 1999 that allowed me to get us a helicopter, the helicopter being useful not for exploring by the air, because you don't see anything from the air.

PP: Because it's all overgrown, right?

GD: Exactly. All you see are undulating expanses of trees. But the distance is so vast, as we had seen year after year after year, expedition after expedition, as we'd been led further and further north, until in 1993, when we got to the plateau of Pantiacolla, by the time we got there, following the Incan road of stone, we realized that it's such a distance from Cuzco that by the time you get there you're just about out of time, resources, equipment and energy. So that's what a helicopter is useful for, to take you closer to the exploration zone so you can start doing what you need to do to with energy and time. That's what did it for us in 1999. Then in 2000, we didn't get funds sufficient for a helicopter, but in 2000, unlike most trips, a couple of Italian adventurous fellows came with me and shared the costs, which helped. At

the end of 2004, the filmmaker who had been working with me, Garrett Strang from Bethesda, Maryland, presented my materials and he got from Eastern Mountain Sports their full funding, so that allowed us again to hire another helicopter and totally outfit us with so much equipment we had more than enough.

PP: Right on. That's a change, eh? Now if I skip around and sound like I'm not following a specific thread, please bear with me. Robert Marx and Richard Nisbet[3] have both reported finding what looks for all the world like wheels in the New World, pre-Columbian wheels.

GD: Who?

PP: Robert Marx, author of *In Quest of the Great White Gods: Contacts Between Old and New World from the Dawn of History*, a world famous underwater explorer and adventurer, and Richard Nisbet, who is a contributor to the anthology in which this interview is being published. Nisbet runs a Web site by the same name as his contribution, *Ancient Walls*, and has taken a lot of amazing photographs of various sites with South American megalithic architecture.[4] He has some photos on his Web site of what looks exactly like a large stone wheel. Robert Marx describes finding something very similar sounding, what appeared to be four three-foot large stone wheels, while walking along an ancient elevated Mayan *sacbe* (pathway) in Quintana Roo, Mexico, but was also lost and thirsty and trying to find his way back to civilization at the time, so neglected to get photographs of his find. Nisbet, on the other hand, obtained a few amazing photos of his discovered wheel—like stone sculpture, and while pointing out that it doesn't appear to be useable due to a large crack running through it, still, it's significantly anomalous to make one wonder about the whole "did the New World have or even use wheels" issue. Have you yourself ever come across anything like this, wheels or what appear to be wheels created prior to the arrival of the conquistadors and other Old World explorers who have up until now been credited with bringing the wheel to the New World?

GD: No.

'93 Tree—Paulino Mamani.

of Peru. While the Department of Cuzco has a lot of unexplored areas, nonetheless, because of having more contact, more on-going, long-term contact with gringos and explorers and scientists and visitors and etc., it didn't buy the whole class-conflict kind of thing that sold more easily in the departments that were more, in a certain sense, backwards in terms of outside contact and influence and so more susceptible to the radical class conflict message of Sendero Luminoso, the rebel group known as the "Shining Path." There's less of that anyway in the Department of Cuzco; then you add to it the fact that the guys that I would always be with—Goyo and Paulino Mamani—are the most knowledgeable, strongest, most widely known and respected in the area, so they always know well ahead of time what's what, so it was only in that one year, 1991, that things got hot—not in the jungle, also the fact that where we go when we get out of the highlands, where we go there's no politics because it's so remote and there's no population

Now, you think the so-called "Pyramids of Parotoari" are really natural formations and not jungle-covered ruins at all, is that correct? Because there's been a lot of speculation over the years, ever since the first satellite photos were released and attention was drawn to the mysterious "dots," as they were also called by some researchers.

PP: Ok, that was quick. You travel a lot using your Peruvian friend Goyo Toledo as a guide, but I notice that during your 1991 expedition to the Petroglyphs of Pusharo, you mentioned something about political unrest keeping you from your initially planned expedition. Do you often have problems like that, running into either rebels, or narco-traffickers, or right-wing paramilitaries while exploring?

GD: Well, there are no right-wing paramilitaries there, even during the worst of it. During the worst years there were renegade policemen and Sendero Luminoso. But we never had a problem per se because for one thing, the Department of Cuzco—they call the states there departments—the whole Department of Cuzco was more immune to the Sendero Luminoso's influence than other parts

base—but anyway, during that particular year, during 1991, the thought was OK, in the highland province of Calca, it has become sort of a hot zone with political problems there, so that's why we decided OK, let's go to the lower altitude jungle that we can get to without going through the political highlands. We can just go by vehicle, then get on a peki-peki, the motorized canoes they use on the Rio Alto Madre de Dios, so decided this would be a good opportunity to make a study of the Petroglyphs of Pusharo, to see first-hand what they are and see what we could do to give some insight into what they might mean.

PP: Now, you think the so-called "Pyramids of Parotoari" are really natural formations and not jungle-covered ruins at all, is that correct? Because

Satellite photo of alleged Pyramids of Parotoari.

Paulino Mamani at the alleged Pyramids of Parotoari.

there's been a lot of speculation over the years, ever since the first satellite photos were released and attention was drawn to the mysterious "dots," as they were also called by some researchers. There have been some pretty self-confident statements as to their provenance by people who are only looking at photographs taken from the air, not after having put their feet to the jungle floor and actually visiting the site as you have, not an easy jaunt through the forest but rather an extremely difficult push through a not-entirely friendly jungle, right? But, having done so yourself, having made the hazardous trek to visit and examine first-hand the enigmatic "dots," you've come away convinced that they are merely oddly-shaped hillocks instead of ruins? You believe them to be natural, not man-made at all?

GD: Yes I do.

PP: I mean, you've actually been to the "dots" and climbed them, and are totally convinced of that?

GD: That's right.

PP: What is the Explorers Club?

GD: The Explorers Club is an international organization dedicated to scientific exploration of all aspects of the earth and natural history as well. It was founded in 1904 by seven gentlemen, and its early presidents included Frederick A. Cook, Robert E. Peary and Vilhjalmur Stefansson.

PP: Oh, I see, you are talking about the famous Explorers Club, the one with its main office, or headquarters rather, here in New York City, right?

GD: Exactly. Really, it was also associated with the pre-existing organization, the Arctic Club, whose members became absorbed into the Explorers Club a few years after its founding. So it's got its headquarters there in Manhattan and now has a bit over 3,000 members worldwide, divided into different categories—Member, Fellow and a new category called "Friends of the Explorers Club."

PP: You do hold some sort of office in the Explorers Club, isn't that so? Your title is what exactly?

GD: I'm a Fellow of the Club, and Chairman of the New England Chapter of the Explorers Club.

PP: When reading some of the stories about your explorations, reading about such adventures as passing over pongos, or as you put it, "impossibly deep gorges," using ropes, it seems that Indiana Jones doesn't have much on your regular, routine expeditions, does he? When you go out, you're making it rough, aren't you? You aren't going to places where there's a convenience store or bodega at the bottom of the hill, you're far out in the boondocks.

GD: Right. Where we go and what we do is not chosen at all for adventure travel, it's not chosen because it's got breath-taking views or an interesting hike or anything like that. It's the area you have

> **Where we go and what we do is not chosen at all for adventure travels, it's not chosen because it's got breath-taking views or an interesting hike or anything like that. It's the area you have to go through to get from point A to point B, to get from here to there and explore, then find what's there.**

to go through to get from point A to point B, to get from here to there and explore, then find what's there. I have people all the time contacting me, saying they want to go with me. Usually, when I explain the details and tell them what it's really like, I don't hear back from them. But the main thing is they don't really want to go through what is required—I mean, they want some adventure and exploration, but in order to go where we go you really have to be either masochistic or so totally obsessed and devoted to the particular goal of in this lifetime having something to say and something worthwhile to write about the whole concept of Paititi and the lost sites of the Inca there. If you didn't have that it would turn out to be a total drag. It's one thing to spend a day or two just putting one foot in front of the other, itchy with bug bites and dirty and wet and tired for hour after hour after hour; but then, after its gone on for days, and a couple weeks or more, it can get to be such that it's too much even for myself. But I just happen to be there to do what I have to do, so I do it. A lot of it is, I mean, it's a cliché, the old "99 percent perspiration, one percent inspiration," but it really is 99 percent drudgery for that one percent when you do discover something and all of a sudden you find energy you never thought you had in order to measure it and film it and photograph it—but the getting there is not necessarily a fun time. And the trek back is even worse, because you are already totally drained, and all the mystery is behind you.

PP: This may very well be my silliest question of the interview, but what sort of bug repellent do you take with you and does it work very well or at all? Because I noticed when reading up on your adventures online that you talk a lot about sweat bees and bugs, and how your endurance really can't take it anymore because the bugs are too much.

GD: No, that kind of question isn't silly at all, those are the real nuts and bolts questions. I take a variety of stuff, because you need a variety of different things. Then when it comes right down to it, many are the times that you realize that, screw it, whatever I use only works for a very short while anyway. I'll have with me some that have a very high percentage of DEET, some that have less percentage of DEET—because if you have too high a percentage of DEET, then that itself has its own possible bad side effects—to those with much lower percentages of DEET, to those that are a hundred percent herbal, with citron and aloe so I can really slather them on. It's really using a combination. Sometimes one will seem to be working for a while, then stop working, so you put on another, or put on a combination of them. You end up getting uncomfortably bitten anyway, because even if you just get a couple bites a day you wind up with quite a collection.

PP: I read a review you wrote a few years ago now, of *The Celestine Prophecy*, and you did not like that book at all, and seemed unhappy with it as a whole, taking issue with a variety of things involving both the story and the author himself. I must admit that I have not read the book so cannot state an opinion about it either way, but I can say that the promotional material for the book made it sound completely unattractive to me. Why didn't you like it, and why do you suppose it sold so well?

GD: Good question. I didn't like it because for me it had what is the thing that most turns me off with anything. What it had that most turns me off about something is when something is a fraud, when something is untrue, when something portrays itself as something that it's not. It was obvious to me, knowing Peru and knowing the area, and to anyone else I know who does know Peru and is a fan of Peru and a fan of the true marvels, the true magical wonders that it does have, this guy had never, obviously never been to Peru nor even ever been to any third-world country, that what he was portraying was his idea of it, what he thought it would be, like the American Southwest. If he'd put it out saying it was an allegorical tale that would be one thing, but the way it was marketed, the way it was described on the cover, everything about it was designed to make people kind of think that it was real, that he was relaying something that he really did. So when reading it I came to see—not to mention it was the most cornily written, silly, badly written thing—all of its facts, figures, all of its portrayal of the people, everything about it was absolutely silly and without any basis in real fact or real experience. The real irony was, here he is, making up all this stuff, which didn't in even one one millionth portray the real, true magic and wonder that Peru, and Machu

GD: Chewing.

PP: Excuse me, yes, chewing coca. You are up in pretty high altitude areas, which chewing coca helps deal with, right? Chewing coca leaves is a totally normal and accepted social practice in many areas of Peru, right?

GD: Correct.

PP: I'm not talking about taking or doing cocaine, it's a totally different thing, right?

GD: It's not in the least the same. It's always dangerous to mention, because in some quarters anything at all having to do with drugs is always totally misunderstood. But coca in places like Peru and Bolivia is no different, except more profound, than the use of coffee is here. Many people here would never think of going off to the office or to work or whatever it is they do without

> It's always dangerous to mention, because in some quarters anything at all having to do with drugs is always totally misunderstood. But coca in places like Peru and Bolivia is no different, except more profound, than the use of coffee is here.

Picchu, really have. So it was that fraudulence that really turned me off. But the reason I think it was so popular really shows that so many college-educated people in the U.S. are really totally uneducated and pie-in-the-sky when it comes to other cultures in other countries and what life there is really like. It fit into that stereotype of the mystical ones, going there and how it's the mystical ones that are really the good guys, and soldiers and priests are the evil ones, doing their thing, trying to hide the secrets the hero was trying to get a hold of; so I think it really showed the naïveté, in my estimation, of the New Age crowd and that's why it was such a big hit.

PP: You mention eating coca leaves while on expeditions a lot in your writings.

their cup of coffee, and that's how it's used there, but even more profoundly, more reverentially because there's a whole social, religious kind of meaning and intent to it. When you run into someone there, you sit down, with someone in the highlands, you sit down, you share. You put your coca in a particular form, five perfectly formed leaves together and hand it to them—that's called Kintu. It's a form of respect. So when someone offers you coca leaves in Kintu, in that particular form, it means I really want to relate to you as a human being and let's swap tales of our lives together. Or it might mean "I respect you." A husband and wife might do it together, or on an expedition we'll do it with each other to say, "hey, I dig being with you."

PP: That's very cool. I saw a television show recently, I believe on History Channel or perhaps National Geographic Channel, about a U.S. archaeologist out hunting ancient ruins in the most out of the way reaches of Peru, and when he approached a lone farmer or shepherd watching over his fields or flock, he'd pull out a bag of coca leaves, explaining to the camera that this is just how it is done in Peru, that everyone shares their coca with one another, that everyone uses it to both deal with the altitude but more as a social interaction, a way to break the ice as it were, to show respect as you say. My next question is on a completely different topic. Do you believe in astral traveling, as reported by your friend Goyo?

GD: Believe in what?

PP: Astral traveling. You mentioned in one of your stories your friend Goyo had said something about seeing some ancient ruins on the top of a mountain while traveling astrally.

He said that he had, while under the influence of ayahuasca, that he'd flown to the top of Apu Catinti, this mountain which is a legendary peak. There is a legend that said it would offer clues to the location of Paititi.

GD: That's right. He said that he had, while under the influence of ayahuasca, that he'd flown to the top of Apu Catinti, this mountain which is a legendary peak. There is a legend that said it would offer clues to the location of Paititi. We did end up climbing Apu Catinti, reaching the peak for the first time anyone ever succeeded in doing so, in 1986, but unfortunately, while at the base of the hills and mountains around there, there were Inca ruins, atop Apu Catinti there was no sign that anyone had ever reached the top, not even the Incas.

PP: That's too bad that you found no ruins there. But you do believe there's something to astral traveling, and using ayahuasca for visionary purposes?

GD: Well, let's say I don't discount it but it's one of those things I don't necessarily believe in it. I

believe it is possible. I myself used to do what people would call astral projection back when I was young, an adolescent, and a younger adult, until I learned that if you—because it can be so scary—until I learned that if you sleep on your side or stomach it's much less likely to happen than if you lie on your back.

PP: Oh, so you were doing it by accident? You were doing it while sleeping? Yeah, my girlfriend does that. Sometimes, and I think it happens when she's sleeping on her back.

GD: Even with that, it may be that it's astral projection but there are other theories to it, like it's a hypnogogic state, where we think we're doing it but we really aren't.

PP: What are your thoughts on a program like MIT's Ulysses Project, in which students are urged to pick a continent and plan an expedition for themselves, then write and report on their adventures? Have you worked with them at all?

GD: Not only that, but, when was it, in 1991, we were contacted by them and so we had a sort of joint relationship with them, our New England chapter did. We helped form their exploration group there. I remember going and giving a slide presentation to the group there at MIT but I haven't heard from them since so don't know what their status is.

PP: Did you actually go on an expedition with them?

GD: No, we just reached a point of us interfacing with them, me going over and giving the slide show and meeting with the people who really wanted to get it going and giving them tips on how to keep an exploration group going. It's been since 2001, really.

PP: I understand you and your partner, Paulino Mamani, are featured in an episode of the History Channel's program, "Digging for the Truth." What was the focus of that episode?

GD: The focus of the episode was really to present something of the Paititi quest. The format of the

> **To an extent, exploration has always been something that, even though there are times when things seem pretty mundane and people aren't that interested, but has always more or less been something that you can interest people in.**

show is that the host, a gentleman by the name of Josh Bernstein, meets up with people who are experts in the field, and questions them and they go with him and turn him on to this and that, but it's really a portrayal of his journeys looking into these mysterious kinds of things.

PP: Now is this the expedition whereby you were able to obtain all this extra equipment and the like?

GD: No, this had nothing to do with that. No, the one where we had all that equipment was back in June 2004. It was our—Paulino and my—expedition where we found and identified the furthest Incan ruins directly to the north of Cuzco.

PP: This happened when? What year was this?

GD: This was June of last year, 2004. And then in December when I was brought down to Peru to interface with this Josh Bernstein and be a part of his looking for El Dorado/Paititi kind of thing.

PP: What do you think of all these television shows about ancient civilizations and ancient mysteries, this sort of thing? Do you think there is a growing curiosity about our past and a distrust of any pat establishment view, or is mass media only making apparent an interest that's always been there, that the people have always had but the people are now becoming aware of because there's such a wider mass media.

GD: To an extent, exploration has always been something that, even though there are times when things seem pretty mundane and people aren't that interested, but has always more or less been something that you can interest people in. I remember

when I was a kid, one of the first things that turned me on was a show on TV called *Expedition*, a documentary that was on each week. I think that the shows that are on these days really run the gamut. Some of them appear to be real attempts to look into a subject and really try and determine what it was like, who were these people and what were they like, and others can run all the way up to silly Indiana Jones wannabe kind of things.

PP: Do you think civilization in South America is older than most mainstream archaeology gives it credit for?

> I think that as far as the dates given to many, many cultures and the advent of many technological and cultural events, that most dates should be earlier than they are, so, I think that the more investigation that is done, especially in South America, the older the dates will become, the further they will have to push them back.

GD: I think that as far as the dates given to many, many cultures and the advent of many technological and cultural events, that most dates should be earlier than they are, so, I think that the more investigation that is done, especially in South America, the older the dates will become, the further they will have to push them back. Another thing I think is that huge question mark will come up, the question mark of the Bering Strait migrations. Sure, a large part of the population of the Americas came across the Bering Straits, but you have so many pieces of real evidence that really run totally contrary to that being the one and only way that ancient man got here. The further south you go, many times the older the dates become for many sites.

PP: That actually leads to my next and, I think, final question. Do you think contact between South America and east and west Old Worlds went both ways, or do you put any stock in those theories at all? Do you think there might have been any contacts at all between ancient Africa and ancient South America, or the Polynesians and South America, or China and South America? Do you see any credence to those theories at all?

GD: I think that more and more mainstream, if you want to call it mainstream, well, let's just say more and more archaeology, anthropology and history, are finally starting to modify themselves on certain subjects which had been taboo but should not have been so, because there being taboo subjects in science is an abomination. One of those taboos, which was a way to instantly ruin your reputation, was to even entertain the thought of pre-Columbian trans-Atlantic contacts. Now it's coming around that people are recognizing that it is very possible that it wasn't necessarily independent invention when it comes to pyramids and all kinds of forms throughout the world, which also had been attributed, if not to independent invention, to the Jungian prototypes that are in all human minds, while to me it always seemed more likely that there were these contacts. Now I'm glad to say that people who had been dyed-in-the-wool, don't-even-entertain-that-thought independent inventionists, are starting to broaden their view. One of the worst methods they used to maintain their orthodoxy, the politically correct one, was by automatically claiming that you were insulting Native Americans, that you were automatically assuming they were too stupid to do these things by themselves, if you entertained the idea of pre-Columbian contacts. But it was nothing of the kind. One of the real ironies of this is that one of the prime movers behind the current reassessment, comes from many of the Native Americans themselves, who are saying "hey no, it's not an insult to us, we were a part of the world culture, too."

PP: I do have one more question for you, Greg. Will Paititi, as a place, with a capital "P," ever be found? Do you think you'll ever reach that goal, and say, "you know what, I've found Paititi and now I can relax, I've accomplished my goal?" Or do you think there's always going to be a search?

Greg Deyermenjian at ancient Incan site in the high-altitude jungles of Mameria.

GD: I think there will always be a search. I think we will always find more and more important sites, but these sites will then possibly be indications of there being something always further on. In this lifetime I can't imagine being able to cover all that territory I see before me, when I'm there and we're looking off from where we were in June last year, from Ultimo Punto, the furthest reach of the Incas yet found, and yet there were range after range after range of jungle-covered mountains still heading off to the north. Plus, on this map I have open right in front of me, there are plenty of areas, totally blank, marked "Datos Insuficientes," or "insufficient data." So I think that while the goal should be to identify it as definitively as possible, I think it's going to go on.

PP: I did just think of one other thing. On your Web site, titled *Search for Paititi*, you have some photos of an ancient Incan stone road. Have you reached the end of it yet?

I think we will always find more important sites, but these sites will then possibly be indications of there being something further on. In this lifetime I can't imagine being able to cover all that territory I see before me, when I'm there and we're looking off from where we were in June last year, from Ultimo Punto, the furthest reach and yet there were range after range after range of jungle-covered mountains still heading off to the north.

Yet I know from personal experience, and from the personal experiences of people who are truly intrepid individual explorers who just go off on their own, that so many parts of the world are so remote, so uncomfortable, that require such dedication and even obsession to want to travel to there, that there are still vast tracts on our earth that are yet to be explored and have yet to reveal their secrets.

GD: Well, no. That's one of the things that we have to do. We had to abandon the attempt in 1999, because in trying to follow it directly it was like trying to follow the Nile from its mouth to its source, like when the Arabs would say if you want to find the source start at the beginning and walk to the end; well, the reality is that the going gets too difficult and you can't do that. Same thing with this. We have to figure ways to get around and reconnoiter it, and come up on it again closer to wherever it leads to.

PP: So you do plan on going back again for another expedition soon?

GD: Oh yeah, I plan and hope to be back again this year.

PP: In the summertime?

GD: Yes, because that's the dry season.

PP: Is there anything you'd like to add that I haven't covered, anything you'd like to say in particular?

GD: Yeah. I wrote an editorial once with this title for our chapter and also sent into the New York headquarters, under the title *Is There Anything Left to Explore?* One of the things that I hear from the people who are within the august exploration societies is that "well, now that everything on the earth has been mapped, and satellite photographed, the only things left to explore are under the sea, and Antarctica and outer space." Yet I know from personal experience, and from the personal experiences of people who are truly intrepid individual explorers who just go off on

their own, that so many parts of the world are so remote, so uncomfortable, that require such dedication and even obsession to want to travel to there, that there are still vast tracts on our earth that are yet to be explored and have yet to reveal their secrets. The impressions one gets from their easy chair or their computer screens is very different from the impression one gets once they actually get out into the field.

PP: OK, thanks very much for speaking with me Greg, and good luck on all your future expeditions. It was very nice speaking with you.

GD: You're welcome, and it was nice speaking to you too, Preston.

References:

www.paititi.com

www.explorers.org

www.neexplorersclub.org

www-tech.mit.edu

www.shipwreckconference.com/conference_bios_marx_projects.htm

1. Edited by *Underground!* contributor and world explorer David Hatcher Childress.
2. Named after Eric Shipton and Bill Tillman.
3. See *Ancient Walls* by Richard Nisbet in this anthology.
4. Many of which are also reproduced in his contribution to this volume.

Mickey Z.

SOURCE OF THE BLOOD:

NAZI GERMANY'S SEARCH FOR ITS ARYAN ROOTS

Archaeology is the search for fact, not truth. If it is truth you are interested in, Dr. Tyree's philosophy class is right down the hall... We do not follow maps to buried treasure and X never, ever marks the spot. 70 percent of all archaeology is done in the library, research, reading. We cannot afford to take mythology at face value.

— Indiana Jones in *Indiana Jones and the Last Crusade* (1989)

WITH RARE EXCEPTIONS, humans are not driven to commit atrocities. With rare exceptions, humans can be driven to commit atrocities. "People often are conscripted into armies, but sometimes they enlist with gusto," explains Steven Pinker, director of the Center of Cognitive Neuroscience at the Massachusetts Institute of Technology. "Jingoism," Pinker declares, "is alarmingly easy to evoke."

In the case of Nazi Germany, it appears the propagandists themselves began their march toward genocide by inventing a past so mythical it could sway an entire nation.

"I have come to believe that men kill in war because they do not know their real enemy and because they are pushed into a position where they must kill," proposes peace activist Thich Nhat Hanh. "We are taught to think that we need a foreign enemy. Governments work hard to get us to be afraid and to hate so we will rally behind them. If we do not have an enemy, they will invent one in order to mobilize us."

In the case of Nazi Germany, it appears the propagandists themselves began their march toward genocide by inventing a past so mythical it could sway an entire nation. Even the leaders themselves couldn't tell fantasy from reality.

BACK TO THULE

"More than a political party, the Nazi party was very much a cult," says author Jonathan Vankin. "Like most demagogic religious sects, its rank and file was spellbound with the courage of demented convictions, and its leadership was financed and

> "The legend of 'Thule' was a variation on the Atlantis myth," Vankin explains. "Thule was supposed to be a nation of superbeings with a utopian civilization. It flourished until 850,000 years ago, when it was wiped away by a cataclysmic flood."

supported by powerful people whose main interest was accumulating more power. The finely tuned machine of brainwashing, fanaticism and secrecy is perfect for that purpose."

The "demagogic religious" sect that reached prominence in pre-war Germany was the Thule Society which, according to journalist Peter Reydt, "believed in the greatness of German history, reaching back to [A.D.] 9, when the Teutonic tribes defeated the Roman army. It promoted the superiority of the Aryan race, an ancient northern European people."

Friedrich Nietzsche's notion of the Übermensch (superman) endured many interpretations... one of which involved a racially superior people— called "Aryans"— who once inhabited northern Europe. This idea would eventually find a murderous home in the architects of the Nazi regime.

It began in 1900, when German occultists formed a society called the Order of New Templars (ONT). "Eight years later," says Vankin, "another occultist formed a group called Armanen. They took the swastika as the Armanen emblem."

"An ancient Indian symbol of good luck, the swastika was also the traditional symbol of Thor, the Norse god of thunder," writes Robin Cross of Channel4.com. In 1920, a Thule Society member suggested to Hitler that he adopt the swastika as the Nazi Party symbol. "Hitler placed it on a white circle against a red background, to compete with the hammer and sickle of the Communist Party," Cross explains.

The ONT and Armanen merged in 1912 and became known as the Germanen-Orden. Six years after that, some members of the Orden created Thulegesellschaft, the Thule Society. "The legend of 'Thule' was a variation on the Atlantis myth," Vankin explains. "Thule was supposed to be a nation of superbeings with a utopian civilization. It flourished until 850,000 years ago, when it was wiped away by a cataclysmic flood." The Thuleans,

so the legend went, brought destruction upon themselves by mating with a lower race.

The Holy Grail for the modern Thuleans was, well, the Holy Grail.

The legend of the Holy Grail—written in 1185—told of a vessel alleged to contain the wine of the Last Supper along with the blood of the crucified Christ. "Supposedly Joseph of Arimathea confiscated it and then used it to collect blood from Christ's wound as he hung on the cross," writes psychologist Katherine Ramsland at CrimeLibrary.com. "Joseph then took the cup to England to hide it in a secret place—Avalon—and it became the ambition of King Arthur's knights to find it and make it the center of their enterprise."

The quest for the grail is history's definitive treasure hunt... and it would seduce both Adolf Hitler and Heinrich Himmler.

HIMMLER'S ROUNDTABLE

Hitler's involvement with the Thule Society is believed to date back to his World War I years in the German Army—but this association intensified in 1919 when he met Dietrich Eckart, a wealthy and persuasive member of the Thule Society's innermost circle. Hitler biographer Wulf Schwarzwaller calls this meeting "more decisive than any other" in the future dictator's life. "Eckart molded Hitler, completely changing his public persona," Schwarzwaller writes.

As Vankin documents, Dietrich Eckart issued this command from his deathbed in December 1928: "Follow Hitler! He will dance but it is I who have called the tune."

Hitler's dance partner was Heinrich Himmler, who he appointed Reichsführer of the SS (an abbreviation of Schutzstaffel, "protection squadrons") in 1929. Until that point, the SS was little more than Hitler's personal bodyguards. Himmler, says Christopher Hale, author of

Himmler's Crusade: The Nazi Expedition to Find the Origins of the Aryan Race, "set about transforming an insignificant cadre into a new Aryan aristocracy."

Already a member of the Thule Society, Himmler joined the Nazi Party in 1925. His fascination with Thulian theories is often overshadowed by his heinous deeds and thus downplayed by historians—but it nonetheless influenced the shape and scope of the Final Solution.

"The truth is that Himmler's enthusiasms about lost civilizations, prehistoric archaeology, the Holy Grail and, especially, the origins of the 'Indo-Germanic' races were intricately interwoven with racial 'theories' that demanded the elimination of the unfit," says Hale.

Yes, it all comes back to the Grail. For what would a reincarnation of past Aryan glory be without the restoration of its most sacred symbol?

"Himmler saw the potential of archaeology as a political tool," Dr. Henning Hassmann of the Archaeological Institute in Dresden explained. "He needed archaeology to provide an identity for his SS. Himmler also believed that archaeology had a certain pseudo-religious content. There were excavations; there were myths and legends, a feeling of superiority. They believed by drawing on the power of prehistory they would achieve success in the present day."

The year 1935 saw Himmler take his obsessions to another level, establishing Das Ahnenerbe (the Ancestral Heritage Society), a new

The truth is that Himmler's enthusiasms about lost civilizations, prehistoric archaeology, the Holy Grail and, especially, the origins of the "Indo-Germanic" races were intricately interwoven with racial "theories" that demanded the elimination of the unfit.

Himmler built the SS to 300,000 strong by 1939 and presented its members as examples of racial purity. "To a remarkable degree, Himmler's ideas had been formed not only by politicians but by anthropologists and biologists," adds Hale.

"In World War II, the SS was the principal enforcer of Nazi racial doctrine," says Cross. "They staffed the Reich's concentration and extermination camps, where they conducted cruel experiments to demonstrate 'Aryan' racial superiority, and formed the core of the Einsatzgruppen (special formations) that were responsible for cleansing eastern Europe of Jews."

To Himmler, the men in the SS were acting in the tradition of his beloved Teutonic knights and kings, and Wewelsburg Castle was designed to be their Camelot. "Rooms were dedicated to figures of Nordic history and mythology like King Arthur," says Reydt. "Himmler's room was dedicated to King Heinrich I, founder of the first German Reich. Himmler believed himself to be the reincarnation of Heinrich. Another room was set aside to house the Holy Grail, which was to be searched for all over the world."

branch of the SS designed to be staffed by academics, thus raising Nazi propaganda to the status of objective truth—or so he hoped. "The Ahnenerbe organized expeditions into many parts of the world—to Iceland in search of the Grail, to Iran to find evidence of ancient kings of pure Aryan blood, to the Canary Islands to seek proof of Atlantis," Reydt says.

Their most ambitious destination was Tibet.

IT'S THE VRIL THING

The 1938 Nazi expedition to Tibet had roots that went all the way back to 1923 when Hitler was doing time in Landsberg Prison. "Hitler immersed himself in the writings of Professor Karl Haushofer," says Cross. Haushofer was the founder of the Vril Society, which sought "contacts with subterranean super-beings to learn from them the ancient secrets of Thule." The word "vril," coined by an English novelist named Edward Bulwer-Lytton, in his 1871 science fiction novel *The Coming Race,* referred to a psychokinetic power possessed by those in a master race.

> **"Hitler immersed himself in the writings of Professor Karl Haushofer,"** says Cross. Haushofer was the founder of the Vril Society, which sought "contacts with subterranean super-beings to learn from them the ancient secrets of Thule."

"The French author Louis Jacolliot furthered the myth in *Les Fils de Dieu* (The Sons of God) (1873) and *Les Traditions indo-européeenes* (The Indo-European Traditions) (1876)," writes Alexander Berzin in his article, *The Nazi Connection with Shambhala and Tibet*. "In these books, he linked vril with the subterranean people of Thule. The Thuleans will harness the power of vril to become supermen and rule the world."

Haushofer viewed central Asia as the origin of the Aryan race, and therefore the key to the harnessing of the power of vril. Since Tibetans, long dominated by both the British and the Chinese, were not averse to making nice with the Germans (and their Japanese allies), the Ahnenerbe set out on an expedition led by German hunter and biologist, Ernst Schäfer.

"One of the members of the Nazi expedition was the anthropologist Bruno Beger, a supporter of the theory that Tibet was home to the descendants of a 'northern race,'" says Cross. Beger's "scientific investigation" of the Tibetan people led him to conclude that they represented "a staging post between the Mongol and European races," and could play "an important role in the region, serving as an allied race in a world dominated by Germany and Japan."

The following year, the Second World War officially commenced and, of course, that domination would not become a reality. Even so, the Ahnenerbe remained active amidst the global conflict. "Entire contents of museums, scientific collections, libraries and archaeological finds were looted and shipped to Berlin or the Wewelsburg. Himmler and Sievers created a special unit—the "Sonderkommando Jankuhn"—to supervise the plunder," Reydt reports. "Professors, doctors and scholars were now directly integrated into the Nazi murder machine."

NEVER AGAIN?

With the benefit of hindsight, we can look down our collective noses at the transparency of Nazi Germany's propaganda ploys, supernatural dabblings and nationalist naïveté, but to do so would be to ignore the long—and current—history of similar tactics used to demonize humans and hence justify often brutal and relentless military attacks and economic domination.

Contemplate these three statements:

"The Antichrist is probably a Jew alive in Israel today."

"Communism was the brainchild of German-Jewish intellectuals."

"The Almighty does not hear the prayer of a Jew."

This is not more from chauvinistic Nazi lore, but rather the words of Reverend Pat Robertson—a high-profile televangelist with a considerable amount of political clout in the U.S. today.

> **Long before Hitler had even seen a swastika, Teddy Roosevelt said: "Democracy has justified itself by keeping for the white race the best portions of the earth's surface."**

Long before Hitler had even seen a swastika, Teddy Roosevelt said: "Democracy has justified itself by keeping for the white race the best portions of the earth's surface."

"I am strongly in favor of using poisoned gas against uncivilized tribes." Not Mengele—but instead, Winston Churchill. In 1937, as Himmler

> **With the idea that blessings from Christ himself enveloped them, the Nazis felt justified to go on a massive killing spree against those who "contaminated" them.... Theirs was a holy mission and nothing they could do in its service was wrong.**

was cultivating his vision of a superior race, the much-revered Churchill had this to say about Palestinians: "I do not agree that the dog in a manger has the final right to the manger even though he may have lain there for a very long time. I do not admit that right. I do not admit for instance, that a great wrong has been done to the Red Indians of America or the black people of Australia. I do not admit that a wrong has been done to these people by the fact that a stronger race, a higher-grade race, a more worldly wise race to put it that way, has come in and taken their place."

Such language would be later appropriated by Israelis like Golda Meir who declared, "There was no such thing as Palestinians; they never existed." Menachem Begin readily admitted the existence of Palestinians but paradoxically called them both "beasts walking on two legs" and "cockroaches."

Native Americans, African slaves, Filipinos during the Spanish-American War, the Japanese in World War II—the list goes on right up to Muslims today, proving that it doesn't require mystical Master Race theologies to justify the slaughter of our fellow humans.

"Searching for lost Aryans or the Holy Grail or Atlantis may seem harmless enough, but German occultism was founded on a racial vision of history," concludes Christopher Hale. "It validated German national identity by conjuring up a bogus yet seductive ancestral past. By taking this chimerical past literally, men like Heinrich Himmler were able to infuse policies of racial purification with an irresistible potency. As a result, occultism facilitated murder. The ground loam of pseudo-Darwinian civilization, led the 'scientists' of the SS to the killing fields of the concentration camps."

"With the idea that blessings from Christ himself enveloped them, the Nazis felt justified to go on a massive killing spree against those who 'contaminated' them," says Channel4.com's Ramsland. "Theirs was a holy mission and nothing they could do in its service was wrong."

With all brands of fundamentalism currently running roughshod over the planet and dictating global policy, how many of us can see past the comforting myths and soothing justifications to recognize the homicidal thirst for power lurking below?

References:

Alexander Berzin, "The Nazi Connection With Shambhala and Tibet." May 2003. www.berzinarchives.com

Robin Cross, "The Nazi Expedition." www.channel4.com

Christopher Hale, *Himmler's Crusade: The Nazi Expedition to Find the Origins of the Aryan Race*. New York: Bantam, 2004.

Katherine Ramsland, "All About Evil and Its Manifestations." www.crimelibrary.com

Peter Reydt, "Nazism and the Myth of the 'Master-Race.'" September 23, 1999. www.wsws.org

Jonathan Vankin, *Conspiracies, Cover-Ups and Crimes: Political Manipulation and Mind Control in America*. St. Paul: Paragon, 1991.

Michael Arbuthnot

TEAM ATLANTIS

ATLANTIS IS a nebulous concept. There is capital "A" Atlantis and lowercase "a" Atlantis. Many people enthralled by the legend believe that capital "A" Atlantis is an archaeological reality. They believe it was a physical place that once ruled the Mediterranean and dominated the Athenians circa 10,000 B.C. Now Atlantis lies submerged beyond the Pillars of Hercules, home only to ghosts and creatures of the deep; however, with the proper time, money, equipment and skilled professionals, capital "A" Atlantis can be located, studied and transitioned from legend to legacy.

It is the proverbial Garden of Eden or Utopia. The name itself evokes visions of a perfect world and a place of mystery beyond imagination.

Lowercase "a" atlantis is something entirely different. It is also a place, yet located in the realm of the human mind. It is the proverbial Garden of Eden or Utopia. The name itself evokes visions of a perfect world and a place of mystery beyond imagination. Lowercase "a" atlantis belongs to everyone, not bound by the rigors of science nor defined by tangible data. This atlantis is whatever it wants to be, limited only by the minds conceiving it. As long as people daydream, lowercase "a" atlantis will live on.

So, then, what is Team Atlantis? Like the ambiguity of "atlantis" itself, the answer depends upon who you ask. Each member of the team is likely to offer his or her own unique definition of Team Atlantis (TA). However, as the pragmatic founder of the organization, I will offer my definition herein. Simply put, TA is a multi-disciplinary research outfit whose mission is to explore archaeological mysteries with an emphasis on those enigmas associated with underwater contexts. Underwater archaeological topics usually have a terrestrial association or some connection to a terrestrial site or sites. As a result, land sites are also fair game to our research endeavors.

Team Atlantis expands and contracts depending on the task at hand, always offering a variety of perspectives and an open mind. Although contention is frequent among the group, we remain united in the belief that paradigms do not have to shift one funeral at a time. The engine that drives the research machine is entertainment, and TA also functions as a multi-level production and attractions company providing high-energy adventure content for both the Internet and television. Moreover, we currently offer patrons spectacular underwater experiences via submersible rides in Mexico. Get ready—tours are on the way.

Using the name "Atlantis" has unquestionably been the most controversial aspect of the TA operation. Many archaeologists have pondered how a commercial research outfit can use the name "Atlantis" in its title, especially since Atlantis has been a subject of debate since the birth of modern archaeology. Although some TA enthusiasts truly seek to find Plato's lost continent, I interpret the name differently. I consider "Atlantis" a metaphor that bespeaks the potential of submerged prehistoric archaeological sites, some of which may demonstrate a relatively sophisticated maritime technology dating to the Late Pleistocene (circa 10,000 B.C.). I also acknowledge the possibility that there may be truth to Plato's tale; that capital "A" Atlantis might exist, but it is not the focus of my research. Instead, I am presently interested in another fascinating mystery—the peopling of the New World.

invisible in the archaeological record. This absence of evidence encourages archaeologists (especially terrestrial ones) to favor one mechanism of culture change over others. In other words, without evidence of culture contact, one might assume the appearance of similar cultural traits in distant locations is the result of independent invention, as opposed to other, presently more controversial mechanisms for culture change, such as diffusion or migration. This is just one example of how our limited knowledge of submerged prehistoric sites has potentially influenced our perception of the Late Pleistocene.

To better grasp why diffusion and migration are such controversial theoretical mechanisms for culture change in the early Twenty-First Century, a discussion of their historical context is warranted. In the early and middle Nineteenth Century, American settlers were moving westward in an

---

Suffice it to say, submerged prehistoric sites have great potential to shed light on questions concerning the peopling of the New World.

Many archaeological sites in the New World were inundated by rising sea levels as glaciers and icecaps melted at the terminal Pleistocene. As a result, our perception of Late Pleistocene cultural adaptation is biased. We have been limited to examining previously land-locked sites because Late Pleistocene coastal sites (with rare exception) are now located underwater, thus, difficult to find and excavate. It is reasonable to assume that our knowledge of Late Pleistocene coastal transportation routes, settlement patterns, maritime adaptation and marine exploitation strategies is incomplete at best. Suffice it to say, submerged prehistoric sites have great potential to shed light on questions concerning the peopling of the New World.

Our inability to access submerged prehistoric sites has likely biased our theoretical perspective on culture change as well. For example, trade between coastal communities was likely occurring along near-shore sea routes during the Late Pleistocene when sea levels were lower. However, evidence of their modes of transportation is virtually

effort to settle vast expanses of land in America's plains regions. As they moved west over the Appalachian Mountains, settlers stumbled upon amazing earthworks and mounds, as well as hostile native peoples. Although naturalists like William Bartram, Reverend James Madison and Dr. James McCulloh believed these artifacts to be the work of American Indians, other individuals like Benjamin Barton, Governor De Witt Clinton and Amos Stoddard proposed counter-theories. Some of these fanciful theories credited the earth mounds to the Danes, Vikings and the Welsh. Other, even more preposterous theories were proposed suggesting the artifacts were built by members of a mysterious lost civilization. Josiah Priest's *American Antiquities and Discoveries in the West* (1833) claimed that the remains were built by a lost race of civilized "Moundbuilders" who were exterminated with the arrival of the Indians.[1] These theories were quickly accepted by the Eurocentric public and helped to fuel racist views that conveniently suited the westward-bound pioneers. The Indians were viewed as bloodthirsty savages who were robbers of land and life. These feelings of racial superiority justified the eradication of the Indians by the pioneers, as well as the reappropriation of their native land.

Even noteworthy researchers like Ephraim G. Squier and Edwin H. Davis initially favored the lost moundbuilder theory. In the newly found Smithsonian Institute's first publication, *Ancient Monuments of the Mississippi Valley* (1848), Squire and Davis proposed that the ancient Ohio moundbuilders had probably relocated to Mexico after encountering the Native Americans.[2] In 1949, Squier did a study of several mounds in western New York and discovered evidence to indicate the Iroquois were responsible for the mounds in that region. This epiphany caused

surveys of native populations. In an effort to account for cultural similarities among diverse populations, the evolutionists championed the theory of "Psychic Unity," which generally countered theories of diffusion and migration.[5] But during the late Nineteenth Century, increasing faith in diffusion and migration as processes for cultural change, and a growing skepticism in psychic unity theory, led the German ethnologist and geographer, Friedrich Ratzel to write such books as *Anthropogeographic* and *The History of Mankind*. Ratzel argued that important inventions, like the bow and arrow, had likely been invented just once. As a consequence of this notion, diffusion created culture areas, which could be interpreted from the archaeological record.[6]

In an effort to account for cultural similarities among diverse populations, the evolutionists championed the theory of "Psychic Unity," which generally countered theories of diffusion and migration.

Squier to reconsider his opinions and abandon the lost moundbuilder theory.

During the mid-Nineteenth Century other researchers, like Samuel Haven and Henry Schoolcraft, also favored a model of cultural continuity for the earthworks. These conclusions were based on strong skeletal and ceramic evidence.[3] However, it wasn't until the 1890s that the ethnologist Cyrus Thomas finally put an end to the lost moundbuilder theory. After extensive mound excavations sponsored by the Bureau of Ethnology, Cushing published his findings in their Twelfth Annual Report. Not only did Cushing find evidence of cultural continuity linking the mounds to the contemporary Native Americans, but he also suggested that the ancestors of different extant indigenous groups had been responsible for different mounds. This hallmark resolution secured a victory for cultural continuity and a triumph over racism.[4]

While archaeologists argued over the origins of New World structures in the mid-Nineteenth Century, cultural evolutionists like Lewis Henry Morgan and Edward B. Tylor conducted ethnographic

Ratzel's theories influenced a young Franz Boas, who then brought the concepts of diffusion and ethnographic culture to the United States. Culture history in Europe and the United States then followed very different developments. In short, Europeans were more interested in chronological variation, while American archaeologists focused primarily on geographical variation. Franz Boas called for a return to historical particularism, an inductive approach to culture history.[7] Although this investigative framework initially condoned diffusion as a model to explain cultural similarity, ironically the methods he employed led to a denial of those same principles. It was an event of methodological nihilism.

In the period to come, known as the Classificatory-Historical period (1914-1940), Boas and his contemporaries, including Max Uhle, Manuel Gamio, N. C. Nelson and others, adopted new analysis techniques, which had been developing in Europe. Stratigraphic, seriational and classificatory methods were revealing sequences, chronologies and illustrating culture change in new and profound ways. It was the revelation of internal culture

Many Native American groups and researchers alike interpret theories of diffusion as degradation to indigenous populations and their inherent capabilities, although nothing about theories of diffusion or migration suggests such notions.

change, combined with the increasing antiquity of native North American cultures, that influenced Boas to reject diffusion.[8] He felt one could explain culture change as the result of unique and natural responses to environmental conditions. According to Boas, such changes were not occurring within a unilinear or evolutionary system.[9] In 1925, Boas declared that "diffusion is finished," and so it was.[10] Boas' opinions were widely acknowledged and accepted by the scientific community. He has been labeled the "Father of North American Anthropology," and with his decree a new paradigmatic precedent was established.

The widespread acceptance of culture continuity by archaeologists, along with Boas' influential rejection of diffusion, has had a caustic impact on theories of culture contact, diffusion and migration within the North American archaeological paradigm. Nowadays, theories in support of such models for culture change are often dismissed due to a lack of collaborative evidence and/or a perceived threat to indigenous innovation and development. Many Native American groups and researchers alike interpret theories of diffusion as degradation to indigenous populations and their inherent capabilities, although nothing about theories of diffusion or migration suggests such notions. For instance, the acceptance of widespread diffusion in ancient Europe has never been tied to theories of racial superiority or dominance. Rather, it is the context of the historical development of these theories in North America, as well as a reaction to past and present political problems in the United States, that continue to suppress serious consideration of diffusion and migration theories in the New World. This wholesale denial and political lumping has been detrimental despite a vast abundance of evidence to the contrary.

Another important factor in the general denial of diffusion and migration theories is the scientific community's general lack of confidence in prehistoric humans' capabilities and technologies. For the past 40 years, archaeologists have supported a model for the peopling of the Americas that is restricted in breadth due to a preconceived image of the immigrants themselves. In other words, because of scientists' assumptions about Late Pleistocene technologies, alternative speculation has been grossly dismissed. The prevailing model for the peopling of the New World states that roughly 13,500 years ago, big game hunters from Asia crossed the Bering Land Bridge, traversed the Ice Free Corridor (through what is now Canada) pursuing game, and rapidly made their way to South America (within 2,000 years). This model envisions the Asian immigrants as fur-clad, caveman-like automatons with little technological know-how beyond simple lithic tool making. Consequently, this popular image has been uniformly applied to humans of the Late Pleistocene worldwide, but without comprehensive evidential support. This outright assumption, however, is contrary to substantial evidence in other parts of the world. For example, the possibility that the New World's first inhabitants had ocean-going sea vessels has been widely rebuked. However, there is indisputable evidence that ocean travel was taking pace in far more remote times. It is generally acknowledged that prehistoric humans reached Australia at least 40,000 years ago. It does not seem like a stretch of the imagination to suggest that 30,000 years later humans in Asia had such maritime technologies; however, until recent years this notion has been rejected.

Archaeologists are empirically limited to tangible data, which is typically limited to non-perishable materials. In the opinion of this author, a reason why archaeologists continue to underestimate the capabilities and technologies of early humans is because much interpretation is reliant on recovered lithic remains. This fact has influenced many archaeologists to conclude that chipped stone tools were the primary tool-type utilized by Late Pleistocene populations. However, simply because lithics are easily recovered from the field, this does not necessarily mean that chipped stone was the primary technology possessed by Late Pleistocene immigrants to the New World. For example, it is believed that the lack of prehistoric remains in Asia may be a result of widespread use of bamboo in ancient times. Bamboo and other organic materials are quickly lost from the archaeological record. Relative to this discussion, rafts or sea going vessels constructed of reeds, bamboo, or other perishable materials will be difficult to recover from the field; however, the absence of such objects in the archaeological record should not be considered evidence of absence. In fact, some of the most compelling evidence in support of pre-Columbian diffusion from Asia to the Americas suggests transoceanic or coastal seafaring.

Since the burgeoning of North American archaeology over 200 years ago, the study has witnessed major paradigm shifts over a variety of important issues. Many of the questions that once divided the discipline have been settled and stable consensuses reached. However, it is the unresolved issues that continue to promote dialogue and debate between different schools of thought. The ultimate goal of the parties in contest is paradigmatic unity which, in turn, leads to the birth of scientific dogma. Yet, it is the fact that unresolved issues persist that keeps the imaginations of men alive, and it is the quest to answer these questions that keeps Team Atlantis engaged.

Over the years TA has embarked on a variety of fascinating adventures to exotic locations. Our efforts have shed light on the geodetic placement of the Giza pyramids and have established that Cat Island's Long Rocks in the Bahamas are natural. We found no evidence indicating that Japan's undersea castle [off Yonaguni in the East China Sea] is a castle at all, but we identified great potential off the sandy beaches of Mexico's eastern peninsula. Through the years we have tackled each adventure with open minds and have applied multi-working hypotheses. We have allowed ourselves to speculate and acknowledge differences of opinion and perspective. Although it was rare for consensus among team members, the desire for truth and the thirst for adventure unified us along the way.

Team Atlantis might serve as an escape from the drudgery of everyday life, or a sojourn into the realm of high-energy adventure in search of clues to unlock the secrets of yesterday.

Team Atlantis is both an idea, and the individuals that manifest that abstraction. The idea of Team Atlantis is defined by the vicarious adventurer who monitors our expeditions posted on the Web site (teamatlantis.com). To this individual, perhaps a high school student or stockbroker, Team Atlantis is a portal that sheds light on humanity's ancient and mysterious past, and helps to make sense of the present. Team Atlantis might serve as an escape from the drudgery of everyday life, or a sojourn into the realm of high-energy adventure in search of clues to unlock the secrets of yesterday. Whatever the reason, the TA organization has something to offer to everyone. So then, back to the question: What is Team Atlantis? The answer is up to you, as its definition is limited only by the breadth of one's imagination.

1. Bruce G. Trigger, *A History of Archaeological Thought*. New York: Cambridge University Press, 1989. p. 104-5.

2. Ibid.

3. Gordon R. Willey and Jeremy A. Sabloff, *A History of American Archaeology*. New York: W. H. Freeman, 1998. p. 42-46.

4. Ibid., p. 47-49

5. Paul Bohannan and Mark Glazer, eds., *High Points in Anthropology*. 2nd Ed. New York: McGraw-Hill, Inc., 1988.

6. Trigger, p. 151.

7. Wiley and Sabloff, p. 91.

8. Trigger, p. 187.

9. Wiley and Sabloff, p. 96-100.

10. Fred Eggan, "The History of Social/Cultural Anthropology." *Perspectives on Anthropology* 1976, American Anthropological Association, no. 10, 1977. p. 4.

Troy Lovata

SHOVEL BUM—

THE LIFE ARCHAEOLOGIC

"SHOVEL BUM" IS A SLANG term referring to archaeology field workers who perform the hands-on tasks out where the tools meet the dirt. *Shovel Bum* is a zine which some of those very workers have written and illustrated, since 1997, about their lives. Shovel bums are the most numerous variety of archaeologist; and yet their viewpoint is rarely discernable in scholarly texts.

Shovel Bum[1] tells two stories. One is a tale of what it takes to move dirt, uncover artifacts, contemplate the past and pay the rent. This is the story of individuals who rarely get mentioned by name, but who—as archaeologist Dr. Patty Jo Watson observed—form "an archaeological proletariat, who do most of the field and laboratory work carried out in this country."[2] Theirs are indeed intriguing, important and underreported stories. *Shovel Bum* not only captures their points of view, but it chronicles how archaeology is actually practiced. It presents the process behind bold claims about the past and behind spectacular artifacts. *Shovel Bum*'s very existence helps explain the state of the discipline. To understand what *Shovel Bum* is about is to know who's who, how decisions are made, and who gets to make them.

Shovel Bum began when archaeology field tech Trent "T-Bone" de Boer sat down during a cultural resource survey in the hinterlands of Arkansas, and sketched comics in his field notebook about

Cover of *Shovel Bum*.

his daily routines. He considered how his chosen work affected his actions: who he talked to, how he dressed, what he ate and where he slept. Trent contemplated the limitations of what disciplinary traditions would allow him to discuss in specific situations; such as what does and doesn't go into an archaeological report. He photocopied the results and started handing them out to friends, archaeologists and lay people. Trent, like most archaeologists, was often asked about the practice of archaeology and hoped his sketches would help explain his career. Slowly people took notice of his work, traded copies with an even wider set of acquaintances, and mentioned his work in serious graduate school classes. Other archaeologists realized that he presented a narrative that mirrored their own lives; which was little recorded, although often mentioned in back rooms and over drinks. These archaeologists began comparing his takes to their experiences. Some felt an urge to respond in kind; and pictures and words started arriving. With each new issue something more was discussed, more people were involved and more stories were told. Individual archaeologists were interacting with each other not because they worked in the same region, studied under the same mentors, examined similar artifacts or asked the same questions about the past. Rather, they were forming relationships outside the typical routes of professional networking, because the very act of doing archaeology had itself shaped their lives. Doing archaeology as a job changes not only one's perspective on the past, but one's lifestyle.

ZINES AND WHY THERE'S ONE WITH A VIEW FROM THE SHOVEL HANDLE

Shovel Bum is a zine. It's important to understand what this moniker means, because it explains why there's a sometimes humorous, sometimes snide, hand-illustrated publication concerning the workings of archaeology. "Zine" is derived from fanzine, which is itself a contraction of fan magazine.[3] Fanzines were amateur publications—as opposed to professional magazines with paid

minds. In the 1970s, following the blossoming of the underground press movement, fanzines grew to include music and movie genres such as slasher horror flicks and punk rock. These were a direct response to a perceived lack of adequate representation in the mainstream press for these genres.[5] Then, sometime early in the Reagan years, many people found a voice that had less to do with fan fawning, and more to do with a connection to personal self-sufficiency and alternatives to the passive consumption of mass media.[6] When this was combined with the advent of cheap computers, accessible desktop publishing and widely available photocopiers, zines grew into their own.[7]

Zines are a means to record personal perspectives outside the confines of market and profit motive, as opposed to magazines produced with the intention of filling a marketing niche or selling advertising space.[8] Zine perspectives range from politics, to cultural scenes, to diary-like chronicling of the mundane activities of day-to-day life. Zines usually start with the work of an individual with individual interests and individual stories to tell.[9] Yet, zines are significant because, when they last beyond a couple issues, communities form. At this point, people apart from the founder or publisher become contributors. Not just ideas, but physical things are shared. Professor Stephen Duncombe notes that, "the form of the zine lies somewhere between a personal letter and a magazine."[10] Letter writing is an apt metaphor for the community zines can build because people interact and relationships are formed through creative production. After reading a zine, many people respond by crafting something of their own. They don't simply discuss what they've found in print. They often

The voice of an archaeology worker, expressed through a zine, illuminates how the discipline functions.

contributions—originally produced by science fiction fans and dating back to the golden age of 1930s and 1940s pulp sci-fi.[4] Fanzines were a medium in which fans could share their own stories, offer critical commentary, discuss the nuances and rules of sci-fi, and form a community of like

send in a submission or even publish their own zine in response.[11] Constructive replies typically include letters to the editor. But replies can extend much further and build far stronger links between people when the response is creatively demanding enough to include hand-drawn pictures or a

Shovel bums choose to pursue archaeology as a career. Yet it is also a reality that the majority of what archaeologists actually do is very different from what they're prepared to do by school or what they might emulate from the discipline's past and present giants.

revealing personal narrative; which includes one fessing up to both the good and bad within themselves.[12] Zines are ephemeral and rarely meet a strict publishing schedule. Nevertheless, the cycle of reading and response is powerful enough to truly form community bonds.

Shovel Bum is a zine about work, and work is not a solitary undertaking. There's a tradition in the genre of zines to contemplate and write about work. How one is able to talk about their work shows much about how a field operates. Employment simply takes up too much of most people's lives to escape the introspective eye that zines offer.[13] The voice of an archaeology worker, expressed through a zine, illuminates how the discipline functions.

Duncombe notes that many zines approach work from the perspective that, "most people work for somebody else, producing or serving something over which they have little say, and doing it in a way that gives them little satisfaction."[14] Archaeology as work is varied enough for this to occasionally both ring very true and occasionally fail to adequately describe the role of Watson's "archaeological proletariat."[15] Shovel bums choose to pursue archaeology as a career. Yet it is also a reality that the majority of what archaeologists actually do is very different from what they're prepared to do by school or what they might emulate from the discipline's past and present giants. This is not to say that one career path is absolutely preferable, just that there are noticeable differences between the academic as scholar, the academic as student, the field worker as manager and the field worker as technician.[16] *Shovel Bum* is often about negotiating these differences.

The ability to work not just to pay the bills, but to interact with something as enticing as the past attracts many. Archaeology can be an extremely satisfying profession. However, shovel bums are the students and technicians who generate primary data and write field reports, but don't always get to decide what data is worth looking for and don't always get first, or even third, author credit. Moreover, archaeologists at all levels are often the last to decide where they physically work. Archaeologists do actually work for someone else; whether it be an educational institution with its administrators and regents, a contract firm with its accountants and profit motive, or any of the myriad other positions with their particular limitations. What's in *Shovel Bum* is what doesn't get published into much of the rest of professional archaeological discourse. *Shovel Bum* recognizes that someone else may be controlling the money, that archaeologists are employees and that people's lives are affected not just by the choice to do archaeology, but by the realities of the discipline.

The first page of the first issue of *Shovel Bum*. Trent de Boer originally drew this in his field notebook to explain to friends and family what doing archaeology actually entailed.

Dr. Ian Hodder noted a decade ago that modern archaeological writing leaves out significant descriptions of what happened in the process of uncovering the past.[17] His examination of the last two hundred years of archaeological writing shows a trend away from "emphasis on the 'I', the actor, dialogue, narrative sequence and interpretation tied to the contingent context of discovery..."[18] Modern archaeologists communicate with each other and understand the past primarily through the written word.[19] Yet Dr. Hodder has found that professional discourse is now a very formalized means of communication, in which:

> The writing has become increasingly distant, objective, impersonal and universal. We have become blind to the fact that we are writing. It appears as if self-evident data are described in neutral terms. The description is undated, timeless and beyond history.[20]

individuals who actually moved the dirt. The examples of professional writing that Hodder examined from archaeology's distant past do make subjective note of time, date and circumstance.[25] However, the laborers who took shovels in hand are unnamed figures, sometimes not even referred to as individuals. They lack the opportunity to describe what it was like to uncover evidence and what choices they made in their labors, much less discuss what it meant to be ordered to dig.

Shovel Bum views archaeology as work, differently from what has come before and much of what is currently considered the discipline's standard. Dr. Hodder explains that archaeology's early writing took the form of correspondence and letters filled with the subjectivity of first person accounts.[26] This is an interesting comparison to Duncombe's observation that zines like *Shovel Bum* are something akin to a personal letter.[27] Jeremy Bushnell observes that "providing 'human context' is one of

---

Archaeology's formalized structures of communication tend to neglect the collective nature of research; and the fact that numerous individuals contributed to the collection, interpretation and publication of any story about the past.

There are legitimate reasons why this format developed, such as standardizing or coding data for use by others.[21] But that doesn't account for all that has changed. Dr. Hodder[22] and Dr. Jeremy Sabloff[23] show that it isn't just the rigorous application of scientific discipline that has formalized writing. Professional communication within archaeology is more detached than it used to be.

Archaeology's formalized structures of communication tend to neglect the collective nature of research; and the fact that numerous individuals contributed to the collection, interpretation and publication of any story about the past.[24] However, one way in which modern professional writing doesn't differ from its past is that authorship is cited and credit is given primarily to the individuals in charge. Narrative accounts are first-person descriptions attributed to the director and not the

the things that zines do best, and *Shovel Bum* is no exception."[28] However, *Shovel Bum* is also distinct because is doesn't just provide the context through which one can better understand artifacts or the story of the past. It presents narratives from a different class of archaeologists. It is a consideration of the context of discovery in its own right. In fact, its view that archaeology is actually work, and that doing such work will shape one's entire lifestyle, separates *Shovel Bum* from other forms of disciplinary expression. There have been other attempts to express how archaeology functions or how it affects those who work at it. Others have tried in their own way to capture some picture of what goes on. These are usually "state of the field type" articles like Dr. Stephen Black's 1995 review of Texas archaeology.[29] But *Shovel Bum* is different from this. *Shovel Bum* exists, in part, because a few archaeologists have

William Lipe has observed that, "the benefits of archaeological research are often not directly accessible to the public because the work is highly technical, and research results are generally published in books and articles written primarily for other archaeologists."

found a way to interact with each other based on what it means to work in their profession.

THE NARRATIVE THAT MATTERS

One can see why *Shovel Bum* exists, and why it matters that it exists. Works like *Shovel Bum*, which present a narrative of discovery and employment, are necessary to satisfy the discipline's responsibilities to itself and the public it serves. The topics it explores are often accounts of the day-to-day and the seemingly mundane in contrast to the allure of shiny artifacts, the exotica of peoples who behaved quite differently than we do, or mysteries of why entire cultures underwent change. The chronicling of quotidian events is crucial for the discipline as it tries to explain itself to a wider audience. The day-to-day account is crucial for the accuracy and authority it provides.

There are few professionals who would doubt archaeology's self interest in successfully communicating with the public. Professor Simon James[30] and Dr. Jeremy Sabloff[31] are but two of the many archaeologists who note that the preservation of sites and artifacts, the opportunity to present findings, and the economic basis of archaeology all require an ability to positively influence a wide audience. Without successful public outreach, the funding dries up and research grinds to a halt.[32] But there is more than a self-interest in public communication—there is a responsibility to participate in a public archaeology because shovel bum and project director alike serve those outside their field. Archaeologists Poirier and Feder are right to claim it requisite that professionals cultivate "an archaeology open and accessible to the public, not just paid for by them."[33] The past is a resource held by professionals in the public trust and this creed is enshrined in professional codes of conduct.[34]

Archaeologists study the lives of real people. Therefore, they rarely face a disinterested public because everyone has direct connection, both legally[35] and emotionally,[36] to some part of the past. Public opinion surveys have repeatedly confirmed the high level of interest in not just the past, but archaeology as a discipline that explains the past.[37] Archaeologist Stephen Williams does not overstate himself when declaring that, "all in all, we have a good product to sell—archaeology is a fascinating subject and viewed as such by millions of people."[38]

But neither the high-minded sentiment of a resource held in the public trust, nor the self-interest in being able to keep doing this exciting job, means that attempts at a public archaeology are particularly successful. William Lipe has observed that, "the benefits of archaeological research are often not directly accessible to the public because the work is highly technical, and research results are generally published in books and articles written primarily for other archaeologists."[39] Government archaeologist Frances McManamon reminds us that, "the shorthand of archaeological jargon and densely written professional material makes poor fare for reaching out to anyone."[40] Moreover, professional codes of conduct only deem it necessary that archaeologists publicly present their findings.[41] Neither these codes or many archaeologists themselves have recognized the necessity to widely report not just what was uncovered, but the process by which one operates.

Researchers like William Lipe note that, "the dynamic character of archaeological research has the potential to help make archaeology more interesting to the public."[42] Simply explaining how archaeology operates drives much of the relationship between professional and public. The previously mentioned opinion polls are telling. Archaeologists are popular because people want to know something not only about the past, but how they came to understand it.[43] Yet without a narrative of what archaeologists do, there is a failure to connect. Archaeologist Nicole Boivins declares that:

> **People use images as a stockpile of memes with which we can approach new situations and compare to what we already know. Archaeologists are no different. Archaeologists judge the validity of claims about the past based on the images produced.**

Archaeology *is* an interesting subject...How can such dried up and shriveled accounts have been born of a tree that is so majestic and exotic? How is it that individuals who regularly visit exotic locales, who pay live witness to the extravagances of beauty and horror that typify the human species, who pursue the mysteries and unearth that which has been lost forever, who operate at the crux of the coming together of a babbling multitude of diverse disciplines...how is it that they of all people can produce as their end results and final conclusions such desiccated and anemic summaries? Surely the sin of dullness is a hundred-fold multiplied when it is perpetrated by the archaeologist.[44]

Peter Young, publisher of the popular magazine *Archaeology*, offers a similar sentiment when he suggests that archaeologists need to be better storytellers. He laments the fact that too many manuscripts arrive at his office "bone dry and bloodless."[45] Peter Young's advice to writers is to "keep it personal without being egocentric," because "readers are interested in you and the story that is unfolding; they should be led through your material..."[46] They should be given a narrative.

Quality storytelling and interesting descriptions of work in progress are powerful steps in public communication. *Shovel Bum* is significant because it has generated positive reviews for the way it tells stories.[47] But Archaeologist Chris Stevens, in reply to Nicole Boivins' lament on the sins of boring writing, makes a valid point when he notes that exciting stories go only so far.[48] If successfully generating public interest was a goal unto itself, *Shovel Bum* isn't big enough to matter. In fact, something much larger is at stake. Without a discussion of how archaeology gets done—including the mundane tribulations, the complaints about the system, the alternating cycles of boredom and awe in the process of discovery, and the gripes about colleagues—the discipline risks its ability to speak with authority about the past. Without a successful presentation of means and methods archaeology risks losing out to, among others, the Creationists, pseudoscientists and New Age theorists. These are real threats to the field's ability not only to thrive, but meet its responsibilities to the past.[49] William Lipe notes that most of archaeology's failings to counter fantastic and false claims are directly related to an inability to show the public how the past is constructed.[50] This includes disagreements as well as the changes both the discipline and individuals go through. William Stiebing Jr. observes that:

Anthropologists, archaeologists and historians should learn from [the] controversy over evolution and creationism, for the average lay person doesn't really understand the methodology of the social sciences either. Laymen think of the past in terms of "facts." By digging in the ground or rummaging through old documents, scholars discover these "facts." But few people understand the details of how this process works...If we spent a little more time making our methodology understandable, maybe the public would be able to recognize the problems that characterize cult archaeology without professional help.[51]

WORDS CAN BE FUNNY, PICTURES CAN BE IMPORTANT

Shovel Bum's pages are filled with a unique discussion of what it means to do archaeology. This makes it important. But its not just what's discussed that makes it matter—its how the discussion is presented. *Shovel Bum* uses a lot of pictures along with its words—funny pictures. It is comic, illustrated, irreverent and downright humorous: haiku odes to the broken down motels that archaeologists stay in, contemplating the coolness of driving up to camp in a garbage truck, considering what robot diggers would look like, filling out Mad Libs about faulty field vehicles. Drawings of stick figure quality with just enough hair-related attributes to identify the real people behind them. One-inch square thumbnails of motel room accidents. A photograph of *Shovel Bum* covers plastered over the service entrance of the American Museum of Natural History. These images are of an "I know that" quality that drives the readers of *Shovel Bum* to participate in the creative cycle of response and reply that underlies a zine built community.

Archaeologists are a visual lot. They make sketches in their field notes that are both necessary (think soil profiles) and otherwise (consider the caricatures of the boss's hippy haircut and shaggy mustache). Archaeologists are entranced by the physical shape of artifacts and their appearance as potent symbols of the past.[52] People use images as a stockpile of memes with which we can approach new situations and compare to what we already know.[53] Archaeologists are no different. Archaeologists judge the validity of claims about the past based on the images produced. Scholars like Dr. Stephanie Moser[54] and Dr. Simon James[55] are but two who have documented a tendency to discuss the past with the subtle subtext of images that shape one's opinions about what is right and what is wrong. Publisher Mitch Allen observes that, even when archaeologists don't have useful drawings or explanatory pictures, they still submit piles of photographs along with every manuscript.[56]

Yet, for all the attraction to images, the academic environment of archaeology actually neglects, if not acts prejudiced against, visual communication. The same people who document the power of pictures repeatedly note that such power is discounted and ignored.[57] Archaeologist Brian Molyneaux observes that in the rush to describe the past in the elite jargon of detached, objective wording, professionals have the propensity to consider images the domain of children and the uneducated.[58] Some may like what they see. Some may note that such pictures have captured something all too human and fragile about the discipline. But, even though the ability to create such images requires careful preparation and understanding of professional issues, many continually fail to appreciate how necessary images are.

A page by Trent de Boer from the "Shovel Bum Joins the Army" theme issue, which deals with the travails of doing archaeology on the large tracts of land owned by the Department of Defense and federal government. Not only do these properties encompass many important archaeology sites, they're littered with countless un-exploded bombs, shells and ammunition.

Comics are powerful. Their ability to amplify by simplifying, to distill an essence of an issue and to juxtapose important concepts is perhaps unrivaled.[59] Archaeologist Bill Sillar has shown how devastatingly effective the juxtaposition of a simple cartoon about prehistory against many, many pages of critical text can be at exposing fallacious thinking.[60] So many of Gary Larson's "Far Side" cartoons were taped upon so many archaeologist's office doors because they were so efficient at capturing the basest of instincts.

Of course, it's not just any kind of image that exhibits such power. It's the funny or satirical images that shake us. Archaeologists Philip Rahtz and Ian Burrows have declared that "archaeology is too important a subject not to be joked about."[61] They understand that there's nothing like an amusing and satirical cartoon to reach a tentative audience, make a serious point palatable, critique earlier people and institutions, or expose intolerant theory for what it is. Bill Sillar explains that, "humor is a rhetorical weapon from which there is no easy defense," because it opens your eyes to new viewpoints by, "asking you to look at the familiar from a different angle, frequently inviting you to laugh at what you might otherwise take for granted, or pass by unnoticed."[62] Self parody and satire are as important as clear narratives in countering the processes of ambivalent elitism and the vilification of the establishment as dogmatic, thus allowing cult archaeology, New Age theories and pseudoscientific explanations about the past to thrive.[63] By laughing at ourselves, we are more human and reachable. By laughing at themselves archaeologists show how laughable notions are that they're closed minded academics, colonial plunderers, treasure happy gold diggers or cultural scrooges who covet and hide the truth. Dictators of all stripes are unable to laugh at themselves.

to tell an individual story in an intimate format. As youth they know what a zine can offer. This is why Nicole Boivins feels that those on the low end of the academic totem pole (graduate students, young researchers and the like), "who have the least vested interest in maintaining the status quo," are the most likely to make archaeology and archaeological writing interesting.[64] She notes that though one would expect that longstanding and tenured academics can get away with advocating change—they could offer interesting formulations and radical critique because they're more established than people under review and moving from job to job—the system is just too entrenched for the elders to act. Anthropologist Julie Chu has produced a particularly vivid portrait of how youth use zines to claim a place within the media environment. She explains how, "the media as an environment for youths looks tremendously different and *richer* when zine publishers' own perceptions are center

> They know what mainstream domination means and respect the ability to tell an individual story in an intimate format. As youth they know what a zine can offer. This is why Nicole Boivins feels that those on the low end of the academic totem pole (graduate students, young researchers and the like), "who have the least vested interest in maintaining the status quo," are the most likely to make archaeology and archaeological writing interesting.

YOUTH

In the end, a lot of what *Shovel Bum* is able to do is connected to youth. Its writers can discuss the way archaeology functions and look critically at what they're doing because they're new enough to the field to still compare it to what they've done before. They're close enough to being—if not still are—students and therefore they're practiced at asking "why?" Shovel bums are open to building a network with each other because they know what it's like to be excluded from decision making and the means of production. They know what mainstream domination means and respect the ability

stage."[65] Her work shows that zines can make things relevant and make things happen for a young generation.[66] Julie Chu perceptively asks not how people can dictate to the next generation, but, "how *we* can involve *ourselves* in the projects young people are initiating on their own."[67]

But labeling *Shovel Bum*, or any other zine, as simply a product of youth is too dismissive. I've heard people write off *Shovel Bum* as a graduate school lark. I've heard them imply that comics and humor are not what professionals do. This type of criticism is blindly dismissive. It's the kind of trivialization of any writing not expressively dry and detached that Dr. Jeremy Sabloff sees as squashing archaeology's ability to thrive.[68] Sabloff has been the editor of a peer-reviewed, traditional journal and has served on many tenure committees; and he notes that too many of these established academic mechanisms are far too dismissive of alternative paths of communication that occasionally reach broad audiences.[69] It's true that Trent "T-Bone" de Boer, along with many other contributors, was in graduate school when *Shovel Bum* got underway. But that was nearly eight years ago. Today, Trent is a supervising archaeologist for the State of Washington with a Master's degree and years of experience in a field in which few last beyond their second season. Other contributors hold doctorates and professorships at a flagship state university. I bring these facts up not to brag about accomplishments, but to point out that contributions to *Shovel Bum* are still arriving when all oould have easily moved on to more familiar academic writing. The zine still feels worthwhile. Professor Stephen Duncombe may explain some of this sentiment when he notes that:

> The reality of work in a capitalist society may be dispiriting, but people are not so easily dispirited. Between the cracks of the system new—and very old—ideas and ideals of what work should be emerge. Zines are a medium through which to express these new ideals but, more important, they are actual embodiments of a type of work and creation that runs counter to the norm within our capitalist society.[70]

These are pretty high ideals to live up to. But the stories of how the past is uncovered, and the stories of those who do the work, are too important to neglect.

Acknowledgement: I would like to acknowledge the valuable assistance of Todd Lovata and Trent de Boer in the preparation of this text.

1. The comic/zine by this title. - Ed.

2. P. J. Watson, "A Parochial Primer: The New Dissonance as Seen From the Midcontinental United States." In *Processual and Postprocessual Archaeologies: Multiple Ways of Knowing the Past*, Robert W. Preucel, ed. Center for Archaeological Investigations, Southern Illinois University at Carbondale, 1991. p. 273.

3. Mike Gunderloy and Janice C. Goldberg, *The World of Zines: A Guide to the Independent Magazine Revolution*. New York: Penguin Books, 1992. p. 2.

4. F. A. Wright, *From Zines to Ezines: Electronic Publishing and the Literary Underground*. Doctoral Dissertation in the Department of English. Ohio: Kent State University, 1991. p. 41.

5. Phil Stoneman, *Fanzines: Their Production, Culture and Future*. Master's Thesis in Publishing Studies, University of Stirling, Scotland, 1991. p. 24.

6. Stephen Duncombe, *Notes From Underground: Zines and the Politics of Alternative Culture*. London: Verso, 1997. p. 40.

7. Chris Dodge, "Zines and Libraries: Pushing the Boundaries." *Wilson Library Bulletin*, 1995. 69(9):26-30. p. 27.

8. Ibid., p. 26.

9. Duncombe, pp. 9-10.

10. Ibid., p. 10.

11. Stoneman, p. 34.

12. Wright, p. 48.

13. Duncombe, pp. 73-74.

14. Ibid., p. 74.

15. Ibid.

16. S. A. Russell, *When the Land Was Young: Reflections on American Archaeology*. Lincoln: University of Nebraska Press, 1996. p. 130-131.

17. Ian Hodder, *Theory and Practice in Archaeology*. London: Routledge, 1995. p. 264-265.

18. Ibid., p. 268.

19. Nicole Boivin, "Insidious or Just Boring? An Examination of Academic Writing in *Archaeology*." *Archaeological Review From Cambridge*, 1997. 14(2):105-125. p. 105.

20. Hodder, p. 269.

21. Chris Stevens, "Is Academic Archaeological Writing Boring? Maybe. Uninteresting? Never." *Archaeological Review From Cambridge*, 1997. 14(2):127–140. p. 130–132.

22. Hodder, p. 264-265.

23. Jeremy Sabloff, "Distinguished Lecture in Archaeology: Communication and the Future of American Archaeology." *American Anthropologist*, 1999. 100(4):869–875. p. 871.

24. Hodder, p. 269.

25. Ibid., p. 263, 267.

26. Ibid., p. 265.

27. Duncombe, p. 10.

28. J. P. Bushnell, *Shovel Bum* #3. Invisible City Productions, Zine Reviews, February 2000. www.invisible-city.com/zines/reviews200.htm#shove3

29. S. L. Black, "(Texas) Archaeology 1995." *Bulletin of the Texas Archeological Society*, 1995. 66:17-45.

30. S. James, "'But Seriously Though, Folks' Humor, Archeology and Communication: The View From the Trenches," *Archaeological Review From Cambridge*, 1997. 11(2):299-309. p. 306.

31. Sabloff, p. 873.

32. Peter Young, "The Archaeologist as Storyteller," in *Public Benefits of Archeology*. Barbara Little, ed. Gainesville: University Press of Florida, 2002. p. 240.

33. D. A. Poirier and K. L. Feder, "Sharing the Past With the Present." *CRM*, 1995. 18(3):3-4. p. 4.

34. K. W. Kintigh, "SAA Principles of Archaeological Ethics." *SAA Bulletin*, 1996. 14(3):5. p. 17.

35. Carol Carnett, *Legal Background of Archaeological Resources Protection*. Technical Brief No. 11, U.S. Department of the Interior, National Park Service, Washington, D.C. 1991. p. 11.

36. Barbara Bender, *Stonehenge: Making Space*. Oxford: Berg, 1998. p. 64.

37. Kenneth Feder, "Cult Archaeology and Creationism: A Coordinated Research Project." In *Cult Archaeology and Creationism*. F. B. Harrold and R. A. Eve, eds., Iowa City: University of Iowa Press, 1995; T. R. Lovata and A. V. Benitez, "Does Anyone Really Know What You're Up To?: An Archaeological Survey." Presented at the 64th Annual Meeting of the Society for American Archaeology, Chicago, March 29, 1999; David Pokotyol and Neil Guppy, "Public Opinion and Archaeological Heritage: Views From Outside the Profession." *American Antiquity*, 1999. 64(3):400-416.

38. Steven Williams, "Fantastic Archaeology: What Should We Do About It?" in *Cult Archaeology and Creationism*, F. B. Harrold and R. A. Eve, eds. Iowa City: University of Iowa Press, 1987. p. 131.

39. William D. Lipe, "Public Benefits of Archaeological Research." In *Public Benefits of Archeology*. Barbara Little, ed., Gainesville: University Press of Florida, 2002. p. 20.

40. Francis P. McManamon, "Why Consult?" *Common Ground*, Summer/Fall 1992. p. 2.

41. Kintigh, p. 17.

42. Lipe, p. 24.

43. William H. Stiebing, Jr., "The Nature and Dangers of Cult Archaeology." In *Cult Archaeology and Creationism*, F. B. Harrold and R. A. Eve, editors. Iowa City: University of Iowa Press, 1997. p. 9.

44. Boivin, p. 110.

45. Young, p. 240.

46. Ibid., p. 242.

47. Bushnell.

48. Stevens, pp. 130, 137.

49. Sabloff, pp. 869, 873.

50. Lipe, pp. 24, 26.

51. Stiebing, pp. 8-9.

52. M. Warburton and P. J. Duke, "Projectile Points as Cultural Symbols." In *Beyond Subsistence: Plains Archaeology and the Post-Processual Critique*. P. G. Duke, ed. Tuscaloosa: University of Alabama Press, 1995. pp. 211-213.

53. Stephen Greenblatt, *Marvelous Possessions: The Wonder of the New World*. Chicago: University of Chicago Press, 1992. pp. 6-7.

54. Stephanie Moser, *Ancestral Images*. Ithaca: Cornell University Press, 1998. p. 18.

55. Simon James, "Drawing Inferences: Visual Reconstructions in Theory and Practice." In *The Cultural Life of Images*. B. L. Molyneaux, ed. London: Routledge, 1997. p. 34.

56. Mitch Allen, "Field Guide to Archaeological Publishing." *The SAA Archaeological Record*, 2003. 3(1):5-6. p. 6.

57. R. Bradley, "To See is to Have Seen." In Molyneaux, p. 62.

58. Molyneaux, p. 6-7.

59. T. R. Lovata, *An Exploration of Archaeological Representation: People and the Domestic Dog on the Great Plains of North America*. Doctoral Dissertation in the Department of Anthropology, University of Texas, Austin, 2000. p. 7-8.

60. B. Sillar, "Digging for a Laugh: Archaeology and Humor." *Archaeological Review From Cambridge*, 1992. 11(2):203-211. p. 209-210.

61. P. Rahtz and I. Burrows, "Archaeology is Too Important a Subject Not to be Joked About," *Archaeological Review From Cambridge*, 1992. 11(2):373-387. p. 373.

62. Sillar, p. 205-206.

63. Stiebing, p. 4-6.

64. Boivin, p. 15.

65. Julie Chu, "Navigating the Media Environment: How Youth Claim a Place Through Zines," *Social Justice*, 1997. 24(3):71-85. p. 83.

66. Ibid., pp. 77-78.

67. Ibid., pp. 82-83.

68. Sabloff, p. 874.

69. Ibid., pp. 873-874.

70. Duncombe, p. 94.

Will Hart

ARCHAEOLOGICAL COVER-UPS:

A PLOT TO CONTROL HISTORY?

The scientific establishment tends to reject, suppress or ignore evidence that conflicts with accepted theories, while denigrating or persecuting the messenger.

THE BRAIN POLICE AND THE BIG LIE

Any time you allege that a conspiracy is afoot, especially in the field of science, you are treading thin ice. We tend to be very skeptical about conspiracies—unless the Mafia or some Muslim radicals are behind the alleged plot. But the evidence is overwhelming and the irony is that much of it is in plain view.

The good news is that the players are obvious. Their game plan and even their play-by-play tactics are transparent, once you learn to spot them. However, it is not so easy to penetrate through the smokescreen of propaganda and disinformation to get to their underlying motives and goals. It would be convenient if we could point to a plumber's unit and a bald-faced liar like Richard Nixon, but this is a more subtle operation.

The bad news: The conspiracy is global, and there are many vested interest groups. A cursory investigation yields the usual suspects—scientists with a theoretical axe to grind, careers to further and a status quo to maintain. Their modus operandi is "The Big Lie"—and the bigger and more widely publicized, the better. They rely on invoking their academic credentials to support their arguments, and the presumption is that no one has the right to question their authoritarian pronouncements that:

1. There is no mystery about who built the Great Pyramid or what the methods of construction were, and the Sphinx shows no signs of water damage;

2. There were no humans in the Americas before 20,000 B.C.;

3. The first civilization dates back no further than 6000 B.C.;

4. There are no documented anomalous, unexplained or enigmatic data to take into account;

5. There are no lost or unaccounted-for civilizations.

Let the evidence to the contrary be damned!

PERSONAL ATTACKS: DISPUTE OVER AGE OF THE SPHINX AND GREAT PYRAMID

In 1993, NBC in the USA aired *The Mysteries of the Sphinx*, which presented geological evidence showing that the Sphinx was at least twice as old (9,000 years) as Egyptologists claimed. It has become well known as the "water erosion controversy." An examination of the politicking that Egyptologists deployed to combat this undermining of their turf is instructive.

> **That was a curious accusation that took the matter off the professional level and put the whole affair on a personal plane. It did not address the facts or issues at all, and was highly unscientific.**

Self-taught Egyptologist John Anthony West brought the water erosion issue to the attention of geologist Dr. Robert Schoch. They went to Egypt and launched an intensive on-site investigation. After thoroughly studying the Sphinx first hand, the geologist came to share West's preliminary conclusion and they announced their findings.

Dr. Zahi Hawass, the Giza Monuments chief, wasted no time in firing a barrage of public criticism at the pair. Renowned Egyptologist Dr. Mark Lehner, who is regarded as the world's foremost expert on the Sphinx, joined his attack. He charged West and Schoch with being "ignorant and insensitive." That was a curious accusation that took the matter off the professional level and put the whole affair on a personal plane. It did not address the facts or issues at all, and was highly unscientific.

But we must note the standard tactic of discrediting anyone who dares to call the accepted theories into question. Shifting the focus away from the issues and "personalizing" the debate is a highly effective strategy—one which is often used by politicians who feel insecure about their positions. Hawass and Lehner invoked their untouchable status and presumed authority. (One would think that a geologist's assessment would hold more weight on this particular point.)

> *Science is a method that anyone can learn and apply. It does not require a degree to observe and record facts and think critically about them, especially in the non-technical social sciences. In a free and open society, science has to be a democratic process.*

A short time later, Schoch, Hawass and Lehner were invited to debate the issue at the American Association for the Advancement of Science. West was not allowed to participate because he lacked the required credentials.

This points to a questionable assumption that is part of the establishment's arsenal: Only degreed scientists can practice science. Two filters keep the uncredentialed, independent researcher out of the loop: credentials and peer review. You do not get to the second unless you have the first.

Science is a method that anyone can learn and apply. It does not require a degree to observe and record facts and think critically about them, especially in the non-technical social sciences. In a free and open society, science has to be a democratic process.

Be that as it may, West was barred. The elements of the debate have been batted back and forth since then, without resolution. It is similar to the controversy over who built the Giza pyramids and how.

This brings up the issue of the Big Lie and how it has been promoted for generations in front of God and everyone. The controversy over how the Great Pyramid was constructed is one example. It could be easily settled if Egyptologists wanted to resolve the dispute. A simple test could be designed and arranged by impartial engineers that would either prove or disprove their long-standing disputed theory—that it was built using the primitive tools and methods of the day, circa 2500 B.C.

Why hasn't this been done? The answer is so obvious, it seems impossible: They know that the theory is bogus. Could a trained, highly educated scientist really believe that 2.3 million tons of stone, some blocks weighing 70 tons, could have been transported and lifted by primitive methods? That seems improbable, though they have no compunction against lying to the public, writing textbooks and defending this theory against alternative theories. However, we

All that Egyptologists have ever done is bat down alternative theories using underhanded tactics. It is time to insist that they prove their own proposals.

must note that they will not subject themselves to the bottom-line test.

We think it is incumbent upon any scientist to bear the burden of proof of his/her thesis; however, the social scientists who make these claims have never stood up to that kind of scrutiny. That is why we must suspect a conspiracy. No other scientific discipline would get away with bending the rules of science. All that Egyptologists have ever done is bat down alternative theories using underhanded tactics. It is time to insist that they prove their own proposals.

PRESSURE TACTICS: THE ICA STONES OF PERU

Now we turn to another, very different case. In 1966, Dr. Javier Cabrera received a stone as a gift from a poor local farmer in his native Ica, Peru. A fish was carved on the stone, which would not have meant much to the average villager, but did mean a lot to the educated Dr. Cabrera. He recognized it as a long-extinct species. This aroused his curiosity. He purchased more stones from the farmer, who said he had collected them near the river after a flood.

Dr. Cabrera accumulated more and more stones, and word of their existence and potential import reached the archaeological community. Soon, the doctor had amassed thousands of "Ica stones." The sophisticated carvings were as enigmatic as they were fascinating. Someone

Someone had carved men fighting with dinosaurs, men with telescopes and men performing operations with surgical equipment. They also contained drawings of lost continents.

Why would scientists try to hide the truth and avoid any test of their hypotheses? Their motivations are equally transparent. If it can be proved that the Egyptians did not build the Great Pyramid in 2500 B.C. using primitive methods, or if the Sphinx can be dated to 9000 B.C., the whole house of cards comes tumbling down. Orthodox views of cultural evolution are based upon a chronology of civilization having started in Sumeria no earlier than 4000 B.C. The theory does not permit an advanced civilization to have existed prior to that time. End of discussion. Archaeology and history lose their meaning without a fixed timeline as a point of reference.

Since the theory of "cultural evolution" has been tied to Darwin's general theory of evolution, even more is at stake. Does this explain why facts, anomalies and enigmas are denied, suppressed and/or ignored? Yes, it does. The biological sciences today are based on Darwinism.

had carved men fighting with dinosaurs, men with telescopes and men performing operations with surgical equipment. They also contained drawings of lost continents.

Several of the stones were sent to Germany and the etchings were dated to remote antiquity. But we all know that men could not have lived at the time of dinosaurs; *Homo sapiens* has only existed for about 100,000 years.

The BBC got wind of this discovery and swooped down to produce a documentary about the Ica stones. The media exposure ignited a storm of controversy. Archaeologists criticized the Peruvian government for being lax about enforcing antiquities laws (but that was not their real concern). Pressure was applied to government officials.

The farmer who had been selling the stones to Cabrera was arrested; he claimed to have found them in a cave but refused to disclose the exact location to authorities, or so they claimed.

This case was disposed of so artfully that it would do any corrupt politician proud. The Peruvian government threatened to prosecute and imprison the farmer. He was offered, and accepted, a plea bargain; he then recanted his story and "admitted" to having carved the stones himself. That seems highly implausible, since he was uneducated and unskilled and there were 11,000 stones in all. Some were fairly large and intricately carved with animals and scenes that the farmer would not have had knowledge of without being a paleontologist. He would have needed to work every day for several decades to produce that volume of stones. However, the underlying facts were neither here nor there. The Ica stones were labeled "hoax" and forgotten.

The case did not require a head-to-head confrontation or public discrediting of non-scientists by scientists; it was taken care of with invisible pressure tactics. Since it was filed under "hoax," the enigmatic evidence never had to be dealt with, as it did in the next example.

scientific community went off the Richter scale. NBC was deluged with letters from irate scientists who called the producer "a fraud" and the whole program "a hoax."

But the scientists went further than this—a lot further. In an extremely unconscionable sequence of bizarre moves, they tried to force NBC not to rebroadcast the popular program, but that effort failed. Then they took the most radical step of all: They presented their case to the federal government and requested the Federal Communications Commission to step in and bar NBC from airing the program again.

This was not only an apparent infringement of free speech and a blatant attempt to thwart commerce, it was an unprecedented effort to censor intellectual discourse. If the public or any government agency made an attempt to handcuff the scientific establishment, the public would never hear the end of it.

The letter to the FCC written by Dr. Allison Palmer, president of the Institute for Cambrian Studies, is revealing:

We have no idea how many enigmatic artifacts or dates have been labeled "error" and tucked away in storage warehouses or circular files, never to see the light of day.

CENSORSHIP OF "FORBIDDEN" THINKING: EVIDENCE FOR MANKIND'S GREAT ANTIQUITY

The case of author Michael Cremo is well documented, and it also demonstrates how the scientific establishment openly uses pressure tactics on the media and government. His book *Forbidden Archeology* examines many previously ignored examples of artifacts that prove modern man's antiquity far exceeds the age given in accepted chronologies.[1]

The examples which he and his co-author present are controversial, but the book became far more controversial than the contents when it was used in a documentary.

In 1996, NBC broadcast a special called *The Mysterious Origins of Man*, which featured material from Cremo's book. The reaction from the

At the very least, NBC should be required to make substantial prime-time apologies to their viewing audience for a sufficient period of time so that the audience clearly gets the message that they were duped. In addition, NBC should perhaps be fined sufficiently so that a major fund for public science education can be established.

I think we have some good leads on who the "Brain Police" are. And I really do not think "conspiracy" is too strong a word—because for every case of this kind of attempted suppression that is exposed, ten others are going on successfully. We have no idea how many enigmatic artifacts or dates have been labeled "error" and tucked away in storage warehouses or circular files, never to see the light of day.

The problem for researchers concerned with establishing humanity's true history is that the goals of nationalists or ethnic groups who want to lay claim to having been in a particular place first, often dovetail with the goals of cultural evolutionists.

DATA REJECTION: INCONVENIENT DATING IN MEXICO

Then there is the high-profile case of Dr. Virginia Steen-McIntyre, a geologist working for the U.S. Geological Survey (USGS), who was dispatched to an archaeological site in Mexico to date a group of artifacts in the 1970s. This travesty also illustrates how far established scientists will go to guard orthodox tenets.

McIntyre used state-of-the-art equipment and backed up her results by using four different methods, but her results were off the chart. The lead archaeologist expected a date of 25,000 years or less, and the geologist's finding was 250,000 years or more.

The figure of 25,000 years or less was critical to the Bering Strait "crossing" theory, and it was the motivation behind the head archaeologist's tossing Steen-McIntyre's results in the circular file and asking for a new series of dating tests. This sort of reaction does not occur when dates match the expected chronological model that supports accepted theories.

Steen-McIntyre was given a chance to retract her conclusions, but she refused. She found it hard thereafter to get her papers published, and she lost a teaching job at an American university.

GOVERNMENT SUPPRESSION AND ETHNOCENTRISM: AVOIDING ANOMALOUS EVIDENCE IN NZ, CHINA AND MEXICO

In New Zealand, the government actually stepped in and enacted a law forbidding the public from entering a controversial archaeological zone. This story appeared in the book *Ancient Celtic New Zealand*, by Mark Doutré.

However, as we will find (and as I promised at the beginning of the article), this is a complicated conspiracy. Scientists trying to protect their "hallowed" theories while furthering their careers are not the only ones who want artifacts and data suppressed. This is where the situation gets sticky.

The Waipoua Forest became a controversial site in New Zealand because an archaeological dig apparently showed evidence of a non-Polynesian culture that preceded the Maori—a fact that the tribe was not happy with. They learned of the results of the excavations before the general public did, and complained to the government. According to Doutré, the outcome was "an official archival document, which clearly showed an intention by New Zealand government departments to withhold archaeological information from public scrutiny for 75 years."

The public got wind of this fiasco, but the government denied the claim. However, official documents show that an embargo had been placed on the site. Doutré is a student of New Zealand history and archaeology. He is concerned because he says that artifacts proving that there was an earlier culture which preceded the Maori are missing from museums. He asks what happened to several anomalous remains:

> Where are the ancient Indo-European hair samples (wavy red brown hair), originally obtained from a rock shelter near Watakere, that were on display at the Auckland War Memorial Museum for many years? Where is the giant skeleton found near Mitimati?

Unfortunately this is not the only such incident. Ethnocentrism has become a factor in the conspiracy to hide mankind's true history. Author Graham Hancock has been attacked by various ethnic groups for reporting similar enigmatic findings.

The problem for researchers concerned with establishing humanity's true history is that the goals of nationalists or ethnic groups who want to lay claim to having been in a particular place first, often dovetail with the goals of cultural evolutionists.

Archaeologists are quick to go along with suppressing these kinds of anomalous finds. One reason Egyptologists so jealously guard the Great Pyramid's construction date has to do with the issue of national pride.

The case of the Takla Makan Desert mummies in western China is another example of this phenomenon. In the 1970s and 1980s, an unaccounted-for Caucasian culture was suddenly unearthed in China. The arid environment preserved the remains of a blond-haired, blue-eyed people who lived in pre-dynastic China. They wore colorful robes, boots, stockings and hats. The Chinese were not happy about this revelation and they have downplayed the enigmatic find, even though Asians were found buried alongside the Caucasian mummies.

National Geographic writer Thomas B. Allen mused in a 1996 article about his finding a potsherd bearing a fingerprint of the potter. When he inquired if he could take the fragment to a forensic anthropologist, the Chinese scientist asked whether he "would be able to tell if the potter was a white man." Allen said he was not sure, and the official pocketed the fragment and quietly walked away. It appears that many things get in the way of scientific discovery and disclosure.

The existence of the Olmec culture in Old Mexico has always posed a problem. Where did the Negroid people depicted on the colossal heads come from? Why are there Caucasians carved on the stele in what is Mexico's seed civilization? What is worse, why aren't the indigenous Mexican people found on the Olmec artifacts? Recently a Mexican archaeologist solved the problem by making a fantastic claim: that the Olmec heads—which generations of people of all ethnic groups have agreed bear a striking resemblance to Africans— were really representations of the local tribe.

STORMTROOPERS FOR DARWINISM

The public does not seem at all aware of the fact that the scientific establishment has a double standard when it comes to the free flow of information. In essence, it goes like this: Scientists are highly educated, well trained and intellectually capable of processing all types of information, and they can make the correct critical distinctions between fact and fiction, reality and fantasy. The unwashed public is simply incapable of functioning on this high mental plane.

The noble ideal of the scientist as a highly trained, impartial, apolitical observer and assembler of established facts into a useful body of knowledge seems to have been shredded under the pressures and demands of the real world. Science has produced many positive benefits for society; but we should know by now that science has a dark, negative side. Didn't those meek fellows in the clean lab coats give us nuclear bombs and biological weapons? The age of innocence ended in World War II.

That the scientific community has an attitude of intellectual superiority is thinly veiled under a carefully orchestrated public relations guise. We always see Science and Progress walking hand in hand. Science as an institution in a democratic society has to function in the same way as the society at large; it should be open to debate, argument and counter-argument. There is no place for unquestioned authoritarianism. Is modern science meeting these standards?

In the fall of 2001, PBS aired a seven-part series titled *Evolution*. Taken at face value, that seems harmless enough. However, while the program was presented as pure, objective, investigative science journalism, it completely failed to meet even minimum standards of impartial reporting. The series was heavily weighted towards the view that the theory of evolution is "a science fact" that is accepted by "virtually all reputable scientists in the world," and not a theory that has weaknesses and strong scientific critics.

The series did not even bother to interview scientists who have criticisms of Darwinism: not "creationists" but bona fide scientists. To correct this deficiency, a group of 100 dissenting scientists felt compelled to issue a press release, "A Scientific Dissent on Darwinism," on the day the first program was scheduled to go to air. Nobel nominee Henry "Fritz" Schaefer was among them. He encouraged open public debate of Darwin's theory.

> **Darwin's theory of evolution is the only theory routinely taught in our public school system that has never been subjected to rigorous scrutiny; nor have any of the criticisms been allowed into the curriculum.**

Some defenders of Darwinism embrace standards of evidence for evolution that as scientists they would never accept in other circumstances.

We have seen this same "unscientific" approach applied to archaeology and anthropology, where "scientists" simply refuse to prove their theories, yet appoint themselves as the final arbiters of "the facts." It would be naïve to think that the scientists who cooperated in the production of the series were unaware that there would be no counter-balancing presentation by critics of Darwin's theory.

Richard Milton is a science journalist. He had been an ardent true believer in Darwinian doctrine until his investigative instincts kicked in one day. After 20 years of studying and writing about evolution, he suddenly realized that there were many disconcerting holes in the theory. He decided to try to allay his doubts and prove the theory to himself by using the standard methods of investigative journalism.

Milton became a regular visitor to London's famed Natural History Museum. He painstakingly put every main tenet and classic proof of Darwinism to the test. The results shocked him. He found that the theory could not even stand up to the rigors of routine investigative journalism.

The veteran science writer took a bold step and published a book titled *The Facts of Life: Shattering the Myths of Darwinism*. It is clear that the Darwinian myth had been shattered for him, but many more myths about science would also be crushed after his book came out. Milton says:

> I experienced the witch-hunting activity of the Darwinist police at first hand—it was deeply disappointing to find myself being described by a prominent Oxford zoologist [Richard Dawkins] as "loony," "stupid" and "in need of psychiatric help" in response to purely scientific reporting.

(Does this sound like stories that came out of the Soviet Union 20 years ago when dissident scientists there started speaking out?)

Dawkins launched a letter-writing campaign to newspaper editors, implying that Milton was a "mole" creationist whose work should be dismissed. Anyone at all familiar with politics will recognize this as a by-the-book Machiavellian "character assassination" tactic. Dawkins is a highly respected scientist, whose reputation and standing in the scientific community carries a great deal of weight.

According to Milton, the process came to a head when the *London Times Higher Education Supplement* commissioned him to write a critique of Darwinism. The publication foreshadowed his coming piece: "Next Week: Darwinism—Richard Milton goes on the attack." Dawkins caught wind of this and wasted no time in nipping this heresy in the bud. He contacted the editor, Auriol Stevens, accused Milton of being a "creationist," and prevailed upon Stevens to pull the plug on the article. Milton learned of this behind-the-scenes backstabbing and wrote a letter of appeal to Stevens. In the end, she caved in to Dawkins and scratched the piece.

Imagine what would happen if a politician or bureaucrat used such pressure tactics to kill a story in the mass media. It would ignite a huge scandal. Not so with scientists, who seem to be regarded as "sacred cows" and beyond reproach. There are many disturbing facts related to these cases. Darwin's theory of evolution is the only theory routinely taught in our public school system that has never been subjected to rigorous scrutiny; nor have any of the criticisms been allowed into the curriculum.

This is an interesting fact, because a recent poll showed that the American public wants the theory of evolution taught to their children; however, "71 percent of the respondents say biology

We outlined some of those taboo subjects at the beginning of the article; now we should add that it is also "unwholesome" and "unacceptable" to engage in any of the following research pursuits: paranormal phenomena, UFOs, cold fusion, free energy and all the rest of the "pseudo-sciences."

teachers should teach both Darwinism and scientific evidence against Darwinian theory." Nevertheless, there are no plans to implement this balanced approach.

It is ironic that Richard Dawkins has been appointed to the position of professor of the public understanding of science at Oxford University. He is a classic "Brain Police" stormtrooper, patrolling the neurological front lines. The Western scientific establishment and mass media pride themselves on being open public forums devoid of prejudice or censorship. However, no television program examining the flaws and weaknesses of Darwinism has ever been aired in Darwin's home country or in America. A scientist who opposes the theory cannot get a paper published.

The Mysterious Origins of Man was not a frontal attack on Darwinism; it merely presented evidence that is considered anomalous by the precepts of Darwin's theory of evolution.

Returning to our bastions of intellectual integrity, Forest Mims was a solid and skilled science journalist. He had never been the center of any controversy, and so was invited to write the most-read column in the prestigious *Scientific American*, "The Amateur Scientist," a task he gladly accepted. According to Mims, the magazine's editor Jonathan Piel then learned that he also wrote articles for a number of Christian magazines. The editor called Mims into his office and confronted him.

"Do you believe in the theory of evolution?" Piel asked.

Mims replied, "No, and neither does Stephen Jay Gould."

His response did not affect Piel's decision to bump Mims off the popular column after just three articles.

This has the unpleasant odor of a witch-hunt. The writer never publicly broadcast his private views or beliefs, so it would appear that the "stormtroopers" now believe they have orders to make sure "unapproved" thoughts are never publicly disclosed.

TABOO OR NOT TABOO?

So, the monitors of "good thinking" are not just the elite of the scientific community, as we have seen in several cases; they are television producers and magazine editors as well. It seems clear that they are all driven by the singular imperative of furthering "public science education," as the president of the Cambrian Institute so aptly phrased it.

However, there is a second item on the agenda, and that is to protect the public from "unscientific" thoughts and ideas that might infect the mass mind. We outlined some of those taboo subjects at the beginning of the article; now we should add that it is also "unwholesome" and "unacceptable" to engage in any of the following research pursuits: paranormal phenomena, UFOs, cold fusion, free energy and all the rest of the "pseudo-sciences." Does this have a familiar ring to it? Are we hearing the faint echoes of religious zealotry?

Who gave science the mission of engineering and directing the inquisitive pursuits of the citizenry of the free world? It is all but impossible for any scientific paper that has anti-Darwinian ramifications to be published in a mainstream scientific journal. It is also just as impossible to get the "taboo" subjects even to the review table, and you can forget about finding your name under the title of any article in *Nature* unless you are a credentialed scientist, even if you are the next Albert Einstein.

To restate how this conspiracy begins, it is with two filters: credentials and peer review. Modern science is now a maze of such filters set up to promote certain orthodox theories and at the same time filter out that data already prejudged to be unacceptable. Evidence and merit are not the guiding principles; conformity and position within the established community have replaced objectivity, access and openness.

Modern science is now a maze of such filters set up to promote certain orthodox theories and at the same time filter out that data already prejudged to be unacceptable.

Scientists do not hesitate to launch the most outrageous personal attacks against those they perceive to be the enemy. Eminent paleontologist Louis Leakey penned this acid one-liner about *Forbidden Archeology*: "Your book is pure humbug and does not deserve to be taken seriously by anyone but a fool." Once again, we see the thrust of a personal attack; the merits of the evidence presented in the book are not examined or debated. It is a blunt, authoritarian pronouncement.

---

1. See Michael Cremo's article *Human Devolution* in this volume.—Ed.

7

RESOURCES

Preston Peet

EDITOR'S NOTE

THIS BOOK HAS BROUGHT together many of the leading voices engaged in theorizing and speculating about our ancient history and pre-history. It is hoped that you, the reader, will be inspired to do further reading on your own, to seek out alternative explanations and ideas about who we human beings are and where we came from. It's important to understand that there are little to no set facts about our past. There are as many unanswered questions about human beginnings and our becoming the social, culture-building and destroying beings we are today, with some cultures thriving and some expiring along the way, as there are theories to explain them.

That being said, there are new discoveries made every day that do appear to lead to solid, incontrovertible answers about our past, answers that seem obvious and confirmed today but might very well be disproved again tomorrow by some new astonishing discovery or archaeological find. Each day new voices and new theories are added to the mix, new researchers, philosophers, explorers, archaeologists, anthropologists, theologians, shovel bums and outright wackos and weirdos too, all proposing their own interpretations of the evidence at hand. All are busy studying, figuring, analyzing, digging and, most importantly for this discussion, almost all of them are writing too. They write and they publish, whether it be in glossy, hardcover coffee-table books about *the greatest* archaeological finds ever, published by mainstream corporations, or eccentric alternative viewpoints about ancient high technologies and sunken worlds—including Atlantis, oft-scoffed at, but searched for nonetheless, by countless respectable men and women throughout the past—published through private vanity presses or small alternative publishing houses. The paradigm concerning our past is always shifting, is never stagnant—over time any radical new and immediately ridiculed idea might become the standard of the day.

With this in mind, I've put to paper a selection of titles from my own library of books and magazines (along with a few of my favorite Web sites too), about ancient civilizations, astonishing archaeology and hidden history, a short list of resources for readers to search out once finished with the selection of articles contained within *Underground!—The Disinformation Guide to Ancient Civilizations, Astonishing Archaeology and Hidden History*. There are plenty of blank spaces still left on maps of the planet earth (as explorer Greg Deyermenjian told me when I interviewed him about his past and future expeditions in Peru), vast areas remote, uninhabited and unexplored, regions where there may be lost cities or ancient civilizations' foundations waiting to be found which will give us the definitive answers to our questions about who we are and why we are here.

The following writers and researchers have attempted to fill in some of those blank spaces with what they feel is the truth, or at least, the most likely version of what they think might be the truth. Many of them have contributed work to this anthology. Right or wrong, they are all thought-provoking and will lead the reader on one adventure after another through the history of our species. Ask your favorite bookseller for these authors and titles (or go online and search out their books and visit the few Web sites included here). This is by no means a comprehensive list of all the writers and all the books and other sources that deal with our ancient and shrouded past (nor are all the books written by each writer listed here necessarily represented—most have written many more books than could possibly be listed in the space I have here) but it's a good start for those readers interested in more than pat explanations that deny and rob us much of any mystery or spice about our distant past, our mysterious origins and beginnings, our development and the extensive, enigmatic traces left behind by our so-called "primitive" ancestors.

BOOKS

Paul G. Bahn, ed., *100 Great Archaeological Discoveries*. New York: Barnes and Noble Books, 1995.

Robert Bauval and Adrian Gilbert, *The Orion Mystery: Unlocking The Secrets Of The Pyramids*. New York: Crown Publishers Inc., 1994.

Trent de Boer, *Shovel Bum: Comix Of Archaeological Field Life*. Walnut Creek: AltaMira, 2004.

Colonel Alexander Braghine, *The Shadow Of Atlantis*. Kempton: Adventures Unlimited Press, 1997.

John G. Burke, *Cosmic Debris: Meteorites In History*. Berkeley: University of California Press, 1986.

David Hatcher Childress, *Lost Cities of China, Central Asia and India*. Kempton: Adventures Unlimited Press, 1985.
Lost Cities and Ancient Mysteries of South America. Kempton: Adventures Unlimited Press, 1986.
Lost Cities of Ancient Lemuria and the Pacific. Kempton: Adventures Unlimited Press, 1988.
Lost Cities and Ancient Mysteries of Africa and Arabia. Kempton: Adventures Unlimited Press, 1989.
Lost Cities of North and Central America. Kempton: Adventures Unlimited Press, 1992.
Lost Cities of Atlantis, Ancient Europe, and the Mediterranean. Kempton: Adventures Unlimited Press, 1996.
Far Out Adventures: The Best Of World Explorer Magazine. Kempton: Adventures Unlimited Press, 1997.

Barbara Hand Clow, *Catastrophobia: The Truth Behind Earth Changes in the Coming Age of Light*. Rochester: Bear and Company, 2001.

William R. Corliss, *Ancient Man: A Handbook of Puzzling Artifacts*. Glen Arm: The Sourcebook Project, 1978.
Ancient Infrastructure: Remarkable Roads, Mines, Walls, Mounds, Stone Circles—A Catalog of Archeological Anomalies. Glen Arm: The Sourcebook Project, 1999.
Archeological Anomalies: Small Artifacts, Bone, Stone, Metal Artifacts, Footprints, High Technology—A Catalog of Archeological Anomalies. Glen Arm: The Sourcebook Project, 2003.

Michael A. Cremo and Richard L. Thompson, *Forbidden Archaeology: The Hidden History of the Human Race*. Los Angeles: Bhaktivedanta Book Publishing, Inc., 1993.
The Hidden History of the Human Race: The Condensed Version of Forbidden Archaeology. Los Angeles: Bhaktivedanta Book Publishing, Inc., 1996.

Joan d'Arc, *Phenomenal World: Remote Viewing, Astral Travel, Apparitions, Extraterrestrials, Lucid Dreams and Other Forms of Intelligent Contact in the Magical Kingdom of Mind-at-Large*. Escondido: The Book Tree, 2000.

Mike Dash, *Borderlands: The Ultimate Exploration of the Unknown*. Woodstock: Overlook Press, 1999.

L. Sprague De Camp and Willy Ley, *Lands Beyond: A Fascinating Expedition Into Unknown Lands*. New York: Rinehart & Co, 1952.

Christopher Dunn, *The Giza Power Plant: Technologies of Ancient Egypt*. Rochester: Bear and Company, 1998.

George Erikson and Ivar Zapp, *Atlantis in America: Navigators of the Ancient World*. Kempton: Adventures Unlimited Press, 1998.

Brian Fagan, *New Treasures of the Past: New Findings That Deepen Our Understanding Of The Archaeology Of Man*. New York: Barnes and Noble, Inc., 2004.

Rand and Rose Flem-Ath, *When the Sky Fell: In Search of Atlantis*. New York: St. Martin's Press, 1995.

Charles Fort, *The Complete Books of Charles Fort: The Book of the Damned / Lo! / Wild Talents / New Lands*. New York: Dover, 1974.

Neil Freer, *Breaking The Godspell: The Politics Of Our Evolution*. Phoenix: Falcon Press, 1987.

Adrian G. Gilbert and Maurice M. Cotterell, *The Mayan Prophecies*. Shaftesbury: Element, 1995.

Peter Haining, *Ancient Mysteries*. London: Sidgwick & Jackson, 1977.

Graham Hancock, *Fingerprints of the Gods: The Evidence of Earth's Lost Civilization*. New York: Crown Trade Paperbacks, 1995.
    Underworld: The Mysterious Origins of Civilization. New York: Crown Publishers, 2002.

Murry Hope, *The Sirius Connection: Unlocking The Secrets of Ancient Egypt*. Shaftesbury: Element, 1996.

Constance Irwin, *Fair Gods and Stone Faces: Ancient Seafarers and the New World's Most Intriguing Riddle*. New York: St. Martin's Press, 1963.

Peter James and Nick Thorpe, *Ancient Inventions*. New York: The Ballantine Publishing Group, 1996.

Peter James and Nick Thorpe, *Ancient Mysteries*. New York: The Ballantine Publishing Group, 1997.

Kenneth Rayner Johnson, *Armageddon 2000: Countdown to Doomsday?* London: Creation Books, 1995.

Frank Joseph, *The Destruction of Atlantis: Compelling Evidence of the Sudden Fall of the Legendary Civilization*. Rochester: Bear and Company, 2002.
    Survivors of Atlantis: Their Impact on World Culture. Rochester: Bear and Company, 2004.

Christopher Knight and Alan Butler, *Civilization One: The World Is Not as You Thought It Was*. London: Watkins Publishing, 2004.
    and Robert Lomas, *Uriel's Machine: Uncovering the Secrets of Stonehenge, Noah's Flood and the Dawn Of Civilization*. New York: Barnes and Noble, 2004.

Donna Kossy, *Strange Creations: Aberrant Ideas of Human Origins From Ancient Astronauts to Aquatic Apes*. Los Angeles: Feral House, 2001.

Alan and Sally Landsburg, *In Search Of Ancient Mysteries*. New York: Bantam Books, Inc., 1974.
    The Outer Space Connection. New York: Bantam Books, Inc., 1975.

Gregory L. Little, John Van Auken and Lora Little, eds., *Mound Builders: Edgar Cayce's Forgotten Record of Ancient America*. Memphis: Eagle Wing Books, Inc., 2001.

Robert F. Marx with Jennifer G. Marx, *In Search of the Great White Gods: Contact Between the Old and New World From the Dawn Of History*. New York: Crown Publishers Inc., 1992.

Gavin Menzies, *1421: The Year the Chinese Discovered America*. New York: William Morrow, 2003.

Richard W. Noone, *5/5/2000: Ice—The Ultimate Disaster*. New York: Three Rivers Press, 1982.

Stephen Oppenheimer, *Eden in the East*. London: Weidenfeld & Nicolson, 1998.

Dan Russell, *Shamanism and the Drug Propaganda: Patriarchy and the Drug War*. Camden: Kalyx.com, 1998.

Peter Russell, *From Science to God: A Physicist's Journey Into the Mystery of Consciousness*. Novato: New World Library, 2002.

Robert M. Schoch, PhD, with Robert S. McNally, *Voices of the Rocks: A Scientist Looks at Catastrophes and Ancient Civilizations*. New York: Harmony Books, 1999.
    Voyages of the Pyramid Builders: The True Origins of the Pyramids From Lost Egypt to Ancient America. New York: Jeremy P. Tarcher/Penguin, 2003.
    Pyramid Quest: Secrets of the Great Pyramid and the Dawn of Civilization. New York: Jeremy P. Tarcher/Penguin, 2005.

Robert B. Stacy-Judd, *Atlantis: Mother of Empires.* Kempton: Adventures Unlimited Press, 1999.

Robert Temple, *The Sirius Mystery: Was Earth Visited by Intelligent Beings From a Planet in the System of the Star of Sirius?* Rochester: Inner Traditions, 1987.
   Netherworld: Discovering the Oracle of the Dead and Ancient Techniques of Foretelling the Future. London: Arrow, 2003.

Peter Tompkins, *Secrets of the Great Pyramid: The Adventures and Discoveries of the Explorers and Scientists Who, For Two Thousand Years, Have Been Probing the Mystery of the Great Pyramid of Cheops.* New York: Harper Colophon, 1971.
   Mysteries of the Mexican Pyramids. New York Harper & Row, 1976.

Peter Tompkins, *The Magic of Obelisks.* New York: Harper & Row, 1981.

John White, *Pole Shift: Scientific Predictions and Prophecies About the Ultimate Disaster.* Virginia Beach: A.R.E. Press, 1980.

Colin Wilson, *From Atlantis to the Sphinx: Recovering the Lost Wisdom of the Ancient World.* New York: Fromm International Publishing, 1997.
   and Rand Flem-Ath, *The Atlantis Blueprint: Unlocking the Ancient Mysteries of a Long-Lost Civilization.* New York: Delta Trade Paperbacks, 2002.

Damon Wilson, *Lost Worlds: Unlock the Earth's Hidden Secrets.* London: Robinson Publishing Ltd., 1998.

Assorted Contributors, *The Search for Lost Origins.* Livingston: Atlantis Rising Books, 1996.

MAGAZINES

Ancient American: Archaeology of the Americas Before Columbus

Archaeology Magazine: A Publication of the Archaeological Institute of America

Atlantis Rising

Legendary Times: Timeless Mysteries Of The World

National Geographic

World Explorer

WEB SITES

www.legendarytimes.com

www.iwaynet.net/~wdc/home.htm

www.ancientamerican.com

paranormal.about.com/od/ancientanomalies

www.altarcheologie.nl

www.atlantisrising.com

www.catastrophism.com/intro

www.farshores.org

www.mcremo.com

www.forteantimes.com

www.lostartsmedia.com/mysteryofamerica.html

www.lost-civilizations.net

www.morien-institute.org/histchan.html

www.myrine.at/Malta

www.mysteriousworld.com

www.s8int.com

www.pgorman.com

www.sacredsites.com

www.science-frontiers.com

www.world-mysteries.com

ARTICLE HISTORIES

1—"Human Devolution" by Michael A. Cremo is adapted from the introduction to *Human Devolution: A Vedic Alternative to Darwin's Theory*, Torchlight Publishing, Badger, California, 2003.

2—"Consider the Kali Yuga" by John Anthony West was first published in Italian in the Italian Magazine *Hera*, in 2004. It is published for the first time in English in this anthology.

3—"Ocean Origins of Indian Civilization" by N. S. Rajaram was written especially for publication in this anthology.

4—"Deus Noster, Deus Solis: Our God, God of the Sun" by Acharya S was written especially for publication in this anthology.

5—"Mysterious Origins—Are Humans Just a Happy Accident?" by Dave Dentel was written especially for publication in this anthology, developed from two columns Dave Dentel crafted earlier for the daily newspaper where he works, the *York Daily Record/York Sunday News*. Those first two columns commented on a controversy sparked when the school board in Dover, Pennsylvania, voted to include the teaching of Intelligent Design theory in biology class as an alternative to Darwinism. The school board's decision not only provoked a lawsuit by the American Civil Liberties Union, it also garnered international media coverage.

6—"Ancient Walls" by Richard Nisbet is included (in an expanded version) on a CD-ROM that accompanies the book *Cusco Tales*, also by Richard Nisbet, published by PH Publishing, 1993.

7—"Along the 33rd Degree Parallel: A Global Mystery Circle" by Gary A. David is published for the first time in this anthology.

8—"Did the Incas Build Machu Picchu" by David Hatcher Childress was originally published in *World Explorer* magazine, vol. 3, no. 6, 2004, p. 33-48.

9—"Summary of *Atlantis and the Old Ones: An Investigation of the Age of Civilization*" by Colin Wilson is a summary of Wilson's book of the same title, to be published by Bear and Co., Rochester, Vermont, in the fall of 2005. It is published for the first time in this anthology.

10—"The Meaning of the Pyramids" by Robert M. Schoch, with Robert S. McNally, was published on Dr. Schoch's Web site robertschoch.homestead.com, but a version of the article also appeared on the History News Network (see hnn.us/articles/1230.html).

11—"The Secret Land" by Roy A. Decker was written especially for publication in this anthology.

12—"Lingering Echoes: Athens, Jerusalem" by Robert Merkin was written especially for this anthology.

13—"Underworld: Confronting Yonaguni" by Graham Hancock is chapter 27 of his book *Underworld: The Mysterious Origins of Civilization*, published by Crown Publishers, New York, New York, 2002.

14—"Sacred Geography: Cosmic and Cometary Induced Cataclysms, and the Megalithic Response" by Martin Gray was written especially for this anthology.

15—"Atlantis in America: A Summing Up—Awaiting the New Paradigm" by George Erikson, with Ivar Zapp, is chapter 14 of his book *Atlantis in America—Navigators of the Ancient World*, published by Adventures Unlimited Press, Kempton, Illinois, 1998.

16—"Nan Madol: The Lost Civilization of the Pacific" by Frank Joseph was written especially for publication in this anthology.

17—"Underworld: Confronting Kerama" by Graham Hancock is chapter 29 of his book *Underworld: The Mysterious Origins of Civilization*, published by Crown Publishers, New York, 2002.

18—"The Giza Power Plant" by Christopher Dunn is reworked from an article prepared for the magazine *Atlantis Rising* after his book *The Giza Power Plant: Technologies of Ancient Egypt* was published in 1998.

19—"Aviation in Antiquity?" by Erich von Däniken was originally published in *Legendary Times* magazine, vol. 2, no. 6, 2000.

20—"The Constantine Conspiracy" by Crichton E. M. Miller was written especially for this anthology.

21—"The Ancient of Days: Deity or Manna-Machine?" by George T. Sassoon was originally written at the behest of James R. Lewis of Santa Barbara, California between four and five years ago, who put it online for the express purpose of disseminating the information, and was picked up and published in *Legendary Times* magazine, vol. 2, no. 5, 2000. It has been adapted from its original form especially for this anthology.

22—"The Giant Flying Turtles of Guatemala" by Giorgio A. Tsoukalos was originally published in *Legendary Times* magazine, vol. 4, no. 1, 2002.

23—"Ancient Scientific Instruments" by William R. Corliss is taken from his book *Archeological Anomalies: Small Artifacts—Bone, Stone, Metal Artifacts, Footprints, High Technology. A Catalog of Archeological Anomalies*, published and distributed by The Sourcebook Project, Glen Arm, Maryland, 2003.

24—"Creation of a Gifted People: The Mayan Calendar" by Sharon Secor was written especially for publication in this anthology.

25—"Ancient Wisdom and the Great Sphinx of Giza" by Robert M. Schoch is a slightly modified version of a piece which originally appeared as an invited article in the *Psychic Reader*, vol. 28, no. 10, October 2003, pp. 10-11; see www.berkeleypsychic.com.

26—"Where is the Holy Grail?" by Reverend Ron Sala was written especially for this anthology.

27—"Journey to Bubastis" by Richard Cusick was written especially for this anthology.

28—"Gnosis: The Plants of Truth" by Dan Russell was excerpted from *Shamanism and the Drug Propaganda: Patriarchy and the Drug War*, published by Kalyx.com, Camden, New York, 1998.

29—"A Conversation With Greg Deyermenjian: Lost Cities Sought, Lost Cities Found" by Preston Peet was written especially for this anthology.

30—"Source of the Blood: Nazi Germany's Search for its Aryan Roots" by Mickey Z. was written especially for this anthology.

31—"Team Atlantis" by Michael Arbuthnot is published for the first time in this complete form in this anthology, with small portions of it previously posted online at the Team Atlantis Web site (www.teamatlantis.com).

32—"Shovel Bum—A Life Archaeologic" by Troy Lovata was originally published as a previous version of this essay, entitled "Putting *Shovel Bum* in Context: Why a View From the Shovel Handle Matters," in *Shovel Bum: Comix of Archaeological Field Life*, Trent de Boer, editor, by AltaMira Press, 2004.

33—"Archaeological Cover-Ups: A Plot to Control History?" by Will Hart was originally published in *Nexus*, vol. 9, no. 3, April-May 2002. It was also published in *Ancient American* magazine in 2003.

CONTRIBUTOR BIOGRAPHIES

Michael Arbuthnot holds a Master's degree in anthropology from Florida State University, where he specialized in underwater archaeology and graduated Magna Cum Laude. He now makes a living as a professional archaeological consultant in Florida and periodically teaches as an adjunct professor of archaeology and Mesoamerican civilizations at Flagler College in St. Augustine. In 1996, Michael founded Team Atlantis Productions. As Creative Director for Team Atlantis, he has been traveling to exotic locations worldwide (Egypt, Japan, Yucatan, Bahamas, Gulf of Mexico, etc.) exploring underwater archaeological sites and their related enigmas. Michael is a member of many professional organizations and affiliations, including: the Register of Professional Archaeologists (RPA); the Florida Archaeological Council (FAC); the Southeastern Archaeological Conference (SEAC); the Florida Anthropological Society (FAS); the American Academy of Underwater Sciences (AAUS); the Western Dredging Association (WEDA) and the St. Augustine Archaeological Association (SAAA). He is the author of many published articles, papers and reports, as well as an authority on the topic of submerged prehistoric archaeological sites.

David Hatcher Childress was born on June 1, 1957, in Poitiers, France. He studied archaeology, journalism, philosophy and history at the University of Montana, and studied in universities around the world, in Taipei, Taiwan; Nepal, Kathmandu; Dharamsala, Himachal Pradesh; Khartoum, Sudan; Nairobi, Kenya and at the University of Beijing. Since his school days, David has roamed the world on one expedition or adventure after another: He explored Afghanistan just prior to the Soviet Invasion; Looted Idi Amin's House during the Ugandan Civil War; was arrested twice in Zambia as being alternately a spy for Idi Amin and a spy for Rhodesia. After being told he would spend the rest of his life in prison, he managed to talk his way out; hitchhiked on yachts in the Indian Ocean for six months and is one of the few people in the world to ever reach the Ghost Island of Aldabra in the remote Indian Ocean; searched for lost cities in the Maldives and Sri Lanka; is one of the first people to trek through the lost Tibetan Kingdom of Zanskar; hitchhiked and traveled through China for three months, as one of the first individuals to be allowed to travel through China alone and at age 26 authored and published his first book, *A Hitchhiker's Guide to Africa and Arabia*. David is the owner and founder of Adventures Unlimited Travel, a unique

Archaeological Adventure Tour Company offering trips and expeditions around the world, is the author of several books about lost cities and civilizations, and owns the Adventures Unlimited Press book publishing company. He also founded the monthly *World Explorer* magazine, covering ancient mysteries, cryptozoology, ancient and modern explorations, enigmatic archaeology and much more.

William R. Corliss is a native of Connecticut, where he graduated from Stamford High School in 1944. He spent the next two years in the US Navy electronics program, ending up with a Seabee battalion in the Philippines repairing the havoc left behind by the Japanese. Under the GI Bill, he graduated from Rensselaer Polytechnic Institute in physics in 1950. An M.S. (physics) followed in 1953 from the University of Colorado. After eight years in the aerospace industry, he began writing full-time in 1963. He is the author of 65 books, including *Propulsion Systems for Space Flight* (1960); *Man and Atom* (co-authored with Nobelist Glenn Seaborg (1971); and the latest, *Science Frontiers II: More Anomalies and Curiosities of Nature* (2004). Corliss is the sole proprietor of the Sourcebook Project (www.science-frontiers.com).

Michael A. Cremo is a researcher in human origins for the Bhaktivedanta Institute, the science studies branch of the International Society for Krishna Consciousness. The purpose of the Institute is to examine scientific questions in light of India's Vedic wisdom. He has presented papers at meetings of the World Archeological Congress, European Association of Archeologists, the International Congress for History of Science, and the International Union of Prehistoric and Protohistoric Sciences. He has given invited lectures at the Royal Institution in London, the Russian Academy of Sciences in Moscow, the Bulgarian Academy of Sciences in Sofia, and at other scientific institutions, conferences and universities worldwide. Cremo is, with Richard Thompson, author of the book *Forbidden Archeology*, a comprehensive survey of archeological evidence consistent with Vedic accounts of extreme human antiquity. The abridged popular edition of *Forbidden Archeology*, titled *The Hidden History of the Human Race*, has been translated into 20 languages, including Portuguese. Cremo's latest book is *Human Devolution: A Vedic Alternative to Darwin's Theory*.

Richard Cusick is a senior editor at *High Times* magazine. He has written over 100 articles for a variety of publications, *including High Times Goldmine, Gadfly, Smug, Tattoo, Grow America, Downtown* (NYC) and the *Newark Evening News*. He was associate editor of *Gauntlet* from 1995 to 1997. In 1997-1998, his weekly "Pot Page" column appeared in the *Aquarian Weekly* and *Downtown*. In the 1980s, Cusick was vice president of operations for the ICI Mortgage Corporation. He owned and operated Wooga Central, an independent comic book company, where he wrote and designed the signature title, *Something Different*. He was ad director of the *Aquarian Weekly, Smug* and, most recently, *High Times*, from 1999 to 2003, and *High Times Grow America* in 2004.

Erich von Däniken was born on April 14, 1935, in Zofingen, Switzerland, and educated at the College St-Michel in Fribourg, where already as a student he occupied his time with the study of the ancient holy writings. While acting as the managing director of a Swiss Five-Star Hotel, he wrote his first book, *Chariots of the Gods?*, which was an immediate bestseller in the United States, Germany and, later, in 38 other countries. Von Däniken's latest book was just translated and published as *The Gods Were Astronauts: Evidence of the True Identities of the Old "Gods."* Von Däniken's books have been translated into 28 languages, and have sold 60 million copies worldwide. From his books two full-length documentary films have been produced: *Chariots of the Gods* and *Messages of the Gods*. Von Däniken is a member of the Swiss Writers Association, the German Writers Association, and the International PEN-Club. Today, von Däniken lives in the small mountain-village of Beatenberg in Switzerland (40 miles from Bern, above the city of Interlaken). Together with two committees he realized the fantastic "Mysteries of the World" theme park, Mystery Park. Von Däniken is the founder of the committees, and also the vice president of the joint-stock company. Mystery Park opened its gates in May 2003 in Interlaken, Switzerland. In 1998, Erich von Däniken, together with Giorgio A. Tsoukalos and Ulrich Dopatka, co-founded the A.A.S.R.A. (Archaeology, Astronautics and SETI Research Association) which publishes the English journal *Legendary Times*, reporting about the latest research in the ancient astronaut field. For more info, or how you too can join the movement, please go to legendarytimes.com. Erich von Däniken has been married to Elisabeth Skaja since 1960. He has one daughter, Cornelia (born 1963), and two grandchildren. Von Däniken is a hobby-chef and a lover of Bordeaux wines.

Gary A. David is an independent researcher living in rural Arizona. David's book *The Orion Zone: Ancient Star Cities of the American Southwest* was published in early 2005 by Hayriver Press. This book describes the Arizona Orion Correlation of ancient Hopi villages. He recently published articles in *Ancient American* and *Atlantis Rising* magazines. Mr. David has also served as a college instructor, with a Master's degree in English literature from the University of Colorado. For more articles on "The Orion Zone" or to order the book, go to azorion.tripod.oom. David can be contacted by e-mail at islandhills@cybertrails.com.

Roy A. Decker is a 47-year-old freelance writer who is a native of northeast Pennsylvania. Roy and his wife, Beth, who is a photographer, also have a home in Arizona. They frequently collaborate on projects, with dozens of published articles on ancient Carthage and lost treasures, both in magazines and on the Internet. Roy is currently working on his new book, *The Secret of Carthage*. Roy's many interests include history, lost civilizations, gold prospecting, raising Percheron horses, archaeology, traveling and collecting ancient coins and weapons.

David Dentel, a journalist, has won awards for editorial writing and newspaper page design. He holds a Master's degree in literature, an interest that ultimately fueled his inquiries into the most intriguing narrative of all: the story of human origins. He and his wife, Kate, live in York, Pennsylvania.

Christopher Dunn has an extensive background as a craftsman, starting his career as an indentured apprentice in his hometown of Manchester, England. Recruited by an American aerospace company, he immigrated to the United States in 1969. Over the past 44 years, Dunn has worked at every level of high-tech manufacturing from machinist, toolmaker, programmer and operator of high-power industrial lasers, Project Engineer and Laser Operations Manager. For the past ten years, he has served in a senior management position with a Midwest aerospace manufacturer. Dunn's pyramid odyssey began in 1977, after he read Peter Tompkins' book *Secrets of the Great Pyramid*. His immediate reaction after learning of the Great Pyramid's precision and design characteristics was to consider that this edifice might have had an original purpose that differed from conventional opinion. After further research and study of source material on various theories, Dunn concluded that it must have originally been built to provide a highly technical society with energy—in short, it was a very large machine. Discovering the purpose of this machine and documenting his case has taken the better part of 20 years of research and, following the 1998 publication of Dunn's book *The Giza Power Plant*, his research continues. Dunn has published over a dozen magazine articles, including the much-quoted "Advanced Machining in Ancient Egypt" in *Analog*, August 1984, and has had his research referenced in several other books on Egypt. In the United States he has appeared discussing his research on PAX Television, the Travel Channel, Discovery Channel, the Learning Channel and Lifetime Television.

George Erikson is the co-author of *Atlantis in America: Navigators of the Ancient World* (with Professor Ivar Zapp of the University of Costa Rica). As an anthropologist he has published several important works in oral traditions of pre-Columbian Mesoamericans, including the highly acclaimed *Maria Sabina: Her Life & Chants*, of which the *Los Angeles Times* said, "For authenticity, this oral autobiography of 80-year-old Mazatec Shaman Maria Sabina puts Castaneda's Don Juan to shame." Erikson and Zapp, in their Atlantis in America, present evidence of stone structures that re-enact myths of destruction and foundation. Colin Wilson, author of the worldwide bestseller *The Outsider*, commented, "Groundbreaking. Remarkable. Manna from heaven!" Colin and his co-author Rand Flem-Ath devoted most of chapter six of their recent *The Atlantis Blueprint* (Delacorte, 2001) to Erikson, Zapp and the spheres of Costa Rica. Andrew Collins, author of *Gateway to Atlantis* (*Atlantis In Cuba*) and *From the Ashes of Angels* wrote, "...(*Atlantis In America*) is a cornucopia of new ideas regarding the origins of Mesoamerican civilization and the

Atlantean tradition. Its clues on ancient navigation could provide vital keys in understanding trans-oceanic contact prior to the Age of Columbus." In their December, 2002 Italian language edition *Edizioni Piemme* called *Le Strade di Atlantide* (*Atlantis in America*), "Un Best Seller provocatorio e intrigante."

Martin Gray is an anthropologist and photographer specializing in the study of sacred sites and pilgrimage traditions around the world. During a 25-year period, Martin Gray traveled widely in 90 countries to study and photograph more than 1,200 holy and magical places of prehistoric, historic and contemporary cultures. Martin is an expert in the subjects of sacred geometry, geomancy, archaeoastronomy, ecopsychology and earth mysteries. More than eight million people have visited Martin's Web sites www.sacredsites.com and www.magicplanet.org. In 2004, National Geographic published The *Geography of Religion* and Martin Gray was the principal photographer.

Graham Hancock is the author of the major international bestsellers *The Sign and The Seal*, *Fingerprints of the Gods*, *Keeper of Genesis*, *The Mars Mystery*, *Heaven's Mirror* and *Underworld*. His books have sold more than five million copies worldwide, have been translated into 27 languages and include five number one bestsellers in the UK. His public lectures and TV appearances, including the three-hour Learning Channel series *Quest for the Lost Civilization* (1998) and *Flooded Kingdoms of the Ice Age* (2002), have put his ideas before audiences of tens of millions. He has become recognized as an unconventional thinker who raises legitimate questions about humanity's history and prehistory and offers an increasingly popular challenge to the entrenched views of orthodox scholars.

Will Hart is a journalist, photographer and author with publishing credits in such diverse magazines as *Wild West*, *Nature Photographer*, *Nexus* and *New Dawn*, and is a regular contributor to *Atlantis Rising*. Inner Traditions published Hart's first book, *The Genesis Race*, to excellent reviews. Will is an ardent conservationist, independent historian and enjoys sharing his views and knowledge on such talk shows as *Coast-to-Coast*, *Dreamland* and many others.

Frank Joseph is the editor-in-chief of *Ancient American*, a popular science magazine describing overseas visitors to the Americas before Columbus. Joseph's *Destruction of Atlantis* is published in ten foreign language editions. His other published books include *Survivors of Atlantis*, Edgar Cayce's *Atlantis and Lemuria*, *The Atlantis Encyclopedia* and *Synchronicity and You*. He is an "honorary professor of archaeology" at Japan's Savant Institute.

Dr. Troy Lovata began as a shovel bum and has gone on to become an assistant professor with the honors program at the University of New Mexico. He holds doctorate and Master's degrees in anthropology, with a concentration on archaeology, from the University of Texas, and a bachelor's degree in anthropology from Colorado State University. His research examines cultural change and how material culture persists through time. He has practiced fieldwork primarily in the Great Plains and Rocky Mountain regions of the American West, and is currently researching *Torreons*—stone structures with roots in Medieval Iberia built by Spanish settlers in New Mexico. His book, *Inauthentic Archaeologies*, is scheduled for publication by Left Coast Press in 2006.

Robert Aquinas McNally is a writer and poet whose early education in classical Latin blossomed into a lifelong fascination with ancient civilization and mythology. His books include *Voyages of the Pyramid Builders*, *Voices of the Rocks* and *Pyramid Quest*, with Robert M. Schoch.

Robert Merkin is a novelist and journalist; his novels are *The South Florida Book of the Dead*, about drug smuggling, and *Zombie Jamboree*, about enlisted soldiers during the Vietnam War. His travel writing has appeared in the *Washington Post* and the *New York Times*. He and his wife Cynthia live in western Massachusetts. His interests include drug policy and prison reform, homeless and veterans' advocacy, active volcanoes, the Canadian Arctic, trains, sea travel, astronomy and science. For several years he was partially composed of titanium; for a few days, he was less than number one on the food chain. For two hours he was Iceland's Least Wanted. His blog is vleeptron.blogspot.com.

Crichton E. M. Miller was born in Scotland, August 25, 1949. Miller has worked in the Royal Air Force as an air traffic controller, for Allied Dunbar as a sales manager and at Guardian Royal Exchange, as their northern regional sales manager. Married and a parent of six children, Miller discovered an ancient instrument in 1997 that could explain the design of ancient constructions, star cultures, astronomy, astrology and ocean navigation. Crichton was granted two British Patents on the instrument in 2001 and 2002. Crichton's work is the first practical theory that provides the essential link between ancient spirituality and modern scientific investigation, and he fervently hopes that his discovery may be of real service to humanity. Crichton's discovery is published in many magazines, newspapers and Web sites throughout the world. They include *Practical Boat Owner*, *Hera* magazine, *Atlantis Rising*, *Ancient American* and *The Coventry Evening Telegraph*. The author has appeared on Teidi Television, Talk Radio, BBC Radio Scotland and Earth Changes Television. His Web site, www.crichtonmiller.com, produces over 300 new visits a day from over 70 countries worldwide, with many visits from mostly U.S. education establishments.

Richard Nisbet has been a theatre and film director, an audio studio owner, a semi-professional equestrian, a writer and a teacher. For 30 years he has had a passionate interest in the stoneworks of the Incas. He has a deep knowledge of this incredible civilization's rise and ultimate conquest by the Spanish. His photographs of the Inca monuments go back to 1975. He has also written the book *Cusco Tales*, best described as a slice of life of today's Cusco (www.cuscotales.com). He divides his time between Cusco and Santa Monica, CA. He continues to study and write, and is now hosting tours to Cusco, Machu Picchu and important points between. He can be contacted at rnisbet@yahoo.com.

Preston Peet is an accomplished author, actor, DJ, musician, psychonaut, and explorer. Editor of both this anthology and *Under the Influence: The Disinformation Guide to Drugs*, editor of DrugWar.com, a long-time contributor to *High Times* magazine, and contributing editor to Disinformation's website [disinfo.com], not to mention author of over 100 articles and stories published in too many publications to list here, Preston has been known to take the more adventurous path when it comes to new experiences, whether they be drug-related or sexual, or other, in nature. Born Tracy Rich in Ft. Meyers, Florida on September 11, 1966, and given up at birth, lived in numerous foster homes, picked the name Preston at age three and was eventually adopted by the Peet family at age five. Preston has lived in the swankiest digs and the muddiest streets in cities around the world, including Sarasota, Orlando, Tampa, and Tallahassee, Florida; Atlanta, Georgia; Paris, France; Las Navas del Marqés, Spain; Bergen, Norway; Rotterdam and Amsterdam, Netherlands; and London, England. Upon arrival in New York City, Preston went from kicking cold turkey while squatting on the SUNY Purchase campus, to living strung out in Central Park and on the streets of Manhattan's Lower East Side, and now, with his life somewhat together, shares a small apartment in Manhattan with his beautiful vegan muse, soul-mate, and lover, Vanessa Cleary, and, at the moment, nine rescued cats. Preston is always on the lookout for ever more knowledge and experience, and is helping bring peace and adventure back in vogue.

Dr. Navaratna S. Rajaram is a mathematician, linguist and historian who, after a 20-year career as an academic and industrial researcher in the United States, turned his attention to history, in which he has several notable achievements. He collaborated with the renowned Vedic scholar Dr. Natwar Jha on the decipherment of the 5,000-year-old Indus script leading to their epoch-making work *The Deciphered Indus Script*. In May 1999, Rajaram deciphered the newly discovered sample of what has been called the "world's oldest writing," showing it to be related to the *Rigveda*. Most recently, by a detailed study of human population genetics, he has shown that the people of India are not recent immigrants but have lived in the region for tens of thousands of years. He sees history as an extension of natural history, rather than as a field for political theories or attaching labels to stereotype people and cultures in the guise of scholarship.

Dan Russell, a 1970 graduate of the City University of New York, is the owner of Kalyx.com, a chain of Internet retail stores. He is also the author of two well-reviewed books, *Shamanism and the Drug Propaganda* and *Drug War*.

Acharya S is an archaeologist, classicist, historian, mythologist, linguist and member of the American School of Classical Studies at Athens, Greece. She has served as a trench master on archaeological excavations in Corinth, Greece and in Connecticut. Acharya has traveled extensively around Europe, and she speaks, reads and/or writes Greek, French, Spanish, Italian, German and Portuguese to varying degrees. She has also cross-referenced the Bible in the original Hebrew and ancient Greek. Acharya is the author of the best-selling and controversial *The Christ Conspiracy: The Greatest Story Ever Sold* and the follow-up blockbuster *Suns of God: Krishna, Buddha and Christ Unveiled*. Acharya S has appeared on dozens of radio programs for almost a decade. Her Web site is truthbeknown.com, and she may be contacted at acharya_s@yahoo.com

Reverend Ron Sala, who holds a Master of Divinity from New York Theological Seminary, is minister of the Unitarian Universalist Society in Stamford, Connecticut, where he lives with his wife and fellow minister ReBecca Ames Sala. He is an activist for such causes as drug policy reform, marriage equality, peace and workers' rights. He was the 2000 recipient of Unitarian Universalists for the Ethical Treatment of Animals' Albert Schweitzer Award and is a frequent contributor to the Stamford Advocate. He is also a York Rite Freemason.

George T. Sassoon is a linguist and computer expert, with a degree in Natural Sciences from Cambridge University, and serves as a consultant to the electronics and computer industries. He has published numerous technical articles and co-authored two books with Rodney Dale, *The Manna-Machine* and *The Kabbalah Decoded*. George T. Sassoon is one of the world's leading experts on Ark of the Covenant studies and Grail mythology. Mr. Sassoon divides his time between his estates in Wiltshire, England and the Isle of Mull, Scotland. Though both *The Mana-Machine* and *The Kabbalah Decoded* are both currently out of print, both are obtainable at wwwlib.umi.com/bod.

Robert M. Schoch, a full-time faculty member at the College of General Studies at Boston University since 1984, earned his PhD in geology and geophysics at Yale University. Schoch has been quoted extensively in the media for his pioneering work recasting the date of the Great Sphinx and is the author, with Robert Aquinas McNally, of *Voices of the Rocks: A Scientist Looks at Catastrophes and Ancient Civilizations*, *Voyage of the Pyramid Builders: The True Origins of the Pyramids from Lost Egypt to Ancient America* and *Pyramid Quest: Secrets of the Great Pyramid and the Dawn of Civilization*. Schoch was featured on the Emmy Award-winning documentary *The Mystery of the Sphinx*. Schoch's Web site can be visited at: www.robertschoch.net

Sharon Secor is a freelance writer living in upstate New York. Her journey into freelance writing was inspired by Christine de Pisa (1364-1429), a widow and writer of social commentary who, in addition to being one of France's earliest well-known female authors, was able to support her children through her writing. Secor read her first college level psychology textbook in the fourth grade, along with the feminist literature of the era, beginning what has proved to be a lifelong passion for the humanities and social sciences. Ms. Secor is working towards completing a double major in Journalism and Spanish—preparation for writing about social and economic issues in Latin America as influenced by increased industrialization and the global marketplace. She plans to write for both English and Spanish language markets. As an anarchist and single parent, she also devotes her time to practicing resistance and raising revolutionaries.

Giorgio A. Tsoukalos is the Chairman of the A.A.S.R.A. (Archaeology, Astronautics and SETI Research Association) and the Publisher and Editor in Chief of the A.A.S.R.A.'s official quarterly, *Legendary Times*. The A.A.S.R.A. was founded on June 17, 1998 by Giorgio A. Tsoukalos, Ulrich Dopatka and Erich von Däniken. Born in Lucerne, Switzerland, Giorgio A. Tsoukalos is fluent in five languages: English, German, French, Italian and Greek. He is also proficient in Spanish. Giorgio is of Greek and Austrian origin and grew up near Zurich, Switzerland, spending his summers sailing the Greek Isles and his winters skiing in Innsbruck, Austria. He was educated at Institut Montana, an international boarding school in the heart of Switzerland on top of the Alps, and has acquired a bachelor's degree in Sports Information & Communications at Ithaca College, NY. He has conducted and participated in several adventurous, hair-raising, swashbuckling expeditions to the remote corners of the world. In his quest to uncover the truth he has traveled hundreds of thousands of miles, seeking out strange archaeological artifacts and monuments that will further strengthen the A.A.S.R.A.'s research. Over the years, he has gained first hand access to, photographed and measured ancient artifacts and other archaeological relics not currently accessible to the general public. Most of those findings have been published in the pages of *Legendary Times*. Mr. Tsoukalos has been a guest on numerous television specials, DVD featurettes, radio programs and has given many lectures all over the world about ancient astronauts at seminars, conferences, meetings and to corporations.

John Anthony West is a writer and independent Egyptologist who has been studying and writing about ancient Egypt for nearly three decades. He is the foremost exponent of the "Symbolist" school of Egyptology—which sees (and demonstrates) an ancient sacred science where modern academics see mainly superstition. West's work redating the Great Sphinx of Giza via geology (proving that it must be at least 10,000 years old or older) was the subject of a 1993 NBC special, *The Mystery of the Sphinx*, hosted by Charlton Heston. Viewed by 30,000,000 people, this was one of the most successful documentaries ever shown, and it has escalated into a heated international scholarly controversy. West won an Emmy in 1993 for Best Research for his work on the video, and the show itself was one of four nominated for Best Documentary Program. The BBC subsequently produced its own version of the show for its prestigious and popular science series *Timewatch*. Re-titled *Age of the Sphinx*, the show recorded the second highest ratings of any *Timewatch* episode and generated still further controversy in the English press. West's non-fiction books include *Serpent in the Sky: The High Wisdom of Ancient Egypt* (a detailed examination of the symbolist interpretation of Egypt), *The Traveler's Key to Ancient Egypt* and *The Case for Astrology*. He has also written a book of short stories, a novel, plays and film scripts. His essays and criticism have appeared in the *New York Times*, Conde Nast's *Traveler*, and many other general interest and specialized publications in America and abroad. He is presently at work (in collaboration with Robert M. Schoch, principal scientific investigator) on a book devoted to his work on the Great Sphinx.

Colin Wilson was born of working class parents in Leicester, England, in 1931. In spite of an early ambition to become a scientist, he decided to become a writer after he left school at 16. During the following years he worked at a variety of jobs, including ditch digging and farm laboring, while working on his first novel, *Ritual in the Dark*, about a sex killer based on Jack the Ripper, in the Reading Room of the British Museum. When the novelist Angus Wilson, then assistant superintendent of the Reading Room, offered to read it, Wilson decided to fill in slack time by writing a non-fiction book about misfits of genius; *The Outsider* came out when he was 24 and made him world famous. After his second book was attacked as harshly as the first had been praised, he moved to a remote cottage in Cornwall with his girlfriend Joy, and went on writing—novels, philosophy, criminology, books on the paranormal—well over a hundred books to date. Writing about ancient civilizations in the 1990s, he became convinced that human intellectual achievement dates back over a hundred thousand years.

Mickey Z. — What can you say about a self-educated kickboxing instructor who lectures on foreign policy at MIT in his spare time, has five books published and can sometimes be seen on C-Span? *Newsday* calls Mickey Z. a "professional iconoclast." *Time Out* says he's a "political provocateur." To Howard Zinn, he's "iconoclastic and bold." A native of Astoria in the New York City borough of Queens, Mickey regularly writes for several online publications, including *Press Action*, *ZNet*, *Counterpunch*, *Street News* and *Dissident Voice*, in addition to print media such as *Veg News* and *New York Press*. Mickey can be found on the Web at www.mickeyz.net.

Preston Peet

ACKNOWLEDGMENTS

WITHOUT meeting and falling in love with Vanessa Cleary, I would not have been able to publish this book, or anything else I've published over the years. "Behind every good (or successful) man stands a good woman," the saying goes in so many words, but in my particular case, that "good woman" stands right alongside me, encouraging, prodding, pushing and pulling me, acting as my muse, my inspiration, my grounding force of positive energy and love. For her I give thanks on a daily basis to whatever powers that be for her coming into my life. I will always appreciate that she stayed, and am grateful and thankful for the chance to share my life and my heart with such a beautiful, caring, kind and loving partner. Vanessa, thank you from the bottom of my heart.

Thank you Gary, Richard, Jason, Ralph, Maya, Jacob, David, Liz and everyone else at the Disinformation Company, for your enthusiastic response to the idea of this book, for your tireless dedication and devotion to getting out to the public-at-large alternative, more often than not controversial and always interesting information to counter the staid, black-and-white worldview the status quo prefers we live in and, last but not least, for your patience and understanding and for giving me yet another opportunity to publish on a topic near and dear to my heart.

I would like to thank my parents and siblings for their love. Graham Hancock gets my heartfelt gratitude and appreciation, not only for his inspiring me with his work on ancient cultures and explorations but, more to the point, because without his agreeing to take part in this project, it might never have happened. Graham's wife, Santha Faiia, gets my enthusiastic thanks as well, for the gracious use of her gorgeous photographs. Peter Gorman gets my thanks for the idea for an article and for his friendship and inspiration. Julian Cope gets my thanks for his inspiration, both in his music and his research and publishing. I thank (and apologize to) Wayne May, publisher of *Ancient American* magazine, for kindly giving me three articles, none of which made it into this anthology but, were things different, would definitely have had prominent placement, and for his quest to understand and present to the public the many enigmas and mysteries of pre-Columbian North America and its peoples. Todd Lovata gets my thanks for introducing me to the world of the *shovel bums*—the most important, underrated workers in the archaeological field, who all too rarely get the credit they deserve for their sweaty, exhausting, backbreaking work literally uncovering our past. Arvind Kumar gets my thanks for introducing me to N. S. Rajaram, a meeting that ended up adding yet another treasure to this anthology. The same goes for Jules Siegel and Ulrich Dopatka, who contributed great articles but for which, in the end, there simply wasn't room. Dimitri, Kurt, Mark and Chris all get my sincere thanks and hugs for their assistance and support in a time of dire need. Coffee gets a nod of appreciation for the same, as well as for inspiration, as does Dan V. My thanks to Maria Monaco for the Christmas gift books, from which I obtained a good quote or three for the introduction to this anthology. Maria also gets, along with Brian Cleary, my deepest, most sincere thanks for the most precious gift in my world. To all my friends and relations I've not named here, please accept my thanks and apologies for not naming each and every one individually, as you are too many to count, though each and every one of you deserve a nod of appreciation.

Last but not least, I'd like to thank all the explorers, questioners, maverick archaeologists, trail blazers, shovel bums, archaeology students, photographers, analysts, speculators, "fringe" characters, researchers, writers and publishers, and everyone else who works endlessly, most often with little financial gain or fame or credit, to bring to light our ancient past—often risking ridicule and even professional careers for positing new ideas, while examining and reporting on the mysteries and wonders of peoples long gone, who accomplished so much but left us such enigmatic, indecipherable records, usually made up of either the merest traces of remains, or massive stone ruins of megalithic proportions, with no texts to explain their construction and reason for being. You are all inspiring adventurers on the forefront of a constantly shifting paradigm concerning our ancient past. To all of you my deepest thanks and appreciation, for examining with such fresh and novel perspectives the unanswered questions and anomalies of our past. Keep digging and speculating, please.

ALSO FROM disinformation®

UNDER THE INFLUENCE
The Disinformation Guide To Drugs
Edited by Preston Peet

In this volume of the oversize Disinformation Guide series of anthologies, editor Preston Peet assembles an all-star cast to lay to rest the specious mis-information peddled by prohibitionists who depend upon the "War on Some Drugs and Users" for their livelihood and power.

Oversized Softcover • 360 Pages
$24.95 ISBN 1-932857-00-1

YOU ARE BEING LIED TO
The Disinformation Guide to Media Distortion, Historical Whitewashes and Cultural Myths
Edited by Russ Kick

This book proves that we are being lied to by those who should tell us the truth: the government, the media, corporations, organized religion, and others who want to keep the truth from us.

Oversized Softcover • 400 Pages
$24.95 ISBN 0-96641007-6

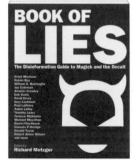

BOOK OF LIES
The Disinformation Guide to Magick and the Occult
Edited by Richard Metzger

Richard Metzger gathers an unprecedented cabal of modern occultists, magicians and forward thinkers in this large format Disinformation Guide. **Book of Lies** redefines occult anthologies, presenting an array of magical essays for a pop culture audience.

Oversized Softcover • 360 Pages
$24.95 ISBN 0-9713942-7-X

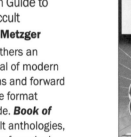

GENERATION HEX
Edited by Jason Louv

If the modern world is crumbling, then magic is what's growing up between the cracks. In **Generation Hex**, editor Jason Louv assembles a collection of dispatches from the edge—a generation of young adults who are inventing and imagining radically new directions for spirituality and human evolution.

Paperback • 288 Pages
$14.95 • ISBN: 1-932857-20-6

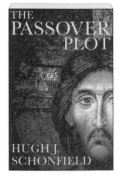

THE PASSOVER PLOT
By Hugh J. Schonfield

This book shows us the historical evidence suggesting that Jesus was a mortal man, a young genius who believed himself to be the Messiah and deliberately and brilliantly planned his entire ministry according to the Old Testament prophecies—even to the extent of plotting his own arrest, crucifixion and resurrection.

Trade Paperback • 288 Pages
$12.95 ISBN: 1-932857-09-5

TURN OFF YOUR MIND
The Mystic Sixties and the Dark Side of the Age of Aquarius
By Gary Lachman

In a well-researched and well-written book author Gary Lachman explores the sinister dalliance of rock's high rollers and a new wave of occultists, tying together John Lennon, Timothy Leary, Mick Jagger, Charles Manson, Anton LaVey and other American cultural icons.

Trade Paperback • 430 Pages
$19.95 ISBN 0-9713942-3-7

http://store.disinfo.com